BEHAVIOR MODIFICATION

WHAT IT IS AND HOW TO DO IT

Garry Martin

University of Manitoba

Joseph Pear

St. Paul's College, Winnipeg, Manitoba

Boston   Columbus   Indianapolis   New York   San Francisco   Upper Saddle River
Amsterdam   Cape Town   Dubai   London   Madrid   Milan   Munich   Paris   Montreal   Toronto
Delhi   Mexico City   Sao Paulo   Sydney   Hong Kong   Seoul   Singapore   Taipei   Tokyo

Executive Editor: Susan Hartman
Editorial Assistant: Mary Lombard
Marketing Manager: Nicole Kunzmann
Senior Production Project
   Manager: Patrick Cash-Peterson
Manufacturing Buyer: Debbie Rossi
Cover Administrator: Joel Gendron
Cover Designer: Joel Gendron
Composition/Full Service Project
   Management: TexTech International
Printer/Binder: Edwards Brothers

> *To*
>
> *Jack Michael, Lee Meyerson, Lynn Caldwell, Dick Powers, and Reed Lawson, who taught us so much and made learning so enjoyable*
>
> *and*
>
> *Toby, Todd, Kelly, Scott, Tana, and Jonathan, who live in a better world because of such dedicated teachers*

Photo Credits: Page 23, Aaron Strong/The Stock Connection; p. 36, Digital Vision/Getty Images; p. 55, Blend Images/Alamy; p. 82 (top left) Yellow Dog Productions/Getty Images Inc; (top right) Laura Dwight/PhotoEdit; (bottom left) Will Faller; (bottom right) Elizabeth Crews Photography; p. 101 (top) Garry Watson/Photo Researchers, Inc.; (middle) Sagfia Fatima/Photonica/Getty Images; (bottom) Bueno Technologies; p. 160 Garry L. Martin; p. 185, Bernd Vogel/Corbis; p. 211 Garry L. Martin; p. 225 (top) Beau Lark/Fancy/Corbis; (bottom) Beau Lark/Fancy/Corbis; p. 249, Skjold Photographs; 301, Image Source/Corbis; and p. 367, Ariel Skelley/Corbis.

Library of Congress Cataloging-in-Publication Data

Martin, Garry
   Behavior modification : what it is and how to do it / Garry Martin Joseph Pear. — 9th ed.
     p. cm.
   ISBN-13: 978-0-205-79272-6
   ISBN-10: 0-205-79272-3
  1. Behavior modification. I. Pear, Joseph, II. Title.
   BF637.B4M37 2011
   155.2'5—dc22

                                     2010013791

10 9 8 7 6 5 4 3 2 1   EB   14 13 12 11 10 9

Allyn & Bacon
is an imprint of

ISBN 10: 0-205-79272-3
ISBN 13: 978-0-205-79272-6

www.pearsonhighered.com

CONTENTS

PREFACE

This ninth edition of *Behavior Modification: What It Is and How to Do It,* like its predecessors, assumes no specific prior knowledge about psychology or behavior modification on the part of the reader. Those who want to know how to apply behavior modification to their everyday concerns—from solving some of their own personal behavior problems to helping children learn life's necessary skills—will find the text useful. Mainly, however, this book is addressed to two audiences: (a) college and university students taking courses in behavior modification, applied behavior analysis, behavior therapy, the psychology of learning, and related areas and (b) students and practitioners of various helping professions (such as clinical psychology, counseling, education, medicine, nursing, occupational therapy, physiotherapy, psychiatric nursing, psychiatry, social work, speech therapy, and sport psychology) who are concerned directly with enhancing various forms of behavioral development.

From our separate experiences over the past 43 years in teaching members of both groups, we are convinced that both groups learn the principles of behavior and how to apply them most effectively when the applications are explained with reference to the underlying behavior principles on which they are based. For this reason, as our title implies, this book deals equally with both the principles and the tactics (i.e., the rules and guidelines for specific applications) of behavior modification.

Our goals and the manner in which we have attempted to achieve them can be summarized as follows:

1. *To teach the elementary principles and procedures of behavior modification.* Thus, we begin with the basic principles and procedures, illustrate them with numerous examples and applications, and increase the complexity of the material gradually. Study Questions distributed throughout each chapter promote the reader's mastery of the material and ability to generalize to situations not described in the text. These questions can also be used for examination purposes in formal courses.

2. *To teach practical how-to skills, such as observing and recording; recognizing instances of reinforcement, extinction, and punishment and their likely long-term effects; interpreting behavioral episodes in terms of behavioral principles and procedures; and designing, implementing, and evaluating behavioral programs.* To accomplish this, we provide Application Exercises that involve other people and teach the reader about analyzing, interpreting, and developing programs for the behavior of others; self-modification exercises, which encourage the reader to analyze, interpret, and develop programs for his or her own behavior; and guidelines for specific applications.

3. *To provide advanced discussion and references to acquaint readers with some of the empirical and theoretical underpinnings of the field.* This material is presented in the "Notes and Extended Discussion" section at the end of each chapter. These sections can be omitted without harm to the continuity of the text. Separate study questions on the Notes are provided for those instructors who wish to use them and as aids for students who wish to broaden their understanding of behavior modification. Instructors can also use information given in the Extended Discussion sections as springboards for lecture material.

4. *To present the material in such a way that it will serve as an easy-to-use handbook for practitioners concerned with overcoming behavioral deficits and excesses in a wide variety of populations and settings.*

The book is divided into six parts:

Part I (Chapters 1 and 2) introduces the behavioral orientation of the book and describes major areas of application of behavior modification techniques for improving a wide variety of behaviors of individuals in diverse settings.

Part II (Chapters 3–16) covers the basic principles and procedures of behavior modification. Each of the chapters begins with a case history drawn from the fields of child development, developmental disabilities, childhood autism, early education, coaching, or normal everyday adult adjustment. Numerous examples of how each principle operates in everyday life and how it can operate to the disadvantage of those who are ignorant of it are also given.

Part III (Chapters 17–19) provides more sophisticated perspectives on the principles discussed in Part II. Chapters 17 and 18 discuss ways in which to combine and apply the principles. Chapter 19 provides a behavioral view of motivation and includes insights on applying various motivational operations. Each of these three chapters also begins with a case history.

Part IV (Chapters 20–22) presents detailed procedures for assessing, recording, and graphing behavior and for evaluating the effects of behavioral treatments using single-subject research designs. Many instructors prefer to present much of this material quite early in their courses—sometimes at the very beginning. Therefore, we have written these chapters so that they can be read independently of the rest of the book; they do not depend on any of the other material. We recommend that students be required to read these chapters prior to carrying out any major projects for their courses.

Part V (Chapters 23–28) deals with how the basic principles, procedures, and assessment and recording techniques are incorporated into effective programming strategies. In keeping with the rigorously scientific nature of behavior modification, we have placed heavy emphasis on the importance of empirically validating program effectiveness.

Part VI (Chapters 29 and 30) expands the reader's perspective of behavior modification. It presents an overview of the history of behavior modification and contains a discussion of the ethical issues in the field. Some instructors might think that these chapters belong near the beginning of the book, and we have written them so that they can be read after Chapter 1. However, we believe that the reader is more prepared to fully appreciate this material after obtaining a clear and thorough knowledge of behavior modification. We placed ethical issues at the end of the text not because we believe that this topic is less important than the others. On the contrary, we stress ethical issues throughout the book, and, thus, the last chapter provides a reiteration and elaboration of our views on this vital subject. We hope that after reading the concluding chapter, the reader will be fully aware that the only justification for behavior modification is its usefulness in serving all humanity in general and its recipients in particular.

CHANGES IN THE NINTH EDITION

First, to help students master the material, we made a pedagogical change: study questions have been placed in three or four small groupings throughout each chapter rather than in one large grouping at the end of each chapter.

Second, in the "Pitfalls" sections of Part II ("Basic Principles and Procedures") of previous editions, we described how lack of knowledge of a principle or procedure could be problematic. In this edition, we identified five specific types of pitfalls, which we illustrate with examples.

Third, in Part II ("Basic Principles and Procedures") of previous editions, we began Chapters 3–16 with a case history to illustrate how the various principles operate in everyday life. In this edition, we added lead cases to Chapters 17, 18, and 19.

Fourth, we renamed Part III (Chapters 17, 18, and 19) "Capitalizing on Antecedent Control Procedures." Those three chapters discuss five different types of antecedent control strategies that can be used for effective behavior modification.

Fifth, we made considerable revisions to the chapter on punishment including an updated discussion on whether punishment should be used.

Sixth, we expanded on the behavioral interpretation of mindfulness in the chapter titled "Cognitive Behavior Therapy, Self-Directed Coping Methods, and ACT" (Chapter 27).

Seventh, we made considerable revisions to Chapter 27 to incorporate recent developments in cognitive behavior therapy and acceptance and commitment therapy.

Eighth, in Chapter 28, we provided an updated overview of behavioral treatments with some of the most common clinical problems of outpatients.

Ninth, we revised Chapter 29, the history chapter, to stand alone because some instructors require their students to read this chapter after Chapter 1.

Tenth, throughout the book, we added examples to better illustrate behavior principles in everyday life, added many new up-to-date references to reflect recent developments in the field, and added a number of new notes to the "Notes and Extended Discussion" sections and deleted old notes when warranted.

Eleventh, we extensively revised and extended the Glossary to help students better understand the technical terms and concepts in the field of behavior modification.

Finally, as the following indicates, all chapters received extensive revision to cover recent developments in this expanding field and to enhance the readability of the text. Some of the specific chapter revisions we made were as follows: In Chapter 1, we expanded the comparison of behavior modification to applied behavior analysis, behavior therapy, and cognitive behavior therapy. In Chapter 2, we clarified the meaning of the terms *developmental disabilities, intellectual disabilities, mental retardation,* and *autism.* To Chapter 3, we added descriptions of five different types of pitfalls of positive reinforcement, that is, different ways that the principle can work against the unwary. To Chapter 4, we added a new lead case illustrating a token reinforcement program with a college student and clarified the definitions and differences between unconditioned reinforcer, conditioned reinforcer, and backup reinforcer. To Chapter 6, we added a section on progressive ratio schedules of reinforcement. In Chapter 7, we refined the definitions of DRL, DRO, DRI, and DRA. We reorganized several sections in Chapter 8 to make it more reader friendly, explained the distinction between a two-term contingency of reinforcement versus a three-term contingency, and clarified the distinction between rule-governed and contingency-shaped behavior. In Chapter 10, we explained the differences between three different types of pitfalls of shaping and how they can work against the unwary. In Chapter 11, we clarified the differences between fading, shaping, and chaining, and explained two different types of pitfalls of chaining. In Chapter 12, we did considerable rewriting to make it more reader friendly, added a section on examples of "therapeutic" punishment, discussed functional communication training and positive behavior support as alternatives to punishment, and rewrote and updated the discussion of whether punishment should be used. In Chapter 14, we clarified definitions of key terms. To Chapter 16, we added behavioral momentum as a strategy for programming operant response generalization. To Chapter 17, we added a new lead case illustrating an effective intervention with a competitive figure skater. To Chapter 18, we added a new lead case that described a mindfulness-based treatment for aggression. To Chapter 19, we added a new lead case involving a motivating operation with a junior high school basketball team and a new table to clarify the distinctions between motivating establishing and abolishing operations and between unconditioned and conditioned motivating operations. In Chapter 20, we clarified the distinction between behavioral and psychodiagnostic approaches to assessment. To Chapter 21, we added a new table to summarize and compare different types of recording strategies. In Chapter 22 (which was Chapter 23 in the 8th edition), we clarified the definitions of different single-subject designs and incorporated discussion of internal and external validity into the body of the chapter (those terms were previously discussed in a note). To Chapter 23 (which was Chapter 22 in the 8th edition), we added a figure and text to clarify the distinctions between the six different types of causes of operant problem behaviors. To Chapter 25, to illustrate various aspects of token economies, including research on the generality of behavior developed in token economies, we added considerable information about and discussion of Achievement Place and the Teaching-Family Model. In Chapter 27, we updated and expanded the discussion of cognitive behavior therapy and acceptance and commitment therapy. In Chapter 28, we updated the overview of behavior therapy treatments with some of the most common clinical problems with outpatients. In Chapter 29, we changed the order in which we discussed some of the historical events to make the exposition flow more naturally. In Chapter 30, we made a number of minor stylistic changes to make the chapter more readable.

INSTRUCTOR'S RESOURCE MANUAL WITH TESTS AND PRACTICA

One of our goals is to help students learn to think about behavior modification critically and creatively. Thus, in the Instructor's Resource Manual to accompany this text, we have included operational definitions of higher-order thinking based on Bloom's taxonomy in the cognitive domain and have applied these definitions to the Study Questions in the text. Taking these thinking levels into account, we have provided an answer key to all of the Study Questions (including those on the "Notes and Extended Discussion" sections), indicating how students are expected to answer these questions on tests and exams in order to achieve a high level of thinking about the material. A pool of multiple-choice and/or true/false questions has also been provided on a chapter-by-chapter basis. Finally, included in the Instructor's Resource Manual are 15 in-class practica or minilab exercises that have been developed and field tested. Each exercise is designed to be completed by a group of two or three students during a regularly scheduled class. After students have studied and have been examined on relevant chapters, completion of a practicum helps them learn to talk about and apply behavior modification principles. Feedback from students indicates that the exercises constitute an excellent teaching tool.

POWERPOINT PRESENTATION

The PowerPoint presentation is an exciting interactive tool for use in the classroom. Each chapter pairs key concepts with images from the textbook to reinforce student learning.

ACKNOWLEDGMENTS

Writing the nine editions of this book was made possible by the help of many individuals. We gratefully acknowledge the cooperation and support of the staff at the Manitoba Developmental Centre and Dr. Carl Stephens and the staff at the St. Amant Centre. Much of the material in this volume was generated while the authors were involved in these institutions; without the support of these staff members, this book would not likely have been written.

Grateful acknowledgment is due to our many students for their constructive feedback on the current and earlier editions. We also thank Jack Michael, Rob Hawkins, Bill Leonhart, and Iver Iversen and his students for their many excellent suggestions for improvements on earlier editions. For this edition, special thanks are due to Kendra Thomson for her cheerful and efficient word processing and to Frances Falzarano for her excellent substantive and stylistic comments.

We are grateful to the following reviewers, whose helpful criticism improved this ninth edition: Ngoc Bui, University of LaVerne; Shirley Albertson Owens, Vanguard University of Southern California; Kirk Lunnen, West Minister College; Page Anderson, Georgia State University; Otto H. MacLin, University of Northern Iowa; Norman Cobb, University of Texas at Arlington; and Thomas Brown, Utica College.

Finally, we express our appreciation to the very capable editorial and production team at Prentice Hall/Pearson Education. In particular, we want to thank *(to be added).*

A research grant from the Canadian Institutes of Health Research (Grant No. MOP-6353) to G. L. Martin facilitated the completion of this book.

TO THE STUDENT

This book is designed to help you learn to talk about and apply behavior modification effectively. You need no prior knowledge about behavior modification to read and understand this text from beginning to end. We are confident that students at all levels—from beginners to advanced—will find the text informative and useful.

Behavior modification is a broad and complex field with many ramifications. Realizing that some students will require or want a deeper knowledge of behavior modification than others, we have separated the more elementary material from the material that demands more thought and study. The former material is presented in the main body of the text. The latter material is presented at the end of each chapter in the section called "Notes and Extended Discussion" (N and ED). The numbers in the margin of the main text refer you to the corresponding numbered passages in the N and ED sections. How you use these sections is up to you and your instructor. You can ignore them altogether and still obtain a good working knowledge of the principles and tactics of behavior modification because the main text does not depend on the material in the N and ED sections. We believe, however, that many students will find these sections very informative and that many instructors will find the material useful in stimulating class discussion and imparting additional background information.

Another major way in which we have attempted to help you learn the material is by providing guidelines on the use of all the behavior modification methods discussed in the text. These guidelines should prove useful as summaries of the material as well as in helping you to actually apply the methods described in the text.

Most chapters also present numerous Study Questions and Application Exercises (including "self-modification" exercises). The study questions are intended to help you check your knowledge of the material when preparing for quizzes and exams. The Application Exercises and the self-modification exercises in them are intended to help you develop the practical skills you will need to complete behavior modification projects effectively.

To help make your study productive and enjoyable, we progress from the simpler and more intrinsically interesting material to the more difficult and complex material. This is also true of the writing style. But a word of caution: *Do not be misled by the seeming simplicity of the earlier chapters.* Students who conclude that they are skilled behavior modifiers after they have learned a few simple behavior modification principles unfortunately end up proving the old maxim that "a little knowledge is a dangerous thing." If we personally had to pick the most important chapter in this book in terms of the knowledge and skills that define a competent behavior modifier, it would probably be Chapter 24. We therefore strongly suggest that you reserve judgment about your abilities as a behavior modifier until you have mastered Chapter 24 and all the preliminary material on which it is based.

We would also point out that—as emphasized in Chapter 30—organizations that regulate behavior modification have appeared and gained in stature and influence in the past few years. If you are considering applying behavior modification on any level, we strongly recommend that you check with the Behavior Analyst Certification Board (www.bacb.com) to determine how you may obtain the necessary qualifications.

With those words of caution, we wish you much success and enjoyment as you pursue your studies in this exciting and rapidly expanding field.

G.L.M.
J.J.P.

TO INDIVIDUALS USING THIS BOOK TO STUDY FOR THE BEHAVIOR ANALYSIS CERTIFICATION BOARD® EXAMINATIONS

For individuals using this book to study for the Board Certified Behavior Analyst® (BCBA®) or the Board Certified Assistant Behavior Analyst® (BCaBA®) exam, the following are the chapters in this book where the content for the task list may be found:

Exam Content Areas from the Task List*	Relevant Chapters
1. Ethical Considerations	30
2. Definition And Characteristics	1, 27, 29
3. Principles, Processes And Concepts	3–16
4. Behavioral Assessment	20–21, 23
5. Experimental Evaluation Of Interventions	22
6. Measurement Of Behavior	1, 7, 20–22
7. Displaying And Interpreting Behavioral Data	1, 20–21
8. Selecting Intervention Outcomes And Strategies	24, 26, 30
9. Behavior Change Procedure	17–19, 25–28
10. Systems Support	2, 16, 25–28

* The full BCBA and BCaBA Behavior Analyst Task List (Third Edition) can be found at www.bacb.com/consum_frame.html

PART I   THE BEHAVIOR MODIFICATION APPROACH

1

Introduction

Many of society's best achievements—from democratic government to dedicated service to the less fortunate, and from great works of art to important scientific discoveries—as well as some of its most pressing health and social challenges—from heart disease to AIDS and from racism to terrorism—are firmly rooted in behavior. According to an article in the *Journal of the American Medical Association,* "modifiable behaviors such as tobacco use, overeating, and alcohol abuse account for nearly one-third of all deaths in the United States" (Loewenstein, Brennan, & Volpp, 2007, p. 2415). These facts led more than 50 scientific organizations in the United States to declare the first 10 years of the new millennium as the Decade of Behavior. But what is behavior? Before attempting an answer, consider the following scenarios:

1. ***Child with Withdrawn Behavior***   A class of nursery school youngsters is in the playground. While most of the children are playing, one little boy who has been diagnosed with autism sits quietly by himself, making no effort to join in the fun. A teacher tries conscientiously, as he has many times before, to coax this child into playing with the others. But the boy steadfastly maintains his social isolation from the other children.
2. ***Tardiness***   Cathy is a 7-year-old girl with very poor visual–motor coordination. She attends a school for children with developmental disabilities. Although she is able to take off her coat and boots and put them in their proper place each morning, she takes a great deal of time to do so, often spending as much as an hour in the coatroom. Her teachers fear that this slowness is interfering with Cathy's development of self-reliance. However, they are at a loss as to what to do about the situation because none of their urgings makes the child move any faster.
3. ***Littering***   Tom and Sally have just arrived at the place where they intend to set up camp and are looking in disgust and amazement at the litter left by previous campers. "Don't they care about the environment?" asks Sally. "If people keep this up," Tom says, "there won't be any nature left for anyone to enjoy." Sadly, they tell each other that something should be done about the problem, but neither can say what would solve it.

4. *Ineffective Studying*   With two term papers due next week and a midterm exam at the same time, Sam is wondering how he is ever going to make it through his first year at university. The week before the exam, he gets practically no sleep because he is cramming every night and just barely manages a C minus on the test. But neither term paper is finished, and he is almost sure to lose marks for lateness even if his professors accept his overdue papers.

5. *Writing a Novel*   Karen works in a bank, but her real ambition is to write a novel. Although most of her evenings and weekends are relatively free, she has not yet begun to write. Instead she spends all of her spare time checking her favorite blogs, text messaging her friends, cooking, exercising, and going out on dates. Unfortunately, it is becoming more and more apparent that Karen's ambition will never be realized.

6. *Speeding*   Accidents frequently occur on the highway approach into Pleasant City. Despite clearly posted signs to reduce speed, many motorists fail to slow down until they are well within the city limits, and there have been quite a few close calls in which cars speeding into the city have just narrowly missed a child. If this continues, eventually some child is going to be seriously hurt or killed.

7. *A Phobia*   Albert is a normal, healthy young man, but he has one quirk: He is terrified of airplanes. If you were to ask him why he is afraid of them, he would not be able to tell you. Rationally, he knows that it is unlikely that anything bad will happen to him when he is in one. His airplane phobia is not only inconvenient but also very embarrassing because his friends do not seem to understand why he will not travel in an airplane to go on vacation with them.

8. *Migraines*   While preparing dinner for her family, Betty was vaguely aware of a familiar feeling creeping up on her. Then, all at once, she felt nauseous. She looked around fearfully, knowing from past experience what to expect. "Tom, Joe," she called to her sons watching TV in the living room, "you'll have to finish fixing dinner yourselves—I'm having another attack." She then rushed up to the bedroom, quickly drew the blinds, and lay down on the bed. Finally, after about 6 hours of almost unbearable pain, her symptoms subsided, and she was able to rejoin her family. But the threat of "another one of Mom's migraines" that could occur again unpredictably at any time still hung over the heads of Betty's family.

9. *Staff Management*   Jack and Brenda were having coffee one morning at the Dairy Queen restaurant they owned. "We're going to have to do something about the evening staff," said Brenda. "When I came in this morning, the ice cream machine wasn't properly cleaned and the cups and lids weren't restocked." "That's only the tip of the iceberg," said Jack. "You should see the grill! Maybe we need some kind of a staff motivation program. We need something!"

10. *Athletic Performance*   A young gymnast performs her routines extremely well at practices. But she's easily distracted at competitions, has trouble focusing on her performance, and usually performs below potential. Neither she nor her coach knows how to solve the problem.

11. *Adapting in a Personal Care Home*   Mary's mom is 88 years old and has lived alone for the past seven years. Unfortunately, it has become increasingly clear that she can no longer care for herself. Mary has made arrangements for her mom to move to a personal care home, but her mom is extremely anxious about "living with strangers." Mary doesn't know how to help her mom cope with the anxiety.

   Close inspection shows that each of these vignettes involves some sort of human behavior. Together, they illustrate the range of problems with which specialists in behavior modification are trained to deal. Each of these types of behavioral problems and many others are discussed in the following pages. Behavior modification, as you will see, is applicable to the entire range of human behavior.

WHAT IS BEHAVIOR?

Before we can talk about behavior modification, we must first ask, what do we mean by **behavior**? Some commonly used synonyms include *activity, action, performance, responding, response,* and *reaction.* Essentially, behavior is anything that a person says or does. Technically, behavior is any muscular, glandular, or electrical activity of an organism. (**Note to reader: Key terms appear in bold type. We encourage you to master their definitions as you encounter them.**) Is the color of someone's eyes behavior? Is blinking behavior? Are the clothes someone is wearing behavior? Is dressing behavior? If you said no to the first and third questions and yes to the second and fourth, we are in agreement. One of the goals of this book is to encourage you to begin thinking and talking very specifically about behavior.

   How about getting an A in a behavior modification course, or losing 10 pounds; are those behaviors? No, those are *products of behavior.* The behavior that produces an A is studying effectively. The behaviors that lead to weight loss are resisting overeating and exercising more.

   Walking, talking out loud, throwing a baseball, yelling at someone—all are *overt* (visible) behaviors that could be observed and recorded by an individual other than the one performing the behavior. As will be discussed in later chapters, the term *behavior* can also refer to *covert* (private, internal) activities that cannot be readily observed by others. All behavior is potentially observable. However, private or covert behaviors do *not* typically refer just to behaviors done in private, such as undressing in one's bedroom with the door locked and the blinds closed. Nor do they usually refer to secretive actions, such as cheating on an exam. Rather, in the field of behavior modification, they more commonly refer to activities that occur "within one's skin" and that therefore require special instruments or procedures for others to observe. For example, just before stepping onto the ice at an important competition, a figure skater might think, "I hope I don't fall," and he or she is likely to feel nervous (increased heart rate, etc.). Thinking and feeling are private behaviors and are discussed further in Chapters 15, 27, and 28. Covert as well as overt behaviors can be influenced by the techniques of behavior modification.

   Sometimes we think in words, called *private self-talk,* as illustrated by the figure skater in the previous paragraph. At other times, we think by imagining. If I were to ask you to close your eyes and imagine a clear, blue sky with a few white fluffy clouds, you would be able to do so. Imagining and private self-talk, in addition to being called *covert behaviors,* are sometimes referred to as *cognitive behaviors.* (Techniques for dealing with cognitive behaviors—called *cognitive behavior therapy*—are discussed in Chapter 27.)

   Characteristics of behavior that can be measured are called *dimensions of behavior.* The *duration* of a behavior is the length of time that it lasts (e.g., Mary studied for 1 hour). The *frequency* of a behavior is the number of instances that occur in a given period of time (e.g., Frank planted five tomato plants in his garden in 30 minutes). The *intensity* or *force* of a behavior refers to the physical effort or energy involved in emitting the behavior (e.g., Mary has a strong grip when shaking hands). Strategies for measuring dimensions of behavior are discussed in Chapter 21.

Study Questions

(Note to reader: You will encounter study questions in each chapter. When you come to a set of questions, we encourage you to (a) pause in your reading of the chapter, (b) prepare answers to those questions, and (c) learn those answers. Doing so will help you to master the content of this book.)

1. What is behavior, generally and technically? Give three synonyms for *behavior.*
2. Distinguish between behavior and products of behavior. Give an example of a behavior and a product of that behavior that are not in this chapter.
3. Distinguish between overt and covert behaviors. Give two examples of each that are not in this chapter.
4. What are cognitive behaviors? Give two examples.
5. Describe two dimensions of behavior. Give an example of each.

SUMMARY LABELS FOR BEHAVIOR

While we have all learned to talk about behavior in various ways, we often do so in quite general terms. Words such as *honest, carefree, hardworking, unreliable, independent, selfish, incompetent, kind, graceful, unsociable,* and *nervous* are summary labels for human actions, but they do not refer to specific behaviors. If, for example, you were to describe a man as nervous, others might know generally what you mean. But they would not know if you were referring to that person's tendency to chew his fingernails frequently, his constant fidgeting when sitting in a chair, the tendency for his left eye to twitch when talking to someone of the opposite sex, or some other behavior. In later chapters, we discuss ways to measure specific dimensions of behavior.

Traditional helping specialists who are not trained as behavior modifiers often use general summary terms such as *intelligence, attitudes,* and *creativity.* Behavior modifiers, on the other hand, talk more precisely about behavior. What do we mean when we say that a person is *intelligent*? To many people, intelligence is something that a person is born with, a sort of "inherited brain power" or innate capacity for learning. But we never observe or directly measure any such thing. On an intelligence test, for example, we simply measure people's behavior—their answers to questions—as they take the test. The word *intelligent* is best used in its adjective form (e.g., "he is an *intelligent* speaker," "his speech is *intelligent*") or its adverb form (e.g., "she writes *intelligently*") to describe how people behave under certain conditions, such as taking a test, not as a noun for some "thing." Perhaps a person described as intelligent readily solves problems that others find difficult, performs well on most course examinations, reads many books, talks knowledgeably about many topics, or gets a high score on an intelligence test. Depending on who uses the word, *intelligence* can mean any or all of these—but whatever it means, it refers to ways of behaving. Therefore, in this book, we avoid using the word *intelligence* as a noun. (For further discussion of a behavioral approach to intelligence, see Williams, Myerson, and Hale, 2008.)

What about an *attitude*? Suppose that Johnny's teacher, Ms. Smith, reports that he has a bad attitude toward school. What does Ms. Smith mean by this? Perhaps she means that Johnny frequently skips school, refuses to do his classwork when he does attend, and swears at the teacher. Whatever she means when she talks about Johnny's "bad attitude," it is clearly his behavior with which she is really concerned.

Creativity also refers to the kinds of behavior that a person is likely to display under certain circumstances. The creative individual frequently emits behaviors that are novel or unusual and that, at the same time, have desirable effects. (For an extensive behavioral approach to creativity, see Marr, 2003.)

Other psychological terms, such as *developmental disabilities* (discussed further in Chapter 2), *autism,* and so on, also are labels for certain ways of behaving. They do not refer to invisible mental abnormalities. How do psychologists and other helping specialists decide that someone has a *developmental disability*? They make the decision primarily because they might observe that the person, at a certain age,

cannot tie shoelaces

is not toilet trained

eats only with fingers or a spoon

performs on psychological tests in such a way that the combined answers yield an IQ score of 75 or less

How do specialists diagnose a child as showing an *autistic disorder*? They make this decision on the basis of certain behaviors that they observe. For example, they might observe that a child

frequently mimics particular questions rather than answering with an appropriate statement (more generally, shows impaired communication);

when called, does not respond, or moves away from the person calling (more generally, shows impaired social behavior);

engages in various self-stimulatory behaviors, such as rocking back and forth, twirling objects with the fingers, or fluttering the hands in front of his or her eyes;

performs much below average on a variety of self-care tasks, such as dressing, grooming, and feeding.

Other summary labels commonly used to refer to psychological problems include *attention-deficit/hyperactivity disorder, anxiety, depression, low self-esteem, road rage, interpersonal difficulties,* and *sexual dysfunction.* Why are summary terms or labels for behavior patterns so frequently used in psychology and in everyday life? First, they may be useful for quickly providing general information about how an individual might perform. We would expect that a 10-year-old child who has been labeled as having a severe developmental disability, for example, would not be able to read even at the first-grade level. Second, the labels may imply that a particular treatment program will be helpful. Someone with road rage might be encouraged to take an anger-management program. Someone who is unassertive might benefit from an assertiveness training course.

However, the use of summary labels also has disadvantages. One is that they may lead to *pseudo-explanations* of behavior (*pseudo* means false). For example, a child who inverts words while reading, such as *saw* for *was*, might be labeled as *dyslexic*. If we ask why the child inverts words, and we are given the answer, "Because he is dyslexic," then the summary label for the behavior has been used as a *pseudo-explanation* for the behavior. (Another name for pseudo-explanation is *circular reasoning*.) A second disadvantage of labeling is that labels can negatively affect the way an individual might be treated. Teachers, for example, may be less likely to encourage children to persist in problem solving if they have been given the label *mentally retarded* (Bromfield, Bromfield, & Weiss, 1988; Bromfield, Weisz, & Messer, 1986). Another disadvantage of labeling is that it may direct our focus to an individual's problem behaviors rather than to her or his strengths. Suppose, for example, that a teenager consistently fails to make his bed but reliably mows the lawn and places the garbage cans on the street on pickup days. If the parents describe their son as lazy, that label may cause them to focus more on the problem behavior than to praise the positive behaviors. In some societies, racial minorities have been given the negative label *lazy* even when they were the ones doing most of the hard physical work in those societies.

In this book, we strongly stress the importance of defining all types of problems in terms of **behavioral deficits** (too little behavior of a particular type) or **behavioral excesses** (too much behavior of a particular type). We do so for several reasons. First, we want to help you to avoid the problems of using general summary labels discussed earlier. Second, regardless of the labels attached to an individual, it is *behavior* that causes concern—and behavior that must be treated to alleviate the problem. Certain behaviors that parents see and hear, or fail to see and hear, cause them to seek professional help for their children. Certain behaviors teachers see and hear prompt them to seek professional help for their students. Certain behaviors that can be seen or heard cause governments to set up institutions, clinics, community treatment centers, and special programs. And certain behaviors that you emit might cause you to embark on a self-improvement program. Third, specific procedures are now available that can be used to improve behavior in schools, in workplaces, and in home settings—in fact, just about anywhere that there is a need to establish more desirable behaviors. These techniques are referred to collectively as *behavior modification*.

Study Questions

6. From a behavioral point of view, to what do terms such as *intelligence* or *creativity* refer? Give an example of each.

7. What are three disadvantages of using summary labels to refer to individuals or their actions? Give an example of each.

8. What is a behavioral deficit? Give two examples that are not in this chapter.

9. What is a behavioral excess? Give two examples that are not in this chapter.

10. Why do behavior modifiers describe behavioral problems in terms of specific behavioral deficits or excesses?

WHAT IS BEHAVIOR MODIFICATION?

The most important characteristic of behavior modification is *its strong emphasis on defining problems in terms of behavior that can be measured in some way and using changes in the behavioral measure of the problem as the best indicator of the extent to which the problem is being helped.*

Another characteristic of behavior modification is that *its treatment procedures and techniques are ways of altering an individual's current environment* to help that individual function more fully. The physical variables that make up a person's environment are called *stimuli* (plural of *stimulus*). More specifically, **stimuli** are the people, objects, and events currently present in one's immediate surroundings that impinge on one's sense receptors and that can affect behavior. For example, the teacher, chalkboard, other students, and the furniture in a classroom are all potential stimuli in a student's environment in a classroom setting. An individual's own behavior can also be a part of the environment influencing that individual's subsequent behavior. When hitting a forehand shot in tennis, for example, both the sight of the ball coming near and the behavior of completing your backswing provide stimuli for you to complete the forehand shot and hit the ball over the net. Things that a therapist might say to a client are also a part of that client's environment. But behavior modification is much more than *talk therapy* or *verbal psychotherapy* (such as psychoanalysis or client-centered therapy). Although both behavior modifiers and "talk" therapists talk to their clients, their approaches to therapy differ in several important ways. One difference between behavior modifiers and talk therapists is that a behavior modifier is frequently actively involved in restructuring a client's daily environment to strengthen appropriate behavior rather than spending a great deal of time discussing the client's past experiences. While knowledge of a client's past experiences might provide some useful information for designing a treatment program, knowledge of the current environmental variables that control the client's behavior is necessary for designing an effective behavioral treatment. Another difference between behavior modifiers and talk therapists is that a behavior modifier frequently gives homework assignments to clients in which they change their own everyday environments for therapeutic purposes. Such homework assignments are discussed in Chapters 26, 27, and 28.

A third characteristic of behavior modification is that *its methods and rationales can be described precisely.* This makes it possible for behavior modifiers to read descriptions of procedures used by their colleagues, replicate them, and get essentially the same results. It also makes it easier to teach behavior modification procedures than has been the case with many other forms of psychological treatment.

As a consequence of the third characteristic, a fourth characteristic of behavior modification is that *the techniques of behavior modification are often applied by individuals in everyday life.* Although, as you will read in Chapters 2, 28, and 30, appropriately trained professionals and paraprofessionals use behavior modification in helping others, the precise description of behavior modification techniques makes it possible for individuals such as parents, teachers, coaches, and others to apply behavior modification to help individuals in everyday situations.

A fifth characteristic of behavior modification is that, to a large extent, *the techniques stem from basic and applied research in the science of learning in general and the principles of operant and Pavlovian conditioning in particular* (e.g., see Pear, 2001). Therefore, in Part II, we cover these principles in considerable detail and show how they are applicable to various types of behavior problems.

Two final characteristics are that *behavior modification emphasizes scientific demonstration that a particular intervention was responsible for a particular behavior change, and it places high value on accountability for everyone involved in behavior modification programs:* client, staff, administrators, consultants, and so on.[1]

Thus, **behavior modification** involves the systematic application of learning principles and techniques to assess and improve individuals' covert and overt behaviors in order to enhance their daily functioning.

WHAT IS BEHAVIORAL ASSESSMENT?

In the preceding section, we said that the most important characteristic of behavior modification is its use of measures of behavior to judge whether or not an individual's behavior had been improved by a behavior modification program. Behaviors to be improved in a behavior modification program are frequently called **target behaviors.** For example, if a university student sets a goal of studying two hours out of class for each hour spent in class, studying is the target behavior.

Behavioral assessment involves the collection and analysis of information and data in order NOTE 1 to (1) identify and describe target behaviors; (2) identify possible causes of the behavior; (3) guide the selection of an appropriate behavioral treatment; and (4) evaluate treatment outcome. One type

---

[1] We thank Rob Hawkins for bringing these last two points to our attention.

of behavioral assessment that has become especially important is termed *functional analysis*. Essentially, this approach (discussed in Chapter 22) involves isolating through experimentation the causes of problem behavior and removing or reversing them. As the interest in behavior modification has expanded during the past five decades, so has the demand for guidelines for conducting behavioral assessments. For more information on behavioral assessment, refer to Chapters 20, 21, and 23, which cover the topic in detail, or the book by Bellack and Hersen (1998).

Study Questions

11. What are stimuli? Describe two examples that are not in this chapter.
12. List seven defining characteristics of behavior modification.
13. Define *behavior modification.*
14. What is meant by the term *target behavior*? Give an example of a target behavior of yours that you would like to improve. Is your target behavior a behavioral deficit to increase or a behavioral excess to decrease?
15. Define *behavioral assessment.*

BEHAVIOR MODIFICATION AND APPLIED BEHAVIOR ANALYSIS

The term **behavior analysis** refers to the scientific study of laws that govern the behavior of human beings and other animals. You might think of behavior analysis as the science on which behavior modification is based. A term that is closely related to behavior modification is *applied behavior analysis*. In fact, some authors maintain that behavior modification and applied behavior analysis are "two terms used to identify virtually identical fields" (e.g., Miltenberger, 2008). Similarly, other writers note that many practitioners who originally referred to themselves as *behavior modifiers* or *behavioral engineers* now refer to themselves as *applied behavior analysts* (Bailey & Burch, 2006). So, what is the difference between behavior modification and applied behavior analysis? To appreciate the difference, you need to consider the historical development of behavior modification and applied behavior analysis.

As described in more detail in Chapter 29, the formative years of behavior modification were the 1950s and 1960s. Some practitioners in that era referred to themselves as *behavior modifiers*. The first book with behavior modification in the title was published in 1965. In 1968, the first issue of the *Journal of Applied Behavior Analysis* was published. In an important editorial article in that issue, Baer, Wolf, and Risley identified the **dimensions of applied behavior analysis** as including: (a) a focus on measurable behavior that is socially significant (e.g., littering, parenting skills, language learning with persons with developmental disabilities); (b) a strong emphasis on the learning principles frequently referred to as *operant conditioning* (described in Chapters 3–13) to develop treatment strategies; (c) an attempt to clearly demonstrate that the applied treatment was responsible for the improvement in the behavior that was measured; and (d) a demonstration of generalizable and long-lasting improvements in behavior. These defining characteristics of applied behavior analysis are very similar to the characteristics of behavior modification we listed in the section "What Is Behavior Modification?" And we, the authors of this book, are very comfortable referring to ourselves either as *behavior modifiers* or *applied behavior analysts*. However, as indicated in the fifth characteristic of behavior modification listed previously, the techniques of behavior modification use the principles of both operant *and* Pavlovian conditioning (described in Chapters 14 and 15) while applied behavior analysis NOTE 2 relies largely on operant conditioning. Moreover, as indicated later in this chapter (and in Chapter 29), the term *behavior modification* encompasses the terms *behavior therapy* and *cognitive behavior therapy.* Thus, although the terms *applied behavior analysis* and *behavior modification* are often used interchangeably, the latter term has acquired a broader meaning.

BEHAVIOR MODIFICATION, BEHAVIOR THERAPY, AND COGNITIVE BEHAVIOR THERAPY

As discussed in Chapter 29, which gives a brief history of behavior modification, the term *behavior therapy* emerged in the late 1950s to refer to treatment procedures based on Pavlovian conditioning to treat anxiety disorders. Subsequently, the term has come to refer to behavior modification carried out on dysfunctional behavior (e.g., anxiety disorders, depression, marital discord) in clinical settings. As discussed in Chapter 27, cognitive therapists in the 1970s began to focus on treating dysfunctional behavior by changing unproductive, debilitating thought patterns that were considered to be responsible for the dysfunctional behavior. This approach came to be referred to as *cognitive behavior modification* or *cognitive behavior therapy.*

To summarize this and the preceding section: Although the terms *applied behavior analysis* and *behavior modification* are sometimes used interchangeably, the latter is a broader term. *Behavior modification* encompasses applied behavior analysis, behavior therapy, and cognitive behavior therapy (the historical use of these and similar terms is discussed in Chapters 27, 28, and 29.) Behavior modification includes all explicit applications of behavior principles to improve an individual's covert and overt behaviors—whether or not in clinical settings and whether or not controlling variables have been explicitly demonstrated. Related terms that you may encounter include *behavior modifier, behavior analyst, behavior manager, behavioral engineer,* and *performance manager.* These terms refer to an individual who deliberately applies behavior principles to improve behavior, whether that individual is a teacher, parent, spouse, peer, roommate, supervisor, colleague, psychologist, psychiatrist, social worker, or person modifying his or her own behavior. It should be noted, however, that persons who apply behavior modification professionally are required to obtain the necessary certifications for their respective professions.

SOME MISCONCEPTIONS ABOUT BEHAVIOR MODIFICATION

You probably encountered the term *behavior modification* before reading this book. Unfortunately, because a number of myths or misconceptions about this area exist, some of what you have heard is likely false. Consider the following statements.

Myth 1: Use of rewards by behavior modifiers to change behavior is bribery.

Myth 2: Behavior modification involves the use of drugs, psychosurgery, and electroconvulsive therapy.

Myth 3: Behavior modification changes only symptoms but doesn't get at the underlying problems.

Myth 4: Behavior modification can be applied to deal with simple problems, such as toilet training children or overcoming fear of heights, but it is not applicable for changing complex problems such as low self-esteem or depression.

Myth 5: Behavior modifiers are cold and unfeeling and don't develop empathy with their clients.

Myth 6:   Behavior modifiers deal only with observable behavior; they don't deal with thoughts and feelings of clients.

Myth 7:   Behavior modification is outdated.

In various sections throughout this book, you will encounter evidence to dispel these myths or misconceptions.

THE APPROACH OF THIS BOOK

The main purpose of this book is to describe behavior modification techniques in an enjoyable, readable, and practical manner. Because it has been written for people in various helping professions as well as for students, we intend to help readers learn not merely about behavior modification but also how to use it to overcome behavioral deficits and excesses.

"Wait a minute," you may say. "From many of your examples it sounds as if this book is intended primarily for people concerned with observable behavior of individuals with severe handicaps." In answer to such an observation, we wish to point out that the behavior modification procedures described in this volume can be used to change any individual's behavior. Even people who are normal or average in most respects usually have some behavior that they would like to improve. Behavior that someone would like to improve can be classified as either behavioral deficits or behavioral excesses and can be overt or covert. Following are examples of each type.

Examples of Behavioral Deficits

1. A child does not pronounce words clearly and does not interact with other children.
2. A teenager does not complete homework assignments, help around the house, work in the yard, or discuss problems and difficulties with her parents.
3. An adult does not pay attention to traffic regulations while driving, thank others for courtesies and favors, or meet his or her spouse at agreed-upon times.
4. A basketball player, encouraged by the coach to visualize the ball going into the net just before a foul shot, is unable to do so.

Examples of Behavioral Excesses

1. A child frequently gets out of bed and throws tantrums at bedtime, throws food on the floor at mealtime, and plays with the buttons on the TV.
2. A teenager frequently interrupts conversations between her parents and other adults, spends hours text messaging and talking on her cell phone, and uses abusive language.
3. An adult watches television continuously, frequently eats candy and other junk food between meals, smokes one cigarette after another, and bites his fingernails.
4. A golfer often thinks negatively (e.g., "If I miss this one, I'll lose!") and experiences considerable anxiety (i.e., heart pounding, palms sweating) just before important shots.

To identify a behavior as excessive or deficient, we must consider the context in which it occurs. For example, a child drawing on paper is showing appropriate behavior, but most parents would consider it a behavioral excess if the child repeatedly draws on the living room wall. A normal teenager might interact appropriately with members of the same sex but be extremely embarrassed and have difficulty talking to members of the opposite sex—a behavioral deficit. Some behavioral excesses—for example, self-injurious behavior—are inappropriate no matter what the context (although with some imagination, one could think of extreme situations in which even self-injurious behavior would be appropriate). In most cases, however, the point at which a particular behavior is considered deficient or excessive is determined primarily by the practices of one's culture and the ethical views of concerned individuals. The relationship between cultural practices, ethics, and behavior modification is discussed in Chapter 30.

To summarize, the behavior modification approach focuses primarily on behavior and involves current environmental (as opposed to medical, pharmacological, or surgical) manipula-   **NOTE 3** tions to change behavior. Individuals who are labeled as having a developmental disability, autism, schizophrenia, depression, or an anxiety disorder, for example, are individuals who show behavioral deficits or excesses. Similarly, individuals who are labeled lazy, unmotivated, selfish, incompetent, or uncoordinated are also individuals who show behavioral deficits or excesses. Behavior modification consists of a set of procedures that can be used to change behavior so that these individuals will be considered less of whatever label has been given them. Some traditional psychologists who are not trained as behavior modifiers have shown an excessive interest in labeling and classifying individuals. Regardless of the label given, however, the behavior of the individuals who are labeled is still there and is still being influenced by their environments. The mother in Figure 1–1, for example, is still concerned about what to do with her child and how to handle the problem. That is where behavior modification comes in.

FIGURE 1–1 The experts "helping" mother with her child?

After the overview in the next chapter, Part II (Chapters 3–16) describes the principles and procedures of behavior modification. In essence, principles are procedures that have a consistent effect and are so simple that they cannot be broken down into simpler ones. Principles are like laws in advanced sciences. Most procedures used in behavior modification are combinations of the principles of behavior modification. These principles are almost never used in isolation from other principles in practical applications, especially with highly verbal individuals. Therefore, to better illustrate the principles under discussion, we have selected relatively simple lead cases for the chapters in Part II. After illustrating the principles involved in such cases, we elaborate on how these principles are used with other types of problems. We also give numerous illustrations of how these principles influence normal behavior in everyday life. Later parts of the book show how highly complex programs are built from the principles and procedures introduced in Part II. In addition to these detailed programming strategies, we describe ethical issues regarding their use. We hope that this book provides satisfactory answers to teachers, counselors, psychologists, students, teenagers, fathers, mothers, and others who say, "Thank you, Ms. or Mr. Expert, but what can I do about it?" (This is the question asked by the mother in Figure 1–1.) We hope also that the book will give introductory students of behavior modification an understanding of why the procedures are effective.

Study Questions

16. What does the term *behavior analysis* refer to?
17. List four dimensions of *applied behavior analysis*.
18. As the terms are used in this book, what is the difference between *applied behavior analysis* and *behavior modification*?
19. In general, what does the term *behavior therapy* mean?
20. In general, what is the focus of *cognitive behavior therapy*?
21. List four myths or misconceptions about behavior modification.

Application Exercises

In most of the chapters of this book, we provide exercises for you to apply the concepts you learned in the chapters. Generally, we present two types of application exercises: (1) exercises that involve the behavior of others and (2) self-modification exercises in which you apply the behavior modification concepts you have learned to your own behavior.

A. EXERCISE INVOLVING OTHERS

Consider someone other than yourself. From your point of view, identify:

1. two behavioral deficits for that person to overcome
2. two behavioral excesses to decrease

For each example, indicate whether you have described:

a. a specific behavior or a general summary label
b. an observable behavior or a covert behavior
c. a behavior or the outcome of a behavior

B. SELF-MODIFICATION EXERCISE

Apply Exercise A to yourself.

Notes and Extended Discussion

1. Behavioral assessment emerged as an alternative to traditional psychodiagnostic assessment in the 1960s. Psychoanalytic approaches to abnormal behavior originated with Sigmund Freud and others who viewed abnormal behavior as a symptom of an underlying mental disturbance in a personality mechanism. A major purpose of traditional diagnostic assessment was to identify the type of mental disorder assumed to underlie abnormal behavior. To help therapists diagnose clients with different types of presumed mental illness, the American Psychiatric Association developed the *Diagnostic and Statistical Manual of Mental Disorders* (*DSM-I*) (American Psychiatric Association, 1952). The manual was later revised as the *DSM-II* in 1968, the *DSM-III* in 1980, the *DSM-III-R* (*R* is for revised) in 1987, the *DSM-IV* in 1994, and the *DSM-IV-TR* (*TR* is for text revision) in 2000. Because they did not agree with Freud's model of abnormal behavior and because there was little evidence that diagnoses based on that model were reliable or valid, behavior modifiers used the first three DSMs very little (Hersen, 1976). However, the *DSM-IV* improved considerably over the earlier manuals in several respects. First, it is based primarily on research rather than on Freudian theory. Second, individual disorders (e.g., obsessive-compulsive disorder, generalized anxiety disorder, major depression) are based on categories of problem behaviors. Third, the *DSM-IV* uses a multidimensional recording system that provides extra information for planning treatment, managing a case, and predicting outcomes. With the improvements in the *DSM-IV* (now the *DSM-IV-TR*), behavior modifiers in a variety of settings are increasingly using it to classify clients. They do so in part because official diagnoses are usually required by clinics, hospitals, schools, and social service agencies before treatment can be offered and because health insurance companies reimburse practitioners on the basis of the diagnoses in the *DSM-IV-TR*. However, it is important to remember that because a *DSM-IV-TR* diagnosis (such as autistic disorder) refers to an individual's behaviors, it is likely to result in labeling the individual (e.g., autistic), which may lead to the disadvantages of labeling mentioned in this chapter. Moreover, in spite of the implication that all individuals with the same label (e.g., autistic) are the same, they are not. To avoid problems associated with labeling, we should use what has come to be referred to as *people first language* when describing individuals with problems. For example, in the case of autism, we should describe the client as a child with autism rather than an autistic child. (As expressed by Malott, 2008, an even better approach would be to refer to the client as a child with autistic behaviors.) Also, in addition to obtaining a *DSM-IV-TR* diagnosis for an individual, we should always conduct detailed behavioral assessments to obtain the necessary information for designing the most effective, individualized treatment program.

2. If you are interested in applied behavior analysis, you might want to visit the website of the Association for Behavior Analysis International (www.abainternational.org), an organization whose mission is "to contribute to the well-being of society by developing, enhancing, and supporting the growth and vitality of the science of behavior analysis through research, education, and practice (*ABAI Newsletter*, 2008, No. 3, p. 1). You might also want to visit the Behavior Analysis Online (BAO) website. BAO is a special interest group of ABAI that is dedicated to educating the public about behavior analysis and is a resource for professionals involved in applied behavior analysis. The BAO website also provides access to eight online journals providing research and applications in various subareas of applied behavior analysis; more journals are planned.

3. Because of this emphasis on the environment, behaviorists are often accused of denying the importance of genetics in determining behavior. This mistaken impression may stem in part from the writings of John B. Watson (1913), who, dissatisfied with the introspective

psychology of his day, argued that the correct subject matter of psychology was observable behavior and only observable behavior. Watson also advocated an extreme form of environmentalism, summarized in the following famous (or infamous) claim:

> Give me a dozen healthy infants, and my own specified world to bring them up in and I'll guarantee to take any one at random and train him to become any type of specialist I might select—doctor, lawyer, artist, merchant-chief, and, yes, even beggarman and thief, regardless of his talents, penchants, tendencies, abilities, vocations, and race of his ancestors. (Watson, 1930, p. 104)

However, Skinner (1974) pointed out that Watson himself admitted that this claim was exaggerated and that he did not disregard the importance of genetics. An appreciation by behavior modifiers of the importance of genetics was indicated by the publication of a miniseries on behavioral genetics in the journal *Behavior Therapy* (1986, Vol. 17, No. 4). Included in the miniseries were articles on cardiovascular stress and genetics, childhood obesity and genetics, smoking and genetics, and alcoholism and genetics (see also Turner, Cardon, & Hewitt, 1995). However, even though the influence of heredity may increase the susceptibility of an individual to certain behavioral problems such as obesity or alcoholism, an individual's environment still plays a major role in the development and maintenance of behaviors that lead to such problems.

Study Questions on Notes

1. What is the full title of the *DSM-IV-TR*? In two or three sentences, what is it?
2. Give five reasons why many behavior modifiers use the *DSM-IV-TR*.
3. What is a potential disadvantage of using the *DSM-IV-TR*?
4. What is meant by "people first language" when describing individuals with problems? Illustrate with an example.
5. Do behavior modifiers deny the importance of genetics? Discuss.

2

Areas of Application: An Overview

The value of behavior modification techniques for improving a wide variety of behaviors has been amply demonstrated in thousands of research reports. Successful applications have been documented with populations ranging from persons with profound learning disabilities to the highly intelligent, from the very young to the very old, and from controlled institutional programs to less controlled community settings. Modified behaviors range from simple motor skills to complex problem solving. Applications of behavior modification are occurring with ever-increasing frequency in areas such as education, social work, nursing, clinical psychology, psychiatry, community psychology, medicine, rehabilitation, business, industry, and sports. This chapter briefly describes major areas of application in which behavior modification has a solid foundation and a promising future.

PARENTING AND CHILD MANAGEMENT

Being a parent is a challenging job. In addition to meeting children's basic needs, parents are totally responsible for their children's initial behavioral development. That responsibility is shared with teachers and others as the children develop through early childhood, adolescence, and into adulthood. There are numerous applications of behavior modification to teach parents ways to improve their child-rearing practices. Behavioral techniques have been applied to help parents teach their children to walk, develop their children's initial language skills, toilet train their children, and influence their children to do household chores (Kendall, 2000; Meadows, 1996). Parents have also been taught behavioral strategies for decreasing problem behaviors, such as nail biting, temper tantrums, aggressive behaviors, ignoring rules, failure to comply with parents' requests, and frequent arguing (Christopherson & Mortweet, 2001; Schaefer & Briesmeister, 1998; Serketich & Dumas, 1996). Allen and Warzak (2000) provided a useful analysis of conditions that strengthen or weaken adherence of parents to effective behavioral programs with their children. Some child and adolescent behavior problems are so complex that, in addition to helping parents work with their children, behaviorally oriented clinical psychologists (called *behavior therapists*; see Chapter 1) treat the problems directly (Blum & Friman, 2000; Christner, Stewart, & Freeman, 2007; Gimpel & Holland, 2003; Hersen & Last, 1999; Wahler, 2007). Also, a program referred to as *Triple P Positive Parenting* is an effective, multilevel parenting program to prevent and offer treatment for severe behavioral, emotional, and developmental problems in children (Graaf, Speetjens, Smit, Wolff, & Tavecchio, 2008). Behavioral strategies have also been developed for helping communities prevent youth violence (Mattaini & McGuire, 2006).

EDUCATION: FROM PRESCHOOL TO UNIVERSITY

Since the early 1960s, behavior modification applications in classrooms have progressed on several fronts. Many applications in elementary school have been designed to change student behaviors that were disruptive or incompatible with academic learning. Out-of-seat behavior, tantrums, aggressive behavior, and excessive socializing have all been successfully dealt with in classroom settings. Other applications have involved modifying academic behavior directly, including oral reading, reading comprehension, composition, spelling, handwriting, and mastering mathematics and science concepts. Considerable success has also been achieved in applications with individuals with special problems, such as learning disabilities, hyperactivity, and attention deficits (Barkley, 1998; Neef & Northup, 2007).

Inroads in the use of behavior modification in physical education have also been made. The progress that has been made includes (a) development of reliable observations for monitoring the behavior of physical education teachers and students to provide usable information on "what's happening in the gym"; (b) increased acceptance by teachers and school administrators of behavioral teaching skills as important components of teacher preparation programs; and (c) increased acceptance of behavioral strategies to help physical educators manage a variety of behavioral difficulties of students (Martin, 1992). For more detailed discussion of behavior modification in physical education, see Siedentop and Tannehill (2000) and Ward (2005).

An important innovation in behavioral approaches to teaching is the Personalized System of Instruction (PSI). It was developed by Fred S. Keller and his colleagues in the United States and Brazil in the 1960s as a behavior modification approach to university teaching (Keller, 1968). Since then it has spread to a wide variety of subject matters and levels of instruction (Keller & Sherman, 1982). The approach has a number of distinctive characteristics that make it possible for teachers to use behavior modification principles to improve classroom instruction. In particular, PSI (also known as the *Keller plan*):

1. identifies the target behaviors or learning requirements for a course in the form of study questions, such as the questions in each chapter in this book
2. requires students to study only a small amount of material before demonstrating mastery, such as the amount of material in one or two chapters that might be studied in a week or two
3. has frequent tests (at least once every week or two) in which students demonstrate their knowledge of the answers to the study questions
4. has mastery criteria so that students must demonstrate mastery at a particular level before going to the next level
5. is nonpunitive in that students are not penalized for failing to demonstrate mastery on a test but simply restudy and try again

6. uses a number of student assistants called *proctors* to score tests immediately and provide feedback to students concerning test performance
7. incorporates a "go-at-your-own-pace" feature in which students are allowed to proceed through the course material at rates that suit their own particular abilities and time demands
8. uses lectures primarily for motivation and demonstration rather than as a major means of **NOTE 1** presenting new information

As originally conceived by Keller (1968), PSI courses can require a good deal of labor to administer, especially with large classes, because of the extensive record keeping that PSI requires. With the rise of computer technology, some instructors have automated much of the PSI procedure to make the approach more efficient. Moreover, some instructors have added electronic backup components, such as videotapes, interactive videodiscs, and computer-delivered tutorials, to increase the efficiency of PSI (Crosbie & Glenn, 1993; Crowell, Quintanar, & Grant, 1981; Hantula, Boyd, & Crowell, 1989; Rae, 1993). In addition, computers enable students to write and submit tests online. Computers allow instructors and proctors to mark tests and provide rapid feedback without the instructor, proctors, and students being in the same location or working on the course at the same time. This can greatly benefit students who are unable to attend classes because of their location, their job, or a disability.

At the University of Manitoba, where it has been used for a number of years in several courses, computer-aided PSI (called *CAPSI*) is popular with both on-campus and off-campus students (Kinsner & Pear, 1988; Pear & Crone-Todd, 1999; Pear & Kinsner, 1988; Pear & Martin, 2004; Pear & Novak, 1996; Springer & Pear, 2008). An innovative feature of CAPSI is the use of students who have mastered a given unit of study material to serve as peer reviewers for that study unit. Studies of CAPSI courses have demonstrated measurable feedback accuracy by peer reviewers and compliance with feedback by students (Martin, Pear, & Martin, 2002a, b). In addition, students in a CAPSI course receive much more substantive feedback than would be possible in a course taught using traditional methods (Pear & Crone-Todd, 2002). A recent study shows that it enhances both learning and critical thinking (Svenningsen, 2009). CAPSI is now used at several universities to teach a variety of courses. (For more information visit www.capsi.org.)

Alberto and Troutman (2008), Cipani (2004a), and Schloss and Schloss (2004) have published excellent how-to descriptions of behavior modification techniques for teachers. Discussion of behavior analysis and school psychology can be found in Ervin and Ehrhardt (2000) and Frederick, Deitz, Bryceland, and Hummel (2003). Discussions of behavioral approaches to college teaching, including PSI, can be found in L. Austin (2000) and Moran and Malott (2004).

Study Questions

1. List five areas in which behavior modification is being applied.
2. List four behaviors of children that have been improved by the application of behavior modification by parents.
3. List four behaviors in education that have been modified with behavior modification.
4. What is PSI, and who was its founder? State eight characteristics of PSI.
5. Briefly describe how PSI has used computer technology. State two benefits of this use of computer technology.

DEVELOPMENTAL DISABILITIES

Beginning in the 1960s, some of the most dramatic successes of behavior modification have oc-curred in applications to individuals with severe behavioral limitations due to atypical develop-ment in childhood. Two types of atypical developments that have received special attention from behavior modifiers are intellectual disabilities and autism. But before discussing these areas, we provide a brief history of the use of several closely related terms that can be somewhat confusing for a first-time reader.

During the latter half of the 20th century, it was common to use the term *mental retardation* to refer to individuals with intellectual impairments, and it was a standard practice for researchers to classify participants as having profound retardation (IQ below 20 or 25), severe retardation (IQ of 20–25 to 35–40), moderate retardation (IQ of 35–40 to 50–55), or mild retardation (IQ of 50–55 to 70–75) (Conyers, Martin, Martin, & Yu, 2002; Hawkins & Cooper, 1990). During the 1990s, a frequently proposed alternative to the term mental retardation was the term *developmental disability* (Warren, 2000), and that term is commonly used by many professionals today instead of *mental retardation*. However, the Developmental Disabilities Bill of Rights Act in the United States (U.S. Congress, 1984) described a developmental disability as a disability that "(A) is at-tributable to a mental or physical impairment or combination of mental and physical impairments; (B) is manifested before the person attains age twenty-two; (C) is likely to continue indefinitely; (D) results in substantial functional limitations in three or more of the following areas of major life activity, (i) self-care, (ii) receptive and expressive language, (iii) learning, (iv) mobility, (v) self di-rection, (vi) capacity for independent living, and (vii) economic self-sufficiency; and (E) reflects the person's need for a combination and sequence of special, interdisciplinary, or generic care, treatment, or other services which are of life-long or extended duration and are individually planned and coordinated" (p. 2664). According to this last description, developmental disability is obviously broader in meaning than mental retardation. In part because of this consideration, the American Association on Intellectual and Developmental Disabilities (AAIDD), formerly the American Association on Mental Retardation (AAMR)—the name change occurred in 2006—indicated in 2007 that the term *intellectual disability* is preferred for the disability historically re-ferred to as *mental retardation*. In consideration of this history, we view developmental disabilities as a broad area that includes the subareas of intellectual disabilities and autism. (For a discussion of these and other subareas of developmental disabilities, see Graziano, 2002.)

Intellectual Disabilities

Although the AAIDD now prefers *intellectual disability*, it defines the term as it previously had defined mental retardation: "a disability characterized by significant limitations both in intellec-tual functioning and in adaptive behavior as expressed in conceptual, social, and practical adap-tive skills. This disability originates before age 18" (AAMR, 2002, p. 8). AAIDD defines *limited intellectual functioning* as an IQ score that is at least 2 standard deviations below the mean of an appropriate assessment instrument, which would be a score of approximately 70 to 75 or below on some IQ tests. This includes approximately 2.3% of the population.

Before the 1960s, few treatment and training programs for all levels of intellectual disabil-ities were available, and those that did exist were mostly limited to the severe and profound levels. Fortunately, three forces materialized during the 1960s and 1970s that collectively revolu-tionized the education of persons with intellectual disabilities. One force comprised individuals called *normalization advocates,* such as Wolfensberger (1972), who argued that persons with intellectual disabilities should be helped to lead the most normative lives possible and that tradi-tional large institutions were simply not normative. The actions of these normalization advocates led to a deinstitutionalization movement and the development of community living options for persons with intellectual disabilities. The second force comprised civil rights advocates and par-ents of persons with intellectual disabilities who secured the legal right of individuals with severe disabilities to receive as normal an education as possible. This meant that educational programs for persons with intellectual disabilities had to be established in public schools. The third force came primarily through the efforts of behavior modifiers who created the technology that made it possible to dramatically improve the behavior of persons with severe and profound intellectual disabilities.

During the ensuing decades, many studies have demonstrated the effectiveness of behav-ioral techniques for teaching persons with intellectual disabilities behaviors such as toileting, self-help skills (i.e., feeding, dressing, and personal hygiene), social skills, communication skills, vocational skills, leisure-time activities, and a variety of community survival behaviors. Reviews of the literature can be found in such sources as Carr, Coriaty, and Dozier (2000), Cuvo and Davis (2000), Didden (2007), Konarski, Favell, and Favell (1997), and Williams (2004); see also issues of the *Journal of Applied Behavior Analysis.*

Autism

Autistic Disorder, often referred to as *autism,* is characterized as a Pervasive Developmental Disorder in the *Diagnostic and Statistical Manual of Mental Disorders, Fourth Edition, Text Revision (DSM-IV-TR)* (American Psychiatric Association, 2000). Two additional pervasive de-velopmental disorders listed in the *DSM-IV-TR* include Asperger's syndrome and Pervasive Developmental Disorder—Not Otherwise Specified. In practice, reference is often made to *Autism Spectrum Disorders (ASDs),* which encompass the preceding three disorders. However, ASD is not officially defined in the *DSM-IV-TR* or in any other international classification code. According to Fombonne (2007), the prevalence of ASDs is now approximately 1 in 150 children.

Children diagnosed with autism are likely to show some combination of impaired social behavior (e.g., not appearing distressed when their mother leaves the room), impaired communi-cation (e.g., meaningless repetition of words or phrases), abnormal play behaviors, and repetitive self-stimulatory behaviors (e.g., spinning objects in front of their eyes). They are also likely to show some behaviors similar to those of children diagnosed with intellectual disabilities by scor-ing much below average on a variety of self-care tasks, such as dressing, grooming, and feeding.

In the 1960s and 1970s, Ivar Lovaas developed behavioral treatments for children with autism. Using an approach he called *early intensive behavioral intervention (EIBI),* Lovaas (1966, 1977) focused on strategies to teach social behaviors, eliminate self-stimulatory behav-iors, and develop language skills. When EIBI was applied to children with autism less than 30 months old, 50% of those children were able to enter a regular classroom at the normal school age (Lovaas, 1987), and the behavioral treatment produced long-lasting gains (McEachin, Smith, & Lovaas, 1993). Although reviewers have criticized the experimental design limitations of the Lovaas study (e.g., Gresham & MacMillan, 1997; Tews, 2007), subsequent research has con-firmed EIBI as the treatment of choice for children with autism in terms of both cost and effec- **NOTE 2** tiveness (Frea & Vittimberga, 2000; Jacobson, Mulick, & Green, 1998; Matson & Smith, 2008; Ghezzi, Williams, & Carr, 1999). An increasing number of government-funded programs are now providing EIBI for children with autism. In Canada, for example, EIBI programs are cur-rently available in 8 of the 10 provinces.

SCHIZOPHRENIA

> People with schizophrenia may hear voices other people don't hear or they may believe
> that others are reading their minds, controlling their thoughts, or plotting to harm them.
> These experiences are terrifying and can cause fearfulness, withdrawal, or extreme ag-
> itation. People with schizophrenia may not make sense when they talk, may sit for
> hours without moving or talking much, or may seem perfectly fine until they talk about
> what they are really thinking. (National Institute of Mental Health, n.d.)

Beginning with a few case studies in the 1950s, major attention was directed to schizophrenia by behavior therapists in the 1960s and early 1970s (Kazdin, 1978). During the late
1970s and early 1980s, however, interest in this area decreased, and only a small number of
articles on behavior modification were published (Bellack, 1986). There is, nevertheless, clear
evidence of the success of behavior modification treatments with this population. Because inadequate social relationships represent a prime contributor to the poor quality of life experienced
by people with schizophrenia, social skills have been one of the behaviors targeted for change.
Available research indicates considerable success in teaching positive social interactions, communication skills, assertiveness skills, and job-finding skills (Bellack & Hersen, 1993; Bellack &
Muser, 1990; Bellack, Muser, Gingerich, & Agresta, 1997). Cognitive-behavioral techniques
have also been used effectively to reduce or eliminate hallucinations or delusions in persons with
schizophrenia (Bouchard, Vallieres, Roy, & Maziade, 1996). These and other studies strongly indicate that behavior therapy can make a significant contribution to the treatment, management, and
rehabilitation of persons with schizophrenia (Beck, Rector, Stolar, & Grant, 2008; McKinney &
Fiedler, 2004; Wilder & Wong, 2007).

BEHAVIOR THERAPY: BEHAVIOR MODIFICATION IN CLINICAL SETTINGS

Chapters 27 and 28 provide a detailed discussion of the treatment of problems such as anxiety
disorders, obsessive-compulsive disorders, stress-related problems, depression, obesity, marital
problems, sexual dysfunction, and habit disorders. More detailed discussion of these and other
areas of clinical treatment can be found in Antony and Barlow (2004), Barlow (2008), Dougher
(2000), Emmelkamp (2004), Hayes and Bissett (2000), Hayes, Follette, and Linehan (2004), and
Hofmann and Otto (2008).

How common is the use of behavior therapy among clinical psychologists? By the early
1980s, at least half of clinical child psychologists followed a behavioral orientation, and behavior therapy had become one of the top two orientations (about on par with psychoanalysis and
other forms of the psychodynamic orientation) for psychologists treating adults (O'Leary, 1984).
While many clinical psychologists are now likely to qualify their orientation as cognitive behavioral rather than purely behavioral (cognitive behavior therapy is discussed in Chapters 27 and
28), the behavioral approach in general continues to grow.

How effective is behavioral treatment for treating psychological problems? Many studies
have demonstrated that there are definite problem areas (e.g., phobias, obsessive-compulsive disorders, depression) for which specific behavioral procedures are demonstrably superior to other
forms of psychotherapy (Barlow, 2008). What about behavior therapy versus drugs for treating
psychological problems? In the provocative book *Taking America off Drugs,* Stephen Ray
Flora (2007) argues that Americans have been deceived into believing that, whatever one's

psychological problem, there is a drug to cure it. In contrast, he argues that most psychological problems, including eating disorders, phobias, obsessive-compulsive disorder, attention-deficit hyperactivity disorder, depression, schizophrenia, sleep disorders, and various sexual disorders, are behaviorally based, not "neurochemical" or "brain based." He argues further that, for such problems, behavior therapy is more effective than drug treatment. Behavioral treatments for clinical disorders are discussed further in Chapters 27 and 28.

Study Questions

6. What is currently the preferred term for the disability historically referred to as *mental retardation*?

7. Name and briefly describe the three forces that have revolutionized the education of persons with intellectual disabilities since the 1960s.

8. List four behaviors in persons with intellectual disabilities that have been modified by behavior modification.

9. List four behaviors in children with autism that have been modified by behavior modification.

10. List four behaviors in people with schizophrenia that have been modified by behavior modification.

11. Briefly, how effective is behavior therapy with psychological problems?

SELF-MANAGEMENT OF PERSONAL PROBLEMS

Recall some of the problems described in Chapter 1. Sam had difficulty studying and finishing his term papers on time. Karen was not able to get started on that novel she wanted to write. And then there was Albert with his phobia of riding in airplanes. Many people would like to change something about themselves. How about you? Would you like to lose a few pounds? Get into an exercise program? Become more assertive? Are there skills you can learn to help you to modify your behavior? A great deal of progress has been made in the area referred to as *self-management, self-control, self-adjustment, self-modification,* or *self-direction.* Successful self-modification requires a set of skills that can be learned. These skills involve ways of rearranging your environment to control your subsequent behavior. Hundreds of successful self-modification projects directed at problems such as saving money, increasing exercise behavior, improving study habits, and controlling gambling have been reported in the psychological literature (Logue, 1995). Self-modification for personal adjustment is described in more detail in Chapter 26. Extensive discussion of this topic can be found in Watson and Tharp (2007).

MEDICAL AND HEALTH CARE

Traditionally, a person who suffered from chronic headaches, a respiratory disorder, or hypertension would never have seen a psychologist for help with the problem. In the late 1960s, however, psychologists working with physicians began using behavior modification techniques to treat these and other medical problems such as seizure disorders, chronic pain, addictive disorders, and sleep disorders (Doleys, Meredith, & Ciminero, 1982). This launched *behavioral medicine,* a broad interdisciplinary field concerned with the links among health, illness, and behavior (Searight, 1998). Behavioral psychologists practicing behavioral medicine work in close consultation with physicians, nurses, dieticians, sociologists, and other specialists on problems that, until recently, have been considered to be of a purely medical nature. Within behavioral medicine, *health psychology* considers how psychological factors can influence or cause illness and how people can be encouraged to practice healthy behavior to prevent health problems (Taylor, 2003). Health psychologists have applied behavioral principles in five major areas. In addition to the following five areas, Nisbet and Gick (2008) suggest that health psychology can help to save the planet.

1. *Direct Treatment of Medical Problems*   Do you suffer from migraine headaches, backaches, or stomach problems? At one time, it was thought that such problems were of purely a medical nature. But sometimes such problems have a learning component. Health psychologists are continuing the late 1960s trend of developing behavioral techniques to treat symptoms such as these directly (Taylor, 2003). One such technique is called *biofeedback,* which consists of providing immediate information to an individual about that person's physiological processes, such as heart rate, blood pressure, muscle tension, and brain waves. Such information helps the individual to gain control over the physiological process that is monitored. Biofeedback has been successfully used to treat a variety of health problems, including high blood pressure, seizures, chronic headaches, irregular heart beat or arrhythmia, accelerated heart rate or tachycardia, and anxiety (Schwartz & Andrasic, 1998; also see p. 131). Behavioral treatments are also being applied to ameliorate symptoms of other medical problems, such as Parkinson's disease (Mohr et al., 1996) and brain injury (Jacobs, 2000).

2. *Establishing Treatment Compliance*   Do you always keep your appointments with the dentist? Do you always take medication exactly as prescribed by your doctor? Many people do not. Because it is behavior, compliance with medical regimens is a natural for behavior modification (Taylor, 2003). Thus, an important part of health psychology is promoting treatment compliance.

3. *Promotion of Healthy Living*   Do you exercise at least three times per week? Do you eat healthy foods and minimize your consumption of saturated fat, cholesterol, and salt? Do you limit your consumption of alcohol? Do you say no to nicotine and other addictive drugs? If you can answer yes to these questions, and if you can continue to answer yes as the years go by, then you can considerably lengthen your life span (see Figure 2–1). As indicated in Chapter 1, preventable behaviors such as smoking, poor dietary habits, and alcohol abuse are the underlying cause of one-third of all deaths in the United States (see the March 2004 issue of the *Journal of the American Medical Association* and the January 2003 issue of *Behavior Modification*). An important area of behavior modification involves the application of techniques to help people manage their own behaviors to stay healthy, such as by eating moderate-size well-balanced meals and exercising frequently (Bandura, 2004; Taylor, 2003).

4. *Management of Caregivers*   Health psychologists are concerned with the behavior not only of the client or patient but also of those who have an impact on the medical condition of the client. Thus, health psychologists deal with the behavior of the client's family, friends, and various medical staff concerned with the client's health. Changing the behavior of physicians, nurses, psychiatric nurses, occupational therapists, and other medical personnel to improve services provided to patients is receiving increased attention (see, e.g., Clarke & Wilson, 2008; Engelman, Altus, Mosier, & Mathews, 2003).

5. *Stress Management*   Like death and taxes, stress is one of the things that you can be sure of encountering in life. *Stressors* are conditions or events (e.g., being stuck in traffic, lacking sleep, exposure to smog, having pending examinations, owing debts, having marital breakdown, and experiencing serious illness or death in the family) that present coping

FIGURE 2–1 Behavioral strategies have been used effectively to help people persist in physical fitness programs.

difficulties. *Stress reactions* are physiological and behavioral responses, such as fatigue, high blood pressure, and ulcers, that can be brought on by stressors. An important area of health psychology concerns the study of stressors, their effects on behavior, and the development of behavioral strategies for coping with stressors (e.g., Lehrer, Woolfolk, & Sime, 2007; Taylor, 2003). Some of these strategies are described in later chapters.

The broad interdisciplinary field of behavioral medicine and the subfield of health psychology have the potential to make a profound contribution to the efficiency and effectiveness of modern medicine and health care. For additional reading in this area, see issues of the *Journal of Behavioral Medicine* and the books by Cummings, O'Donohue, and Ferguson (2003) and Taylor (2003).

GERONTOLOGY

Do you want to know what it's like to be old? Then "you should smear dirt on your glasses, stuff cotton in your ears, put on heavy shoes that are too big for you, and wear gloves, and then try to spend the day in a normal way" (Skinner & Vaughan, 1983, p. 38). Because the elderly are an increasing percentage of the population, more and more individuals must deal on a daily basis with the loss of skills and ability to function independently that occurs with old age or with chronic illness. Once again, behavior modification can make a positive contribution. For example, habitual ways of performing daily routines at home or at work may no longer be possible. New routines must be developed and learned. Anxiety or fear about the possibility of failing to cope also might have to be dealt with. Disruptive behaviors in nursing homes may become a serious concern, and new relationships might need to be developed with professional care staff. Behavioral techniques are being used increasingly to help the elderly and chronic-care patients to solve these problems (Coon & Thompson, 2002; Derenne & Baron, 2002; Dick-Siskin, 2002; Spira & Edelstein, 2006; Wetherall, 2002; Wisocki, 1999).

Study Questions

12. List four behaviors in the area of self-management of personal problems that have been modified by behavior modification.
13. What is health psychology?
14. Describe five areas of application within health psychology.
15. List four behaviors of elderly persons that have been improved with behavior modification.

COMMUNITY BEHAVIORAL ANALYSIS

As discussed in Chapter 29, which gives a brief history of behavior modification, the bulk of the early (1950s) behavioral applications focused on individuals (such as persons with developmental disabilities and psychiatric patients) with severe problems and took place in institutional or highly controlled settings. By the 1970s, however, important behavior modification projects were directed toward such broad objectives as controlling littering in public campgrounds, increasing recycling of returnable soft drink containers, helping community boards to use problem-solving techniques, promoting energy conservation by increasing bus ridership, encouraging welfare recipients to attend self-help meetings, and helping college students live together in a co-operative housing project (for reviews of the early research in these areas, see Geller, Winett, & Everett, 1982; Martin & Osborne, 1980). The scope of behavior modification had clearly expanded from individual problems to community concerns. One of the early studies in this area defined *behavioral community psychology* as "applications to socially significant problems in unstructured community settings where the behavior of individuals is not considered deviant in the traditional sense" (Briscoe, Hoffman, & Bailey, 1975, p. 57).

Glenwick (1990) identified five trends in behavioral community applications. The first is greater involvement of the target populations in all aspects of the intervention process. If, for example, an overall goal in an AIDS treatment program is to increase glove wearing by nurses (see, e.g., DeVries, Burnette, & Redmon, 1991), then the nurses would be fully involved in selecting subgoals, choosing an intervention, and monitoring the results. Second, there is increased fostering of the target individual's personal control (versus control by professionals). In the project with nurses, there might be an emphasis on self-control techniques (described in Chapter 26) to increase their glove wearing rather than relying on their being told to do so by the head nurse. Third, there is increased inclusion of subjective assessments when evaluating treatment outcomes. Objectively, one might assess whether or not the nurses are wearing gloves more often. Subjectively, we would want to know how they feel about the overall program (subjective assessment is discussed further in Chapter 22). Fourth, there is increased emphasis on antecedent events (the intervention with the nurses might rely on posted reminders and the example of senior staff wearing their gloves) versus consequent events (such as praising the nurses for wearing their gloves). (Issues regarding antecedent and consequent events are discussed in Chapters 8, 17, 18, and 19.) Finally, there is greater interdisciplinary collaboration among professionals. For additional readings in community behavioral analysis, see issues of the *Journal of Applied Behavior Analysis*.

BUSINESS, INDUSTRY, AND GOVERNMENT

Behavior modification has also been applied to improve the performance of individuals in a wide variety of organizational settings. This general area has been referred to as *organizational behavior management (OBM)*, which has been defined as the application of behavioral principles and methods to the study and control of individual or group behavior within organizational settings (Frederiksen & Lovett, 1980). Other labels used interchangeably with organizational behavior management include *performance management, industrial behavior modification, organizational behavior modification, organizational behavior technology,* and *organizational behavior analysis*. Like all areas of application in this overview, organizational behavior management is data oriented. It emphasizes specific staff activities that characterize successful performances or produce successful results. It also emphasizes frequent feedback and rewards for employees who show desirable behaviors. Examples of the types of organizations involved range from small businesses to large corporations and from small community centers (note the overlap with behavioral community psychology) to large state hospitals. Thus, OBM is concerned with organizations both small and large, and both private and public.

One of the earliest studies in what was to become the field of OBM was carried out at the Emery Air Freight Company. According to an article "Conversations with B. F. Skinner" in the 1973 issue of *Organizational Dynamics,* the desired behavior—employees' placement of packages in special containers—was increased from 45% to 95% through the use of positive reinforcement in the form of praise from supervisors.

Other studies since then have used behavioral techniques to change behavior in ways that improve productivity, decrease tardiness and absenteeism, increase sales volume, create new business, improve worker safety, reduce theft by employees, reduce shoplifting, and improve management-employee relations. For additional reading in this area, see Austin (2000), Daniels and Daniels (2005), Johnson, Redmon, and Mawhinney (2001), Poling, Dickinson, Austin, and Normand (2000), Reid and Parsons (2000), and issues of the *Journal of Organizational Behavior Management.*

SPORT PSYCHOLOGY

Since the early 1970s, there has been a growing desire on the part of coaches and athletes for more applied sport science research, particularly in the area of sport psychology. *Applied sport psychology* has been defined as the use of psychological knowledge to enhance athletic performance and the satisfaction of athletes and others associated with sports (Blimke, Gowan, Patterson, & Wood, 1984). Behavior modification has made a number of contributions to this area (Martin, 2007; Martin, Thomson, & Regehr, 2004).

Techniques for Improving Skills of Athletes

What is the most effective way to help an athlete learn new skills, eliminate bad habits, and combine simple skills into complex patterns of execution? Considerable research has examined behavior modification techniques for effectively improving athletes' skills (Martin & Tkachuk, 2000), and practical strategies for applying these techniques have been described (Martin, 2007).

Strategies for Motivating Practice and Endurance Training

How can a coach effectively improve attendance at practices, motivate athletes to get the most out of practice time, and organize practices so that there is little downtime? Techniques for solving these types of problems are based on principles described in this book and can readily be learned by coaches (Martin, 2007).

Changing the Behavior of Coaches

Coaches have a very difficult job. From a behavior modification perspective, a coach must effectively instruct, set goals, praise, reprimand, and perform other activities that, collectively, determine his or her effectiveness as a behavior modifier. Numerous research studies have been conducted in this area (Martin & Tkachuk, 2000).

"Sports Psyching" to Prepare for Competition

We have all heard expressions such as "The reason the team lost was that they were psyched out," or "If you want to do your best, you have to get psyched up." While we may have some general ideas as to what these kinds of phrases mean, knowing generally what they mean and learning how to teach psychological coping skills to athletes are two different things. A number of behavioral strategies have been described for helping athletes prepare for serious competition in sport (see recent issues of *The Sport Psychologist* and books by Martin, 2007, and Martin, Toogood, & Tkachuk, 1997).

BEHAVIOR MODIFICATION WITH DIVERSE POPULATIONS

During the past two decades, behavior modifiers have given increased attention to issues of culture, gender, ethnicity, and sexual orientation as variables that can influence the effectiveness of treatment (see, e.g., Borrego, Ibanez, Spendlove, & Pemberton, 2007; Hatch, Friedman, & Paradis, 1996; Iwamasa, 1999; Iwamasa & Smith, 1996; Paradis, Friedman, Hatch, & Ackerman, 1996; Purcell, Campos, & Perilla, 1996). It is helpful, for example, for therapists to know that many clients with Asian cultural backgrounds prefer to be told specifically what to do by the therapist (as opposed to a more nondirective approach) (Chen, 1995). Many clients with Hispanic cultural backgrounds are more likely to comply with specific goal-directed suggestions if those suggestions are preceded by a period of familiarizing "small talk" (Tanaka-Matsumi & Higginbotham, 1994).

A particularly striking example of the importance of understanding the cultural backgrounds of one's clients comes from the Lakota Sioux reservation near the Badlands in South Dakota. Dr. Tawa Witko, a psychologist on the reservation, described the case of an individual who had been diagnosed by another psychologist as schizophrenic. The reason for the diagnosis was that the man heard voices, especially around ceremony times. Dr. Witko explained that if the therapist had dug deeper, she would have found that this phenomenon is common among Native Americans, has spiritual meaning, and does not by itself indicate mental illness (Winerman, 2004).

In some cases, cultural factors might counterindicate teaching a particular behavior. For example, increased eye contact as a target behavior for a social skills training program for some Native Americans might be inappropriate. For the Navajo culture, prolonged eye contact is typically considered to be aggressive (Tanaka-Matsumi, Higginbotham, & Chang, 2002). Readers interested in behavioral treatment with culturally diverse clients are encouraged to examine the special issues on cultural diversity in *Cognitive and Behavioral Practice* (1996, Vol. 3, No. 1) and in *The Behavior Therapist* (1999, Vol. 22, No. 10), and issues of the *Journal of Muslim Mental Health* and the *International Journal of Culture and Mental Health.*

Although information about clients' cultural backgrounds can be helpful for therapists, we must also be sensitive to the dangers of overgeneralizing about any particular cultural group. (Cautions similar to those made in Chapter 1 about the dangers of labeling are relevant here.) To illustrate this point, as Iwamasa (1999) pointed out, the Asian American population comprises over 30 different cultural and ethnic groups, and each has its own primary language, values, lifestyles, and patterns of adaptation to the United States.

Study Questions

16. What is behavioral community psychology?
17. List five current trends in behavioral community applications.
18. List four behaviors in the area of behavioral community psychology that have been modified by behavior modification.
19. Define *organizational behavior management.*
20. List four behaviors in business, industry, or government that have been modified by behavior modification. For each, are you referring to an actual behavior or a product of a behavior?
21. List four general areas of sport psychology in which behavior modification has been applied.
22. Describe how knowledge of a cultural characteristic might be helpful for behavior modifiers working with individuals from different cultures. Give an example.

CONCLUSION

The rise of behavior modification as a successful approach for dealing with a wide range of human problems has been remarkable. Books and journal articles describe behavioral procedures NOTE 3 and research ranging from child raising to coping with old age, from work to leisure activities, and from self-improvement to preserving the environment in which we live. It has been used with a range of people, from those with profound disabilities to those who are gifted. Several thousand books have been published concerning basic, applied, and theoretical issues in behavior modification. At least 31 journals are predominantly behavioral in their orientation. Examples of applications in many of these areas are described and illustrated in the following chapters.

Notes and Extended Discussion

1. Historically, lecturing (in combination with two or three exams per semester) has been the overwhelming method of choice for teaching undergraduates in most universities (Terenzini & Pascarella, 1994). A number of studies have demonstrated that PSI is more effective in enhancing the learning of course material than is the more traditional lecture method (Kulik, Kulik, & Bangert-Drowns, 1990). In fact, PSI has produced a statistically significant average learning advantage of 19 percentile points over traditional approaches (Pascarella & Terenzini, 1991). Course evaluations indicate that most students strongly praise such a system and identify frequent tests or exams as being responsible for generating extensive and well-paced study (Michael, 1991).

2. A common strategy for delivering EIBI to children with autism is called *discrete-trials teaching (DTT)*. It is made up of a series of individual teaching trials that typically last approximately 5 to 20 seconds each. On each trial, an instructor provides an antecedent (an instruction plus prompts to encourage a correct response), the child typically responds, and the teacher provides an immediate and appropriate consequence, such as a reward for correct behavior or saying no following an error. Repetitive DTT trials are typically separated by brief intertrial intervals and presented in blocks of 12 to 20 trials. Researchers have investigated a variety of strategies for teaching staff and parents to implement DTT in EIBI programs (for a review of the teaching strategies, see Thomson, Martin, Arnal, Fazzio, & Yu, 2009). Considering that millions of dollars are being spent on public programs to fund EIBI treatment of children with autism, reviewers of outcome literature (e.g., Matson & Smith, 2008; Perry, Pritchard, & Penn, 2006) have identified several important needs that must be addressed, two of which are (a) quality assessment systems to evaluate the effectiveness of specific components of EIBI interventions and (b) the development of research-based, economical, rapid training procedures for teaching parents and instructors to conduct DTT. A step toward meeting the first need is the development and field-testing of the Discrete-Trials Teaching Evaluation Form (Babel, Martin, Fazzio, Arnal, & Thomson, 2008), and a step toward meeting the second need is the field-testing of a self-instructional manual for teaching DTT to instructors of children with autism (Arnal et al., 2007; Fazzio, Martin, Arnal, & Yu, 2009; Thiessen et al., 2009).

3. Wyatt, Hawkins, and Davis (1986) critiqued the claim by some nonbehavioral psychologists that behaviorism—the philosophy behind behavior modification—is dead. They argued that it is very much alive and growing. Part of the evidence is the abundance of journals that are primarily behavioral in orientation including the following: *Analysis of Gambling Behavior* (2007–); *Behavior Analysts for Social Action* (1980–), originally *Behaviorists for Social Action: Behavior and Social Issues* (1991–); *Behavior Analysis in Practice* (2008–); *Behaviour Change* (1984–), the official journal of the Australian Behavior Modification Association, which changed its name in 1995 to the Australian Association for Cognitive and Behavior Therapy; *Behavior Modification* (1977–); *Behavior Research and Therapy* (1963–); *Behavior Therapy* (1970–); *Behavioral and Cognitive Psychotherapy* (1973–), originally *Behavioral Psychotherapy*; *Behavioral Counseling Quarterly* (1981–); *Behavioral Interventions* (1986–); *Behavioral Processes* (1981–), originally *Behavior Analysis Newsletters*; *Behavioral Residential Treatment* (1986–); *Child and Family Behavior Therapy* (1979–), originally *Child Behavior Therapy*; *Education and Treatment of Children* (1969–), originally *School Applications of Learning Theory*; *European Journal of Behavior Analysis* (2008–); *Japanese Journal of Behavior Therapy* (1976–); *Journal of Applied Behavior Analysis* (1968–); *Journal of Behavior Therapy and Experimental Psychiatry* (1970–); *Journal of Behavior Analysis in Crime and Victim: Treatment and Prevention* (2008–); *Journal of Behavioral Analysis in Health, Sports, Fitness, and Behavioral Medicine* (2008–); *Journal of Behavioral Education* (1991–); *Journal of Early and Intensive Behavioral Intervention* (2007–); *Journal of the Experimental Analysis of Behavior* (1958–); *Journal of Organizational Behavior Management* (1978–); *Journal of Psychopathology and Behavioral Assessment* (1979–), originally *Journal of Behavioral Assessment*; *Journal of Rational-Emotive and Cognitive Behavior Therapy* (1983–); *La Technologie du Comportment* (1977–); *Mexican Journal of Behavior Analysis* (1975–); *Research in Developmental Disabilities* (1987–) (in 1987, *Applied Research in Mental Retardation* [1980–1986] and *Analysis and Intervention in Developmental Disabilities* [1981–1986] were collapsed into one journal); *Scandinavian Journal of Behavior Therapy* (1999–); *The Behavioral Development Bulletin* (2007–); *The Behavior Analyst* (1978–); *The Behavior Analyst Today* (2007–); *The Behavior Therapist*

(1978–); *The International Journal of Behavioral Consultation and Therapy* (2007–); and *The Journal of Speech-Language Pathology and Behavior Analysis* (2007–).

Study Questions on Notes

1. Which is more effective for teaching undergraduates, the traditional lecturing approach or PSI? Justify your choice.
2. What are two important research needs in EIBI programs for children with autism?
3. What is behaviorism? Is it dead, sleeping, or very much alive? Justify your answer.

3

Getting a Behavior to Occur More Often with Positive Reinforcement

"Do you want to sit here, Mommy?"

REINFORCING DARREN'S COOPERATIVE BEHAVIOR[1]

Six-year-old Darren was extremely uncooperative with his parents. In the hope of learning how to deal more effectively with his excessive commanding behavior, Darren's parents took him to the Gatzert Child Developmental Clinic at the University of Washington. As his parents described the problem, Darren virtually "ran the show" at home, deciding when he would go to bed, what foods he would eat, when his parents could play with him, and so on. To obtain direct observations of Darren's behavior, both cooperative and uncooperative, Dr. Robert Wahler asked Darren's mother to spend some time with Darren in a playroom at the clinic. The playroom was equipped with adjoining observation rooms for data recording. During the first two 20-minute sessions, called a baseline phase[2]), Darren's mother was instructed: "Just play with Darren as you might at home." Darren's commanding behavior was defined as any verbal or nonverbal instructions to his mother, such as pushing her into a chair or saying such things as "You go over there and I'll stay here," or "No, that's wrong. Do it this way." Cooperative behavior was defined as any noncommanding statements, actions, or questions, such as, "Do you want to sit here?" while pointing to a chair. To illustrate the consistency of Darren's behavior, Figure 3–1 is a graph of the data collected in consecutive 10-minute intervals. As can be seen, Darren showed a very low rate of cooperative behavior during the baseline sessions. His commanding behavior (not shown in the figure), on the other hand, occurred at an extremely high rate. Following the baseline sessions, Darren's mother was asked to be very positive and supportive of any instances of cooperative behavior shown by Darren. At the same time, she was instructed to completely ignore his commanding behavior. Over the next two sessions, Darren's cooperative behavior steadily increased. (During the same time,

---

[1] This example is based on an article by Wahler, Winkel, Peterson, and Morrison (1965).
[2] A *baseline phase* (discussed further in chapter 23) is a measure of behavior in the absence of a treatment program.

FIGURE 3–1 Darren's cooperative behavior. Each data point (dot) represents the total number of instances of Darren's cooperative behavior during a 10-minute interval within a session. *Baseline* refers to the observation phase prior to the reinforcement program. (Replotted from "Mothers as Behavior Therapists for Their Own Children," by R. G. Wahler, G. H. Winkel, R. F. Peterson, and D. C. Morrison, *Behavior Research and Therapy,* Vol. 3, 1965, Figure 1, p. 117. Copyright © 1965 with permission from Elsevier Science.)

his commanding behavior decreased to near zero.) Further experimentation was done by Dr. Wahler and his colleagues to demonstrate that Darren's improvement resulted from the positive consequences provided by his mother following instances of Darren's cooperative behavior (in conjunction with her ignoring of commanding behavior). ■

POSITIVE REINFORCEMENT

A **positive reinforcer** is a stimulus that, when presented immediately following a behavior, causes the behavior to increase in frequency. The term *positive reinforcer* is roughly synonymous with the word *reward*. Once an event has been determined to function as a positive reinforcer for a particular individual in a particular situation, that event can be used to strengthen other behaviors of that individual in other situations. In conjunction with the concept of positive reinforcer, the principle called **positive reinforcement** states that if, in a given situation, somebody does something that is followed immediately by a positive reinforcer, then that person is more likely to do the same thing again when he or she next encounters a similar situation.

Although everyone has a commonsense notion of rewards, very few people are aware of just how frequently they are influenced by positive reinforcement during every day of their lives. See Table 3–1 for some examples of instances of positive reinforcement. (The terms *positive reinforcement* and *reinforcement* are often used interchangeably.)

The individuals in each of the examples in Table 3–1 were not consciously using the principle of reinforcement; they were just doing what comes naturally. In each example, it might take several repetitions before the reinforced response would show any really obvious increase (that is, an increase that would be noticeable to a casual observer). Nevertheless, the effect is still there.

Think about some of your behaviors during the past hour. Were any of those behaviors followed immediately by reinforcing consequences? In some cases, we may not be aware of these consequences and the effects they are having on our behavior.

TABLE 3–1	Examples of Instances of Reinforcement of Desirable Behaviors		
Situation	**Response**	**Immediate Consequences**	**Long-Term Effects**
1. Mother is busy ironing in the kitchen.	Her 3-year-old daughter begins playing with baby brother.	Mother has just completed her ironing and sits down to play with daughter and baby brother for a brief period.	In the future, the daughter is more likely to play with baby brother when mother is ironing because of the attention given when she began playing with him.
2. While you are waiting in a long line of cars for the light to change at a busy intersection, a car stops in the alley on your right.	You wave to the driver in the alley to pull into the line of traffic in front of you.	The driver nods and waves thanks to you and pulls into the line of traffic.	The pleasant feedback from the driver increases the likelihood that you will be courteous in similar situations in the future.
3. The students in a third-grade class have been given an assignment to complete.	Suzy, who is often quite disruptive, sits quietly at her desk and works on the assignment.	The teacher walks over to Suzy and pats her gently on the shoulder.	In the future, Suzy is more likely to work on the assignments given to her in class.
4. Father and child are shopping in a department store on a hot afternoon and both are very tired.	The child (uncharacteristically) follows father around the store quietly and without complaining.	Father turns to the child and says, "Let's go and buy an ice cream cone and sit down for a while."	On future shopping excursions, the child is more likely to follow father quietly.
5. A woman has just tasted a batch of soup she made, and it tasted very bland.	She adds a little Worcestershire sauce.	"It tastes very tangy, just like minestrone soup," she says to herself.	There is an increased likelihood that, in similar situations in the future, she will add Worcestershire sauce to her soup.
6. A husband and wife are undressing and getting ready for bed.	The husband picks up the wife's underwear and places it in the laundry hamper.	His wife pats him and murmurs her thanks.	On future evenings, the husband is more likely to put his wife's underwear in the laundry hamper.
7. One of the authors of this book is attempting to dictate some material into a tape recorder, but it is not working.	The author jiggles one of the wires attached to the microphone.	The tape recorder starts working.	The likelihood of wire jiggling will increase in similar situations in the future.

Behaviors that operate on the environment to generate consequences and are in turn influenced by those consequences are called **operant behaviors** (or *operant responses*). Each of the responses listed in Table 3–1 is an example of operant behavior. Operant behaviors that are followed by reinforcers are strengthened, and operant behaviors that are followed by punishers (see Chapter 12) are weakened. A different type of behavior—reflexive behavior—is discussed in Chapters 14 and 15.

It is helpful to think about behavior in the same way that we think about other aspects of nature. What happens when you drop a shoe? It falls toward the earth. What happens to a lake when the temperature drops below 0° C? The water freezes. These are things that we all know about and that physicists have studied extensively and formulated into laws, such as the law of gravity. The principle of positive reinforcement is also a law. Scientific psychology has been studying this principle in great detail since the early part of the last century (e.g., Thorndike, 1911), and we know that it is an extremely important part of the learning process. We also know of a number of factors that determine the degree of influence the principle of reinforcement has on behavior. These factors have been formulated into guidelines to be followed when using positive reinforcement to strengthen desirable behavior.

Study Questions

1. What is a baseline? Give an example.
2. What is plotted on the vertical axis in Figure 3–1?
3. What is plotted on the horizontal axis in Figure 3–1?
4. What is a positive reinforcer?
5. What is the principle of positive reinforcement?
6. What is operant behavior? Describe an example, and indicate how the example fits the definition of operant behavior.
7. In what way is positive reinforcement like gravity?
8. Describe an example of positive reinforcement of a desirable behavior that you have encountered. Identify the situation, behavior, immediate consequence, and probable long-term effects (as shown in Table 3–1 on the next page. The example should not be from the text).

FACTORS INFLUENCING THE EFFECTIVENESS OF POSITIVE REINFORCEMENT

1. Selecting the Behavior to Be Increased

The behaviors to be reinforced must first be identified specifically. If you start with a general behavior category (e.g., being more friendly), you should then identify specific behaviors (e.g., smiling) that characterize that category. By being specific in this way, you (a) help to ensure the reliability of detecting instances of the behavior and changes in its frequency, which is the yardstick by which one judges reinforcer effectiveness, and (b) increase the likelihood that the reinforcement program will be applied consistently.

2. Choosing Reinforcers ("Different Strokes for Different Folks")

Some stimuli are positive reinforcers for virtually everyone. Food is a positive reinforcer for almost anyone who has not had anything to eat for several hours. Candy is a reinforcer for most children. On the other hand, different individuals are frequently "turned on" by different things. Consider the case of Dianne, a 6-year-old girl with a developmental disability who was in a project conducted by one of the authors. She was able to mimic a number of words, and we were trying to teach her to name pictures. Two reinforcers commonly used in the project were candy and bites of the child's supper, but neither of these proved effective with Dianne. She spat them out about as often as she ate them. After trying many other potential reinforcers, we finally discovered that allowing her to play with a toy purse for 15 seconds was very reinforcing. As a result, after many hours of training, she is now speaking in phrases and complete sentences. For another child, listening to a music box for a few seconds turned out to be an effective reinforcer after other potential reinforcers failed. These stimuli might not have been reinforcing for everyone, but that is not important. The important thing is to use a reinforcer that is effective with the individual with whom you are working.

It is important to keep in mind that positive reinforcers are events that strengthen a response when they are introduced or added following the response. The removal of an event following a response may also strengthen that response, but this is not positive reinforcement. For example, a parent might nag a teenager to do the dishes. When the child complies, the nagging stops. Although the cessation of nagging when dishwashing occurs may strengthen the dishwashing response, it was the nagging's *removal* (not its introduction) following the response that strengthened it. (This is an example of the principle of **escape conditioning** or **negative reinforcement**, which states that there are certain stimuli, called aversive stimuli, whose removal immediately after the occurrence of a behavior will increase the likelihood of that behavior. This is discussed further in Chapter 13.

Most positive reinforcers can be classified under five somewhat overlapping headings: *consumable, activity, manipulative, possessional,* and *social.* Consumable reinforcers are items that one can eat or drink (i.e., consume), such as candy, cookies, fruit, and soft drinks. Examples of activity reinforcers are the opportunities to watch television, look at a picture book, or even stare out of a window. Manipulative reinforcers include the opportunities to play with a favorite toy, color or paint, ride a bicycle, surf the Internet, or tinker with a tape recorder. Possessional reinforcers are the opportunities to sit in one's favorite chair, wear a favorite shirt or dress, have a private room, or enjoy some other item that one can possess (at least temporarily). Social reinforcers include affectionate pats and hugs, praise, nods, smiles, and even a simple glance or other indication of social attention. Attention from others is a very strong reinforcer for almost everyone (see Figure 3–2).

In choosing effective reinforcers for an individual, it is often helpful to examine a list of reinforcers used by others (see Table 3–2) or to complete a reinforcer survey. An example of such a survey is shown in Figure 3–3.

A considerable amount of trial and error may be involved in finding an appropriate reinforcer for a particular individual. Another method is simply to observe the individual in everyday activities and note those activities engaged in most often. This method uses the **Premack principle** (first formulated by David Premack, 1959), which states that if the opportunity to engage in a behavior that has a high probability of occurring is made contingent on a behavior that has a low probability of occurring, then the behavior that has a low probability of occurring will be strengthened. For example, W. G. Johnson (1971) used this principle to help a depressed 17-year-old college student increase the frequency of positive self-statements. The student was asked to imagine a positive thought (a low-probability behavior) as prompted from a statement on an index card just before each instance of urinating (the high-probability behavior). After a few days, the student spontaneously thought the positive self-statements just before urinating without the necessity of reviewing the index card. After two weeks of this procedure, the student reported that the positive thoughts were occurring at a high rate (and that the depressive thoughts

FIGURE 3–2 Praise is a powerful positive reinforcer for strengthening and maintaining valued behaviors in everyday life.

had completely disappeared). For a discussion of the limitations of the Premack principle, see Timberlake and Allison (1974) and Timberlake and Farmer-Dougan (1991).

It is often quite effective to allow an individual to choose among a number of available reinforcers (DeLeon & Iwata, 1996). Variety is not only the spice of life; it is also a valuable asset to a training program. For example, in a program for a person with developmental disabilities, a tray containing sliced fruits, peanuts, raisins, and diet drinks can be presented as a reinforcer with the instruction to take one item. The advantage of this is that only one of the reinforcers among the selection has to be strong in order for the selection to be an effective reinforcer. If the individual can read or respond to pictures, the names or pictures of the reinforcers can be presented in the form of a reinforcer menu, and the preferred reinforcers can be chosen similarly to

TABLE 3–2 Reinforcers for Employees in a Variety of Work Settings	
Special-Attention Reinforcers Praise Praise in front of others Special work assignments Reserved parking space Choice of office Selection of own office furnishings Invitation to higher-level meetings Choice of work attire Social contacts with others Solicitation of opinions and ideas Choice of work partner Flexible job duties	**Monetary Reinforcers** Promotion Paid days off Company stock Company car Pay for sick days not taken Pay for overtime accumulated Tickets to special events Free raffle or lottery tickets Extra furnishings for office Gift certificates Dinner for family at nice restaurant Personalized license plate Personalized gifts Computer hardware/software upgrade Business cards Expense account
Company-Time Reinforcers Time off for work-related activities Time off for personal business Extra break time Extra meal time Choice of working hours or days off	**Participation Reinforcers** Voice in policy decisions Helping to set standards More responsibility Opportunity to learn new skills

Source: From *Turning Around: The Behavioral Approach to Managing People* (p. 45), by Beverly Potter. All rights reserved. New York: AMACOM, a division of American Management Association. Copyright © 1980. Reprinted with permission.

the way that one would order a meal at a restaurant. Matson and colleagues (1999) described a reinforcer menu that staff might use to select reinforcers for persons with severe and profound developmental disabilities.

No matter how you have selected a potential reinforcer for an individual, it is always the individual's performance that tells you whether you have selected an effective reinforcer. When you are not sure whether a particular item is reinforcing, you can always conduct an experimental test that involves *going back to the definition of a reinforcer given at the beginning of this chapter.* Simply choose a behavior that the individual emits occasionally and that does not appear to be followed by any reinforcer, record how often the behavior occurs without reinforcement over several trials, and then present the item immediately following the behavior for a few additional trials and see what happens. If the individual begins to emit that behavior more often, then your item is indeed a reinforcer. If the performance does not increase, then you do not have an effective reinforcer. In our experience, not using an effective reinforcer is a common error of training programs. For example, a teacher may claim that a particular reinforcement program that is being used is failing. Upon examination, the reinforcer used may turn out not to be a reinforcer for the student. You can never really be sure that an item is a reinforcer for someone until it has been demonstrated to function as such for that person. In other words, an object or event *is defined as a reinforcer only by its effect on behavior.*

This questionnaire is designed to help you find some specific activities, objects, events, or individuals that can be used as reinforcers in an improvement program. Read each question carefully and then fill in the appropriate blanks.

A. Consumable reinforcers: What does this person like to eat or drink?

   1. What things does this person like to eat most?
     a. regular meal-type foods _____
     b. health foods—dried fruits, nuts, cereals, etc. _____
     _____
     c. junk foods—popcorn, potato chips, etc. _____
     d. sweets—candies, ice cream, cookies, etc. _____

   2. What things does this person like to drink most?
     a. milk _____   c. juices _____
     b. soft drinks _____   d. other _____

B. Activity reinforcers: What things does this person like to do?

   1. Activities in the home or residence
     a. hobbies _____
     b. crafts _____
     c. redecorating _____
     d. preparing food or drinks_____
     e. housework _____
     f. odd jobs _____
     g. other_____

   2. Activities in the yard or courtyard
     a. sports_____
     b. gardening_____
     c. barbecue _____
     d. yardwork _____
     e. other_____

   3. Free activities in the neighborhood (window-shopping, walking, jogging, cycling, driving, swinging, teeter-tottering, etc.) _____
     _____

   4. Free activities farther away from home (hiking, snowshoeing, swimming, camping, going to the beach, etc.)
     _____

   5. Activities you pay to do (films, plays, sports events, night clubs, pubs, etc.) _____
     _____

   6. Passive activities (watching TV, listening to the radio, CDs, or an iPod; sitting, talking, bathing, etc.) _____
     _____

C. Manipulative reinforcers: What kinds of games or toys interest this person?

   1. Toy cars and trucks _____
   2. Dolls _____
   3. Wind-up toys _____

FIGURE 3–3 A questionnaire to help an individual identify reinforcers.

    4. Balloons _____

    5. Whistle _____

    6. Jump rope _____

    7. Coloring books and crayons _____

    8. Painting kit _____

    9. Puzzles _____

  10. Other _____

D. Possessional reinforcers: What kinds of things does this person like to possess?

    1. Brush_____

    2. Nail clippers_____

    3. Hair clips _____

    4. Comb_____

    5. Perfume_____

    6. Belt _____

    7. Gloves _____

    8. Shoelaces _____

    9. Other _____

E. Social reinforcers: What kinds of verbal or physical stimulation does this person like to receive from others? (specify who)

    1. Verbal stimulation

      a. "Good girl (boy)" _____

      b. "Good work"_____

      c. "Good job" _____

      d. "That's fine" _____

      e. "Keep up the good work" _____

      f. other_____

    2. Physical contact

      a. hugging _____

      b. kissing _____

      c. tickling _____

      d. patty-cake_____

      e. wrestling _____

      f. bouncing on knee_____

      g. other_____

FIGURE 3–3 (*Continued*)

    If you deliberately use a tangible (or extrinsic) item to reinforce someone's behavior, won't you undermine that person's intrinsic motivation (inner desire or sense of satisfaction) to perform that behavior? Some critics of behavior modification (e.g., Deci, Koestner, & Ryan, 1999) have suggested that you will. Some (e.g., Kohn, 1993) have gone so far as to argue that tangible rewards should never be given because, for example, if a parent gives a child money as a reinforcer for reading, then the child will be less likely to read for reading's sake. However, a careful review of the experimental literature on this topic (Cameron, Banko, & Pierce, 2001) and two experiments (Flora & Flora, 1999; McGinnis, Friman, & Carlyon, 1999) clearly indicates that this view is wrong. Moreover, the notion that extrinsic reinforcers undermine intrinsic motivation flies in the face of common sense (Flora, 1990). If extrinsic reinforcers undermine intrinsic motivation, then those fortunate people who genuinely enjoy their jobs should refuse to be paid (or demand only a minimal subsistence wage) for fear that their paychecks will destroy their enjoyment of their work. It is also worth noting that the extrinsic–intrinsic distinction between reinforcers may not even be valid: All reinforcers involve external (i.e., extrinsic) stimuli and all have internal (i.e., intrinsic) aspects.

Study Questions

9. Why is it necessary to be specific when selecting a behavior for a reinforcement program?

10. After dinner, a teenager begins washing dishes and the parent stops nagging the teenager to do so. Is that an example of positive reinforcement? Explain why or why not, in terms of the definition of positive reinforcement.

11. Describe the Premack principle. Give an example.

12. "It is always the individual's performance that tells you whether or not you have selected an effective reinforcer." Explain what this means.

13. Using the definition of positive reinforcer, describe the steps to test whether a particular item is a reinforcer for someone. Illustrate with an example.

14. Using the definition of positive reinforcer, how might you conduct a test to determine whether the social attention of a particular adult is or is not reinforcing for a withdrawn child?

15. Does extrinsic reinforcement undermine intrinsic motivation? Discuss.

3. Motivating Operations

Most reinforcers will not be effective unless the individual has been deprived of them for some period of time prior to their use. In general, the longer the deprivation period, the more effective the reinforcer will be. Sweets will usually not be reinforcing to a child who has just eaten a large bag of candy. Playing with a purse would not have been an effective reinforcer for Dianne had she been allowed to play with one prior to the training session. We use the term **deprivation** to indicate the time during which an individual does not experience a particular reinforcer. The term **satiation** refers to a condition in which an individual has experienced a particular reinforcer to such an extent that it is temporarily no longer reinforcing. "Enough's enough," as the saying goes.

   Events or conditions—such as deprivation and satiation—that (a) temporarily alter the effectiveness of a reinforcer and (b) alter the frequency of behavior reinforced by that reinforcer are called **motivating operations (MOs)** (the definition is expanded and discussed further in Chapter 19). Thus, food deprivation not only establishes food as an effective reinforcer for the person who is food deprived but also momentarily increases various behaviors that have been reinforced with food. As another example, feeding a child very salty food would be an MO because (a) it would momentarily increase the effectiveness of water as a reinforcer for that child and (b) it would also evoke behavior (e.g., asking for a drink, turning on a tap) that had previously been followed by water. An MO might be thought of as a *motivational variable*—a variable that affects the likelihood and direction of behavior. Because it is genetically determined (i.e., not learned) that food deprivation increases the effectiveness of food as a reinforcer an ingestion increases the effectiveness of water as a reinforcer, these events *unconditioned MOs.* In Chapter 19, we will introduce you to the notion of conditio[?] general terms, MOs might be thought of as motivators. In everyday life, people m depriving one of food motivates that individual to eat. Similarly, they might say that givin[?] dividual salted peanuts motivates the individual to drink.

4. Reinforcer Size

The size (amount or magnitude) of a reinforcer is an important determinant of its effectiveness. Consider the following example. Staff at a large mental hospital discovered that only 60% of the female patients brushed their teeth. When the patients were given a token that could be cashed in later for reinforcing items (cigarettes, coffee, or snacks) for brushing their teeth, those who did so increased to 76%. When the patients were given five tokens for brushing their teeth, the percent who did so increased to 91% (Fisher, 1979). Now consider an example that is more typical of many of our everyday lives. Many teenagers in a northern state such as Minnesota would likely be unwilling to shovel snow from a driveway or sidewalk of a house for 25¢, although many would eagerly do so for $25. As we will discuss further in Chapter 6, the optimum amount of a reinforcer to ensure its effectiveness depends on additional factors, such as the difficulty of the behavior and the availability of competing behaviors for alternative reinforcers. For now, keep in mind that the size of the reinforcer must be sufficient to strengthen the behavior that you want to increase. At the same time, if the goal is to conduct a number of trials during a session, such as in teaching basic language skills to a person with developmental disabilities, the reinforcer on each trial should be small enough to minimize satiation and maximize the number of reinforced trials per session.

5. Instructions: Use of Rules

For a reinforcer to increase an individual's behavior, it is not necessary that the individual be able to talk about or indicate an understanding of why he or she was reinforced. After all, the principle **NOTE 1** has been shown to work quite effectively with animals that cannot speak a human-type language. Nevertheless, instructions should generally be used.

Instructional influences on behavior will be easier for you to understand after reading Chapters 8 and 17. For now, let's view instructions as specific rules or guidelines that indicate that specific behaviors will pay off in particular situations. For example, your instructor might suggest the rule, "If you learn the answers to all of the study questions in this book, you will receive an A in the course."

Instructions can facilitate behavioral change in several ways. First, specific instructions will speed up the learning process for individuals who understand them. For example, beginning tennis players practicing backhand shots showed little progress when simply told to concentrate. However, they showed rapid improvement when told to vocalize the word *ready* when the ball machine was about to present the next ball, the word *ball* when they saw the ball fired from the machine, the word *bounce* as they watched the ball contact the surface of the court, and the word *hit* when they observed the ball contacting their racquet while swinging their backhand (Ziegler, 1987). Second, as indicated earlier (and discussed further in Chapter 17), instructions may influence an individual to work for delayed reinforcement. Getting an A in the course for which you are using this book, for example, is delayed several months from the beginning of the course. Daily rehearsing of the rule, "If I learn the answers to the questions listed in each chapter, I'll likely get an A," may exert some influence over your study behavior. Third (as discussed further in Chapter 8), adding instructions to reinforcement programs may help to teach individuals (such as very young children or persons with developmental disabilities) to follow instructions.

Some critics have accused behavior modifiers of using bribery. Suppose that a gambler offered $5,000,000 to a famous baseball player to strike out during each at-bat in the World Series. Clearly, that fits the definition of *bribery*—a reward or a gift offered to induce someone to commit an immoral or illegal act. Now suppose that a parent offers a child $5 for completing a homework assignment within a set period of time. Is that bribery? Of course not. The parent's offer is the use of instructions about a reinforcement program to strengthen desirable behavior. Similarly, people at most jobs are told ahead of time how much they will be paid for their work, but that is not bribery. Obviously, critics who accuse behavior modifiers of using bribery fail to distinguish between the promise of reinforcers for desirable behaviors versus the promise of reinforcers for immoral or illegal deeds.

6. Reinforcer Immediacy

For maximum effectiveness, a reinforcer should be given immediately after the desired response. In the example in Table 3–1 of the husband picking up his wife's underthings and placing them in the laundry hamper, his wife immediately thanked him. If she had waited until the next morning to do so, her thanks might not have had the same effect. In some cases, it may appear that a behavior is influenced by delayed reinforcement. Telling a child that if she cleans up her room in the morning, her father will bring her a toy in the evening is sometimes effective. Moreover, people do work toward long-delayed goals, such as college degrees. However, it is a mistake to attribute such results just to the effects of the principle of positive reinforcement. It has been found with animals that a reinforcer is unlikely to have much direct effect on a behavior that precedes it by much longer than 30 seconds (Chung, 1965; Lattal & Metzger, 1994; Perin, 1943), and we have no reason to believe that humans are essentially different in this respect (Michael, 1986; Okouchi, 2009).

How is it, then, that a long-delayed reinforcer might be effective with humans? The answer is that there must be certain events that mediate or bridge the gap between the response and the long-delayed reinforcer (see Pear, 2001, pp. 246–249). Consider the case of Fernando. He worked in a factory located on the outskirts of Mexico City.[3] He was 1 of a group of 12 workers who had a chronic problem—they were frequently late for work. Annual bonuses given by the factory to the 40 workers who had the best attendance records had no effect on Fernando. Likewise, disciplinary interviews and one-day suspensions without pay failed to increase the frequency with which he arrived on time. In fact, over a 12-week period Fernando arrived on time less than 80% of the working days (see Figure 3–4, baseline phase). Jaime Hermann, with the support of managers at the factory, decided to implement a treatment program involving positive reinforcers. Jaime explained the procedure individually to Fernando and the other workers who participated in the program. Each day that Fernando punched in on time, he was immediately given a slip of paper indicating that he had earned approximately 2 pesos (which had considerable value for Fernando at the time the study was conducted). At the end of each week, Fernando exchanged his slips for cash. As you can see in Figure 3–4, the program had an immediate effect.

---

[3] This example is based on the article by Hermann, deMontes, Dominiquez, Montes, and Hopkins (1973).

FIGURE 3–4 Fernando's instances of arriving at work on time. Each data point (dot) represents the percentage of total instances that Fernando arrived at work on time during a 2-week period. (Replotted from "Effects of Bonuses for Punctuality on the Tardiness of Industrial Workers," by J. A. Hermann, A. I. Montes, E. Dominguez, F. Montes, and B. L. Hopkins, 1973, *Journal of Applied Behavior Analysis,* Vol. 6, 1973, Figure 2, p. 568. Copyright © 1973. Reprinted by permission.)

Fernando arrived at work on time every day during the first 8 weeks of the program. The program had a similar positive effect on the other 11 workers who had also frequently been late for work. Moreover, additional experimental phases demonstrated that the improvement was due to the treatment.

At first glance, Fernando's improvement may appear to represent a straightforward case of the effects of positive reinforcement. A closer analysis reveals the necessity for an alternative interpretation (Michael, 1986). The response that made it possible for Fernando to arrive on time was leaving for work half an hour earlier in the morning, but that response preceded his receiving the slip of paper (indicating 2 pesos) by much longer than 30 seconds. Did some other variable affect Fernando's behavior? Perhaps just after awaking, Fernando said to himself, "I'm going to leave for work half an hour early to make sure that I earn 2 extra pesos," and these self-statements may have influenced the critical behavior. Although the positive effects of the program were due to the treatment, the treatment was more complex than that of a positive reinforcer increasing the frequency of a response that immediately preceded it.

The **direct effect** of a positive reinforcer is the increased frequency of a response because NOTE 2 it was immediately followed by that reinforcer. The **indirect effect** of a positive reinforcer is the strengthening of a response (such as Fernando leaving for work earlier) that is followed by that reinforcer (earning two pesos) even though the reinforcer is delayed. Delayed reinforcers may have an effect on behavior because of instructions about the behavior leading to the reinforcer and/or because of self-statements (or thoughts) that intervene between that behavior and the delayed reinforcer. On the way to work, for example, Fernando may have been making self-statements (i.e., thinking) about how he would spend his extra pesos. (Other explanations of indirect effects of a positive reinforcer are presented in Chapter 17.)

The distinction between direct and indirect effects of positive reinforcers has important im- NOTE 3 plications for practitioners. If you can't present a reinforcer immediately following the desired behavior, then provide instructions concerning the delay of reinforcement.

Study Questions

16. What do behavior modifiers mean by the term *deprivation*? Describe an example.

17. What do behavior modifiers mean by the term *satiation*? Describe an example.

18. What is a motivating operation? Describe two examples, one of which was not in this chapter.

19. Should you tell an individual with whom you are using reinforcement about the reinforcement program before putting it into effect? Why or why not?

20. If you instruct someone about a positive reinforcement program for that person's behavior, is that bribery? Why or why not?

21. Distinguish between the direct and indirect effects of a positive reinforcer.

7. Contingent Versus Noncontingent Reinforcement

We say that a reinforcer is **contingent** when a specific behavior must occur before that reinforcer will be presented. We say that a reinforcer is **noncontingent** if that reinforcer is presented at a particular time regardless of the preceding behavior. To illustrate the importance of this distinction, consider the following example.[4] Coach Keedwell watched her young swimmers swim a set during a regular practice at the Marlin Youth Swim Club. (A *set* is several lengths of a particular stroke to be swum within a specified time.) She had frequently tried to impress on them the importance of practicing their racing turns at each end of the pool and swimming the sets without stopping in the middle. Following the suggestion of one of the other coaches, she had even added a reward to her practices. During the last 10 minutes of each practice, the swimmers were allowed to participate in a fun activity of their choice (swimming relays, playing water polo, etc.). However, the results were still the same: The young swimmers continued to show a high frequency of improper turns and unscheduled stops during sets.

The mistake made by Coach Keedwell is common among novice behavior modifiers. Incorporating a noncontingent fun activity into practices might increase attendance, but it's not likely to have much effect on practice behaviors. Educators frequently make the same mistake as did Coach Keedwell. They assume that creating a pleasant environment will improve the learning of the students in that environment. However, reinforcers must be contingent on specific behaviors in order for those behaviors to improve. When this was pointed out to Coach Keedwell, she made the fun activity contingent on desirable practice behaviors. For the next few practices, the swimmers had to meet a goal of practicing a minimum number of racing turns at each end of the pool and swimming their sets without stopping to earn the reinforcer at the end of practice. As a result, the swimmers showed approximately 150% improvement. Thus, to maximize the effectiveness of a reinforcement program, be sure that the reinforcers are contingent on specific behaviors that you want to improve.

In addition to not increasing a desirable behavior, a noncontingent reinforcer may increase an undesirable behavior that it happens to follow. Suppose, for example, that, unbeknown to a parent, little Johnny is in his bedroom drawing on the walls with a crayon when the parent calls out, "Johnny, let's go get some ice cream." This accidental contingency might strengthen Johnny's tendency to draw on his walls. That is, behavior accidentally followed by a reinforcer may be strengthened even if it did not actually produce the reinforcer. This is called **adventitious**

---

[4] This example is based on a study by Cracklen and Martin (1983).

reinforcement. Behavior that is strengthened and maintained by adventitious reinforcement is called **superstitious behavior** (Skinner, 1948a). As another example, suppose that a man playing a slot machine tends to cross his fingers because, in the past, doing so was accidentally followed by winning a jackpot. Such behavior would be considered superstitious.

8. Weaning the Learner from the Program and Changing to Natural Reinforcers

The factors just described influence the effectiveness of positive reinforcement while it is being applied in a program. But what happens to the behavior when the reinforcement program terminates and the individual returns to everyday life behaviors? Most everyday behaviors are followed by reinforcers that no one specifically or deliberately programmed to increase or maintain those behaviors. Reading signs is frequently reinforced by finding desired objects or directions. Eating is reinforced by the taste of food. Flipping on a light switch is reinforced by increased illumination. Turning on a water tap is reinforced by the flow of water. Verbal and other social behaviors are reinforced by the reactions of other people. A setting in which an individual carries out normal, everyday functions (i.e., not a situation explicitly designed for training) is referred to as the **natural environment**. Reinforcers that follow behavior in the course of everyday living (i.e., that occur in the natural environment), are called **natural reinforcers**. Reinforcers that are arranged systematically by psychologists, teachers, and others in behavior modification programs are referred to as *arbitrary, contrived,* or **programmed reinforcers**.

After we have strengthened a behavior through proper use of positive reinforcement, it may then be possible for a reinforcer in the individual's natural environment to take over the maintenance of that behavior. For example, sometimes it is necessary to use reinforcers such as edibles to strengthen object naming in children with developmental disabilities. However, when the children leave the classroom and return to their homes, they often say the words that they have learned and receive a great deal of attention from their parents. Eventually, the edibles may no longer be needed to reinforce the children for saying the names of objects. This, of course, is the ultimate goal of any training program. The behavior modifier should always try to ensure that the behavior being established in a training program will be reinforced and maintained in the natural environment. One thing that you can count on is that if a behavior that has been strengthened in a reinforcement program is no longer reinforced at least occasionally (either by arbitrary or natural reinforcers), then that behavior will return to its original level. Because the problem of maintaining desirable behaviors is so important, it is discussed in much more detail in Chapters 6, 7, and 16.

Study Questions

22. When Coach Keedwell required young swimmers to show improved performance in order to earn a fun activity at the end of practice, their performance improved dramatically. Was this a direct effect or an indirect effect of reinforcement? Justify your choice.
23. Describe an example of contingent reinforcement that is not in this chapter.
24. Describe an example of noncontingent reinforcement that is not in this chapter.
25. What is adventitious reinforcement? What is a superstitious behavior? Give an example of each.
26. What do we mean by the *natural environment*? By *natural reinforcers*? By *programmed reinforcers*?
27. Describe three behavioral episodes in this chapter that involved natural reinforcers. Justify your choices.
28. Briefly describe in one sentence each the eight factors that influence the effectiveness of reinforcement.

PITFALLS OF POSITIVE REINFORCEMENT

Those who are well versed in behavior principles, such as positive reinforcement, can use them to bring about desirable changes in behavior. Lack of knowledge of a principle or procedure can be problematic in five distinct ways. In a "Pitfalls" section for each of Chapters 3–13 and Chapter 16, we will consider one or more of these five different types of pitfalls. We now illustrate these pitfalls with respect to the principle of positive reinforcement.

Pitfall Type 1: A Principle Can Be Misused by Someone Who Is Unaware of Using It

Unfortunately, those who are not aware of positive reinforcement are apt to use it unknowingly to strengthen undesirable behavior (see Table 3–3). Many undesirable behaviors are due to the social attention that such behavior evokes from aides, nurses, peers, teachers, parents, doctors, and others. This may be true even in cases when one would least expect it. Consider, for example, children who exhibit extreme social withdrawal. One behavioral characteristic of such children is that they avoid looking at someone who is talking to them. Frequently, they move away from adults. We might conclude that they don't want our attention. Actually, the withdrawn child's behavior probably evokes more social attention than would have been obtained by looking at the adult. In such cases, it is only natural for adults to persist in attempting to get a child to look at them when they speak. Unfortunately, this behavior is likely to reinforce the child's withdrawal behavior. The tendency to shower attention is sometimes maintained by the theory that social interaction is needed to bring a child out of the withdrawn state. In reality, an appropriate treatment might involve withholding social attention for withdrawal behavior and presenting it only when the child engages in some sort of social-interaction behavior—such as looking in the direction of the adult who is attempting the interaction. The hard work of one behavior modifier using appropriate behavior techniques can be greatly hindered, or completely undone, by others who reinforce the wrong behavior. For example, an aide who attempts to reinforce eye contact in a withdrawn child is probably not going to have much effect if other people who interact with the child consistently reinforce the looking-away behavior. In Chapter 23, we discuss methods for assessing whether a problem behavior is being maintained by positive reinforcement and how to treat it if it is.

Pitfall Type 2: A Person May Know the Principle But Not Realize Some Ramification That Interferes with Applying It Effectively

"A little knowledge can be a dangerous thing," as the saying goes. For example, novice behavior modifiers often assume that simply presenting reinforcers noncontingently will strengthen a specific behavior. Coach Keedwell, as described earlier in this chapter, assumed that providing a fun activity at the end of each swimming practice would strengthen desirable swimming behaviors. That didn't occur, however, because the fun activity was not contingent on specific practice behaviors.

Pitfall Type 3: A Principle Can Be Inaccurately Used as an Oversimplified Explanation of a Change in Behavior

Suppose that a college student studies for three hours on Monday evening for an exam, writes the exam on Tuesday, and receives the test with an A on Thursday. To say that the college student

TABLE 3–3	Examples of Positive Reinforcement Following Undesirable Behavior		
Situation	**Response**	**Immediate Consequences**	**Long-Term Effects**
1. A child who has been coloring in a coloring book gets up and looks around the living room.	The child goes over to the TV remote and begins fiddling with the buttons.	Mother immediately comes over to her and says, "I guess you're tired of playing by yourself; let's go for a walk."	The chances of the child fiddling with the TV remote in the future increases because of the attention from mother.
2. While getting ready for work in the morning, a man cannot find his clean shirt.	He yells loudly, "Where in the hell is my shirt?"	His wife immediately finds the husband's shirt.	In the future, the husband is more likely to yell and swear when he can't find his clothes.
3. A father is busy ironing, and his two young children are playing quietly.	One child hits the other over the head with a toy truck.	Father stops ironing and sits down to play with the children for a while.	The child is more likely to hit someone in the future to gain father's attention.
4. Mother and child are shopping in a department store.	Child begins to whine, "I want to go home; I want to go home; I want to go home."	Mother is embarrassed and leaves the store immediately with the child before making her purchases.	The child is more likely to whine in a similar situation in the future.
5. Persons with severe developmental disabilities are eating their meal in the dining room at a group home.	One girl holds up her empty glass and grunts loudly, "Mmmm, mmmm, mmmm."	One of the staff members immediately comes and fills the glass with milk.	The girl is likely to hold up her glass and make similar noises in future situations when she wants milk.
6. Father is watching a Stanley Cup playoff hockey game on TV.	Two of his children are playing in the same room and are being extremely noisy.	Father gives each of them some money so that they will go to the store and not interfere with his TV watching.	The children are more likely to play noisily when father is watching TV in similar situations in the future.
7. At a party, a husband becomes sullen when his wife is dancing flirtatiously with another man.	The husband shows signs of jealousy and angrily leaves the party.	The wife immediately follows him and showers him with attention.	The husband is more likely to leave parties in similar situations in the future.

studied for three hours because of being reinforced later by getting a good grade would be an overly simplistic explanation. There was a long gap in time between the studying and receiving the A. When explaining a behavior, we should always look for immediate consequences that may have strengthened that behavior in the past. With respect to the studying behavior, perhaps the night before the exam the student worried about failing, which caused him or her to feel anxious. Perhaps the immediate consequence of studying was the removal of anxiety (as discussed further in Chapters 13 and 17). Or perhaps immediately after studying, the student thought about the likelihood of getting an A, which helped bridge the gap between the behavior and the reinforcer. As discussed in Chapter 26, reminding oneself of a delayed natural reinforcer for a behavior immediately after it occurs can strengthen that behavior. Remember that when you are attempting to explain the strengthening of a behavior by positive reinforcement, always look for an immediate consequence of that behavior. If a reinforcer is delayed by (as a rule of thumb) more than 30 seconds following a behavior, then offering just positive reinforcement as an explanation of the increase in that behavior may be overly simplistic. (It should be noted, however, that some research shows that, under certain conditions, delayed positive reinforcement can be effective with no apparent stimuli that bridge the gap between the behavior and the reinforcer; e.g., see Stromer, McComas, & Rehfeldt, 2000.)

Pitfall Type 4: Individuals Without Behavioral Knowledge Sometimes Attempt to Explain Behavior or the Lack of It by Inappropriately Giving People a Label

Suppose that a teenager consistently leaves her or his room in a mess, never makes her or his bed, never cleans up in the kitchen after making a snack, rarely studies, and spends many hours each week watching TV or being on Facebook. The teen's parents explain her or his behavior by saying, "She or he is just lazy." A more accurate explanation of her or his behavior would be that the teenager's friends provide frequent reinforcement for interactions on Facebook, the teenager frequently observes enjoyable scenes while watching TV, and she or he has not received much reinforcement from her or his parents for helping around the house or from her or his teachers for studying.

Pitfall Type 5: Some Behavioral Procedures Aren't Applied Because They Are Quite Complex and Require Specialized Knowledge or Training

For example, a parent who is unfamiliar with the principle of positive reinforcement may fail to reinforce a rare instance of a normally inconsiderate child showing polite behavior, thereby missing an opportunity to strengthen that behavior.

GUIDELINES FOR THE EFFECTIVE APPLICATION OF POSITIVE REINFORCEMENT

These summary guidelines are offered to ensure the effective use of positive reinforcement.

1. *Selecting the Behavior to Be Increased*   As indicated earlier in this chapter, the target behavior should be a specific behavior (such as smiling) rather than a general category (such as socializing). Also, if possible, select a behavior that will come under the control of natural reinforcers after it has been increased in frequency. Finally, as shown in Darren's case at the beginning of this chapter, to judge the effectiveness of your reinforcer accurately, it is important to keep track of how often the behavior occurs prior to your program.

2. *Selecting a Reinforcer*
   a. If possible, complete the reinforcer survey presented in Figure 3–3 and select strong reinforcers that
      (1) are readily available.
      (2) can be presented immediately following the desired behavior.

(3) can be used over and over again without causing rapid satiation.

(4) do not require a great deal of time to consume (if it takes half an hour to consume the reinforcer, this minimizes the training time).

b. Use as many reinforcers as feasible, and, when appropriate, use a reinforcer tray or menu.

3. *Applying Positive Reinforcement*

a. Tell the individual about the plan before starting.

b. Reinforce *immediately* following the desired behavior.

c. Describe the desired behavior to the individual while the reinforcer is being given. (For example, say "You cleaned your room very nicely.")

d. Use lots of praise and physical contact (if appropriate and if these are reinforcing to the individual) when dispensing reinforcers. However, to avoid satiation, vary the phrases you use as social reinforcers. Don't always say "Good for you." (Some sample phrases are "Very nice," "That's great," "Super," "Tremendous.")

4. *Weaning the Student From the Program* (discussed more fully in Chapter 16).

a. If during a dozen or so opportunities, a behavior has been occurring at a desirable rate, you might try to gradually eliminate tangible reinforcers (such as treats and toys) and maintain the behavior with social reinforcement.

b. Look for other natural reinforcers in the environment that might also maintain the behavior once it has been increased in frequency.

c. To ensure that the behavior is being reinforced occasionally and that the desired frequency is being maintained, plan periodic assessments of the behavior after the program has terminated.

Study Questions

29. Is it correct to conclude that a withdrawn child necessarily does not like attention from other people? Explain.

30. Describe an example of Pitfall Type 1 that involves a person unknowingly applying positive reinforcement to strengthen an undesirable behavior.

31. State Pitfall Type 2. How did Coach Keedwell exemplify this pitfall?

32. Consider this statement: "A college student was reinforced for studying for three hours on the weekend by getting a good grade on the test the following week." How does this statement exemplify Pitfall Type 3?

33. State Pitfall Type 4, and describe an example.

34. Ideally, what four qualities should a reinforcer have (besides the necessary quality of functioning as a reinforcer)? (See pp. 48–49.)

Application Exercises

A. EXERCISES INVOLVING OTHERS

1. During an hour that you spend with children, how many times do you dispense social approval (nods, smiles, or kind words)? How many times do you dispense social disapproval (frowns, harsh words, etc.)? Ideally, your social approval total at the end of the hour will be four or five times the social disapproval total. We encourage you to continue this exercise until you have achieved this ratio. Several studies have shown this ratio of reinforcers to reprimands to be beneficial (e.g., Madsen & Madsen, 1974; Stuart, 1971; also see Flora, 2000).

2. List 10 different phrases that you might use to express your enthusiastic approval to an individual. Practice varying these phrases until they come naturally to you.

3. Are you aware of how your gestures, expressions, posture, and body language in general affect those around you? Briefly describe five different examples of one or more of these behaviors that you mightshow when expressing your approval to an individual.

B. SELF-MODIFICATION EXERCISES

1. Be aware of your own behavior for five 1-minute periods while behaving naturally. At the end of each minute, describe a situation, a specific behavior, and the immediate consequences of that behavior. Choose behaviors whose consequences seemed pleasant (rather than neutral or unpleasant).

2. Complete the reinforcer questionnaire (Figure 3–3) for yourself.

3. Assume that someone close to you (your husband, wife, friend, etc.) is going to reinforce one of your behaviors (such as making your bed daily, talking in conversation without swearing, or reading pages of this book). Select the two reinforcers from your completed questionnaire that best satisfy the guidelines given previously for *selecting a reinforcer* (p. 48). Indicate how the guidelines have been satisfied.

Notes and Extended Discussion

1. Although it may seem strange to think of people learning without understanding or being reinforced for emitting a certain behavior without being aware of it, this is much easier to understand when we consider the following observations: First, from everyday experience as well as from basic experiments, it is obvious that animals can learn even though they are not able to verbalize an understanding or an awareness of their behavioral changes. Similarly, the behavior of persons with profound developmental disabilities who cannot speak has been shown to be strengthened by reinforcement (see Fuller, 1949). Finally, a number of experiments have demonstrated that normal adult humans can be influenced by reinforcement to show behavioral changes even if they are unable to verbalize them. For example, university students in an experiment were instructed to say words individually and not to use sentences or phrases. When the experimenter nodded and said "Mmm-hmm" following particular types of words (such as plural nouns), the students showed an increased frequency of saying that particular type of word. And yet, when questioned after the experiment, the students were unaware (i.e., were unable to verbalize) that their behavior had been influenced (Greenspoon, 1951).

2. Michael (1986) identified three indicators that a behavior change is due to an indirect versus direct effect of a reinforcer: (a) the critical response precedes the reinforcer by more than 30 seconds (such as in the case of Fernando, in which the critical response was leaving for work earlier than usual); (b) the behavior that is measured shows some increase in strength prior to the first occurrence of the consequence (such as Fernando arriving for work on time the very first morning of the program before he had even received the 2-peso consequence); and (c) a single occurrence of a consequence produces a large change in behavior (such as Fernando maintaining 100% on-time arrivals from the onset of the treatment). In Chapter 17, we discuss in detail strategies that teachers can use to increase the chances of obtaining indirect-acting effects with procedures that involve positive reinforcers.

3. Suppose that you're trying to teach an individual with a severe intellectual disability to open containers. In one condition, on each trial, you give a container to the client and ask him or her to "open it"; if he or she does so, you hand the client an edible as a reinforcer. In the second condition, everything is the same, except that the edible is hidden inside the container and will be discovered if the client opens it. Research indicates that individuals with

severe intellectual disability or autism learn better under the second condition (Koegel & Williams, 1980; Thompson & Iwata, 2000). The authors in these studies describe the first arrangement as an indirect-reinforcement contingency and the second arrangement as a direct-reinforcement contingency. To avoid confusion with what we are calling direct and indirect effects of reinforcers, we suggest that an instance in which a response reveals the reinforcer (such as opening the container revealing the edible hidden within it) be described as a *reinforcer-discovery contingency.*

Study Questions on Notes

1. Discuss evidence that people's behavior can be modified without their being aware of it.
2. What are three indicators that a behavior change is due to an indirect versus a direct effect of a reinforcer?
3. How do some authors use the terms *direct* and *indirect contingencies of reinforcement?* What suggestions do the authors of this text make regarding that usage, and why?

4

Developing and Maintaining Behavior with Conditioned Reinforcement

"Don't be so rude! Be nice!"

ERIN'S POINTS[1] PROGRAM

"Erin, don't be so rude," exclaimed Erin's friend, Carly. "You're so unpleasant to everybody, even your friends. Why don't you try being nice for a change?" As Carly walked away, Erin decided that she had to modify her behavior. She wanted to be nicer to her friends, instead of always making smart comments. But being rude was such a habit that she knew she needed some extra motivation to change. After reading about self-management strategies in her psychology course, she decided to put herself on a points program. She really liked spending time on Facebook or YouTube after doing her homework, but from now on she would have to earn the opportunity to do so. Every time she left her house in the morning, she carried an index card and a pen with her. Each time that she said something nice to her friends, she gave herself a point on the card. Then after finishing her homework that evening, she allowed herself time on Facebook or YouTube according to her "points menu." Her menu looked like this:

2 points	20 minutes of time
4 points	40 minutes of time
6 points	60 minutes of time
More than 6 points	As much time as I want

A week later when Carly and Erin were having lunch, Carly said, "I can't believe how nice you've been lately. It's like you are a different person." Erin replied jokingly, "Yeah, it's that personality operation I had."

---

[1] This case is based on one described by Watson and Tharpe (2007).

UNCONDITIONED AND CONDITIONED REINFORCERS

We have inherited the capacity to be reinforced by some stimuli without prior learning. Such stimuli or events are important for our survival or biological functioning and are called **unconditioned reinforcers**, which are stimuli that are reinforcing without prior learning or conditioning. (They are also called *primary* or *unlearned reinforcers*.) Examples include food for a hungry person, water for a thirsty person, warmth for someone who is cold, and sexual contact for someone who has been deprived of such contact. Other stimuli become reinforcers because of particular learning experiences. These stimuli, called **conditioned reinforcers**, are stimuli that were not originally reinforcing but have become reinforcers by being paired or associated with other reinforcers. (They are also called *secondary* or *learned reinforcers*.) Examples of condi- **NOTE 1** tioned reinforcers include praise, a picture of a loved one, books that we like to read, our favorite television programs, and clothes that make us look good.

When a stimulus becomes a conditioned reinforcer through deliberate association with other reinforcers, the other reinforcers are called **backup reinforcers**. Consider, for example, the type of training conducted with dolphins at Sea World. Early on, the trainer pairs the sound from a hand-held clicker with the delivery of fish to a dolphin. A fish is a backup reinforcer, and after a number of pairings, the clicking sound becomes a conditioned reinforcer. Later, when teaching a dolphin to perform a trick, the sound of the clicker is presented as an immediate conditioned reinforcer, and the clicker sound continues to be intermittently paired with fish.

In this example of training the dolphins, the backup reinforcer—the fish—was an unconditioned reinforcer. However, backup reinforcers for a conditioned reinforcer could also be other conditioned reinforcers. To illustrate, consider Erin's program. The points that she awarded herself were not primary reinforcers. We doubt that she would have worked very hard, if at all, just to obtain them for their own sake. The points were conditioned reinforcers because they were paired with the backup reinforcer, the opportunity to go on Facebook or YouTube. In this example, the backup reinforcer for the points was also a conditioned reinforcer. Erin was not born with Facebook or YouTube being unconditioned reinforcers for her. Rather, these stimuli would have become conditioned reinforcers by being paired with other things such as attention from adults and friends. Thus, backup reinforcers that give a conditioned reinforcer its strength can be either unconditioned reinforcers (such as the fish with the dolphins) or other conditioned reinforcers (such as time spent on Facebook or YouTube).

Study Questions

1. Explain what an unconditioned reinforcer is. Give two examples.
2. Explain what a conditioned reinforcer is. Give and explain two examples.
3. Explain what a backup reinforcer is. Give and explain two examples.
4. What were the backup reinforcers in Erin's program?
5. Describe a target behavior of yours that you would like to improve that might be amenable to a points program like Erin's. What would you use as backup reinforcers for the points?

Tokens as Conditioned Reinforcers

Tokens are conditioned reinforcers that can be accumulated and exchanged for backup reinforcers. A behavior modification program in which individuals can earn tokens for specific behaviors and can cash in their tokens for backup reinforcers is called a **token economy** or a **token system**. For example, a kindergarten teacher might implement a token economy in which the children could earn gold stars for various behaviors, such as one star per child for playing cooperatively during recess and one star per correct answer given in class. At the end of the day, the children might be allowed to cash in their stars for backup reinforcers, such as five stars per child to play a computer game or three stars per child for the class to have an extra 5 minutes of story time. Just about anything that can be accumulated can be used as the medium of exchange in a token economy or system. In some token economies, individuals earn plastic discs (like poker chips), which they can retain until they are ready to cash them in for backup reinforcers. In other token economies, people receive payment as "paper money" on which is written (to control use and facilitate record keeping) the amount earned, the individual's name, the name of the employee who paid the individual, the date, and the task the individual performed to earn the token. In still others, as in Erin's program, individuals receive points, which are recorded on a chart, on an index card, or in a notebook. (Token economies are discussed further in Chapter 25.)

Tokens constitute one type of conditioned reinforcer (Hackenberg, 2009), but stimuli that cannot be accumulated can also be conditioned reinforcers. A common example is praise. A mother who expresses pleasure at her child's good behavior is disposed to smile at, hug, or play with the child. Sometimes a treat, toy, or other things the child enjoys may accompany the mother's praise. Normally, praise is established as a conditioned reinforcer during childhood, but it continues to be maintained as one for adults. When people praise us, they are generally more likely to favor us in various ways than when they do not praise us. Thus, praise is a conditioned reinforcer, but it is not a token reinforcer. A bunch of praise statements cannot be saved up and exchanged for a backup reinforcer.

The main advantage of using tokens or other conditioned reinforcers in a behavior modification program is that they can usually be delivered more immediately than the backup reinforcer can. Hence, they help to bridge delays between behavior and more powerful reinforcers.

Before closing this section, we mention briefly the principle of *conditioned punishment,* which is very similar to that of conditioned reinforcement. Just as a stimulus that is paired with reinforcement becomes reinforcing itself, so a stimulus that is paired with punishment becomes punishing itself. "No!" and "Stop that!" are examples of stimuli that become conditioned punishers because they are often followed by punishment if the individual continues to engage in the behavior that provoked them. Moreover, punishing tokens as well as reinforcing ones are possible. The demerit system used in the military is an example of a punishment token system. There are, however, problems with the use of punishment (see Chapter 12).

Study Questions

6. What are tokens?
7. Explain in two or three sentences what a token economy is.
8. Is money a token? Justify your answer.
9. Give two examples of stimuli that are conditioned reinforcers but not tokens. Explain why they are conditioned reinforcers.
10. Explain what a conditioned punisher is. Give and explain two examples.

FACTORS INFLUENCING THE EFFECTIVENESS OF CONDITIONED REINFORCEMENT

1. The Strength of Backup Reinforcers

The reinforcing power of a conditioned reinforcer depends in part on the reinforcing power of the backup reinforcer(s) on which it is based. For example, because Facebook or YouTube were strong backup reinforcers for Erin, the points functioned as effective conditioned reinforcers.

2. The Variety of Backup Reinforcers

A stimulus can become a conditioned reinforcer because of pairings with a single backup reinforcer. This is illustrated by the example of an ice cream vendor who rings a bell when entering a neighborhood. After a few pairings, the sound of the ice cream vendor's bell will be a conditioned reinforcer for the children in the neighborhood. A conditioned reinforcer that is paired with a single backup reinforcer is called a **simple conditioned reinforcer**. In contrast, a stimulus that is paired with more than one kind of backup reinforcer is referred to as a **generalized conditioned reinforcer**. Early in life, for example, parents feed their infants, wash them, play with them, and meet their needs in many other ways. Because each of these is paired with many kinds of reinforcers, adult attention becomes a powerful generalized conditioned reinforcer. Similarly, money is a powerful generalized reinforcer for us because of its pairings with food, clothing, shelter, transportation, entertainment, and other reinforcers (see Figure 4–1).

   The reinforcing power of a conditioned reinforcer depends in part on the number of different backup reinforcers available for it. This factor is related to the preceding one in that, if many different backup reinforcers are available, then at any given time, at least one of them will probably be

FIGURE 4–1   Why is money a generalized conditioned reinforcer?

TABLE 4–1	Examples of Conditioned Reinforcers

Examples of Simple Conditioned Reinforcers	Examples of Generalized Conditioned Reinforcers	Examples of Unconditioned Reinforcers
Air miles	Money	Food
Being told, "Your order is ready" at a take-out restaurant	Praise	Water
A subway token	A gift certificate for food and beverages at a restaurant	Sex
A coupon for a free hamburger		Physical comfort
		Sleep
		Novelty

strong enough to maintain tokens at a high reinforcing strength for any individual in the program. Examples of simple and generalized conditioned reinforcers are given in Table 4–1.

    A category of stimuli that are not commonly recognized as conditioned reinforcers includes stimuli that have been paired with addictive drugs. These conditioned reinforcers include **NOTE 2** such things as the smell or taste of substances containing the drug (e.g., tobacco) or the sight of the paraphernalia used to prepare or administer the drug.

3. The Number of Pairings with a Backup Reinforcer

A conditioned reinforcer is likely to be stronger if it is paired with a backup reinforcer many times. For example, the expression "good girl" or "good boy" spoken to a very young child immediately following a desirable behavior is likely to be a stronger conditioned reinforcer if that expression has been paired with a hug from a parent many times as opposed to having been paired with a hug from a parent just once (assuming that other backup reinforcers were not involved).

4. Loss of Value of a Conditioned Reinforcer

For a conditioned reinforcer to remain effective, it must, at least occasionally, be associated with a suitable backup reinforcer. In the example of the token program described previously, if the kindergarten teacher discontinued the backup reinforcers for which the stars could be exchanged, the children may have eventually stopped behaving appropriately for which they received the stars.

PITFALLS OF CONDITIONED REINFORCEMENT

In Chapter 3, we introduced five types of pitfalls that work against those who have limited or no knowledge of behavioral principles, and we showed how these principles apply to the principle of positive reinforcement. Here we consider two of those pitfall types with regard to conditioned reinforcement.

Pitfall Type 1

People who are unfamiliar with the principle of conditioned reinforcement may unknowingly misapply it in various ways. One misapplication is the unknown pairing of conditioned reinforcers with stimuli that are meant to be punishing. An example of this misapplication is when an adult frequently scolds a child for behaving inappropriately but (a) never provides any type of "backup punisher" (see Chapter 12) with the scolding, and (b) the scolding is accompanied by other aspects of adult attention (e.g., being close by, being spoken to) that are likely to have acquired conditioned reinforcing value because of previous pairings with reinforcers. The attention that accompanies such negative verbal stimuli may even be highly reinforcing, especially for children or individuals with developmental handicaps who may not receive much attention from adults. Thus, in some situations, scoldings and other negative verbal stimuli (such as "No!") might come to function as conditioned reinforcers, and the individual will behave inappropriately to obtain them.

Indeed, even stimuli that are normally punishing can become conditioned reinforcers through association with powerful primary reinforcers. The classic example is the parent who spanks a child for misbehavior and then, feeling guilty from the ensuing piteous crying, immediately hugs the child and provides a treat. The possible outcome of this unthinking procedure is that the child will develop a "liking for lickings"; that is, the spanking could become a conditioned reinforcer that would maintain, not eliminate, the misbehavior it follows.

Pitfall Type 2

Ceasing to pair a conditioned reinforcer with a backup reinforcer can have unfortunate results for those who are not aware that this will cause a conditioned reinforcer to lose its value. An example of this is a teacher who awards stars as tokens for good behavior but fails to use effective backup reinforcers. The result is that the stars eventually lose whatever reinforcing power they may have had when they were first introduced. Failure to use effective backup reinforcers in token economies can account for the lack of motivation students sometimes show.

GUIDELINES FOR THE EFFECTIVE USE OF CONDITIONED REINFORCEMENT

The following guidelines should be observed in applying conditioned reinforcement.

1. A conditioned reinforcer should be a stimulus that can be managed and administered easily in the situations in which you plan to use it. For example, points were ideally suited for Erin's program.
2. As much as possible, use the same conditioned reinforcers that the individual will encounter in the natural environment. For example, it is desirable in training programs to transfer control from artificial tokens to the monetary economy of the natural environment or to naturally receive praise and attention from others.
3. In the early stages of establishing a conditioned reinforcer, a backup reinforcer should be presented as quickly as possible after the presentation of the conditioned reinforcer. Later, the delay between the conditioned reinforcer and the backup reinforcer can be increased gradually if desired.
4. Use generalized conditioned reinforcers whenever possible; that is, use many different types of backup reinforcers, not just one. In this way, at least one of the backup reinforcers will probably be strong enough at any given time to maintain the power of the conditioned reinforcer.
5. When the program involves more than one individual (as in the program in which the children in the kindergarten class could earn stars), avoid destructive competition for conditioned and backup reinforcers. Giving one person reinforcement to the detriment of another may evoke aggressive behavior in the second individual or cause that individual's

desirable behavior to extinguish. This rule implies in particular to avoid making an issue out of the fact that one individual is earning more conditioned and backup reinforcement than another. Of course, people differ in their abilities, but designing programs in which individuals earn sufficient reinforcement for performing at their own levels can minimize any difficulties that these differences might cause.

6. In addition to the preceding five rules, one should follow the same rules for conditioned reinforcers that apply to any positive reinforcer (Chapter 3). Additional details for establishing token economies are described in Chapter 25.

Study Questions

11. Distinguish between a simple conditioned reinforcer and a generalized conditioned reinforcer. Explain why a generalized conditioned reinforcer is more effective than a simple conditioned reinforcer.
12. Is praise a generalized conditioned reinforcer? Defend your answer.
13. Were the points in Erin's program a generalized conditioned reinforcer? Defend your answer.
14. List three factors that influence the effectiveness of conditioned reinforcers.
15. Explain what causes a conditioned reinforcer to lose its value.
16. Describe two pitfalls of conditioned reinforcement, and give an example of each.

Application Exercises

A. EXERCISES INVOLVING OTHERS

1. What is the probable reinforcer and what behavior does it strengthen in each of the following situations? Are these reinforcers unconditioned or conditioned? Justify your choice in each case.

   a. An individual walks through a park in autumn and admires the beautifully colored leaves on the trees.
   b. A person finishes jogging 3 miles and experiences the runner's "high" (caused by the release of endorphins in the brain).
   c. A teenager finishes mowing the lawn and is allowed to use the family car.
   d. A thirsty child holds a glass of milk and drinks several swallows.

2. Observe four instances that are different from the preceding situations in which people are probably being reinforced, and answer the preceding questions for those instances.

B. SELF-MODIFICATION EXERCISE

1. Identify a behavioral deficiency of yours that you would like to overcome. Next, describe the details of a plausible token system that might be applied by a friend or a relative to help you overcome your behavioral deficiency.

Notes and Extended Discussion

1. How is it that infants appear to learn new words when those words are not immediately followed by an observable reinforcer? A part of the answer lies with automatic conditioned reinforcement—a reinforcing effect produced by a response due to the resemblance of that response to a conditioned reinforcer (Skinner, 1957). Suppose that a parent says, "Say 'ma ma'" to an infant while providing reinforcement (tickling, touching, clapping, etc.). After several such trials, the sounds "ma ma" will become a conditioned reinforcer. Later, when

in the crib alone, the infant may begin saying "ma ma" because of the automatic conditioned reinforcement received from reproducing the same sound. More generally, vocal responses of infants may increase in frequency because the sounds that those vocal responses produce have become conditioned reinforcers and thus automatically strengthen their production responses. Studies have clearly confirmed this role of automatic conditioned reinforcement in early language acquisition (Smith, Michael, & Sundberg, 1996; Sundberg, Michael, Partington, & Sundberg, 1996). Automatic reinforcement appears to be important in not only language acquisition but also the strengthening of a variety of practical and artistic behaviors (Skinner, 1957; Vaughan & Michael, 1982).

2. As is commonly known, what gives cigarettes their reinforcing power is the addictive drug nicotine that is concentrated in tobacco. It is doubtful that anyone would smoke just to experience the smell, taste, and sensations that come from cigarette smoke in the mouth, lungs, and nose. What is perhaps not so well known is that because these stimuli are paired with the reinforcing effects of nicotine in the bloodstream, they become conditioned reinforcers. This has been shown in studies that have compared de-nicotinized cigarettes with standard nicotine-containing cigarettes. Shahan, Bickel, Madden, and Badger (1999) had smokers pull a plunger a number of times to obtain two puffs on a cigarette. The smoker could earn up to eight reinforcements per session. Responding for two different types of cigarettes was compared in this experiment. In some sessions, the smokers responded to standard nicotine-containing cigarettes; in other, randomly alternated, sessions, they responded to de-nicotinized cigarettes. The number of times the smoker had to pull the plunger for each reinforcement steadily increased over each session. The smoker had to make 2 responses to obtain the first reinforcement, 100 to obtain the second, 300 to obtain the third, 1,000 to obtain the fourth, 3,000 to obtain the fifth, 6,000 to obtain the sixth, 12,000 to obtain the seventh, and 24,000 to obtain the eighth. The results showed no detectable difference between the rates of responding to the standard cigarettes and the de-nicotinized cigarettes, although a subsequent preference test showed that the smokers preferred the standard cigarettes. In a related study, Juliano, Donny, Houtsmuller, and Stitzer (2006) looked at the effect of lapses on the cessation of smoking. If during treatment to eliminate smoking a person has a lapse—that is, smokes one or a few cigarettes—the gains made will be reversed in that it will now take longer for that person to eliminate smoking than it would have if the lapse had not occurred. This is because of the reinforcement of smoking during a lapse. What Juliano and her colleagues found is that smoking de-nicotinized cigarettes during a lapse resulted in as much reversal of gains as smoking standard cigarettes did. Thus, in both studies, the conditioned reinforcing effects of the stimuli associated with nicotine appeared to be comparable to the unconditioned reinforcing effects of nicotine. This underscores the point that when treating smoking and other addictions, therapists need to attend to the effects that conditioned reinforcement can have on the progress of the treatment.

Study Questions on Notes

1. How is conditioned reinforcement involved in influencing babies to babble sounds in their native language, even when no adults are around to reinforce this behavior?
2. Discuss how conditioned reinforcement is involved in an addiction such as to nicotine and in making it difficult for people to quit their addiction.

5

Decreasing a Behavior with Extinction

"Louise, let's get rid of your migraines."

LOUISE'S CASE[1]

When Louise was 13 years old, she began complaining about headaches. Over the next few years, she received inordinate amounts of parental, social, and professional attention for her headaches, including comments such as, "You poor dear, that must really hurt," "Let me give you a hug; that might make you feel better," and "I'm so sorry about your headaches—is there anything I can do to help?" In addition, Louise's complaints about headaches often led to her being allowed to stay home from school. These consequences may have reinforced the problem. At 26 years of age, Louise experienced debilitating headaches almost daily. These headaches had typical migraine characteristics—some visual effects (seeing "silver specks") followed by throbbing pain over her temples, nausea, and occasional vomiting. Various treatments had been tried unsuccessfully, including medication, acupuncture, chiropractic, psychotherapy, and electroconvulsive shock. Demerol injections, which she received from her physician approximately three times per week, appeared to provide temporary relief.

Several medical examinations failed to identify an organic basis for Louise's headaches. Following extensive assessment by behavior therapist Dr. Peter Aubuchon, Louise agreed that her migraines might have been learned through their reinforcement and said she would try a behavioral treatment program. First, Louise understood that her physician would no longer provide Demerol. Second, Louise and her husband agreed that he would record her pain behaviors (which were identified as complaints, going to bed, and putting cold compresses on her head). Third, Louise's parents, husband, physician, and nurses at the clinic that she regularly visited all agreed to completely ignore all pain behaviors Louise exhibited. Moreover, these same individuals

---

[1] This case is based on one reported by Aubuchon, Haber, and Adams (1985).

provided praise and other reinforcers for "well" behaviors (such as exercising and performing domestic duties). To ensure her commitment, Louise signed a statement indicating her agreement with this program (such a statement is referred to as a behavioral contract, which is discussed further in Chapters 24 and 26). The results of this program are shown in Figure 5–1. ■

EXTINCTION

There are two types of extinction: operant and respondent. This chapter is concerned with operant extinction (we discuss respondent extinction in Chapter 14). The principle of **extinction** (operant) states that (a) if, in a given situation, an individual emits a previously reinforced behavior and that behavior is not followed by a reinforcer, (b) then that person is less likely to do the same thing again when next encountering a similar situation. Stated differently, if a response has been increased in frequency through positive reinforcement, then completely ceasing to reinforce the response will cause it to decrease in frequency.

Discussions with Louise had indicated that she received a lot of attention for showing overt symptoms of and talking about her headaches. It is possible that this attention was a positive reinforcer in maintaining the high frequency of her pain behaviors. When Louise's pain behaviors no longer received attention, their frequency decreased to a low level. Although extinction was **NOTE 1** an effective treatment for Louise, we don't mean to imply that all pain behaviors are maintained by attention from others. For an evaluation of other factors that may influence behaviors of patients with chronic pain, see Turk and Okifuji (1997).

As with positive reinforcement, very few of us are aware of how frequently we are influenced by extinction every day of our lives. Some examples appear in Table 5–1. In each example, the individuals are simply doing what comes naturally in their daily activities. It might take several

FIGURE 5–1 Mean number of Louise's daily pain behaviors as reported by her spouse. (Reprinted from *Journal of Behavior Therapy and Experimental Psychiatry, 16,* "Can Migraine Headaches Be Modified by Operant Pain Techniques?" by P. Aubuchon, J. D. Haber, and H. E. Adams, p. 262. ©1985, with permission of Elsevier Science Ltd., The Boulevard, Langford Lane, Kidlington OX5 1GB, UK.)

TABLE 5–1   Examples of Extinction

Situation	Response	Immediate Consequences	Long-Term Effects
1. A 4-year-old child is lying in bed at night while the parents are sitting in the living room talking to guests.	The child begins to make loud animal noises while lying in bed.	The parents and guests ignore the child and continue to talk quietly.	The child is less likely to make animal noises in future situations of that sort.
2. The next evening, the same child and parents are having dinner at the dining room table. The child has just finished the main course.	The child holds up her empty plate and yells, "Dessert! Dessert! Dessert!"	The parents continue talking and ignore the child's loud demands.	The behavior of demanding dessert is less likely to occur in similar situations in the future.
3. A husband and wife are standing in the kitchen just after the husband comes home from work.	The husband complains about the traffic.	The wife goes about preparing supper and does not pay attention to his comments about the traffic.	Unproductive complaining by the husband is less likely to occur in that situation in the future.
4. A child in a third-grade classroom has just finished an assignment and raised his hand.	The child begins to snap his fingers.	The teacher ignores the child and responds to those children who raised their hands and are not snapping their fingers.	The child is less likely to snap his fingers in similar situations in the future.
5. A 3-year-old child working on a plastic puzzle is attempting to put a piece in the wrong place.	The child rotates the piece to try to make it fit.	The piece still doesn't fit, no matter how many times the child rotates it.	The likelihood of the child attempting to insert that piece in that position decreases.

repetitions of the behavior occurring and not being reinforced before any really obvious decrease in its frequency occurs. Nevertheless, the effect is still there. Over a number of trials, behaviors that no longer "pay off" gradually decrease. Of course, this is highly desirable in general, for if we persisted in useless behavior, we would quickly disappear as a species.

Keep in mind that extinction is just one of several possible causes of decreases in behavior. Suppose, for example, that the parents of a child who swears a lot decide to implement a program to decrease swearing. Suppose that, over several days, each time the child swears, the parents immediately yell "Stop that!" As a result, swearing is eliminated. In this case, swearing decreased because it was followed by a punisher (a reprimand). Now consider another possibility. Suppose that rather than reprimanding the child following instances of swearing, the parents said to the child, "You have just lost 25¢ of your weekly allowance" and that this procedure eliminated swearing. In this case, the removal of the child's allowance contingent on swearing is referred to as *response-cost punishment* (both reprimands and response-cost punishment are discussed in Chapter 12). Behavior can also decrease because of forgetting. In *forgetting,* a behavior is weakened as a function of time following its last occurrence. (For a behavioral interpretation of memory, see Palmer, 1991.) Extinction differs from each of these in that extinction weakens behavior as a result of being emitted without being reinforced.

Study Questions

1. What are the two parts to the principle of extinction?
2. Is telling someone to stop eating candies and the person stops an example of extinction? Explain why or why not on the basis of the definition of extinction.
3. Is a parent ignoring a child's behavior an example of extinction? Explain why or why not on the basis of the definition of extinction.
4. Suppose that, immediately after an instance of swearing, parents remove a portion of the child's weekly allowance and the result is that swearing decreases. Is this an example of extinction? Explain why or why not.
5. What is the difference between forgetting and extinction?
6. Explain the difference, in terms of procedure and results, between the loss of value of a conditioned reinforcer (see Chapter 4) and the extinction of a positively reinforced behavior.

FACTORS INFLUENCING THE EFFECTIVENESS OF EXTINCTION

1. Controlling Reinforcers for the Behavior That Is to Be Decreased

Consider the case of a 4-year-old girl, Susie, who has developed a great deal of whining behavior, especially in situations in which she wants something. Her mother has decided to ignore this behavior in the hope that it will go away. On three occasions during an afternoon, Mother ignored the behavior until it ceased, and then, following a brief period of no whining, provided Susie with the item she desired. Things seemed to be progressing well until early evening when Father came home. While Mother was in the kitchen, Susie approached her and in a whiny tone asked for some popcorn to eat while watching TV. Although Mother completely ignored Susie, Father entered the room and said, "Mother, can't you hear your child? Come here, Susie, I'll get your popcorn." We are sure that you can now predict the effect this episode will have on Susie's future whining behavior (not to mention Mother's anger toward Father).

    Reinforcers presented by other people or by the physical environment can undo your good **NOTE 2** efforts at applying extinction. Unfortunately, it is often difficult to convince others of this if they are not familiar with the principles of positive reinforcement and extinction. For example, if several nursery school staff are ignoring a child's tantrumming behavior and another staff member enters and says, "Oh, I can get this child to stop crying—here, Tommy, have a candy," then Tommy is likely to stop crying at that moment. But in the long run, his crying may increase in frequency because of that reinforced trial. Because Tommy did stop crying temporarily, however, it would probably be difficult to convince that staff member of the importance of extinction. In such cases, it is necessary either to control the behavior of individuals who might sabotage an extinction procedure or to carry out the procedure in their absence.

2. Extinction of a Behavior Combined with Positive Reinforcement for an Alternative Behavior

Extinction is most effective when combined with positive reinforcement for some desirable alternative behavior (Lerman & Iwata, 1996). Thus, not only were Louise's pain behaviors ignored (extinction), alternative behaviors (exercising, performing domestic duties, etc.) were positively reinforced. The combination of the two procedures probably decreased the frequency of the undesirable behavior much faster (and possibly to a lower level) than would have been the case had the extinction procedure been used alone.

Suppose that a parent wanted to combine extinction of a child's inappropriate crying with positive reinforcement for a desirable alternative behavior. It is often impractical to reinforce a child every few seconds for engaging in some desirable behavior (such as playing quietly) rather than disruptive behavior. It is possible, however, to begin with short intervals of desirable behavior and gradually increase them to longer, more manageable intervals. For example, the child who is engaging in inappropriate crying could be ignored until he had stopped crying and was playing quietly for a period of 10 seconds. At the end of the 10-second interval, he could be reinforced with praise. On subsequent trials, the parent could require successively longer periods of playing quietly—15 seconds, then 25, then a minute, and so on—before presenting reinforcement. It is important that the increase in the requirement of the desirable behavior be very gradual; otherwise, the undesirable behavior is likely to reoccur. Also, care must be taken not to present the reinforcer immediately after the undesirable behavior (e.g., crying) ceases because this would tend to reinforce the undesirable behavior, thereby increasing rather than reducing it.

It is also important during the application of extinction to ensure that the reinforcers that you are withholding are the ones that were actually maintaining the undesirable behavior. Failure to do this would technically not meet the definition of extinction, and the undesirable behavior would not likely decrease, as shown in Figure 5–2.

Extinction is sometimes criticized on the grounds that it is cruel to deprive people of social attention during their time of need (this criticism usually assumes that an individual who is crying, whining, or showing various other behaviors that commonly evoke attention is in a time of need). In some cases, this might be a valid criticism. In many situations, crying does indicate injury, emotional distress, and other forms of discomfort. We suggest that any behavior you are thinking of decreasing must be examined closely in terms of the desirability of decreasing it. If a decrease is desired, extinction frequently is the right procedure.

3. The Setting in Which Extinction Is Carried Out

As indicated previously, one reason for changing the setting in which extinction is carried out is to minimize the possibility that other people will reinforce the behavior you are trying to decrease. Another reason is that it may be socially difficult or even impossible to carry out extinction in certain situations. It would be unwise, for example, for a mother to initiate extinction of her child's temper tantrums in a department store. The nasty looks from other shoppers and store clerks would decrease the chances that the mother would carry through effectively with the procedure. It is important to consider the setting in which extinction will be carried out to (a) minimize the influence of alternative reinforcers on the undesirable behavior to be extinguished and (b) maximize the chances of the behavior modifier persisting with the program.

FIGURE 5–2 An extreme example of why attempts to apply extinction often fail. The actual reinforcer for the behavior must always be withheld.

4. Instructions: Use Rules

Although it is not necessary that an individual be able to talk about or understand extinction, it will probably help to speed up the decrease in behavior if the person is initially told something like this: "Each time you do X, then Y [the reinforcing item] will no longer occur." Consider, for example, the third case described in Table 5–1. Upon arriving home from work each day, the husband complains excessively about the slow traffic. His wife would be adding instructional control to extinction if she said something like, "George, the traffic is the same each day, and it doesn't do any good complaining about it. I love to talk to you about other things. But each time that you come home and complain excessively about the traffic, I'm just going to ignore it." This should cause George's complaining to decrease rapidly, although it may take a few trials. But remember that this procedure is more complex than simple extinction. (Instructional control is discussed further in Chapter 17.)

5. Extinction Is Quicker After Continuous Reinforcement

Let's take another look at the case of Susie's whining behavior. Before Mother decided to implement extinction, what happened when Susie was whining? Sometimes nothing would happen because Mother was busy with other things, such as talking on the telephone. But at other times (often after five or six instances of whining), Mother would attend to Susie and give her what she wanted. This is typical of many reinforcement situations in that Susie's whining was not reinforced following each instance. Rather, her whining was reinforced occasionally, following several instances of it. This is an example of *intermittent reinforcement,* which is discussed in detail in Chapters 6 and 7. It is necessary to mention continuous and intermittent reinforcement here because they can influence the effectiveness of extinction. **Continuous reinforcement** is an arrangement in which each instance of a particular response is reinforced. **Intermittent reinforcement** is an arrangement in which a response is reinforced only occasionally (i.e., intermittently) rather than every time it occurs.

The influence of a reinforcement schedule on subsequent extinction can easily be imagined if you consider a little problem that you may have encountered. Suppose you are writing with a pen that suddenly stops. What do you do? You probably shake it up and down a couple of times and try to write with it a few more times. If it still doesn't write, you throw it away and get another pen. Now suppose that you are writing with another pen. This second pen occasionally skips. You shake it a few times and write some more, and then it misses some more. Each time you shake it, it writes a little more. Now comes the question: In which situation are you likely to persist longer in shaking and attempting to use the pen? Obviously, the second because the pen occasionally quits but it usually writes again.

When a behavior has always been reinforced and then is never reinforced (such as when a pen quits altogether), behavior extinguishes quickly. When intermittent reinforcement has maintained a behavior (such as a pen writing after shaking it), that behavior is likely to extinguish slowly (Kazdin & Polster, 1973).This seemingly simple phenomenon is complex and depends in part on how one measures behavior during extinction (Lerman, Iwata, Shore, & Kahng, 1996; Nevin, 1988). For our purposes, it is sufficient to note that in general, behavior that has been intermittently reinforced extinguishes more slowly than behavior that has been continuously reinforced. Behavior that extinguishes slowly is said to be *resistant to extinction.*

Now let's look closely at Susie's whining. It will likely take longer for extinction to eliminate her whining completely if it sometimes pays off and sometimes does not than if it always paid off before being ignored completely. In other words, extinction is often quicker after *continuous reinforcement* than after *intermittent reinforcement.* If you try to extinguish a behavior that has been reinforced intermittently, you must be prepared for extinction to take longer.

Study Questions

7. If a behavior that was maintained by positive reinforcement is not reinforced at least once in a while, what will happen to the behavior?
8. Why did the mother's attempt to extinguish the child's cookie eating fail (refer to Figure 5–2)?
9. Examine Table 5–1. Which of those examples involve positive reinforcement for an alternative response? For those that do not, indicate how positive reinforcement for an alternative response might be introduced.
10. Why is it necessary to consider the setting as a factor influencing your extinction program?
11. Describe a particular behavior you would like to decrease in a child with whom you have contact. Would your extinction program require a special setting? Why or why not?
12. Define *continuous reinforcement* and give an example.
13. Define *intermittent reinforcement* and give an example.
14. What is the effect of continuous versus intermittent reinforcement on the resistance to the extinction of a behavior?

6. Behavior Being Extinguished May Get Worse Before It Gets Better

During extinction, behavior may increase before it begins to decrease. That is, things may get worse before they get better. An increase in responding during extinction is commonly referred to as an **extinction burst**. Suppose a child in a classroom is constantly raising her or his hand and snapping her or his fingers to gain the teacher's attention. A teacher who keeps track of the frequency of finger snapping for a while and then introduces extinction (that is, ignores the finger snapping) would probably observe an increase in finger snapping during the first few minutes of extinction before the behavior gradually began to taper off. Why? Most of us have learned that if something is no longer paying off, a slight increase in the behavior may be sufficient to again bring the payoff. Well documented in basic research, extinction bursts have also been reported in applied research (Lerman & Iwata, 1995; Lerman, Iwata, & Wallace, 1999). Thus, extinction bursting is something that everyone who attempts to apply an extinction procedure should know. A teacher who decided to introduce extinction following finger snapping and then observed an increase in this behavior during the next few minutes might erroneously conclude that extinction wasn't working and give up in the middle of the program. The effect of this action would be to reinforce the behavior when it gets worse. The rule to follow here is this:

> If you introduce extinction, keep with it. Things usually get worse before they get better, but hang in there; doing so will pay off in the long run.

Exceptions to this rule are situations in which an extinction burst may be harmful. If you can anticipate that possibility, you might take preventive steps. For example, before implementing an extinction program to decrease head banging of a young girl with developmental disabilities, Brian Iwata and his colleagues put a helmet on the girl during extinction sessions so that she would not harm herself during an extinction burst (Iwata, Pace, Cowdery, & Miltenberger, 1994). Alternatively, if you predict that an extinction burst might cause harm, then don't use extinction. Other strategies for decreasing problem behaviors are described in later chapters.

7. Extinction May Produce Aggression That Interferes with the Program

Another difficulty of extinction is that the procedure may produce aggression. Again, we have all experienced this. Probably all of us have had the desire to pound and kick a vending machine that took our money and did not deliver the merchandise. If we reconsider the finger-snapping example, we might at first see some mild aggression. If a teacher ignores a child's finger snapping, the child might start snapping his or her fingers louder and louder and perhaps banging on the desk and yelling "Hey!" This characteristic of extinction has been studied extensively in laboratory situations and has also been reported in applied research (Lerman et al., 1999; Lerman & Iwata, 1996). In studies of extinction of self-injurious behavior, aggression was observed in nearly half of the cases in which extinction was the sole intervention. However, the prevalence of aggression was substantially lower when extinction was implemented as part of a treatment package that included positive reinforcement for an alternative desirable behavior. It is important to minimize aggression not only because it is undesirable but also because it could lead to giving up too soon. This might not only reinforce the undesirable behavior on an intermittent schedule but also reinforce aggression.

Another option would be to conduct an extinction program in a setting in which a certain amount of aggression can be tolerated. If parents decide to apply extinction to decrease a child's tantrumming, for example, they might do so at home after removing any breakable objects. As another example, in an extinction program to decrease aggressive behaviors (scratching, hitting, kicking, and biting) of a boy with a severe developmental disability, Edward Carr and his colleagues had teachers wear protective clothing that consisted of a thick corduroy coat and rubber gloves (Carr, Newson, & Binkoff, 1980).

8. Extinguished Behavior May Reappear After a Delay

Another difficulty of extinction is that a behavior that has disappeared during an extinction session may reappear at the next opportunity after some time has passed. The reappearance of an extinguished behavior following a rest is called **spontaneous recovery**. Let's reconsider the finger-snapping example. Suppose that the teacher initiated an extinction program for finger snapping when the student returned to school after lunch. During the first hour, 10 instances of finger snapping occurred, and the teacher and the other students ignored each. Let's suppose further that there were no instances of finger snapping during the remainder of the afternoon and that the teacher assumed that finger snapping had been successfully extinguished. When the teacher returned to class the next morning, however, another five instances of finger snapping occurred during the first hour of school. This would be spontaneous recovery of finger snapping. Typically, the amount of behavior that recovers spontaneously following a rest is less than the amount that occurred during the previous extinction session. After several additional extinction sessions, spontaneous recovery is usually not a problem. Although these characteristics of spontaneous recovery are well documented in basic research (Pear, 2001), it has not been formally studied in applied research, and very few anecdotal (i.e., informal) reports of spontaneous recovery occurring in applications of extinction (Lerman & Iwata, 1996) have been reported. We highly recommend that the teacher be prepared to continue with the extinction program despite the occurrence of spontaneous recovery.

NOTE 3   To review, in this chapter and Chapter 3, we suggest that if you want behavior to happen more often, reinforce it; if you want behavior to happen less often, ignore it. But beware: There is much more to positive reinforcement and extinction than first meets the eye.

PITFALLS OF EXTINCTION

In Chapter 3, we introduced five types of pitfalls that can work against the unwary. Here we consider two of these pitfall types with regard to extinction.

Pitfall Type 1

As with many natural laws, such as the law of gravity and the principle of positive reinforcement, the principle of extinction operates whether or not we are aware of it. Unfortunately, those who are not aware of extinction are apt to apply it unknowingly to the desirable behavior of friends, acquaintances, family, and others. See Table 5–2 for some examples of how extinction may, in the long run, work to decrease desirable behavior.

Pitfall Type 2

Even when some individuals are knowledgeably applying behavior modification in an effort to help behaviorally deficient individuals, others who are less knowledgeable about extinction may undo their good work. Suppose, for example, that a child in a program for persons with

		Immediate	Long-Term
TABLE 5–2 Examples of Undesirable Instances of Extinction			
Situation	**Responses**	**Consequences**	**Effects**
1. You ask a friend to call you on your cell phone on a particular evening.	Your friend dials your number several times.	Each time the phone rings, you ignore it and continue reading your novel.	Your friend is less likely to attempt to call you when requested to do so.
2. Two staff members are talking to each other in a special education classroom, and a student approaches and stands nearby.	The student stands and waits patiently beside the two staff members for several minutes. Finally, the student interrupts.	The staff members continued talking while the student waited patiently and stopped talking and listened after the student interrupted.	The response of standing beside the staff and waiting patiently is less likely to occur in the future, and the response of interrupting staff is more likely to occur in the future.
3. A man carrying several parcels is walking toward the exit door of a department store. A woman standing by the door sees the man coming.	The woman opens the door for the man.	The man rushes out without saying a word.	The chances of the woman opening the door in similar situations in the future are decreased.
4. A 3-month-old baby is lying quietly in the crib just before feeding time.	The baby begins making cooing sounds (which might be interpreted by eager parents as "mama" or "dada").	The mother, busy preparing a bottle, ignores the child. When the child is picked up later, she is again quiet (or, more likely, crying).	The mother has just missed an opportunity to reinforce noise making that approximates speech. Instead, she reinforced lying quietly (or crying). Therefore, cooing is less likely to occur in the future.

developmental disabilities has been reinforced by an aide for dressing himself. Suppose also that this aide has been transferred or has gone on vacation and is replaced by an aide who is less familiar with the principles of positive reinforcement and extinction. Confronted with one child who dresses himself and many children who cannot, the new aide will likely spend a great deal of time helping the latter children but give little attention to the one child. It is a common human tendency to give plenty of attention to problems and to ignore situations in which things seem to be going well. It is easy to rationalize this selective attention. "After all," the aide may say, "why should I reinforce Johnny for doing something that he already knows how to do?" However, if the child's self-dressing behavior is to be maintained after it has been established, it must be reinforced at least occasionally. Strategies to maintain desirable behavior (and thereby prevent unwanted extinction) are described in Chapter 16.

GUIDELINES FOR THE EFFECTIVE APPLICATION OF EXTINCTION

The following rules are offered as a checklist for effectively using extinction to decrease a particular behavior. As with the guidelines for positive reinforcement in Chapter 3, assume that the user is a parent, teacher, or some other person who is working with individuals with behavior problems.

1. *Selecting the Behavior to Be Decreased*
   a. In choosing the behavior, be specific. Don't expect a major character improvement to take place all at once. For example, do not try to extinguish all of Johnny's trouble-making behavior in a classroom. Rather, choose a particular behavior, such as Johnny's finger snapping.
   b. Remember that the behavior often gets worse before it gets better and that aggressive behavior is sometimes produced during the extinction process. Therefore, make sure that the circumstances are such that you can follow through with your extinction procedure. For example, be very careful if the target behavior is destructive to the individual or others. Will it be harmful for you to persist in your extinction program if the behavior gets worse? You should also consider the setting in which the target behavior is likely to occur. It may be impractical to extinguish temper tantrums in a restaurant because of obvious social pressures that you may be unable to resist. If you are concerned with decreasing a particular behavior but you cannot apply extinction because of these considerations, do not despair. We will describe other procedures for decreasing behavior in Chapters 7, 12, 17, 18, and 23.
   c. Select a behavior for which you can control the reinforcers that are currently maintaining it.

2. *Preliminary Considerations*
   a. If possible, keep track of how often the target behavior occurs prior to your extinction program. During this recording phase, do not attempt to withhold the reinforcer for the undesirable behavior.
   b. Try to identify what is currently reinforcing the undesirable behavior so that you can withhold the reinforcer during treatment. (If this is not possible, then, technically, the program does not have an extinction component.) The reinforcement history of the undesirable behavior might provide some idea of just how long extinction will take.
   c. Identify some desirable alternative behavior in which the individual can engage.
   d. Identify effective reinforcers that can be used for desirable alternative behavior by the individual.
   e. Try to select a setting in which extinction can be carried out successfully.
   f. Be sure that all relevant individuals know before the program starts just which behavior is being extinguished and which behavior is being reinforced. Be sure that all who will be coming in contact with the individual have been prompted to ignore the undesirable behavior and to reinforce the desirable alternative behavior.

3. *Implementing the Plan*
   a. Tell the individual about the plan before starting.
   b. Regarding the positive reinforcement for the desirable alternative behavior, be sure to follow the rules in Chapter 3 for putting the plan into effect.
   c. After initiating the program, be completely consistent in withholding reinforcement after all instances of the undesirable behavior and reinforcing the desirable alternative behavior.

4. *Weaning the Student from the Program* (discussed in more detail in Chapter 16)
   a. After the undesirable behavior has decreased to zero, occasional relapses may occur, so be prepared.
   b. Three possible reasons for the failure of your extinction procedure are
      (1) the attention you are withholding following the undesirable behavior is not the reinforcer that was maintaining the behavior
      (2) the undesirable behavior is receiving intermittent reinforcement from another source
      (3) the desired alternative behavior has not been strengthened sufficiently
      Examine these reasons carefully if it is taking a long time to complete the extinction procedure successfully.
   c. Regarding the reinforcement of the desirable alternative behavior, try to follow the rules in Chapter 3 for weaning the child from the program.

Study Questions

15. What is an extinction burst? Describe an example.
16. What is spontaneous recovery? Describe an example.
17. In a sentence for each, describe eight general factors influencing the effectiveness of extinction.
18. Describe two examples of extinction that you have encountered, one involving a desirable behavior and one involving an undesirable behavior. For each example, identify the situation, behavior, immediate consequence, and probable long-term effects as is done in Tables 5–1 and 5–2. (Your examples should not be from the text.)
19. Briefly describe an example of a pitfall of extinction. Does your example illustrate Pitfall Type 1 or Type 2?
20. Extinction should not be applied to certain behaviors or in certain situations (see p. 70). What types of behaviors and situations would these be? Give an example of a behavior to which extinction should not be applied. Give an example of a situation in which extinction should not be applied.
21. What are three possible reasons for the failure of an extinction program?

Application Exercises

A. EXERCISE INVOLVING OTHERS

Choose a situation in which you can sit and watch an adult interact with one or more children for approximately half an hour. During this period, write the number of times that the adult pays attention to desirable behaviors of the children and the number of times the adult ignores specific desirable behaviors. This will give you some idea of how often we miss opportunities to reinforce the desirable behaviors of those around us.

B. SELF-MODIFICATION EXERCISES

1. Think of something you did today that did not pay off. Give a specific, complete description of the situation and behavior following the examples in Table 5–1.
2. Select one of your behavioral excesses (perhaps one that you listed at the end of Chapter 1). Outline a complete extinction program that you (with a little help from your friends) might apply to decrease that behavior. Make sure that you select a behavior for which the reinforcer that maintains it can be withheld. Make sure that your plan follows the guidelines given for the effective application of extinction.

Notes and Extended Discussion

1. Louise's case raises some intriguing questions. Was it simply her reports of pain that decreased? Did her "feelings" of pain—the actual headaches—also decrease? Although she did not self-monitor headache frequency, Louise reported at a 12-month follow-up that she had experienced only two headaches over the previous several months. Her other behaviors tended to support this: She was able to perform a variety of activities (domestic chores, work, etc.) that she had not been able to do in the past, and she and her husband reported that their marital relationship had greatly improved. As discussed further in Chapters 15, 26, and 27, private behaviors are assumed to be affected by behavioral techniques in the same way as are public behaviors. Perhaps in Louise's case, both public complaints about pain and private pain behavior were decreased as a function of the extinction procedure.

2. One of the greatest hazards an extinction program faces is reinforcement from a well-intentioned person who does not understand the program or its rationale. This obstacle was encountered in one of the earliest reports on the application of extinction to a child's temper tantrums. C. D. Williams (1959) reported the case of a 21-month-old infant who screamed and cried if his parents left the bedroom after putting him to bed at night. A program was initiated in which the parent left the room after bedtime pleasantries and did not reenter it, no matter how much the infant screamed and raged. The first time the child was put to bed under this extinction procedure, he screamed for 45 minutes. By the 10th night, however, he no longer cried but smiled as the parent left the room. About a week later, however, when the parents were enjoying a much-needed evening out, he screamed and fussed after his aunt, the babysitter, had put him to bed. The aunt reinforced the behavior by returning to the bedroom and remaining there until he went to sleep. It was then necessary to extinguish the behavior a second time, which took almost as long as the first time. Ayllon and Michael (1959) observed the undesirable effect of unwanted reinforcement in extinction, which they called *bootleg reinforcement*. A patient in a psychiatric hospital engaged in such annoying psychotic talk (of the type referred to as *delusional*) that other patients had on several occasions beaten her in an effort to keep her quiet. To decrease her psychotic talk, the doctors instructed the nurses to ignore it and to pay attention only to sensible talk. As a result, the proportion of her speech that was psychotic decreased from 0.91 to 0.25. Later, though, it increased to a high level, probably because of bootleg reinforcement from a social worker. This came to light when the patient remarked to one of the nurses, "Well, you're not listening to me. I'll have to go and see [the social worker] again, 'cause she told me that if she listens to my past she could help me."

3. An alternative to extinction for reducing undesirable behavior in persons with developmental disabilities is *noncontingent reinforcement*. For example, suppose that in a treatment center for children with developmental disabilities, Suzy appears to display frequent tantrums because tantrumming usually leads to adult attention. A noncontingent reinforcement program might involve giving Suzy adult attention once every 30 seconds regardless of the behavior that is occurring. In a number of studies, this type of treatment has proven to be effective in decreasing challenging behavior (for a review of such studies, see Tucker, Sigafoos, & Bushell, 1998). A potential criticism of this strategy to decrease behavior is that it might reduce the client's motivation to participate in teaching sessions (considering that a reinforcer is received frequently for essentially doing nothing). In addition, because it acts indiscriminately on any behavior that occurs at a high rate, it can also reduce desirable behavior.

Study Questions on Notes

1. Discuss whether the extinction program with Louise decreased her "feelings" of pain.
2. What is bootleg reinforcement? Give an example.
3. Describe how noncontingent reinforcement might be used to decrease challenging behavior. What is a potential limitation of this approach?

6

Developing Behavioral Persistence Through the Use of Intermittent Reinforcement

"Jan, let's see how many math problems you can do."

IMPROVING JAN'S WORK RATE IN MATH CLASS[1]

Jan was 13-year-old seventh grade student of average intelligence. During math classes, she exhibited a great deal of inattentive behavior and made frequent errors. With the support of her teacher, two behavior modifiers introduced a strategy for improving Jan's work rate. One of them worked with Jan every day during math class, giving Jan a worksheet containing math problems. During the first two days, when Jan completed two problems correctly, the behavior modifier responded with "Good work" or "Excellent job," or some similar positive reaction. During the next two days, the number of problems to be completed before praise was given increased to four. Two days after that, Jan had to complete eight problems correctly before receiving praise. During the final two days, no praise was given until Jan had completed 16 problems.

The praise schedule had a positive effect on Jan's work rate. From the beginning to the end of the study, her rate of correct problem solving tripled, with the highest work rate occurring when Jan was praised following each 16 problems solved. Moreover, by the end of the study, Jan was attending to the task 100% of the time. ∎

---

[1] This case is based on a report by Kirby and Shields (1972).

SOME DEFINITIONS

As stated in Chapter 5, intermittent reinforcement is an arrangement in which a behavior is reinforced only occasionally (i.e., intermittently) rather than every time it occurs. Jan's problem-solving behavior was not reinforced after each math problem that she solved. Instead, she received reinforcement after a fixed number of problem-solving responses had occurred. On this reinforcement schedule, Jan worked at a very steady rate. (*Note: Response rate* and *response frequency* are synonymous terms; although we tended to use the latter in the earlier chapters of this book, we now switch to the former.)

To talk about intermittent reinforcement, we must first define schedule of reinforcement. A **schedule of reinforcement** is a rule specifying which occurrences of a given behavior, if any, will be reinforced. The simplest schedule of reinforcement is continuous reinforcement, which, as indicated Chapter 5, is an arrangement in which each instance of a particular response is reinforced. Had Jan received reinforcement for each problem solved, we would say that she was on a continuous reinforcement schedule. Many behaviors in everyday life are reinforced on a continuous reinforcement schedule. Each time you turn the tap, your behavior is reinforced by water. Each time that you insert and turn the key in the front door of your home or apartment, your behavior is reinforced by the door opening.

The opposite of continuous reinforcement is called *extinction.* As discussed in Chapter 5, on an extinction schedule, no instance of a given behavior is reinforced. The effect is that the behavior eventually decreases to a very low level or ceases altogether.

Between these two extremes—continuous reinforcement and extinction—lies intermittent reinforcement. Many activities in the natural environment are not reinforced continuously. You may not always get a good grade after studying. You have to work for a week before you get your weekly paycheck. Experiments on the effects of various strategies for reinforcing behaviors have been studied under the topic of schedules of reinforcement. The number of such schedules is unlimited. Because each produces its own characteristic behavior pattern, different schedules are suitable for different types of applications. In addition, certain schedules are more practical than **NOTE 1** others (e.g., some are more time consuming or labor intensive than others).

While a behavior is being conditioned or learned, it is said to be in the *acquisition* phase. After it has become well learned, it is said to be in the *maintenance* phase. It is best to provide continuous reinforcement during acquisition and then switch to intermittent reinforcement during maintenance. Intermittent schedules have several advantages over continuous reinforcement for maintaining behavior: (a) The reinforcer remains effective longer because satiation takes place more slowly; (b) behavior that has been reinforced intermittently tends to take longer to extinguish (see Chapter 5); (c) individuals work more consistently on certain intermittent schedules; and (d) behavior that has been reinforced intermittently is more likely to persist after being transferred to reinforcers in the natural environment. In this chapter, we discuss four types of intermittent schedules for increasing and maintaining behavior: ratio, simple interval, interval with limited hold, and duration. Each of these is subdivided into fixed and variable, giving eight basic schedules. (Basic research on these schedules is described in Pear, 2001.)

Before describing the basic schedules of reinforcement, we first distinguish between free-operant procedures and discrete-trials procedures. A *free-operant procedure* is one in which the individual is "free" to respond repeatedly in the sense that there are no constraints on successive responses. For example, if Jan had been given a worksheet containing 12 math problems to solve, she could have worked at various rates (e.g., 1 problem per minute, 3 per minute). In a *discrete-trials procedure,* a distinct stimulus is presented prior to an opportunity for a response to occur and be followed by reinforcement, and the next response cannot occur until another stimulus is presented, and so on. Thus, if Jan's teacher presented a math problem and waited a brief time for Jan to solve it, following which the teacher presented another problem to Jan, and so on, this would be a discrete-trials procedure. You can see that a discrete-trials procedure limits the rate of responding to the rate at which successive stimuli are presented at the beginning of each trial, which is determined by the wait time for a response to occur. When we talk about the characteristic effects of schedules of reinforcement in this chapter, we are referring to free-operant procedures unless otherwise specified. (For discussion discrete-trial teaching, see p. 28.)

Study Questions

1. Define and give an example of *intermittent reinforcement.*
2. Define and give an example of *schedule of reinforcement.*
3. Define and give an example of *continuous reinforcement.*
4. Describe four advantages of intermittent over continuous reinforcement for maintaining behavior.
5. What is a free-operant procedure? Give an example.
6. What is a discrete-trials procedure? Give an example.

RATIO SCHEDULES

In a **fixed-ratio (FR) schedule**, a reinforcer occurs each time a fixed number of responses of a particular type are emitted. The reinforcement schedules for Jan were FR schedules. Recall that early in her program, she had to complete two math problems for each reinforcement, which is abbreviated FR 2. Later she had to solve four problems for reinforcement, which is abbreviated FR 4. Finally, she had to make 16 correct responses, abbreviated FR 16. Note that the schedule was increased in steps. If Jan's responses had been put on FR 16 immediately (i.e., without the intervening FR values), her behavior might have deteriorated and appeared as though it were on extinction. This deterioration of responding from increasing an FR schedule too rapidly is sometimes referred to as *ratio strain*. The optimal response requirement differs for different individuals and for different tasks. For example, Jan increased her response rate even when the FR increased to 16. Other students may have shown a decrease before reaching FR 16. In general, the higher the ratio at which an individual is expected to perform, the more important it is to approach it gradually through exposure to lower ratios. The optimal ratio value that will maintain a high rate of response without producing ratio strain must be found by trial and error.

When introduced gradually, FR schedules produce a high steady rate until reinforcement, followed by a postreinforcement pause. The length of the postreinforcement pause depends on the value of the FR—the higher the value, the longer the pause (Schlinger, Derenne, & Baron, 2008). FR schedules also produce high resistance to extinction (see Chapter 5, p. 66).

NOTE 2   There are many examples of FR schedules in everyday life. If a football coach were to say to the team, "Everybody do 20 push-ups before taking a break," that would be an FR 20. Another example is paying an industrial worker for a specified number of completed parts (called *piece-rate pay*).

With a **variable-ratio (VR) schedule**, a reinforcer occurs after a certain number of a particular response, and the number of responses required for each reinforcer changes unpredictably from one reinforcer to the next. The number of responses required for each reinforcement in a VR schedule varies around some mean value, and this value is specified in the designation of that particular VR schedule. Suppose, for example, that over a period of several months, a door-to-door salesperson averages one sale for every 10 houses called on. This does not mean that the salesperson makes a sale at exactly every 10th house. Sometimes a sale might have been made after calling on five houses in a row. Sometimes sales might occur at two houses in a row. And sometimes the salesperson might call on a large number of houses before making a sale. Over several months, however, a mean of 10 house calls is required to produce reinforcement. A VR schedule that requires an average of 10 responses is abbreviated VR 10. VR, like FR, produces a high steady rate of responding. However, it also produces no or a minimal postreinforcement pause (Schlinger et al., 2008). The salesperson can never predict exactly when a sale will occur and is likely to continue making house calls right after a sale. Three additional differences between the effects of VR and FR schedules are that the VR schedule can be increased somewhat more abruptly than an FR schedule without producing ratio strain, the values of VR that can maintain responding are somewhat higher than FR, and VR produces a higher resistance to extinction than FR schedules of the same value.

The natural environment contains many examples of VR schedules. Asking someone for a date is an example because even the most popular people often have to ask an unpredictable number of different people to obtain an acceptance. Slot machines are programmed on VR schedules: The gambler has no way of predicting how many times he or she must put in money to hit a payoff. Similarly, casting for fish is also reinforced on a VR schedule: One must cast an unpredictable number of times to get a bite.

Ratio schedules—both FR and VR—are used when one wants to generate a high rate of responding and can monitor each response (because it is necessary to count the responses to know when to deliver reinforcement on a ratio schedule). FR is more commonly used than VR in behavioral programs because it is simpler to administer.

A type of reinforcement schedule that is becoming increasingly popular in applied settings is progressive ratio (PR). In fact, the *Journal of Applied Behavior Analysis* devoted its summer 2008 issue to this topic. A PR schedule is like an FR schedule, but the ratio requirement increases by a specified amount after each reinforcer. At the beginning of each session, the ratio requirement starts back at its original value. After a number of sessions, the ratio requirement reaches a level—called the *break point* or *breaking point*—at which the individual stops responding completely. The typical effect of a PR schedule is an increasingly longer pause after each successive reinforcer and an indefinitely long pause at the break point (Schlinger et al., 2008).The main application of PR is to determine how potent or powerful a particular reinforcer is for a particular individual. The higher the reinforcer's break point is for the individual, the more effective the reinforcer is likely to be in a treatment program for that individual (Roane, 2008).

Although the preceding discussion pertains to ratio schedules in a free-operant procedure, ratio schedules have also been studied in discrete-trials procedures. An example of the use of a ratio schedule in a discrete-trials procedure involves a task designed to teach children with developmental disabilities to name pictures of objects. The procedure involves presenting a carefully designed sequence of trials in which the teacher sometimes speaks the name of the picture for the child to imitate and sometimes requires that the child name the picture correctly. Correct responses are reinforced with praise (e.g., "Good!") and a treat. Children make more correct responses and learn to name more pictures when correct responses are reinforced with a treat on a ratio schedule than when they are continuously reinforced with a treat. However, this is true only if the ratio schedule does not require too many correct responses per reinforcement. As the response requirement increases, performance improves at first but then begins to show ratio strain (see Stephens, Pear, Wray, & Jackson, 1975).

Study Questions

7. Explain what an FR schedule is. Describe the details of two examples of FR schedules in everyday life (at least one of which is not in this chapter). Do your examples involve a free-operant procedure or a discrete-trials procedure?

8. What are three characteristic effects of an FR schedule?

9. What is ratio strain?

10. Explain what a VR schedule is. Describe the details of two examples of VR schedules in everyday life (at least one of which is not in the text). Do your examples involve a free-operant procedure or a discrete-trials procedure?

11. Describe how a VR schedule is similar procedurally to an FR schedule. Describe how it is different procedurally.

12. What are three characteristic effects of a VR schedule?

13. Describe two examples of how FR or VR might be applied in training programs. (By *training program,* we refer to any situation in which someone deliberately uses behavior principles to increase and maintain someone else's behavior, such as parents to influence a child's behavior, a teacher to influence students' behavior, a coach to influence athletes' behavior, an employer to influence employees' behavior, etc.) Do your examples involve a free-operant or a discrete-trials procedure?

14. Explain what a PR schedule is and how PR has been mainly used in applied settings.

SIMPLE INTERVAL SCHEDULES

In a **fixed-interval (FI) schedule**, a reinforcer is presented following the first instance of a specific response after a fixed period of time (see Figure 6–1). The only requirement for a reinforcer to occur is that the individual engage in the behavior after reinforcement has become available because of the passage of time. The size of the FI schedule is the amount of time that must elapse before reinforcement becomes available (e.g., if 1 minute must elapse before the behavior can be reinforced, we call the schedule an *FI 1-minute schedule*). Note from Figure 6–1 that although the passage of a certain amount of time is necessary for reinforcement to occur, a response must occur sometime after the specified time interval. Note also that there is no limit on how long after the end of the interval a response can occur in order to be reinforced. Finally, note that a response occurring before the specified interval ends has absolutely no effect on the occurrence of the reinforcer.

The typical effects of an FI schedule are illustrated in the following example. Suppose that two young children play together each morning. About 2 hours after breakfast, a parent has a midmorning snack prepared for them; approximately 2 hours after that, lunch is prepared for them. As the time draws to a close in each 2-hour period, the children begin making more and more frequent trips to the kitchen, each time asking, "Is our food ready yet?" Finally, after 2 hours, it's ready. After eating, they return to their play, and there's a fairly lengthy passage of time before they start to make trips to the kitchen again. The children's behavior of going to the kitchen is characteristic of behavior reinforced on an FI schedule. That is, provided that the individuals don't have access to clocks or others who will tell them the time, then FI schedules produce (a) a rate of responding that increases gradually near the end of the interval until reinforcement and (b) a postreinforcement pause. Note that the word *pause* does not mean that no behavior occurs; it simply means that the behavior of interest, such as the trip to the kitchen, does not occur. The length of the postreinforcement pause depends on the value of the FI—the higher the value (i.e., the more time between reinforcers), the longer the pause. Most of us, however, rely on clocks to tell us when to do things that are reinforced on an FI schedule. We usually

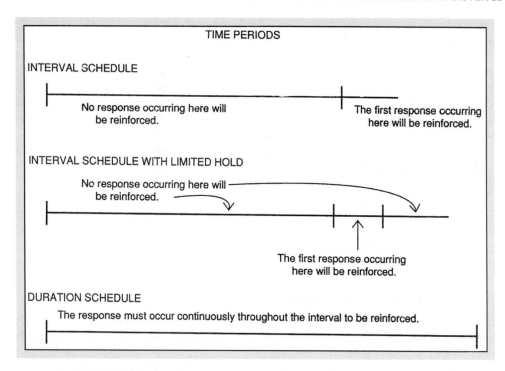

FIGURE 6–1 Diagrams illustrating the differences between the time-based schedules described in the text. In each diagram, the horizontal line represents a period of time.

wait until the reinforcer is available and then make one response and receive it. (But note that the behavior of glancing at a clock or watch follows the typical FI pattern. Can you see why?)

When judging whether a behavior is reinforced on a fixed-interval schedule, you should ask yourself two questions: (a) Does reinforcement require only one response after a fixed interval of time? (b) Does responding during the interval affect anything? If you can answer yes to the first question and no to the second question, your example is an FI. Consider, for example, a college class in which students have a test on the same day of the week. The students' pattern of studying likely resembles the characteristic pattern of responding on an FI schedule in that little or no studying occurs immediately after a test and studying increases as the test day draws near. However, consider the preceding two questions. Can the students wait around until a week has passed, make "one" study response, and receive a good grade? No, a good grade is contingent on studying during the one-week interval. Does responding before the interval ends affect anything? Yes, it contributes to a good grade. Therefore, this is not an example of FI, although it may resemble it in some ways.

A job that pays by the hour is sometimes cited as an example of an FI schedule, but this is not correct because hourly pay assumes that the individual works during the hour. An FI schedule, however, requires only one response at the end of the interval. Picking up one's paycheck is an example of behavior reinforced on an FI schedule in that the check is ready only after a certain period of time, and going to the pay window earlier does not make it ready any sooner.

In a **variable-interval (VI) schedule**, a reinforcer is presented following the first instance of a specific response after an interval of time, and the length of the interval changes unpredictably from one reinforcer to the next. Stated more simply, on a VI schedule, a response is reinforced after unpredictable intervals of time. The lengths of the intervals in a VI schedule vary around some mean value, which is specified in the designation of that particular VI schedule. For example, if a mean of 25 minutes is required before reinforcement becomes available, the schedule is abbreviated VI 25 minutes. VI produces a moderate steady rate of responding and no (or at most a very small) postreinforcement pause. Like the intermittent schedules discussed previously, VI produces a high resistance to extinction relative to continuous reinforcement. However, responding is lower during extinction after VI than it is after FR or VR.

Because letters can be sent or messages left at unpredictable times, checking one's mailbox for mail, one's answering machine for messages, and one's computer for email are examples of VI schedules in the natural environment.

Simple interval schedules are not often used in behavior modification programs for several reasons: (a) FI produces long postreinforcement pauses; (b) although VI does not produce postreinforcement pauses, it does generate lower response rates than ratio schedules do; and (c) simple interval schedules require continuous monitoring of behavior after the end of each interval until a response occurs.

INTERVAL SCHEDULES WITH LIMITED HOLD

When what is called a *limited hold* is added to an interval schedule, it can have a powerful effect on behavior. We'll explain how it works by describing an effective strategy for managing the behavior of kids on a family car trip. It's based on *The Timer Game,*[2] also known as *The Good Behavior Game* (Tingstrom, Sterling-Turner, & Wilczynski, 2006). When one of the author's two boys were children, family car trips were trying. With Mom and Dad in the front seat and the boys in the back seat, nonstop bickering between the boys seemed to rule the day ("You're on my side," "Give me that," "Don't touch me," etc.). After several unpleasant car trips, Mom and Dad decided to try a variation of The Timer Game. First, they purchased a timer that could be set at values up to 25 minutes and produced a "ding" when the set time ran out. At the beginning of the car trip, they announced the new rules to the boys: "Here's the deal. Every time this timer goes 'ding,' if you are playing nicely, you can earn 5 extra minutes for watching late-night TV in the motel room [a powerful reinforcer for the boys in the days before there were DVD players in vehicles]. But if you are bickering, you lose those 5 minutes. We'll play the game until we get there." Thereafter, a parent set the timer at random intervals for the duration of the trip. The results seemed miraculous. From nonstop bickering, the boys switched to mainly cooperative play. Although it required only an instant of cooperative play to earn a reinforcer, the boys never knew when that opportunity might occur. The result: continuous cooperation. The reinforcement schedule applied in this case was a VI with a limited hold.

A *limited hold* is a finite amount of time after a reinforcer becomes available that a response will produce it. A limited hold is essentially a deadline for meeting the response requirement of a schedule of reinforcement. That is, once a reinforcer is set up, its availability is "held" only for a limited period. For the boys in The Timer Game, following a VI, the limited hold was zero seconds because they had to be behaving at the instant the "ding" occurred to receive reinforcement. The addition of a limited hold to an interval schedule is indicated by writing the abbreviation for the schedule followed by "/LH" and the value of the limited hold. For example,

---

[2] This procedure was developed on the basis of a study by Wolf, Hanley, King, Lachowicz, and Giles (1970).

if a limited hold of 2 seconds is added to an FI 1-minute schedule, the resulting schedule is abbreviated FI 1 minute/LH 2 seconds.

Interval schedules with short limited holds produce effects similar to those caused by ratio schedules (including strain if large increases in interval size are introduced abruptly). For small FIs, FI/LH produces effects similar to those produced by FR schedules. VI/LH produces effects similar to those produced by VR schedules. Thus, interval schedules with short limited holds are sometimes used when a teacher wants to produce ratio-like behavior but is unable to count each instance of the behavior, such as when the teacher can monitor the behavior only periodically or at irregular intervals.

In the natural environment, a good approximation of an FI/LH schedule is waiting for a bus. Buses usually run on a regular schedule (e.g., one every 20 minutes). An individual may arrive at the bus stop early, just before the bus is due, or as it is arriving—it makes no difference, for that person will still catch the bus. So far, this is just like a simple FI schedule. However, the bus will wait only a limited time—perhaps 1 minute. If the individual is not at the bus stop within this limited period of time, the bus goes on and the person must wait for the next one. A good approximation of behavior on a VI/LH schedule occurs when we are telephoning a friend whose line is busy. Note that as long as the line is busy, we will not get through to our friend no matter how many times we dial, and we have no way of predicting how long the line will be busy. However, after finishing the call, our friend may leave or receive another call. In either case, if we do not call during one of the limited periods in which the line is free and the friend is at home, we miss the reinforcement of talking to our friend and must wait another unpredictable period before we again have an opportunity to gain this particular reinforcement. See Figure 6–2 for other examples of VI/LH in everyday life.

Interval schedules with short limited holds are common in behavior modification programs. For example, a teacher faced with a classful of rambunctious young students might use a variation of The Timer Game, such as a VI 30 minutes/LH 0 seconds schedule to reinforce in-seat behavior. That is, if the children are working quietly at their seats whenever the timer rings after a variable 30-minute interval, they would receive some desirable item such as points that could be accumulated toward extra free time.

It's also possible to add a limited hold to ratio schedules. For example, if a fitness instructor says to a person who is exercising, "If you do 30 sit-ups in 2 minutes, you can get a drink of water," that would be an FR30/LH 2 minutes. Because ratio schedules already generate high rates of response, it is more common for a limited hold to be added to interval schedules than to ratio schedules.

Note that interval schedules with limited holds are also more common in nature than are interval schedules without limited holds. For example, if you go to the grocery store to pick your favorite fruit before it is ripe, your behavior will not be reinforced by the taste of the fruit, nor will waiting too long after it has ripened reinforce your behavior.

Study Questions

15. What is an FI schedule?
16. What are two questions to ask when judging whether a behavior is reinforced on an FI schedule? What answers to those questions would indicate that the behavior is reinforced on an FI schedule?
17. Suppose that a professor gives an exam to students every Friday. The students' studying behavior would likely resemble the characteristic pattern of an FI schedule in that studying would gradually increase as

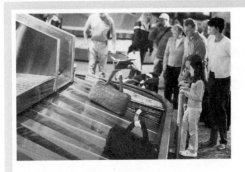

Response: Watching for one's luggage at an airport
Reinforcer: Getting the luggage

Contingency arrangement: After an unpredictable time, luggage appears on the conveyor.

Response: Stacking pieces on a pegboard
Reinforcer: Getting all the pieces stacked
Contingency arrangement: After a fixed number of responses, all the pieces will be stacked.

Response: Taking clothes out of dryer
Reinforcer: Clothes are dry

Contingency arrangement: After a fixed period of time, the first response will pay off.

Response: Watching TV
Reinforcer: Viewing an enjoyable scene
Contingency arrangement: Enjoyable scene occurs unpredictably, and lasts briefly.

FIGURE 6–2 Examples of people responding on intermittent reinforcement schedules.

Friday approaches, and the students would show a break in studying (similar to a lengthy postreinforcement pause) after each exam. But this is not really an example of an FI schedule for studying. Explain why.

18. What is a VI schedule?

19. Explain why simple interval schedules are not often used in training programs.

20. Explain what an FI/LH schedule is, and describe the details of an example from everyday life. (*Hint:* Think of behaviors that occur at certain fixed times, such as arriving for meals, plane departures, and cooking.)

21. Describe how an FI/LH schedule is procedurally similar to a simple FI schedule. Describe how it procedurally differs.

22. Explain what a VI/LH schedule is. Describe the details of two examples that occur in everyday life (at least one of which is not in the text).

23. What are three characteristic effects of a VI/LH schedule?

24. Describe two examples of how VI/LH might be applied in training programs.

25. Describe an example of an FR-LH schedule that is not in this chapter.

DURATION SCHEDULES

In a **fixed-duration (FD) schedule**, a reinforcer is presented only if a behavior occurs continuously for a fixed period of time. The value of the FD schedule is the amount of time that the behavior must be engaged in continuously before reinforcement occurs (e.g., if it is 1 minute, we call the schedule an FD 1-minute schedule). In a **variable-duration (VD) schedule**, a reinforcer is presented only if a behavior occurs continuously for a fixed period of time, and the interval of time from reinforcer to reinforcer changes unpredictably. The mean interval is specified in the designation of the VD schedule. For example, if the mean is 1 minute, the schedule is abbreviated VD 1-minute. Both FD and VD schedules produce long periods of continuous behavior. The FD schedule, however, produces a postreinforcement pause, whereas the VD schedule does not (or, at most, a very short one).

A number of examples of duration schedules occur in the natural environment. For instance, a worker who is paid by the hour might be considered to be on an FD schedule. Melting **NOTE 3** solder might also be an example of behavior on an FD schedule. To melt the solder, one must hold the tip of the soldering iron on the solder for a continuous fixed period of time. If the tip is removed, the solder cools quickly and the person has to start over again and apply heat for the same continuous period. An example of a VD schedule might be rubbing two sticks together to produce fire because the amount of time this takes varies as a function of factors such as the size, shape, and dryness of the sticks. Another example of a VD schedule is waiting for traffic to clear before crossing a busy street.

Behavior modification programs use duration schedules only when the target behavior can be measured continuously and reinforced on the basis of its duration. One should not assume, however, that this is the case for any target behavior. Presenting reinforcement contingent on a child studying or practicing the piano for an hour may work. However, it may also reinforce only sitting at the desk or in front of the piano. This is particularly true of something like studying, for which it is difficult for the parent or teacher to observe whether the desired behavior is occurring (the child may be daydreaming or reading a comic book). Practicing the piano is easier to monitor because the parent or teacher can hear whether the child is doing the lesson.

Eye contact is a behavior that is commonly reinforced on duration schedules in training programs for children with developmental disabilities. Many such children do not make eye contact with others, and any attempt by an adult to initiate this behavior causes the child to quickly avert her or his eyes from the adult. Eye contact is important as a prerequisite to further social development.

Study Questions

26. Explain what an FD schedule is. Describe the details of two examples of FD schedules that occur in everyday life (at least one of which is not in the text).

27. Suppose that each time that you put bread in a toaster and press the lever, 30 seconds passes before your toast is ready. Is this an example of an FD schedule? Why or why not? Would it be an FD schedule if (a) the catch that keeps the lever down doesn't work or (b) the timer that releases it doesn't work? Explain in each case.

28. Explain why FD might not be a very good schedule for reinforcing study behavior.

29. Describe two examples of how FD might be applied in training programs.

30. Explain what a VD schedule is, and describe the details of an example of one that occurs in everyday life.

31. For each of the photos in Figure 6–2, identify the schedule of reinforcement that appears to be operating. In each case, justify your choice of schedule.

OVERVIEW OF EIGHT BASIC INTERMITTENT SCHEDULES FOR INCREASING AND MAINTAINING BEHAVIOR

NOTE 4 Refer to Table 6–1 for the eight basic intermittent schedules we have discussed in this chapter and their characteristic effects. To summarize, the eight basic schedules are: FR, VR, FI, VI, FI/LH, VI/LH, FD, and VD. *Ratio schedules* (FR and VR) make reinforcement contingent on a certain number of responses being completed; *simple interval schedules* (FI and VI) make reinforcement contingent on a response being made after a certain time period has elapsed; *interval schedules with limited hold* (FI/LH and VI/LH) make reinforcement contingent on a response occurring within a limited period of time after reinforcement becomes available; and *duration schedules* (FD and VD) make reinforcement contingent on a response being made for a certain continuous period of time.

Thus, the schedules in each of the categories listed along the side of Table 6–1 have certain requirements that must be met for reinforcement to occur. These requirements are based on either the number of responses (i.e., ratio schedules) or the time plus response(s) (i.e., simple interval schedules, interval schedules with limited hold, and duration schedules).

CONCURRENT SCHEDULES OF REINFORCEMENT

In most situations, we have the option of performing more than just one type of behavior. At home during a particular evening, for example, a student might have the options of watching TV, surfing the Net, doing homework, or talking on the phone. When each of two or more behaviors is reinforced on different schedules at the same time, the schedules of reinforcement that are in effect are called **concurrent schedules of reinforcement**. Considering the concurrent schedules of reinforcement for the same student, in which option is the student likely to engage? In 1961, Richard Herrnstein proposed the matching law, which states that the response rate or the time devoted to an activity in a concurrent schedule is proportional to the rate of reinforcement of that activity relative to the rates of reinforcement on the other concurrent activities. Research has indicated other factors that are likely to influence one's choice when several schedules are available. They are (a) the types of schedules that are operating; (b) the immediacy of reinforcement; (c) the magnitude of reinforcement (e.g., a student might choose to study for an exam worth 50% of the final grade over watching a boring TV show); and (d) the response effort involved in the

TABLE 6–1	Characteristic Effects and Applications of the Basic Intermittent Reinforcement Schedules for Increasing and Maintaining Behavior		
Schedule	**Fixed**	**Variable**	**Application**
Ratio	High steady rate; short postreinforcement pause; high RTE*	High steady rate; no postreinforcement pause; very high RTE	To increase and maintain rate of specific responses that can be easily counted, such as solving addition or subtraction problems correctly or correct repetitions of a sport skill
Simple interval	Gradually increasing rate; long postreinforcement pause; moderate RTE	Moderate steady rate; no postreinforcement pause; moderately high RTE	Not commonly used in behavioral programs
Interval with limited hold	High steady rate (with small intervals); short postreinforcement pause; moderate RTE	High steady rate; no postreinforcement pause; high RTE	To increase and maintain duration or steady rate of behaviors such as on-task behavior of children in a classroom, cooperative behavior of children on a family car trip, or treading water by persons in a swimming class
Duration	Continuous behavior; moderate RTE	Continuous behavior; high RTE	To increase and maintain behaviors that can be monitored continuously and that should persist throughout a period of time, such as practicing the piano

*RTE = resistance to extinction.

different options (Friman & Poling, 1995; Mazur, 1991; Myerson & Hale, 1984; Neef, Mace, & Shade, 1993; Neef, Mace, Shea, & Shade, 1992; Neef, Shade, & Miller, 1994).

An understanding of the research on concurrent schedules is valuable when designing a behavior modification program. Suppose, for example, that you are attempting to decrease an undesirable behavior by reinforcing a desirable alternative behavior. You should ensure that the schedule of reinforcement for the desirable alternative behavior involves more immediate reinforcers, more frequent reinforcement, more powerful reinforcement, and a response of less effort than that which occurs for the undesirable behavior.

PITFALLS OF INTERMITTENT REINFORCEMENT

Pitfall Type 1

The most common pitfall of intermittent reinforcement often traps not only the unwary but also those with some knowledge of behavior modification. It involves what may be described as inconsistent use of extinction. For example, a parent may at first attempt to ignore a child's tantrums. But the child persists, and in despair, the parent finally gives in to the child's demands. Thus, the child obtains reinforcement on a VR or VD schedule, and this leads to further persistent tantrumming in the future. Many times, parents and staff say that they had to give in to the child's demands because "extinction was not working." However, the resulting intermittent reinforcement produces behavior that occurs at a higher rate and is more resistant to extinction than behavior that has been continuously reinforced.

GUIDELINES FOR THE EFFECTIVE USE OF INTERMITTENT REINFORCEMENT

To use intermittent schedules effectively in generating and maintaining desired behaviors, observing the following rules is important:

1. Choose a schedule that is appropriate to the behavior you wish to strengthen and maintain.
2. Choose a schedule that is convenient to administer.
3. Use appropriate instruments and materials to determine accurately and conveniently when the behavior should be reinforced. For example, if you are using a ratio schedule, make sure that you have a counter of some sort—a wrist counter, a calculator, a string of beads, or simply pencil and paper. Similarly, if you are using an interval or duration schedule, make sure that you have an accurate timer appropriate for your schedule. If you are using a variable schedule, make sure that you have arranged to follow a sequence of random numbers that vary around the mean you have chosen.
4. The frequency of reinforcement should initially be high enough to maintain the desired behavior and should then be decreased gradually until the final desired amount of behavior per reinforcement is being maintained. (Recall that for Jan, the FR was at first very small and was then increased.) Always remain at each stage long enough to ensure that the behavior is strong. This is similar to the shaping procedure described in Chapter 10. If you increase the requirement too rapidly, the behavior will deteriorate, and you will have to return to an earlier stage (possibly continuous reinforcement) to recapture it.
5. In language that he or she can understand, inform the individual of the schedule you are using. A number of studies (Pouthas, Droit, Jacquet, & Wearden, 1990; Shimoff, Matthews, & Catania, 1986; Wearden, 1988) indicate that people perform more efficiently if they have specific rules to follow regarding the schedule in effect (see discussion of rule-governed behavior in Chapter 17).

Study Questions

32. What are concurrent schedules of reinforcement? Describe an example.
33. If an individual has an option of engaging in two or more behaviors that are reinforced on different schedules by different reinforcers, what four factors in combination are likely to determine the response that the person will make?
34. Describe how intermittent reinforcement works against those who are ignorant of its effects. Give an example.
35. Name eight schedules of reinforcement used to develop behavior persistence (i.e., the ones described in this chapter).
36. In general, which schedules tend to produce higher resistance to extinction (RTE), the fixed or the variable schedules (see Table 6–1)?

Application Exercises

A. EXERCISE INVOLVING OTHERS

Assume that the following behaviors have been established:

1. dishwashing behavior of roommate or spouse
2. dusting behavior of son or daughter
3. doing mathematics assignments by a student

You now face the task of maintaining them. Following the guidelines for the effective use of intermittent reinforcement, describe in detail the best schedules of reinforcement and how you might apply them for each of these behaviors.

B. SELF-MODIFICATION EXERCISE

Assume that you have been assigned a 200-page book to read in the next few days. Select an appropriate reinforcer for yourself, and identify the best schedule on which to dispense the reinforcer. Describe the reasons for your selections (characteristic effects, ease of application, etc.), and outline the mechanics of how you might implement the program and complete it successfully.

Notes and Extended Discussion

1. The effects of the various schedules of reinforcement have been worked out mainly with animals. The classic authoritative work on this topic written by Ferster and Skinner (1957) deals mostly with pigeons pecking on a response key to obtain reinforcement in the form of access to grain for a few seconds. A number of experiments have been conducted to determine whether humans show the same patterns of responding that other animals do when exposed to basic schedules of reinforcement. In one common procedure, for example, a human volunteer presses a lever to produce points that can be exchanged for money or some other reinforcing item. In many cases, however, humans responding under these conditions do not show the behavior patterns described in this chapter. In particular, humans often do not show decreased response rates and pauses in responding although animals typically do (see Pear, 2001, pp. 74–75).

    One possible reason for these differences between humans and animals has to do with the complex verbal behavior humans have typically been conditioned to emit and to respond to—that is, humans can verbalize rules (as described in Chapter 17) that may influence them to show different behavior patterns than animals show when exposed to various reinforcement schedules (Michael, 1987). Thus, humans may make statements to themselves about the schedule of reinforcement in effect and respond to those statements rather than to the actual schedule itself. For example, humans may tell themselves that the experimenter will be pleased if they respond at a high rate throughout the session—even though the schedule may be one that normally generates a low rate of responding—and this self-instruction may then produce a high rate. Evidence for this view comes from data indicating that the patterns shown by preverbal infants are similar to those shown by animals (Lowe, Beasty, & Bentall, 1983) and gradually become less similar as children become increasingly verbal (Bentall, Lowe, & Beasty, 1985). In addition, instructions can very strongly influence rate and patterns of responding on various schedules of reinforcement (Otto, Torgrud, & Holborn, 1999), especially when the experimenter rather than a computer gives the instructions (Torgrud & Holborn, 1990).

2. An analysis of records kept by novelist Irving Wallace suggests that novel writing follows a fixed-ratio pattern (Wallace & Pear, 1977). Wallace typically stopped writing immediately after completing each chapter of a book he was working on. After a brief pause of a day or so, he resumed writing at a high rate, which he maintained until the next chapter was

completed. In addition, longer pauses typically occurred after a draft of a manuscript was completed. Thus, one might reasonably argue that completed chapters and completed drafts of manuscripts are reinforcements for novel writing and that these reinforcements occur according to FR schedules. Of course, it should be recognized that novel writing is a complex behavior and that other factors are also involved.

3. Evidence supports the position that, when FR and FD both appear to be applicable, the former is preferable. Semb and Semb (1975) compared two methods of scheduling workbook assignments for elementary school children. In one method, which they called "fixed-page assignment," the children were instructed to work until they had finished 15 pages. In the other method, "fixed-time assignment," the children were instructed to work until the teacher told them to stop. The amount of time the children were required to work was equal to the average amount of time they spent working during the fixed-page condition. In both methods, each child who answered correctly at least 18 of 20 randomly selected workbook frames received free time; otherwise, the child(ren) had to redo the entire assignment. On the whole, the children completed more work and made more correct responses under the fixed-page condition than under the fixed-time condition.

4. Schedules of reinforcement can help us understand behavior that has frequently been attributed to inner motivational states. For example, consider the pathological gambler. Because this individual is acting against his or her own best interests, it is sometimes said that the individual has an inner motive of masochism—a need for self-punishment. However, the pathological gambler may be a victim of an accidental adjustment to a high VR schedule. Perhaps when first introduced to gambling, this individual won several large sums in a row. Over time, however, the gambler won bets less frequently and now maintains the gambling at a high rate of very infrequent reinforcers. Similar adjustment to a high VR schedule with a low reinforcement rate can account for highly persistent desirable behavior as well—for example, that of the dedicated student, businessperson, or scientist.

Study Questions on Notes

1. Who wrote the classic authoritative work on schedules of reinforcement, and what is the title of that book?
2. What may account for the failures to obtain the schedule effects in basic research with humans that are typically found in basic research with animals?
3. Describe how FR schedules may be involved in writing a novel.
4. Might it be better to reinforce a child for dusting the living room furniture for a fixed period of time or for a fixed number of items dusted? Explain your answer.
5. Briefly describe how schedules of reinforcement can help us understand behavior that has frequently been attributed to inner motivational states.

7 Intermittent Reinforcement to Decrease Behavior

"Tommy, a little less talking out, please!"

DECREASING TOMMY'S TALKING OUT[1]

Tommy, an 11-year-old boy with a developmental disability, was judged by his teacher to be the most disruptive student in his classroom. He frequently engaged in inappropriate talking and other vocalizations during class. The behavior was troublesome not so much because of its nature but because of the high rate at which it occurred. A program was therefore undertaken to reduce his vocalizations to a less bothersome level.

The undesirable behavior, "talking out," was given the following precise behavioral definition: "talking to the teacher or classmates without the teacher's permission; talking, singing, or humming to himself; and making statements not related to the ongoing class discussion." A practice teacher located in the back of the room recorded Tommy's talk outs during one 50-minute session per day. A second trained observer also recorded Tommy's talk outs to ensure the accuracy of the observations.

In phase 1 of the program, the behavior was recorded for 10 sessions. It was found that Tommy averaged about one talk out every 9 minutes (or about 0.11 per minute). In phase 2, Tommy was told the definition of a talk out and instructed that he would be allowed 5 minutes of free play time at or near the end of the day if at the end of the 50-minute session he had made three or fewer talk outs (i.e., fewer than about one every 17 minutes). At the end of each session, the teacher told Tommy whether he had met the requirement, but during the session, he was never told the number of talk outs recorded.

---

[1] This case is based on Deitz and Repp (1973).

This procedure was quite effective. During phase 2, which lasted 15 sessions, Tommy aver-aged about one talk out every 54 minutes (0.02 per minute). Moreover, he never exceeded the upper limit of three per session.

In the third and final phase, the reinforcement schedule was removed, and Tommy was told that he would no longer receive free time for low rates of talk outs. Over the eight sessions of this phase for which data were taken, his rate of talking out increased to an average of one every 33 minutes (0.03 per minute). Although this rate was higher than the rate during the treatment pro-cedure (phase 2), it was still a great deal lower than the rate before the procedure was intro-duced (phase 1). Thus, the treatment had a beneficial effect even after it was terminated. ■

THE SCHEDULES IN THIS CHAPTER

The schedules of reinforcement in the previous chapter are used to increase and maintain appro-priate behavior. The schedules in this chapter, as illustrated by Tommy's case, are used to de-crease and/or eliminate responding that is inappropriate (see O'Brien & Repp, 1990).

DIFFERENTIAL REINFORCEMENT OF LOW RATES

Differential reinforcement of low (DRL) rates is a schedule of reinforcement in which a rein-forcer is presented *only* if a particular response occurs at a low rate. One type of DRL, called **limited-responding DRL**, specifies a maximum allowable number of responses during a certain time interval in order for a reinforcer to occur. This was the type of schedule used with Tommy. In that case, an interval (50 minutes) was specified and reinforcement occurred at the end of the

NOTE 1   interval if it contained fewer than a specified number of responses (three talk outs).

The maximum allowable number of responses in limited-responding DRL for reinforcement to occur can be specified for an entire session or for separate intervals throughout a session. For example, it would have been possible to divide Tommy's 50-minute session into three intervals, each approximately 17 minutes long, and to give Tommy reinforcement at the end of each interval in which a limit of one talk out occurred.

Limited-responding DRL is useful when two conditions hold: (a) some of the behavior is tolerable but (b) less of it is better. In Tommy's case, the teacher believed that three talk outs per session would not be too disruptive; no doubt she would have preferred none at all, but she did not wish to impose too stringent a requirement on Tommy. Therefore, Tommy would hear that he had earned his 5 minutes of free time by making three, two, one, or zero talk outs during any given session.

A second type of DRL, called **spaced-responding DRL**, requires that a specified behavior not occur during a specified interval, and after the interval has passed, an instance of that behav-ior must then occur in order for a reinforcer to occur.. In other words, instances of a specific be-havior must be spaced out over time. Spaced-responding DRL is useful when the behavior wanted to reduce is actually desirable provided that it does not occur at too high a rate. For example, a student who always calls out the correct answer deprives classmates of the chance to respond to the teacher's questions. Naturally, we would not wish to eliminate this child's correct answering. We would hope, however, to reduce the calling out behavior. We might do this by placing the behavior on the following type of DRL schedule: Any target response that occurs after 15 minutes of the previous target response is immediately reinforced; any target response that occurs within 15 minutes of the previous target response is not reinforced. Note that a target response before the interval has passed causes the timing of the interval to start over again. This procedure is called a *spaced-responding DRL 1-response/15-minute schedule.* This type of schedule requires that responses be emitted for reinforcement to occur. On the limited-responding schedule used with Tommy, the individual need not respond at all to obtain reinforcement.

Another example of the use of spaced-responding DRL is the reinforcement of slow speech in a student who speaks too rapidly. The student would be asked questions such as "How are you?" or "Where do you live?" for which standard responses are reinforced—but only if they encompass a certain minimum time period whose length is determined by what the teacher regards as a normally acceptable rate of speech. Thus, the sequence of respond–wait–respond is reinforced (provided that the wait is long enough). As another example, Lennox, Miltenberger, and Donnelly (1987) used a spaced-responding DRL to decrease the eating rate of three individuals with profound developmental disabilities who ate their meals at such a rapid rate that it was considered unhealthy.

Study Questions

1. Describe briefly, point by point, how Tommy's talking out in class was reduced.
2. Explain, in general, what a DRL schedule is. Give an example of one that occurs in everyday life.
3. Define *limited-responding DRL,* and give an example.
4. Define *spaced-responding DRL,* and give an example.
5. How is a spaced-responding DRL procedurally similar to and different from an FI schedule?
6. What is a procedural difference between a spaced-responding DRL and an FD schedule?
7. Describe in some detail two examples (at least one of which is not in the text) of how DRL would be useful in treating a behavior problem.

DIFFERENTIAL REINFORCEMENT OF ZERO RESPONDING

Tommy's teachers were willing to put up with a certain amount of talking out. But consider the case of Gerry, a 9-year-old boy of normal intelligence who scratched and rubbed his skin so severely that he produced open sores all over his body. Because of this problem, he had spent most of his time in hospitals and had never attended school. A DRL procedure would not have been appropriate because none of Gerry's skin scratching and rubbing behavior was tolerable. The procedure that was used is referred to as DRO (pronounced "dee-arr-oh"). **Differential reinforcement of zero responding (DRO)** is a schedule in which a reinforcer is presented *only* if a specified response does *not* occur during a specified period of time. Note that a target response before the interval has passed causes the timing of the interval to start over again. Working with the nurses in the hospital, researchers (Cowdery, Iwata, & Pace, 1990) began with a schedule referred to as *DRO 2 minutes.* If scratching occurred during the 2-minute interval, the interval started again. However, if scratching did not occur (i.e., was at a zero rate), Gerry was given tokens that he could later exchange for access to TV, snacks, video games, and various play materials. Over several days, the DRO interval was increased to 4 minutes, then to 8 minutes, then to 15 minutes, and eventually to 30 minutes. Although DRO was initially applied in brief sessions, it was subsequently extended to the entire day. Eventually, Gerry was discharged from the hospital, and his parents continued to use the procedure at home.

Technically, when Gerry was reinforced on DRO 30 minutes, he would have received a token for doing anything other than scratching. For this reason, a DRO is sometimes referred to as *differential reinforcement of other responding.* Practically, however, we're sure that Gerry would not have been allowed to do "anything" other than scratching. If, for example, he began breaking windows instead of scratching, we're sure that the behavior modifiers would have intervened. DRO schedules have been used successfully to decrease a variety of target behaviors, such as inappropriate behaviors in classrooms (Repp, Deitz, & Deitz, 1976), bedtime thumb-sucking in children (Knight & McKenzie, 1974), and self-injurious behavior of persons with developmental disabilities (Mazaleski, Iwata, Vollmer, Zarcone, & Smith, 1993).

If an undesirable behavior occurs often and for long intervals, beginning with a DRO of short duration would be wise. For example, DRO 5 minutes might be used to eliminate tantrum behavior. This procedure could be carried out by resetting a stopwatch to zero each time a tantrum occurred and allowing it to "tick off" seconds when the tantrum stopped. Reinforcement would occur when a continuous 5 minutes had elapsed with no tantrumming. When the nonoccurrence of the behavior is under good control of this contingency, the schedule should be increased—for example, to DRO 10 minutes. The size of DRO should continue to be increased in this fashion until (a) the behavior is occurring very rarely or not at all and (b) a minimum amount of reinforcement is being given for its nonoccurrence.

DIFFERENTIAL REINFORCEMENT OF INCOMPATIBLE BEHAVIOR

When applying a DRO, some behavior is occurring when the reinforcer is received. Even though Gerry wasn't scratching, for example, he was doing something when the 30-minute interval passed and he was given a token. An alternative is to specify explicitly an incompatible response that is to be reinforced in eliminating a particular target response. By an incompatible response, we mean a response that cannot be emitted at the same time as the target response. For example, sitting and standing are incompatible behaviors. If we decide to decrease a target response by withholding reinforcers for it (if we know their source and block them) and by reinforcing an incompatible response, the schedule is referred to as **differential reinforcement of incompatible (DRI) behavior**. Suppose you are a grade school teacher who wants to eliminate the running-around-the-room behavior of one of your students with attention-deficit hyperactivity disorder. One possibility would be to put the behavior on a DRO schedule; however, it might be replaced by an incompatible behavior that is also undesirable—for example, lying on the floor. To avoid this, you might use DRI instead of DRO by specifying the incompatible behavior that is to be reinforced. You might, for example, reinforce sitting quietly. An even better choice would be completing schoolwork because this behavior is more useful to the child. As another example, Allen and Stokes (1987) applied DRI successfully to strengthen the behavior of being still and quiet while children were being treated in a dentist's chair. See Table 7–1 for other examples of potential incompatible behaviors for target behaviors.

TABLE 7–1	Examples of Incompatible Behaviors for Target Behaviors
Target Behaviors to Decrease	**Incompatible Behaviors to Increase**
Driving after excessive alcohol consumption	Taking a taxi or asking a friend to drive
Biting fingernails	Keeping hands below shoulders
Swearing	Talking without swearing
Arriving late to classes	Arriving to classes on time

Study Questions

8. Explain what a DRO schedule is. Give an example of one that occurs in everyday life.
9. Describe in some detail two examples (at least one of which is not in this chapter) of how a DRO might be useful in treating behavior problems.
10. What two words does the *O* in DRO stand for? Explain your answer.
11. Explain what a DRI schedule is. Give an example.
12. Why might a DRI schedule sometimes be chosen instead of a DRO schedule?

DIFFERENTIAL REINFORCEMENT OF ALTERNATIVE BEHAVIOR

An alternative to DRI is the **differential reinforcement of alternative (DRA) behavior**, which is a procedure that involves the extinction of a problem behavior combined with reinforcing a behavior that is topographically dissimilar to but not necessarily incompatible with the problem behavior (Vollmer & Iwata, 1992; Vollmer, Roane, Ringdahl, & Marcus, 1999). Consider the case of Kyle, a 4-year-old boy with severe developmental disabilities. During training sessions, Kyle was frequently aggressive and attempted to hit, scratch, or kick the therapist. To decrease this behavior, Vollmer et al. implemented a DRA. During training sessions, they reinforced compliance with performing various requested tasks and ignored aggressive behavior. Note that this was a DRA instead of a DRI in that Kyle was physically able to be compliant and still show aggression. The DRA nevertheless was effective in decreasing Kyle's aggression as well as increasing his compliance.

The use of DRA to eliminate an undesirable behavior is essentially what we recommended in Chapter 5 when we stated, "Extinction is most effective when combined with positive reinforcement for some desirable alternative behavior." In fact, DRA (and the other schedules discussed in this chapter) will likely be very effective if you use the reinforcer that was maintaining the undesirable behavior; techniques for identifying that reinforcer are described in Chapter 23. The choice of schedule for reinforcing the alternative behavior should be based on considerations discussed in Chapter 6.

Before closing this section, we should point out that there is some question as to whether DRI and DRA really are more effective than simple extinction in reducing or eliminating undesirable behavior (e.g., see Johnston, 2006). Until this issue is resolved, however, we stand by the preceding recommendations as the safer course to follow. In addition, although DRI and DRA have the disadvantage of being more complicated to administer than simple extinction, they have the advantage of developing new or strengthening old desirable behavior.

PITFALLS OF SCHEDULES FOR DECREASING BEHAVIOR

Pitfall Type 1

A pitfall that is unique to DRL is the tendency to unknowingly reinforce a desirable behavior on a DRL, thereby causing that desirable behavior to occur at a low rate rather than reinforcing the behavior on a schedule that would maintain that behavior at a high rate. Understanding this pitfall may help us to appreciate how underachievers are frequently generated in our society.

Consider what happens when a child starts performing well in school. At first, the teacher is quite impressed and enthusiastically reinforces the behavior. However, as the rate of the behavior increases, the teacher gradually becomes less impressed. The teacher thinks that this is "obviously a bright child" and so expects a high rate of good behavior. Thus, the rate of reinforcement gradually decreases, perhaps to zero, as the rate of the behavior increases. Eventually, the child learns that more reinforcement occurs when performance is at a low rate because the teacher is more impressed with good behavior when it occurs infrequently than when it occurs frequently. Some children show only occasional flashes of brilliance in school instead of using their full potential. To avoid this type of inadvertent DRL schedule, teachers should define precisely the behavior they want to maintain at a high rate and reinforce it on an appropriate schedule.

Pitfalls of DRO and DRI are similar to the pitfalls already discussed for reinforcement (Chapter 3) and extinction (Chapter 5).

GUIDELINES FOR THE EFFECTIVE USE OF INTERMITTENT SCHEDULES TO DECREASE BEHAVIOR

1. Decide which type of schedule should be used to reduce the target behavior. Use limited-responding DRL if some of the target behavior is tolerable, but the less the better. Use spaced-responding DRL if the behavior is desirable as long as it does not occur too rapidly or too frequently. Use DRO if the behavior should be eliminated and there is no danger that the DRO procedure might result in the reinforcement of an undesirable alternative behavior. Use DRI or DRA if the behavior should be eliminated and there is a danger that DRO would strengthen undesirable alternative behavior.

2. Decide what reinforcer to use. In general, the procedure will be most effective if the reinforcer is the one maintaining the behavior that you want to reduce and if the reinforcer can be withheld for that behavior (see Chapter 23).

3. Having chosen which schedule to use and a reinforcer, proceed as follows.
   a. If a limited-responding DRL schedule is to be used:
      (1) Record as baseline data the number of target responses per session for several sessions or more to obtain an initial value for the DRL schedule that will ensure frequent reinforcement.
      (2) Gradually decrease the responses allowed on the DRL in such a way that reinforcement occurs frequently enough throughout the procedure to ensure adequate progress by the student.
      (3) Gradually increase the size of the interval to decrease response rate below that obtained with (2).
   b. If a spaced-responding DRL schedule is to be used:
      (1) Record baseline data over several sessions or more, determine the average time between responses, and use this average as the starting value of the DRL schedule.
      (2) Gradually increase the value of the DRL schedule in such a way that reinforcement occurs frequently enough throughout the procedure to ensure adequate progress by the student.
   c. If DRO is to be used:
      (1) Record baseline data over several sessions or more to obtain an initial interval for the DRO.
      (2) Use DRO starting values that are approximately equal to the mean value between instances of the target behaviors during baseline.
      (3) Gradually increase the size of the interval in such a way that reinforcement occurs frequently enough to ensure adequate progress by the student.

    d. If DRI is to be used:

        (1) Choose an appropriate behavior to strengthen that is incompatible with the behavior to be eliminated.

        (2) Take baseline data of the appropriate behavior over several sessions or more to determine how frequently the appropriate behavior should be reinforced to raise it to a level at which it will replace the inappropriate behavior.

        (3) Select a suitable schedule of reinforcement for increasing the appropriate behavior (see Chapter 6).

        (4) While strengthening the incompatible behavior, apply the guidelines for the extinction of the problem behavior, as described in Chapter 5.

        (5) Gradually increase the schedule requirement for the appropriate behavior in such a manner that it continues to replace the inappropriate behavior as the reinforcement frequency decreases.

    e. If DRA is to be used, follow all of the guidelines listed for DRI except that the behavior to be strengthened does not have to be incompatible with the behavior to be eliminated.

4. If possible, inform the individual in a manner that he or she is able to understand of the procedure that you are using.

Study Questions

13. What is the difference between DRI and DRA?

14. What happens if the frequency of reinforcement on DRL, DRO, DRI, or DRA is too low or is decreased too rapidly?

15. Describe a pitfall of DRL for people who are ignorant of its effects. Give an example.

16. Explain how the effects of DRL, DRO, DRI, and DRA differ from the effects of the intermittent-reinforcement schedules discussed in Chapter 6.

Application Exercises

A. EXERCISES INVOLVING OTHERS

1. For each of the two types of DRL schedules cited in Study Questions 3 and 4, describe a possible application in training programs for children with developmental disabilities. Describe in detail how you would program and administer DRL in these situations.

2. Describe two possible applications of DRO in programs of early childhood education. Describe in detail how you would program and administer DRO in these situations.

B. SELF-MODIFICATION EXERCISE

Describe in some detail how you might use one of the schedules in this chapter to reduce one of your own behaviors that you would like to occur less frequently.

Note and Extended Discussion

1. One might think that the 5 minutes of free play that occurred near the end of the day functioned as a reinforcer for decreasing Tommy's talk outs much earlier in the day. Recall from Chapter 3, however, that the direct effects of reinforcement operate only over very short intervals. Therefore, Tommy's improvement cannot be attributed to the direct effect of the free play near the end of the school day as a reinforcer for the behavior of working quietly in the classroom. Rather, when Tommy was working quietly, the immediate consequence was probably praise and attention from the teacher, who might have said, "You're doing great, Tommy; keep it up and you'll earn another 5 minutes of free play. Just think of how much fun you're going to have." The praise may have been a reinforcer for Tommy's improved performance. In addition, immediately after a few minutes of working quietly, Tommy might have told himself how much fun he was going to have during his extra play time. This rehearsal of a rule (as discussed earlier and further explained in Chapter 17) may have helped to bridge the time gap between the occurrence of desirable behavior during the 50-minute session and the extra playtime that occurred on a much-delayed basis. Tommy's saying the rule was eventually reinforced by the occurrence of the free play because the free play confirmed the rule, and confirmation of a rule is typically a reinforcer.

Study Questions on Note

1. What might account for the effectiveness of the delayed reinforcement contingency applied to Tommy's talk outs?
2. We have suggested that covertly saying a rule to himself may have reinforced Tommy's decreased talk outs. On what schedule was saying the rule likely reinforced? Explain. (*Hint:* It was not the free play itself that reinforced saying the rule because the free play did not depend directly on whether Tommy said the rule. It was the confirmation of the rule that reinforced saying it.)

8

Doing the Right Thing at the Right Time and Place: Stimulus Discrimination and Stimulus Generalization

"Children, please work at your desks."

LEARNING TO FOLLOW TEACHER'S INSTRUCTIONS[1]

The teacher in a regular third-grade class in an Auckland suburban elementary school had a problem. When she was giving instructions to the class, she wanted the children to listen attentively from their seats. At other times she wanted them to work quietly on their own. But 9 of the 34 children posed special problems of inattention and poor in-seat behavior. These youngsters frequently argued, shouted, hit and kicked other youngsters, banged on furniture, and left the classroom without permission. They did listen attentively and work quietly occasionally but not often and usually not when the teacher wanted them to. This was clearly a situation in which the desired behavior (listening attentively or working quietly) was in the children's repertoire (i.e., they could do it), but it did not occur at the desired times.

On several mornings, observers recorded the on task behavior of the nine problem children during teacher instruction when they were to remain silently in their seats and attend to the teacher and during work period when they were to write a story, draw a picture, or perform other

_____

[1] This example is based on a study by Glynn and Thomas (1974).

activities prescribed by the teacher. The problem children were typically on task less than 50% of the time. The teacher then introduced a procedure for getting the desired behavior to occur at the desired time during an oral and written language lesson from 9:30 to 10:20 every morning. She made a large chart, on one side of which was printed in red letters:

> *LOOK AT THE TEACHER*
>
> *STAY IN YOUR SEAT*
>
> *BE QUIET*

On the other side, in green letters, was

> *WORK AT YOUR PLACE*
>
> *WRITE IN YOUR BOOKS*
>
> *READ INSTRUCTIONS ON THE BLACKBOARD*

At various times, one side of the chart or the other was showing. The children were each given a 10 × 12-inch card with several rows of squares on it, one row for each day of the week, and the definitions of on task behaviors during teacher instruction and during work periods were explained to them. The children were told that a "beep" would sound several times throughout the lesson, and they were to mark themselves on task by placing a check mark in one of the squares if they were "doing what the chart says" when a beep occurred. The beeps occurred an average of once every 2 minutes. The children were also told that at the end of the lesson, they would be able to cash in each check mark for one minute of free play time in a nearby room that contained a variety of games and toys. The program was introduced for all of the children in the class, although data were taken only on the nine problem children. In very short order, the sign telling them what to do exerted strong control over their behavior, influencing them to perform the desired behavior at the desired times. The program increased the on task behavior of the nine problem children to approximately 91%. ■

LEARNING TO RESPOND AT THE RIGHT TIME AND PLACE

As you have seen in previous chapters, behavior is strongly affected by its consequences. Behavior that is reinforced increases. Behavior that is not reinforced decreases. However, any behavior is valuable only if it occurs at the right times and in appropriate situations. For instance, at an intersection, it is desirable to stop the car when the light is red, not when the light is green. Executing a perfect double back flip will earn you valuable points in a gymnastics routine, but it probably won't have the same effect in your first corporate-level job interview. As we acquire new behaviors, we also learn to produce those behaviors at the right time and place. How do we learn to do this successfully?

To understand the process, we must first recognize that there are always other people, places, or things that are around when behavior is reinforced or extinguished. For example, when Johnny is playing outside with his friends, laughter and attention are likely to reinforce his swearing. When Johnny is sitting at the dinner table at Grandpa and Grandma's on Sunday, his swearing is not likely to be reinforced and may even be punished. After several such experiences, the people and things that were around during reinforcement and extinction come to cue the behavior. Johnny's swearing becomes highly probable in the presence of the kids on the street and very improbable in his grandparents' house.

Any situation in which behavior occurs can be analyzed in terms of three sets of events: (a) the stimuli that exist just prior to the occurrence of the behavior, called *antecedent stimuli* (such as the presence of friends or the dinner table at Grandma and Grandpa's house just before Johnny swore), (b) the behavior itself (Johnny's swearing), and (c) the consequences of the behavior (either approval from Johnny's friends or disapproval from Grandma and Grandpa). Recall from Chapter 1 that *stimuli* are the people, objects, and events currently present in one's immediate surroundings that impinge on one's sense receptors and that can affect behavior. Visual objects, such as books, clothing, furniture, lights, people, pets, and trees, are all potential stimuli as are all types of sounds, smells, tastes, and physical contacts with the body. Any stimulus can be an antecedent or a consequence of a behavior. Identifying the antecedents and consequences of a behavior is sometimes referred to as an *ABC (antecedents, behavior, and consequences) assessment.*

When a behavior is reinforced in the presence of a particular stimulus but not others, that antecedent stimulus begins to exert control over the occurrence of that behavior. For example, at the end of the program at the Auckland elementary school, when the children saw the signs saying LOOK AT THE TEACHER and so on in big red letters, they listened carefully to what the teacher had to say because doing so had been reinforced in the presence of that antecedent stimulus. We say that the stimulus had come to exert control over the behavior. When a particular behavior is more likely to occur in the presence of a particular stimulus but not others, we say that the behavior is under the control of that stimulus.

We use the term **stimulus control** to refer to the degree of correlation between the occurrence of a particular stimulus and the occurrence of a subsequent response. **Good** or **effective stimulus control** refers to a strong correlation between the occurrence of a particular stimulus and a particular response; that is, when the stimulus occurs, the response is likely to follow. For example, suppose that you have just put money into a vending machine and are looking for your favorite candy bar. You see the name of that bar beside a particular button, and you press that button. The sign exerted good stimulus control over your button-pressing behavior. Similarly, at the end of the program in the lead example for this chapter, the signs LOOK AT THE TEACHER and so on exerted good stimulus control over the children's behavior of paying attention.

While some stimuli are consistent predictors that a particular behavior will be reinforced, other stimuli are consistent predictors that a particular behavior will not be reinforced. An Out of Order sign on a vending machine is a cue that the behavior of inserting money into the machine will not be reinforced. The appearance of an empty cup is a cue that raising the cup to your lips will not result in a drink. Through experience, we learn to refrain from performing certain behaviors in the presence of certain stimuli because we have learned that those behaviors will go unreinforced. Thus, there are two types of controlling stimuli, which are described next.

TYPES OF CONTROLLING STIMULI: S^Ds AND S^Δs

A **discriminative stimulus** or S^D (pronounced "ess-dee") is a stimulus in the presence of which a response will be reinforced. Loosely speaking, an S^D is a cue that a particular response will pay off. An S^Δ (pronounced "ess-delta") is a stimulus in the presence of which a response will not be reinforced. Loosely speaking, an S^Δ is a cue that a particular response will *not* pay off. An S^D might be called a *stimulus for reinforcement,* and an S^Δ might be called a *stimulus for extinction.*

In our example of Johnny's swearing, the stimulus of the other kids is an S^D for the response of swearing because their laughter and attention reinforced that response. The stimulus of

Grandpa and Grandma is an S^Δ for the response of swearing because it was not reinforced in their presence. This can be diagrammed as follows:

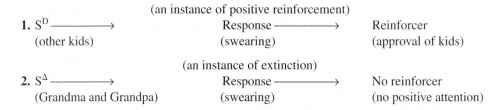

(an instance of positive reinforcement)

1. S^D ⟶   Response ⟶   Reinforcer
    (other kids)   (swearing)   (approval of kids)

(an instance of extinction)

2. S^Δ ⟶   Response ⟶   No reinforcer
    (Grandma and Grandpa)   (swearing)   (no positive attention)

A stimulus can simultaneously be an S^D for one response and an S^Δ for another; that is, in the presence of a particular stimulus, one response may be reinforced while another may not be reinforced (e.g., see Figure 8–1). For instance, if you are eating dinner with friends and someone asks you, "Please pass the pepper," that statement is an S^D for your response of passing the pepper, and it is an S^Δ for you to pass the salt. As another example, when the teacher in the Auckland classroom presented the signs LOOK AT THE TEACHER and so on, that stimulus was an S^D for the children's on task behavior (staying in their seats and attending to the teacher), and it was an S^Δ for their off task behavior (running around the room, etc.). This may be diagrammed as follows:

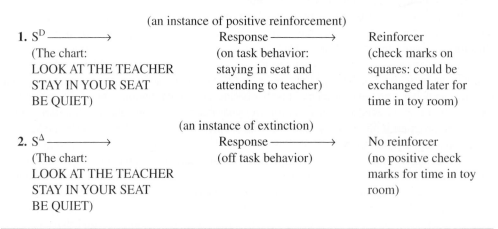

(an instance of positive reinforcement)

1. S^D ⟶   Response ⟶   Reinforcer
    (The chart: (on task behavior: (check marks on
    LOOK AT THE TEACHER   staying in seat and   squares: could be
    STAY IN YOUR SEAT   attending to teacher)   exchanged later for
    BE QUIET)   time in toy room)

(an instance of extinction)

2. S^Δ ⟶   Response ⟶   No reinforcer
    (The chart: (off task behavior)   (no positive check
    LOOK AT THE TEACHER   marks for time in toy
    STAY IN YOUR SEAT   room)
    BE QUIET)

Study Questions

1. What is a stimulus? Give two examples that are not from the text.
2. What is an ABC assessment?
3. Define *stimulus control*.
4. What is good stimulus control? Describe an example that is not in this chapter.
5. Define S^D and give an example. Identify both the S^D and the response in the example.
6. Define S^Δ and give an example. Identify both the S^Δ and the response in the example.
7. What is the difference between a stimulus and a discriminative stimulus?
8. Describe an example (not from this chapter) of a stimulus that is an S^D for one behavior and an S^Δ for a different behavior.
9. Identify examples of S^Ds and S^Δs as follows: two S^Ds from Table 3–1, two S^Ds from Table 3–3, two S^Δs from Table 5–1, and two S^Δs from Table 5–2.

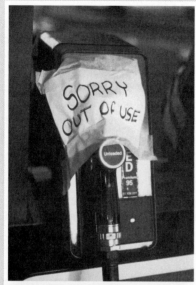

The sign is an S^Δ for inserting money, and an S^D to seek out a different machine (one that is not out of order).

The sign is an S^D for a female to enter the bathroom and an S^Δ for a male to enter.

The sign is an S^D for driving in the direction of the arrow, and an S^Δ for driving in a direction against that signified by the arrow.

FIGURE 8–1   Many stimuli are simultaneously an S^D for one response and an S^Δ for a different response, although such stimuli do not always control the appropriate responses.

Source: 8-1c, "You May Not Tie An Alligator to a Fire Hydrant: 101 Dumb Laws"

STIMULUS DISCRIMINATION

Stimulus discrimination training refers to the *procedure* of reinforcing a response in the presence of an S^D and extinguishing that response in the presence of an S$^\Delta$. After sufficient stimulus discrimination training, the *effects* can be described as (1) **good stimulus control**—a strong correlation between the occurrence of a particular stimulus and a particular response, or (2) a **stimulus discrimination**—a response occurs to an S^D, not to an S$^\Delta$. In the example with the teacher in the Auckland classroom, the children received discrimination training as diagrammed on p. 100. The result was stimulus control: The printed signs came to exert control over their appropriate behavior.

STIMULUS GENERALIZATION

Stimulus generalization refers to the *procedure* of reinforcing a response in the presence of a stimulus or situation and the *effect* of the response becoming more probable in the presence of another stimulus or situation. In other words, instead of discriminating between two stimuli and responding differentially to them, an individual responds in the same way to two different stimuli. Thus, stimulus generalization is the opposite of stimulus discrimination. There are several reasons for the occurrence of stimulus generalization.

Unlearned Stimulus Generalization Due to Considerable Physical Similarity

People and animals are likely to perform a behavior in a new situation if that situation is similar to the one in which they learned the behavior. Consider a case that is familiar to many parents: an infant learns to say "doggie" to a large, hairy, four-legged creature with floppy ears and a friendly bark. Later, the infant sees a different kind of large dog and says "doggie." It is fortunate that we have evolved in this way. Imagine what life would be like if you could not perform a newly learned skill in a new situation that was somewhat different from the circumstances in which you originally learned the skill. You would have to relearn how to cook in each new kitchen; you would have to relearn to ski on each new slope; you would have to relearn to dance to each new song. Fortunately, we have evolved so that the more physically similar two stimuli are, the more stimulus generalization will occur between them.

Learned Stimulus Generalization Involving Minimal Physical Similarity

Suppose that a child learns to say "dog" to a large German shepherd. Would the child also spontaneously say "dog" to a tiny Chihuahua? Probably not. Although the dogs have some limited physical similarity, they are very different in many respects. Stimulus generalization is not likely to occur in the latter case until the child has learned the stimulus class dog. A more common word for stimulus class is *concept*.

The members of some stimulus classes or concepts have many characteristics in common. A **common-element stimulus class** is a set of stimuli, all of which have one or more physical characteristics in common. Behavior modifiers generally refer to such a set of stimuli as a *stimulus class*. We use the term *common-element stimulus class* to distinguish it from a *stimulus equivalence class,* discussed later. For example, cars have four wheels, windows, a steering wheel, and so forth. When a child learns to say the word *car* when seeing a particular one, the child is likely to show unlearned stimulus generalization and be able to identify other cars. For other concepts, however, their members have only limited physical characteristics in common, and some learning is likely required for stimulus generalization to occur. To teach a child the concept red, you might reinforce the response *red* to many different red-colored objects and extinguish that response to objects that are not red. Eventually, the child would learn to recognize a red pencil and a red automobile as both being red, even though the pencil and the automobile are very different in other respects. As another example, to teach the concept of wetness, you would reinforce the response *wet* to many different wet objects and extinguish that response (and reinforce the response *dry*) to dry objects.

When an individual emits an appropriate response to all members of a common-element stimulus class and does not emit that response to stimuli that do not belong to the class, we say that the individual generalizes to all members within a common-element stimulus class or concept, such as recognizing red objects as red, and discriminating between common-element stimulus classes such as between red objects and blue objects. When an individual responds in this way, such as to the concept red, we say that the individual is showing *conceptual behavior.*

It is important to note that verbal behavior is not necessarily involved in conceptual behavior. Pigeons, although nonverbal, can readily learn a surprising range of concepts. By presenting slides to them and reinforcing pecks at slides that are exemplars of a particular concept while withholding reinforcement for pecks at slides that are not exemplars of that concept, researchers have taught pigeons the concepts such as person and tree as well as some number concepts such as 16 versus 20 (Herrnstein & deVilliers, 1980; Herrnstein & Loveland, 1964; Herrnstein, Loveland, & Cable, 1976; Honig & Stewart, 1988; Lubow, 1974; Vaughan & Herrnstein, 1987). The proof that the pigeons have learned a concept (such as fish) is that they respond correctly to types of fish that they have never seen before.

Learned Stimulus Generalization Due to Stimulus Equivalence Classes

Suppose that you are shown a number of items such as a carrot, a calculator, a pea, a pencil, and a carton of milk. You are asked to identify the food items. Obviously, you will be able to do so. You would be showing conceptual behavior with respect to the concept food, yet nothing about a carrot, a pea, and a carton of milk is physically similar. You have learned that these items belong to a **stimulus equivalence class**, a set of completely dissimilar stimuli that an individual has learned to group or match together. (*Stimulus equivalence classes* are sometimes referred to simply as *equivalence classes,* although the former term is preferred because of the potential confusion of the latter with the mathematical meaning of the term *equivalence class.*) Behavioral researchers have typically studied the formation of stimulus equivalence classes during matching-to-sample training. Consider the following experiment for teaching the stimulus equivalence class 3 to a young child. In Phase I, the child is given a number of trials with Training Panel 1 (see Figure 8–2). Across trials, the positions of ∴, IV, and 7 are randomly alternated. Using appropriate prompting and reinforcement, the child is taught to match 3 to ∴. Then Phase II proceeds similarly, but with Training Panel 2, and the child is taught to match ∴ to III. Now comes a test to see whether the child has learned the stimulus equivalence class. The child is shown the Test Panel and asked to match III to 4, 6, or 3. In this experiment, the child will likely match III to 3. The III and the 3 have become members of a stimulus equivalence class, even though those two stimuli were never previously paired. The members of this stimulus equivalence class are functionally equivalent in the sense that they all control the same behavior.   NOTE 1

As we grow up, we acquire many stimulus equivalence classes in which all members of a class control the same response but in which the members of the class are physically very different.

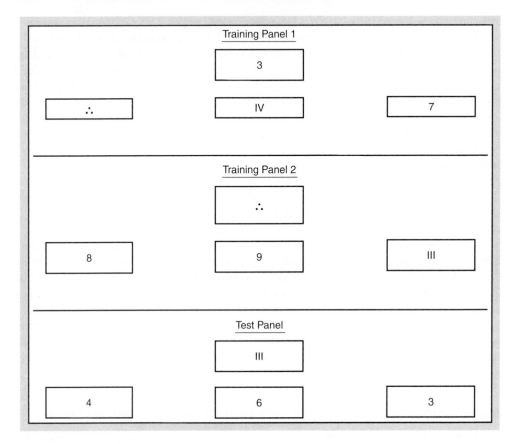

FIGURE 8–2 Visual displays in a stimulus equivalence experiment.

When a new behavior becomes conditioned to one member of a stimulus equivalence class, other members of the class are likely to control that behavior without training. In everyday speech, we would say that the members of a stimulus equivalence class mean the same thing or share a common meaning (as when we learn the different representations for the number 3, the different words for drinking utensil, that *mammal* indicates animals such as cows, whales, and bats, and that *fruit* indicates plants such as apples, pears, and strawberries). Each of these stimulus equivalence classes is also referred to as a *concept.*

NOTE 2

    Note that what may be a common-element stimulus class for some individuals is a stimulus equivalence class for others. For example, the tomato is a member of the common-element stimulus class fruit for botanists and a member of the stimulus equivalence class vegetable for cooks. For zoologists, the concept mammal is a common-element stimulus class, whereas for the average nonbiologist, it is a stimulus equivalence class. Thus, a biologist would be more likely to correctly generalize to new instances of the concept mammal than a nonbiologist would.

    In summary, if a response that has been reinforced to one stimulus occurs to a different stimulus (due to unlearned generalization, the learning of a common-element stimulus class, or the learning of a stimulus equivalence class), we say that *stimulus generalization* has occurred. But note that not all instances of stimulus generalization are favorable. For example, a child might learn to say "doggie" to a hairy four-legged creature and later say "doggie" when seeing a cat. In these (and thousands of other) instances, it is necessary to teach discriminations as described in the next section. (Strategies for improving generalization are discussed further in Chapter 16.)

Study Questions

10. Describe the stimulus discrimination training procedure, and give an example.
11. State the two effects of stimulus discrimination training.
12. Define *stimulus generalization,* and give an example.
13. In a sentence, state the difference between an instance of stimulus discrimination and an instance of stimulus generalization.
14. What do we mean by *common-element stimulus class*? By *conceptual behavior*? Describe an example of each.
15. Describe how you might teach the concept of honest to a child. Would your program teach a child to be honest? Why or why not?
16. What do we mean by *stimulus equivalence class*? Describe an example.
17. What is a primary distinction between stimulus generalization involving common-element stimulus classes and stimulus generalization involving stimulus equivalence classes?

FACTORS DETERMINING THE EFFECTIVENESS OF STIMULUS DISCRIMINATION TRAINING

1. Choosing Distinct Signals

If it is important to develop stimulus control of a particular behavior, it is often desirable to identify controlling S^Ds that are very distinctive. For example, the teacher in the Auckland school used large, red letters for the sign that prompted the students to listen and look at the teacher and large, green letters for the sign that prompted the students to work at their desks.

When considering a stimulus to be set up as an S^D for the behavior of another person, you might ask yourself the following questions.

1. Is the stimulus different from other stimuli along more than one dimension? That is, is it **NOTE 3** different in location, size, color, and sensory modality (vision, hearing, touch, etc.)?
2. Is the stimulus one that can be presented only or at least mainly on occasions when the desired response should occur to avoid confusion with the occurrence of the stimulus on other occasions?
3. Is the stimulus of the type that the probability of the person attending to it when it is presented is high?
4. Are there any undesirable responses that might be controlled by the chosen stimulus? (If some undesirable response follows the stimulus, it will interfere with the development of new stimulus control of the desired response.)

Careful attention to these questions will increase the chances that your stimulus discrimination training will be effective.

2. Minimizing the Opportunities for Error

During discrimination training, a response to an S^Δ or a failure to respond to an S^D is typically referred to as an *error*. Consider the example of a child learning to pick up a phone when it rings but not to when it is silent. The responses of picking up the phone if it is silent or failure to pick up the phone when it rings would be errors. Stimulus control can be developed most effectively when the behavior modifier minimizes the possibility of errors. For example, a parent who is teaching a child to answer the phone appropriately might move the phone out of reach if it is not ringing and add verbal prompts of this sort: "Now remember, we don't pick up telephones when they are not ringing. We only answer them just after they've begun to ring." Then, as soon as the phone rings (a call made specifically for training purposes), the parent might immediately place the phone in front of the child and say, "The phone is ringing. Now you should answer it."

At this point, you might be thinking, "But often we want to teach people to respond to subtle cues. Why should we then maximize distinctive signals?" Let's simply reply that choosing distinctive cues and minimizing errors will lead to more rapid stimulus control than might otherwise occur. In Chapter 9, we discuss techniques for gradually introducing discriminations involving subtle cues. For the moment, it is important to keep in mind that efforts to choose distinctive signals and to minimize errors will lead to the development of effective stimulus control more quickly and with less frustration than attempting to develop discriminations that involve subtle cues.

3. Maximizing the Number of Trials

In general, it is well accepted that a number of reinforced trials are necessary to develop consistent behaviors in persons with developmental disabilities and other individuals who are behaviorally deficient. What many people forget is that this is often true for all of us when we are acquiring new discriminations. Suppose, for example, that, after a few months of marriage, one of the partners presents subtle cues that he or she is not in the mood for lovemaking. What that partner must realize is that the other person may not learn to respond to subtle cues, or even obvious cues, with just one or two trials. After a number of instances of reinforcement for correct responding to the S^Ds and extinction for responses to the S^Δs, those S^Ds and S^Δs will likely control the response on subsequent trials.

4. Using Rules: Describe the Contingencies

In Chapter 3, we introduced you to contingent versus noncontingent reinforcement. In general, a *contingency* is an if-then type of arrangement. For example, *if* you press the button on the water fountain, *then* a stream of water will appear. We say that the appearance of the water is contingent upon the button-pressing response. This would be an example of a two-term (behavior-consequence) contingency. If we describe both the antecedents and the consequences of a behavior, then we would be identifying a three-term contingency. As Skinner (1969, p. 7) stated,

> An adequate formulation of the interaction between an [individual] and [his or her] environment must always specify three things: (1) the occasion upon which a response occurs; (2) the response itself; and (3) the reinforcing consequences. The interrelationships among them are the "contingencies of reinforcement."

The development of stimulus control often involves trial and error with three-term contingencies—several trials of positive reinforcement for a behavior in the presence of an S^D

and several trials of that behavior going unreinforced in the presence of an S^{Δ}. Johnny's swearing, for example, came under the control of the other kids as S^Ds (and came not to occur in the presence of Grandma and Grandpa as S^{Δ}s) through trial and error. Behavior that develops because of its immediate consequences is referred to as **contingency-shaped behavior**. Thus, Johnny's swearing illustrates contingency-shaped behavior. However, the children in the Auckland classroom did not take a few trials to show evidence of stimulus control. During the very first session after the teacher had explained the new set of classroom rules, the children showed an immediate increase in on task behavior in the presence of the appropriate signs (LOOK AT THE TEACHER and so on). Thus, the behavior of the children in the Auckland school illustrates what is called *rule-governed behavior*. A **rule** (from a behavioral perspective) describes a *situation* in which a *behavior* will lead to a *consequence*. Thus, a rule describes a three-term contingency of reinforcement. **Rule-governed behavior** is behavior that is controlled by the statement of a rule. When you wish to develop good stimulus control over a particular behavior, you should always provide the individual with a rule or set of rules stating what behaviors in what situations will lead to what consequences. Because of our complex conditioning histories for following instructions, the addition of a set of rules to a stimulus discrimination program may lead to instantaneous stimulus control. For example, if a father were to tell his 16-year-old son, "You can use the family car each Saturday night, but only if you mow the lawn each Friday," then the son is likely to comply with the rule on the first opportunity. (Use of rules is discussed further in Chapter 17.)

PITFALLS OF STIMULUS DISCRIMINATION TRAINING

Pitfall Type 1

Any effective method can be misapplied inadvertently by the unwary, and stimulus discrimination training is no exception. One of the authors observed an example of this with a 7-year-old boy with developmental disabilities who banged his head against hard surfaces unless an adult was holding his hand. As soon as the adult dropped the child's hand and moved away, he would immediately dive to the floor and begin banging his head hard enough to cause considerable bleeding. This behavior occurred only when the child was standing on a hard surface (floor or concrete). It did not occur when he was standing on a rug or on grass. The reason for this is easy to see. An adult would not come running to give him attention if he banged his head on a soft carpet or on grass because he would not injure himself when he did that. Of course, the adult had no choice but to give him attention when he banged his head on hard surfaces. Adults had inadvertently taught the boy the following discrimination.

1. S^D ⟶ hard surface   Response ⟶ banging head   Reinforcer attention from adults

2. S^{Δ} ⟶ soft surface   Response ⟶ banging head   No reinforcer no attention from adults

Examples of situations in which people inadvertently teach others to respond inappropriately to particular cues are numerous. Behavioral episodes of the following sort are common in many households with young children. Terri, a 3-year-old girl, is playing with the remote control for the TV set. Mother says quietly, " Terri, please leave that alone." Terri continues to fiddle with the remote control. A few minutes later, Mother yells a little louder and a little less politely,

"Terri, put that down." Terri continues to fiddle with the remote, rapidly changing channels, which is a reinforcer for her. A minute or two later Mother says, this time loudly and with a threatening look, "Terri, for the last time, leave the remote alone and get away from the TV set before I get really mad!" Terri finally moves away from the TV set and Mother says, "Now, that's better, Terri. Mommy likes it when you do what I tell you; why didn't you do that in the first place?" It is probably obvious to you that Mother has just reinforced Terri for responding to her third-level threats. The discrimination Terri is learning is that of waiting until Mother is really angry and threatening before attending to her requests.

If you feel that you have to tell an individual something many times before the person responds, or that nobody listens to you, or that others are not doing the right thing at the right time and place, you should closely examine your interactions with these individuals for instances of misapplication of stimulus discrimination training.

GUIDELINES FOR EFFECTIVE STIMULUS DISCRIMINATION TRAINING

1. ***Choose Distinct Signals***   Specify the S^Ds and at least one S^Δ. (In other words, specify conditions under which the behavior should and should not occur.)
2. ***Select an Appropriate Reinforcer***   See Figure 3–3.
3. ***Develop the Discrimination***
   a. Arrange for several reinforced responses in the presence of the S^D.
      (1) Specify clearly in a rule the S^D–desirable response–reinforcer sequence. Help identify the cues that indicate that the behavior will be reinforced versus the cues that indicate that the behavior will not be reinforced, and use instructions when appropriate to teach the person to act in a particular way under one set of circumstances but not under another.
      (2) Keep verbal cues constant initially.
      (3) Post the rules in a conspicuous place, and review them regularly.
      (4) Recognize that stimulus control over the behavior will not develop if the individual is not attending to the cues; therefore, use prompts (discussed further in Chapter 9) to emphasize the cues.
      (5) To teach the individual to act at a specific time, present prompts for correct performance just before the action is to occur.
   b. When the S^Δ is presented, make the change from the S^D very obvious and follow the rules for extinction for the behavior of concern. Stimuli that can acquire control over behavior include such things as location of training place; physical characteristics and location of furniture, equipment, and people in the training room; time of day of training; and sequence of events that precede and accompany training. A change in any of these may disrupt stimulus control.
4. ***Weaning the Individual from the Program***   (discussed in more detail in Chapter 16).
   a. If the behavior occurs in the right place at the right time at a desirable rate during a dozen or so of the opportunities for the behavior and if it is not occurring in the presence of the S^Δ situations, it might be possible to gradually eliminate contrived reinforcers and maintain the behavior with natural reinforcers.
   b. Look for other natural reinforcers in the environment that might maintain the behavior once it is occurring in the presence of S^Ds, and not in the presence of S^Δs.

   c. After the program is terminated, plan periodic assessments of the behavior to ensure that it is occasionally being reinforced and that the desired frequency of the behavior is being maintained in the presence of the S^Ds.

Study Questions

18. When you are considering the selection of a stimulus to be set up as an S^D, what four questions might you ask yourself about that stimulus? (See p. 105.)
19. Describe a stimulus that you would like to establish as an S^D for a behavior of yourself or a friend, and describe the behavior. Then, for that stimulus, answer the four questions that you asked yourself in Question 18.
20. What do we mean by an error in stimulus discrimination training?
21. In general, what is a contingency? Describe an example that is not in this chapter.
22. What is a three-term contingency of reinforcement? Describe an example that is not in this chapter.
23. From a behavioral perspective, what is a rule?
24. With examples, distinguish between rule-governed and contingency-shaped behavior.
25. Was the children's high on task behavior to the posted rule in the Auckland classroom likely rule governed or contingency shaped? Justify your choice.
26. Describe an example of how ignorance of stimulus discrimination training may lead parents or other caregivers to develop an undesirable behavior in a child or adult in their care.

Application Exercises

A. EXERCISES INVOLVING OTHERS

1. Identify five situations in which you presented an S^D that controlled the behavior of another person. Clearly identify the general situation, the controlling S^D, the behavior controlled, and the reinforcers.
2. Describe five situations in which you presented an S^Δ to some other person. Clearly identify the general situation, the S^Δ, the behavior for which your stimulus was an S^Δ, and the consequences. Indicate whether the S^Δ controlled the behavior appropriately.

B. SELF-MODIFICATION EXERCISES

1. Describe a recent situation in which you generalized in a desirable way. Clearly identify the behavior, the situation in which the behavior was initially reinforced (the training situation), and the situation to which the behavior generalized (target situation).
2. Describe a recent situation in which you generalized in an undesirable way (in other words, had an undesirable outcome). Again, identify the behavior, training situation, and target situation.
3. Choose an excessive behavior of yours that you might like to decrease. Carefully monitor those situations in which the behavior occurs and does not occur over a two- or three-day period. Clearly identify the controlling S^Ds, and, if possible, some controlling S^Δs for the behavior. Such information will prove to be extremely helpful if you decide to set up a self-control program after completing this book.
4. On the basis of the material you have read thus far in this book, describe in detail how you might set up a program to control your study behavior to improve your learning of the discriminations that are necessary in mastering the remainder of the material in this book. (*Hint:* Consider stimulus control, reinforcement, extinction, incompatible behaviors, and schedules of reinforcement.)

Notes and Extended Discussion

1. Technically, stimulus equivalence requires the demonstration of three relationships: reflexivity, symmetry, and transitivity (Dymond & Rehfeldt, 2000; Sidman, 1994). Reflexivity simply involves recognizing instances of a stimulus. In other words, a child is able to match 3 to 3, ∴ to ∴, and III to III. Now consider the top panel in Figure 8–2. Suppose that, after training, the child has learned to correctly press the panel ∴ when shown 3. We then place ∴ in the top panel and then randomly place 3 with the other two choices. The child has demonstrated symmetry by choosing 3 when shown ∴. Transitivity is demonstrated when the child passes the test in the third panel shown in Figure 8–2. In other words, as a result of learning to match A to B and B to C, an individual now matches C to A without specific training to do so.

2. Following Skinner's (1957) publication of a behavioral account of language, some psycholinguists have argued that operant conditioning is inadequate to explain a child's acquisition of her or his native language (Brown, 1973; Chomsky, 1959; Pinker, 1994). Their argument is based largely on the view that children learn more about language than is directly trained or directly reinforced. However, through automatic conditioned reinforcement (described in Note 1 of Chapter 4), infants are able to emit vocal behaviors that have not been directly reinforced. And through stimulus equivalence training, children learn that physically different sounds that are members of the same stimulus equivalence class "mean" the same thing as other sounds. Such factors can explain how individuals can produce a new sentence they have never heard before, and experimental analysis of these factors can provide empirical support for a behavioral view of language development (Stromer, Mackay, & Remington, 1996).

3. Some forms of stimulus control are more complex than a single stimulus (such as a green light or a sign in a window) controlling a single response (such as crossing a street or going into a shop to buy something). One complex type of stimulus control, called *contextual control,* occurs when the general setting or context may alter the manner in which an individual responds to particular stimuli. For example, when you drive in Great Britain, the highway dividing line is an S^D to steer to the left of it, whereas when you drive in Canada, it is an S^D to steer to the right of it. In this example, the country in which you are driving is the context that determines how a particular stimulus controls your behavior. Knowledge of contextual control can be important in designing effective behavioral treatments. For example, Haring and Kennedy (1990) found a procedure that was effective in reducing the self-stimulating behavior of a girl with autism in the classroom was not effective in a recreational setting; and, conversely, a procedure that was effective in reducing her self-stimulatory behavior when she was doing leisure activities was not effective in reducing it when she was performing classroom tasks.

Study Questions on Notes

1. Using examples, explain what is meant by *reflexivity, symmetry,* and *transitivity.*
2. How have studies of stimulus equivalence provided support for a behavioral view of language development?
3. What is meant by the term *contextual control*? Illustrate with an example.
4. Just before starting to cross a street, a pedestrian from England visiting Canada observed that the street was clear to the right, stepped into the street, and was struck by a car. Explain how lack of contextual control was involved in this accident.

9 Changing the Control of a Behavior with Fading

"Peter, what's your name?"

TEACHING PETER HIS NAME[1]

Peter, diagnosed with autism, possessed an extensive vocal mimicking repertoire. He could repeat many of the words other people said but had little other verbal behavior. He would imitate many words, even when it was not appropriate. For example, when asked, "What's your name?" he would reply, "Name." Sometimes he would repeat the entire question, "What's your name?" This was a problem of stimulus control in that questions (stimuli) evoked mimicking responses rather than appropriate answers.

A university student named Veronica taught Peter to respond appropriately to the question, "What's your name?" as follows. First, Veronica identified an effective reinforcer. Because Peter had been taught to work for plastic chips that could be exchanged for treats such as candy and popcorn, Veronica decided to use the chips as reinforcers.

Peter sat at a small table in a quiet room, and Veronica sat across from him. In a very soft whisper, Veronica asked, "What's your name?" Then very loudly and quickly, before Peter could respond, she shouted, "PETER!" Of course, Peter mimicked the word "Peter," and Veronica reinforced this with "Good boy!" and a chip. You may wonder how this could represent any progress because the boy was still only mimicking. However, over several trials, Veronica began asking the question "What's your name?" more loudly and supplying the answer "Peter" more quietly. On each trial, she continued to reinforce the correct response—"Peter." Eventually, Veronica asked loudly, "What's your name?" and simply mouthed the word "Peter." Nevertheless, the boy responded with the correct answer, "Peter." Over several trials, Veronica ceased mouthing the correct answer, but Peter still responded correctly to the question "What's your name?" ■

---

[1] This case is taken from Martin, England, Kaprowy, Kilgour, and Pilek (1968).

FADING

Fading is the gradual change over successive trials of an antecedent stimulus that controls a response so that the response eventually occurs to a partially changed or completely new stimulus.

Peter would at first say his name only when it was said to him. Through a fading process, the stimulus control over the response "Peter" was gradually transferred from the antecedent stimulus "Peter" to the antecedent stimulus "What's your name?" One might ask whether Peter knew that he was saying his own name. To phrase this question more behaviorally, would Peter have consistently responded correctly when asked other questions involving his name? For example, would he have consistently answered "Peter" when shown his reflection in the mirror and asked, "Who's that?" Probably not. However, teaching him to respond appropriately to "What's your name?" was an important start to teaching him to answer other questions involving his name and to his knowing that he was saying his name.

Fading is involved in many everyday situations in which one person teaches a behavior to another person. Parents are likely to fade out their help and support when a child is learning to walk or to ride a bicycle. A dance instructor might use less and less hand pressure to guide a student through new dance steps. And as a teenager progresses in drivers' education, the driving instructor is likely to provide fewer and fewer hints regarding traffic regulations.

In any situation in which a stimulus exerts strong control over a response, fading can be a very useful procedure for transferring the control of that response to some other stimulus. **Errorless discrimination training**, sometimes referred to as **errorless learning**, is the use of a fading procedure to establish a stimulus discrimination so that no errors occur. The discovery and development of fading techniques have led to some changes in educators' views regarding the learning process. At one time, it was believed that people had to make mistakes while learning in order to know what *not* to do. However, errorless transfer of a discrimination can occur, and it has at least three advantages over procedures involving trial and error. First, errors consume valuable time. Second, if an error occurs once, it tends to occur many times, even though it is being extinguished. (Remember from Chapter 5 that during extinction, things may get worse before they get better.) Third, the nonreinforcement that occurs when errors are being extinguished often produces emotional side effects such as tantrums, aggressive behavior, and attempts to escape from the situation.

The authors have used fading procedures in many learning situations in our programs with persons with developmental disabilities including autism and with very young children. In teaching these learners to name a shirt, for example, teachers might proceed according to the following steps:

1. *Point to your shirt and say "shirt."* Keep doing this until the learner consistently mimics "shirt" a number of times, and immediately reinforce each correct response. The learner must be able to mimic this particular word and be able to look at any item you point to.
2. *When the learner consistently mimics "shirt," present the stimulus that you want to control the response and at the same time gradually fade out saying "shirt."* That is, you might say, "What's this? Shirt" while pointing to the shirt. In response, the learner usually mimics "shirt." Over several trials, gradually decrease the intensity of saying "shirt" to zero so that the learner eventually responds with the answer "shirt" to the stimulus of someone pointing at a shirt and asking, "What's this?" Again, each appropriate response is to be reinforced.

Fading can also be used to teach tracing, copying, and drawing shapes (e.g., circles, lines, squares, and triangles), numerals, and letters of the alphabet. To teach a child to trace a circle, the teacher might begin with a large number of sheets with a heavily dotted circle on each of them. The teacher places a pencil in the child's hand, says "Trace the circle," and then guides the child's hand so that the pencil traces the circle by connecting the dots. Immediately after this, the child receives a reinforcer. After several trials, the teacher fades out the pressure of her hand as a cue controlling the child's tracing by

1. lightly holding the child's hand for several trials
2. touching her fingertips to the back of the child's hand for several trials
3. pointing to the item to be traced
4. finally, simply giving the instruction, "Trace the circle." (Steps 1, 2, and 3 are always accompanied by this instruction.)

Once the teacher has taught the child to trace, the child can be taught to draw or copy by the teacher's fading out the dotted cues that guide the tracing. For example, the teacher might use a sheet on which there are several dotted circles. The circles progress from a heavily dotted circle on the left to a circle with very few dots on the right. The teacher points to the most heavily dotted circle and instructs the child, "Trace the circle here." The desired response is reinforced, and the procedure is repeated with the more lightly dotted circles. On subsequent steps, the dots can be faded out completely so that the child will draw a circle in their absence. It is then a simple matter to fade in the instruction "Draw a circle" to this newly acquired response. The instruction "Copy a circle" said while the teacher points to a circle can also be faded in and come to control the response. Learning to copy many different shapes in this fashion will eventually enable the child to copy shapes not previously copied.

DIMENSIONS OF STIMULI FOR FADING

In general, a *dimension* of a stimulus is any characteristic that can be measured on some continuum. As illustrated by the preceding examples, fading occurs along dimensions of stimuli, such as the loudness of the question that Veronica presented to Peter, the pressure of a teacher's hand that guides a child's printing, and the clarity of dots that a child might be expected to trace. Thus far, we have talked of fading across very specific stimulus dimensions, but fading can also occur across changes in a general situation or setting. In one of the authors' programs with children with autism, a group of children was expected to respond appropriately in a classroom setting (Martin et al., 1968). However, the children were very disruptive, especially in a group situation, and could not be placed directly into a classroom setting. So, the desired behavior for each child was obtained in an individual situation that was then faded into the classroom setting.

The initial training sessions were conducted in a small room in which there were several chairs and tablet-arm desks. Each day two or three university students worked individually with two or three children on a one-to-one basis. The procedures involved eliminating tantrums through extinction and reinforcing sitting attentively, exhibiting appropriate verbal behavior, drawing, copying, and displaying other desirable behaviors. Each child's desk was placed against the wall in such a fashion that it was difficult for the child to leave the situation.

Within one week, the children learned to sit quietly, attend to the university students, and imitate words. Stimulus control was established between the general training situation and the children's attentiveness. But the goal was to teach the children to function appropriately in a regular classroom situation with one teacher at the front of the class. If the classroom situation had been switched to after the first week, much inattentiveness and disruptive behavior would no doubt have occurred. Over a period of four weeks, the training situation gradually changed from one small room with three children and three university students to a standard-sized classroom with seven students and one teacher.

One dimension was the physical structure of the room. The children were moved from the small room to the regular large classroom. This was done by first placing the three tablet-arm desks against the wall of the regular classroom, just as we had done in the small room. The three chairs that the university students sat in were also moved to the regular classroom. The rest of the classroom was empty. Over several days, the tablet-arm desks were gradually moved away from the wall and toward the center of the room until, finally, the three desks were side by side. Additional desks and furnishings were added one at a time until the children were finally sitting in desks in a normally furnished classroom.

The second dimension was the number of children per teacher. Fading along this dimension was carried out at the same time that fading along the first dimension took place. At first, one university student worked with one student for several sessions. The university student then worked with two students, alternating questions between them for several sessions. In this fashion, the student–teacher ratio was increased gradually until only one teacher worked with the seven children in a classroom situation.

Study Questions

1. Define *fading* and give an example of it.
2. Define *errorless discrimination training.*
3. Why is establishing a stimulus discrimination without errors advantageous?
4. What is meant by a dimension of a stimulus? Describe an example.
5. Identify three stimulus dimensions along which fading occurred in the examples cited in the first two sections of this chapter.
6. Describe an example from this chapter in which the training situation remained constant but a specific stimulus dimension was faded.
7. Describe an example from this chapter in which the general training situation was faded.
8. Describe how you might use fading to teach your pet to perform a trick.
9. Assume that you have an 18-month-old child who imitates the word *chip.* Describe in detail how you might use fading to teach your child to correctly identify a chip (i.e., a potato chip) when you point to it and ask, "What's that?"

FACTORS INFLUENCING THE EFFECTIVENESS OF FADING

1. The Final Desired Stimulus

The *final desired stimulus* should be chosen carefully. It is important to select it so that the occurrence of the response to that particular stimulus is likely to be maintained in the natural environment. Some fading programs make the error of stopping with a stimulus that does not include some aspect of the situation that the learner will frequently encounter in the natural environment. In Peter's case, it would have been easy for Veronica to stop training at the second to last step, at which Veronica asked loudly, "What's your name?" and then mouthed the word "Peter." However, when others approached Peter in his natural environment and asked "What's your name?" they would not likely mouth "Peter." Therefore, Veronica conducted the last step of the program, in which Peter responded correctly to the question "What's your name?" completely on his own.

2. The Starting Stimulus: A Prompt

At the beginning of a fading program, it is important to select a *starting stimulus* that reliably evokes the desired behavior. In the task of teaching Peter his name, Veronica knew that Peter would mimic the last word of a question when that word was spoken loudly. Therefore, the starting stimulus with Peter was the question, "What's your name?" said very softly and followed quickly by the shouted word, "Peter!" The shouted word "Peter" prompted him to give the correct answer. A **prompt** is a supplemental antecedent stimulus provided to increase the likelihood that a desired behavior will occur, but that is not the final desired stimulus to control that behavior.

INSTRUCTOR BEHAVIORS AS PROMPTS   It is helpful to distinguish between several types of instructor behaviors that can be used as prompts. *Physical prompts* (also called *physical guidance*) consist of guiding the learning through touch. Parents frequently use physical guidance to help their children learn new behavior, such as holding their hands while teaching them to walk. Beginning dancers, martial arts students, and novice golfers often find a guiding hand to be help- **NOTE 1** ful. *Gestural prompts* are certain motions that a teacher makes, such as pointing to the correct cue or making signals directed to the learner without touching him or her. A teacher, for example, might extend a hand in a palm-downward motion as a prompt for children to talk softly. *Modeling prompts* occur when the correct behavior is demonstrated (modeling is discussed further in Chapter 18). A swimming coach might model the correct arm movements for the freestyle stroke for young swimmers. A golfing instructor might model the correct way to grip a golf club for a group of beginning golfers. *Verbal prompts* are verbal hints or cues. A driving instructor might use verbal prompts by telling a student driver to "check over your left shoulder before pulling out." Parents frequently use verbal prompts when teaching their children how to dress themselves (e.g., "Now pull the sweater over your head.").

ENVIRONMENTAL ALTERATIONS AS PROMPTS   *Environmental prompts* consist of alterations of the physical environment in a manner that will evoke the desired behavior. Someone attempting to eat healthily, for example, might put a bowl of fresh fruit in easy reach while keeping junk food out of sight in a difficult-to-reach cupboard. As another example, a student might ensure that a study area contain only objects and materials related to studying.

Technically speaking, all of the categories of prompts are parts of the environment for a learner. However, to distinguish instructor-behavior prompts from other aspects of the physical environment, we define each category of the prompts as described earlier.

EXTRA-STIMULUS VERSUS WITHIN-STIMULUS PROMPTS   Instructor-behavior prompts and environmental prompts can be further subdivided into extra-stimulus prompts and within-stimulus prompts. An *extra-stimulus prompt* is something that is added to the environment to make a correct response more likely. Suppose that a parent wanted to teach a child to place a knife, fork, and spoon appropriately when setting a table for dinner. One option would be for the parent to point to the appropriate location of each utensil as it was named and placed. Pointing would be an extra-stimulus instructor-behavior prompt, and it would be faded over trials. Alternatively, the parent might draw a knife, fork, and a spoon in their appropriate locations on a placemat and require the child to place the utensils appropriately. The line drawings would be an extra-stimulus environmental prompt and could gradually be erased over trials. A *within-stimulus prompt* is an alteration of the S^D or the S^Δ to make their characteristics more noticeable and therefore easier to discriminate. In the table-setting example, training might be initiated with a normal fork and knife in their normal positions with a large wooden spoon as the training item. This would be a within-stimulus environmental prompt. The initial focus would be on teaching the child to place the spoon in the correct position. Over trials, the size of the spoon could be faded back to normal. This process could then be repeated with the knife and the fork until the child sets the table correctly. A within-stimulus prompt could also involve teacher behavior. A teacher trying to teach a child to respond appropriately to two words that sound similar, such as pen and pencil (both include the "pen" sound), might initially exaggerate differences in the sounds of the words when asking for either a pen ("PEN!") or a pencil ("pen-CIL!") and then gradually fade the sounds to their normal pitch and loudness. The different types of prompts are listed in Table 9–1. Several studies have indicated that within-stimulus prompt fading is more effective than extra-stimulus prompt fading with children with developmental disabilities including autism (Schreibman, 1975; Witt & Wacker, 1981; Wolfe & Cuvo, 1978).

A behavior modifier may provide any or all of these types of prompts to ensure the correct response. Suppose a teacher wishes to develop appropriate stimulus control by the instruction "Touch your head" over the response of a learner touching her head. The behavior modifier might initiate training by saying "Touch your head. Raise your hand and put it on your head like this" while touching his own head. In this example, "Raise your hand and put it on your head like this" is a verbal prompt, and the teacher's action of putting his hand on his head is a modeling prompt. Selecting several kinds of prompts that together reliably produce the desired response will minimize errors and maximize the success of the fading program.

Fading Steps

NOTE 2

When the desired response is occurring reliably to the prompts given at the onset of the training program, the prompts can then be gradually removed over trials. The steps through which prompts are to be eliminated should be carefully chosen. Unfortunately, effective use of fading is somewhat of an art. It is very important to monitor the learner's performance closely to determine the speed at which fading should be carried out. Fading should be neither too fast nor too slow. If the learner begins to make errors, the prompts may have been faded too quickly or through too few fading steps. It is then necessary to backtrack until the behavior is again well established before continuing with fading. However, if too many steps are introduced or too many

TABLE 9–1   Types of Prompts
Instructor-Behavior Prompts
Physical guidance—physically assisting the learner
Gestures—pointing or motioning
Modeling—demonstrating the correct behavior
Verbal—using words as hints or cues, giving instructions
Environmental Prompts
Environmental—rearranging the physical surroundings
Extra-Stimulus Versus Within-Stimulus Prompts
Extra-stimulus—adding another stimulus to make a correct response more likely
Within-stimulus—making the S^D or the S^Δ more noticeable and easier to discriminate

prompts are provided over a number of trials, the learner might become overly dependent on the prompts. Consider the example of teaching a child to touch her head when asked to do so. If the teacher spends a great many trials providing the prompt of touching his own head, the child may become dependent on it and attend much less to the instruction, "Touch your head."

PITFALLS OF FADING

Pitfall Type 1

Just as other behavior principles and procedures can be applied unknowingly by those who are not familiar with them, so can fading be misused. However, it appears to be more difficult to misuse fading inadvertently because the necessary gradual change in cues rarely occurs by chance.

The case of the child who banged his head on hard surfaces (described in Chapter 8) might be an example of the effects of the misuse of fading. Suppose that the child began attracting attention initially by hitting his head on soft surfaces, such as grass. At first, this behavior may have caused adults to come running to see whether the child had injured himself. When they eventually learned that no injury resulted from this behavior, they ceased providing him attention. The child may then have progressed to hitting his head with the same force but on slightly harder surfaces, such as carpeted floors. For a while, this perhaps increased the amount of attention elicited from adults, but this amount may eventually have decreased when the adults learned that the child did not injure himself in this way. Only when the child graduated to hitting his head on surfaces such as hard floors and even concrete, which caused real and serious self-injury, did the adults give him continued attention. Note that throughout this example, a gradual change occurred in the stimulus (the type of floor surface), evoking the undesired behavior; eventually, the behavior was evoked by the most undesirable stimulus possible. Thus, this example fits the technical definition of fading.

GUIDELINES FOR THE EFFECTIVE APPLICATION OF FADING

1. *Choose the Final Desired Stimulus*   Specify very clearly the stimuli in the presence of which the target behavior should eventually occur.
2. *Select an Appropriate Reinforcer*   See Chapter 3.
3. *Choose the Starting Stimulus and Fading Steps*
   a. Specify clearly the conditions under which the desired behavior now occurs—that is, what people, words, physical guidance, and so forth, presently are necessary to evoke the desired behavior.
   b. Specify specific prompts that will evoke the desired behavior.
   c. Specify clearly the dimensions (such as color, people, and room size) that you will fade to reach the desired stimulus control.
   d. Outline the specific fading steps to be followed and the rules for moving from one step to the next.
4. *Put the Plan Into Effect*
   a. Present the starting stimulus and reinforce the correct behavior.
   b. Across trials, the fading of cues should be so gradual that there are as few errors as possible. However, if an error occurs, move back to the previous step for several trials and provide additional prompts.

c. When the desired stimulus control is obtained, review the guidelines in previous chapters for weaning the learner from the program (a topic that is discussed in more detail in Chapter 16).

Study Questions

10. What do we mean by *final desired stimulus*? Give an example.
11. What do we mean by *starting stimulus*? Give an example.
12. Define *prompt*. Describe an example that is not from this chapter.
13. Define the four major categories of teacher-behavior prompts. Give an example of each.
14. Define *environmental prompt*, and describe an example that is not from this chapter.
15. Define *within-stimulus prompt*, and describe an example that is not from this chapter. Does your example involve a teacher-behavior prompt or an environmental prompt?
16. Define *extra-stimulus prompt*, and describe an example that is not from this chapter. Does your example involve a teacher-behavior prompt or an environmental prompt?
17. How many reinforced trials should occur at any given fading step before the stimuli of that particular step are changed? (*Hint:* What suggestions were made in the examples in this chapter?)

Application Exercises

A. EXERCISES INVOLVING OTHERS

1. Suppose that a 3-year-old child has reached the stage at which she is beginning to wander away from her front yard. The child has already learned some speech, and you wish to teach her to answer the question "Where do you live?" Outline a fading program you could use to teach the answer to this question; indicate what you would use as a reinforcer, the number of trials you would have at each fading step, and so forth.
2. You want to instruct a child with severe developmental disabilities or a very young normal child to eat with a spoon. Name and describe the categories of prompts that you would use. Describe how each of the prompts would be faded.

B. SELF-MODIFICATION EXERCISE

Suppose that you detest certain vegetables from the cabbage family—such as broccoli—but research studies have convinced you that you can reduce your chances of heart disease and cancer by eating more of these vegetables. Outline a fading program that you could use to increase the amount of broccoli or other such vegetables that you eat. (*Hint:* Your program should not—at least in the long run—increase your fat intake because that would defeat its purpose.)

Notes and Extended Discussion

1. The use of physical guidance raises a potential ethical issue. Suppose that in a program for persons with developmental disabilities, a teacher decides to use physical guidance. Suppose further that an individual client resists being guided. Physical guidance in that instance would therefore be viewed as somewhat intrusive or restrictive. However, as indicated in the discussion of ethical guidelines in Chapter 30, when behavior modifiers do use physical guidance, the least intrusive and restrictive interventions possible should be chosen. The teacher applying physical guidance in this instance should ensure that doing so meets appropriate ethical guidelines and accreditation standards. This issue is discussed further in Chapter 30.

2. The four methods of removing prompts gradually are (a) decreasing assistance, (b) increasing assistance, (c) graduated guidance, and (d) time delay. All of the examples of this chapter illustrate decreasing assistance in which a starting stimulus that evokes the response is gradually removed or changed until the response is evoked by the final desired stimulus. Increasing assistance takes the opposite approach. The teacher begins with the final desired stimulus and introduces prompts only if the learner fails to respond appropriately to the final desired stimulus. The level of the prompts gradually increases during a trial in which the learner failed to respond at the preceding level until eventually the learner responds to the prompt. Graduated guidance is similar to the method of decreasing assistance except that the teacher's physical guidance is gradually adjusted from moment to moment within a trial as needed and then is faded across trials. For example, the teacher may grasp the learner's hand firmly at the beginning of the trial and gradually reduce the force on the learner's hand as the trial progresses. With time delay, the final desired stimulus and the starting stimulus are presented together at first; then, rather than change the starting stimulus, the time interval between the final desired stimulus and the starting stimulus is gradually increased until eventually the individual is responding only to the final desired stimulus. Many studies have indicated little or no difference in the effectiveness of these different prompt-removal methods (for a review, see Demchak, 1990).

Study Questions on Notes

1. Describe a plausible example in which use of physical guidance in a teaching program might require ethical approval. Why would ethical approval be required?
2. Which of the prompt-removal procedures fit the definition of fading given at the beginning of this chapter, and which do not? Explain.

10 Getting a New Behavior to Occur with Shaping

"Frank, did you do your jogging?"

IMPROVING FRANK'S EXERCISING[1]

After taking early retirement at the age of 55, Frank decided to make some changes in his life. But he wasn't sure where to start. Knowing that he needed to change some of his long-standing habits, he enrolled in a behavior modification course at the local community college. Next, on the advice of his doctor, he resolved to begin a regular exercise program. Frank had been a "couch potato" all of his adult life. He typically came home from work, grabbed a can of beer, and parked himself in front of the television set. Frank launched his exercise program with a pledge to his wife that he would jog a quarter of a mile each day. But after a couple of attempts, he returned to his couch-potato routine. He had expected too much too soon. He then decided to try a procedure called shaping that he had studied in his behavior modification course. The following three stages summarize that procedure.

1. Specify the final desired behavior. *Frank's goal was to jog a quarter of a mile each day. However, for a chronic nonexerciser, this was more than could be expected.*
2. Identify a response that could be used as a starting point in working toward the final desired behavior. *Frank decided that he would put on his sneakers and walk around the outside of the house once (approximately 30 yards). Although this was a long way from a quarter of a mile, it was a start.*
3. Reinforce the starting response; then reinforce closer and closer approximations until eventually the desired response occurs. *Frank decided to use the opportunity to drink a beer as a reinforcer. He explained his program to his wife and asked her to remind him that he had to complete his exercise before he could have a beer. After the first approximation had occurred*

---

[1] This case is based on one described by Watson and Tharp (1997).

on several successive afternoons, Frank increased the requirement to walking around the house twice (approximately 60 yards). A few days later, the distance was increased to walking around the house four times (approximately 120 yards), then six times (180 yards), then farther and farther until the distance was approximately a quarter of a mile, and then finally to jogging that distance. By reinforcing successive approximations to his goal, Frank reached the point where he jogged a quarter of a mile regularly. (The application of behavior modification techniques to improve self-control is discussed further in Chapter 26.) ■

SHAPING

In the previous two chapters, we described how stimulus discrimination training and fading could be used to establish appropriate stimulus control over a behavior provided that the specific behavior occurred occasionally. But what if a desired behavior never occurs? In that case, it is not possible to increase its frequency simply by waiting until it occurs and then reinforcing it. However, a procedure called *shaping* can be used to establish a behavior that the individual never performs. The behavior modifier begins by reinforcing a response that occurs with more frequency than zero and at least remotely resembles the final desired response. Frank, for example, was first reinforced for walking once around his house because this behavior occurred occasionally and remotely approximated his nonexistent behavior of jogging a quarter of a mile. When this initial response is occurring at a high frequency, the behavior modifier stops reinforcing it and begins reinforcing a slightly closer approximation of the final desired response. In this way, the final desired response is eventually established by reinforcing successive approximations to it. **Shaping** can be defined as the development of a new behavior by the reinforcement of successive approximations of that behavior and the extinction of earlier approximations of that behavior until the new behavior occurs. Shaping is sometimes referred to as the *method of successive approximations*.

The behaviors that an individual acquires during a lifetime develop from a variety of sources and influences. Sometimes a new behavior develops when an individual performs some initial behavior and the environment then reinforces slight variations in that behavior across a number of trials. Eventually, that initial behavior may be shaped so that the final form no longer resembles it. For example, most parents use shaping in teaching their children to talk. When an infant first begins to babble, some of the sounds remotely approximate words in the parents' native language. When this happens, the parents usually reinforce the behavior with hugs, caresses, kisses, and smiles. The sounds "mmm" and "daa" typically receive exceptionally large doses of reinforcement from English-speaking parents. Eventually *ma-ma* and *da-da* occur and are strongly reinforced, and the more primitive mmm and daa are subjected to extinction. At a later stage, reinforcement is given after the child says "mommy" and "daddy," and ma-ma and da-da are extinguished.

The same process occurs with other words. First, the child passes through a stage in which very remote approximations of words in the parents' native language are reinforced. Then the child enters a stage in which "baby talk" is reinforced. Finally, the parents and others require the child to pronounce words in accordance with the practices of the verbal community before reinforcement is given. For example, a child who says "wa-wa" at an early stage is given a glass of water, and if she is thirsty, this action reinforces the response. At a later stage "watah" rather than wa-wa is reinforced with water. Finally, the child must say "water" before water reinforcement will be given.

Of course, this description greatly oversimplifies the way in which a child learns to talk. However, it serves to illustrate the importance of shaping in the process by which normal children gradually progress from babbling to baby talk and finally to speaking in accordance with prevailing social conventions. Other processes that play important roles in speech development are discussed elsewhere in this text, for example, automatic reinforcement in Chapter 4, stimulus equivalence in Chapter 8, and fading in Chapter 9.

The five aspects or dimensions of behavior that can be shaped are topography, frequency, duration, latency, and intensity (or force). *Topography* is the spatial configuration or form of a particular response (i.e., the specific movements involved). Printing a word and writing the same word are examples of the same response made with two different topographies. Topography shaping occurs, for example, when teaching a child to switch from a printing response to a writing response, shaping a child's saying, "Mommy" instead of "Mama," learning to ice skate with longer and longer strides rather than short choppy steps, and shaping the proper finger movements for eating with chopsticks. An example of an early study involving topography shaping involved teaching a child to wear his glasses by reinforcing successive approximations of touching them, picking them up, putting the glasses up to his face, and finally wearing them (Wolf, Risley, & Mees, 1964).

We sometimes refer to the frequency or duration of a particular behavior as the *amount* of that behavior. The *frequency* of a behavior is the number of instances that occur in a given period of time. Examples of frequency shaping include increasing the number of steps (the distance) that Frank walked in his exercise program and increasing the number of repetitions that a golfer practices a particular golf shot. The frequency of a response may also be reduced by shaping as in a behavior modification program in which a patient with multiple sclerosis learned through shaping to gradually increase the time between and hence decrease the frequency of bathroom visits (O'Neill & Gardner, 1983). The *duration* of a response is the length of time that it lasts. Examples of duration shaping include lengthening the time spent studying before taking a break and gradually adjusting the duration of stirring pancake batter until it achieves just the right consistency.

Latency is the time between the occurrence of a stimulus and the response evoked by that stimulus. A common term for latency is reaction time. On the popular TV quiz show *Jeopardy!* the time from the presentation of the host's verbal stimulus until a contestant presses a button is the contestant's latency of responding to that particular stimulus. In a race, the time between firing the starter's pistol and the runner leaving the blocks is the latency of the runner's response to the firing of the starting pistol. Latency shaping might enable the runner to react more quickly or the *Jeopardy!* contestant to press the button faster.

The *intensity* or force of a response refers to the physical effect the response has or potentially has on the environment. For an example of shaping force, consider a farm boy whose job is to pump water out of a well with an old-fashioned hand pump. When the pump was first installed, it was freshly oiled, and when the boy applied a certain amount of force to the handle, it moved up and down very easily and water flowed. Suppose, however, that with lack of regular oiling, the pump has gradually acquired a little rust. Each day the boy applies approximately the amount of force he applied on the first day. When applying that force is no longer reinforced by the flow of water because the addition of rust has made the pump handle more difficult to move, the boy will likely apply a little more force and find that it pays off. Over several months, the boy's behavior is gradually shaped so that he presses very hard on the first trial, a terminal behavior quite different from the initial behavior. Other examples of intensity shaping include learning to shake hands with a firmer grip and learning to apply the right amount of force when scratching to relieve an itch without damaging one's skin. An example of intensity shaping in a behavior modification program involved teaching a socially withdrawn girl whose speech was barely audible to speak louder and louder until she was speaking at normal voice volume (Jackson & Wallace, 1974). See Table 10–1 for a summary of the dimensions of behavior.

TABLE 10–1	Dimensions of Behavior That Can Be Shaped	
Dimension	**Definition**	**Example**
Topography (form)	Physical movements involved in the behavior	Extent of follow through on a tennis serve
Amount: frequency	Number of instances of the behavior in a given time	Number of dishes washed in 5 minutes
Amount: duration	Continuous amount of time that the behavior lasts	Length of time treading water
Latency	Time between the controlling stimulus and the behavior	Time between the question "What time is it?" and the response of looking at your watch
Intensity (force)	Amount of energy expended on the behavior	Force of a punch in boxing

Shaping is so common in everyday life that people are seldom even aware of it. Sometimes the shaping procedure is applied systematically as in Frank's case, sometimes nonsystematically **NOTE 1** as when parents shape correct pronunciation of words spoken by their children; sometimes shaping occurs from consequences in the natural environment as when a cook gradually perfects the method for flipping pancakes.

Care should be taken to avoid confusing shaping with fading. Both are procedures of gradual change. However, as described in Chapter 9, fading involves reinforcement of a specific response in the presence of slight changes in a stimulus so that the stimulus gradually comes to resemble the stimulus that will control the response. Shaping, on the other hand, involves reinforcement of slight changes in a behavior so that it gradually comes to resemble the target behavior. Thus, *fading involves the gradual change of a stimulus while the response stays about the same; shaping involves the gradual change of a response while the stimulus stays about the same.*

Study Questions

1. Identify the three basic stages in any shaping procedure as presented at the beginning of this chapter, and describe them with an example (either Frank's case or an example of your own).
2. Define *shaping*.
3. What is another name for shaping?
4. Explain how shaping involves successive applications of the principles of positive reinforcement and extinction.
5. Why bother with shaping? Why not just learn about the use of straightforward positive reinforcement to increase a behavior?
6. In terms of the three stages in a shaping procedure, describe how parents might shape their child to say a particular word.
7. List five dimensions of behavior that can be shaped. Give two examples of each.
8. Describe a behavior of yours that was shaped by consequences in the natural environment, and state several of the initial approximations.
9. Distinguish between shaping and fading.

FACTORS INFLUENCING THE EFFECTIVENESS OF SHAPING

1. Specifying the Final Desired Behavior

The first stage in shaping is to identify clearly the final desired behavior, which, as described in Chapter 1, is often referred to as the *target behavior*. In Frank's case, the final desired behavior was jogging a quarter of a mile each day. With a definition as specific as this, there was little possibility that Frank or his wife would develop different expectations regarding his performance. If different people working with the individual expect different things, or if one person is not consistent from one training session or situation to the next, progress is likely to be delayed. A precise statement of the final desired behavior increases the chances for consistent reinforcement of successive approximations of that behavior. The final desired behavior should be stated in such a way that all of the relevant characteristics of the behavior (its topography, amount, latency, and intensity) are identified. In addition, the conditions under which the behavior is or is not to occur should be stated, and any other guidelines that appear to be necessary for consistency should be provided.

2. Choosing a Starting Behavior

Because the final desired or target behavior does not occur initially and because it is necessary to reinforce some behavior that approximates it, you must identify a *starting behavior*. This should be a behavior that occurs often enough to be reinforced within the session time, and it should approximate the final desired behavior. For example, Frank's behavior of walking around the house once is something that he did periodically. This was the closest approximation that he regularly made with respect to the goal of jogging a quarter of a mile.

In a shaping program, it is crucial to know not only where you are going (the target behavior) but also the level at which the individual is currently performing. The purpose of the shaping program is to get from one to the other by reinforcing successive approximations from the starting point to the final desired behavior even though they might be very dissimilar. For example, in a classic study, Isaacs, Thomas, and Goldiamond (1960) applied shaping to redevelop verbal behavior in a catatonic schizophrenic man who had been mute for 19 years. Using chewing gum as a reinforcer, the experimenter took the patient through the shaping steps of eye movement toward the gum, facial movement, mouth movements, lip movements, vocalizations, word utterance, and, finally, understandable speech.

3. Choosing the Shaping Steps

Before initiating the shaping program, it is helpful to outline the successive approximations through which the person will be moved in the attempt to approximate the final desired behavior. For example, suppose that the final desired behavior in a shaping program for a child is saying *daddy*. It has been determined that the child says *daa*, and this response is set as the starting behavior. Let's suppose that we decide to go from the initial behavior of saying daa through the following steps: saying *da-da, dad, dad-ee,* and *daddy*. To begin, reinforcement is given on a number of occasions for emitting the initial behavior (daa). When this behavior is occurring repetitively, the trainer moves to step 2 (da-da) and reinforces that approximation for several trials. This step-by-step procedure continues until the child finally says *daddy*.

NOTE 2   How many successive approximations should there be? In other words, what is a reasonable step size? Unfortunately, there are no specific guidelines for identifying the ideal step size.

In attempting to specify the behavioral steps from the starting behavior to the target behavior, behavior modifiers might imagine what steps they would go through. Also it is sometimes helpful to observe others who can already perform the target behavior and to ask them to perform the initial and subsequent approximations. Whatever guidelines or guesses are used, it is important to try to stick to them yet be flexible if the trainee does not proceed quickly enough or is learning more quickly than had been expected. Some guidelines for moving through the behavioral program are offered in the following section.

4. Moving Along at the Correct Pace

How many times should each approximation be reinforced before proceeding to the next approximation? Again, there are no specific guidelines for answering this question. However, there are several rules of thumb to follow in reinforcing successive approximations of a final desired response:

a. Reinforce an approximation at least several times before proceeding to the next step. In other words, avoid underreinforcement of a shaping step. Trying to go to a new step before the previous approximation has been well established can result in losing the previous approximation through extinction without achieving the new approximation.

b. Avoid reinforcing too many times at any shaping step. Item *a* cautions against going too fast. It is also important not to progress too slowly. If one approximation is reinforced for so long that it becomes extremely strong, new approximations are less likely to appear.

c. If you lose a behavior because you are moving too fast or taking too large a step, return to an earlier approximation where you can pick up the behavior again. You also may need to insert an extra step or two.

These guidelines may not seem very helpful. On the one hand, it is advisable not to move too fast from one approximation to another; on the other hand, it is advisable not to move too slowly. If we could accompany these guidelines with a mathematical formula for calculating the exact size of the steps that should be taken in any situation and exactly how many reinforcements should be given at each step, the guidelines would be much more useful. Unfortunately, the experiments necessary for providing this information have not yet been conducted. The behavior modifier should observe the behavior carefully and be prepared to make changes in the procedure—changing the size of, slowing down, speeding up, or retracing steps—whenever the behavior does not seem to be developing properly. Shaping requires a good deal of practice and skill if it is to be performed with maximum effectiveness.

Study Questions

10. What do behavior modifiers mean by the term *target behavior* in a shaping program? Give an example.
11. What do behavior modifiers mean by the term *starting behavior* in a shaping program? Give an example.
12. How do you know you have enough successive approximations or shaping steps of the right size?
13. Why is it necessary to avoid underreinforcement at any shaping step?
14. Why is it necessary to avoid reinforcing too many times at any shaping step?

PITFALLS OF SHAPING

Pitfall Type 1

As with other procedures and natural processes, shaping operates whether we are aware of it or not. Unfortunately, those who are not aware of shaping may unknowingly apply it to develop un- desirable behavior of friends, acquaintances, family members, and others. See Figure 10–1 for an example of this.

NOTE 1

Consider another example of this pitfall. In Chapter 9, we described how the inadvertent misapplication of fading by those unwary of the procedure could lead to a child who bangs his head against hard surfaces. This could also happen through the inadvertent misapplication of shaping by those unwary of it. Suppose, for example, a small child receives very little social

FIGURE 10–1 A misapplication of shaping.

attention from family members when he performs appropriate behavior. Perhaps one day the child accidentally falls and strikes his head lightly against a hard floor. Even if the child is not injured seriously, a parent may come running quickly and make a big fuss over the incident. Because of this reinforcement and because anything else the child does that is appropriate seldom evokes attention, he is likely to repeat the response of striking his head lightly against the floor. The first few times this occurs, the parent may continue to reinforce the response. Eventually, however, seeing that the child is not really hurting himself, the parent may stop reinforcing it. Because the behavior has now been placed on extinction, the *intensity* of the behavior may increase (see Chapter 5). That is, the child may begin to hit his head more forcefully, and the slightly louder thud will cause the parent to come running again. If this shaping process continues, the child will eventually hit his head with sufficient force to cause physical injury. It is extremely difficult, if not impossible, to use extinction to eliminate such violently self-destructive behavior. It would have been best never to have let the behavior develop to the point at which the child's parents were forced to continue reinforcing it and increasing its strength.

Many undesirable behaviors commonly seen in children with special needs—for example, violent temper tantrums, constant fidgeting, injuring other children, voluntary vomiting—are often products of the inadvertent application of shaping. It is possible that these behaviors can be eliminated by a combination of extinction of the undesirable behavior and positive reinforcement of the desirable behavior. Unfortunately, this is often difficult to do because (a) the behavior is sometimes so harmful that it cannot be allowed to occur even once during the period in which extinction is to take place and (b) adults who are ignorant of behavior principles sometimes unknowingly foil the efforts of those who are conscientiously attempting to apply these principles.

In Chapter 23, we describe how to diagnose and treat problem behaviors that may have been developed inadvertently through shaping. As in medicine, however, the best cure is prevention. Ideally, all persons responsible for the care of other persons will be so thoroughly versed in behavior principles that they will refrain from shaping undesirable behavior.

Pitfall Type 4

(See Chapter 3 for the five types of pitfalls.) A child who has not learned to talk by a certain age may be labeled as intellectually disabled or autistic. It is possible that there are individuals with intellectual disabilities or autism whose deficiency exists not because of any genetic or physical defect but simply because they were never exposed to effective shaping procedures. Many variables can prevent a physically normal child from receiving the shaping that is necessary to establish normal behaviors. For an excellent discussion of how delays in acquiring age-appropriate language skills develop in preschool children with no known genetic or physical defects that might cause the delayed behavior, see Drash and Tudor (1993).

Pitfall Type 5

Another type of pitfall is the failure to apply shaping to develop desirable behavior. Some parents, for example, may not be responsive enough to their child's babbling behavior. Perhaps they expect too much at the beginning and do not reinforce extremely remote approximations of normal speech. Some parents, for example, seem to expect their tiny infant to say "Father!" right off the bat and are not impressed when the child says "da-da." The opposite type of problem also exists. Instead of not giving enough reinforcement for babbling, some parents may overreinforce babbling. This could result in a child whose speech consists entirely of baby talk at an age when most children have mastered their culture's speech patterns.

GUIDELINES FOR THE EFFECTIVE APPLICATION OF SHAPING

1. *Select the Target Behavior*
   a. Choose a specific behavior (such as working quietly at a desk for 10 minutes) rather than a general category (e.g., "good" classroom behavior). Shaping is appropriate for changing amount, latency, and intensity of behavior, as well as for developing new behavior of a different topography (form). If the target behavior is a complex sequence of activities (such as making a bed) that can be broken down into sequential steps, and if the program amounts to linking the steps together in a particular order, it is not a shaping program. Rather, the target behavior needs to be developed by chaining (see Chapter 11).
   b. If possible, select a behavior that will come under the control of natural reinforcers after it has been shaped.

2. *Select an Appropriate Reinforcer* See Figure 3–3 and the "Guidelines for the Effective Application of Positive Reinforcement," pp. 48–49.

3. *The Initial Plan*
   a. List successive approximations to the target behavior, beginning with the starting behavior. To choose the starting behavior, find a behavior already in the learner's repertoire that resembles the target behavior most closely and that occurs at least once during an observation period.
   b. Your initial steps or successive approximations are usually "educated guesses." During your program, you can modify these according to the learner's performance.

4. *Implementing the Plan*
   a. Tell the learner about the plan before starting.
   b. Begin reinforcing immediately following each occurrence of the starting behavior.
   c. Never move to a new approximation until the learner has mastered the previous one.
   d. If you are not sure when to move the learner to a new approximation, utilize the following rule. Move to the next step when the learner performs the current step correctly in 6 of 10 trials, usually with 1 or 2 trials less perfect than desired and one or two trials in which the behavior is better than the current step.
   e. Do not reinforce too many times at any one step, and avoid underreinforcement at any one step.
   f. If the learner stops working, you may have moved up the steps too quickly, the steps may not be the right size, or the reinforcer may be ineffective.
      (1) First, check the effectiveness of your reinforcer.
      (2) If the learner becomes inattentive or shows signs of boredom, the steps may be too small.
      (3) Inattention or boredom may also mean you have progressed too rapidly. If so, return to the previous step for a few more trials and then try the present step again.
      (4) If the learner continues to have difficulty, despite retraining at previous steps, add more steps at the point of difficulty.

Study Questions

15. Give an example of Pitfall Type 1 in which shaping might be accidentally applied to develop an undesirable behavior. Describe some of the shaping steps in your example.
16. State Pitfall Type 5 (see Chapter 3, p. 48).

17. Give an example of Pitfall Type 5 in which the failure to apply shaping might have an undesirable result.
18. Give an example from your own experience of a target behavior that might best be developed through a procedure other than shaping (see Guideline 1a, p. 128).
19. State a rule for deciding when to move the learner to a new approximation (see p. 128).
20. Why do we refer to positive reinforcement and extinction as principles but to shaping as a procedure? (*Hint:* See Chapter 1, p. 12.)

Application Exercises

A. EXERCISE INVOLVING OTHERS

Think of a normal child between the ages of 2 and 7 with whom you have had contact (e.g., a sister, brother, or neighbor). Specify a realistic target behavior of that child that you might try to develop by utilizing a shaping procedure. Identify the starting point you would choose, the reinforcer, and the successive approximations you would go through.

B. SELF-MODIFICATION EXERCISES

1. Take a close look at many of your own skills—for example, personal interaction, lovemaking, and studying. Identify two specific skills that were probably shaped by others, either knowingly or unknowingly. Identify two specific behaviors that were probably shaped by the natural environment. For each example, identify the reinforcer and at least three approximations that you likely performed during the shaping process.

2. Select one of your behavioral deficits, perhaps one that you listed at the end of Chapter 2. Outline a complete shaping program that with a little help from your friends you might use to overcome that deficit. Make sure that your plan follows the guidelines for the effective application of shaping discussed in this chapter.

Notes and Extended Discussion

1. Shaping appears to be useful in modifying not only external behavior but also internal behavior. For example, R. W. Scott and colleagues (1973) demonstrated that shaping could be used to modify heart rate. In this study, the device monitoring heart rate was hooked up to the video portion of a TV set that the individual watched. Although the sound portion of the TV was on continuously, the video portion appeared only when the individual's heart rate changed by a few beats per minute from its previous level. When the subject's heart rate remained at a new level for three consecutive sessions, the video portion was used to reinforce a further change in heart rate. In one case involving a psychiatric patient suffering from chronic anxiety and manifesting a moderately elevated heart rate, the investigators shaped several decreases in the individual's heart rate. Interestingly, when the individual's heart rate had been decreased to a lower level, reports from his ward indicated that "he seemed less 'tense' and 'anxious'" and that "he made fewer requests for medication."

   In other studies, information about a person's physiological processes, such as heart rate or muscle tension, is displayed on a screen or in some way made immediately available to the individual. Such techniques, which are referred to as *biofeedback,* enable individuals to gain control over the physiological processes being monitored. Clinical applications of biofeedback have been successful in reducing epileptic seizures by helping individuals learn to control electrical brain activity associated with their seizures and reducing blood pressure, thereby enabling hypertensive patients to use less medication, and reducing chronic headaches, accelerated heart rate, and anxiety (Schwartz & Andrasic, 1998).

2. How fast should you move from one step to the next? How large should step size be? One reason there are no specific answers to these questions is the difficulty of measuring specific step sizes and consistently reinforcing responses that satisfy a given step size. Human judgment is simply not fast enough or accurate enough to ensure that any given shaping procedure is being applied consistently in order to make comparisons between it and other consistently applied shaping procedures. This is particularly true when topography is the aspect of behavior that is being shaped. Computers, however, are both accurate and fast and may therefore be useful in answering fundamental questions concerning which shaping procedures are most effective (Midgley, Lea, & Kirby, 1989; Pear & Legris, 1987). For example, using two video cameras that were connected to a microcomputer programmed to detect the position of a pigeon's head within a test chamber, Pear and Legris demonstrated that a computer can shape where the pigeon moves its head.

In addition to providing a methodology for studying shaping, these studies suggest that computers may be able to shape some kinds of behavior as effectively as humans. For example, a device that shapes movements may help a person regain the use of a limb that has been paralyzed from a stroke or accident (e.g., see Taub et al., 1994).

Such a device would have the advantage over a human shaper in its precision, its ability to provide extremely rapid and systematic feedback, and its patience (i.e., computers are nonjudgmental and untiring).

3. Rasey and Iversen (1993) provided a good laboratory demonstration of a potential maladaptive effect of shaping. They reinforced rats with food for extending their noses over the edge of a platform on which the rats were standing. Over trials, the rats were required to extend their noses farther and farther over the edge before receiving reinforcement. Eventually, each rat extended its nose so far over the edge that it actually fell off the platform. A net under the platform kept the rat from being injured; however, this experiment demonstrates that animals, and probably humans as well, can be shaped to engage in behavior that is harmful to them.

Study Questions on Notes

1. Describe how Scott and colleagues used shaping to decrease the heart rate of a man suffering from chronic anxiety.
2. What is biofeedback?
3. Describe how computer technology might be used to shape specific limb movements in a paralyzed person.
4. Describe how computer technology might be used to study shaping more accurately than can be done with the usual noncomputerized shaping procedures.
5. Describe an experiment demonstrating that maladaptive behavior can be shaped.

11

Getting a New Sequence of Behaviors to Occur with Behavioral Chaining

"Steve, your preputt routine is inconsistent."

TEACHING STEVE TO FOLLOW A CONSISTENT PREPUTT ROUTINE[1]

Steve was a young professional golfer on the Canadian PGA Tour who, although playing well, had not yet won a professional tournament due in part to inconsistent putting. He knew that professional golfers have a more consistent preputt routine than skilled amateur golfers, and that skilled amateur golfers have a more consistent preputt routine than less skilled amateur golfers. Steve realized that his own preputt routine was not as consistent as it might be. He did not always check the slope of the putting green from both sides of the ball before putting. If it was an especially important putt, he tended to stand over the ball for a longer period of time than usual before stroking it toward the hole. Other inconsistencies also occurred from one instance of putting to the next during a competitive round. He concluded that his inconsistent preputt routine could be contributing to inconsistent putting.

The first step to establishing a consistent sequence of responses during his preputt routine was to list the specific steps that he wanted to follow on each occasion. They were as follows:

1. When approaching the ball, forget about the score and think only about the putt at hand.
2. Go behind the hole, look back at the ball, and check the slope of the green in order to estimate the speed and path of the putt.
3. Move behind the ball, look toward the hole, and recheck the slope.

---

[1] This example is based on a consultation with G. Martin (1999).

4. *While standing behind the ball, pick a spot to aim at, take two practice strokes, and visualize the ball rolling in the hole.*
5. *Move beside the ball, set the putter down behind the ball, and adjust it so that it is aiming at the desired spot.*
6. *Adjust your feet so that they are parallel to the putting line, grip the putter in the usual way, and say, "Stroke it smooth."*
7. *Look at the hole, look at the ball, look at the spot, look at the ball, and stroke the putt.*

The training procedure involved 10 trials. On each trial, Steve performed all seven steps of the preputt routine while practicing a short putt on the practice green. The reason he practiced the routine on short putts rather than long ones was that he wanted each sequence to be followed by the reinforcer of making the putt. On each trial, a friend checked off the steps as they were performed. If he missed a step, his friend prompted him to perform it before continuing to the next step. After completing the 10 trials, Steve and his friend played a practice round of golf during which his friend prompted him to complete the preputt routine on every putt. During subsequent tournament rounds, Steve asked his caddy to remind him to follow his preputt routine. Three weeks later Steve won his first tour event. While a number of factors undoubtedly contributed to his win, Steve felt that one of them was his improved putting as the result of his more consistent preputt routine. ∎

BEHAVIORAL CHAINING

A **behavioral chain**, also called a **stimulus-response chain,** is a consistent sequence of stimuli and responses that occur closely to each other in time and in which the last response is typically followed by reinforcement. In a behavioral chain, each response produces a stimulus that serves as an S^D for the next response (and, as will be discussed later, a conditioned reinforcer for the previous response). What Steve had acquired in learning to follow a consistent preputt routine was a behavioral chain. The first stimulus (S^D_1) for the entire sequence was the sight of his ball on the putting green as he walked toward it. The response (R_1) to that stimulus was "I'm going to focus just on this putt." This statement was the cue (S^D_2) to go behind the hole, look back at the ball, and check the slope of the green in order to estimate the speed and path of the putt (R_2). The resulting visual stimuli (and perhaps certain internal stimuli we might call "an image of the putt and speed of the ball") was the cue (S^D_3) to walk behind the ball and look toward the hole to observe the slope of the green from that angle (R_3). In this way, each response produced the cue or stimulus for the next response until the entire chain was completed and Steve experienced the reinforcement of making the putt. The reason for calling this procedure a *stimulus-response chain* can be seen by writing it out as follows:

$$S^D_1 \rightarrow R_1 \rightarrow S^D_2 \rightarrow R_2 \rightarrow S^D_3 \rightarrow R_3 \ldots S^D_7 \rightarrow R_7 \rightarrow S^+$$

The stimulus–response connections are the "links" that hold the chain together. As the saying goes, "A chain is only as strong as its weakest link." Similarly, if any response is so weak that it fails to be evoked by the S^D preceding it, the next S^D will not be produced and the rest of the chain will not occur. The chain will be broken at the point of its weakest link. The only way to repair the chain is to strengthen the weak stimulus–response connection by means of an effective training procedure.

The symbol S^+ at the far right of the diagram symbolizes the positive reinforcer that follows the last response in the chain. It designates the "oil" that one must apply regularly to keep the chain rust free and strong. The reinforcer at the end of a chain maintains the stimuli in the chain as effective S^Ds for the responses that follow them (and as will be described later, as effective conditioned reinforcers for the responses that precede them).

Not All Behavioral Sequences Are Behavioral Chains

Many behavioral sequences that you perform in everyday life are behavioral chains. Playing a particular song on a musical instrument, brushing your teeth, lacing and tying your shoes, and making a sandwich are all behavioral chains. However, not all behavioral sequences are behavioral chains. Studying for an exam, writing an exam, and attending the next class to get a grade represent a sequence of behavior that a college student performs. But this general sequence consists of a variety of activities (reading, memorizing, writing, etc.) with many breaks in the action (studying, then sleeping, then going to class, etc.). It is not made up of a consistent series of stimuli and responses that occur closely in time and for which each stimulus (except the last) is an S^D for the next response.

Study Questions

1. Briefly describe the chaining procedure used to teach Steve to perform a consistent preputt routine.
2. Describe or define *behavioral chain,* and give an example other than those in this chapter.
3. Why do you suppose a behavioral chain is called a *chain*?
4. Distinguish between a behavioral sequence that is a chain and one that is not a chain. Describe an example of a behavioral sequence that is not a chain, and explain why it is not one.

METHODS FOR TEACHING A BEHAVIORAL CHAIN

The three major methods of teaching a behavioral chain are the total-task presentation method, the backward-chaining method, and the forward-chaining method. With the **total-task presentation** method, an individual attempts all of the steps from the beginning to the end of the chain on each trial and continues with total task trials until that person learns the chain (see Figure 11–1). Prompting is provided at each step as needed, and a reinforcer follows the correct completion of the last step. Using this strategy, Steve learned to follow a consistent preputt routine. As another example, Horner and Keilitz (1975) used total task presentation to teach adolescents with developmental disabilities to brush their teeth.

With the **backward chaining** method, the last step is taught first, then the next-to-last step is taught and linked to the last step, then the third-from-last step is taught and linked to the last two steps, and so on, progressing backward toward the beginning of the chain (see Figure 11–1). Backward chaining gradually constructs the chain in a reverse order from that in which the chain is performed. Backward chaining has been used in numerous programs, including teaching various dressing, grooming, work, and verbal behaviors to individuals with developmental disabilities (e.g., Martin, England, & England, 1971). To teach Craig, a boy with a developmental disability, to put on a pair of slacks, for example, the instructor broke down the task into the seven steps illustrated in Figure 11–2. The instructor then conducted a baseline assessment to determine the type of prompt needed for Craig to perform each step correctly. Training began with the last step (Step 7). Craig's instructor helped him put on the slacks except for the response at

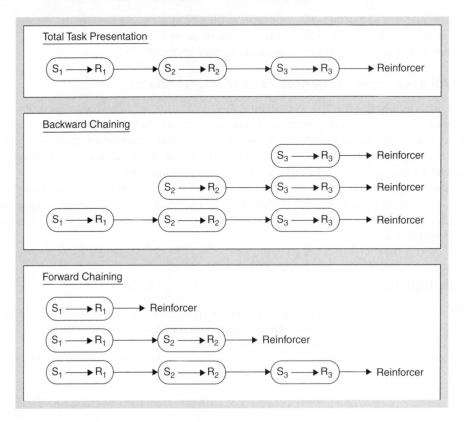

FIGURE 11–1   A diagram of the three major chaining methods.

Step 7. Several training trials were then conducted to teach Craig the response at Step 7. As Figure 11–2 documents, over several trials, prompts were faded until Craig could do up the zipper by himself. When Craig had learned this, his instructor then started him from Step 6 and taught him to finish from there. When Craig could perform the last two steps without errors, training trials began at Step 5. With the slacks down around his ankles, he was taught to pull them all the way up (Step 5), which was the S^D for him to perform Step 6. Performing Step 6 provided the S^D to perform Step 7. On each trial, Craig completed all of the steps learned previously. Training proceeded in this way, one step added at a time, until Craig could perform all seven steps. Throughout training, individual steps performed correctly were reinforced with praise, and the completion of Step 7 on each trial was followed by an edible treat as an unconditioned or primary reinforcer (see Chapter 4).

Students of behavior modification often find backward chaining strange when they first read about it, apparently because the name suggests that an individual learns to perform the chain backward. Naturally, this is not true. There is a very good theoretical rationale for using backward chaining. Consider the example of teaching Craig to put on a pair of slacks. By starting with Step 7, the response of "doing up the zipper" was reinforced in the presence of the fastened snap above the zipper. Therefore, the sight of the snap fastened became an S^D for Step 7, doing up the zipper. Also, the sight of the snap fastened was paired with the reinforcers

TASK	Putting on slacks	Scoring System											
CLIENT	Craig	3 = without prompts											
REINFORCERS	praise & edible	2 = verbal prompt											
		1 = gestural/imitative prompts											
		0 = physical guidance											

S^D s	Responses	Baseline	Training Trials									
1. "Put on your slacks."	Taking slacks from dresser drawer	2										
2. Slacks in hands	Hold slacks upright with front facing away from client	1										
3. Slacks held upright	Put one leg in slacks	1										
4. One leg in slacks	Put other leg in slacks	1										
5. Both legs in slacks	Pull slacks all the way up	2									2	3
6. Slacks all the way up	Do up the snap	0					0	1	2	3	3	3
7. Snap done up	Do up the zipper	0	0	1	2	3	3	3	3	3	3	3

FIGURE 11–2 A simple task analysis and data sheet for teaching a person with a developmental disability to put on slacks.

(praise and an edible) that Craig received after doing up the zipper. Therefore, on the basis of the principle of conditioned reinforcement, the sight of the fastened snap also became a conditioned reinforcer for whatever preceded it. After several trials at Step 7, Craig's instructor went on to Step 6. The behavior of fastening the snap produced the sight-of-the-fastened-snap stimulus. The sight of the fastened snap had become a conditioned reinforcer, and it immediately followed performing Step 6. Thus, when one uses backward chaining, the reinforcement of the last step in the presence of the appropriate stimulus, over trials, establishes that stimulus as a discriminative stimulus for the last step and as a conditioned reinforcer for the next-to-last step. When the step before the last is added, the S^D in that step also becomes a conditioned reinforcer, and so on. Thus, the power of the positive reinforcer that is presented at the end of the chain is transferred up the line to each S^D as it is added to the chain. In this way, backward chaining has a theoretical advantage of always having a built-in conditioned reinforcer to strengthen each new response that is added to the sequence. In chains taught by total task presentation and forward chaining (described next), each stimulus (after the first) also eventually functions as an S^D for the next response and as a conditioned reinforcer for the previous **NOTE 1** response. In backward chaining, as described, however, these two functions are developed very systematically.

The **forward chaining** method teaches the initial step of the sequence first, then teaches and links together the first and second steps, then the first three steps, and so on until the entire chain is acquired (see Figure 11–1). For example, Mahoney, VanWagenen, and Meyerson (1971) used forward chaining to toilet train children who were normal and others who were developmentally disabled. The components of the chain included walking to the toilet, lowering the pants, sitting on or standing facing the toilet (as appropriate), urinating, and pulling up the pants. Training began with the first step, and after a step was mastered, the next step was introduced. Each step was reinforced until the next step was introduced.

At least partly because backward chaining resembles a reversal of the natural order of things, forward chaining and total-task presentation are used more often in everyday situations by individuals not trained in behavior modification. Among the many examples that can be cited to illustrate forward chaining, consider the way in which a child might be taught to pronounce a word such as *milk*. She or he might be first taught to say "mm," then "mi," then "mil," and finally "milk."

The three major chaining methods are outlined in Table 11–1. Which is most effective? Bellamy, Horner, and Inman (1979) concluded that total-task presentation has several practical advantages over the other chaining formats for teaching persons with developmental disabilities. Total-task presentation requires the instructor to spend less time in partial assembly or disassembly to prepare the task for training; it appears to focus on teaching response topography and response sequence simultaneously and, therefore, should produce results more quickly; and it appears to maximize the learner's independence early in training, especially if some steps are already familiar

TABLE 11–1 An Outline of the Three Major Chaining Methods
For All Methods
• Do a task analysis.
Total-Task Presentation
• The learner attempts every step on each trial, so that all unmastered steps are taught concurrently.
• The instructor provides prompts and praise for all unmastered steps.
• A reinforcer is presented following the last step.
• Training continues in this way until all steps are mastered.
Forward Chaining
• Starting with the first one, the step must be mastered before proceeding to the next one.
• The instructor provides prompts and a reinforcer for the step that is being taught.
• On each trial, all previously mastered steps are required.
• In this way, one step is learned at a time, progressing forward to the last step.
Backward Chaining
• Starting with the last step, it must be mastered before proceeding to the next-to-last step.
• The instructor provides prompts for the step that is being taught.
• On each trial, all previously mastered steps are required, and the last step is followed by a reinforcer.
• In this way, one step is learned at a time, progressing backward to the first step.

to him or her. Moreover, several studies have demonstrated that total-task presentation is at least as good as, or better than, backward chaining or forward chaining for teaching various tasks to persons with developmental disabilities (Martin, Koop, Turner, & Hanel, 1981; Spooner, 1984; Yu, Martin, Suthons, Koop, & Pallotta-Cornick, 1980).

Which is the method of choice for individuals who do not have developmental disabilities? For relatively simple tasks with a small number of steps, such as the preputt routine for Steve, total-task presentation is probably the method of choice. For more complex tasks, however, either backward or forward chaining is likely to be more effective. For example, in teaching a complex sequence of dive bombing to pilots, Bailey, Hughes, and Jones (1980) found backward chaining to be more effective than total-task presentation. In an experiment to teach introductory psychology students to perform a musical task on a keyboard for which they were scored for both melodic and timing errors, backward chaining and forward chaining were both more effective than total-task presentation, and forward chaining was more effective than backward chaining on most measures (Ash & Holding, 1990). Also, using backward chaining to teach certain tasks may be more practical. When giving driving instructions, for example, it is highly advisable to teach the use of the brake before teaching the use of the accelerator.

Study Questions

5. Briefly describe the total-task presentation chaining method.
6. Briefly describe the backward chaining method.
7. Briefly describe the forward chaining method.
8. Describe how each of the three major chaining methods could be used to teach bed making.
9. In a chain, a given stimulus is both an S^D and a conditioned reinforcer. How can this be? Explain with an example.
10. Which of the major chaining methods do the authors recommend for teaching persons with developmental disabilities, and for what four reasons?

CHAINING COMPARED WITH FADING AND SHAPING

Behavioral chaining, fading, and shaping are sometimes called *gradual change* procedures because each involves progressing gradually through a series of steps to produce a new behavior, new stimulus control over a behavior, or a new sequence of stimulus–response steps. Clearly understanding the distinctions among the three gradual change procedures is important.

Shaping steps consist of reinforcing closer and closer approximations to the final desired response (see Chapter 10). Fading steps consist of reinforcing the final desired response in the presence of closer and closer approximations to the final desired stimulus for that response (see Chapter 9). Chaining steps usually consist of reinforcing more and more of the specific stimulus–response links that compose the chain. An exception to this is the method of total-task presentation; in this case, all links are taught right from the beginning of training, and shaping or fading may be used to develop the responses or to bring them under the control of their appropriate stimuli. Because shaping or fading is used, the procedure is still a gradual change procedure. Table 11–2 summarizes some of the similarities and differences of the three procedures as they are typically applied.

TABLE 11–2	Similarities and Differences Among Shaping, Fading, and Chaining		
	Shaping	**Fading**	**Chaining**
Target behavior	New behavior along some physical dimension such as topography, amount, or intensity	New stimulus control of a particular behavior	New consistent sequence of stimuli and responses
General training environment	Often involves an unstructured environment in which the learner has the opportunity to emit a variety of behaviors	Typically involves a structured environment because the stimuli must be controlled precisely	Typically involves a semistructured or structured environment because the stimuli and responses must be sequenced precisely
Other procedural considerations	Involves successive applications of reinforcement and extinction	Involves successive applications of reinforcement; if extinction has to be used, fading has not proceeded optimally	Frequently involves verbal and physical prompts and/or physical guidance combined with fading and/or shaping at some of the steps

FACTORS INFLUENCING THE EFFECTIVENESS OF BEHAVIORAL CHAINING

1. The Task Analysis

For maximum effectiveness of behavioral chaining, the behavioral sequence must be broken down into manageable components, and the proper order of the components must be maintained. The process of breaking down a task into smaller steps or component responses to facilitate training is called a **task analysis**. Some examples of complex skills that have had task analyses performed on them are apartment-upkeep skills (Williams & Cuvo, 1986), menstrual care skills (Richman, Reiss, Bauman, & Bailey, 1984), tennis skills (Buzas & Ayllon, 1981), play execution of the offensive backfield on a youth football team (Komaki & Barnett, 1977), leisure skills (Schleien, Wehman, & Kiernan, 1981), and pedestrian skills for walking safely through traffic (Page, Iwata, & Neef, 1976).

As with the selection of shaping steps (discussed in Chapter 10), the selection of chaining steps or components is somewhat subjective. The components should be simple enough to be learned without great difficulty. If you want a child to learn proper toothbrushing, it would be a mistake to consider the task to be learned as putting toothpaste on the brush, brushing, and rinsing. For the child to master the chain, each of these components should be subdivided into smaller components. The components should also be selected so that there is a clear-cut stimulus signaling the completion of each component. These stimuli will then become conditioned reinforcers for the responses preceding them and S^Ds for the subsequent responses in the chain. For example, in teaching proper hand washing, you might select putting water in the sink as one of the components. It would be important to specify a particular level of water in the sink and perhaps even make a mark (at least temporarily) at that level to provide a very clear stimulus that terminates the end of this particular component (which you might define as holding the water taps on until the water reaches the desired level).

After completing your task analysis, review each of the controlling stimuli or S^Ds for each response in the sequence. Ideally, each S^D should be clearly distinct from the other S^Ds. Having similar stimuli control different responses increases the chance for the learner's error and confusion. If, in your task analysis, two of the controlling stimuli are quite similar and there appears to be nothing you can do about it, then consider artificially coding one of the stimuli in some way to make acquisition of the chain easier.

2. Independent Use of Prompts by Learners

As was the case with Steve, many individuals can use prompts independently to guide the mastery of a chain of behaviors. For learners able to read, a *written task analysis* might effectively prompt them to appropriately complete behavior chains (see, e.g., Cuvo, Davis, O'Reilly, Mooney, & Crowley, 1992). If the learners are unable to read, a series of *picture prompts* might guide them. For example, Thierman and Martin (1989) prepared a picture-prompt album to guide adults with severe intellectual disabilities to complete behavior chains that improved the quality of their household cleaning. The learners were taught to look at the picture of an appropriate step, perform that step, and then transfer a self-monitoring adhesive dot to indicate that the step had been completed. The strategy proved to be quite effective. Another strategy that involves independent use of prompts to guide completion of behavioral chains involves reciting *self-instructions*. Individuals with developmental disabilities have been taught to recite self-instructions to prompt correct completion of vocational tasks (Salend, Ellis, & Reynolds, 1989), completion of math problems correctly (Albion & Salzburg, 1982), and sorting letters into boxes correctly (Whitman, Spence, & Maxwell, 1987).

3. A Preliminary Modeling Trial

In some cases, such as with persons with developmental disabilities or young children, it may be desirable to model the entire sequence while verbally describing the performance of each step (see, e.g., Griffen, Wolery, & Schuster, 1992). (Guidelines for modeling are described in Chapter 18.) If only one sample of the training task is available, the task must be disassembled after the modeling trial and the components rearranged for the learner to perform the task. Otherwise, the learner can be taught using alternative samples of the task.

4. Training the Behavioral Chain

Training should start with a request to begin work and to complete the step(s) of the task. The step or steps to begin depend on whether you use total-task presentation, backward chaining, or forward chaining. If at any step the learner stops responding or appears distracted, you should first provide a pacing prompt such as "What's next?" or "Carry on." If the learner performs a response incorrectly or fails to begin responding at any step within a reasonable period of time, you should proceed with error correction. Provide the necessary instruction or physical guidance to help the learner perform that step correctly. After an error is corrected, go on to the next step.

5. Ample Social and Other Reinforcers

Sometimes a natural reinforcer that follows the completion of a chain will be sufficient to maintain it. This was the case with Steve. When teaching behavioral chains to persons with developmental disabilities or young children, however, it is often desirable to immediately praise the correct completion of each step during early training trials (see, e.g., Koop, Martin, Yu, & Suthons, 1980). In addition, providing a primary or unconditioned reinforcer (such as an edible) contingent upon successful completion of the last step in the chain is often desirable. As the learner becomes more skillful in performing the steps, praise and other reinforcers can be gradually eliminated. Additional strategies for maintaining behavioral chains that have been mastered are described in Chapter 16.

6. Assistance at Individual Steps

Depending on the details of the task analysis, providing some additional instruction or physical assistance in correcting errors may be necessary. Across successive trials, this extra assistance should be faded as quickly as possible. Not providing assistance to the point of creating a dependency in the learner is important. That is, be careful not to reinforce errors or waiting for your help at particular steps.

Study Questions

11. Distinguish among the types of target behavior typically established by shaping, fading, and chaining.
12. Suppose that you want to teach a teenager to change a tire on a car. Would you use shaping or chaining? Justify your choice.
13. What is meant by the term *task analysis*? Describe a plausible task analysis appropriate for teaching a 3-year-old child the chain of tying a knot in a shoelace.
14. Briefly describe three strategies to help individuals use prompts independently to guide the mastery of a chain of behaviors.

PITFALLS OF BEHAVIORAL CHAINING

Pitfall Type 1

Relatively simple undesirable responses are often established inadvertently in the administration of positive reinforcement by the unwary, as are chains with one or more undesirable components. A behavioral chain that has some components that are functional in producing the reinforcer and at least one component (called a *superstitious component*) that is not is called an **adventitious chain**. (See also adventitious reinforcement in Chapter 3, pp. 44–45).

A common kind of undesirable adventitious chaining occurs when an inappropriate and nonfunctional response precedes one or more appropriate responses that are reinforced; both the inappropriate and appropriate responses are thereby strengthened. An example of this type of chaining is the distracting habit of frequently saying "like" or "uh" while talking that some speakers exhibit. A similar although somewhat more serious example is making bizarre facial expressions prior to each utterance.

Other examples of Pitfall Type 1 involve self-control problems that plague many people. The undesirable behavioral chains that characterize such problems are not adventitious chains because all of the components are functional in producing reinforcement. However, one or more of the components of the chain are undesirable. Consider the problem of overeating. Although undoubtedly a variety of possible reasons for overeating exists, one of the more frequent causes may be the inadvertent development of undesirable behavioral chains. For example, it has been observed that some overweight people eat very rapidly. An examination of the behavioral sequence involved suggests the following chain: loading food onto the utensil, placing food in the mouth, reloading the utensil while chewing the food, simultaneously swallowing the food while raising the next load of food to the mouth, and so forth. This behavioral chain can be broken successfully by extending the chain and introducing delays. A more desirable chain might be the following: loading food onto the utensil, placing food in the mouth, putting down the utensil, chewing the food, swallowing, waiting three seconds, reloading the utensil, and so on. In other words, in the undesirable chain, the person gets ready to consume the next mouthful before even finishing the present one. A more desirable chain separates these components and introduces brief delays.

Another undesirable behavioral chain that is manifested by some overweight people consists of watching TV until a commercial comes on, going to the kitchen during the commercial, getting a snack, and returning to the TV program (which, along with the taste of the food, reinforces getting the snack). A variety of procedures can solve such self-control problems, and these are discussed more fully in Chapter 26. The point to remember here is that undesirable behaviors are frequently components of unintentionally developed behavioral chains.

Pitfall Type 2

Some seemingly sound behavior modification procedures can promote undesirable chaining if the behavior modifier is not careful. A project by Olenick and Pear (1980) to teach names of pictures to children with developmental disabilities illustrated this. The children were given a question trial in which they were shown a picture to be named and were asked, "What's this?" Correct responses were reinforced. If the children made an error, they were then given an imitation trial in which the instructor presented the question and then immediately modeled the answer (e.g., "What's this? Cat."). Olenick and Pear observed that some children made a large number of errors even when it appeared that they could name the pictures appropriately. The researchers suggested that for these youngsters, a chain had developed in which errors on question trials were reinforced by imitation trials because an easier response (imitation) was reinforced on these trials. Olenick and Pear solved this problem by lowering the reinforcement rate for correct responses on imitation trials while maintaining a high reinforcement rate for correct responses on question trials.

GUIDELINES FOR THE EFFECTIVE USE OF BEHAVIORAL CHAINING

Observe the following rules when teaching behavioral chains.

1. *Do a Task Analysis.* Identify the units of the chain that are simple enough for the learner to learn without great difficulty.
2. *Consider Strategies (e.g., Pictures) for Independent Use of Prompts by Learners.*
3. *If Necessary, Do a Preliminary Modeling Trial.*
4. *Teach the Units in the Proper Sequence.* Otherwise, poor stimulus control will develop: When one step is completed, it will not necessarily be a discriminative stimulus for the next step but may control some other step (as when a young child learns to count incorrectly, for example, 1, 2, 4, 3).
5. *To Expedite Learning, Use a Fading Procedure to Decrease Extra Help That the Learner May Need to Perform Some of the Steps.*

6. *When Using Backward or Forward Chaining, Make Sure That on Each Trial, the Individual Performs the Entire Set of Components Learned up to That Point.*
7. *Early in Training, Use Ample Reinforcement for Correct Performance of Individual Steps.* Gradually decrease this reinforcement as the learner becomes more skillful.
8. *Make Sure That the Reinforcement Provided at the End of the Chain Conforms to the Guidelines for the Effective Application of Positive Reinforcement Given in Chapter 3.* The more effective this terminal reinforcement, the more stable is the chain of responses. This does not mean, however, that once a chain is developed, it must be reinforced each time it occurs in order to be maintained. After a chain has been taught, it can be viewed as a single response, which could, if desired, be put on any intermittent reinforcement schedule.

Study Questions

15. What is an adventitious chain?
16. How is an adventitious chain similar to and different from superstitious behavior? (See pp. 44–45 and p. 140.)
17. Describe an example of an adventitious chain that is not from this chapter. Clearly identify the superstitious component.
18. Give an example of a Pitfall Type 1 of chaining other than an adventitious chain. Explain how this pitfall could be avoided.

Application Exercises

A. EXERCISES INVOLVING OTHERS

1. Describe how you might use behavioral chaining to teach a child to lace his or her shoes.
2. Describe how you might use behavioral chaining to teach a child to tie a knot.
3. Describe how you might use behavioral chaining to teach a child to tie a bow.
4. Try out your chaining programs in Application Exercises 1–3 and see how they work.

B. SELF-MODIFICATION EXERCISE

Identify a behavioral deficit of yours that might be amenable to a chaining procedure. Describe in detail how you might use the guidelines for the effective use of chaining to overcome this deficit.

Note and Extended Discussion

1. The theory that the stimuli in a chain function as conditioned reinforcers for the preceding responses and as S^Ds for the subsequent response has appealed to many behavior analysts because of its elegant simplicity. However, basic research with animals over the past 50 plus years has shown this theory to be an oversimplification (see, e.g., Fantino, 2008). The earlier stimuli in a long behavioral chain take on another function besides that of being conditioned reinforcers and S^Ds. Indeed, if the conditioned reinforcers occur a long enough time before the primary or unconditioned reinforcer (see Chapter 4) at the end of the chain, they actually become S^Δs. To be more precise, as the temporal distance (i.e., the distance in time)

of the stimuli in a behavioral chain from the primary reinforcer increases, the more their quality of being S^Ds decreases and the more they begin to take on the property of S^Δs. This is so because as their distance in time from primary reinforcement increases, the more they become associated with the absence of primary reinforcement. In other words, in considering the strength of an S^D on the basis of the conditioned reinforcer that follows it, one also has to consider its weakness as an S^D—or, more technically, its inhibitory potential—as a function of its distance in time from primary reinforcement. This inhibitory function may offset whatever advantage backward chaining may have in providing conditioned reinforcement, which may be why applied studies have typically found no superiority of backward chaining over forward chaining (e.g., Ash & Holding, 1990; Batra & Batra, 2005/2006; Hur & Osborne, 1993; Walls, Zane, & Ellis, 1981).

Study Question on Note

1. Explain how the theory that the stimuli in a behavioral chain are conditioned reinforcers for the preceding responses and S^Ds for the subsequent responses is an oversimplification.

12 Eliminating Inappropriate Behavior Through Punishment

"Ben, don't be so aggressive."

ELIMINATING BEN'S AGGRESSIVENESS[1]

Ben was a 7-year-old boy enrolled in a public school program for severely disturbed children. He had been diagnosed as a child with developmental delay, and the staff in the school had noticed an increase in his frequency of hitting other children and the staff. In fact, during baseline observations over approximately 3 weeks, the frequency of Ben's hits averaged about 30 per day. Something had to be done. The staff decided to examine whether making required exercise contingent on Ben's hitting would decrease it.

A number of precautions were taken to ensure that the contingent exercise would not be detrimental to Ben's health and would be ethically acceptable. The procedures were explained thoroughly to the parents, and parental consent was obtained for Ben's participation in the program. The procedures were also reviewed and approved by the ethical review board of the school district in which the program was conducted.

The program was conducted at Ben's school throughout the school day. On the day that the contingent exercise was introduced, Ben's first hit was followed by the nearest adult saying, "Ben, no hitting. Stand up and sit down 10 times." The adult then held Ben's hand and lifted it over his head to prompt standing up and then pulled his upper body forward to prompt sitting down, at the same time saying "Stand up, sit down" each time. Although Ben showed some verbal resistance to the exercise on a few occasions, physical prompting was necessary only on the first few training trials. On subsequent days, only verbal reminders were necessary to prompt the exercise task. From an average of approximately 30 hits per day during baseline, Ben's hits

---

[1] This example is based on an article by Luce, Delquadri, and Hall (1980).

dropped to 11 on the first day of the program, 10 on the second day, 1 on the third day, and either zero or 1 thereafter.

After two weeks of the procedure, the staff stopped applying the contingent exercise to see what would happen to Ben's hits. The frequency of hits remained low for 4 days but then began to increase over the next 4 days. The staff reinstituted the contingent exercise and observed an immediate drop in the frequency of hitting to near zero. Ben could run about and interact with other children and no longer showed the distressful aggressiveness characteristic of his past behavior. ■

THE PRINCIPLE OF PUNISHMENT

A **punisher** is a stimulus whose presentation immediately after a behavior causes that behavior to decrease in frequency. Punishers are sometimes referred to as *aversive stimuli,* or simply *aversives.* Once an event has been determined to function as a punisher for a particular behavior of an individual in a particular situation, that event can be used to decrease other behaviors of that individual in other situations. Associated with the concept of a punisher is the principle of **punishment**: If, in a given situation, someone does something that is immediately followed by a punisher, then that person is less likely to do the same thing again when she or he next encounters a similar situation. In Ben's case, contingent exercise was a punisher for his hitting.

Note that the technical meaning of the word *punishment* for behavior modifiers is quite specific and differs from the meaning of the word that most people know. Consider, for example, a common use of the word *punishment* in our culture: Sending a person to prison is seen as punishment for committing a crime. But going to prison is not likely to be an *immediate* consequence of committing the crime. Also, many individuals believe that prison is or should be a form of *retribution* that is given because the individual *deserves* it in some moral sense. Moreover, sending a person to prison is often viewed as a *deterrent* to other potential wrongdoers. For behavior modifiers, however, the word *punishment* does not mean any of these things; it is simply a technical term referring to the application of an immediate consequence following an individual's specific behavior in a specific situation that has the effect of decreasing the likelihood of future instances of that individual engaging in that specific behavior in that specific situation. This is not to deny that some consequences of the legal system may function as punishment in this technical sense, such as when someone immediately receives a traffic ticket for speeding. However, legal consequences for crimes often do not function as punishment in the technical sense and are generally not thought of in that limited way by legislators, law enforcement officials, members of the legal professions, and the general public.

Like positive reinforcement, punishment affects our learning throughout life. The immediate consequences of touching a hot stove teach us not to do that again. Early in life, the pain from a few falls helped to teach us better balance. However, it is important to recognize that some controversy regarding the deliberate use of punishment exists within the field of behavior modification. We return to this issue later in this chapter after discussing the different types of punishment and the factors that influence the effects of punishment in suppressing behavior.

Study Questions

1. Briefly describe how Ben's aggressive behavior was eliminated.
2. How was stimulus control an important part of the punishment contingency for Ben?

3. What is a punisher? Describe an example in which you identify both the response and the punisher.
4. State the principle of punishment.
5. How does the meaning of the word *punishment* for behavior modifiers differ from the meaning of that word for most persons?

TYPES OF PUNISHERS

Many kinds of events, when delivered as immediate consequences for behavior, fit the definition of punisher as given here. Most of these events can be classified in the following categories (see Van Houten, 1983): (a) pain-inducing punisher, (b) reprimand, (c) timeout, and (d) response cost. Although there is some overlap among these categories, they provide a convenient way in which to organize punishment procedures. We now consider each category in turn.

Pain-Inducing Punisher

A **pain-inducing punisher**, also referred to as a *physical punisher,* is a stimulus immediately following a behavior that activates pain receptors or other sense receptors that typically evoke feelings of discomfort. Examples include spankings, pinches, electric shock, ammonia vapor, cold baths, very loud or harsh sounds, prolonged tickling, and hair tugging. Such stimuli or events are called **unconditioned punishers**, which are stimuli that are punishing without prior learning.

Reprimand

A **reprimand** is a strong negative verbal stimulus immediately contingent on behavior. An example would be a parent saying, "No! That was bad!" immediately after a child emits an undesirable behavior, Reprimands also often include a fixed stare and, sometimes, a firm grasp. In Chapter 4 we noted that a stimulus that is a punisher as a result of having been paired with another punisher is called a **conditioned punisher**. It is likely that the verbal component of a reprimand is a conditioned punisher. It is possible that other components, such as the firm grasp, are unconditioned punishers. In some cases, the effectiveness of reprimands has been increased by pairing them with other punishers. For example, Dorsey, Iwata, Ong, and McSween (1980) paired reprimands with a water-mist spray to suppress self-injurious behavior in individuals with developmental disabilities. This caused the reprimands to become effective not only in the original setting but also in a setting where the mist had not been used.

Timeout

A **timeout** is a period of time immediately following a particular behavior during which an individual loses the opportunity to earn reinforcers. There are two types of timeout: exclusionary and nonexclusionary. An **exclusionary timeout** consists of removing an individual briefly from a reinforcing situation immediately following a behavior. Often a special room, called a *timeout room,* is used for this purpose. It is bare of anything that might serve as a reinforcer and may be padded to prevent self-injury. The period in the timeout room should not be very long; about 5 minutes is usually quite effective (Brantner & Doherty, 1983; Fabiano et al., 2004). Also, ethical considerations—such as whether the ends justify the means; see Chapter 30—and practical considerations (such as avoiding lengthy timeouts that take the individual away from a learning environment) must also be contemplated in selecting a particular timeout duration. A **nonexclusionary timeout** consists of introducing into the situation, immediately following a behavior, a stimulus associated with less reinforcement. Foxx and Shapiro (1978) reported an example of this. Children in a classroom wore a ribbon that was removed for a short time when a child was disruptive. When not wearing the ribbon, the child was not allowed to participate in classroom activities and was ignored by the teacher.

Response Cost

Response cost involves the removal of a specified amount of a reinforcer immediately following a behavior (Reynolds & Kelley, 1997). Response cost is sometimes used in behavior modification programs in which learners earn tokens as reinforcers (Kazdin, 1977a). Working in a classroom setting, for example, Sullivan and O'Leary (1990) showed that loss of tokens (each of which could be exchanged for 1 minute of recess) for off task behavior successfully decreased it. Note that response cost differs from a timeout in that, when response cost is administered, the individual does not temporarily lose the opportunity to earn reinforcers. Response cost is also not to be confused with extinction. In an extinction procedure, a reinforcer is withheld following a previously reinforced response. In response cost, a reinforcer is taken away following an undesirable response.

Examples of response cost in everyday life are library fines, traffic tickets, and charges for overdrawn bank accounts. However, these punishers are not typically applied immediately following the offending behavior. Just as we distinguished between the direct-acting effect and the indirect-acting effect of positive reinforcement in Chapter 3, we make a similar distinction with respect to punishment. The *direct-acting effect* of punishment is the decreased frequency of a response because of its immediate punishing consequences. The *indirect-acting effect* of punishment is the weakening of a response that is followed by a punisher even though the punisher is delayed. Suppose that a person speeds through an intersection, is caught by photo radar, and receives a ticket in the mail a week later. Although that procedure may reduce the person's future speeding, it involves much more than the principle of punishment. Delayed punishers may have an effect on behavior because of instructions about the behavior leading to the punisher, because of self-statements ("thoughts") that intervene between that behavior and the delayed punisher, or because of immediate conditioned punishers that intervene between the behavior and the delayed backup punisher. It is a mistake to offer punishment as an overly simplistic explanation of a decrease in behavior when the punisher does not follow the behavior immediately. Explanations of the indirect-acting effect of punishment are discussed further in Chapter 17.

Study Questions

6. Define *unconditioned punisher,* and give an example of it.
7. Describe or define four different types of punishers, and give an example of each.
8. Under which of the four categories of punishment would you put the type of punishment used with Ben? Justify your choice.
9. Define *conditioned punisher,* and give an example that is not in this chapter.
10. Distinguish between an exclusionary and nonexclusionary timeout.
11. What is a common example of response-cost punishment that parents apply to their children?
12. State the procedures for extinction, response cost, and exclusionary timeout.
13. Distinguish between the direct-acting and indirect-acting effect of punishment. Give an example of each.
14. What are three reasons that could explain the effectiveness of a delayed punisher in decreasing a behavior?

FACTORS INFLUENCING THE EFFECTIVENESS OF PUNISHMENT

1. The Conditions for a Desirable Alternative Response

To decrease an undesirable response, it is generally considered to be maximally effective to increase some desirable alternative response that will compete with the undesirable behavior to be eliminated (see, e.g., Thompson, Iwata, Connors, & Roscoe, 1999; for an alternative view, see Johnston, 2006).

You should attempt to identify S^Ds that control the desirable behavior and present these to increase the likelihood that the desirable behavior will occur. To maintain the desirable behavior, you should also have effective positive reinforcers that can be presented on an effective schedule (see, e.g., Figure 12–1).

2. Cause of the Undesirable Behavior

To maximize the opportunity for the desirable alternative behavior to occur, anyone attempting a punishment procedure should also minimize the causes of the undesirable behavior. This implies two things. First, the person should try to identify and eliminate the current S^Ds for the undesirable behavior. Second, the person should try to identify and eliminate existing reinforcers that are maintaining the undesirable behavior. Identifying the antecedents and consequences of a behavior is referred to as a *functional assessment* and is discussed in more detail in Chapter 23.

It is important to emphasize that punishment may often not be necessary. Minimizing the causes of the undesirable behavior while maximizing the conditions for a desirable alternative behavior may cause the desirable behavior to compete so strongly with the undesirable behavior that it is greatly reduced or completely suppressed without the use of punishment.

3. The Punishing Stimulus

If punishment is to be used, it is important to be sure that the punisher is effective. In general, the more intense or strong the punishing stimulus, the more effective it will be in decreasing the undesirable behavior. However, the intensity of the punisher that is needed to be effective depends

FIGURE 12–1   An example of the reinforcement of a desirable alternative behavior.

on the success in minimizing the causes of the undesirable behavior while maximizing the conditions for a desirable alternative behavior. Even a mild punisher, such as a reprimand, can be effective if the reinforcer for the undesirable behavior is withheld following instances of the behavior and if a desirable alternative behavior is reinforced with a strong reinforcer. For example, Thompson et al. (1999) evaluated the effects of reprimands and brief manual restraint as mild punishers contingent on the self-injurious behavior of four individuals who had been diagnosed with developmental disabilities. In all cases, the mild punishers produced greater response suppression when access to a reinforcer for desirable alternative behavior (manipulation of leisure materials) was available.

Contingent exercise turned out to be a very suitable punisher for Ben. It was highly effective, could be presented immediately following the undesirable behavior, and could be presented in a manner so that it was in no way paired with positive reinforcement. The care and attention that the staff gave to choosing the actual exercise task obviously paid off. The staff chose the task because it could be prompted by a voice command from a staff member, it could be carried out in a variety of settings, and it appeared to tire Ben quickly without causing any unnecessary strain.

Rather than selecting just one punisher, it may be more effective to select several that vary over successive instances of the undesirable behavior. For example, Charlop, Burgio, Iwata, and Ivancic (1988) applied a reprimand, physical restriction, timeout, or loud noise as a punisher following aggression and self-stimulation by children with developmental disabilities. In some sessions, only one of the punishers was applied. In other sessions, the four punishers were varied while still administering just one at a time. The children showed less aggression and self-stimulation during sessions when the teacher varied the punishers.

4. Antecedents (Including Verbal Rules) for Punishment

You will recall from Chapter 8 that an S^D is a stimulus in the presence of which a response will be reinforced. Similarly, an S^{Dp} is a stimulus in the presence of which a response will be punished.[2] When we were children, many of us learned that asking our parents for something when they were in a bad mood often led to a reprimand. The parental behaviors characteristic of "being in a bad mood" constituted an S^{Dp}. Research on the effects of S^{Dp}s has shown that if in the presence of an S^{Dp} a punisher is consistently applied following a response, then that response is less likely to occur when the S^{Dp} is encountered (e.g., O'Donnell, Crosbie, Williams, & Saunders, 2000).

Beginning students of behavior analysis often confuse an S^{Dp} with an S^Δ. Suppose, for example, that each time that a child swore, the parents deducted 25 cents from the child's allowance and that as a result of this contingency, the swearing decreased. In this example, the sight of the parents would be an S^{Dp} for swearing. If, on the other hand, the parents simply ignored the child when swearing (i.e., withheld their attention as a reinforcer), and the swearing decreased, then the sight of the parents would be an S^Δ for swearing. In both scenarios, the presence of the parents would eliminate the swearing. However, the causes of the behavior change are different.

As we described for positive reinforcement and extinction, adding rules to a punishment program will probably help to decrease the undesirable behavior and increase the desirable alternative behavior more quickly (see, e.g., Bierman, Miller, & Stabb, 1987). Also, as stressed in Chapter 3,

---

[2] We acknowledge Jennifer O'Donnell (2001) for introducing the symbol S^{Dp}.

emphasizing the beha*vior*, not the beha*ver*, is very important. The behavior, not the individual, is undesirable. Appropriate use of rules is discussed further in Chapter 17.

5. Delivery of the Punisher

To increase the effectiveness of punishment when delivering it, several guidelines should be followed.

GUIDELINE 1: THE PUNISHER SHOULD BE PRESENTED IMMEDIATELY FOLLOWING THE UNDESIRABLE BEHAVIOR   If the punisher is delayed, a more desirable behavior may occur prior to the use of the punisher, and this behavior may be suppressed to a much greater extent than the undesirable behavior. The classic example of this is the mother who asks her husband after he returns home from work to punish their child, who has misbehaved earlier in the day. This request is doubly disastrous. First, the child receives the punisher even though she or he may now be engaging in good behavior. Second, the father is punished for coming home from work. We do not mean to imply that delayed punishment is completely ineffective. As we point out in our discussion of rule-governed behavior in Chapter 17, most humans are adept at bridging rather large time gaps between their behavior and its consequences. Even so, immediate punishment is more effective than delayed punishment.

GUIDELINE 2: THE PUNISHER SHOULD BE PRESENTED FOLLOWING EVERY INSTANCE OF THE UNDESIRABLE BEHAVIOR   Occasional punishment is not as effective as punishment after every instance of the undesirable behavior (see, e.g., Kircher, Pear, & Martin, 1971; Lerman, Iwata, Shore, & DeLeon, 1997). If behavior modifiers are unable to detect most instances of the behavior to be punished, they should have serious doubts about the value of implementing a punishment procedure for two reasons. First, occasions in which a behavior modifier is unable to detect instances of the undesirable behavior may be occasions in which the undesirable behavior is positively reinforced, which would maintain its strength. Second, punishment procedures have negative side effects (to be discussed later), and it may be unethical to implement a procedure that may not be effective when that procedure also has negative side effects.

GUIDELINE 3: THE DELIVERY OF THE PUNISHER SHOULD NOT BE PAIRED WITH POSITIVE REINFORCEMENT   This requirement often presents difficulties when the punisher is delivered by an adult and the individual being punished receives very little adult attention. If a child has received a lot of loving attention from an adult during a period of time prior to the occurrence of the undesired behavior and the adult immediately presents a strong verbal reprimand following the undesirable behavior, the verbal reprimand is likely to be punishing. However, if that reprimand is the only adult attention that the child has received for an extended period of time, such attention may reinforce the undesirable behavior.

GUIDELINE 4: THE PERSON ADMINISTERING THE PUNISHER SHOULD REMAIN CALM WHEN DOING SO   Anger and frustration on the part of the person administering the punisher may reinforce the undesirable behavior or inappropriately alter the consistency or intensity of the punisher. A calm, matter-of-fact approach helps ensure that a punishment program will be followed consistently and appropriately. This also makes clear to the recipient that punishment is not being administered out of anger or for other irrelevant reasons. For a review of research on factors affecting the effectiveness of punishment, see Lerman and Vorndran (2002).

Study Questions

15. If you do a good job of attending to the first two factors influencing the effectiveness of punishment, you may not have to apply punishment. Discuss.
16. What are two conditions under which a mild punisher can be effective?
17. What steps might you follow to experimentally determine whether a verbal reprimand was a punisher for a particular child?
18. Compare S^D to S^{Dp}. Give an example of each.
19. Compare S^{Δ} to S^{Dp}. Give an example of each.
20. What are four guidelines in regard to delivering a punisher?
21. We suggested that if behavior modifiers are unable to detect most instances of a behavior to be punished, they should have serious doubts about the value of implementing a punishment procedure.
    a. What two reasons can you cite to support this suggestion?
    b. What alternative means of managing the situation are available to the behavior modifier (see Chapters 5 and 7)?

SOME EXAMPLES OF THERAPEUTIC PUNISHMENT

Behavioral journals describe numerous reports of the deliberate use of punishment as a treatment strategy, sometimes referred to as *therapeutic punishment*, with individuals who have severe behavioral challenges. We will describe several examples.

An example of possibly life-saving therapeutic punishment is the treatment of a 6-month-old baby who was admitted to a hospital because of a failure to gain weight (Sajwaj, Libet, & Agras, 1974). Sandra was underweight and undernourished, and death was a distinct possibility. Preliminary observations indicated that, a few minutes after being given milk, Sandra would begin ruminating, or bringing up the milk and reswallowing it, and would continue this for about 20 to 40 minutes. Because some of the regurgitated milk would spill out of her mouth, she apparently lost most of the milk she had consumed. Sajwaj and his colleagues decided to administer lemon juice as a punisher of Sandra's ruminating behavior. During treatment, her mouth was filled with lemon juice immediately after staff members detected the vigorous tongue movements that reliably preceded her rumination. After 16 feedings with lemon juice punishment, the rumination had decreased to a very low level. To ensure that the improvement was due to the treatment program, Sajwaj and his colleagues suspended the use of lemon juice for two feedings. The result was a dramatic increase in rumination. Following additional treatment, Sandra was discharged to foster parents, who maintained the treatment until it was no longer necessary.

Another example of therapeutic punishment involves a severe case of bruxism—the constant grinding of one's teeth. Gerri was a 16-year-old girl with profound intellectual disability who had been grinding her teeth almost ever since her permanent teeth had grown in. Her teeth were severely worn and were in danger of being lost. Behavior analysts were consulted about the problem (Blount, Drabman, Wilson, & Stewart, 1982). After considering a variety of reinforcement procedures and rejecting them for various reasons, they settled on a mild pain-inducing punishment procedure. Each time Gerri audibly ground her teeth, a staff member touched her face with an ice cube for a few seconds. Gerri's teeth grinding decreased considerably within the first few days of treatment, and after 2 months of this procedure, her bruxism had almost completely ceased.

As another example, consider Tom, a 15-year-old with profound intellectual disability who suffered from pica, which is eating inedible or non-nutritive substances. Tom had a tendency to eat whatever he could get his hands on, including cigarette butts, plastic objects, pieces of hair, paint chips, dirt, sand, and bits of paper. Pica has been associated with lead poisoning, intestinal blockage, intestinal perforation, and intestinal parasites. To treat Tom's pica, Johnson, Hunt, and Siebert (1994) taught him to eat only items that were placed on a bright yellow plastic placemat. Each time that Tom complied, he experienced the natural reinforcement of the good taste for eating the items on the placemat and was enthusiastically praised by the staff at the institution where he lived. Ingesting items that were not on the placemat was immediately followed by a punisher—Tom's face was washed with a cool damp cloth for 15 seconds. The procedure effectively eliminated Tom's pica.

Some individuals with intellectual disabilities or autism repeatedly engage in severe self-injurious behavior—damaging their vision by gouging their eyes, damaging their hearing by clapping their hands against their ears, causing tissue damage and bleeding by banging their heads on hard objects or tearing at their flesh, becoming malnourished by inducing vomiting after eating—that places them in great danger of disabling or killing themselves. A number of studies in the literature demonstrate that these behaviors can be suppressed by pain-inducing punishment (see, e.g., Favell et al., 1982; Linscheid, Iwata, Ricketts, Williams, & Griffin, 1990; Linscheid, Pejeau, Cohen, & Footo-Lenz, 1994). Once the self-injurious behavior is suppressed, positive reinforcement is then used to maintain the desirable alternative behavior, but this cannot be done until the self-injurious behavior has been controlled.

The preceding examples involve pain-inducing punishers. There are also many reports of therapeutic punishment with children involving response-cost, timeout, and reprimand punishers. For example, in a preschool classroom, children could earn tokens (stars) for a variety of desirable behaviors, and the tokens could be cashed in at the end of each session for various reinforcers such as gummi bears and jelly beans (Conyers et al., 2004). In some sessions, there were no consequences for disruptive behaviors, but in other sessions, disruptive behaviors were followed by token loss (response-cost punishment). The response-cost procedure was effective for decreasing disruptive behavior. As another example, Mathews et al. (1987) taught mothers to use a reprimand combined with a time-out to decrease dangerous behaviors (e.g., touching an electrical cord outlet) of their 1-year-old children. A mother would praise her child for playing appropriately, and say "No" and place the child in a playpen for a brief period immediately contingent upon the occurrence of a dangerous behavior. The intervention effectively decreased the dangerous behavior for all of the children.

As these and other examples illustrate, in some situations, applications of punishment by parents, teachers, and others appear to be in the best interests of the persons who receive it. Nevertheless, because of the potential harmful side effects of punishment, considerable controversy exists over whether behavior modifiers should design and implement therapeutic punishment programs. Before discussing the controversy, we review the potential harmful side effects of punishment.

POTENTIAL HARMFUL SIDE EFFECTS OF PUNISHMENT

1. *Aggressive Behavior* Punishment tends to elicit aggressive behavior. Experiments with animals show that painful stimuli cause them to attack other animals—even though these other animals had nothing to do with inflicting these stimuli (Azrin, 1967). Some research suggests that this finding also applies to humans (Berkowitz, 1988, 1989). Thus, we should not be surprised to observe individuals who have just been punished attacking other individuals.

2. *Emotional Behavior* Punishment can produce undesirable emotional side effects, such as crying and general fearfulness. These side effects not only are unpleasant for all concerned but also frequently interfere with desirable behavior—especially if it is of a complex nature.

3. *Escape and Avoidance Behavior*   Punishment may cause the situation and people associated with the aversive stimulus to become conditioned punishers. For example, if, while teaching a child to read, you punish him or her whenever he or she makes a mistake, anything associated with this situation—such as printed words, books, the person who delivers the punishment, the type of room in which the punishment occurs—will tend to become punishing. The child may attempt to escape or avoid these stimuli (see Chapter 13). Thus, instead of helping the individual to learn, punishment may drive him or her away from everything having to do with the learning situation.

The punisher need not be particularly strong to have the undesirable effects just mentioned. For example, a teacher we know used a timeout chair as a punisher for students in her first-grade class. For some unknown reason—perhaps it had something to do with the fact that the chair was black and the teacher told rowdy children to go sit in the "black chair"—the chair became frightening to the students. Years later, former students who came back to visit the teacher mentioned how fearful they had been of the "black chair," even though nothing bad ever happened to them when they sat there. When the teacher discovered the problem with the chair, she changed her procedure. The chair is no longer black, and she now calls it the "calming-down chair," and she periodically demonstrates its benign qualities to her students by sitting in it herself when she feels the need to calm down![3]

4. *No New Behavior*   Punishment does not establish any new behavior; it only suppresses old behavior. In other words, punishment does not teach an individual what to do; at best, it teaches only what *not* to do. For example, the main defining characteristic of persons with developmental disabilities is that they lack behavior that the majority of people have. The primary emphasis for these individuals, then, should be on establishing new behavior rather than on merely eliminating old behavior. Reinforcement is required to accomplish this.

5. *Modeling of Punishment*   Children often model or imitate adults. If adults apply punishment to children, the children are apt to do the same to others. Thus, in punishing children, we may inadvertently be providing a model for them to follow in presenting aversive stimuli toward others (Bandura, 1965, 1969). For example, children who were taught a game in which they were fined for incorrect behavior fined other children to whom they taught the game (Gelfand et al., 1974).

6. *Overuse of Punishment*   Because punishment often results in rapid suppression of undesirable behavior, it can tempt the user to rely heavily on it and neglect the use of positive reinforcement for desirable behavior. However, the undesirable behavior may return after only a temporary suppression, or some other undesirable behavior could occur. The person administering punishment may then resort to progressively heavier doses, thereby creating a vicious circle with disastrous effects.

Study Questions

22. In two or three sentences, describe either the case of the lemon juice therapy with Sandra or the ice cube therapy with Gerri.
23. What is pica? What factors influencing the effectiveness of punishment did Johnston et al. incorporate into their treatment for pica?
24. Briefly describe the procedure that Mathews et al. taught mothers to decrease dangerous behaviors of their 1-year-old children. Was the timeout component exclusionary or nonexclusionary? Justify your choice.
25. Cite six potential harmful side effects of the application of punishment.

---

[3] We thank Fran Falzarano for this example.

SHOULD PUNISHMENT BE DELIBERATELY USED?

NOTE 1   The deliberate use of corporal punishment has always been highly controversial, even before the advent of behavior modification, but the controversy intensified during the 1980s and 1990s. As reviewed by Feldman (1990), two opposing positions emerged. On the one hand, the right-to-effective-treatment position is that a client's right to effective treatment might in some cases dictate the use of quicker-acting punishment procedures rather than slower-acting procedures involving positive reinforcement of alternative behavior (see Van Houten et al., 1988). On the other hand, the freedom-from-harm position is that nonaversive methods for eliminating unacceptable behavior are always at least as effective as punishment and that, therefore, using pain-inducing punishment is never justified (see Guess, Helmstetter, Turnbull, & Knowlton, 1986). During the 1980s and 1990s, advocates of this latter position described a variety of al-

NOTE 2   ternatives to punishment for treating challenging behavior. For example, Carr and Durand (1985) observed that some children with developmental disabilities emitted self-injurious behavior to obtain caregiver attention. They developed a procedure called *functional communication training* in which the children were taught a simple communicative response (e.g., ringing a bell) as an alternative to self-abuse to obtain staff attention. The self-injurious behavior was effectively eliminated. In 1990, Horner et al. described an approach called *positive behavior support* (*PBS*) that emphasized nonaversive approaches for treating individuals who exhibit challenging behavior. PBS has gathered a number of adherents and now includes an organization that holds an annual conference and produces the *Journal of Positive Behavior Interventions* and a number of other publications. (For a discussion of PBS, see Anderson & Freeman, 2000; Bambara & Kern, 2005; Carr & Sidener, 2002; Filter, 2007; Johnston, Foxx, Jacobson, Green, & Mulick, 2006.) Moreover, a number of organizations concerned with helping people have formulated official statements against at least some uses of punishment. For example, the Practice Directorates of the American Psychological Association and the National Association of School Psychologists provided testimony to the United States Congress in support of an amendment banning the use of corporal punishment for emotionally disturbed children ("P.D. Supports Ban on Corporal Punishment," 1990). In 1990, the American Association on Mental Retardation adopted a policy statement condemning "aversive procedures which cause physical damage, pain, or illness" and "procedures which are dehumanizing—social degradation, verbal abuse and excessive reactions" (p. 5).

So what is the current status of the controversy? On the one hand, during the last decade of the 20th century, the proportion of published articles reporting the use of punishment-based procedures decreased (Pelios, Morren, Tesch, & Axelrod, 1999). On the other hand, it has been recognized that some individuals do not show significant decreases in challenging behavior when given nonpunitive interventions alone but do improve when punishment is added to their programs (e.g., Hagopian et al., 1998; Hanley, Piazza, Fisher, & Maglieri, 2005). For an excellent recent review of the controversy, see Vause, Regehr, Feldman, Griffiths, & Owen, 2009).

Now let's reconsider the question of whether punishment should be deliberately used. Before doing so, we reemphasize a point made earlier in this chapter: We are not talking about the concept of punishment as many people think of it. That is, we are *not* talking about punishment of an individual as retribution, as a deterrent to others, or as a delayed consequence for misbehavior. Rather, we are talking about the technical use of consistently presenting an immediate punisher following a problem behavior and doing so in full consideration of the factors influencing the effectiveness of punishment as discussed previously. Moreover, because punishment can have a number of potentially harmful side effects, *we recommend that behavior modifiers consider designing punishment programs only when:*

- The behavior is very maladaptive, and it is in the client's best interest to bring about rapid behavior change.
- Clear steps are taken to maximize the conditions for a desirable alternative response and to minimize the causes of the response to be punished before resorting to punishment.
- The client or the client's parent or guardian provides informed consent (see Chapter 30).
- The intervention meets ethical standards (see Chapter 30).
- Punishment is applied according to clear guidelines (see pp. 156).
- The program includes safeguards to protect the client (see Chapter 30).

PITFALLS OF PUNISHMENT

Pitfall Type 1

People who are not aware that they are doing so often apply punishment. A common example is criticizing or ridiculing a person for inadequate behavior. Criticism and ridicule are generally punishing, and they will likely suppress future instances of that behavior. Yet the inadequate behavior that is criticized and ridiculed may be an approximation of more adequate behavior. Suppressing it could destroy the individual's opportunity to obtain the more desired behavior through the use of shaping. In everyday language, the individual becomes discouraged and gives up in his or her attempt to develop adequate behavior. In addition, because he or she may attempt to escape from and avoid the person administering the criticism and ridicule (see Chapter 13), that person will lose a great deal of potential reinforcing effectiveness.

Another example of someone applying punishment without being aware of it is the person who says "That was good, but. . . ." Suppose that a teenager helps a parent with the dishes and the parent replies, "Thanks for helping, but next time don't be so slow." We are sure that, based on the foregoing discussion, you can describe a much more effective and pleasant way for the parent to react.

Pitfall Type 2

Sometimes an individual thinks that she or he is applying a punisher but in fact is applying a reinforcer. For example, an adult may say "No! Naughty child! Stop that!" to a child who is engaging in an undesirable behavior. The child may immediately cease the undesirable behavior, and the adult might then conclude that the reprimand was an effective punisher. However, someone who tracked the frequency of that undesirable behavior might find that the reprimand was not a punisher but in fact a reinforcer. The child may have stopped temporarily because, having obtained the attention of the adult, he or she can then engage in other behavior that will maintain the adult's attention. Several studies indicate that reprimands can function as positive reinforcers and that the long-term frequency of the undesirable behavior that evoked the reprimand is therefore likely to increase (e.g., Madsen, Becker, Thomas, Koser, & Plager, 1970). This is not to say that reprimands are never punishing. As in our previous discussion of reprimands, they can be effective punishers. Situations in which they are most effective, however, seem to be those in which they are consistently backed up by another punisher, the causes of the undesirable behavior have been minimized, and the conditions for a desirable alternative behavior have been maximized (Van Houten & Doleys, 1983).

GUIDELINES FOR THE EFFECTIVE APPLICATION OF PUNISHMENT

The rules for the effective use of punishment are probably violated more than those for other principles. Therefore, extra care must be taken when designing a behavior modification program involving punishment. The conditions under which it is to be applied must be stated clearly, written down, and followed consistently.

1. *Select a Response*   Punishment is most effective with a specific behavior, such as jumping on the arm of the chair, rather than a general category of behavior (such as wrecking furniture).

2. *Maximize the Conditions for a Desirable (Nonpunished) Alternative Response*
   a. Select a desirable alternative behavior that competes with the behavior to be punished so that the alternative behavior can be reinforced. If possible, select a behavior that the natural environment will maintain after the termination of your reinforcement program.
   b. Provide strong prompts to increase the likelihood that the desirable alternative behavior will occur.
   c. Reinforce the desirable behavior with a powerful reinforcer on an appropriate schedule.

3. *Minimize the Causes of the Response to Be Punished*
   a. Try to identify and eliminate as many as possible of the S^Ds for the undesirable behavior early in the training program.
   b. Try to eliminate any possible reinforcement for the undesirable behavior.

4. *Select an Effective Punisher*
   a. Choose an effective punisher that can be presented immediately following the undesirable behavior.
   b. The punisher should be one that will not be paired with positive reinforcement following the undesirable behavior.
   c. Select a punisher that can be presented following every instance of the undesirable behavior.

5. *Present Clear S^{Dp}s*
   a. Tell the learner about the plan before starting.
   b. Give a clear "warning" or "reminder" (e.g., "Wait for mommy before crossing").

6. *Deliver the Punisher*
   a. Present the punisher *immediately* following the response to be decreased.
   b. Present the punisher following *every* instance of the response to be decreased.
   c. Take care not to pair punishment of the undesirable behavior with reinforcement for that behavior.
   d. Administer the punisher in a calm and matter-of-fact manner.

7. *Take Data*   In all programs involving punishment, careful data should be taken on the effects of the program.

Study Questions

26. Briefly describe the right-to-effective-treatment and freedom-from-harm positions in regard to the deliberate use of punishment treatment procedures.
27. Describe an example of functional communication training.
28. List six conditions that should be met for behavior modifiers to design punishment programs.
29. In view of the controversy regarding the use of punishment, do you agree with the way punishment was used with Ben? Defend your answer.
30. Describe an example of how punishment is applied by people who are not aware that they are doing so.

Application Exercises

A. EXERCISES INVOLVING OTHERS

1. Consider the behavior of speeding (driving a car in excess of the speed limit) in our culture.

   - Briefly outline the current reinforcement and punishment contingencies with respect to speeding.
   - Compare the current punishment contingencies for speeding with the guidelines for the effective application of punishment procedures. Identify those guidelines that lawmakers and law enforcers ignored.

2. Consider the behavior of littering the highways in your area. Answer the questions for this behavior that you answered for speeding in Application Exercise 1.

B. SELF-MODIFICATION EXERCISE

Choose a behavior of yours that you would like to decrease. Describe in detail a punishment program that, with the help of a friend, would likely decrease that behavior. (Make the program as realistic as possible, but do not apply it.) Your punishment program should be consistent with all of the guidelines for the effective application of punishment.

Notes and Extended Discussion

1. The issue of spankings by parents has made headlines in many newspapers, including the *New York Times* and *USA Today*. We hasten to point out, however, that discussion of the use of punishment by parents need not imply corporal punishment (for a review of corporal punishment by parents, see Gershoff, 2002). Rather, punishment can involve timeout, response cost, or reprimands. Also, we want to reemphasize that any discussion of punishment should be done with full consideration of the behavioral approach to punishment used in this chapter. In that sense, there are situations in which application of punishment by parents would likely be in the best interests of their children, as in the case of a child who frequently runs into a busy street, sticks metal objects into electrical outlets, or eats paint chips off walls. However, before applying punishment, parents should become knowledgeable concerning the factors that influence the effectiveness of punishment. An excellent source for parents is the book by Cipani (2004) that describes myths about punishment, basic principles of punishment, and guidelines for responsible use of punishment by parents.

2. Several authors have described methods, such as an approach called *gentle teaching* (McGee, Menolascino, Hobbs, & Menousek, 1987), that they claim can effectively replace all forms of aversive control. For the most part, the methods described are based on the behavior principles discussed in Chapters 3–11 of this text. Although these authors provide many good examples of alternatives that should be tried before resorting to aversive methods, it is not clear that the methods they propose can effectively replace aversive methods in all cases. Moreover, several authors (e.g., Bailey, 1992; Jones & McCaughey, 1992) have identified several important limitations of this approach. What is clear is that the decision to use or not use pain-inducing punishment in a particular case requires considerable professional training and expertise and should not be made by unqualified individuals (Griffith & Spreat, 1989).

Study Question on Notes

1. Do you think parents should use punishment? Discuss.

13

Establishing Behavior by Escape and Avoidance Conditioning

"Jason, that's bad for your health!"

CURING JASON'S SLOUCHING[1]

Jason was a model employee. An attendant at the Anna State Hospital, he was hardworking, punctual, and well liked by the patients. Unfortunately, Jason constantly slouched while he worked. At first thought, slouching might not seem to be a serious problem, but slouching by staff presented an inappropriate role model for the psychiatric patients at the hospital. Poor posture by such individuals frequently discourages social acceptability when they return to the community. Moreover, many medical authorities believe that good posture benefits health.

Fortunately for Jason, some psychologists at the hospital were conducting research on behavioral engineering—the use of an apparatus to manage contingencies to change behavior. Jason agreed to wear a specially designed shoulder harness that held an elastic cord across his back. The elastic cord was wired to a small tone generator and a clicker. When Jason wore a shirt and sweater over the harness, it was completely concealed from view. Here's how the apparatus worked: When Jason slouched, the elastic cord stretched, producing a clicking sound. Three seconds later, a loud aversive tone sounded and remained on until Jason stopped slouching. Thus, by exhibiting good posture after the tone came on, Jason would escape the sound of the tone because it would turn off. If he continued to display good posture, he would avoid the tone altogether. The results were dramatic. Before Jason wore the apparatus, he slouched almost 60% of the time, but when he wore it, he slouched only 1% of the time. When Jason removed the apparatus, his slouching did recover somewhat (to approximately 11%), but the clear demonstration of the effects of the apparatus gave him hope that he could cure his slouching habit. ∎

---

[1] This case is based on Azrin, Ruben, O'Brien, Ayllon, and Roll (1968).

ESCAPE CONDITIONING

Three behavioral principles were used in Jason's case: escape conditioning, avoidance conditioning, and punishment. The principle of **escape conditioning** (also called **negative reinforcement**) states that the removal of certain stimuli (called **aversive stimuli**) immediately after the occurrence of a behavior will increase the likelihood of that behavior. In the escape procedure used with Jason, the removal of the loud tone following the response of showing good posture increased the probability that he would show good posture each time the tone was presented.

Escape conditioning is similar to punishment in that both involve the use of an aversive stimulus. While escape conditioning and punishment are therefore similar, they differ procedurally in terms of both the antecedents and the consequences of behavior. With regard to antecedents, the aversive stimulus (the loud tone in Jason's case) used in escape conditioning must be present prior to an escape response, whereas the aversive stimulus (also called the *punisher*) is not present prior to a response that is punished. With regard to consequences, escape conditioning removes the aversive stimulus immediately following a response whereas punishment presents the aversive stimulus (or punisher) immediately following a response. In terms of results, the punishment procedure *decreases* the likelihood of the target response whereas the escape conditioning procedure *increases* the likelihood of the target response.

Another name for escape conditioning is *negative reinforcement* (Skinner, 1953). The word *reinforcement* indicates that it is analogous to positive reinforcement in that both strengthen responses. The word *negative* indicates that the strengthening effect occurs because the response leads to the removal (the taking away or subtraction) of an aversive stimulus.

Escape conditioning is common in everyday living. In the presence of a bright light, we have learned to escape the intensity of the light by closing our eyes or squinting. When a room is too cold, we escape the chill by putting on an extra sweater (see Figure 13–1). When it is too hot, we escape the heat by turning on a fan or air conditioner. If a street crew is repairing the street outside your room, you might close the window to escape the noise. See Table 13–1 for other examples of escape conditioning.

Study Questions

1. Define *escape conditioning,* and describe how it was used with Jason.
2. How is escape conditioning similar to punishment? In what two procedural ways do they differ? How do their effects differ?
3. In what two procedural ways is escape conditioning different from positive reinforcement? How are their effects similar?
4. Describe two examples of escape conditioning in everyday life, one of which is not in this chapter.
5. What is another name for escape conditioning, and why is it called that?

AVOIDANCE CONDITIONING

Escape conditioning has the disadvantage that the aversive stimulus must be present for the desired response to occur. In the escape procedure used with Jason, the loud tone was on before he showed good posture. Therefore, escape conditioning is generally not a final contingency for maintaining behavior but is preparatory training for avoidance conditioning. Thus, Jason was influenced by avoidance conditioning after he had demonstrated escape behavior.

FIGURE 13–1   Escape conditioning is strengthened by dressing warmly in the winter.

The principle of **avoidance conditioning** is a contingency in which a behavior prevents an aversive stimulus from occurring thereby resulting in an increase in the frequency of that behavior. During the avoidance procedure used with Jason, good posture prevented the tone from occurring. Note that both escape conditioning and avoidance conditioning involve the use of an aversive stimulus. And with both, the likelihood of a behavior increases. However, one difference between escape and avoidance conditioning is that an escape response removes an aversive stimulus that has already occurred while an avoidance response prevents an aversive stimulus from occurring at all. Keeping this in mind will help you to distinguish between instances of escape versus instances of avoidance. Suppose you are walking down the aisle of a shopping mall and someone whom you dislike steps in front of you and begins talking. You make an excuse that you are late for an appointment and must leave and you walk away. That is an instance of escape conditioning because the aversive stimulus was there and you responded to escape from it. Now suppose that the next day, you are once again walking in that shopping mall and you see the person whom you dislike come out of a store some distance away, but that person hasn't yet seen you. You duck into a store to avoid an unpleasant confrontation. That is an instance of avoidance conditioning.

A second difference between escape and avoidance conditioning is that the latter often involves a **warning stimulus** (also called *conditioned aversive stimulus*), which is a stimulus that signals a forthcoming aversive stimulus. In the example at the shopping mall, the sight of the person you dislike some distance away was a warning stimulus, and you ducked into the store to

NOTE 1

TABLE 13–1	Examples of Escape Conditioning		
Aversive Situation	**Escape Response by Individual**	**Removal of Aversive Situation**	**Long-Term Effect**
1. A child sees an adult with a bag of candies. The child begins to scream, "Candy, candy, candy."	To terminate the screaming, the adult gives the screaming child a candy.	The child stops screaming.	In the future, the adult is more likely to give in to the screaming child to escape the screaming (and the child is likely to scream to get candy, a positive reinforcer).
2. A teacher presents prompts every 30 seconds to a child with developmental disabilities.	The child begins to tantrum.	The teacher gives the child a break from the training program.	The child is likely to tantrum when presented with frequent prompts from the teacher.
3. A nonverbal child has had shoes put on her that are too tight and are pinching her toes.	The child makes loud noises in the presence of an adult and points to her toes.	The adult removes the shoes (and perhaps puts on larger shoes).	The child is likely to make loud noises and point to her sore feet (or other areas of pain) more quickly in similar situations in the future.
4. A jogger experiences a sensation of sore lips while jogging on a windy day.	The jogger puts lip balm on his lips.	The sensation of soreness ceases.	The jogger is likely to use lip balm to soothe sore lips.
5. A zookeeper encounters a pile of smelly dung on the floor of a monkey cage.	The zookeeper walks away without cleaning it up.	The zookeeper escapes the aversive smell.	In the future, the zookeeper will likely walk away from smelly dung on the floor of the monkey cage.

avoid that person. The clicking of the apparatus when Jason slouched was a warning stimulus—it signaled the occurrence of the tone 3 seconds later. Jason quickly learned to show good posture at the sound of the clicker to avoid the backup aversive stimulus, the loud tone. This type of avoidance conditioning, which includes a warning signal that enables the individual to discriminate a forthcoming aversive stimulus, is called *discriminated avoidance conditioning*.

Because the clicking became a conditioned punisher through pairings with the backup aversive stimulus, the procedure used with Jason also included a punishment component. If he showed poor posture, then clicking—a conditioned punisher—would occur. Thus, when Jason began wearing the apparatus, escape conditioning strengthened good posture, avoidance conditioning maintained it, and poor posture was immediately punished. It's no wonder that the results were so dramatic.

Avoidance conditioning is also common in everyday living. Students learn to give the right answers on tests to avoid poor grades. Our legal system is based largely on avoidance conditioning. We pay our taxes to avoid going to prison. We put money in parking meters to avoid getting a ticket. We pay our parking fines to avoid a court summons. See Table 13–2 for other examples of avoidance conditioning.

Behavioral theoreticians have debated the theoretical explanation for avoidance responding. The increase in positively reinforced responses and escape responses and the decrease in punished responses are all explained by their immediate stimulus consequences. However, the consequence of an avoidance response is the nonoccurrence of a stimulus. How can the nonoccurrence of something cause a behavior? Because theoreticians tend to dislike paradoxes such as this, behavioral theoreticians have asked themselves the following question: Are there immediate consequences that perhaps are easily overlooked by the casual observer but that might nevertheless maintain avoidance responses?

There appear to be several possibilities. One possibility in discriminated avoidance conditioning is that the avoidance response is strengthened because it immediately terminates the warning stimulus. For example, recall that in Jason's case, the loud tone was the backup aversive stimulus. Because clicking was paired with the tone, clicking became an aversive stimulus. When Jason showed good posture in the presence of the clicking, the immediate result was that the clicking ceased. Although Jason's good posture was an avoidance response with respect to the tone, it was an escape response with respect to the clicking. This type of explanation might enable us to account for the first example of avoidance conditioning in Table 13–2.

A second possible explanation of discriminated avoidance conditioning is that, in some cases, the avoidance response enables a person to immediately escape from anxious feelings.

TABLE 13–2   Examples of Avoidance Conditioning

Situation	Warning Stimulus	Avoidance Response	Immediate Consequence	Aversive Consequence Avoided
1. While driving, you are exceeding the speed limit.	You notice a police car just ahead.	You immediately turn down a side street.	You no longer see the police car.	You avoid receiving a speeding ticket.
2. A child playing in her front yard hears the neighbor's dog barking (the dog had previously scared the child by barking loudly).	The child feels anxious.	The child goes into her house.	The child feels less anxious.	The child avoids hearing loud barking.
3. One of the authors is about to leave his office to go home.	He remembers that his son is practicing his drumming at home.	He phones home to ask his son to stop practicing.	Thoughts of encountering loud drumming cease.	He avoids experiencing extremely loud drumming when he enters his house.

This is illustrated by the second example in Table 13–2. Hearing the dog's barking caused the child to feel anxious. Immediately following the avoidance response, she felt less anxious. The possibility that avoidance responses occur because they enable us to escape from anxiety is discussed further in Chapter 15.

A third possible explanation is that in some cases, the avoidance response enables a person to immediately escape from unpleasant thoughts. This might explain the avoidance response in the third example in Table 13–2. Perhaps thoughts of experiencing his son's loud drumming were aversive, and these thoughts immediately ceased following the phone call. Or perhaps the explanation of that example may involve rule-governed control over behavior, discussed in Chapter 17. While such explanations are plausible, they are speculative. You can see why behavior modifiers are puzzled about how to explain avoidance responding in terms of immediate stimulus consequences.

Study Questions

6. Define *avoidance conditioning,* and describe how it was used with Jason.
7. Give another name for warning stimulus.
8. What is the name of the type of avoidance conditioning that involves a warning stimulus?
9. How is a warning stimulus like an S^D? How is it different?
10. How is a warning stimulus different than an S^{Dp} (see Chapter 12)?
11. What are two procedural differences between escape conditioning and avoidance conditioning?
12. Describe two examples of avoidance conditioning in everyday life, one of which is not in this chapter.
13. Describe three types of immediate consequences that might maintain avoidance responses.

PITFALLS OF ESCAPE AND AVOIDANCE CONDITIONING

Pitfall Type 1

People often unknowingly strengthen others' undesirable behavior by allowing such behavior to lead to escape or avoidance of aversive stimuli. This is illustrated by Example 2 in Table 13–1 (and demonstrated by Lalli et al., 1999). Observations of family interactions by Snyder, Schrepferman, and St. Peter (1997) indicated that parents of children labeled as antisocial frequently strengthened aggressive behavior in their children by backing off or giving in when the aggressive behavior occurred. Parents may inadvertently establish inappropriate verbal behavior with a child who desperately promises, "I'll be good; I won't do it again," to escape or avoid punishment for some infraction of parental authority. When such pleas are successful, the pleading behavior is strengthened and thus increased in frequency under similar circumstances, but the undesirable behavior the parent meant to decrease may have been affected very little or not at all. Verbal behavior having little relation to reality may be increased while the undesirable target response may persist in strength.

Another example of this pitfall sometimes can be seen when prisoners learn to make the "right" verbal statements to obtain early parole. Parole boards often have difficulty determining when it is only the verbal behavior of prisoners that has been modified, not their antisocial behaviors (e.g., assaults). Apologies, confessions, and the "guilty look" characteristic of transgressors in all walks of life can be traced to similar contingencies. Lying or misrepresenting the facts is a way of avoiding punishment if one can get away with it. (Other examples of undesirable behavior maintained by escape conditioning are presented in Chapter 23.)

A second variety of Pitfall Type 1 is the inadvertent establishment of conditioned aversive stimuli to which an individual then responds in such a way as to escape or avoid them. For example, if a coach yells at, criticizes, and ridicules athletes, the athletes may show improved skills primarily to avoid or escape the coach's wrath. But in the process, the coach has become a conditioned aversive stimulus for the athletes, so that they are now likely to avoid the coach off the athletic field. If the coaching tactics become too aversive, everything associated with the sport will become aversive, and some team members might even quit it entirely.

A third variety of Pitfall Type 1 is that in some situations, a person might be inadvertently influenced by escape and avoidance conditioning to positively reinforce the undesirable behavior of others. An example with regard to escape conditioning is the first example in Table 13–1. An example with regard to avoidance conditioning is the reinforcement of a threat because it prevents the more aversive behavior that might follow, such as when a parent gives a child a candy because the child threatens to cry if candy is not forthcoming.

GUIDELINES FOR THE EFFECTIVE APPLICATION OF ESCAPE AND AVOIDANCE CONDITIONING

Any person who applies escape and avoidance conditioning should observe the following rules:

1. *Given a Choice Between Maintaining Behavior on an Escape or an Avoidance Procedure, the Latter Is to Be Preferred*   There are two reasons for this. First, in escape conditioning, the backup aversive stimulus must be present prior to the target response, whereas in avoidance conditioning, the backup aversive stimulus occurs only when the target response fails to occur. Second, in escape conditioning, the target response does not occur when the backup aversive stimulus is not present, whereas in avoidance conditioning, responding decreases very slowly when the backup aversive stimulus may no longer be forthcoming.

2. *The Target Behavior Should Be Established by Escape Conditioning Before It Is Put on an Avoidance Procedure*   In the case at the beginning of this chapter, Jason learned how to escape the loud noise prior to learning how to avoid it.

3. *During Avoidance Conditioning, a Warning Stimulus Should Signal the Impending Aversive Stimulus*   This enhances conditioning by providing a warning that failure to respond will result in aversive stimulation. An example is the printed word VIOLATION on a parking meter's time indicator, which indicates that the motorist may receive a parking ticket if he or she does not put a coin in the meter. The clicker served a similar function for Jason, indicating that the tone would occur 3 seconds later unless he showed good posture. And if Jason showed good posture during the 3 seconds, he could avoid the loud tone. Similarly, putting a coin in a parking meter removes the VIOLATION sign and prevents getting a ticket.

4. *Escape and Avoidance Conditioning, Like Punishment, Should Be Used Cautiously*   Because these procedures involve aversive stimuli, they can result in harmful side effects, such as aggression, fearfulness, and a tendency to avoid or escape any person or thing associated with the procedure.

5. *Positive Reinforcement for the Target Response Should Be Used in Conjunction with Escape and Avoidance Conditioning*   This will not only help to strengthen the desired behavior but also will tend to counteract the undesirable side effects mentioned. The procedure used with Jason would probably have worked even better if positive reinforcement for good posture had been added to it. (This was not done because the experimenters were interested only in the escape and avoidance procedures.)

6. *As with All Procedures Described in This Text, the Individual Concerned Should Be Told—to the Best of His or Her Understanding—About the Contingencies in Effect*
Again, as with all of these procedures, however, instructions are not necessary for escape and avoidance conditioning to work. **NOTE 2**

Study Questions

14. Briefly describe an example of how people unknowingly strengthen others' undesirable behavior by allowing such behavior to lead to escape or avoidance of aversive stimuli.

15. Describe an example of the inadvertent establishment of conditioned aversive stimuli, which then causes individuals to avoid or escape those stimuli.

16. Explain with an example of your own why an individual might unknowingly positively reinforce the undesirable behavior of another individual. (*Hint*: See the first example in Table 13–1.) Clearly identify the behavior principles involved.

17. Explain how escape conditioning might influence an adult to unknowingly positively reinforce a child's extreme social withdrawal.

Application Exercises

A. EXERCISE INVOLVING OTHERS

Successful avoidance behavior means that an individual probably has been conditioned to respond to a warning signal in such a way as to avoid the occurrence of a backup aversive stimulus. This means that the avoidance behavior might persist even if the environment has changed so that the backup aversive stimulus will no longer be presented regardless of the individual's behavior. Describe an example you have observed in someone other than yourself that illustrates this effect.

B. SELF-MODIFICATION EXERCISE

Construct a table similar to Table 13–1 in which you present five examples of escape conditioning that have influenced your behavior. Present each example in terms of the categories of aversive situation, escape response, removal of aversive stimulus, and probable long-term effects on the escape response.

Notes and Extended Discussion

1. Not all types of avoidance conditioning involve a warning stimulus. One type that does not is known as *Sidman avoidance* (after Murray Sidman, who studied this type of avoidance extensively with lower organisms; e.g., Sidman, 1953). In a typical Sidman avoidance conditioning experiment with a laboratory rat, a brief electric shock is presented every 30 seconds without a preceding warning stimulus. If the rat makes a designated response, the shock will be postponed for 30 seconds. Under these conditions, the rat will learn to make the appropriate avoidance response on a regular basis and will be relatively shock free. Sidman avoidance conditioning is also referred to as *nondiscriminated, noncued,* or *free-operant avoidance conditioning*. Sidman avoidance has been demonstrated with humans (Hefferline, Keenan, & Harford, 1959) and appears to underlie some everyday preventive behaviors. For example, many older model cars have no warning light to indicate when the windshield wiper fluid container is almost empty. Nevertheless, to avoid running out of fluid, many drivers of these cars regularly refill the container before it is empty. (However, as discussed in Chapter 17, this behavior might also be explained as rule-governed behavior.

2. Even animals whose nervous systems are quite different from ours show escape and avoidance conditioning. For example, the hermit crab—an animal that carries around or "wears" a discarded sea shell it has found—will leave its shell and tend to select another shell rather than returning to its original shell if it has received a small electric shock in the original shell (Elwood & Appel, 2009).

Study Questions on Notes

1. What is Sidman avoidance conditioning?
2. Explain how applying sunscreen or insect repellent might be an example of Sidman avoidance. Give another example from everyday life. (*Hint:* Some common computer applications have built-in timers that fit the definition of Sidman avoidance conditioning.)
3. Describe how avoidance conditioning has been demonstrated in the hermit crab. Did this study also demonstrate escape conditioning? Explain.

14 Procedures Based on Principles of Respondent Conditioning

"I hate that word!"

MAKING WORDS "UNPLEASANT"[1]

Sue was a student in first-year psychology at Arizona State University. As a participant in an experiment, she had been asked to memorize a list of words that were presented to her one at a time. Sitting as comfortably as one can be with electrical wires attached to one's ankle and wearing headphones, Sue read the words as they were presented: "chair," "smile," "small," "large" (ZAP! CLANG! Sue was startled by the feeling of a mild electric shock to her ankle and a loud clang she heard through the headphones). Sue continued to memorize the words on the list. The word large *appeared several times, and each time it was paired with the mild shock and the loud sound. During the experiment, the shock and the sound caused Sue to feel anxious as measured by her galvanic skin response (GSR), an increase in the electrical conductivity of the skin that occurs during a sweat gland reaction. As a result of pairing the word* large *with the mild shock and the loud sound, hearing the word* large *by itself now caused Sue to feel anxious. Afterward, when Sue was asked to rate the pleasantness of the words on the list, she rated* large *as more unpleasant than the other words.*

    Note: *During a debriefing session, Sue learned the purposes of the experiment. She also discovered that saying the word* large *many times without pairing it with the mild shock and the loud tone caused that word to gradually lose its unpleasantness.* ■

OPERANT VERSUS RESPONDENT BEHAVIOR

The principles and procedures described in the previous pages of this book are mainly those of **operant conditioning**, which is the process of strengthening a behavior by reinforcing it or

---

[1] This example is based on an experiment by Staats, Staats, and Crawford (1962).

weakening it by punishing it (Skinner, 1938). In other words, operant behavior is behavior that is modified by its consequences. As you have seen, consequences that cause a behavior to increase are called *reinforcers,* and those that cause it to decrease are called *punishers*. Behaviors that operate on the environment to generate consequences, and are in turn controlled by those consequences, are called **operant behaviors**. Examples include putting gas in your car, asking for directions, writing an exam, turning on a TV set, and making breakfast.

Although operant principles have widespread applicability, some behavior does not seem to fit the model of operant conditioning. Some of our behaviors, like Sue's anxious feelings and GSR to the mild shock and loud clang, seem to be reflexive, and are called **respondent behaviors**, which are behaviors elicited by prior stimuli and are not affected by their consequences. Examples include salivating when smelling dinner cooking, feeling frightened when watching a scary movie, blushing when told that your fly or blouse is undone, and becoming sexually aroused when watching X-rated movies. A different set of principles seems to apply to respondent behaviors. In this chapter, we briefly describe these principles and how they differ from those of operant conditioning. In addition, we highlight some of the applications of these principles.

PRINCIPLE OF RESPONDENT CONDITIONING

Respondent conditioning, defined below, is based on *unconditioned reflexes*. An **unconditioned reflex** is a stimulus–response relationship in which a stimulus automatically elicits a response apart from any prior learning. Examples of such reflexes are shown in Figure 14–1.

The reflexes in Figure 14–1 are unconditioned because the stimuli elicit the responses without prior conditioning; in other words, they are "hard wired," or inborn. A stimulus that elicits a response without prior learning or conditioning is called an **unconditioned stimulus (US)**. A response elicited by an unconditioned stimulus is called an **unconditioned response (UR)**. In the experiment with Sue, the mild shock and loud sound were USs, and Sue's anxious feeling and GSR to the shock were URs.

Respondent Conditioning

Each of the responses in Figure 14–1 has stimuli that do not elicit it. In that sense, such stimuli are considered neutral. For example, assume that a particular stimulus (such as the opening motif of Beethoven's Fifth Symphony) is neutral with respect to the response of salivation in the sense that it does not elicit a salivation in a particular individual. The principle of **respondent conditioning** states that if a stimulus (e.g., the opening motif of Beethoven's Fifth Symphony) is followed closely in time by a US (e.g., food in the mouth) that elicits a UR (e.g., salivation), then the previously neutral stimulus (the opening motif of Beethoven's Fifth Symphony) will also tend to elicit that response (salivation) in the future. Of course, it may take more than just one pairing of the opening motif of Beethoven's Fifth Symphony with food before it would elicit any noticeable amount of salivation. Figure 14–2 illustrates respondent conditioning. *Respondent conditioning* is also called *Pavlovian conditioning* (after Ivan Pavlov, the Russian physiologist who studied it) or *classical conditioning* (because it was the first type of conditioning to be identified), and we use these three terms interchangeably.

A **conditioned reflex** is a stimulus–response relationship in which a stimulus elicits a response because of prior respondent conditioning. If a salivation response were in fact conditioned to the opening motif of Beethoven's Fifth Symphony, that stimulus–response relationship

---

UNCONDITIONED REFLEX

Unconditioned Stimulus ················>	Unconditioned Response
Digestive system	
Food ··································>	salivation
Bad food ······························>	sickness, nausea
Object in esophagus ···················>	vomiting
Reproductive system	
Genital stimulation ···················>	vaginal lubrication, penile erection, orgasm
Nipple stimulation ····················>	milk release (in lactating women)
Circulatory system	
High temperature ······················>	sweating, flushing
Sudden loud noise ·····················>	blanching, pounding heart
Respiratory system	
Irritation in nose ····················>	sneeze
Throat clogged ························>	cough
Allergens ·····························>	asthma attack
Muscular system	
Low temperature ·······················>	shivering
Blows or burns ························>	withdrawal
Tap on patellar tendon ················>	knee jerk
Light to eye ··························>	pupil constriction
Novel stimulation ·····················>	reflexive orienting
Infant reflexes	
Stroking the cheek ····················>	head turning
Object touches lips ···················>	sucking
Food in mouth ·························>	swallowing
Object in the hand ····················>	grasping
Held vertically, feet touching ground ··········>	stepping

FIGURE 14–1 A partial list of unconditioned reflexes.

Source: John D. Baldwin and Janice I. Baldwin, *Behavior Principles in Everyday Life,* 2nd ed. 1986, p. 44. Reprinted by permission of Prentice Hall, Inc., Upper Saddle River, NJ.

would be referred to as a *conditioned reflex.* The stimulus in a conditioned reflex is called a **conditioned stimulus (CS),** defined as a stimulus that elicits a response because that stimulus has been paired with another stimulus that elicits that response. The response in a conditioned reflex is referred to as a **conditioned response (CR),** defined as a response elicited by a conditioned stimulus. For example, the opening motif of Beethoven's Fifth Symphony became a CS, and salivation to the opening motif was a CR. In the experiment with Sue, the word *large* became a CS eliciting an anxious feeling and a GSR as CRs. You can see how respondent conditioning might explain your reactions to certain words (such as *cancer*) or even to a single letter (such as F on an exam). As indicated by Sue's rating of the word *large* as unpleasant, such pairings contribute to the meaning of words on a personal level (Staats, 1996; Tyron & Cicero, 1989).

Respondent Conditioning

Procedure: Pair neutral stimulus and unconditioned stimulus.

Many
pairings
{ NS (sound of classical music)

US (food in mouth) ——→ UR (salivation)

Result: Neutral stimulus acquires ability to elicit response.

CS (sound of classical music) ——→ CR (salivation)

Note: NS = neutral stimulus
US = unconditioned stimulus
UR = unconditioned response
CS = conditioned stimulus
CR = conditioned response

FIGURE 14–2 Model for respondent conditioning.

Factors Influencing Respondent Conditioning

Several variables influence the development of a conditioned reflex. First, *the more the number of pairings of a CS with a US, the more likely is the ability of the CS to elicit the CR* until a maximum strength of the conditioned reflex has been reached. If a child was frightened several times by the loud barking of a dog, the sight of the dog will elicit a stronger fear than if the child had been scared by the dog only once.

Second, *stronger conditioning occurs if the CS precedes the US by about half a second rather than by a longer time or rather than following the US.* Conditioning in the latter case, called *backward conditioning,* is difficult to attain. If a child sees a dog and the dog immediately barks loudly, the sight of the dog is likely to become a CS with fear as a CR for the child. If, however, the child hears the loud barking of a dog hidden from view and a few seconds later sees a dog trot around the corner of a building, the fear caused by the loud barking is not likely to be conditioned to the sight of the dog.

Third, *a CS acquires a more likely ability to elicit a CR if the CS is always paired with the US than if it is only occasionally paired with the US.* If a couple consistently lights a candle in the bedroom just before having sex but not at other times, the candlelight is likely to become a CS eliciting sexual arousal. If they light a candle in the bedroom every night but have sex there only one or two nights each week, then the candlelight will be a weaker CS for sexual arousal.

Fourth, *when several neutral stimuli precede a US, the stimulus that is most consistently associated with the US is the one most likely to become a strong CS.* A child may experience thunderstorms in which dark clouds and lightning are followed by loud claps of thunder, which cause fear. On other occasions, the child sees dark clouds but there is no lightning or thunder. The child will acquire a stronger fear of lightning than of the dark clouds because lightning is more consistently paired with thunder.

Fifth, *respondent conditioning will develop more quickly and strongly when the CS or US or both are intense rather than weak* (Lutz, 1994; Polenchar, Romano, Steinmetz, & Patterson, 1984). A child will acquire a stronger fear of lightning if the lightning is exceptionally bright and the thunder is exceptionally loud than if either or both are relatively weak.

Study Questions

1. To what does the term *operant conditioning* refer?
2. What are operant behaviors? Give three examples.
3. What are respondent behaviors? Give three examples
4. Define *unconditioned reflex*. Give three examples.
5. State the principle of respondent conditioning. Clearly diagram an example of respondent conditioning that is not in the text. What is another name for respondent conditioning?
6. Define *conditioned reflex,* and describe an example.
7. Define and give an example of the following: *unconditioned stimulus, unconditioned response, conditioned stimulus,* and *conditioned response*.
8. In a sentence for each, briefly describe five variables that influence the development of a conditioned reflex.

HIGHER-ORDER CONDITIONING

Suppose that someone is conditioned to salivate to the opening motif of Beethoven's Fifth Symphony by following it with food a great many times. The opening motif of Beethoven's Fifth Symphony will thus have become a CS for salivation. Now let's suppose that, over several trials, just before presenting the opening motif of Beethoven's Fifth Symphony by itself, we turn on a yellow light. The light is a neutral stimulus for salivation and is never paired with food. However, after a number of pairings of the light with the music (an established CS for the response of salivation), the light itself will come to elicit salivation. The procedure in which a neutral stimulus becomes a conditioned stimulus by being paired with another conditioned stimulus instead of with an unconditioned stimulus is known as **higher-order conditioning**. The pairing of the music with the food is referred to as conditioning of the *first order*. Pairing the light with the music is referred to as conditioning of the *second order*. Although third-order conditioning has been reported (Pavlov, 1927), higher-order conditioning beyond the second order appears to be difficult. The model for higher-order conditioning is presented in Figure 14–3.

Let's see how higher-order conditioning might apply in everyday life. Suppose that a child experiences painful stimuli several times, such as from touching a hot stove on one occasion and a sharp thorn on another. Each painful stimulus can be considered a US causing fear as a UR. Let's suppose further that, just before each painful experience, a parent yelled, "Watch out! You'll hurt yourself!" This warning from the parent is likely to become a CS eliciting fear. Suppose also that the parent later utters the same warning when the child climbs on a ladder, stands on a chair, or climbs onto the kitchen counter. Pairings of the warning with these other activities might influence the child to develop a general fear of heights through higher-order conditioning. The conditioning stages were as follows: First, the warnings were followed by painful stimuli; second, being in high places was followed by warnings. Result: Being in a high place now elicits a response (fear) similar to that elicited by painful stimuli.

RESPONDENT EXTINCTION

Once respondent conditioning occurs, does it stay with us forever? Not necessarily. It may be reversed through the principle of **respondent extinction**, which involves the procedure of presenting a CS while withholding the US with the result that the CS gradually loses its capability of

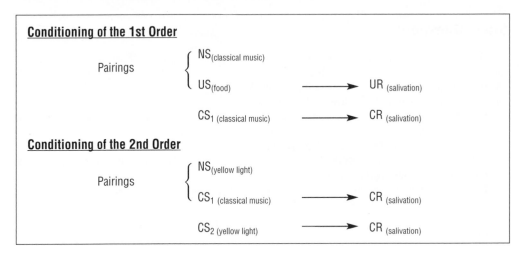

FIGURE 14–3   Model for higher-order conditioning.

eliciting the CR. Suppose that a child reaches out to touch a large dog just as the dog barks very loudly, scaring the child. As a function of the pairing of the loud bark with the sight of the big dog, the sight of the dog alone now elicits crying and trembling. This is a Pavlovian conditioned response that we label *fear*. Now suppose that the parent takes the child to a dog show. Although there are lots of large dogs around, they have been trained to walk and sit quietly while on display. Repeated contact with these dogs (without pairings with barking) will help the child overcome the fear of seeing dogs. That is, the sight of dogs loses its capability of functioning as a CS to elicit the fear reaction as a CR. Many of the fears that we acquire during childhood—fears of the dentist, the dark, lightning, and so on—undergo respondent extinction as we grow older as a function of repeated exposure to these things in the absence of dire consequences. Figure 14–4 illustrates respondent extinction. And luckily for Sue, after encountering the word *large* several times without further pairings with the shock and tone, it gradually lost its ability to elicit anxiety.

Respondent extinction is the reason that higher-order conditioning is difficult to obtain beyond the second order. In the example cited in Figure 14–3, when conditioning of the second order is attempted, CS_1, the opening motif of Beethoven's Fifth Symphony, is no longer paired with food, the US. Thus, the opening motif of Beethoven's Fifth Symphony is undergoing extinction as a CS and the salivation elicited by the opening motif of Beethoven's Fifth Symphony is weaker than the salivation originally elicited by food.

COUNTERCONDITIONING

Recall from Chapter 5 that operant extinction proceeds more quickly and effectively if an alternative response is reinforced. A similar rule holds for respondent extinction: A conditioned response may be eliminated more effectively if a new response that is incompatible with the conditioned response is conditioned to the conditioned stimulus at the same time that the former conditioned response is being extinguished. This process is called **counterconditioning**. Stated technically, a CS will lose its ability to elicit a CR if that CS is paired with a stimulus that elicits a response that is incompatible with the CR. To illustrate this process, let's reconsider the example of a child who

---

Respondent Extinction

Procedure: Present conditioned stimulus repeatedly without further pairings with the unconditioned stimulus.

Repeated   CS (sight of
trials   dog) ⟶ CR (fear)

Result: Conditioned stimulus loses ability to elicit conditioned response.

Stimulus (sight of
dog) ⟶ no fear reaction

FIGURE 14–4   Model for respondent extinction.

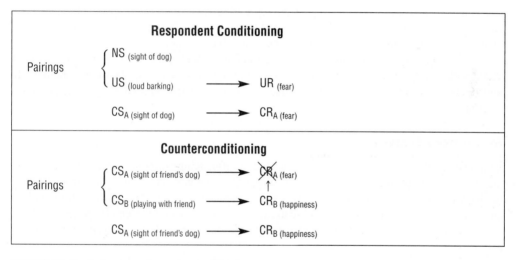

FIGURE 14–5   A diagram of counterconditioning.

acquired a fear of the sight of dogs. Let's suppose that the child likes playing with a friend who has become a CS eliciting feelings of happiness as a CR, and let's suppose that the friend has a friendly dog who doesn't bark loudly. As the child plays with the friend and the friend's dog, some of the positive emotions elicited by the friend will become conditioned to the friend's dog. These positive conditioned emotional responses will help counteract the negative conditioned emotional responses previously elicited by dogs and thus more quickly and more effectively eliminate the negative responses. Figure 14–5 illustrates counterconditioning.

COMMON RESPONDENTLY CONDITIONED RESPONSES

Through evolution, humans are born with numerous unconditioned reflexes, such as those listed in Figure 14–1. Such reflexes are important to our survival, reproduction, and day-to-day biological functioning. We are also evolved with a susceptibility to Pavlovian conditioning. The fact that reflexive responses can be conditioned to previously neutral stimuli is biologically adaptive. Our capability of being conditioned to salivate at the sight of food, for example, prepares us to digest our food more rapidly than would occur if Pavlovian conditioning were not possible. Let's consider in more detail some major categories of conditioned reflexes.

Digestive System

The salivation reflex is only one of the digestive reflexes that are susceptible to Pavlovian conditioning. A student experiences butterflies in the stomach before giving a talk in class. After experiencing chemotherapy, some patients feel nauseous while waiting in the treatment room for therapy to begin. An extremely frightening experience, such as being threatened by a knife-wielding intruder, can cause anxiety defecation.

Circulatory System

Increased heart rate and blood flow are involved in many conditioned reflexes. Feeling embarrassed in a social setting, overhearing risqué topics discussed, experiencing socially inappropriate thoughts—all have become CSs, causing blushing in many individuals as blood flows to the outer layers of the skin. The circulatory system is involved in conditioned reflexes, such as when you are all alone in a house and an unexpected knock on the door causes your heart to pound. The circulatory system is also involved in sexual stimulation, such as when nude photographs elicit increased heart rate and increased blood flow to the genital areas, causing penile or clitoral erection.

Respiratory System

Pavlovian conditioning has also been implicated in influencing coughing, sneezing, and asthma attacks—reflexes of the respiratory system. Suppose a person's aunt, who visits rarely, happens to visit when that person suffers an asthma attack. The aunt might become a CS for the coughing and wheezing characteristic of an asthmatic reaction. Dekker and Groen (1956) reported that asthmatic responses have been elicited by such CSs as the sight of horses, caged birds, goldfish, and police vans.

Other Systems

Other organ systems of the body—such as the urinary and reproductive systems—are also susceptible to Pavlovian conditioning. And, of course, the nervous system is involved in all conditioning.

A Variation of Factors Influencing Respondent Conditioning

When one of the authors was 16 years old, he had an encounter with lemon gin at a party. Except for the occasional bottle of beer, he was an inexperienced alcohol drinker. The first few sips of lemon gin were quite enjoyable and produced no immediate reaction of drunkenness. In approximately 15 minutes, he had drunk several ounces of lemon gin. Approximately an hour later, he became violently ill. Since that time, the smell or taste of lemon gin causes instant nausea. Even the thought of it causes his stomach to start complaining. In this example, the large amount of lemon gin in the stomach was a US causing nausea as a UR. Even though the smell and taste of lemon gin were paired with the reflexive responses of nausea and vomiting just once, and even though there was a long delay between the previously neutral stimuli (the taste and smell of lemon gin) and the experience of nausea, Pavlovian conditioning occurred. The taste and smell of lemon gin became a CS for the sickness reflex, and a *conditioned taste aversion,* in this case, a dislike for lemon gin, was established. The phenomenon of conditioned taste aversion is an exception to the rule that respondent conditioning is ineffective if there is a long delay between the CS and the US. Evolution has apparently provided for a long delay between the CS and US to be effective in this case because of the time that toxic substances take to have an effect on the body. It is also an exception to the need for many conditioning trials in order for a strong conditioned reflex to be formed because just one ingestion of a toxic substance can be extremely harmful or even fatal.

Seligman (1971) coined the term *biological preparedness* to refer to the predisposition of members of a species to be more readily conditioned to some neutral stimuli as CSs than to others. As an example of biological preparedness, humans will more quickly learn fears to stimuli that may have posed a threat to survival, such as snakes and insects, than to stimuli that were likely nonthreatening in our ancestors' history, such as pictures of flowers (Ohman, Dimberg, & Ost, 1984). Conditioned taste aversion is another example of biological preparedness. Having evolved the strong tendency for taste to be conditioned to nausea greatly decreases the chances that one will repeatedly consume food that causes illness and perhaps death.

Study Questions

9. Diagram an example of higher-order conditioning.
10. State the procedure and result of the principle of respondent extinction. Describe an example that is not in this chapter.
11. Describe the process of counterconditioning. Describe an example of counterconditioning that is not in this chapter.
12. Describe three examples of your own conditioned reflexes, one for each of these categories: digestion, circulation, and respiration. Make sure the stimuli in your examples are CSs, not USs.
13. Describe an example of a conditioned taste aversion.
14. Why do you suppose that we have evolved so that we are susceptible to conditioned taste aversion?
15. What is biological preparedness? Give an example.
16. Discuss whether all stimuli are equally capable of becoming CSs.

RESPONDENT AND OPERANT CONDITIONING COMPARED

Respondent and operant conditioning procedures appear to influence two different kinds of behaviors (Pear & Eldridge, 1984). Nevertheless, the procedures have a number of parallels. Let's examine some of the differences and similarities.

Responses

Respondent behaviors are reflexive in that they occur automatically to prior stimuli and are typically referred to as *involuntary.* Few people, for example, are able to blush, salivate, or produce tears on command. Good actors may appear to do this, but they often use special tricks—such as surreptitiously pulling out one of their nose hairs to elicit tears, as Marlon Brando was said to have done. Operant behavior, in contrast, is controlled by consequences and is sometimes referred to as *voluntary*. When asked to do so, for example, physically intact people can readily stand up, sit down, talk, whisper, and so on. Reflexive responses usually involve smooth muscles and glands that are important in the functioning of internal bodily processes, such as relaxation before sleeping or arousal when exposed to a threatening situation. Operant behavior usually involves skeletal muscles and is generally important in enabling us to interact with the external environment.

Reinforcement

The Pavlovian conditioning procedure consists of pairing a neutral stimulus (NS) with a US (or with a CS in the case of higher-order conditioning) *before* the response. The result of Pavlovian reinforcement is that the NS (now called a CS) acquires the capability to elicit the response (now called a CR). The operant conditioning procedure consists of the presentation of a positive reinforcer or the removal of an aversive stimulus immediately *following* a response. The result is that the operant behavior increases in frequency.

Extinction

The Pavlovian extinction procedure involves the presentation of a CS without further pairings with the US. The result is that the CS loses the capability of eliciting the CR. The operant extinction procedure involves withholding a reinforcer following a previously reinforced response. The result is that the response decreases in frequency.

CSs and S^{D}s

CSs are like S^{D}s in that both produce responses that have been conditioned to them. The conditioning procedures that establish them differ, however. In addition, the ways in which CSs and S^{D}s produce their responses differ. Responses produced by CSs frequently seem to be more automatic or consistent. To capture this difference, standard behavioral terminology refers to CSs as *eliciting* the responses conditioned to them, whereas S^{D}s are said to *evoke* the responses conditioned to them. In addition, operant behavior is sometimes said to be *emitted* by an individual, whereas respondent behavior is *elicited* by a stimulus. Throughout the text, we have been consistent in the use of the terms *elicit, evoke,* and *emit.*

APPLICATIONS OF RESPONDENT CONDITIONING

NOTE 1   Applications of respondent conditioning and extinction have involved controlling allergies, immune system function, reactions to drugs, sexual arousal, nausea, blood pressure, thoughts, and emotions (especially fear and anxiety). In Chapter 28, we discuss applications of respondent principles to treat phobias. In this section, we illustrate its application to several other types of problems.

Aversion Therapy

Certain kinds of positive reinforcers can be very troublesome. People who find fattening foods overly reinforcing tend to eat too many and become overweight. Similarly, people who find cigarettes, alcohol, and other harmful commodities overly reinforcing tend to indulge in them to the detriment of their health and well-being. People who obtain sexual reinforcement in socially unacceptable ways—for instance, by seducing children—tend to endanger others by exposing them to harmful experiences and themselves by risking imprisonment and other social sanctions.

Aversion therapy was developed largely as an attempt to counteract the power of trouble-some reinforcers (those that tend to be overindulged in or that harm others). Before describing some of the methods of aversion therapy, we should caution the reader that their safe and effective use requires special expertise. These procedures, as the label *aversion therapy* implies, involve the use of aversive stimulation. As you have seen in Chapter 12, the use of aversive stimulation has potential harmful side effects. It should be used only by qualified experts.

Basically, aversion therapy involves the repeated pairing (i.e., over a number of trials) of a troublesome reinforcer with an aversive event. The rationale of aversion therapy is countercondi-tioning; that is, it is assumed that the undesirable reinforcer should then become less reinforcing because it will come to elicit a response similar to that elicited by the aversive stimulus.

For example, in the treatment of alcoholism, a client may be given the drug disulfiram fol-lowed by an alcoholic drink. Alcohol interacts with disulfiram to produce nausea and other ex-tremely unpleasant effects. Thus, the sight, smell, and taste of the drink are followed closely by a negative reaction that includes nausea. This pairing of alcohol with nausea is repeated over a number of sessions. Eventually, the alcohol itself will tend to elicit nausea, which may cause the client to avoid alcohol. How well the therapy works in any given case depends on other factors. These include whether the client continues taking the drug after termination of treatment and on operant processes operating in the natural environment, such as whether the client receives social reinforcement for subsequently choosing nonalcoholic over alcoholic beverages at parties, restaurants, and bars.

In a study in which alcoholics experienced the pairing of alcohol drinking with disulfiram but no other treatment, fewer than 1% of the clients continued to take the drug after release from a hospital (Lubetkin, Rivers, & Rosenberg, 1971). In another study, only 7% of the patients con-tinued to take disulfiram after one year (Ludwig, Levine, & Stark, 1970). An aversion-conditioning component involving disulfiram, however, proved to be a valuable addition to a program for treating alcoholics that included a multiple-component behavior therapy program with proce-dures directed to job finding, marital counseling, social and recreational programming, and a buddy system (Azrin, 1976; Azrin, Sisson, Meyers, & Godley, 1982). Similar results have been obtained for cigarette smoking. The aversion-conditioning procedure in this case involved re-quiring subjects to smoke one cigarette after another rapidly until nausea occurred. In this way, the smell and flavor of cigarettes were paired with an aversive stimulus (nausea). This procedure, called *rapid-smoking aversion therapy,* caused short-term cessation of smoking but did not show successful long-term effects (Danaher, 1977). When the rapid-smoking aversion procedure was added to a behavioral counseling program for quitting smoking, however, both short-term and long-term results were better than with the behavior counseling program alone (Tiffany, Martin, & Baker, 1986).

Aversion therapy commonly uses symbolic representations (such as pictures) of the trou-blesome reinforcers rather than the actual reinforcers themselves. This is largely a matter of con-venience. Slides, videotapes, or computer disks containing pictures of a wide variety of troublesome reinforcers can easily be stored in the therapist's office. Moreover, it is relatively easy to make new stimuli appropriate to individual cases. These stimuli can then be presented at specified intervals and for specified durations and can be associated with the onset or termination of the aversive stimulus in a precisely controlled manner. In addition, their use precludes various problems that would arise if the actual undesirable reinforcers were used during therapy. To give an extreme example, one obviously would not use real children in treating a child molester. It is generally acceptable, however, to use pictures of children in various poses, but therapists should consult the laws of the jurisdiction in which they are working before using this type of procedure.

Although aversion therapy appears to be a valuable addition to multiple-component programs for treating various problems such as excessive alcohol drinking and cigarette smoking, it is not widely used. As Wilson (1991) indicated, its limited use stems from ethical concerns about the use of aversive stimulation in treatment, the expense typically associated with the continual supervision of a therapist or in a hospital that the treatment requires, and the fact that there is a fairly high dropout rate from treatments by clients using aversion therapy.

Treatment of Chronic Constipation

An example of respondent conditioning of a desirable response is the treatment for chronic constipation developed by Quarti and Renaud (1964). Defecation, the desired response in cases of constipation, can be elicited by administering a laxative. However, reliance on such drugs to achieve regularity is not the healthiest solution because of undesirable side effects. Quarti and Renaud had their clients administer to themselves a distinctive electrical stimulus—a mild, nonpainful electric current—immediately prior to defecating. Defecation (UR) was initially elicited by a laxative (US), and then the amount of the drug was gradually decreased until defecation (CR) was elicited by the electrical stimulus (CS) alone. Then, by applying the electrical stimulus at the same time each day, several of the clients were eventually able to get rid of the electrical stimulus because the natural environment stimuli characteristically present at that time each day acquired control over the behavior of defecating. Thus, these clients achieved regularity without the continued use of artificial stimulation (also see Rovetto, 1979).

Treatment of Nocturnal Enuresis (Bed-Wetting)

NOTE 2

Another example of respondent conditioning of a desirable response is the bell-pad treatment for nocturnal enuresis (bed wetting; Scott, Barclay, & Houts, 1992). One possible explanation for nocturnal enuresis, a problem that is rather common in young children, is that pressure on the child's bladder while asleep and having to urinate does not provide sufficient stimulation to awaken the child. A device that seems to be effective for many enuretic children consists of a bell connected to a special pad under the bottom sheet on the child's bed. The apparatus is wired so that the bell sounds (US) and awakens (UR) the child as soon as the first drop of urine makes contact with the pad. Eventually, in many cases, the child will awaken before urinating because the response of waking up has been conditioned to the stimulus of pressure on the bladder. When that happens, the behavioral chain of getting up, walking to the bathroom, and urinating in the toilet should be positively reinforced. (For a review of treatments for enuresis and encopresis, see Williams, Jackson, & Friman, 2007.)

Study Questions

17. Describe three differences between operant responses and respondent responses.
18. Describe the procedures and results of both operant and respondent reinforcement.
19. Describe the procedures and results of both operant and respondent extinction.
20. In what way are CSs and S^Ds similar? In what two ways are they different?
21. For what general type of problem is aversion therapy used? Give three examples of such problems (one of which is not in this chapter).
22. Describe the basic procedure and rationale of aversion therapy. Give an example of aversion therapy.
23. Why should only competent professional practitioners use aversion therapy?

24. Describe a respondent conditioning procedure for treating constipation. Identify the US, UR, CS, and CR.

25. Describe a respondent conditioning component of a procedure for treating nocturnal enuresis. Identify the US, UR, CS, and CR.

Application Exercises

A. EXERCISE INVOLVING OTHERS

Interview a relative, friend, or acquaintance regarding something that elicits feelings of fear or nausea in that person but does not do so in most people. Determine whether that person can recall events that may have led to this unusual reaction. Are these events consistent with the description of respondent conditioning in this chapter? Discuss.

B. SELF-MODIFICATION EXERCISE

Cut a fresh lemon into four wedges. Each day, over a period of 4 days, squeeze the juice from one wedge into the same distinctive cup. Drink the juice (unsweetened) from the cup, and store the remaining wedges in the fridge for the next day's trial. Over the trials, note and describe any reactions you have that could be due to respondent conditioning as described in this chapter.

Notes and Extended Discussion

1. Pavlovian conditioning procedures may affect the functioning of our immune system. Ader and Cohen (1982) found with rats that pairing saccharine with an immune-suppressive drug established saccharine as a conditioned stimulus that elicits immune suppression. Other studies have also demonstrated classical conditioning of various aspects of immune responses in other species (Ader & Cohen, 1993; Maier, Watkins, & Fleshner, 1994; Turkkan, 1989). For a human example, consider that a standard treatment for cancer, chemotherapy, involves chemical agents that are immunosuppressive. In a study in which repeated chemotherapy was done in the same room in the same hospital setting for women suffering from ovarian cancer, the women eventually displayed immunosuppression after simply being brought to that room of the hospital prior to receiving chemotherapy (Bovjberg et al., 1990). This exciting area of research on the effects of conditioning processes on the functioning of the body's immune system is called *psychoimmunology* or *psychoneuroimmunology* (Daruna, 2004).

2. In a case study with a 15-year-old female resident of Boys' Town, Friman and Vollmer (1995) demonstrated that a urine alarm may also be used effectively with diurnal enuresis (daytime wetting). The moisture-sensitive part of the alarm system was attached to the girl's underwear and the alarm was attached unobtrusively to her outer clothing. Although the procedure was successful almost immediately, it appears that its success was based on escape and avoidance rather than respondent conditioning. This was indicated in part by the fact that whenever the alarm sounded, the child seemed embarrassed and quickly left for the bathroom. Thus, her reduced wetting may have been under the control of aversive social stimuli that occurred when the alarm sounded.

Study Questions on Notes

1. Describe the field of psychoimmunology. What is its potential applied importance?
2. Discuss how different behavior principles may be responsible for the success of a urine alarm with nocturnal and diurnal enuresis.

15

Respondent and Operant Conditioning Together

"I have to finish my term paper!"

RESPONDING TO MEET DEADLINES

Rick was a student in a second-year psychology course at the University of Manitoba. At the beginning of the course, students had been assigned a paper that was due by midterm. Like many students, Rick liked to party. A week before the paper was due, Rick still hadn't started to work on it. Five days before the due date, he started to get a little concerned. But when his friends asked him to go to a bar, he thought, "What the heck, I've got five days left." At the bar he told his friends, "Don't call me for the next 4 days. I have to finish a major paper." Although Rick started on his paper the next day, the deadline was fast approaching. As each day passed, he felt increasingly nervous about the likelihood of finishing it on time. Fortunately, after three late nights in a row, he finished the paper. Rick felt a huge weight lifted from his shoulders. ■

OPERANT–RESPONDENT INTERACTIONS

In Chapters 3–13, we talked about principles of operant conditioning. In Chapter 14, we talked about principles of respondent conditioning. This may have given you the impression that the two types of conditioning occur sequentially. However, any given experience is likely to include both respondent and operant conditioning occurring concurrently. Let's consider Rick's case. Like all of us, Rick probably had a history of being punished for failing to meet deadlines. Punishment elicits feelings of anxiety, a respondent reaction. As a consequence of prior pairings with punishment, stimuli associated with missing a deadline were likely CSs eliciting anxiety as a CR in Rick. The closer to the deadline, the stronger would be the CSs associated with missing the deadline, and hence the stronger would be the CR of anxiety. What about working on the term paper—how does it fit into this picture? The relevant responses (looking up references, reading background material, taking notes, etc.) are operant responses. As these responses occurred and Rick began to see that he would meet the deadline, the anxiety decreased. Thus, stimuli associated with the deadline likely caused Rick to feel anxious, a respondent response, and responding to meet the deadline, operant responses, were maintained by the negative reinforcement of the decrease in Rick's anxiety. While other factors were undoubtedly influencing Rick's behavior, the preceding analysis illustrates how both operant and respondent conditioning may have occurred concurrently and interacted.

Here is another example of a behavioral sequence that involves both respondent and operant conditioning. A small child runs to pet a large dog. Never having had any reason to fear dogs, the child shows no fear now. Suppose, however, that the dog playfully jumps and knocks the child down. Quite naturally, the child will begin crying because of the pain and surprise of this rough treatment. With respect to this behavioral sequence, illustrated in Figure 15–1, first consider how it is an instance of respondent conditioning. A stimulus (sight of dog) that was previously not a CS for a particular response (crying and other types of fear behavior) has come to be one because it was paired with a US (suddenly being knocked down) that did elicit that response.

FIGURE 15–1 A behavioral sequence that involves both respondent and operant conditioning, and that leads to the development of a stimulus as a conditioned punisher.

Now let's consider how that behavioral sequence involved an instance of operant conditioning. The operant response of the child approaching the dog was followed by a punisher (the child was knocked down). Consistent with the principle of punishment, the child is less likely to approach large dogs in the future. Moreover, the sight of a large dog nearby is likely to be a conditioned punisher (because of a pairing with being knocked down).

A result of this operant and respondent conditioning interaction is that it will likely cause the child to escape or avoid large dogs in the future. That is, if the child sees a large dog nearby, it will likely be a CS eliciting anxiety. If the child runs away, the anxiety is likely to decrease. Thus, running away from large dogs is likely to be maintained by negative reinforcement or escape conditioning in that the child will escape both the sight of the dog close by (a conditioned aversive stimulus) and the feelings of anxiety.

Both operant and respondent conditioning also occur in behavioral sequences involving positive reinforcers. As you can see in the behavioral sequence illustrated in Figure 15–2, the sound of the bell will become both a CS for a respondent response and an S^D for an operant response.

FIGURE 15–2 A behavioral sequence that includes both operant and respondent conditioning, and that leads to the development of a stimulus as a conditioned reinforcer.

Study Questions

1. Explain why, for most of us, an approaching deadline likely functions as a CS eliciting anxiety as a CR.
2. Describe how respondent and operant conditioning interacted to influence Rick to get his term paper done by the deadline.
3. Describe a behavior sequence that involves an aversive stimulus and that includes both respondent conditioning and operant conditioning. Diagram the respondent conditioning and the operant conditioning components.
4. Describe a behavioral sequence that involves a positive reinforcer and that includes both respondent and operant conditioning. Diagram the respondent conditioning and the operant conditioning components.

In the lead cases in Chapters 3–13, we focused on operant behavior. In the lead cases in Chapters 14 and 15, we focused on respondent behavior. However, each of the individuals in those cases likely experienced both respondent and operant conditioning in those situations. Although we, as behavior modifiers, chose to focus on one or the other, we should not lose sight of the fact that both are involved in most situations, and complete behavioral explanations sometimes necessitate consideration of both (see Pear & Eldridge, 1984). One area in which it is necessary to consider both respondent and operant conditioning is in the study of emotions.

RESPONDENT AND OPERANT COMPONENTS OF EMOTIONS

Emotions play an important role in our lives. To fully understand this important topic, we examine the role of respondent and operant conditioning in four areas: (a) the reaction that one feels during the experience of an emotion (such as the "queasiness" in the pit of one's stomach before an important job interview); (b) the way that one learns to outwardly express or disguise an emotion (such as clasping one's hands tightly to hide nervousness); (c) how one becomes aware of and describes one's emotions (for example, "I'm nervous" as opposed to "I'm angry"); and (d) some causes of emotions.

The Respondent Component: Our Feelings

The respondent component of emotions involves primarily the three major classes of respondents discussed in Chapter 14—reflexes of the digestive system, the circulatory system, and the respiratory system. These reflexes are controlled by the part of our nervous system referred to as the *autonomic nervous system*. What happens inside you in a moment of great fear? Your adrenal glands secrete adrenaline into your bloodstream, which physically arouses and mobilizes your body for action. Your heart rate increases dramatically (circulatory system). At the same time, you breathe more rapidly (respiratory system), providing an increased supply of oxygen to the blood. This oxygen surges through your body with the increased heart rate, supplying more oxygen to your muscles. You may begin to sweat, which acts as a cooling mechanism in preparation for increased energy output of the body. At the same time that these changes are occurring, you may get a queasy feeling in your stomach (digestive system). Blood vessels to the stomach and intestines constrict, and the process of digestion is interrupted, diverting blood from your internal organs to your muscles. Your mouth becomes dry as the action of the salivary glands is impeded. You might even temporarily lose bowel or bladder control (a reaction that for our primative ancestors lightened their bodies in preparation for flight and tended to distract their pursuers). These internal reactions prepare the body for fighting or fleeing. They clearly had survival value in our evolutionary history, but they may not always be useful in modern society.

The autonomic nervous system is not involved in all respondent behaviors. Some skeletal reflexes are respondent behaviors. In studies of unconditioned reflexes of newborn infants, loss of support, loud sounds, or pushes are USs that elicit the URs of a sudden catching of breath, a clutching or grasping response, puckering of lips, and crying that we label as *fear*. Hampering an infant's movements is a US that elicits the URs of crying, screaming, and body stiffening that we label as *anger*. Tickling, gentle rocking, and patting appear to be USs for the URs of smiling, gurgling, and cooing, labeled as *happiness*. Cross-cultural evidence suggests that these reflexive reactions may be universal (Ekman, 1972). We learn to describe these physiological components of our emotions as our *feelings*.

Although the exact number of inherited emotional reflexes must await further research, there is no doubt about the importance of respondent conditioning for attaching physiological components of emotions to new stimuli. Nearly every organ and gland controlled by the autonomic nervous system is susceptible to respondent conditioning (Airapetyantz & Bykov, 1966). When experimenters have demonstrated respondent conditioning of emotions with humans, they have often relied on the visible signs of the physiological changes to demonstrate that learning has occurred. Consider a classic experiment by John B. Watson and Rosalie Rayner (1920). They were interested in demonstrating that fears could be learned through Pavlovian procedures. They conducted their experiment with a normal 11-month-old infant called Albert in the report. He was in a hospital where the study was done because his mother was a wet-nurse there. During preliminary observations, it was demonstrated that Albert was not afraid of a variety of items that were placed near him while he was happily playing on a rug on the floor. The experimenters also demonstrated that the noise from striking a steel box with a hammer would elicit a fear reaction. They introduced a white rat to which Albert had previously shown no fear, and while Albert was watching the rat closely, one of the experimenters banged the bar with the hammer just behind Albert's head. The loud noise caused a startle reaction, crying, and other fearful behavior in Albert. Over two separate sessions approximately 1 week apart and after a total of seven pairings of the loud noises with the white rat, Albert showed a strong fear reaction to the rat. Whenever the rat appeared, Albert cried, trembled, and showed the facial expression for fear. When other items—namely, a rabbit, a dog, and a seal fur coat—that bore some similarity with the white rat were introduced, Albert showed fear reactions to them. Since he had not shown fear toward these items before the loud noise had been paired with the white rat, it appeared that the fear established to the white rat had spread to these items as well. Unfortunately, Albert left the hospital before Watson and Rayner had a chance to extinguish the fear. However, Mary Cover Jones (1924) followed up some of Watson's suggestions and demonstrated the elimination of a child's fear of white rabbits with a counterconditioning procedure that involved pairing a white rabbit with food. It would be considered unethical today to subject infants to aversive stimuli for experimental purposes. Procedural questions about the Watson and Rayner study have also been raised (Harris, 1979). Nevertheless, the finding that fears are influenced by reflexive learning is well established. (For a discussion of how contemporary learning principles and research can account for the cause of anxiety disorders, see Mineka & Zinbarg, 2006.)

The feelings associated with other emotions are also influenced by respondent conditioning. At a family reunion, for example, family members experience many happy moments. A few weeks later, when viewing the photos taken at the reunion, the pictures will likely be CSs eliciting "happy" feelings. But there is more to emotions than the autonomic responses that we feel. Let's see how operant conditioning is also involved.

Operant Components: Our Actions, Descriptions, and Awareness

When you experience an emotion-causing event, your body responds with an immediate physiological reaction and accompanying facial expression. Then what happens? That depends on your operant learning experiences. In a situation that causes anger, one person might clench her fists and swear (see Figure 15–3) while another person in that same situation might breathe heavily and walk away. Albert initially showed the respondent components of fear by crying and trembling (as well as the internal reaction mentioned earlier in this chapter). However, he also showed operant fear responses. When the white rat was presented, Albert crawled away as fast as he could. Because the operant component of emotions depends on each individual's conditioning history, these secondary displays of emotion vary from person to person and from culture to culture. Fans at a sporting event in North America are likely to show their displeasure for unsportsmanlike play by booing while fans in Europe do so by whistling. We learn to display our emotions in ways that have been modeled and operantly reinforced in the past.

Operant conditioning is also involved when we are taught to be aware of and describe our emotions. As we grow up, people around us teach us to label our emotions. Depending on our behavior, moms and dads ask questions such as, "Why are you so angry?" or "Aren't you having fun?" or "How are you feeling?" From such experiences, we learn about "being angry," "feeling happy," and "feeling sad." By age 9, most children have learned to recognize a large number of emotional expressions in themselves and others (Izard, 1991). Nevertheless, many emotions are not easily described or defined. We can account for this difficulty to some extent by considering the multiple sources of control over the naming of behavior that we describe as emotional. Suppose you see a girl's brother grab her toy train and the girl run after him screaming. You might conclude that the girl is angry. The next day, when coming out of your house, you see the same girl screaming and running after her brother. You might again conclude that she is angry. However, in the second instance, the children could simply be enjoying a game of tag. Thus, when labeling emotions, we don't always have access to the emotion-causing events, the inner

FIGURE 15–3 Withholding reinforcers following a previously reinforced response can cause anger. What are some operant and respondent components of anger?

feelings, and the relevant operant behaviors. This contributes to inconsistencies in the way that we talk about emotions.

Some Causes of Emotions

Presentation and withdrawal of reinforcers and presentation and withdrawal of aversive stimuli produce at least four major emotions. Presentation of reinforcers produces the emotion called *joy*. Getting an A on an exam, receiving a compliment, cashing your paycheck, and watching a funny movie all involve the presentation of positive reinforcers. Withholding or withdrawing reinforcers produces the emotion called *anger*. All of us have experienced such anger-causing events as putting our money in a vending machine that takes it but fails to produce the goods, being kept waiting in the doctor's office, using a pen that stops writing in the middle of a quiz, and having a ticket line close just before you get to the window to buy a ticket. The presentation of aversive stimuli produces the emotion called *anxiety*. Approaching scary-looking strangers in a dark alley, seeing a car drive directly toward you at a high speed, or hearing a dog bark right behind you are all likely to cause you to feel anxious. Finally, withdrawal of aversive stimuli produces an emotion that is called *relief*. When a woman receives the results from a test of a lump on her breast or a man receives the results of an assessment of an enlarged prostate, each is likely to feel relief if she or he is told that the problem is not cancer.

Emotions can occur on a continuum from very mild to very strong. Presentation of reinforcers, for example, can cause emotions ranging from mild pleasure to ecstasy. Withdrawal of reinforcers can cause emotions ranging from mild annoyance to rage. Presentation of aversive events can cause emotions ranging from mild apprehension to stark terror. And the effects of withdrawal of aversive stimuli might range from mild relief to intense relief verging on an emotional collapse. Other emotions might represent a mixture of some of these basic emotions (see, e.g., Martin & Osborne, 1993).

To summarize, many of our emotions are caused by either the presentation or withdrawal of reinforcers or aversive stimuli. Our emotions have three important characteristics: (a) the autonomic reaction that you feel during the experience of an emotion (typically accompanied by visible signs, such as frowns or smiles), which is influenced by respondent conditioning; (b) the way that you learn to express an emotion overtly (such as shouting, jumping up and down), which is influenced by operant conditioning; and (c) the way that you become aware of and describe your emotions, which is also influenced by operant conditioning. In Chapters 27 and 28, we discuss examples of how respondent and operant conditioning have been used to change troublesome emotions.

Study Questions

5. Describe several physiological activities that we experience in a moment of great fear.
6. Describe unconditioned reflexes that appear to characterize emotions of fear, anger, and joy.
7. In the experiment with Albert, what was the US? the UR? the CS? the CR?
8. Cross-cultural studies of emotions suggest that emotions are both universal and culture specific. How can we explain this apparent contradiction?
9. Describe the procedures that are major causes for each of the emotions of joy, anger, anxiety, and relief.
10. In a sentence for each, summarize three important characteristics that make up our emotions, and name the type of conditioning involved in each characteristic.

RESPONDENT AND OPERANT COMPONENTS OF THINKING

Like emotions, much of what we call "thinking" in everyday language involves both respondent and operant conditioning.

A Respondent Component: Our Imagery

Try the following exercise. Close your eyes and imagine that you are sitting on a lawn chair on a warm summer day. You look up and see the clear blue sky. Imagine a few white fluffy clouds drifting slowly along. Chances are that you will be able to form a clear image of the blue sky and the white fluffy clouds—so clear that you can almost see the colors. Thus, one type of thinking appears to consist of imagining in response to words—imagining so vividly that it can sometimes seem like the real thing. This probably comes about through respondent condition- **NOTE 1** ing. If you actually look at a clear blue sky, the color elicits activity in the visual system much as food elicited salivation in Pavlov's dogs. As you grew up, you experienced many trials in which the words "blue sky" were paired with actually looking at and seeing a blue sky. As a consequence, when you close your eyes and imagine that you are looking at a blue sky with white fluffy clouds, the words likely elicit activity in the visual part of your brain so that you experience the behavior of "seeing" the actual scene. This has been referred to as *conditioned seeing* (Skinner, 1953). In a broader sense, we might think of conditioned sensing. That is, just as we acquire conditioned seeing through experience, we also acquire conditioned hearing, conditioned smelling, and conditioned feeling. Consider the example described by Martin and Osborne (1993) in which an individual experienced numerous passionate sexual encounters with a partner who consistently used a very distinctive perfume. One day when someone wearing that same perfume walked past that individual in a department store, he immediately imagined seeing the partner (conditioned seeing), felt "tingly" all over (conditioned feeling), and even imagined that he heard the partner's voice (conditioned hearing). This sort of thing is also a part of what goes on during fantasy (Malott & Whaley, 1983). To experience a fantasy or to read or listen to a story is, in some sense, to be there. It's as though you can see what the people in the story see, feel what they feel, and hear what they hear. We are able to do this because of many instances of conditioned sensing. Our long histories of associating words with actual sights, sounds, smells, and feelings enable us to experience the scenes that an author's words describe. The internal actions that occur when we're thinking are real—we're really seeing, feeling, or hearing when we respond to the words (Malott & Whaley; Pear, 2001, pp. 108–109). This is not to say that everyone experiences the same conditioned sensory responses; they are undoubtedly unique to each individual.

An Operant Component: Our Self-Talk

Imaging (conditioned seeing) and other types of conditioned sensing constitute one type of thinking. Another type of thinking is self-directed verbal behavior, or self-talk. As we indicated in earlier chapters, our verbal behavior is taught to us by others through operant conditioning. We learn to speak because of effective consequences for doing so. As children, we learn to ask for such things as our favorite foods and the opportunity to watch our favorite cartoons. We also learn to say things that please our parents and other adults. Much of our thinking is verbal behavior. We learn to think out loud as children because it helps us to perform tasks more efficiently (Roberts, 1979). When children first start attending school, they often say rules out loud to themselves to adjust to difficult tasks (Roberts & Tharp, 1980). When they are about 5 or 6 years old, however, they also begin to engage in subvocal speech in the sense that their self-talk begins to occur below the spoken level (Vygotsky, 1978).

We learn to talk silently to ourselves at a very early age largely because we encounter punishers when we think out loud (Skinner, 1957). For example, teachers in school request children to think quietly because thinking out loud disturbs the other students. Naturally distressed reactions from others teach us to keep certain thoughts to ourselves. When you are introduced to the hostess at a party, your first reaction might be, "Wow, what an ugly dress!" But you probably won't say it out loud; instead, you'll just "say it to yourself" or "think" it. (Other reasons for silent self-talk are that it requires less effort and can occur more rapidly than overt self-talk.)

PRIVATE THOUGHTS AND FEELINGS: MORE RESPONDENT–OPERANT INTERACTIONS

Much of what we call "thinking" and "feeling" in everyday life goes on at a level that is not observable by others. As indicated in Chapter 1, we refer to such activity as *covert* or *private*. Although private behavior is more difficult to "get at," behavior modifiers assume that in other respects it is the same as public behavior; that is, that the principles and procedures of operant and respondent conditioning apply to private behavior.

Often an instance of what we would refer to as private behavior includes both respondent and operant components of thinking and emotions. To illustrate, consider the following example (described by Martin & Osborne, 1993). One of the authors grew up on a farm just outside of a small town. He attended school in the town, and it was very important to him to be accepted by the town children. One of the town kids, Wilf, frequently teased him about being a "farmer." "Hey, gang," Wilf would say, "Here comes Garry the farmer. Hey, Garry, do you have cow dung on your boots?" Now imagine that it's Saturday afternoon and Garry and his family are getting ready to go to town. Garry is going to the Saturday afternoon matinee at the Roxy Theatre with the rest of the gang, which is a big deal because they didn't have TV on the farm. Garry says to himself, "I wonder if Wilf will be there" (operant thinking). Garry can picture Wilf clearly (conditioned seeing) and can imagine Wilf teasing him about being a farmer (both operant thinking and conditioned hearing). Thoughts of the aversive experience elicit unpleasant feelings (a reflexively learned response). Garry reacts by paying special attention to his appearance in the hope that appearing "citified" will give Wilf nothing to say.

Consider some additional examples of private behavior that involve respondent and operant components of thinking and emotions. Imagine a lineman in football preparing to go after the opposing quarterback just before the ball is snapped. The lineman thinks "I'm all over him! I'll tear his head off! This guy is history!" That kind of self-talk (operant thinking) is likely to help the lineman feel aggressive (a respondent emotion). Or consider a sprinter who thinks "explode" while waiting in the blocks for the starter's pistol to sound; or a figure skater who says to herself during her program, "Graceful, feel the music" to help create the proper mood for the music and the choreography. In instances like these, the operant self-talk serves as a CS to elicit certain feelings—the respondent component of emotions.

You can see that, contrary to the impression given by many introductory psychology texts, behavior modifiers do not ignore what goes on inside a person. Although it is true that the great majority of studies in behavior modification have been concerned with observable behavior, many behavior modifiers have taken an interest in dealing with private behavior. As illustrated by the work of Joseph Cautela and his colleagues, thinking and feeling as private behaviors are proper subject matter for behavior modifiers and can be readily dealt with in terms of operant and respondent conditioning principles (e.g., Cautela & Kearney, 1993). In Chapters 27 and 28, we'll describe behavioral strategies for overcoming troublesome thoughts and feelings.

Study Questions

11. Describe an example of respondent thinking that is not in this chapter.
12. Describe an example of operant thinking that is not in this chapter.
13. When behavior modifiers speak of private behavior, to what are they referring?
14. What basic assumption do the authors of this text make about public and private behavior?
15. Describe a behavior not described in this chapter that illustrates how operant thinking might function as a CS to elicit the respondent component of an emotion.
16. Discuss whether behavior modifiers deny the existence and importance of thoughts and feelings.

Application Exercises

A. EXERCISE INVOLVING OTHERS

Pick an emotion (e.g., anger), and observe the operant displays of that emotion in two people you know. Are their operant components of that emotion similar or different?

B. SELF-MODIFICATION EXERCISE

Consider an emotion that you frequently experience. Describe how experiencing that emotion includes both respondent and operant responses.

Note and Extended Discussion

1. A number of behavioral techniques rely on imagery. In Chapter 28, we describe how Wolpe used imagery in systematic desensitization. Another procedure involving imagery is called *covert sensitization* (Cautella, 1966), which is essentially a form of aversion therapy (see Chapter 14) in which a troublesome reinforcer is paired repeatedly with an aversive stimulus. Recall that aversion therapy is based on counterconditioning—it is assumed that the troublesome reinforcer will become less reinforcing because it will come to elicit a response similar to that elicited by the aversive stimulus. In covert sensitization, the client imagines both the troublesome reinforcer and the aversive stimulus. This procedure is so named because the pairing of the stimuli occurs only in the client's imagination (in other words, it is covert) and the anticipated result of this covert pairing process is that the undesirable reinforcer becomes aversive (i.e., the client becomes sensitized to it).

The procedure has been used with clients who wish to give up smoking, as described by Irey (1972). During a particular trial, the client might be instructed to vividly imagine lighting a cigarette after dinner in a restaurant, inhaling, and then suddenly becoming so violently ill that he vomits all over his hands, his clothes, the tablecloth, and the other people at the table. He continues to vomit and then, when his stomach is empty, to gag while the other people in the restaurant stare at him in disgust. In short, the scene is made extremely realistic and aversive. When the client feels the maximum degree of aversiveness, he is instructed to imagine turning away from his cigarette and immediately beginning to feel better. The scene concludes with the client washing up in the bathroom without his cigarettes and feeling tremendous relief. Research on covert sensitization can be found in Cautela and Kearney (1993).

Study Questions on Note

1. What is the rationale of covert sensitization?
2. Describe in some detail a plausible example of covert sensitization.

16

Transferring Behavior to New Settings and Making It Last: Generality of Behavioral Change

"Hi, there. I have a nice surprise for you in my car."

TEACHING STAN TO PROTECT HIMSELF[1]

During recess time, 4-year-old Stan was playing with a toy near the edge of his preschool playground, unaware that a stranger was observing him. No teacher was in sight. Gradually, the stranger approached until he was standing beside Stan.

"Hi, there," said the stranger, "What's your name?"

"Stan," the boy replied.

"Nice day, isn't it, Stan?"

The stranger engaged Stan in small talk. Then, casting his eyes around the school yard, the stranger casually asked, "Stan, how would you like to go for a walk with me?"

The stranger seemed friendly and Stan was used to taking directions from adults. He stood up and approached the stranger. Just then, a teacher appeared and the stranger quickly moved away.

An attempted child abduction? Not exactly. The stranger was actually an assistant in an experiment designed to study a method of teaching self-protection to young children, and Stan was being tested to determine his suitability for the experiment. He and two other children (Patti and John), who also appeared susceptible to the lures often used by child molesters, were included in the experiment. The children were tested several times to verify that they would go with a

---

[1] This case is based on an experiment by Poche, Brouwer, and Swearingen (1981).

stranger who approached them using any of several kinds of lures (e.g., "Your teacher said it was all right for you to come with me" and "I have a nice surprise in my car. Would you like to come and see it?"). Then training began. Two adult trainers acted out a scene in which one trainer approached the other and used one of the lures. The other trainer responded with "No, I have to go ask my teacher," and ran toward the school building. The child was then instructed to respond in the same way as the second trainer to the lure of the first trainer and, contingent on doing so, was provided with social reinforcement (e.g., praise) that was occasionally followed with material and activity reinforcement (e.g., stickers, playing on the swings).

Responses were trained to one lure per day. When a child consistently responded correctly to the first lure, responding was trained to a second lure, and then to a third lure. In addition to the lures being varied in this manner, the exact location of each session on the school grounds was also varied by approximately 75 feet. After training was completed, each child was tested in a community setting to determine whether the response established during training would be performed in a novel setting. All three children responded correctly to the lures in that setting. After 12 weeks, Stan and Patti were tested again in the community setting. Stan continued to respond perfectly, whereas Patti made the correct verbal response but stayed in the vicinity of the stranger. ■

GENERALITY

A behavior change is said to have *generality* when the trained behavior transfers from the training situation to the natural environment, when training leads to the development of new behavior that has not been specifically trained, or when the trained behavior is maintained in the natural environment over time (Baer, Wolf, & Risley, 1968). Before examining strategies for programming for generality of behavior change in these three ways, it will be helpful to review stimulus generalization (which we introduced in Chapter 8) and response generalization. In the following discussion, we will be referring to operant behavior unless otherwise indicated.

Stimulus Generalization

Stimulus generalization refers to the *procedure* of reinforcing a response in the presence of a stimulus or situation, and the *effect* of the response becoming more probable in the presence of another stimulus or situation. As discussed in Chapter 8, stimulus generalization occurs for several reasons. First, the more physically similar two stimuli are, the more stimulus generalization will occur between them (e.g., two similar-looking berries). This is an inherited (unlearned) characteristic. Second, stimulus generalization might occur from one stimulus to another because we have learned that the two stimuli are members of a common-element stimulus class—a set of stimuli that have some physical characteristic in common (e.g., a house with green shutters and a girl with green socks). Third, stimulus generalization might occur from one stimulus to another because we have learned that the stimuli are members of an equivalence class—a set of completely dissimilar stimuli that an individual has learned to group or match together (e.g., the words *mutt* and *pooch* and a picture of a dog). Such stimuli are functionally equivalent in that they control the same behavior and whatever change occurs to the behavior controlled by one will have a similar effect on the behavior controlled by the others. Both common-element stimulus classes and stimulus equivalence classes are called *concepts*.

The first sentence in the preceding paragraph describes stimulus generalization of operant conditioning. Respondent stimulus generalization happens when a respondent CR occurs to a new stimulus; it is discussed later in this chapter.

Response Generalization

Response generalization occurs when a behavior becomes more probable as a result of the reinforcement of another behavior. Like stimulus generalization, response generalization occurs for several reasons.

UNLEARNED RESPONSE GENERALIZATION DUE TO CONSIDERABLE PHYSICAL SIMILARITY OF RESPONSES   The more physically similar two responses are, the more unlearned response generalization will occur between them. If you learn a forehand shot in racquetball, chances are that you would be able to perform a forehand shot in squash or tennis. The responses involved are very similar. Likewise, you will probably find roller blading easier to learn if you have already learned to ice skate because the responses involved in the two activities are similar.

LEARNED RESPONSE GENERALIZATION BASED ON MINIMAL PHYSICAL SIMILARITY OF RESPONSES   Just as there are large classes of stimuli that share a common characteristic although they differ in many other characteristics, there are also widely different responses that share a common characteristic. Learned response generalization can occur within such response classes. For example, a child who has learned to add *s* to the ends of words pertaining to more than one object or event may show response generalization even when it is grammatically incorrect (e.g., saying "foots" instead of "feet" while looking at a picture of two feet). In Stan's case, if a stranger tried to lure Stan, and he said, "No, I have to ask my mother" instead of "my teacher," this would be an example of learned response generalization because the two sentences are different but have a common grammatical structure and share some of the same words.

LEARNED RESPONSE GENERALIZATION DUE TO FUNCTIONALLY EQUIVALENT RESPONSES
Different responses that produce the same consequences are called *functionally equivalent responses*. You might show response generalization because you have learned functionally equivalent responses to a stimulus. If you are asked to start a fire, you might obtain and strike a match, flip a cigarette lighter, place a stick in an existing fire to start a new fire, or perhaps even rub two sticks together. As another example, a child who learns to "be honest" might tell the truth, return valued articles left or dropped by others, and refrain from copying another student's answers. All of these responses are functionally equivalent in the sense that they are likely to bring praise from various members of the child's community.

Study Questions

1. Define *stimulus generalization* and give an example that is not in this chapter.
2. Explain the difference between stimulus generalization and stimulus discrimination. Describe examples illustrating the difference.
3. Distinguish between unlearned stimulus generalization and learned stimulus generalization involving a common-element stimulus class. Give an example of each.
4. What is a primary distinction between stimulus generalization involving a common-element stimulus class and stimulus generalization involving an equivalence class?
5. Define or describe *unlearned response generalization* due to physical similarity of responses, and give an example.
6. Define or describe *learned response generalization* based on minimal physical similarity of responses, and give an example.
7. Describe an example of learned response generalization due to functionally equivalent responses.

FACTORS INFLUENCING THE EFFECTIVENESS OF PROGRAMMING GENERALITY OF OPERANT BEHAVIOR

In discussing generality, we distinguish two situations: (a) the *training* situation in which the behavior is initially strengthened and (b) the *target* situation—a situation in which we want generality to occur. The target situation is usually, but not necessarily, the natural environment. Because programming for generality is somewhat different for operant and respondent behavior, we shall consider each separately. *Programming for generality* of operant behavior change includes strategies of programming for stimulus generalization, response generalization, and behavior maintenance.

Programming Operant Stimulus Generalization

NOTE 1

The initial occurrence of stimulus generalization depends critically on the physical similarity between the training and target situations. The more similar the situations are, the more stimulus generalization and, hence, the less discrimination there will be between them.

TRAIN IN THE TARGET SITUATION   Thus, the first effort of the behavior modifier attempting to program stimulus generalization should be to make the final stages of the training situation similar to the target situation in as many ways as possible. Other things being equal, the best way in which to do this is to train in the target situation itself. Suppose that a parent wants to teach a child to count out the correct amount of change for purchasing a bag of candy. The ideal place to do this would be in a store that sells candy. (Of course, some preliminary training in a more controlled setting might be necessary.)

VARY THE TRAINING CONDITIONS   This might be done by conducting training sessions with relatively little control over the stimuli in the presence of which correct responses are reinforced. If behaviors are brought under the control of a wider variety of stimuli during training, then the probability of some of those stimuli being present in the target situation increases. Thus, in the lead case for this chapter, no attempt was made to control background stimuli, such as playground and traffic noise, as might be done in more basic research.

PROGRAM COMMON STIMULI   A third tactic is to program common stimuli deliberately by developing the behavior to specific stimuli that are present in both the training and target settings. For example, Walker and Buckley (1972) described a program in which social and academic classroom behaviors were taught to children in a remedial classroom. Stimulus generalization to the regular academic classroom was ensured by using the same academic materials (i.e., common stimuli) in both classrooms.

A useful strategy for programming common stimuli is to bring the desired behavior under the control of instructions or rules that an individual can rehearse in novel situations (Guevremont, Osnes, & Stokes, 1986; Stokes & Osnes, 1986). Stan might have been taught the rule, "If someone I don't know approaches me in the schoolyard, I should run into the school building." Rehearsal of an appropriate rule in novel settings might lead to desired behavior even though the stimuli in the novel settings are physically dissimilar to the stimuli that were present during training. For example, if Stan is in his yard and a stranger approaches him, he might run into his house as a result of saying the rule. (Rule control over behavior is discussed further in Chapter 17.)

When an individual is taught to emit desired behavior to a few specific stimuli in the training situation and then to take those stimuli to target situations, the individual might be said to be using a self-mediated physical or verbal stimulus. Martin (2007) described how a young figure skater used this strategy to transfer skilled skating performance from practices to competitions. The young skater was able to land her double axel consistently at practices but often missed it at competitions because the jump was rushed in the excitement of the moment. To solve the problem, she inserted into her routine the word *easy* (said very slowly and stretched out) just before stepping onto her takeoff foot as a prompt to control the speed of the takeoff. Using this key word consistently at practices and then at competitions improved her execution during competitions. (Also see Stokes & Osnes, 1989.)

TRAIN SUFFICIENT STIMULUS EXEMPLARS   A fourth tactic, which Stokes and Baer (1977) considered to be one of the most valuable for programming generality, is called *training sufficient stimulus exemplars*. This technique increases the probability of appropriate generalization to new stimuli and situations because of the large number and variety of stimuli and situations to which training has occurred. Thus, Stan's training occurred in several different places in the schoolyard and with several different lures.

Horner and colleagues described a variation of training sufficient stimulus exemplars that they referred to as *general case programming* (Horner, Sprague, & Wilcox, 1982). With this approach, the teacher begins by identifying the range of relevant stimulus situations to which a learner will be expected to respond and the response variations that might be required. Then, during training, the learner's behavior and acceptable variations are brought under the control of samples of the range of relevant stimuli. Sprague and Horner (1984) used this approach to teach adolescents with developmental disabilities to use vending machines by introducing them to a variety of different machines and the responses needed to use them. This approach was very effective in producing generalization to enable the learners to subsequently operate any available vending machine with which they came in contact.

Programming Operant Response Generalization

It appears that there has been less concern in the literature for programming response generalization than for programming stimulus generalization. Nevertheless, there are some strategies for programming response generalization, two of which are described next.

TRAIN SUFFICIENT RESPONSE EXEMPLARS   A strategy for programming response generalization is similar to that of training sufficient stimulus exemplars to establish stimulus generalization. This is referred to as *training sufficient response exemplars* (Stokes & Baer, 1977). Guess, Sailor, Rutherford, and Baer (1968) taught a girl with a developmental disability to use plural nouns correctly in speech with this technique. With prompting and reinforcement, they first NOTE 2 taught the girl to name objects correctly in the singular and the plural when presented with one object (e.g., cup) and two objects (e.g., cups). They continued in this way until, after a number of exemplars of the correct singular and plural labels had been taught, the girl appropriately named new objects in the plural even though only the singular labels for these objects had been taught. Thus, the girl showed response generalization.

VARY THE ACCEPTABLE RESPONSES DURING TRAINING   Another strategy is to vary the responses that are acceptable during training. For example, in developing creativity, Goetz and Baer (1973) reinforced children during block building in a nursery school setting for any response that was different from prior block-building responses. This tactic led to an increase in the children's creative block building.

CAPITALIZE ON BEHAVIORAL MOMENTUM   A third strategy for programming response generalization is to capitalize on *behavioral momentum,* which is a momentary increase in the probability of some response occurring as a result of one or more functionally equivalent responses having been reinforced. Consider the problem of overcoming noncompliance with children. Compliance with instructions can include a variety of functionally equivalent responses. Thus, to increase the probability that a child will follow instructions that the child normally does not follow, it is often effective first to give instructions that the child is likely to follow and to reinforce compliance with those instructions. If the instructions that the child is less likely to follow are then given soon after this, the chances are greatly increased that the child will follow them (Mace & Belfiore, 1990; Mace et al., 1988; Singer, Singer, & Horner, 1987).

NOTE 3

Study Questions

8. When discussing programming of generality of behavior, what do we mean by the training situation versus the target situation?
9. List the three aspects of programming for behavioral generality. Describe an example of each aspect.
10. Briefly describe how the experiment to teach self-protection skills to children demonstrated behavioral generality.
11. Briefly list four tactics for programming operant stimulus generalization. Give an example of each.
12. Which of the strategies for programming operant stimulus generalization capitalizes on stimulus generalization due to physical similarity? Justify your choice.
13. How might the teaching of a rule facilitate operant stimulus generalization? State the general factor for programming for generalization that seems to be operating, and illustrate with an example.
14. Describe the example of a self-generated mediator of generalization involving the figure skater.
15. Describe the generalization strategy referred to as *general case programming.* Describe an example.
16. Briefly list three tactics for programming operant response generalization. Describe an example of each.
17. What is the meaning of the term *behavioral momentum*? Describe an example.

Programming Operant Behavior Maintenance

It is one thing to program stimulus generalization to a new setting or response generalization for new behaviors. It's another thing for a therapeutic behavioral change to last in those new settings or with those new behaviors. Maintenance depends critically on whether the behavior will continue to be reinforced. There are four general approaches to the problem of achieving behavior maintenance.

BEHAVIORAL TRAPPING: ALLOW NATURAL CONTINGENCIES OF REINFORCEMENT TO TAKE EFFECT   A **behavioral trap** is a contingency in which a behavior that has been developed by programmed reinforcers is "trapped" (i.e., maintained) by natural reinforcers. (Baer & Wolf, 1970; Kohler & Greenwood, 1986). Using a behavioral trap can be a very effective way to program behavior maintenance. This approach requires the behavior modifier to realistically identify contingencies in the natural environment and then to tailor the target behavior so that it will be trapped by those contingencies. Talking is an obvious example of behavior that is heavily reinforced in most social environments. After speech has been established in a training situation, it may continue unabated in the natural environment because of the natural contingencies of reinforcement for it there. Indeed, it often seems necessary only to establish vocal imitation and a few object-naming responses for the natural contingencies of reinforcement to take over and develop functional speech behavior. Behavioral trapping might be involved in overcoming a child's shyness. Playing with other children is a behavior that might gradually be shaped in a shy child. Once this behavior is strongly established, however, the behavior modifier probably will not have to worry about reinforcing it further. The other children will take care of that in the course of their play, for, indeed, that is what social play is all about. See Figure 16–1 for another example of behavioral trapping.

FIGURE 16–1 An example of behavioral trapping.

CHANGE THE BEHAVIOR OF PEOPLE IN THE NATURAL ENVIRONMENT   A second approach to the problem of achieving lasting generality is usually more difficult than the first. It involves actually changing the behavior of people in the target situation so that they will maintain a learner's behavior that has generalized from the training situation. In following this approach, it is necessary to work with people in the target situation—parents, teachers, neighbors, and others who have contact with the target behavior. The behavior modifier must teach these individuals how to reinforce the learner's behavior if it is desirable or how to extinguish it if it is undesirable. The behavior modifier must also occasionally reinforce the appropriate behavior of these individuals—at least until there is contact with the learner's improved target behavior, which will then ideally reinforce their continued application of the appropriate procedures.

As an example of this second approach, consider the case of a child who has shown a high frequency of tantrumming. Perhaps this is the child's sole means of gaining attention and other reinforcers in the home. There is little doubt that more desirable behaviors could be established in a training situation, but such behaviors would not be maintained in the home situation unless the contingencies operating there were changed. A behavior modifier called in on this case might therefore adopt the following plan. In a training situation designed to teach the child to play with toys rather than to tantrum, the behavior modifier would first adjust the desired behavior to an appropriate schedule—for instance, VI/LH with infrequent reinforcement because it will not be practical for the parents to give extremely frequent reinforcement in the home environment. Having accomplished this, the behavior modifier would then show the mother how to keep accurate records of the child's desirable and undesirable behavior. Next the mother, with the help and prompting of the behavior modifier, would frequently reinforce the child for playing with toys in the living room. Gradually, the mother would decrease the frequency of reinforcement to have more time for activities that did not involve the child. She could use a kitchen timer to remind herself to reinforce the child. Throughout this procedure, the behavior modifier would frequently reinforce the mother for appropriately managing and recording the child's behavior. Then the behavior modifier would fade out of the situation by visiting less and less frequently to check the mother's records. However, if the program deteriorated, the behavior modifier would temporarily stop the fading process and spend enough time in the training situation to correct matters. Ideally, the mother's behavior of appropriately reinforcing the target behavior would eventually be maintained by the child's good play behavior and decreased whining, crying, and tantrumming.

USE INTERMITTENT SCHEDULES OF REINFORCEMENT IN THE TARGET SITUATION   After a behavior has generalized to a target situation, it may be desirable to reinforce the behavior deliberately in the target situation on an intermittent schedule for at least a few reinforced trials. The intermittent schedule should make that behavior more persistent in the target situation and thereby increase the probability of the behavior lasting until it can come under the control of natural reinforcers.

GIVE THE CONTROL TO THE INDIVIDUAL   An area within behavior modification concerns helping individuals to apply behavior modification to their own behavior. This area, which has been referred to as *self-management, self-modification,* or *behavioral self-control,* has produced many books containing easy-to-follow "how-to" procedures that help individuals to manage their own behavior. This area is discussed more fully in Chapter 26. Giving control to the individual to maintain behavior in the target situation might occur in one of two major ways. First, it might be possible to teach an individual to assess and record instances of his or her own generalized behavior and apply a specific reinforcement procedure to that behavior. Second, as Stokes and Baer (1977) suggested, it might be possible to teach an individual to *recruit a natural community of reinforcement* to maintain the generalized responding. For example, Hildebrand, Martin, Furer, and Hazen (1990) taught workers with developmental disabilities in a sheltered workshop to meet a productivity goal and then to call a staff member's attention to their good work. This led to increased reinforcement for the workers from the staff, which in turn helped to maintain the workers' higher level of productivity.

PROGRAMMING GENERALITY OF RESPONDENT BEHAVIOR

As indicated previously, programming for generality of operant behavior involves strategies to bring about stimulus generalization, response generalization, and behavior maintenance. When dealing with respondent behavior, stimulus generalization is also important. When extinguishing a phobia, for example, one would not want to decrease the fear to only one specific stimulus (see Figure 16–2). For many treatments involving respondent conditioning, however, we are typically concerned primarily with maintaining the conditioned reflex over time. To see why this is so, let's review a couple of examples of respondent conditioning from Chapter 14. In that chapter, the results of a respondent conditioning program for constipation was a conditioned reflex in which a particular time of day became a CS causing a bowel movement as a CR. In each case, having the adults experience a bowel movement upon arising in the morning was desirable. Would they have wanted stimulus generalization to occur so that bowel movements were elicited at other times during the day? No, that would have been very inconvenient. Was it important to program response generalization so that a wide variety of bowel movements were elicited by the CS of a specific time of day? No, that would not have been adaptive.

Let's consider another example from Chapter 14 in which, after conditioning, pressure on a child's bladder in the middle of the night became a CS causing awakening as a CR so that the child could subsequently go to the bathroom to urinate rather than wetting the bed. Would it have been desirable for stimulus generalization to occur so that only a slight amount of pressure would cause awakening? No—the amount of pressure just before having to urinate was the ideal CS, and that's what was trained. Was it necessary to program response generalization of awakening? No, as long as awakening occurred at the right time, the manner in which it occurred did not seem to be important. As these examples illustrate, programming stimulus and response generalization is often not of concern in behavior management programs involving conditioned reflexes.

It is important, however, that desirable conditioned reflexes be maintained over time. If a CS is presented without further pairings with a US, the CS will lose its ability to elicit the CR. Thus, in programs involving respondent conditioning, it is sometimes necessary to periodically pair the CS with the US so that the CS will continue to elicit the desired response over time.

PITFALLS OF GENERALITY

Pitfall Type 1

A behavior learned in a situation in which it is appropriate may show stimulus generalization to a situation in which it is inappropriate. A conspicuous example of this can often be seen among individuals with developmental disabilities involving greetings and displays of affection. Of course, it is highly desirable for these behaviors to occur under appropriate circumstances, but when an individual walks up to and hugs a total stranger, the results can be less than favorable. The solution to this problem is to teach the individual to discriminate between situations in

FIGURE 16–2   An example of a failure to program stimulus generalization of a respondent behavior.

which different forms of greetings and expressions of affection are appropriate and situations in which they are inappropriate.

Another example of inappropriate stimulus generalization of a desirable behavior may be the destructive competitiveness demonstrated frequently by some individuals and occasionally by all of us. Such behavior may stem in part from the strong reinforcement given in our culture for winning in sports. As the saying goes, "It may be true that wars have been won on the playing fields of Eton, but they have also been started there."

A second variety of Pitfall Type 1 is the stimulus generalization of an undesirable behavior from the situation in which it developed to a new situation for which it is also undesirable. Suppose that an overly protective grandparent while supervising a grandchild who is learning how to walk provides a great deal of attention each time the child falls. As a result, falling increases in frequency. When the child returns to the parents, the excessive falling might generalize to their presence as well.

A third variety of Pitfall Type 1 involves response generalization, the strengthening of an undesirable response that can lead to an increased frequency of similar undesirable responses. An example can be seen when a child is reinforced for emitting a swearword, perhaps by an adult who is amused by this "cute" behavior, and that child emits subsequent variations of that word.

Pitfall Type 5

(To review this pitfall, see p. 48.) Sometimes individuals fail to program for desirable generalization. An illustration of this can be seen in the study habits of students who cram the night before an examination. They memorize certain verbal chains in response to certain prompts and questions. What they frequently fail to consider is the importance of bringing their knowledge of the material under broader stimulus control than just one or two questions. Many people have had the same experience with learning a second language. Both authors took a second language during 4 years of high school but at the end of that time were still incapable of speaking the second language. They had a certain repertoire for answering questions on exams, translating English articles into the second language, and translating articles in the second language into English, but these repertoires had not been brought under the stimulus control of a typical conversational setting.

Another example of lack of programming for stimulus generalization of desirable behaviors can be seen in the interaction between some parents and their children. In various social situations, such as restaurants, some parents do not present the same stimuli to their children, or provide the same contingencies of reinforcement, that they present at mealtimes in the home situation. Consequently, the children do not generalize table manners and good behaviors that occur at home to the restaurant or other social settings. It is not uncommon to hear a parent lament, "I thought I taught you how to be a good child, and now look at you." We hope that after reading this book and performing the study questions and study exercises, the same parents would do a much better job of programming stimulus generalization. If not, you would hear us lament, "I thought I taught you how to be a good behavior modifier, and now look at you!"

The pitfalls for programming maintenance of behavior change concerning schedules of reinforcement were described in Chapters 6 and 7.

GUIDELINES FOR PROGRAMMING GENERALITY OF OPERANT BEHAVIOR

To ensure stimulus and response generalization from the training situation to the natural environment and to ensure behavior maintenance, the behavior modifier should observe the following rules as closely as possible:

1. Choose target behaviors that are clearly useful to the learner because these are the behaviors that are most likely to be reinforced in the natural environment.

2. Teach the target behavior in a situation that is as similar as possible to the environment in which you want the behavior to occur.

3. Vary the training conditions to maximally sample relevant stimulus dimensions for transfer to other situations and to reinforce various forms of the desirable behavior.

4. Establish the target behavior successively in as many situations as is feasible, starting with the easiest and progressing to the most difficult.

5. Program common stimuli (such as rules) that might facilitate transfer to novel environments.

6. Vary the acceptable responses in the training settings.

7. Gradually reduce the frequency of reinforcement in the training situation until it is less than that occurring in the natural environment.

8. When changing to a new situation, increase the frequency of reinforcement in that situation to offset the tendency of the learner to discriminate the new situation from the training situation.

9. Ensure sufficient reinforcement for maintaining the target behavior in the natural environment. This rule requires especially close attention in the early stages of transferring the target behavior from the training situation to the natural environment. Add reinforcement as necessary, including reinforcement to those (such as parents and teachers) who are responsible for maintaining the target behavior in the natural environment, and then decrease this reinforcement slowly enough to prevent the target behavior from deteriorating.

Study Questions

18. Define *behavioral trapping,* and describe an example.

19. Briefly describe four tactics for programming operant behavior maintenance. Give an example of each.

20. Briefly explain why considerations regarding generality of respondent behavior differ from those regarding operant behavior.

21. Give two examples of Pitfall Type 1 involving stimulus generalization, one of which involves generalization of a desirable behavior to an inappropriate situation and the other involves generalization of an undesirable behavior.

22. Give an example of a Pitfall Type 1 involving response generalization.

23. State Pitfall Type 5 (see Chapter 3, p. 48).

24. Describe an example of Pitfall Type 5 that involves failure to program for desirable generalization.

Application Exercises

A. EXERCISE INVOLVING OTHERS

Choose one of the cases described in the previous chapters in which there was no effort to program generality. Outline a specific plausible program for producing generality in that case.

B. SELF-MODIFICATION EXERCISES

1. Describe a recent situation in which you generalized in a desirable way. Clearly identify the behavior, the training situation (in which the behavior was initially reinforced), and the test situation (to which the behavior generalized).

2. Describe a recent situation in which you generalized in an undesirable way (in other words, the outcome was undesirable). Again, identify the behavior, training situation, and test situation.

3. Consider the behavior deficit for which you outlined a shaping program at the end of Chapter 10.

Assuming that your shaping program will be successful, discuss what you might do to program generality. (See the factors influencing the effectiveness of generality that were discussed in this chapter.)

Notes and Extended Discussion

1. In a study by Welch and Pear (1980), objects, pictures of the objects, and photographs of the objects were compared as training stimuli for naming responses in four children with severe developmental disabilities in a special training room. It was found that three of the four children displayed considerably more generalization to the objects in their natural environment when they were trained with the objects rather than the pictures or photographs of the objects. The fourth child, who was also the most proficient linguistically, displayed substantial generalization regardless of the type of training stimulus used. A follow-up study by Salmon, Pear, and Kuhn (1986) indicates that training with objects also produces more generalization to untrained objects in the same stimulus class than does training with pictures. The results suggest that parents and teachers of children with severe developmental disabilities should use objects as training stimuli as much as possible whenever generalization to those objects is desired.

2. This instance of response generalization (as is true with the examples given on p. 193) is somewhat more complex than our straightforward definition given at the beginning of this chapter. It does appear, in this example, that the reinforcement of a specific response has increased the probability of similar responses. The new form of the response (the plural for a new object), however, is also occurring to a new stimulus (the plurality of the new object itself). Thus, stimulus generalization is also involved. For a discussion of difficulties in defining response generalization, see the *Journal of Organizational Behavior Management*, 2001, 21(4).

3. The term *behavioral momentum* has come to have a dual meaning (Pear, 2001, p. 172; Plaud & Gaither, 1996). As stated in the body of this text, it refers to a momentary increase of the probability of some response occurring as the result of one or more functionally equivalent responses having been reinforced. But it also refers to a theory about the persistence of behavior in a given situation when there is a disruption to that behavior. According to the theory, the more reinforcement that has occurred in a given situation, the more resistant to disruption that response will be in that situation (see, e.g., Mace, McCurdy, & Quigley, 1990). This fact has at least two practical implications: (a) As we pointed out in Chapter 6, a response that has been intermittently reinforced will take longer to be decreased by extinction than will a response that has been continuously reinforced. However, according to the theory, this is only because the change from CRF to extinction is more disruptive than is the change from intermittent reinforcement to extinction. Thus, according to the theory, a response that has been continuously reinforced will be more resistant to other forms of disruption (Nevin, 1992). (b) One way to decrease a response is to present reinforcement noncontingently (i.e., independent of responding) (Tucker, Sigafoos, & Bushell, 1998). However, this method of decreasing a response results in more reinforcement in the situation,

thus making the response more resistant to disruption, according to the theory. Although the theory of behavioral momentum is still controversial and requires further testing, support for it is growing (Nevin & Grace, 2000).

Study Questions on Notes

1. What rule for programming stimulus generalization is exemplified by the study in which object and picture names were taught to children with developmental disabilities? Explain.
2. Describe the two ways in which the term *behavioral momentum* has been used in the behavioral literature.
3. Explain at least one practical implication of behavioral momentum with regard to response disruption.

PART III

CAPITALIZING ON ANTECEDENT CONTROL PROCEDURES

17 Antecedent Control: Rules and Goals

"What if I don't skate well?"

HELPING SUSAN TO SKATE WELL[1]

Susan, a 12-year-old figure skater competing in the novice category, was standing beside her sport psychologist and coach just off the ice surface, waiting for her turn to skate her short program in the Provincial Figure Skating Championship. Showing signs of extreme nervousness, Susan turned to her sport psychologist and expressed her concerns: "I hope I don't fall on my double axel. I hope I don't come in last. What if I don't skate well?" Her sport psychologist could see that Susan's negative self-talk was causing her to feel anxious, and her anxiety was likely to interfere with her skating well. But there was no time to go through a lengthy behavior modification program. The psychologist said to Susan, "I want you to repeat after me, and focus on what it is that you are saying: 'I've landed all of my jumps in practice and I can land them all here.'" Susan repeated the words. "If I take it one step at a time, and if I focus on the things that I do when I'm skating well at practices, I will skate well here." Again, Susan repeated the words. "I'll smile, have fun, and play to the judges." After Susan repeated the last statement, her psychologist asked her to practice a relaxation technique called deep center breathing, in which she breathed low down in her abdomen, and quietly said "r-e-l-a-x" each time she exhaled. The combination of the positive self-talk and the deep center breathing strategy helped Susan to feel considerably calmer and more confident. At that moment, the skater before her finished skating her program. Shortly thereafter Susan stepped on the ice, skated to her start position, and performed well. ∎

---

[1] This case is based on Martin and Toogood (1997).

ANTECEDENT CONTROL

Because our behavior of responding to various antecedent stimuli (people, places, words, smells, sounds, etc.) has been reinforced, those stimuli exert control over our behavior whenever they occur. Before designing a lengthy behavior modification program involving strategies like shaping and chaining, it's important to ask, "Can I capitalize on existing forms of stimulus control?" Susan's sport psychologist did not go through a lengthy shaping process to modify her self-statements. Instead, the psychologist capitalized on her reinforcement history of responding to instructions. Treatment packages that focus on the manipulation of antecedent stimuli—also called *antecedents*—fall into the categories of rules, goals, modeling, physical guidance, situational inducement, and motivation. We discuss the first two categories in this chapter and the others in the next two chapters.

RULES

As described in Chapter 8, a **rule** describes a *situation* in which a *behavior* will lead to a *consequence*. Speaking loosely, it is a statement that a specific behavior will "pay off" in a particular situation. When we were infants, rules were meaningless. As we grew older, we learned that following rules often led to rewards (e.g., "If you eat all your vegetables, you can have dessert.") or enabled us to avoid punishers (e.g., "If you're not quiet, I'll send you to your room."). Thus, a rule can function as an S^D—a cue that emitting the behavior specified by the rule will lead to the reinforcer identified in the rule, or a cue that not following the rule will lead to a punisher (Skinner, 1969; Vaughan, 1989). (As described in Chapter 19, rules can also function as motivating operations.)

Sometimes rules clearly identify reinforcers or punishers associated with following the rules, as illustrated in the foregoing examples. In other cases, consequences are implied. A parent saying to a child in an excited voice, "Wow! Look at that!" looking in the indicated direction will likely enable the child to see something interesting. Reinforcers are also implied for rules stated in the form of advice. For example, the advice "You should get a good education" typically implies that doing so will lead to a well-paying job. On the other hand, rules given in the form of a command or a threat imply that noncompliance will be punished. For example, the command "Don't touch that vase" implies that touching it will lead to an unpleasantness such as a reprimand.

Rules that do not identify all three aspects of a contingency of reinforcement are referred to as *partial rules*. The examples of partial rules in the preceding paragraph focused on the behavior. Other partial rules identify the antecedent (school zone sign) while the behavior (drive slowly) and the consequence (avoid hitting a child) are implied. In other instances, partial rules identify the consequences (e.g., "98% payout") while the antecedent ("at this casino") and the behavior (put money in the slot machines) are implied. Because of our various learning experiences, partial rules also control our behavior.

Contingency-Shaped Versus Rule-Governed Behavior

While attending church with his parents, Bobby whispers funny comments to his sister. She ignores him and his mom gives him a firm look. In the future, Bobby is less likely to whisper comments in church. Now suppose that Bobby whispers funny comments to his teammates on the pee-wee hockey team while his coach is trying to explain how to execute a play. Bobby's teammates laugh, and his whispering is strengthened in that setting. In these examples, we would refer to Bobby's whispering as **contingency-shaped behavior**—behavior that develops because of its immediate consequences. Suppose at the start of the next practice, Bobby's coach says, "Bobby, if you listen carefully and don't whisper when I'm talking to the team, we'll have an extra 5 minutes of scrimmage at the end of practice." During the practice, Bobby frequently repeats the rule, makes it through the practice without whispering, and earns the reinforcer. In this example, listening attentively without whispering while the coach is talking to the team is **rule-governed behavior**—behavior controlled by the statement of a rule.

Contingency-shaped behavior involves immediate consequences and is typically strengthened gradually through "trial and error"—or, to be more precise, through immediate reinforcement and nonreinforcement. Bobby's whispering initially came under the control of his teammates as S^Ds through several trials involving immediate reinforcement for whispering and nonreinforcement for other behavior. His whispering in church gradually decreased in the presence of his sister and parents as S^Δs after several trials of extinction in their presence. Rule-governed behavior, in contrast, often involves delayed consequences and frequently leads to immediate behavior change. When Bobby's coach gave him a rule concerning not whispering at practices, Bobby's behavior improved immediately. It did not take a few trials to show evidence of stimulus control, even though the reinforcer for following the rule was delayed until the end of practice.

Knowledge of rule-governed behavior enables us to more fully explain some applications we presented earlier that involved indirect effects of reinforcers. Recall the case of Fernando in Chapter 3. When Fernando was told that he would be given a slip of paper that could be exchanged for 2 pesos contingent upon arriving at work on time, he was never again late for work throughout the duration of the study. This was not an example of the direct effects of reinforcement because the reinforcer of 2 pesos occurred well after the behavior of leaving earlier for work. Instead, it was likely Fernando's rehearsal of a rule (e.g., "If I leave earlier, I will arrive on time and I will earn 2 extra pesos") that controlled his behavior of leaving half an hour earlier in the morning.

Often behavior that might seem to be strengthened by the direct effects of reinforcement might result, at least partly, from the existence of rule-governed behavior. For example, the child who has just cleaned her room and is told, "Good girl for cleaning your room," might tend to engage in this behavior more frequently. The stimulus "Good girl for cleaning your room" seems to be acting as a reinforcer in this instance. But the child has also been given a rule—namely, "If I clean my room, I'll be a good girl"—which tends to exert rule-governed control over the room-cleaning behavior in the future quite apart from the reinforcing effect of praise. This is one reason why we would not use "Good girl for cleaning your room" as a reinforcer for the child doing her homework.

Study Questions

1. Define *rule* and give an example that is not in this chapter.
2. Describe an example of a rule that was stated by the figure skater just before competing.
3. A teacher of a second-grade class complains to you, "When I tell the children to stay at their desks and work, they never listen to me." Describe the contingencies that are likely operating with respect to that rule given by the teacher to the kids in the class.

4. Describe an example of a partial rule that is not in this chapter. What aspects of the three-term contingency does your partial rule identify? What are the missing parts that the partial rule implied ?
5. Define *contingency-shaped behavior,* and give an example.
6. Define *rule-governed behavior,* and give an example.
7. Describe two common differences between rule-governed and contingency-shaped behavior.
8. Give an example of an indirect effect of a reinforcer for your behavior.

When Rules Are Especially Helpful

In several chapters, we have asserted that behavior modification programs should always include instruction in the form of rules, even with individuals with limited verbal skills. And in Chapter 30, we discuss ethical reasons why behavior modification programs should be clearly explained to all clients. However, including rules in a behavior modification program in some specific situations with verbal people is especially effective (Baldwin & Baldwin, 1998; Skinner, 1969, 1974).

WHEN RAPID BEHAVIOR CHANGE IS DESIRABLE   Correct use of rules can often produce behavior change much more rapidly than shaping, chaining, or trial and error. The sport psychologist helping Susan at the figure skating competition essentially gave her a rule: "If I focus on the things that I think about when I'm skating well at a practice, then I'll land all the elements in my program, just like I do at practice." Rehearsing the rule helped Susan focus on the cues that normally enabled her to land her jumps. The rule might also have functioned as a CS to elicit the relaxed feelings that were typically experienced at practices and that might have been part of the contextual stimuli that controlled good skating.

WHEN CONSEQUENCES ARE DELAYED   Suppose that a parent wants to encourage a child to study for an hour or so each evening during the week. A suitable reinforcer might be allowing the child to stay up late on the weekend to watch a movie. However, movie watching on Friday night is long delayed from studying for an hour on Monday. By adding the rule, "If you study for an hour each night this week, you can watch the late movie on Friday night," the parent has increased the chances of the delayed reinforcer having an effect on the desired behavior.

WHEN NATURAL REINFORCERS ARE HIGHLY INTERMITTENT   Suppose that salespeople in a department store are working on a commission during times when sales are slow. Making a sale is immediately reinforced by the fact that it gives the salesperson who makes it more money. However, the salespeople must approach many customers before a sale is made. In other words, the schedule of reinforcement is very lean, so ratio strain might occur. The store manager might increase their persistence by encouraging the salespeople to rehearse the rule, "Be persistent! The very next customer might mean a sale."

WHEN BEHAVIOR WILL LEAD TO IMMEDIATE AND SEVERE PUNISHMENT   Rules can help people learn appropriate behavior when learning "the hard way" could be costly. For example, surprising though it might seem, some students are genuinely unaware that copying parts of a textbook word for word on a term paper without acknowledging the source is unacceptable. All students should be taught, long before they ever reach college, the rule, "Copying from a source without giving credit is plagiarism and can lead to serious academic penalty."

Why Rules Control Our Behavior

It's easy to understand why people would learn to follow rules that describe direct-acting consequences. Following the rule "Try this new flavor of ice cream; I think you'll like it" will be reinforced immediately by the taste of the ice cream. Failure to follow the rule "Move back from the
campfire or you might get burned" could lead to an immediate punisher. But why do we follow
rules that identify very delayed consequences? There are several possibilities.

First, although the reinforcer identified in a rule might be delayed for an individual, other
people might provide other immediate consequences if the individual follows or does not follow
the rule. In the example of the parent who provides the rule, "If you study for an hour each night
this week, you can watch the late movie on Friday night," the parent might also say, immediately
after an instance of studying on Monday night, "Good for you. Keep it up and you'll be able to
stay up late on Friday."

Second, an individual might follow a rule and then immediately make reinforcing statements. In the case of Fernando in Chapter 3, after complying with the rule of leaving half an hour
earlier for work in the morning, Fernando might have speculated about what he might buy with
the extra pesos that he would earn. (Self-reinforcement is discussed further in Chapter 26.)
Alternatively, failure to comply with a rule might lead to immediate self-punishment.

A third possibility is that our operant–respondent interactions (see Chapter 15) give us a reinforcement history so that following rules is automatically strengthened and failure to follow rules is
automatically punished. Suppose you give yourself the rule, "I'd better start studying my behavior
modification text now or I'll fail the exam tomorrow." Perhaps because of your history of being
punished for failing to meet deadlines, such a statement might increase the aversiveness of stimuli
associated with not studying for the exam, which would elicit some anxiety. When you comply with
the rule, your anxiety decreases and your rule following is maintained by escape conditioning. In
everyday language, rehearsal of the deadline causes you to feel anxious, but responding to the rule to
meet the deadline then makes you feel a lot better (Malott, 1989). Of course, whether such automatic
consequences will continue to influence your rule following will depend on the extent to which you
continue to experience punishment for noncompliance with rules and failure to meet deadlines.

Although we have given many examples illustrating how rules generally enhance the
development and maintenance of behavior, it is important to realize that exceptions to this generalization exist. Rules introduce extra stimuli and responses that, in some circumstances, can have
the net effect of interfering with contingency-shaped behavior. A person trying to verbalize and
follow rules might, in these circumstances, become somewhat like the proverbial centipede that
tied itself in knots trying to think about how it walked.

Effective and Ineffective Rules

We have said that a rule is a cue that behaving as specified in the rule will lead to a reinforcer or
escape from or avoidance of an aversive stimulus. But all rules are not created equal. Some rules
are more likely to be followed than others. Let's look at five conditions that affect the likelihood
of rule-following behavior.

SPECIFIC VERSUS VAGUE DESCRIPTIONS OF BEHAVIOR   A rule that describes behavior
specifically is more likely to be followed than a rule that describes a behavior vaguely. Telling
young figure skaters, for example, that they will become better skaters if they work hard at practices is less effective than telling them, "If you complete at least 60 jumps and spins during each
45-minute practice, you will become a better skater."

SPECIFIC VERSUS VAGUE DESCRIPTIONS OF CIRCUMSTANCES   A rule that describes specific circumstances in which the behavior should occur is more likely to be followed than a rule that describes the circumstances vaguely or not at all. Telling a young child, for example, "Remember to say 'please'" is less effective than telling the child, "Remember to say 'please' when you ask for something."

PROBABLE VERSUS IMPROBABLE CONSEQUENCES   Rules are likely to be followed if they identify behavior for which the consequences are highly probable even though they might be delayed. Suppose that a parent tells a teenage child, "Mow the lawn on Monday and I'll give you $20 on Saturday." Assuming that the parent always follows up on such rules, we can then assume that it is highly likely that the teenager will mow the lawn on Monday. If the teenager does so, receiving the $20 the following Saturday is a certainty. Conversely, rules are likely to be ineffective if they describe low-probability outcomes for behavior even if those outcomes are immediate when they occur (Malott, 1989, 1992). To illustrate this point, most people know that wearing a lifejacket when canoeing could save their lives. And most people know that wearing a helmet when bike riding could prevent brain damage from a serious accident. So, why do many people go canoeing without a lifejacket or bike riding without a helmet? One reason (that does not necessarily involve rules) might be that desirable safety behavior in such instances leads to fairly immediate punishers (e.g., the lifejacket and the helmet are hot and uncomfortable). Another reason is that such rules (i.e., to wear a lifejacket while canoeing and a helmet while bike riding) involve low-probability consequences. Many people have gone canoeing without ever upsetting the canoe. And having never experienced a serious bicycle accident, the bike rider thinks that an accident that would cause brain damage is unlikely. We are not suggesting that rules should not be used in such situations. The bike rider should be encouraged to rehearse before getting on a bike, "If I wear my helmet, I reduce the possibility of serious injury." However, for a rule to be effective when it describes improbable or low-frequency consequences, it might need to be supplemented by other behavior management strategies, such as modeling (see Chapter 18), self-monitoring (see Chapter 26), or behavioral contracting (see Chapter 26).

SIZEABLE CONSEQUENCES VERSUS SMALL BUT CUMULATIVELY SIGNIFICANT CONSEQUENCES   Rules that describe sizeable consequences are likely to be effective. In the lawn-mowing example just cited, $20 was a sizeable consequence for that teenager. However, a rule is less likely to be effective if the consequence is small after each instance of following the rule. Suppose an individual resolves, "I'm going to stop eating desserts" and "I'm going to exercise three times a week." Why are such rules often ineffective? One reason that does not necessarily involve rules is that there are direct-acting consequences that support behavior that is incompatible with following the rule. Eating a dessert is immediately reinforced by the delicious taste. And exercising often involves fairly immediate punishers (boredom, discomfort, and tiredness). Another reason that such rules are ineffective is that the supportive consequences of a single instance of following such a rule are too small to be noticeable and are only cumulatively significant (Malott, 1989, 1992). (Other possibilities are discussed in Chapter 26.) That is, it's not the excess weight from the single extra dessert that's a problem; it's the increased weight that occurs when you have the extra dessert on many occasions (see Figure 17–1). Likewise, a single instance of exercising won't produce observable benefits. It's the accumulation of the benefits of exercising on many occasions that is eventually noticeable. Rules that describe small consequences that are harmful or beneficial only after they have accumulated, and therefore only after a long delay, are likely to be ineffective unless complemented by some of the self-management strategies described in Chapter 26.

FIGURE 17–1 Why are some rules (such as resisting extra dessert) so difficult to follow?

DEADLINES VERSUS NO DEADLINES   Suppose that a preschool teacher says to a child, "If you put all the toys away, I'll bring you a treat next week." Is the child likely to put the toys away for such a delayed reinforcer? What if the teacher says to the child, "If you put all the toys away *right now,* I'll bring you a treat next week." Would specifying "right now" make a difference? Surprisingly, it would. Braam and Malott (1990) found that with 4-year-old children, rules to perform behavior with no deadline and a one-week delay of the reinforcer were relatively ineffective while rules to perform behavior *with a deadline* and a one-week delay of a reinforcer were quite effective. Very early in life we learn that meeting deadlines is likely to be reinforced and failing to meet them leads to unpleasantness.

To summarize, rules that describe *specific circumstances* and *deadlines* for *specific behavior* that will lead to *sizeable* and *probable outcomes* are often effective even when the outcomes **NOTE 1** are delayed. Conversely, rules that describe the behavior and the circumstances for it vaguely, that do not identify a deadline for the behavior, and that lead to small or improbable consequences for the behavior are often weak or ineffective.

Guidelines for Using Rules Effectively

Here are some general guidelines for the effective use of rules.

1. The rules should be within the understanding of the individual to whom they are applied.
2. Rules should clearly identify:
   a. the circumstances in which the behavior should occur
   b. the specific behavior in which the individual is to engage
   c. a deadline for performing the behavior
   d. the specific consequences involved in complying with the rule, and/or
   e. the specific consequences for not complying with the rule.

3. Rules should describe probable and sizeable outcomes rather than improbable and small outcomes. (Rules that describe improbable and/or small consequences might need to be supplemented by some of the procedures described in Chapter 26.)

4. Complex rules should be broken into easy-to-follow steps.

5. Rules should be delivered in a pleasant, courteous, unemotional manner.

6. Fading of rules should be used as necessary to allow other stimuli that are present to take control of the behavior.

Study Questions

9. Using examples, briefly describe four situations in which the addition of rules to a behavior modification program might be especially helpful.

10. Describe, using examples, three explanations for why we might follow rules that identify very delayed consequences.

11. Explain (in terms of contextual stimulus control, as described in Note 3 of Chapter 8) why the tone of voice of someone giving you instructions might determine whether you will follow the instructions.

12. How might we explain the behavior of someone who fails to wear a helmet when riding a bicycle even though that person knows that wearing a helmet could prevent brain damage from an accident?

13. How might we account for the relative ineffectiveness of such rules as "I'm going to stop eating sweets"?

14. In a couple of sentences, distinguish between rules that are often effective versus rules that are often weak or ineffective in controlling behavior.

GOALS

A *goal* is a level of performance that an individual or group attempts to achieve. In industrial and organizational settings, goal-setting programs have led to improved performance in such areas as truck loading, safety behavior, customer service, and typing (Locke & Latham, 1990). In sports, goal-setting programs have led to improvements in such areas as laps completed in running, foul shots in basketball, serves in tennis, and accuracy in archery (Gould, 1998).

In everyday language, goals are considered to be motivational (discussed further in Chapter 19). They are seen as committing an individual to the effort and dedication that are necessary to achieve success; they give a sense of purpose and help to keep the person on target. From a behavioral perspective, a goal is a rule. If a basketball player says, "I'll go to the gym and practice shooting foul shots until I can make 10 in a row," that player has identified the circumstances (at the gym), the behavior (practicing foul shots), and the reinforcer (making 10 in a row, plus the implied reinforcer of scoring a higher percentage of foul shots in games). And like the use of rules, goal setting is often applied to influence individuals to improve performance when reinforcers are delayed (e.g., a bonus in a work setting is received well after the work has been completed) or are immediate but highly intermittent (e.g., the basketball player initially making only 1 of every 30 foul shots).

Although goal setting might be viewed as making and using a rule, the circumstances in which one might apply goal setting are often somewhat different than those described in the previous section. We previously suggested that it is possible to capitalize on stimulus control by using rules to bring about instant behavior change. The sport psychologist, for example, was concerned with helping Susan "on the spot" rather than giving her a long-term objective to work toward. Goal setting, in contrast, is often used to influence individuals to work toward some objective over a period of time or during a number of practice opportunities. We wouldn't expect the basketball player to immediately meet the goal of making 10 foul shots in a row. Nevertheless, setting a practice goal in that type of situation is likely to lead to faster performance improvement than if the player just practiced shooting foul shots without a particular goal in mind.

Effective and Ineffective Goal Setting

The efficacy of goal setting as a performance improvement strategy is well established provided that a number of conditions are met (Gould, 1998). We might distinguish two types of goals: (a) goals for behavior and (b) goals for the products or outcomes of behavior. Examples of the former are eating a healthier diet and exercising more. An example of the latter is losing 10 pounds.

SPECIFIC GOALS ARE MORE EFFECTIVE THAN VAGUE GOALS   Rather than a goal of having a better relationship, a couple might agree to spend half an hour of quality time together or to tell each other daily at least three things that they appreciate about their relationship. It would be more effective for an individual considering dieting to have as a goal to lose 10 pounds rather than saying that the goal is to lose some weight. Similarly, saying that you want to save a specific percentage of your take-home pay would likely be more effective than the goal of wanting to save some money.

GOALS WITH RESPECT TO LEARNING SPECIFIC SKILLS SHOULD INCLUDE MASTERY CRITERIA   A **mastery criterion** is a specific guideline for performing a skill so that if the guideline is met, the skill is likely to be mastered. This means that an individual who has met a mastery criterion for a skill has learned it well enough to perform it correctly upon demand or when it is necessary to do so. Examples of mastery criteria for learning athletic skills might include making six 4-foot putts in a row in golf, hitting 10 backhands in a row down the line in tennis, or making 10 foul shots in a row in basketball. Examples of mastery criteria for academic skills are reciting the periodic table or a Shakespearean sonnet three times in a row without making a mistake.

GOALS SHOULD IDENTIFY THE CIRCUMSTANCES UNDER WHICH THE DESIRABLE BEHAVIOR SHOULD OCCUR   A goal for a wrestler to practice takedowns is somewhat vague. A goal to practice arm-drag take downs until three in a row occur adds a quantity dimension but still does not indicate the circumstances under which the behavior should occur. A goal to practice arm-drag takedowns until three in a row occur on an opponent offering moderate resistance identifies the circumstances surrounding the performance. Similarly, a goal to give a talk to an audience of 30 strangers is different from a goal to give the same talk to two friends.

REALISTIC, CHALLENGING GOALS ARE MORE EFFECTIVE THAN DO-YOUR-BEST GOALS
The phrase *just do your best* is often said by coaches to young athletes just before a competition, by parents to their children who are about to perform in a concert, by teachers to students before taking tests, and by employers to employees doing their jobs. A number of studies, however, have demonstrated that do-your-best goals are not nearly as effective as are specific goals for improving performance. Perhaps do-your-best goals are ineffective because they are vague. Or perhaps individuals who are instructed to simply do your best set relatively easy goals, and, as Locke and Latham suggested (1990), difficult or challenging goals might produce better performance.

From a behavioral perspective, an instructor who identifies a specific goal for a learner is more likely to consistently provide reinforcement for meeting the goal than is an instructor who simply gives the learner a do-your-best goal. The reason for this is that the instructor and the learner might disagree as to whether or not the learner did his or her best. After all, the judgment of whether a goal is easy or difficult is somewhat subjective because our information about someone's physiological and behavioral capabilities is always incomplete. The accuracy of that judgment might be maximized, however, by considering the individual's current level of performance and the range of performance on similar tasks by others of similar ability.

PUBLIC GOALS ARE MORE EFFECTIVE THAN PRIVATE GOALS Consider the following experiment with three groups of students who were all given the same booklet of material to study. The first group of students participated in a public goal-setting program. Each student set a goal concerning the amount of time he or she would study and the score that he or she hoped to receive on a test to be given at the end of the program. These students announced their goals to other members of their group. The second group of students practiced private goal setting. They were treated the same as the first group except that they kept their goals to themselves. The third group of students was not asked to set any goals; it was a control group. These students were simply given the material to study for the same amount of time as the first group with the knowledge that they would receive a test at the end of the experiment. The results: The public goal-setting group scored an average of 17 percentage points higher on the test than either of the other two groups, who performed at about the same level (Hayes et al., 1985). Similar results on the effects of public goals versus private goals were found by Seigts, Meertens, and Kok (1997). Hayes and colleagues theorized that setting a public goal results in a public standard against which performance can be evaluated and that it also implies social consequences for achieving or not achieving the goal.

Although goals that someone else knows about might be more likely to be met than private goals that nobody knows about, the public component must be practiced with some caution. Suppose that you recommend goal setting as a part of a behavior modification program to help someone exercise consistently. If you recommend that the exerciser share the goals with another person, that person should be someone who is likely to prompt the exerciser with gentle reminders when goals are not met and who will offer encouragement when progress is satisfactory. That person should not be someone who will send the exerciser on a heavy guilt trip for not meeting the goals. (This issue is discussed further in Chapter 30.)

GOAL SETTING IS MORE EFFECTIVE IF DEADLINES ARE INCLUDED Each of us has a history of positive reinforcement for meeting various deadlines and for encountering aversive consequences when we don't meet them. Capitalizing on this history increases the effectiveness of goal setting. Suppose that you set a goal for yourself during the coming year of emailing friends and relatives more often. You are more likely to meet that goal if you resolve that by February 1, you'll have emailed a specific number of individuals, by March 1 you'll have emailed so many more, and so on.

GOAL SETTING PLUS FEEDBACK IS MORE EFFECTIVE THAN GOAL SETTING ALONE Goals are more likely to be met if feedback indicates the degree of progress toward the goal. One way of providing feedback is to chart the progress being made. As discussed in Chapter 20, individuals who chart their progress toward a goal are likely to find improvements in the chart to be reinforcing. Another way to provide feedback is to break long-term goals into a number of short-term goals. Suppose that a couple decides to repaint their entire house, inside and out. Short-term goals might include painting the bedroom by the end of February, then the living room by the end of March, and so on.

GOAL SETTING IS MOST EFFECTIVE WHEN INDIVIDUALS ARE COMMITTED TO THE GOALS

Goals are likely to be effective only if the individuals involved have a continuing commitment to them. By *commitment,* we mean statements or actions by the learner indicating that the goal is important, the learner will work toward it, and the learner recognizes the benefits of doing so. One way of gaining commitment is to have the learner participate in the goal-setting process. Research indicates that self-selected goals are at least as effective as those that are externally imposed (Fellner & Sulzer-Azaroff, 1984).

Guidelines for Goal Setting

Many individuals attempt to capitalize on goal setting with New Year's resolutions. However, this is not necessarily the best time for setting goals due to competing festive activities. In addition, the stimuli present on January 1 are likely to be quite different from stimuli present during other times of the year. This would be unlikely to result in good generalization. Also, if goal setting occurs only on New Year's Day, then by definition, it occurs only once a year, whereas goal setting is more effective when it can be practiced a number of times throughout the year. Moreover, there are clearly ways of setting goals that are more effective than the kinds of New Year's resolutions that people typically make. If your goals are vague or do-your-best goals with no deadlines or timelines for meeting them and without a feedback mechanism for monitoring progress, they are not likely to have much effect on behavior. If, however, you practice goal setting according to the following guidelines, your goals are more likely to be effective in modifying your behavior.

1. Set goals that are specific, realistic, and challenging.
2. Identify the specific behaviors and the circumstances in which they should occur to meet the goals.
3. Be clear about the specific consequences that might occur for meeting or not meeting the goal.
4. Break long-term goals into several short-term goals.
5. If the goal is complex, devise an action plan for meeting it.
6. Set deadlines for goal attainment.
7. Ensure that individuals involved are committed to the goals.
8. Encourage the learner to share the goals with a friendly supporter.
9. Design a system for monitoring progress toward goals.
10. Provide positive feedback as progress toward goals is achieved.

Study Questions

15. In general, what do we mean by the word *goal*? Describe an example of a behavioral goal that is not in this chapter. Describe an example of an outcome goal that is not in this chapter.
16. Is goal setting different from using rules? Discuss.
17. Briefly list six of the eight conditions that summarize effective versus ineffective goal setting as a behavior modification strategy.

18. What is a mastery criterion? Describe an example that is not in this chapter.
19. From a behavioral perspective, why might realistic, challenging goals be more effective than do-your-best goals?
20. From a behavioral perspective, why might public goals be more effective than private goals?
21. What do the authors mean by *commitment* in the context of goal setting?

Application Exercises

A. EXERCISES INVOLVING OTHERS

1. Choose a behavior that a parent might want to change in a child so that there is no obvious immediate, natural reinforcer for that behavior. Describe how the parent, following the guidelines for using rules effectively, might capitalize on rule-governed behavior to bring about a desired outcome.
2. Consider a practice setting for a youth sport with which you are familiar. Describe how a coach might use goal setting to influence desirable practice behavior of an athlete in that setting. Indicate how the coach has followed the guidelines for goal setting.

B. SELF-MODIFICATION EXERCISES

1. Consider the guidelines for using rules effectively. Now consider a behavior that you could physically perform. Identify a rule with respect to that behavior, and structure the contingencies according to the guidelines for using rules effectively.
2. Identify a behavior of yours that was probably contingency shaped. It might be something like riding a bicycle, balancing on one foot, eating with chopsticks, whistling a short tune, or flipping flapjacks. Devise a measure (e.g., number of errors) of how well you perform the behavior, and using the measure, record your performance of the behavior on several trials. Next write out a set of rules for performing the behavior, and again perform and record the behavior on several occasions, carefully following the rules. According to your measure, how did the addition of rules affect your performance? Interpret your finding.

Note and Extended Discussion

1. For persons who suffer from insomnia, one option is to treat the problem with drugs. Another option is behavioral sleep therapy, which relies on rule-governed behavior (Smith et al., 2002). Behavioral sleep therapy includes the following rules: (1) Exercise regularly, but not in the late evening; (2) relax before bedtime; (3) don't consume caffeine or alcohol late in the evening; (4) go to bed only when you are feeling sleepy; (5) if sleep has not occurred within 10 minutes, leave the bedroom and read a book until you feel sleepy; (6) avoid non-sleep activities in bed; (7) get up at the same time each morning, regardless of the time that you go to bed. In a review of 21 studies of a total of 470 participants with insomnia, behavioral sleep therapy was more effective than pharmacological treatment on all measures. This indicates that behavior therapy should be a first-line treatment for chronic insomnia.

Study Question on Note

1. List five rules that are a part of behavioral sleep therapy.

18 Antecedent Control: Modeling, Physical Guidance, and Situational Inducement

"James, feel the soles of your feet."

A MINDFULNESS-BASED INTERVENTION FOR AGGRESSION[1]

James, a 27-year-old man with mild intellectual disability, had alternated between group home placement and a psychiatric hospital for many years. He preferred to live in a group home, but his aggressive behavior resulted in regular readmissions to a psychiatric hospital. Although a variety of aggression management treatments had been tried, none had been successful. As a last resort, after spending 12 months as an inpatient without achieving much control over his verbal and physical aggression, James agreed to try a mindfulness-based self-control strategy. Mindfulness (discussed further in Chapter 27) involves becoming fully aware of one's sensations, thoughts, feelings, and observable behavior on a moment-to-moment basis.

Following a procedure called Soles of the Feet, James learned to divert his attention from whatever was making him angry at a particular moment by focusing on the soles of his feet. Doing so enabled James to feel calm, smile, and walk away from the anger-causing situation. To teach James to practice this strategy, the therapist used modeling and role-playing. During therapy sessions, James would be standing or sitting but always with his feet flat on the floor. The therapist would then remind James of an incident in which he was angry and verbally or physically aggressive toward a person who made him angry. When James showed signs of anger, such as rapid breathing, the therapist would say, while modeling the behavior being described, "Feel the soles of your feet. Slowly, move your toes, and feel your socks. Can you feel them? Now move the heels

---

[1] This case is based on a report by Singh, Wahler, Adkins, and Myers (2003).

217

of your feet against the back of your shoes. Feel your heels rubbing your shoes. Keep breathing slowly, and pay attention to the soles of your feet until you feel calm. Now smile, and walk away from the situation, like I'm doing." The therapist and James would then walk away from each other smiling. The therapist provided this type of training during 30-minute role-playing sessions held twice a day for 5 days. This was followed by homework practice assignments for another week. Then James was instructed to use the procedure to control his verbal and physical aggression in actual situations. The procedure was very effective. Before treatment, James had averaged approximately 10 instances of serious verbal aggression and 15 instances of physical aggression per month. Following treatment, James met the requirement of 6 months of aggression-free behavior in the psychiatric hospital before being returned to the group home. He then successfully lived in the group home with no aggressive behavior during a one year follow-up. ■

CAPITALIZING ON EXISTING STIMULUS CONTROL

As we indicated in the previous chapter, behavior modification programs should include instructions in the form of rules that can be followed easily. Sometimes, however, instructions are not enough so it is necessary to introduce other types of antecedent stimuli, as was done with James. This chapter describes these additional strategies for capitalizing on existing forms of stimulus control.

MODELING

Modeling is a procedure by which a sample of a given behavior is demonstrated to an individual to induce that individual to engage in a similar behavior. As is true for rules, modeling can be quite powerful. You may convince yourself of this by performing the following simple experiments:

1. For an entire day, speak only in a whisper and note how often people around you also whisper.
2. Yawn conspicuously in the presence of other people and note their frequency of yawning.
3. Stand on the corner of a street where there are lots of pedestrians and look at the sky for an hour, and note how many people stop and also look at the sky.

In each case, compare the data obtained with data gathered under comparable circumstances when the behavior is not being modeled.

As with rules, the general public so commonly uses modeling that few people think of it as a behavior modification procedure. Parents use it rather unsystematically, but quite effectively, in many cases, to teach politeness, caring, language, and many other behaviors to their children. When a dog walks by a parent and a 2-year-old child, the parent, while looking at the dog, might say, "Look at the dog. Can you say 'dog'?" When showing a child how to make a sandwich, a parent might say "Do it like this" while modeling the desired behavior. Modeling affects the behavior of individuals of all ages, not just young children. When teenagers first enter high school, they see how the older students dress and talk, and they soon dress the same way and use the same expressions. All of us in our daily lives have frequent opportunities to observe the actions of others, and we frequently imitate their behaviors.

What determines whether we will imitate the behavior of a model? Although several possible explanations exist, clearly our history of reinforcement and punishment for imitating others NOTE 1 is an important factor. Also, because each of us has had different experiences, the specific variables that determine which models and modeled behaviors are S^Ds for imitation vary somewhat from person to person. Nevertheless, several general factors influence the effectiveness of modeling as a behavior modification technique for most people (Bandura, 1986). The following rules capitalize on these factors.

ARRANGE FOR PEERS TO BE MODELS   People are more likely to imitate those who are similar to them in various ways (age, socioeconomic status, physical appearance, etc.). Friends and peers are more likely to be imitated than are strangers or individuals outside one's peer group. Thus, whenever possible, use peers as models in your behavior modification programs. Consider the case of an extremely withdrawn nursery school child who almost never interacts with other children. You might arrange for the child to observe several instances of another child joining in the activities of a group of children. The group should be responding to the model in a reinforcing manner (such as by offering her play material, talking to her, and smiling). To ensure that the modeling occurs under opportune circumstances and in a suitable fashion, it may be necessary to instruct certain children to perform as models and to instruct the children in the group to behave in a conspicuously reinforcing manner to the models. It is sometimes convenient and effective to videotape a number of such episodes for viewing by socially withdrawn children (see O'Connor, 1969). The presentation of modeling scenes through films, videos, and other media is called *symbolic modeling.* Studies show that symbolic modeling can sometimes be as effective as the real thing (e.g., see Poche, Yoder, & Miltenberger, 1988).

ARRANGE FOR THE MODELED BEHAVIOR TO BE SEEN TO BE EFFECTIVE   Suppose that you want to improve your debating skills. Are you more likely to imitate the discussion strategies of friends who consistently get their points across or friends who consistently lose arguments? Clearly, the competence of the model in obtaining desired consequences is a factor that determines the effectiveness of modeling as a behavior modification technique. Even with children, peers who are more proficient at obtaining consequences for various behaviors are more likely to be imitated (Schunk, 1987). Therefore, to capitalize on this factor when using modeling in your behavior modification program, arrange for the learner to observe the model emit the desired behavior and receive reinforcement.

Social psychologists have long known that high-status and highly prestigious persons are more likely to be imitated than individuals of lower status or prestige (e.g., Asch, 1948; Henrich & Gil-White, 2001). This might be interpreted as a subcategory of the competence factor. A popular teenager is likely to be imitated by peers who frequently observe the popular teenager receiving many positive consequences for various behaviors.

USE MULTIPLE MODELS   Sarah, a 35-year-old real estate salesperson and part-time student, drank beer regularly with six other women at a local tavern on Friday afternoons. All of them were taking a course on behavior modification, but Sarah was unaware that her own drinking behavior was being studied. Over several sessions of baseline, it was established that Sarah invariably drank about 72 ounces of beer in an hour. Then the experimental phases of the study began. During the first experimental phase, one of the other women modeled a drinking rate of half of Sarah's. Sarah's drinking was not affected. During the second experimental phase, her drinking was not affected when two of the other women modeled drinking rates half of hers. However, when in the third experimental phase, four other women modeled drinking rates that were half of Sarah's, her drinking rate reduced by half (DeRicco & Niemann, 1980). This study illustrates that the number of people modeling a particular behavior is a factor in determining whether that behavior will be imitated.

COMBINE MODELING WITH RULES   Modeling is likely to be most effective when combined with rules and other behavioral strategies. The following excerpt from a therapy session illustrates this (Masters, Burrish, Hollon, & Rimm, 1987, pp. 100–101). The client was being treated for difficulty asking for a date. In the excerpt, the client is rehearsing effective date-asking behavior. Note how the therapist combines instruction and shaping with modeling.

CLIENT: By the way (*pause*) I don't suppose you want to go out Saturday night?

THERAPIST: Up to actually asking for the date, you were very good. However, if I were the woman, I think I might have been a bit offended when you said, "By the way." It's like your asking her out is pretty casual. Also, the way you phrased the question, you are kind of suggesting to her that she doesn't want to go out with you. Pretend for the moment I'm you. Now, how does this sound: "There's a movie at the Varsity Theater this Saturday that I want to see. If you don't have other plans, I'd very much like you to go with me."

CLIENT: That sounded good. Like you were sure of yourself and liked the woman too.

THERAPIST: Why don't you try it?

CLIENT: You know that movie at the Varsity? Well, I'd like to go, and I'd like you to go with me on Saturday, if you don't have anything better to do.

THERAPIST: Well, that certainly was better. Your tone of voice was especially good. But the last line, "if you don't have anything better to do," sounded like you don't think you have much to offer. Why not run through it one more time?

CLIENT: I'd like to see the show at the Varsity, Saturday, and, if you haven't made other plans, I'd like you to go with me.

THERAPIST: Much better. Excellent, in fact. You were confident, forceful, and sincere.

This example also illustrates a technique referred to as **behavioral rehearsal** or **role-playing** in which a client rehearses particular behaviors (plays a role) in a practice setting to increase the likelihood that the client will follow those behaviors appropriately in the real world. In the preceding example, the client rehearsed asking for a date. Role-playing was also used with James to teach him to focus on the soles of his feet as an alternative to aggression. A combination of instructions, modeling, behavioral rehearsal, and consequence management has been used to enhance performance in a variety of areas, such as social skills training (Huang & Cuvo, 1997), assertion training (Schroeder & Black, 1985), and anger management training (Larkin & Zayfert, 1996).

Guidelines for Using Modeling

The following are some general guidelines for the effective use of modeling. It may not be possible to follow all of them in every situation, but the more that are followed, the more effective the modeling is likely to be.

1. Select models who are friends or peers of the learner and who are seen by the learner as competent individuals with status or prestige.
2. Use more than one model.
3. The complexity of the modeled behavior should be suitable for the behavioral level of the learner.
4. Combine rules with modeling.

5. Have the learner watch the model perform the behavior and be reinforced (preferably by natural reinforcers).

6. Design the training so that correct imitation of the modeled behavior will lead to a natural reinforcer for the learner. If this is not possible, arrange for reinforcement for correct imitation of the modeled behavior.

7. If the behavior is quite complex, then the modeling episode should be sequenced from very easy to more difficult approximations for the learner.

8. To enhance stimulus generalization, the modeling scenes should be as realistic as possible.

9. Use fading as necessary so that stimuli other than the model can take control over the desired behavior.

Study Questions

1. Define *modeling*. How was it incorporated into the therapy sessions with James?

2. List four strategies that you might follow to influence the effectiveness of modeling as a behavior modification technique.

3. Describe two recent situations in which you were influenced by modeling to emit a behavior. For each instance, describe whether the four factors that influence the effectiveness of modeling were present.

4. What does *symbolic modeling* mean? Describe how this might explain how a city-dwelling child might learn to fear snakes.

5. Describe the specific steps you might go through in using modeling to overcome the extreme withdrawal behavior of a nursery school child who never interacts with other children. Identify the basic principles and procedures being applied in your program.

6. In the dialogue between the client and the therapist concerning the client's difficulty in asking for dates, briefly describe
   a. how modeling was involved
   b. how instructions were involved
   c. how shaping was involved

7. Define or describe behavioral rehearsal (or role-playing), and give an example.

PHYSICAL GUIDANCE

Physical guidance is the application of physical contact to induce an individual to go through the motions of a desired behavior. Some familiar examples are a dance instructor leading a pupil through a new dance step, a golf instructor holding a novice's arms and moving the novice through a proper swing, and a parent holding a child's hand while teaching the child to cross the street safely. Physical guidance is always only one component of a teaching procedure. Both the dance instructor and the golf instructor will also use instruction (telling the student what to do and giving pointers), modeling (demonstrating the appropriate physical postures and motions), and reinforcement for correct responses or approximations to them (such as "Much better!" or "Excellent!"). Likewise, the parent teaching safe street crossing will use rules (e.g., by saying, "Look both ways") and modeling (looking both ways in an exaggerated manner).

Some uses of physical guidance in behavior modification programs were given in Chapter 9— for example, using physical guidance and fading to teach a child to touch her or his head upon request. Physical guidance is generally used as an aid in teaching individuals to follow instructions or imitate a modeled behavior so that instruction or modeling can then be used without physical guidance to establish other behaviors. In one procedure for teaching instruction following, a child is placed in a chair opposite the teacher. At the beginning of a trial, the teacher says, "Johnny, stand up," and then guides the child to his feet. Reinforcement is then presented immediately, as though the child himself had performed the response. Next, the teacher says, "Johnny, sit down," and gently presses him back on the chair. Again, immediate reinforcement is presented. The process is repeated over trials while physical guidance is faded out (see Kazdin & Erickson, 1975). After this set of instructions is learned, another set (such as "Come here" and "Go there") is taught using a similar procedure. Less and less physical guidance may be required to teach successive instruction following until eventually even fairly complex instruction following can be taught with little or no physical guidance.

As in teaching instruction following, the teacher who uses physical guidance to teach a child to imitate a model starts with a few simple imitations (such as touching one's head, clapping one's hands, tapping the table, standing up, and sitting down) and adds new imitations as the previous ones are learned. At the beginning of each trial, the teacher says, "Do this" while modeling the response and guiding the child to perform the response. Correct responses are reinforced and physical guidance is faded out over trials. This facilitates the development of **generalized imitation** by which an individual, after learning to imitate a number of behaviors (perhaps with some shaping, fading, physical guidance, and reinforcement), learns to imitate a new response on the first trial without reinforcement (Baer, Peterson, & Sherman, 1967).

Another common application of physical guidance is in helping individuals to overcome fears. Helping an individual who is terrified of water might involve gradually leading the individual by the hand into the shallow end of a swimming pool and providing support while the individual floats. The least fear-provoking aspects of a situation should be introduced first and the more fear-provoking aspects added later in a gradual manner. One should never try to force an individual to do more than the individual feels comfortable doing. The more fearful the individual is, the more gradual the process should be. In the case of a very fearful individual, one may have to spend several sessions simply sitting with the individual on the edge of the pool. (Use of modeling and other procedures to help a client overcome extreme fears is discussed further in Chapter 28.)

Guidelines for Using Physical Guidance

Some general guidelines for the effective use of physical guidance follow.

1. Ensure that the learner is comfortable and relaxed while being touched and guided. Some initial relaxation training may be necessary to accomplish this.
2. Determine the stimuli that you want to control the behavior and ensure that they are conspicuously present during physical guidance.
3. Consider using rules or cue words during physical guidance so that they may eventually control the behavior. For example, when teaching a novice right-handed golfer the proper shoulder turn during a golf swing, the instructor might say the cue words, "Left shoulder to chin, right shoulder to chin," while guiding the novice through the backswing and the downswing.
4. Reinforcement should be given immediately after the successful completion of the guided response.
5. Physical guidance should be sequenced gradually from very easy to more difficult behavior for the learner.
6. Use fading so that other stimuli can take control over the behavior.

Study Questions

8. What does the term *physical guidance* mean? How does it differ from gestural prompting (see p. 115)?

9. Identify a behavior that you were influenced to perform as a result of physical guidance. Describe how physical guidance was involved.

10. What is generalized imitation? Describe an example.

SITUATIONAL INDUCEMENT

Largely because of our similar histories of reinforcement and punishment, numerous situations and occasions in society control similar behavior in many of us. The interiors of certain public buildings, such as churches, museums, and libraries, tend to suppress loud talking. Parties tend to evoke socializing and jovial behavior. Catchy melodies prompt humming and singing. Audience laughter, real or artificial, induces many people to continue watching TV sitcoms.

The term *situational inducement* refers to the influence of a behavior by using situations and occasions that already exert control over the behavior. Such techniques no doubt predate recorded history. Gatherings involving singing and dancing probably served to strengthen a sense of community in ancient tribes, just as they do today in almost all cultures. Monasteries and convents have been used for centuries to promote spiritual behavior by providing an environment conducive to reading religious texts and meditating. Supermarkets and department stores use many situational features to induce buying. Among these are the ways in which the products or pictures of the products are prominently and attractively displayed. Fine restaurants provide relaxing atmospheres to induce leisurely enjoyment of a full-course meal. Fast-food restaurants where many people are waiting for tables might play fast music to induce rapid eating.

Examples of situational inducement can also be found in the home. Many people prominently display items such as interesting *objets d'art* to stimulate conversation when guests arrive. If a guest seems about to mishandle one of these conversation pieces, the host may use situational inducement by handing the potential offender a drink.

Situational inducement has been used in a number of imaginative and effective ways in behavior modification programs to help increase or decrease target behaviors or to bring them under appropriate stimulus control. Examples can be discussed under four somewhat overlapping categories: (a) rearranging the existing surroundings, (b) moving the activity to a new location, (c) relocating the people, and (d) changing the time of the activity.

Rearranging the Surroundings

An interesting example of rearranging the surroundings occurred in a case reported by the pioneering behaviorist Israel Goldiamond (1965). He was consulted by a couple having a problem in their relationship.[2] When they were at home together, the husband could not refrain from screaming at his wife about her once having gone to bed with his best friend. One of the therapy goals decided on was to replace screaming with civilized conversational behavior. Goldiamond reasoned that the husband's screaming had probably come under the control of the S^Ds in the home environment and that one way to weaken the behavior in that situation would be to change

---

[2] For additional discussion of behavior therapy for couples, see Chapter 28.

those S^{D}s. He therefore instructed the couple to rearrange the rooms and furniture in the house to make it appear considerably different. The wife went one step further and bought herself a new outfit. Goldiamond then provided for the reinforcement of civilized conversation in the presence of these new cues that were not associated so strongly with screaming. (How he did this is explained in the next section.) It was important to make these changes as quickly as possible because if screaming occurred too often in the presence of these new stimuli, they might become S^{D}s for screaming just as the old stimuli had.

Another example of rearranging the surroundings is altering the items in one's room to promote better and more persistent studying behavior. A student might turn on more lights, use a brighter light bulb, clear the desk of irrelevant material, move the bed as far as possible from the desk, and have the desk facing away from the bed. Better yet, the bed should not be in the same room as the desk because the bed is an S^D for sleeping. To prevent nonstudy behaviors from being conditioned to the new stimuli, the student should engage only in studying behavior in the rearranged environment (see Goldiamond, 1965).

Moving the Activity to a New Location

In the case reported by Goldiamond, rearranging the furniture eliminated some but not all of the S^{D}s that evoked the husband's screaming. Goldiamond therefore arranged for the interaction between the spouses to initially be moved to a new location. He instructed the couple that, after rearranging the furniture in their home, they were to immediately go to a place that would induce civilized conversation. It was hoped that this behavior would continue until they returned home and then would come under the control of the new stimuli in the home.

To quote from Goldiamond's report (1965, p. 856),

> Since it was impossible for [the husband] to converse in a civilized manner with his wife, we discussed a program of going to one evening spot on Monday, another on Tuesday, and another on Wednesday.
>
> "Oh," he said, "you want us to be together. We'll go bowling on Thursday."
>
> "On the contrary," I said, "I am interested in your subjecting yourself to an environment where civilized chit-chat is maintained. Such is not the case at a bowling alley."
>
> I also asked if there was any topic of conversation which once started would maintain itself. He commented on his mother-in-law's crazy ideas about farming. He was then given an index card and instructed to write "farm" on it and to attach some money to that card. The money was to be used to pay the waitress on Thursday, at which point he was to start the "farm" discussion which hopefully would continue into the taxi and home.

Changing the location of the activity is one approach to improving studying (see Figure 18–1). A student using this approach should select a place that is conducive to studying and has distinctive stimuli that are not associated with any behavior other than studying. A reserved carrel in a university library is ideal for this, although other well-lit, quiet areas with adequate working space would be suitable. Depending on how deficient the student's study behavior is, it may be necessary to combine relocating the activity with some of the basic procedures discussed in Part II of this text. For severe deficiencies, behavior incorporating good study skills should first be shaped and then placed on either a low-duration or a low-ratio schedule in the special studying area. The value of the schedule should then be increased gradually so that the behavior will eventually be

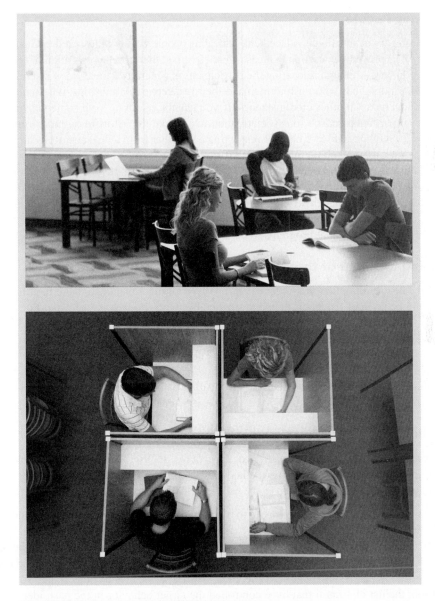

FIGURE 18–1 Examples of situational inducement.

maintained at the desired level. Appropriate reinforcement such as coffee with a friend should be arranged to occur immediately after the schedule requirement has been met. A student who experiences a tendency to daydream or to engage in other nonstudy behavior while in the studying area should do a little more productive studying and then leave immediately so that daydreaming does not become conditioned to the stimuli in the studying area. Similarly, the husband in the case reported by Goldiamond was instructed to go to the garage and sit on a specially designated "sulking" stool whenever he felt a tendency to sulk—this being a behavior that was threatening the recently strengthened conversational behavior after screaming had been eliminated.

Relocating People

The third category of situational inducement, relocating people, was not illustrated in Goldiamond's case study. The procedures used in that case were effective; therefore, a separation of the spouses was not necessary. Although relocating the participants is generally a measure of last resort when dealing with individuals who wish to maintain their respective relationships, it is sometimes the most practical tactic in other circumstances. If you cannot get along with someone with whom you have no particular reason to associate, then why make the effort to be more compatible? Both of you would probably be happier respecting each other from a distance. Relocating people can also be used to bring about the opposite effect, that is, to bring people together. For example, getting dates is a problem for many college students. To deal with this problem, therapists often recommend that clients increase their nondating contacts with others who may be candidates for dating. Teachers often change seating arrangements to relocate students whose close proximity leads to various types of disruptions. This is usually much easier than designing and carrying out reinforcement or punishment programs to eliminate undesirable interactions.

Changing the Time of the Activity

The final category of situational inducement involves taking advantage of the fact that certain stimuli and behavioral tendencies change predictably with the passage of time. For example, couples may find that sexual activity is better for them in the morning than at night. Changing the time of an activity has been used effectively in weight-control programs. People who cook for their families sometimes put on excess weight by "nibbling" while preparing meals and then sitting down for a full-course dinner. Rather than forgoing dinner with one's family, a partial solution to this problem is to do the preparation shortly after having eaten the previous meal while the tendency to eat is still relatively weak (see LeBow, 1981, 1989).

Guidelines for Using Situational Inducement

Situational inducement covers a broad set of procedures. Its use, therefore, is considerably less straightforward than is that of the other methods discussed in this chapter. In short, a good deal of imagination is typically required if it is to be used effectively. We suggest the following guidelines.

1. Clearly identify the desired behavior to be strengthened and, if appropriate, the undesirable behavior to be decreased.
2. Brainstorm all possible environmental arrangements in the presence of which the desired behavior has occurred in the past or is likely to occur. Remember, situations and controlling stimuli can be anything—people, places, times, days, events, objects, and so on.
3. From the list of stimuli that have controlled the target behavior in the past, identify those that could be easily introduced to control the target behavior.
4. Arrange for the learner to be exposed to the stimuli that control the target behavior in the desired way and to avoid locations and arrangements that do not have this control.
5. Make sure that undesirable behavior never occurs in the presence of situations introduced to strengthen desirable behavior.
6. When the desirable behavior occurs in the presence of the new arrangement, be sure that it is reinforced.
7. Use fading to bring the behavior under desired stimulus control.

Study Questions

11. What do we mean by the term *situational inducement*? Which term given previously in this book has essentially the same meaning (see p. 115)?

12. Describe each of the four categories of situational inducement.

13. Give an example from your own experience of each of the four categories of situational inducement.

14. For each of the following examples, identify the category of situational inducement in which it might best be placed and indicate why.

    a. On Saturday afternoon, an exercise buff can't seem to get the energy to lift weights. To increase the likelihood of weight lifting, the exercise buff places the weights in the center of the exercise room, turns on the TV to a sporting event, and opens a copy of *Muscle Beach* magazine to the centerfold showing a famous bodybuilder.

    b. It is said that Victor Hugo, a renowned writer, controlled his work habits in his study by having his servant take his clothes away and not bring them back until the end of the day (Wallace, 1971, pp. 68–69).

    c. To stop drinking, an alcoholic surrounds herself or himself with members of Alcoholics Anonymous and stops seeing her or his old drinking buddies.

    d. A couch potato has decided to jog a mile every night before going to bed. Alas, "the road to hell [or perhaps to heart attack] is paved with good intentions." Late nights, good TV, wine with dinner, and other delights take their toll. Three months later, the couch potato is still overweight and out of shape because of many missed jogging nights. The couch potato takes a friend's advice to change the routine and begins jogging each day immediately upon arriving home and before eating dinner.

    e. After many interruptions while working on this book at the university, the authors began working at one of their homes.

15. According to the proposed guidelines for the use of rules, modeling, and physical guidance,

    a. what behavior principle is used with all three procedures?

    b. what two other behavioral procedures are likely to be used with all three procedures?

Application Exercises

A. EXERCISE INVOLVING OTHERS

Outline a program that a parent might follow to teach a 2-year-old child to respond consistently to the instruction, "Please bring me your shoes." Indicate how your program might use rules, modeling, and physical guidance, and how it follows the guidelines for the effective application of each.

B. SELF-MODIFICATION EXERCISE

Select two of your behaviors from the following list:

  1. doing the dishes or putting them in the dishwasher immediately after a meal

  2. getting up when the alarm sounds

  3. feeling happy

  4. cleaning up your bedroom twice per week

  5. doing some exercises daily

  6. increasing your studying

Describe how you might influence each behavior by combining at least four of the following tactics: rules, modeling, physical guidance, rearranging the existing surroundings, moving the activity to a new location, relocating people, and changing the time of the activity. Make your suggestions highly plausible in regard to the situation.

Note and Extended Discussion

1. Historically, learning by imitation has been given an important place in a number of different psychological theories, not just behavioristic ones. In Freudian (psychoanalytic) theory, a male child typically develops "male" behavior patterns through identification with his father, and a female child develops "female" behavior patterns through identification with her mother. Thus, the absence of a strong male figure with whom to identify could (in Freudian theory) lead to feminine traits—even homosexuality—in a boy who identifies excessively with his mother. Gestalt psychologists considered imitative learning to be innate in higher species and attempted to show, for example, that chimpanzees could learn to solve problems by watching other chimpanzees solve them. Bandura (1977) defined *observational learning* (also called *vicarious learning*) as the increase or decrease of behavior that is similar to that of a model as a result of watching the model's behavior be reinforced or punished. Bandura believes that this type of learning can occur without external reinforcement for the observer. If so, then it seems that we would have to add observational learning as a basic type of learning. Many behavioral psychologists, however, believe that the behavioral learning principles described in Chapters 3–15 of this book can account for behavior acquired through observation.

   There are several processes by which observational or imitative behavior might be learned. First, an individual is frequently reinforced after emitting behavior that is similar to behavior that another individual has emitted. Other people's actions tend to become S^Ds for engaging in similar actions. For example, a child who watches someone open a door to go outside receives the reinforcement of going outside after performing the same action. Second, to the extent that other people are reinforcing to us, their actions acquire conditioned reinforcing properties. We receive conditioned reinforcement when we perform the same actions. A third possibility is that once we have learned to imitate simple responses, we can then imitate more complex behaviors, provided that these are composed of the simpler responses. For example, once a child has learned to imitate "al," "li," "ga," and "tor" as single syllables, or as units of various words, the child can then imitate the word *alligator* upon hearing it for the first time (Skinner, 1957). A fourth possibility is that imitative behavior is not just a set of separate stimulus–response relationships but is itself an operant class of responses. In other words, it is possible that once a child is reinforced for imitating some behaviors, the child will then tend to imitate other behaviors even though they contain no elements in common with the imitative behaviors that were reinforced. As indicated earlier in this chapter, this is referred to as *generalized imitation*. For more detailed interpretations of vicarious or imitative learning from a contemporary behavioral approach, see Masia and Chase (1997) or Pear (2001, pp. 95–100).

Study Questions on Note

1. How did Bandura define *observational learning*? What is another name for observational learning?
2. Describe four processes by which imitative behavior might be learned, and give an example of each.

19 Antecedent Control: Motivation

"OK, team! Here's how you can earn an Eagle Effort award."

COACH DAWSON'S MOTIVATION PROGRAM[1]

"Let's see a little concentration out there. You should hardly ever miss layups in drills!" shouted Jim Dawson at basketball practice. Jim was coach of the Clinton Junior High basketball team in Columbus, Ohio. He was concerned about the players' performance during a series of drills that he used to open each practice. There was also an attitude problem. "Some of them just aren't team players," he thought to himself. "Some of them really have a bad attitude."

With the help of Daryl Siedentop of The Ohio State University, he worked out a motivational system in which players could earn points for performance in layup drills, jump-shooting drills, and free throw drills at daily practice. In addition, they could earn points for being a "team player" by making supportive comments to teammates. Points were deducted if Coach Dawson saw a lack of hustle or a bad attitude. Student volunteers who served as managers for the team recorded the points. This motivational system was explained in detail to the players beforehand. At the end of a practice, the coach praised players who earned more points than they had in the previous practice as well as players who earned a large number of points. In addition, players who earned a sufficient number of points had their names posted conspicuously on an "Eagle Effort" board in the hall leading to the gymnasium. These players were also honored with an "Eagle Effort" award at a postseason banquet. Overall, the program was highly effective. Performance in layup drills improved from an average of 68% to an average of 80%. Jump-shooting performance improved from 37% to 51%. Free throw shooting at practices improved from 59% to 67%. However, the most dramatic improvement was in the "team player" category. The number of supportive comments made by the players to teammates increased to such an

---

[1] This example is based on a report by Siedentop (1978).

229

extent that the managers could not monitor them all. In addition, at first most of the supportive comments sounded "pretty phony," according to Coach Dawson, but over the season, they became increasingly sincere. By the end of the season, the players were exhibiting behavior reflective of a positive attitude to a remarkable extent. In Coach Dawson's words, "We were more together than I ever could have imagined." ■

A TRADITIONAL VIEW OF MOTIVATION

Consider the behavior of Susie and Jack, two children in third grade at an elementary school. Susie consistently completes homework assignments, works hard during various classroom activities, listens attentively to the teacher, and is polite with the other children. According to Susie's teacher, "Susie is a good student *because* she's highly motivated." Jack, on the other hand, is the opposite. Jack rarely completes homework assignments, fools around while the teacher is talking, and doesn't appear to apply himself. Jack's teacher believes that Jack lacks motivation. As illustrated by these examples, many people conceptualize motivation as some "thing" within us that causes our actions. Consistent with this traditional view, *Webster's Unabridged Dictionary* defines *motive* as "some inner drive that causes a person to act in a certain way." Moreover, many introductory psychology texts describe motivation as the study of inner drives, needs, and wants that cause our actions.

A conceptual or logical problem with the traditional view of motivation is that it involves circular reasoning. This inner thing called *motive, drive,* and so on is usually inferred from the very behavior that it is supposed to explain. Why does Susie work hard? Because she is highly motivated. How do we know she's highly motivated? Because she works hard. In addition to this circularity, conceptualizing motivation as an internal cause of behavior has several practical problems. First, the suggestion that the causes of behavior are inside of us rather than in the environment might influence some to ignore the principles for changing behavior described in earlier chapters and the enormous amount of data demonstrating that application of those principles can effectively modify behavior. Second, conceptualizing motivation as an internal cause of behavior may influence some to blame the individual for substandard performance by attributing this to a lack of motivation, or laziness, rather than trying to help such individuals to improve their performance. Third, conceptualizing motivation as an internal cause of behavior may influence some to blame themselves for failures to emit various behaviors (e.g., "I just can't get motivated to go on a diet") rather than examining potential self-management strategies (see Chapter 26) for improving their performance.

Study Questions

1. How do many people who are not behaviorists or behavior modifiers conceptualize motivation? Illustrate with an example.
2. What is a conceptual problem with the traditional view of motivation? Illustrate with an example.
3. Describe three practical problems with conceptualizing motivation as an internal cause of behavior.
4. If by "motivating someone to do something" we mean nothing more than manipulating antecedent conditions to influence that person to behave in a certain way, list each of the strategies presented in Chapters 17 and 18 to accomplish that task.

A BEHAVIORAL VIEW OF MOTIVATION

It's one thing for a person to *know how* to emit a given behavior; it's another thing for that person to *want* to emit that behavior. Traditional psychological theories of motivation have addressed the "processes of wanting" by postulating inner drives. However, rather than taking this approach, behavioral psychologists have adopted the concept of a motivating operation, as introduced and developed by the pioneering behaviorist Jack Michael (1982, 1993, 2000, 2007). We touched on the concept of motivating operation in Chapter 3, but now we discuss it more in depth. A **motivating operation (MO)** is an event or operation that (a) temporarily alters the effectiveness of a reinforcer or punisher (a value-altering effect) and (b) influences behavior that normally leads to that reinforcer or punisher (a behavior-altering effect) (Laraway, Snycerski, Michael, & Poling, 2003). Let's first examine MOs involving reinforcers. Consider, for example, the unconditioned reinforcer of food. When we are food deprived, food is a powerful reinforcer, and we are likely to engage in various food-seeking behaviors. Just after eating a big meal, however, food temporarily loses its effectiveness as a reinforcer, and we are less likely to engage in food- **NOTE 1** seeking behaviors. Thus, deprivation and satiation of food are MOs.

MOs also affect punishers. Consider the punisher of time out discussed in Chapter 12. Suppose that at Little League baseball practices, Coach Jackson typically requires a player to sit in the dugout alone for 5 minutes as a time out contingent for swearing, throwing bats, and other misbehavior. Suppose also that at one particular practice, Coach Jackson announced that players could earn points for performing well (catching the ball, getting a hit, etc.), and that the five players with the most points would each be awarded a ticket to attend a major league baseball game. This announcement immediately made points a reinforcer for the players. In addition, it increased the effectiveness of the time out as a punisher because the players could not earn points if they were sitting in the dugout for misbehavior.

You can see from these examples that there are two main types of MOs: A **motivating establishing operation (MEO)** is an event or operation that temporarily increases the effectiveness of a reinforcer or punisher and that increases the likelihood of behaviors that lead to that reinforcer or decreases the likelihood of behaviors that lead to that punisher. A **motivating abolishing operation (MAO)** is an event or operation that temporarily decreases the effectiveness of a reinforcer or punisher and decreases the likelihood of behaviors that normally lead to that reinforcer or increases the likelihood of behaviors that normally lead to that punisher. Food **NOTE 2** deprivation is an MEO. Food satiation is an MAO. The announcement of Coach Jackson's points program was an MEO for points because it increased their reinforcing effectiveness and an MEO for time out because it increased its effectiveness as a punisher.

Unconditioned Versus Conditioned Motivating Operations

In addition to distinguishing between MEOs and MAOs, we also distinguish between unconditioned and conditioned motivating operations (Michael, 1993); see Figure 19–1. With *unconditioned motivating operations* (*UMOs*), the value-altering effect is innate. Thus, deprivation of food is an *unconditioned motivating establishing operation* (*UMEO*) because it increases the effectiveness of food as a reinforcer without prior learning. Satiation is an *unconditioned motivating abolishing operation* (*UMAO*) because it decreases the effectiveness of food as a reinforcer without prior learning. The behavior-altering effect of UMOs, however, is learned. For example, when someone is hungry, the behaviors of looking in the refrigerator or going to a fast-food outlet are

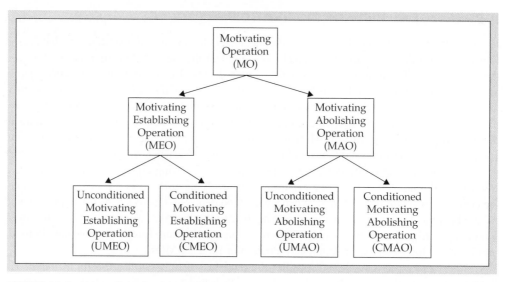

FIGURE 19–1 Types of motivating operations.

NOTE 3 learned behaviors. Other UMEOs include deprivation of water, sleep, activity, oxygen, and sexual stimulation. Satiation of each of these are UMAOs.

Some MOs alter the effectiveness of consequences as reinforcers or punishers because of prior learning. Such MOs are called *conditioned motivating operations* (*CMOs*). Coach Dawson's announcement of the program with the basketball players was an MEO because it established the points as reinforcers for the players and it increased the likelihood of desirable practice behaviors to earn those reinforcers. More specifically, his announcement of the program was a conditioned motivating establishing operation (CMEO) because it established points as conditioned reinforcers from prior learning. The announcement would not have worked as a motivating operation if the players had not previously learned to respond to such announcements.

Martin (2007) described the strategy that a young competitive golfer used to motivate himself to practice putting. The golfer used imagery to create pressure games. When practicing putting, the golfer would frequently imagine that he was leading the tournament on the final day of the U.S. Open. For each of 18 practice putts, he would pretend that he needed the putt to maintain the lead. In this example, by using the imaginary pressure game, the golfer was administering a CMEO to himself. The pressure game increased the conditioned reinforcing value of making a putt and increased the likelihood of focusing appropriately to make the putt.

As indicated previously, the value-altering effect of a UMO is innate while the behavior-altering effect is learned. However, with CMOs, both the value-altering and the behavior-altering effects are due to learning. As Sundberg (2004) pointed out, many of the topics discussed under motivation in introductory psychology books, such as "acquired drives" or "social motives," involve CMOs.

CMEOs and S^Ds

When considering stimulus control over behavior, it is easy to confuse the concept of discriminative stimulus, or S^D, and the concept of CMEO. Knowledge of both is important in being able to reliably and effectively use either as antecedent variables to influence behavior. An S^D is a stimulus that has been correlated with the availability of a reinforcer for a particular behavior. To influence an individual's behavior by presenting an S^D, that individual must have been deprived of the reinforcer associated with responding to that S^D. In everyday language, an S^D is a cue that tells you what to do to get what you already want. Suppose that a family is camping on a cold fall evening. A parent might say to a shivering child, "Move your sleeping bag closer to the campfire and you'll feel warmer." This statement would be an S^D for the child to move the sleeping bag closer to the campfire. Warmth was obviously a reinforcer for the shivering child. A CMEO is a motivator that momentarily increases the value of a conditioned reinforcer and increases the likelihood of behavior that has led to that reinforcer in the past. In everyday language, a CMEO is a cue that makes you want something and tells you what to do to get it. Suppose a parent says to his teenage daughter, "Each time that you mow the lawn, you can earn 3 points, and each time that you trim the hedges you can earn 2 points. When you accumulate 20 points, you can use the family car for a weekend." In this example, the rule given by the parent is a CMEO. The rule established points as conditioned reinforcers for the teenager and told her how to earn them.

CMAOs and S^Δs

The distinction between S^Δ and conditioned motivating abolishing operation (CMAO) is analogous to the distinction between S^D and CMEO. An S^Δ is a stimulus in the presence of which a response has not been reinforced. It is also assumed that the individual has been deprived of that particular reinforcer. In everyday language, an S^Δ is a cue that tells you that emitting a particular behavior will not lead to something that you want. Suppose that while shopping with their child in the past, parents had purchased candy when the child screamed, "I want candy." Suppose further that, at the beginning of a shopping excursion, the same parents tell their child, "We're not going to buy you candy when you scream." If the parents stick to this rule, this instruction would be an S^Δ for screaming. In contrast, a CMAO is a stimulus that momentarily decreases the value of a conditioned reinforcer and decreases the likelihood of behavior that has led to that reinforcer in the past. In everyday language, a CMAO influences someone to no longer want a particular consequence and decreases behavior that would lead to that consequence. Suppose that Charlie shopped at a particular grocery store because purchases were accompanied by coupons that could be cashed in for movie tickets. One day the store announced that in the future, the coupons would be exchanged only for country-western CDs. Charlie, who is not a country-western fan, begins to shop at another store. The store's announcement was a CMAO for Charlie, decreasing the value of the coupons and decreasing the behavior that had led to obtaining those coupons.

Study Questions

5. Define *motivating operation*. Describe an example that illustrates both aspects of the definition.
6. In what two ways are motivating establishing operations and motivating abolishing operations different?
7. Are the value-altering and behavior-alternating effects of unconditioned motivating operations learned or innate? Discuss with reference to an example.
8. Are the value-altering and behavior-alternating effects of CMOs learned or innate? Discuss with reference to an example.
9. Would you describe Coach Dawson's explanation of the points program to the basketball players as a UMEO or a CMEO? Justify your choice.

10. Suppose that a football team has been practicing for an hour in the hot sun without water. The coach says to one of the players, "Here are the keys to my car. Get the bottles of water from the trunk." Would this request be classified as an S^D or a CMEO for getting the water? Justify your choice.

11. Suppose that a pianist sets a goal for practicing a piece: "Before I can stop practicing, I have to play this piece through 10 times in a row without making a mistake." Is that goal best conceptualized as an S^D or a CMEO? Justify your choice.

SOME APPLICATIONS OF MOTIVATING OPERATIONS

Teaching Mands to Children with Autism

Considerable success has been achieved in a number of language intervention programs for children with autism and other developmental disabilities by combining intensive behavioral interventions with Skinner's (1957) analysis of verbal behavior (Sundberg & Michael, 2001; Sundberg & Partington, 1998; Verbeke, Martin, Thorsteinsson, Murphy, & Yu, 2007). Skinner was interested in studying the verbal behavior of individual speakers rather than the grammatical practices of a verbal community. He defined *verbal behavior* as behavior that is reinforced through the mediation of another person when the person providing the reinforcement was specifically trained to provide such reinforcement. Verbal behavior is contrasted with nonverbal behavior, which is behavior that is reinforced through contact with the physical environment. Skinner distinguished among several types of basic verbal responses, three of which were echoics, tacts, and mands. Skinner's definitions are technical, but roughly, an **echoic** is a vocal imitative response that is developed and maintained by social reinforcement. If a parent says, "Say 'water,'" and the child says "water" and receives praise, the child's response "water" is an echoic. A **tact** is a naming response that is developed and maintained by social reinforcement. If the parent points to a glass of water and asks, "What's that?" and the child says "water" and receives praise, the child's response "water" is a tact. A **mand** is a verbal response that is under the control of a motivating operation and is reinforced by the corresponding reinforcer or removal of the corresponding aversive stimulus. If a child is thirsty and asks a parent for "water," the child's response "water" is a mand. The same spoken word, *water,* is considered to be a different verbal response (e.g., an echoic, a tact, or a mand) depending on its controlling variables.

Observations suggest that a mand is the first type of verbal behavior acquired by a child (Bijou & Baer, 1965; Skinner, 1957). Therefore it is natural to start with mands when training verbal behavior. MOs have been used effectively in mand training programs for children with autism and developmental disabilities (Sundberg & Michael, 2001). Structured mand training typically begins by teaching a child to mand a reinforcer (such as a specific food or a favorite toy) that has high motivational value. To teach the child to mand for juice, the parent might give the child a sip of juice on the first trial. Next, in full view of the child, the parent might hide the juice under the table and ask the child, "What do you want? Say 'juice.'" If the child responds correctly, the child would be given another sip of juice. At this point, as you probably have discerned, the child is showing echoic behavior. On subsequent trials while hiding the juice, the parent would simply say, "What do you want?" and would reinforce asking for juice. After a certain amount of this type of training, the child is likely to generalize the behavior of saying "juice" to other situations when motivated for juice. Sundberg and Partington (1998) and Sundberg (2004) described additional strategies for using MOs for mand training.

NOTE 4

Motivating Seat Belt Use Among Senior Drivers

Pleasant Oaks is a residential senior community in Virginia. The seniors living there have an enjoyable lifestyle including frequent car trips to nearby Charlottesville. Many of those at Pleasant Oaks were acutely aware that automobile accidents are the leading cause of accidental death among individuals between the ages of 65 and 74. Although injuries, hospitalizations, and deaths are significantly fewer among drivers who wear safety belts, 30% of the drivers and passengers entering and leaving Pleasant Oaks did not buckle up. Brian, Amanda, and Daniel Cox of the University of Virginia Health Sciences Center decided to implement a simple procedure to try to encourage more residents of Pleasant Oaks to wear their seat belts. On stop signs located at the exits of the community scattered around Pleasant Oaks, these researchers placed the message, "BUCKLE UP, STAY SAFE" on permanent, aluminum vinyl-lettered signs. Because feeling safe is an important concern for seniors, the researchers hypothesized that the signs would function as a CMEO to increase the reinforcing value of wearing a fastened seat belt and therefore would increase the behavior of buckling up. They were right. Following installation of the signs, the percentage of seniors who buckled up increased from 70% to 94%. Six months after installation of the signs, 88% of the seniors continued to use seat belts appropriately (Cox, Cox, & Cox, 2000).

Decreasing Self-Injurious Behavior Maintained by Attention

Brenda was a 42-year-old woman with profound intellectual disability who lived in a public residential facility for persons with developmental disabilities. She had a long history of self-injurious behavior (SIB), including severe head banging and head hitting. Observations indicated that her SIB was maintained by reactions of well-meaning staff. After an instance of SIB, a staff member might say, "Brenda, don't do that, you'll hurt yourself." To treat Brenda's SIB, Timothy Vollmer and colleagues introduced a program that included an MAO for staff attention. During treatment sessions, a schedule of noncontingent reinforcement in which attention was initially provided every 10 seconds was arranged. This satiated Brenda on attention, and her SIB that had been previously reinforced by attention immediately dropped to a very low level. Extinction was also a part of the treatment in that the SIB was no longer followed by attention. Over several sessions, the frequency of noncontingent attention gradually decreased from its initial rate of six instances per minute to a final rate of one instance every 5 minutes. SIB remained at a very low level. Similar results were obtained with two other individuals (Vollmer, Iwata, Zarcone, Smith, & Mazaleski, 1993).

MOTIVATING OPERATIONS AND BEHAVIOR MODIFICATION

In this chapter, we discussed an antecedent variable—MOs—that temporarily alter the effectiveness of consequences as reinforcers or punishers and that thereby temporarily alter the occurrence of behavior influenced by such consequences. Consideration of MOs in the design of behavior modification programs is likely to enhance their effectiveness.

Study Questions

12. Define *echoic,* and describe an example that is not in the book.
13. Define *tact,* and describe an example that is not in the book.

14. Define *mand,* and describe an example that is not in the book.
15. Using an example, describe how a motivating operation might be incorporated into mand training with a child.
16. How was a CMEO used to motivate seat belt use among senior drivers?
17. How was an MAO applied to decrease the self-injurious behavior of a woman with profound intellectual disability?

Application Exercise

SELF-MODIFICATION EXERCISE

Suppose that you want to increase the frequency of your studying. Several strategies might help motivate you to master the answers to the study questions in this book. (a) Post the dates beginning now and ending with the final exam for the course, and cross off each day as it passes. (b) Arrange to study with a friend on a regular basis. (c) Sign a contract with a friend or relative that stipulates that you will be given certain reinforcers if you meet certain study objectives. (d) Rearrange your study environment to present cues for studying and to eliminate cues for incompatible behaviors (such as watching TV). Pick three strategies and briefly describe each of them. Indicate whether each of the strategies involves presentation of an S^D, S^Δ, CMEO, or CMAO. In each case, justify your choice.

Notes and Extended Discussion

1. As Poling (2001) has pointed out, it is important to keep in mind that a given MO is likely to affect many behaviors, and a given behavior is likely to be affected by many MOs. Consider, for example, the MEO of food deprivation. Food deprivation not only increases the reinforcing value of food and leads to various food-seeking behaviors but also increases the reinforcing value of a broad range of abused drugs and could lead to increased drug use. It also increases the reinforcing value of water and thus increases water intake (Poling). Thus, for the MO concept to be maximally useful as a behavior management tool, researchers must examine ways for isolating MOs that affect important behaviors in predictable ways.

2. As described in Chapter 29, two major texts in the history of applied behavior analysis in the 1950s were *Principles of Psychology* (Keller & Schoenfeld, 1950) and *Science and Human Behavior* (Skinner, 1953). Both texts discussed a behavioral approach to the topic of motivation and considered variables such as deprivation and satiation. Keller and Schoenfeld introduced the term *establishing operation* to refer to such variables. By the 1970s, however, behavior modification texts (e.g., Fantino & Logan, 1979; Martin & Pear, 1978; Powers & Osborne, 1976; Whaley & Malott, 1971) no longer emphasized the topic of motivation. Beginning in the 1980s, Michael argued in a series of papers (1982, 1988, 1993, 2000, 2007) that behaviorally oriented psychologists needed to give more weight to the topic of motivation. Michael adopted Keller and Schoenfeld's term *establishing operation.* Because establishing operations as defined by Michael included *increasing* (i.e., establishing) the effectiveness of reinforcers as well as *decreasing* (i.e., abolishing) the effectiveness of reinforcers, Michael and colleagues (Laraway et al., 2003) proposed changing the term *establishing operation* to *motivating operation* and analyzed motivating operations as establishing or abolishing operations. Those are the terms that with one slight modification we have adopted in this book. We have inserted the word *motivating* before *establishing* and *abolishing* to indicate what has been established or abolished. For example, instead of

conditioned establishing operation (*CEO*), we use the term *conditioned motivating establishing operation* (*CMEO*). For a detailed discussion of the history of the treatment of motivation in applied behavior analysis, see Sundberg (2004). For a discussion of the application of motivating operations in organizational behavior management, see Agnew (1998) and Olsen, Laraway, and Austin (2001). For a discussion of the role of motivating operations in the treatment and prevention of problem behavior, see McGill (1999) and a special section of the *Journal of Applied Behavior Analysis* (Winter 2000).

3. Ingestion or injection of drugs also functions as a motivating operation (Pear, 2001, p. 281). Amphetamines, for example, function as a UMAO to decrease the reinforcing effectiveness of food; aphrodisiacs function as a UMEO to increase the reinforcing effectiveness of sexual stimulation. In this book, however, we focus on motivational variables that are located in the individual's external environment.

4. If you are familiar with Skinner's (1957) analysis of verbal behavior, you will recognize that when a parent asks "What do you want?" and a child replies "Juice," the child's response might be an *intraverbal*—a verbal response under the control of a preceding verbal stimulus with no point-to-point correspondence between the stimulus and the response. The child's response "Juice" is, however, at least partly a mand because it is under the control of a specific deprivation state. Thus, overlap among the different categories of verbal behavior can occur. In training mands, some intraverbal training may be necessary to begin. Ideally, the child will eventually learn to make requests without requiring an antecedent verbal stimulus to prompt the request. At that point, the child will be emitting pure mands.

Study Questions on Notes

1. What psychologist influenced a renewed emphasis on the concept of motivation by behaviorally oriented psychologists in the 1980s?
2. Describe an example illustrating that a given MO may affect the value of more than one reinforcer and may influence the occurrence of many behaviors.
3. Describe an example that illustrates how a drug might function as an MO. What subtype of MO would it be (see Figure 19-1)? Justify your answer.
4. Distinguish between an echoic and an intraverbal. Illustrate each with an example that is not in the text.

20 Behavioral Assessment: Initial Considerations

Throughout this book, numerous examples illustrate the effectiveness of behavior modification procedures. Many of these examples are accompanied by graphs showing the changes (increases or decreases) that occurred in behavior when particular procedures were applied. Some of the graphs also include follow-up observations indicating that the improvements were maintained after the programs had terminated. The graphs were presented not just to make it easier for you to understand the material; precise records of behavior represent an inseparable part of behavior modification procedures. Indeed, some people have gone so far as to say that the major contribution of behavior modification has been the insistence on accurately recording specific behaviors and making decisions on the basis of recorded data rather than merely on the basis of subjective impressions.

As indicated in Chapter 1, the behaviors to be improved in a behavior modification program are frequently called target behaviors. **Behavioral assessment** involves the collection and analysis of information and data in order to (a) identify and describe target behavior; (b) identify possible causes of the behavior; (c) select appropriate treatment strategies to modify the behavior; and (d) evaluate treatment outcome.

MINIMAL PHASES OF A PROGRAM

A successful behavior modification program typically involves four phases during which the target behavior is identified, defined, and recorded: (a) a screening or intake phase, (b) a preprogram assessment phase, (c) a treatment phase, and (d) a follow-up phase. In this section, we give a brief overview of these phases.

Screening or Intake Phase

The initial interactions between a client and a practitioner or an agency constitute the *intake phase.* During this phase, a client typically completes an *intake form,* which requests general information: the client's name, address, date of birth, marital status, and so forth. It also asks the client to state the reason for seeking service from that agency or practitioner.

One function of the screening phase is to determine whether a particular agency or behavior modifier is the appropriate one to deal with a potential client's behavior (Hawkins, 1979). If not, the results of this phase should indicate the agency or practitioner who should work with the client. For example, a center for children with learning difficulties might screen a child to determine whether the child's academic skills are unusual enough to require some sort of program not ordinarily provided by the school. A second function is to inform the client about the agency's or practitioner's policies and procedures related to service provision. A third function is to screen for the presence of a crisis condition (child abuse, suicide risk, etc.) that might require immediate intervention. A fourth function of the screening phase is to gather sufficient information through client interview and psychological tests (such as intelligence tests) to diagnose the client according to the standardized categories of mental disorder, such as those listed in the *Diagnostic and Statistical Manual of Mental Disorders, 4th ed., Text Revision* (American Psychiatric Association, 2000), also known as the *DSM-IV-TR*. As indicated in Note 1 of Chapter 1, clinics, hospitals, schools, and other agencies might require such diagnoses before treatment can be offered, and health insurance companies might require them before treatment can be paid for. A fifth function of the screening phase is to provide specific information about which behavior(s) should be assessed. To achieve this initial assessment, behavior modifiers use all of the above information plus other information such as teachers' reports, various traditional test results, and other assessment devices to aid in pinpointing specific target behaviors to address.

Preprogram Assessment Phase

During the *assessment* phase, the behavior modifier assesses the target behavior to determine its level prior to the introduction of the program or treatment and analyzes the individual's current environment to identify possible controlling variables of the behavior to be changed.

The need for a preprogram assessment phase follows from the importance that behavior modifiers place on directly measuring the behavior of concern and using changes in the measure as the best indicator that the problem is being helped as explained in Chapter 1. If a child is having difficulty in school, for example, the behavior modifier would be especially interested in obtaining a baseline of specific behavioral excesses or deficits that constitute the problem (e.g., a reading deficiency or disruptive behavior). Further details about the sources of information for the preprogram assessment phase are given later in this chapter.

Treatment Phase

After making a precise preprogram assessment, a behavior modifier will design a program to bring about the desired behavior change. In educational settings, such a program is typically referred to as a *training* or *teaching program*. In community and clinical settings, the program is referred to more often as an *intervention strategy* or a *therapy program*.

Behavior modification programs typically provide for frequent observation and monitoring of the behavior of interest during training or treatment. In some cases, the difference between behavior modification and other approaches on this point is primarily a matter of degree. Traditional educational practices typically involve periodic assessment during the teaching program for the purpose of monitoring the students' performance. Certain clinical treatment programs involve client assessment at various intervals. Moreover, some programs that have been labeled behavior modification have consisted primarily of before-and-after measures and have lacked precise, ongoing recording during treatment. Nevertheless, behavior modifiers emphasize and practice, to a degree rarely found in other approaches, frequent monitoring of the behavior throughout the application of the specific treatment or intervention strategies. In addition, behavior modifiers strongly emphasize changing the program if the measurements taken indicate that the desired change in behavior is not occurring within a reasonable period of time.

Follow-Up Phase

Finally, the *follow-up phase* is conducted to determine whether the improvements achieved during treatment are maintained after the program's termination. When feasible, this will consist of precise observation or assessment in the natural environment or under circumstances in which the behavior is expected to occur.

Study Questions

1. What does the term *target behavior* mean? Illustrate with an example from an earlier chapter.
2. Define *behavioral assessment*.
3. List the four phases of a behavior modification program.
4. What are the five functions of the intake phase of a behavior modification program?
5. What two things typically occur during the assessment phase of a behavior modification program?
6. In what types of settings are the terms *training program, therapy program,* and *intervention strategy* typically used?
7. What is the purpose of the follow-up phase of a behavior modification program?

SOURCES OF INFORMATION FOR PREPROGRAM ASSESSMENT

Defining target behaviors clearly, completely, and in measurable terms is an important prerequisite to the design and implementation of behavior modification programs. Behavioral assessment procedures for collecting information to define and monitor target behaviors fall into three categories: indirect, direct, and experimental.

Indirect Assessment Procedures

In many situations in which a behavior modification program might be applied, the behavior modifier (e.g., a nurse, a teacher, a parent, a coach) can directly observe the behavior of interest. However, suppose that you are a behavior therapist who, like other professional therapists, sees clients in your office at regularly scheduled appointment times. It might be impractical for you to observe clients regularly in the situations in which the target behaviors occur. Moreover, what if some of your clients wanted to change some of their thoughts and feelings that others couldn't observe? (As discussed in Chapters 15 and 27, behavior modifiers regard thoughts and feelings as private or covert behaviors.) For such changes, behavior therapists have made considerable use of indirect assessment procedures. The most common are interviews with the client and significant others, questionnaires, role-playing, information obtained from consulting professionals, and client self-monitoring. Indirect assessment procedures have the advantages of being convenient, not requiring an inordinate amount of time, and potentially providing information about covert behaviors. However, they suffer from the disadvantages that those providing information might not remember relevant observations accurately or have biases that would influence them to provide inaccurate data.

INTERVIEWS WITH THE CLIENT AND SIGNIFICANT OTHERS   Observation of an initial interview across a random sample of behavior therapists and therapists of other orientations would show many commonalities. When first meeting a therapist, many clients are anxious, so the therapist typically does most of the initial talking. The therapist might begin by briefly describing the types of problems with which he or she typically works. The therapist might then ask a number of simple questions concerning the client's background or might ask the client to complete a simple demographic referral form. The therapist might next invite the client to describe, in general terms, what the problem is (see Table 20–1). During initial interviews, behavior therapists and traditional therapists typically use similar techniques (being a good listener, asking open-ended questions, requesting clarification, and acknowledging the validity of the client's feelings and problems) to help the client feel at ease and to gain information about the problem.

In interviewing the client and significant others (spouse, parents, or anyone else directly concerned with the client's welfare), behavior therapists attempt to establish and maintain rapport with the client and the significant others just as traditionally oriented therapists do. This relationship can be facilitated by the therapist's being especially attentive to the client's description of the problem while refraining from expressing personal values that might unduly influence the client, showing empathy by communicating some understanding of the client's feelings, and emphasizing the confidentiality of the client–therapist relationship (Sarwer & Sayers, 1998).

Some behavior therapists keep the discussion during the initial interview at a general level. Others lead the discussion more directly to the presenting problem. Although individual differences exist among behavior therapists in this respect, most focus discussion on the specific behaviors that characterize a client's problem(s) relatively soon in the therapeutic relationship. This can be done by asking a number of questions about a problem and its controlling variables (see, e.g., Sarwer & Sayers, 1998). At some point in the interviewing process, the behavior therapist will (a) help the client identify major problem areas, (b) select one or two problem areas for initial treatment focus, (c) translate the problem areas into specific behavioral deficits or excesses, (d) attempt to identify controlling variables of the problem behavior, and (e) identify some specific behavioral objectives for treatment. Specific behavioral questionnaires and role-playing are often used to facilitate this process.

TABLE 20–1	Examples of Questions a Behavior Therapist Typically Asks During an Intake Interview

1. What seems to be the problem?
2. Can you describe what you typically say or do when you experience the problem?
3. How often does the problem occur?
4. For how long has the problem been occurring?
5. In what situations does the problem typically occur? In other words, what sets it off?
6. What tends to occur immediately after you experience the problem?
7. What are you typically thinking and feeling when the problem occurs?
8. How have you tried to deal with the problem thus far?

QUESTIONNAIRES   A well-designed questionnaire provides information that might be useful in assessing a client's problem and developing a behavioral program tailored to the client. A large number of such questionnaires are available; for example, Fischer and Corcoran (1994) published a collection of more than 300 questionnaires to help assess a wide range of problems. Several types of questionnaires are popular with behavior therapists:

> *Life history questionnaires* provide demographic data such as marital status, vocational status, and religious affiliation, and background data such as sexual, health, and educational histories. A notable example is *The Multimodal Life History Inventory* (Lazarus & Lazarus, 2005). *Self-report problem checklists* have the client indicate those problem(s) from a detailed list that apply to him or her. Such questionnaires are particularly useful in helping the therapist completely specify the problem or problems for which the client is seeking therapy (Jensen & Haynes, 1986). An example is the *Behavior Self-Rating Checklist* (Upper, Cautela, & Brook, 1975). Another example is the behavioral checklist shown in Figure 20–1, which was developed by the first author for sport psychology con-   NOTE 1
> sultation with figure skaters. For a comprehensive discussion of the issues involved in self-report, see Stone et al. (2000).

> *Survey schedules* provide the therapist information needed to conduct a particular therapeutic technique with the client. The questionnaire shown in Figure 3–3 provides information useful in applying positive reinforcement procedures. Other types of survey schedules are designed to provide information preparatory to using other behavioral procedures. Different types of survey schedules can be found in Cautela (1977, 1981).

> *Third-party behavioral checklists* or *rating scales* permit significant others and professionals to subjectively assess the frequency and quality of certain client behaviors. An example of such a checklist for use with individuals with developmental disabilities is the *Objective Behavioral Assessment of the Severely and Moderately Mentally Handicapped: The OBA* (Hardy, Martin, Yu, Leader, & Quinn, 1981). The OBA enables third-party informants who are familiar with the client's behavior to rate whether the client can perform a variety of tasks such as putting on a shirt or tying shoelaces. Incidentally, the OBA can also be used as a direct observation instrument.

ROLE-PLAYING   If it is not feasible for the therapist to observe the client in the actual situation in which the problem occurs, an alternative is to re-create that situation or at least certain crucial aspects of it in the therapist's office. That, essentially, is the rationale behind role-playing—the client and therapist enact interpersonal interactions related to the client's problem (as described in Chapter 18). For example, the client might enact being interviewed for a job with the therapist playing the role of the interviewer. Role-playing is frequently used both in assessing a problem and in treating it (see, e.g., p. 220).

INFORMATION FROM CONSULTING PROFESSIONALS   If other professionals (physicians, physiotherapists, teachers, nurses, social workers) have been dealing with the client in any way related to the problem, the therapist should obtain relevant information from them. A client's problem might be related to a medical factor about which his or her physician could provide important information for dealing with it. Before requesting such information, the client must give permission.

CLIENT SELF-MONITORING   Self-monitoring—the direct observation by the client of his or her own behavior—is the next best thing to the therapist's direct observation. We mention it under

Name _____	Date _____								
Would you say you need help or need to improve:	Check here if not sure	Definitely no		To some extent		Definitely yes			
Regarding Free Skating Practices, to:									
1. Set specific goals for every practice?	____	1	2	3	4	5			
2. Arrive at every practice totally committed to do your best?	____	1	2	3	4	5			
3. Consistently be stretched and warmed up <u>before</u> stepping on the ice at practice?	____	1	2	3	4	5			
4. Be more focused when doing your jumps and spins? (Answer "yes" if you often just do the jumps or spins in a haphazard way without trying to do your best.)	____	1	2	3	4	5			
5. Stay positive and not get down on yourself when you're having a bad practice?	____	1	2	3	4	5			
6. Make better use of <u>full</u> practice time?	____	1	2	3	4	5			
7. Overcome fear of doing difficult jumps?	____	1	2	3	4	5			
8. Improve consistency of jumps you can already land?	____	1	2	3	4	5			
9. Feel more confident about your ability to do difficult jumps?	____	1	2	3	4	5			
10. Not worry about what other skaters are doing?	____	1	2	3	4	5			
11. Figure out how to monitor progress on a new jump that you are learning, so that you don't get discouraged when progress seems slow?	____	1	2	3	4	5			
12. Do more <u>complete</u> program run-throughs (where you try everything in your program)?	____	1	2	3	4	5			
13. Keep track of your % landed during program run-throughs?	____	1	2	3	4	5			
14. Make better use of video feedback when learning a new jump?	____	1	2	3	4	5			
15. Push harder while stroking, in order to get in better shape?	____	1	2	3	4	5			
16. Keep a written record of your progress in meeting your goal?	____	1	2	3	4	5			

FIGURE 20–1 A questionnaire to assess areas in need of help during a seasonal sport psychology program for figure skaters.

indirect assessment procedures because the therapist does not observe the behavior directly. Thus, as with the other indirect assessment procedures, the therapist cannot have as much confidence in the observations as would be the case if a trained observer had made them.

Except for covert behavior, behaviors that might be self-monitored are the same as those that a trained observer would observe directly. These are described in Chapter 21. Self-monitoring might also aid the discovery of the causes of the problem behavior, as discussed in Chapter 23. Additional examples of self-monitoring are provided in Chapter 26.

Would you say you need help or need to improve:	Check here if not sure	Definitely no	To some extent	Definitely yes
Regarding Free Skating at a Competition, to:				
1. Stay confident at practices when you see what the other skaters are doing?	_____	1 2	3 4	5
2. At practices, forget about other skaters and just focus on your own skating?	_____	1 2	3 4	5
3. Avoid putting extra pressure on yourself when you see what other skaters are doing at practices?	_____	1 2	3 4	5
4. Learn how <u>not</u> to worry about other skaters?	_____	1 2	3 4	5
5. Learn how <u>not</u> to worry about where you will place?	_____	1 2	3 4	5
6. Have a better time management plan for the entire competition so you are well organized, eat healthy, and get lots of rest?	_____	1 2	3 4	5
7. Skate as well during a competition as during the last 2 or 3 weeks before the competition (in other words, skate up to your potential)?	_____	1 2	3 4	5
8. Stay loose (not too tense) during the last ½-hour or so before the 6' warmup?	_____	1 2	3 4	5
9. Stay loose (not too tense) during the 6' warmup?	_____	1 2	3 4	5
10. Stay loose (not too tense) after the 6' warmup while waiting for your turn?	_____	1 2	3 4	5
11. Stay loose (not too tense) when you go on the ice for your turn?	_____	1 2	3 4	5
12. Feel confident about your skating while stretching before the 6' warmup?	_____	1 2	3 4	5
13. Not be psyched out by other skaters?	_____	1 2	3 4	5
14. Feel confident about your skating during the 6' warmup?	_____	1 2	3 4	5
15. Feel confident about your skating after the 6' warmup, while waiting for your turn to skate?	_____	1 2	3 4	5
16. Take it one element at a time during your program (& not get ahead of yourself or think only about difficult elements)?	_____	1 2	3 4	5
17. Concentrate on easy elements as well as hard ones?	_____	1 2	3 4	5
18. Stay positive and skate well for the rest of your program, even if you fall?	_____	1 2	3 4	5

FIGURE 20–1 *Continued*

Direct Assessment Procedures

In each of the case histories at the beginning of Chapters 3–14, other individuals directly observed and precisely defined a client's specific behavior(s). Observation of a person's behavior by another individual constitutes a direct assessment procedure. The main advantage of direct assessment procedures is that they are more accurate than indirect assessment procedures.

Disadvantages of direct assessment procedures are that they are time consuming, require that observers be appropriately trained, and cannot be used to monitor covert behaviors. Chapter 21 is devoted to a discussion of direct assessment procedures.

Experimental Assessment Procedures

Experimental assessment procedures are used to clearly reveal the antecedent and consequent events that control and maintain problem behavior. Such procedures are referred to as *experimental functional analyses* or more simply as *functional analyses*. They are used to demonstrate that the occurrence of a behavior is a function of certain controlling variables. Functional analysis is discussed in detail in Chapter 23.

Computer-Assisted Data Collection

Computer technology increasingly is being used to facilitate data collection (Haynes, 1998; Thompson, Felce, & Symons, 2000). Computers greatly increase the efficiency and accuracy of the collection and analysis of direct observation and self-monitoring data (Farrell, 1991). Examples of computerized observation systems for direct assessment procedures have been described by Brown et al. (2006), Bush and Ciocco (1992), Hile (1991), McIver, Brown, Pfeiffer, Dowda, and Pate (2009), and Richard and Bobicz (2003). Brown et al. and McIver et al. described highly sophisticated hand-held systems in which an observer moves a light pen over various bar codes to enter the occurrence of different categories of children's physical activity in real time. For an overview of a number of computerized systems used for collecting observational data, see Kahng and Iwata (2000). Hand-held computers have also been used to facilitate client self-monitoring. For example, in a study by Taylor, Fried, and Kenardy (1990), clients used hand-held computers to record panic and anxiety symptoms, cognitive factors, and settings. In a study by Agras, Taylor, Feldman, Losch, and Burnett (1990), obese clients used hand-held computers to monitor their weight, caloric intake, exercise, daily goals, and goal attainment. Devices that automatically collect and record behavior are also being developed and used in applied settings. An example is the accelerometer, which is used for measuring and storing data on physical activity (Sirard & Pate, 2001). The device, which is typically worn at waist level, detects, measures, and records accelerations of the body.

Study Questions

8. What is prerequisite to the design and implementation of a behavior modification program?
9. Briefly distinguish between direct and indirect assessment procedures.
10. Describe two circumstances that might lead to the use of indirect assessment procedures.
11. Briefly describe the advantages and disadvantages of indirect assessment procedures.
12. List the five main types of indirect assessment procedures.
13. List and describe briefly four types of questionnaires used in behavioral assessments.
14. Briefly describe the advantages and disadvantages of direct assessment procedures.

DATA! DATA! DATA! WHY BOTHER?

Accurate data are recorded for a number of reasons. One reason is that, as indicated at the beginning of this chapter, an accurate behavioral preprogram assessment helps the behavior modifier to decide whether he or she is the appropriate one to design a treatment program. Considerations relevant to this are described in more detail in Chapter 24.

A second reason is that an accurate baseline will sometimes indicate that what someone thought to be a problem is actually not one. For example, a teacher might say, "I don't know what to do with Johnny; he's always hitting the other kids." But after taking a baseline, the teacher might discover that the behavior actually occurs so rarely that it does not merit a special program. Both of the authors have experienced this phenomenon more than once. Others have, too, as illustrated by the following example from Greenspoon (1976):

> The reliance on casual observation led a woman to complain to a psychologist that her husband rarely talked to her during mealtime. She said that his failure to talk to her was becoming an increasing source of annoyance to her and she wanted to do something about it. The psychologist suggested that she prepare a chart and record on the chart the number of times that he initiated a conversation or responded to the verbal behavior that she emitted. She agreed to the suggestion. At the end of a week, she called back to inform the psychologist that she was surprised and pleased to report that she had been in error. It turned out that her husband both initiated conversation and responded to her verbal emissions at a very high rate. (p. 177)

A third reason is that data collected during the preprogram assessment phase often helps the behavior modifier identify both the causes of a behavior and the best treatment strategy. For example, determining whether a behavioral excess of an individual is reinforced by the attention of others, whether it enables the individual to escape from the demands of an unpleasant task, or whether some other variable controls it can be helpful for discovering potential reinforcers and designing an effective intervention program. As mentioned, using information from a baseline to analyze the causes of behavior is referred to as a *functional assessment*; it is discussed further in Chapter 23.

A fourth reason for collecting accurate data throughout a program is that it provides a means for clearly determining whether the program is producing the desired change in behavior. Sometimes people claim that they do not need to record data to know whether a desirable change in behavior has occurred. No doubt this is often true. A mother obviously needs no data sheet or graphs to tell her that her child is completely toilet trained. But not all cases are so clear-cut—at least not immediately. Suppose that a child is acquiring toileting behavior very slowly. The parent might think that the program is not working and abandon it prematurely. With accurate data, this type of mistake can be avoided. This point is well illustrated by the following case.[1] Dr. Lynn Caldwell was consulted by a woman whose 6-year-old son was, in her words, "driving me up a wall with his constant slamming of the kitchen door every time he goes out of the kitchen." Dr. Caldwell asked the mother to obtain a baseline of the target behavior by tallying each instance of it on a sheet of paper attached to the refrigerator. Over a 3-day period, the total number of door slams was 123. Dr. Caldwell then instructed the mother to provide approval each time the boy went through the door without slamming it. However, she was to administer a brief time out each time he slammed the door. He was to go back and remain for 3 minutes in whichever room he had just left, and the mother was to ignore him during that time and then require him to

---

[1] This case was described by Lynn Caldwell at the first Manitoba Behavior Change Conference, Portage la Prairie, Manitoba, Canada, 1971.

proceed through the door without slamming it. After applying this procedure for three days, the mother brought the tally sheet to Dr. Caldwell. "This behavior modification stuff doesn't work," she complained, pointing to the large number of tally marks on the data sheet. "He's just as bad as he ever was." When the tally marks were counted, however, there were only 87 of them over the 3 days of treatment, compared with the 123 that were entered over the 3 days of baseline. Encouraged by this observation, the mother continued the program, and the behavior quickly dropped to an acceptable level of about five per day.

Without accurate data, one might also make the opposite type of error. One might conclude that a procedure is working and continue it when in fact it is ineffective and should be abandoned or modified. For example, Harris, Wolf, and Baer (1964) described the case of a boy in a laboratory preschool who had the annoying habit of pinching adults. His teachers decided to use a behavior modification procedure to encourage him to pat rather than pinch. After the procedure had been in effect for some time, the teachers agreed that they had succeeded in reducing pinching by substituting patting. When they looked at the data recorded by an outside observer, however, they saw clearly that, although patting was considerably above the level it had been during the baseline recordings, pinching had not decreased from its baseline level. Perhaps concentrating on the procedure or the patting so diverted the teachers that they had failed to notice the pinching as much as they had before introducing the procedure. In any case, had it not been for the recorded data, the teachers probably would have wasted a great deal more time and effort than they did on an ineffective procedure.

A fifth reason for accurately recording behavior is that publicly posted results—preferably in the form of a graph or a chart—can prompt and reinforce behavior modifiers for carrying out a program. In training centers for persons with developmental disabilities, for example, staff often become more conscientious in applying procedures when up-to-date charts or graphs clearly showing the effects of the procedures are posted conspicuously (e.g., see Hrydowy & Martin, 1994). Parents and teachers alike might find that their efforts to modify children's behavior are strengthened by graphic representation of the behavior.

A final reason for recording data is that the displayed data might lead to improvements by the learner separately from any further treatment program. This is an example of a phenomenon known as *reactivity* (Tyron, 1998): When people know that their behavior is being observed either by others or by self-recording, their observed behaviors might change. For example, students who graph their own study behavior (e.g., by daily recording the number of paragraphs or pages studied or the amount of time spent studying) might find increases in the graph to be reinforcing (see Figure 20–2). Data that are presented appropriately can be reinforcing even to young children. For example, an occupational therapist at a school for children with handicaps once consulted one of the authors concerning a 7-year-old girl who each morning took an excessive amount of time taking off her outside garments and hanging them up. It appeared that the teachers could not be persuaded to stop attending to the child when she was in the coatroom. The author suggested that the therapist somehow attempt to influence the child with a graph of the amount of time she spent in the coatroom each morning. The procedure that the therapist devised proved to be as effective as it was ingenious.[2] A large chart was hung on the wall. The chart was colored green to represent grass, and a carrot patch was depicted near the bottom of it. Days were

---

[2] We are grateful to Nancy Staisey for providing us with the details of this procedure.

FIGURE 20–2 Monitoring and charting performance can serve at least six functions. Can you name them?

indicated along the bottom of the chart and the amount of time in the coatroom was indicated along the side. Each day, a circle was marked on the chart to indicate the amount of time spent in the coatroom in the morning, and a small paper rabbit was attached to the most recent circle. Using simple language, the therapist explained the procedure to the child and concluded by saying, "Now let's see if you can get the bunny down to eat the carrots." When the rabbit was down to the level of the carrots, the child was encouraged to keep it there. "Remember, the longer the bunny stays in the carrot patch, the more it can eat." A follow-up showed that the improved behavior persisted over a period of one year.

Behavior modifiers were not the first to discover the usefulness of recording one's behavior to help modify it. As with many other supposedly "new" psychological discoveries, the real credit should perhaps go to the writers of great literature. For example, novelist Ernest Hemingway used self-recording to help maintain his literary output. One of his interviewers reported the following (Plimpton, 1965, p. 219):

He keeps track of his daily progress—"so as not to kid myself"—on a large chart made out of the side of a cardboard packing case and set up against the wall under the nose of a mounted gazelle head. The numbers on the chart showing the daily output of words differ from 450, 575, 462, 1250, back to 512, the higher figures on days Hemingway puts in extra work so he won't feel guilty spending the following day fishing on the gulf stream.

Author Irving Wallace also used self-recording even before he was aware that others had done the same. In a book touching on his writing methods (1971, pp. 65–66), he made the following comment.

I kept a work chart when I wrote my first book—which remains unpublished—at the age of nineteen. I maintained work charts while writing my first four published books. These charts showed the date I started each chapter, the date I finished it, and number of pages written in that period. With my fifth book, I started keeping a more detailed chart which also showed how many pages I had written by the end of every working day. I am not sure why I started keeping such records. I suspect that it was because, as a free-lance writer, entirely on my own, without employer or deadline, I wanted to create disciplines for myself, ones that were guilt-making when ignored. A chart on the wall served as such a discipline, its figures scolding me or encouraging me.

See Wallace and Pear (1977) for examples of his charts.

Study Questions

15. Give six reasons for collecting accurate data during an assessment or baseline phase and throughout a program.
16. What error does the case of Dr. Caldwell and the door slammer's mother exemplify? Explain how accurately recorded data counteracted this error.
17. What error does the case of the boy who went around pinching adults exemplify? Explain how accurately recorded data counteracted this error.
18. What does *reactivity* mean in behavioral assessment? Illustrate with an example.
19. Briefly describe the details of the clever graphing system devised for the child who got the rabbit to the carrot patch.
20. Briefly describe how Ernest Hemingway and Irving Wallace used self-recording to help them maintain their writing behavior.

BEHAVIORAL ASSESSMENT COMPARED TO TRADITIONAL ASSESSMENT

As indicated in Chapter 2, a major purpose of traditional psychodiagnostic assessment is to identify the type of mental disorder presumed to underlie abnormal behavior. Behavioral assessment began to emerge during the 1960s and 1970s in response to criticisms made by behaviorally oriented psychologists against the underlying assumptions of traditional psychodiagnostic assessment approaches (Nelson, 1983). Barrios and Hartmann (1986) described some differences in the aims, assumptions, and applications of the behavioral and traditional approaches to assessment (see the summary in Table 20–2).

TABLE 20–2	Some Differences Between Behavioral and Psychodiagnostic Approaches to Assessment	
Behavioral Approach	**Psychodiagnostic Approach**	
Basic Assumptions		
—Performance on a checklist is a sample of a person's response to specific stimuli —Covert behaviors (thoughts and feelings) are like overt behaviors (in terms of their controlling variables) and are not accorded special status	—Test performance is viewed as a sign of an enduring, intrapsychic trait, or person variable —Covert behaviors (e.g., cognitions) are viewed as fundamentally different from overt behaviors	
Goals of Assessment		
—To identify behavioral excesses or deficits —To identify environmental causes of current problem behaviors	—To diagnose or classify individuals —To identify intrapsychic or trait causes of behavior	
Methods of Assessment		
—Preference for direct observation of specific Behaviors	—Direct assessment of intrapsychic factors and underlying traits is impossible (by definition)	
Frequency of Assessment		
—Preference for continuous assessments before, during, and after application of intervention	—Typically pre- and posttreatment assessments based on standardized tests	

Study Questions

21. How does a behavioral approach differ from a traditional approach to assessment in terms of a basic assumption about performance on a test or a checklist?
22. Describe two differences in the goals of a behavioral approach to assessment compared to a traditional approach.
23. Describe a difference between the method of a behavioral approach compared to a traditional approach to assessment.

Note and Extended Discussion

1. Martin, Toogood, and Tkachuk (1997) developed a manual of self-report problem checklists for sport psychology consultation. For example, the sport psychology checklist for basketball players asks such questions as: "Would you say that you need to improve at tuning out negative thoughts, staying relaxed, and not getting too nervous just before or during a game?" and "Do you need to improve at identifying and reacting to your opponents' weaknesses and making adjustments as the game progresses?" The manual includes self-report problem checklists for 21 sports. Each checklist contains 20 items to identify areas in which an athlete might need to improve before or during competitions, 5 items to identify areas in which an athlete might need to improve on postcompetition evaluations, and 17

items to identify areas in which an athlete might need to improve at practices. These behavioral checklists are not like traditional psychological tests such as the Wexler Adult Intelligence Scale (Wexler, 1981) or the 16-Personality Factor Inventory (Cattell, Eber, & Tatsuoka, 1970). Behavioral checklists do not have norms, nor are they designed to measure character or personality traits. Rather, such behavioral assessment tools provide information necessary to design effective interventions for remediating deficits or excesses in specific situations with individual athletes. While formal research on these tools has been limited, those checklists that have been formally researched have shown high test–retest reliability and high face validity (Leslie-Toogood & Martin, 2003; Lines, Schwartzman, Tkachuk, Leslie-Toogood, & Martin, 1999). Feedback from athletes and sport psychology consultants who have used various checklists in the manual mentioned here has been uniformly positive concerning their value in obtaining useful behavioral assessment information.

Study Questions on Note

1. What is the major purpose of sport-specific behavioral checklists?
2. What are two differences between behavioral checklists and traditional psychological tests?

21 Direct Behavioral Assessment: What to Record and How

Suppose that you have chosen a particular behavior to modify. How do you directly measure, assess, or evaluate that behavior? As mentioned in Chapter 20, behavior modifiers prefer direct to indirect measurement. In measuring behavior directly, six general characteristics should be considered: topography, amount, intensity, stimulus control, latency, and quality.

CHARACTERISTICS OF BEHAVIOR TO BE RECORDED

Topography of Behavior

As indicated in Chapter 10, the **topography** of a response is the specific movements involved in making the response. Suppose that a teacher wants to shape arm raising by a child with developmental disabilities as a means of obtaining attention in a classroom. The teacher might first identify the measurable levels of arm raising described in Table 21–1 and then proceed with a shaping program based on those levels. An observer would be fairly accurate in recording instances of these topographies during the shaping process.

    Picture prompts are sometimes useful for helping observers to identify variations in the topography of a response. One of the authors developed detailed checklists with picture prompts for evaluating swimming strokes of young competitive swimmers. See Figure 21–1 for the backstroke checklist.

Amount of Behavior

Two measures of the amount of a given behavior are frequency and duration.

FREQUENCY OF BEHAVIOR   **Frequency (or rate) of behavior** refers to the number of instances of a behavior that occurs in a given period of time. If you wanted to improve the practice performance of young figure skaters, you might examine the frequency with which they performed various jumps and spins. That was the approach taken by Michelle Hume, a figure skating coach at **NOTE 1**

TABLE 21–1	Levels of Arm Raising from Poor Quality to Good Quality
1. While sitting at a table and resting both arms on the table,	the student raises an arm so that the hand and forearm are approximately 2 inches off the table.
2. While sitting at a table and resting both arms on the table,	the student raises an arm so that it is approximately at her chin level.
3. While sitting at a table and resting both arms on the table,	the student raises an arm so that it is approximately at her eye level.
4. While sitting at a table and resting both arms on the table,	the student raises an arm so that her hand is slightly above her head.
5. While sitting at a table and resting both arms on the table,	the student raises an arm so that it is pointing upward with her hand 6 inches above her head, but her elbow is still bent.
6. While sitting at a table and resting both arms on the table,	the student raises an arm so that it is pointing straight above her head.

St. Anne's Figure Skating Club in Manitoba, (Hume et al., 1985). Coach Hume first defined jumps and spins in such a way that student observers could decide when either of those responses occurred. A *jump* was defined as any occasion when a skater jumped in the air so that both skates left the ice, a minimum of one complete revolution occurred in the air, and the skater landed on one foot, facing in the opposite direction without falling. A *spin* was defined as spinning on one skate for a minimum of three revolutions while maintaining a balanced, stationary position. When the observers knew what behaviors to look for, Coach Hume's next step was to take a baseline of the number of jumps and spins each individual skater performed during several practices. The observers used the data sheet shown in Figure 21–2.

In many situations, an individual does not have the time or a helper to take data using paper and pencil. Fortunately, other ways of measuring quantity require minimal time. One such method is to use a golf counter. With these counters, you can count up to 99 simply by pressing a button for each instance of the behavior. You could also use an electronic calculator and press +1 each time an instance of the behavior occurs; the calculator keeps track of the total. As described in the previous chapter, hand-held computers are used to record more than one behavior or the behavior of more than one individual and the times at which each instance of behavior occurs (Brown et al., 2006; McIver, Brown, Pfeiffer, Dowda, & Pate, 2009; Paggeot, Kvale, Mace, & Sharkey, 1988; Repp, Karsh, Felce, & Ludewig, 1989). For detailed guides to counting and recording responses, other topics relating to measuring and graphing behavioral outcomes and using the results to make clinical decisions, see Hawkins, Mathews, and Hamdan (1999) and Thompson, Felce, and Symons (2000).

The baseline performance of one of the figure skaters in Coach Hume's program can be seen in Figure 21–3. This type of graph is called a *frequency graph*. Each data point represents the total number of elements (jumps plus spins) completed by a skater during a practice session. Following baseline, a chart prepared for each skater contained a checklist of all jumps and spins that he or she should be practicing. These charts were posted at the side of the rink. Pointing to the charts, Coach Hume said to the skaters: "Each practice session, do the first three elements on your chart and then record them here. Then practice the next three elements and record them. Continue in this way until you've practiced all the elements. Then go through the whole routine again until the end of practice. At the end of practice, I will check your charts to see how you are

FIGURE 21–1 Checklist for the backstroke.

Date: January 3 Student: Kathy				Observer: Bill K.
			Observation	
	Instances	Total	Time	Additional Comments
Jumps:	++++ ++++ ++++ ++++ ++++ ++++ ++++ ++	35	25 min	Kathy spent 5 minutes chatting with other skaters
Spins:	++++ ++++ ++++	15	20 min	

FIGURE 21–2 A sample data sheet for recording jumps and spins at figure skating practices.

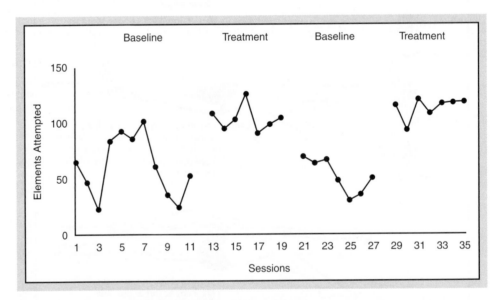

FIGURE 21–3 Frequency graph of the number of elements (jumps and spins) per session performed by a figure skater during baseline and treatment (self-recording).

doing." The self-charting program combined with positive feedback from Coach Hume at the end of each practice was effective in improving the number of jumps and spins performed (see Figure 21–3). Interestingly, when charting and coach feedback were discontinued, performance decreased to near baseline levels. When charting and coach feedback were reinstated, performance once again improved.

Sometimes a frequency graph is not the most informative way to present data. Consider a study by Mulaire-Cloutier, Vause, Martin, and Yu (2000). These researchers examined the effects of giving persons with severe intellectual disabilities a choice versus no choice of work tasks. During the first of three daily sessions, each participant was given a choice of which of two tasks to work on. In the remaining two daily sessions, the participants were randomly given either the the task they had preferred on the first session or the less preferred task. Because the participants were nonverbal and could not describe how they felt about the different tasks, one dependent measure was a happiness indicator. This consisted of behaviors such as smiling, laughing, and yelling while smiling. A frequency graph of the happiness indicators displayed by one of the participants in the three conditions is shown in Figure 21–4A. Because of the small and somewhat inconsistent effects of the three conditions, it's difficult to see clear differences between the conditions in that figure.

Now look at Figure 21–4B. This figure is based on the same data as the frequency graph in Figure 21–4A. However, Figure 21–4B is a *cumulative graph.* In this type of graph, each response for a condition during a session is cumulated or added to the total responses of all previous sessions for that condition. Consider, for example, the happiness indicators during the no-choice less preferred task (the bottom line). The first three sessions had no happiness indicators, and the cumulative total of zero was therefore plotted corresponding to sessions 1, 2, and 3. The fourth session had 3 happiness indicators, yielding a cumulative total of 3 plotted for session 4. The fifth session had 2 happiness indicators, which, added to the previous total of 3, made a total of 5 happiness indicators, and that cumulative total was plotted for session 5. During session 6, 5 happiness indicators were added, yielding a cumulative total across the first six sessions of 10 happiness indicators, and a data point was therefore placed at 10 for session 6. In this way, the performance during any one session of a condition was added to the total performance during all previous sessions of that condition and then graphed on the cumulative record.

Note that on a cumulative graph, the average slope of the line over an interval indicates how many responses occurred during that period of time. In other words, the slope of the line in a cumulative graph indicates the rate of the response. The low slope of the line during the no-choice less preferred condition indicates a low rate of happiness indicators. The highest slope during the choice condition indicates the highest rate of happiness indicators. Another feature of a cumulative graph should be noted: The line can never decrease. If a participant is not performing at all as during the first three sessions of the no-choice less preferred condition, no response is cumulated with what is already there, and the line is flat. In short, a steep line indicates a high rate of responding; a flat line indicates zero responding.

A cumulative graph is usually preferred over a frequency graph when comparing two or more behaviors or conditions and when the differences are small. You can see that differences in the frequency of happiness indicators between the choice, no-choice preferred, and no-choice less preferred tasks are difficult to detect when plotted as frequency graphs in Figure 21–4A. However, when those same data are plotted cumulatively in Figure 21–4B, the gradual spread of the cumulative results shows clear differences between the three conditions. Requiring the workers to function at the less preferred task produced the lowest overall rate of happiness indicators while allowing the workers to choose among tasks produced the highest rate of happiness indicators.

It is sometimes convenient to design a recording sheet that also serves as a final graph. Consider the case of a child who frequently swore at the teacher and teacher's aides in the classroom. The teacher decided to record this behavior using the chart shown in Figure 21–5. Each time the teacher or teacher's aides observed an instance of swearing, they were to ignore the child and go to the front desk and place an X in the appropriate place on the chart.

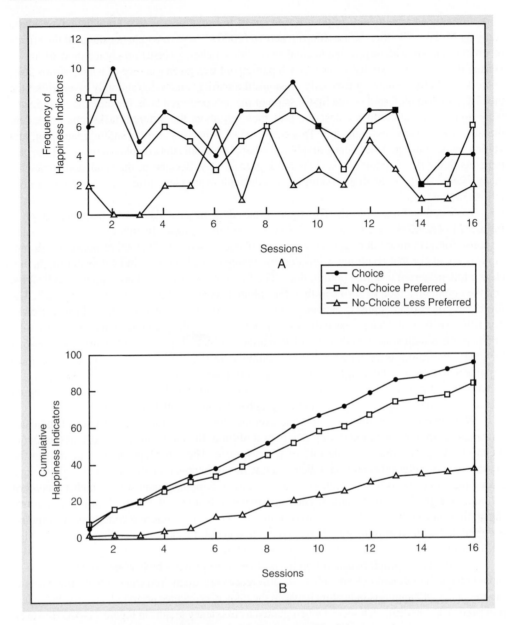

FIGURE 21–4   A frequency graph **(A)** and a cumulative graph **(B)** of the same data.

The instances of swearing were recorded up the side of the graph and the days of the program were recorded across the bottom (see Figure 21–5). Each time an instance of swearing occurred, the staff would simply add an X for the appropriate day to the number of Xs that were already on the chart for that particular day. The graph shows clearly that many instances of swearing occurred during the first 10 days. Apparently, something other than attention from the teacher or teacher's aides was maintaining the behavior. On day 11, as the double vertical line in the chart indicates, the child was placed on the following differential reinforcement of other

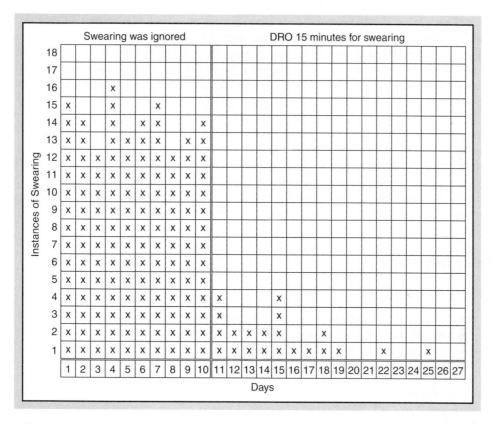

FIGURE 21–5 Jackie's swearing behavior. Each X represents one swear word.

behavior (DRO) schedule: Reinforcement occurred at the end of each 15-minute period in which swearing did not occur. The result can be clearly seen: Swearing showed an immediate drop and eventually decreased to zero. (*Note:* These data are hypothetical and are presented to illustrate the plotting procedure.) This type of graph is useful for those who do not have the time to rechart their behavior tallies from their data sheet to a graph.

Each instance of a behavior that is recorded in terms of frequency, such as jumping or spinning as defined for the figure skaters, is a separate, individually distinct behavior that is easy to tally in a given period of time. Behavior modifiers have recorded the frequency of such behaviors as saying a particular word, swearing, throwing objects, completing arithmetic problems, chewing mouthfuls of food, taking puffs on a cigarette, and exhibiting nervous twitches. Each of these behaviors has characteristics so that successive occurrences of the given behavior are relatively brief and the amount of time that it takes to perform the behavior is about the same from one occasion to the next.

DURATION OF BEHAVIOR   While frequency or rate is a common measure of the amount of behavior, the relative duration of a behavior or, more precisely, the sum of its durations divided by total time, is also sometimes important in measuring amount. The **relative duration of behavior** is the length of time that it occurs within some period. In dealing with a behavior such as temper tantrumming, you may be more concerned with its duration than with its frequency. In fact, frequency can be ambiguous when trying to apply it to something like temper tantrums

(Pear, 2004). What should we count as a separate response? Each cry, scream, or kick on the floor? Or should we count each episode of tantrumming as a separate response? Because it's usually difficult to answer these questions, we can generally avoid them by focusing on the duration of tantrumming. Other examples of behaviors for which duration may be more appropriate than frequency are listening attentively, sitting in one's seat in a classroom, watching television, talking on the telephone, and taking coffee breaks.

If you are concerned with keeping track of the relative duration of some activity over successive sessions or days, you might easily tabulate and present these data for effective visual display on a combined data sheet/graph. For example, an individual concerned with monitoring TV watching might prepare a chart showing cumulative minutes of TV watching up the side and days across the bottom. The slope of this graph would indicate the relative duration of the person's TV watching, just as the slope of a cumulative frequency graph indicates response rate. Duration of behavior is measured using timers, stopwatches, or clocks.

Study Questions

1. What does the *topography* of a behavior mean? Describe an example that is not in this chapter.
2. Name two common measures of the overall amount of a given behavior.
3. What does the *frequency* of a behavior mean? Describe an example that is not in this chapter.
4. Describe three ways to keep track of the number of times a certain response occurs during a day.
5. Make a frequency graph and a cumulative graph of the following instances of a behavior that were observed during successive sessions: 3, 7, 19, 0, 0, 0, 27, 12, 12, 6.
6. Describe at least four ways in which a cumulative graph of a set of data differs from a frequency graph of the same data.
7. On a cumulative graph, what can you infer from the following?
   a. a high or steep slope
   b. a low slope
   c. a flat line
8. What two characteristics do behaviors recorded in terms of frequency usually show?
9. What do we mean by the *relative duration* of a behavior? Give and explain an example in which relative duration might be more appropriate than frequency.

Intensity of Behavior

Sometimes we are concerned with measuring the intensity, magnitude, or force of a response. Assessments of intensity often utilize instrumentation. For example, when voice loudness is the behavior of concern, decibel level can be measured by a device called a *voice meter*. To measure the strength of grip pressure (such as during a handshake), a device called a *dynamometer* can be used. Measures of force are common in the skills involved in various sports. Machines are now available that assess how hard a pitcher can throw a baseball or a hockey player can shoot a hockey puck. The speed of an object as determined with such devices is used to infer the force with which it was propelled.

Stimulus Control of Behavior

We often assess a behavior in terms of the conditions under which it might be observed to occur. As we pointed out in Chapter 8, the term **stimulus control** refers to the degree of correlation between a stimulus and a response. An example of an assessment instrument that evaluates stimulus control is the Assessment of Basic Learning Abilities (ABLA) test developed by pioneering behaviorists Nancy Kerr and Lee Meyerson. The ABLA assesses the ease with which persons with intellectual disabilities are able to learn six stimulus-discrimination levels: *Level 1, imitation,* a tester puts an object into a container and asks a client to do likewise; *Level 2, position discrimination,* a tester presents a red box and a yellow can in fixed left-right positions and requires a client to consistently place an object in the container on the left; *Level 3, visual discrimination,* when the red box and the yellow can are presented in randomized left-right positions, a client is required to consistently place a neutral nonmatching object in the yellow can independent of its position when the teacher says, "Put it in"; *Level 4, visual match-to-sample,* a client demonstrates visual match-to-sample behavior if, when she or he is allowed to view the yellow can and the red box in randomized left-right positions and is then presented a yellow cylinder or a red cube sequentially, she or he consistently places the yellow cylinder in the yellow can and the red cube in the red box; *Level 5, auditory discrimination,* when presented with the yellow can and the red box in fixed left-right positions, a client is under the control of auditory cues when consistently putting a nonmatching object in the appropriate container when the tester randomly says, "red box" or "yellow can"; and *Level 6, auditory-visual combined discrimination,* the client correctly puts a nonmatching object into the yellow can or the red box when the position of the containers and the tester's request for one or the other are randomly alternated.

During the assessment of each ABLA level, correct responses are reinforced. and incorrect responses are followed by an error-correction procedure. Testing at a level continues until a client meets a pass criterion of eight consecutive correct responses or a failure criterion of eight cumulative errors. Research on the ABLA test indicates that the six levels are ordered in difficulty from Levels 1 (easier) to 6 (most difficult) and that it is a valuable tool for teachers and rehabilitation workers for selecting and sequencing training and work tasks for persons with profound, severe, and moderate intellectual disabilities (Martin, Thorsteinsson, Yu, Martin, & Vause, 2008; Vause, Yu, & Martin, 2007). For example, a client who passes ABLA Level 4 is able to readily learn socially useful identity matching tasks such as sorting socks into pairs or restocking a salad bar at a fast-food restaurant.

Behavior modification programs concerned with the development of preverbal and verbal skills are typically preceded by behavior assessments of the stimulus control of the client's verbal behavior. Tests are available to determine the conditions under which clients will emit appropriate requesting behavior, echoic behavior, or object identification (i.e., mands, echoics, or tacts, as described in Chapter 19; also see Marion et al., 2003). In many training programs, the critical measure of behavior is whether the client identifies some pictorial or printed stimulus correctly (see, e.g., Verbeke, Martin, Yu, & Martin, 2007). In such cases, the client's identification response is said to be controlled by the stimulus that the client is identifying. For that matter, any kind of test in which a person answers questions is a test of the stimulus control of behavior. Such tests assess whether the correct answers are under the control of the questions.

Latency of Behavior

The **latency** of a behavior is the time between the occurrence of a stimulus and the beginning of that behavior. For example, although a child in a classroom might work effectively once started, when first given a task, the child seems to fool around forever before starting. This child has a long latency getting started. Like duration, latency is assessed using timers, stopwatches, or clocks.

Quality of Behavior

Concern about the quality of a behavior is frequently encountered in everyday life. Teachers might describe the quality of a child's handwriting as good, average, or poor. In judgmental sports such as diving, gymnastics, and figure skating, athletes receive points based on the quality of their performances. We all make resolutions to do various activities "better." But quality is not a characteristic additional to those mentioned previously. Rather, it is a refinement of one or more of them. Sometimes differences in judgments of quality are based on topography, as when a figure skating jump that is landed on one foot is considered better than one that lands on two feet. Sometimes it is a combination of frequency and stimulus control. For example, someone who is a good student is most likely to show a high frequency of studying and answering test questions correctly. A child who is said to be "good" shows a high frequency of minding or following instructions from parents and teachers. In terms of latency, a runner who leaves the blocks very quickly after the firing of the starter's pistol might be considered to have a "good" start, while a runner who shows a longer latency had a "poor" start. Thus, quality of response is essentially an arbitrary designation of one or more of the previously mentioned characteristics of behavior that has some functional or social value.

Study Questions

10. What is another word for the *intensity* of a response? Describe an example in which it would be important to measure the intensity of a behavior.
11. Define *stimulus control,* and give an example.
12. Name the six levels that the ABLA assesses.
13. Describe the details of the stimulus control assessed by Level 4, visual match-to-sample discrimination.
14. Describe the details of the stimulus control that the ABLA test assesses with Level 6, auditory-visual combined discrimination.
15. What do we mean by the *latency* of a response? Describe an example that is not in this chapter.
16. Using an example, explain how the quality of a behavior is a refinement of one or more of the other dimensions of behavior.

STRATEGIES FOR RECORDING BEHAVIOR

One could attempt to observe and record any given target behavior whenever it occurs. In most cases, this is simply impractical. A more practical alternative is to designate a specific period of time in which to observe and record the behavior. Of course, the period in which observations may be made should be chosen because the behavior is particularly likely to occur or is of particular concern during that period, such as a training session, a mealtime, or a recess time. The three basic techniques for recording behavior during a specific observation period are continuous recording, interval recording, and time sampling.

Continuous recording is the recording of every instance of a behavior during a designated observation period. A continuous recording system is commonly used when successive responses are quite similar in duration, such as the number of cigarettes smoked, instances of a child pinching another child, or frequency of saying *ain't*. But what if successive responses are of variable duration, such as time spent watching TV or on Facebook or exhibiting off-task behavior in a classroom? In such cases, interval recording is commonly used.

Interval recording logs the behavior as either occurring or not occurring during short intervals of equal duration (e.g., intervals of 10 seconds) during the specified observation period (such as 30 minutes). The two types of interval recording procedures are partial interval and whole interval. *Partial-interval recording* records the target behavior a maximum of once per interval regardless of how many times the behavior occurs during each interval and regardless of the behavior's duration. An observer might use a tape recorder or other device that plays a pre-recorded audible signal such as a beep to indicate the end of one interval and the start of the next. Suppose that two behaviors of a child in nursery school that are of concern are the child's frequent inappropriate touching and loud vocalizations. The two behaviors are to be recorded independently. For each behavior, if an instance occurs once during a 10-second interval, a tally is made on the data sheet (for a sample data sheet, see Figure 21–6). If several instances of a behavior occur during a 10-second interval, the observer still makes only one tally. As soon as the beep is heard, indicating the start of the next 10-second interval, the behavior is again recorded if it occurs. *Whole-interval recording* notes the target behavior as occurring during an interval only if it persists throughout the entire interval. This type of interval recording is less commonly used than partial-interval recording. Behavior recorded with either a partial-interval or a whole-interval recording procedure is typically graphed in terms of the percentage of observation intervals in which the behavior is recorded as occurring.

Time-sampling recording scores a behavior as occurring or not occurring during very brief observation intervals that are separated from each other by a much longer period of time. For example, a parent of a preschool child might be concerned about the frequency of the child's sitting and rocking back and forth (a self-stimulation behavior). It might be useful to have records of when this behavior occurs and how as long as it occurs throughout the child's waking hours, but in general this is not realistic. An alternative is for the parent to seek out the child once every hour and make a note of whether the child shows any sitting and rocking behavior during a 15-second observation interval. Each observation interval is separated from the next by approximately 1 hour. This type of observational technique enables one observer to record one or more behaviors of one or more individuals even though the observer has many other commitments

FIGURE 21–6 Sample data sheet for interval recording.

DATE _____							
	Behavior			**Location**			**Comments**
Time	Sitting	Standing	Rocking	Kitchen	Living Room	Bedroom	
8:00 AM							
9:00							
10:00							
11:00							
12:00 PM							
1:00							
2:00							
3:00							
4:00							
5:00							
6:00							
7:00							
8:00							
9:00 PM							

FIGURE 21–7   A time-sampling data sheet for recording behavior of a child who frequently sits and rocks.

during the day. An example of a data sheet for time sampling appears in Figure 21–7. A special case of time sampling is referred to as *momentary time sampling* in which a behavior is recorded as occurring or not occurring at specific points in time, such as every hour on the hour rather than during specific brief intervals. (For a comparison of mometary time-sampling and partial-interval recording, see Meany-Daboul, Roscoe, Bourret, & Ahearn, 2007.)

Often observers use a recording procedure with features of both interval recording and time-sampling recording. For example, an observer might watch the learner for a specified interval (say, 10 seconds) and then record the behavior during the next 10 seconds. This strategy of *observe* (for 10 seconds) and *record* (for 10 seconds) would continue over a given period of time (for instance, half an hour). In this way, one observer may record the behavior of several learners. In such a case, the observer might watch one learner for 10 seconds and then record a behavior as occurring or not occurring, watch another learner for 10 seconds and record a behavior as occurring or not occurring, and so forth, until all learners have been observed once. All of them would then be observed a second time, a third time, and so forth, throughout the observation period. Such a procedure would likely be referred to as an *interval-recording procedure,* although, strictly speaking, it could also be described as time sampling with a very brief time between observation intervals. For a summary of the recording strategies just discussed, see Table 21–2.

TABLE 21–2	Summary of Types of Recording Strategies	
Type	**Observation Intervals**	**Criteria for Recording**
Continuous	Equal to the observation period	Record every instance of the behavior.
Partial interval	Short and of equal lengths within an observation period	Record behavior as having occurred once in an interval if it occurred at least once during the interval.
Whole interval	Short and of equal lengths within an observation period	Record behavior as having occurred once in an interval if it occurred throughout that interval.
Time sampling	A short interval within a much larger observation period (which typically is repeated)	Record behavior as having occurred once in an interval if it occurred at least once during the interval.
Momentary time sampling	The observation interval reduced to a single point in time	Record behavior as having occurred during the observation period if it was occurring at the momentary observation point.
Combined interval time sampling	Small intervals of equal length within an observation period	Record behavior only during some portion of the intervals (e.g., once every 4 intervals).

Study Questions

17. Define *continuous recording*. Describe an example that is not in this chapter.
18. Define *interval recording*. Distinguish between the partial-interval recording system and the whole-interval recording system.
19. When would one likely select a continuous recording system?
20. When would one likely select an interval-recording system over a continuous recording system?
21. Define *time-sampling recording*. Describe an example that is not in this chapter.
22. Briefly describe momentary time-sampling recording.

ASSESSMENT OF THE ACCURACY OF OBSERVATIONS

Hawkins and Dotson (1975) identified three sources of error that can affect the accuracy of observations. First, the *response definition* might be vague, subjective, or incomplete, so that the observer has problems in making accurate observations. Second, the *observational situation* might be such that an observer has difficulty detecting the behavior because of distractions or other obstructions to the observing process or because the behavior is too subtle or complex to be observed accurately in that situation. Third, the *observer* might be poorly trained, unmotivated, or biased. We might add two other possible sources of error: poorly designed *data sheets* and cumbersome *recording procedures*. Because any one or a combination of these sources of error might be present in any behavior modification project, behavior modifiers frequently conduct **interobserver reliability (IOR)** estimates. Two independent observers might record observations of the same behavior of the same individual during a given session. They are careful not to influence or signal each other while they are recording or to peek at each other's observations. The question is, given their best efforts while using the available behavior definitions and recording procedures and considering their training, how closely will their scores compare? Several IOR procedures can evaluate this, but two are more common than the others.

To illustrate one common IOR procedure, we return to the example of the observer recording the number of elements (jumps plus spins) of figure skaters. Suppose that a second observer stands on the opposite side of the ice rink from the first observer. The second observer is familiar with the definitions of jumps and spins and uses a data-recording sheet identical to that used by the first observer. At the end of the session, the first observer recorded 20 elements, and the second observer recorded 22 elements. This can be converted to an IOR estimate by dividing the smaller number by the larger number and multiplying by 100%: IOR equals 20 divided by 22 times 100% equals 91%. Now it is important to ask what this IOR score means. It means that the two observers agreed quite closely (almost 100%) on the total *number* of elements. It does not mean that they agreed on 20 specific elements; the second observer counted 2 extra to make 22. It is quite possible that one observer recorded an element that the second observer missed. The second observer could then have counted an element that the first observer missed. This could have gone on throughout the session, in which case the two observers would have disagreed completely on specific individual responses. Nevertheless, their close agreement on the total gives us confidence that the actual total was close to the number that each observer tallied despite the possible disagreements on individual cases. This approach of counting two totals and then dividing the smaller by the larger and multiplying by 100% is quite common when two observers are counting the frequency of a particular response over a period of time.

The other common IOR procedure is used with interval recording. Recall that interval-recording procedures can record one and only one response during each brief period of time (usually 5 or 10 seconds) over an extended observation period (see Table 21–2). If we have two independent observers recording the same behavior and each is using an interval-recording procedure, then the question is how their successive intervals compare with regard to those that contain a response versus those that do not. Let's suppose that two observers are recording two types of social interaction for one child. The behaviors are defined as touching another child and vocalizing in the direction of the other child. Their interval scores are shown in Figure 21–6.

As you can see, both observers counted the same number of instances of touching: 18. However, the two observers agreed on only 16 of these 18 instances. Each counted two instances that the other missed, yielding a total of four disagreements. If we used the procedure described previously, we would obtain an IOR of 100%. However, in the second procedure, the IOR is obtained by dividing the number of intervals on which the two observers agree that the behavior occurred by the total number of intervals on which either recorded a behavior (agreements divided by agreements plus disagreements on the occurrence of a behavior) and multiplying by NOTE 2   100%. Thus, in this instance, the second procedure would yield an IOR of 80%.

Typically, by convention, IOR scores between 80% and 100% are considered acceptable in behavior modification programs. Potential variation in computational procedures, however, renders the final IOR value potentially misleading when considered by itself. We suggest that readers of behavior modification literature consider the response definitions, observer-training procedures, recording system, method of calculating IOR, and the final IOR value as a total package when judging the reliability of reported data. Defects in any of these might make the results suspect.

Study Questions

23. Describe five sources of error in recording observations.
24. In a sentence or two, explain what we mean by *interobserver reliability*. (Describe it in words, but don't give the procedures for calculating IORs.)
25. Using the procedure described in the text for computing IORs with interval data, compute an IOR for the data of vocalizing as recorded by observers 1 and 2 (Figure 21–6). Show all of your computations.
26. According to convention, what is an acceptable IOR in a behavior modification program? What does *convention* mean?

Application Exercises

A. EXERCISE INVOLVING OTHERS

Select a behavioral deficit or excess that was modified successfully (e.g., Peter's tantrums) as described in one of the other chapters. For that behavior:

1. Design a plausible data sheet, including a column for sessions and a column for the instances of behavior per session.
2. Prepare a summary of some representative data (real or hypothesized), and write it in your data sheet.

3. Graph your data in a frequency graph.
4. Graph your data in a cumulative graph.

B. SELF-MODIFICATION EXERCISE

Select one of your own behavioral excesses or deficits. For that behavior, answer Items 1 to 4 in the previous exercise.

Notes and Extended Discussion

1. When the observational method affects the behaviors being observed, we say that the observation is *obtrusive*. To record observations *unobtrusively* means that the observations do not cause those being observed to deviate from their typical behavior. Our observations should not influence the behavior we are observing. You can ensure that your observations are unobtrusive in several ways. One possibility is to observe the behavior from behind a one-way window, as illustrated in the case of Darren in Chapter 3. Another possibility is to inconspicuously observe individuals from a distance. This strategy was used to study the drinking habits of patrons in bars in a mid-size U.S. city (Sommer, 1977). Another method is to have a confederate make observations while working side by side with a client in a normal work setting (Rae, Martin, & Smyk, 1990). Other alternatives include recording the behavior with a hidden camera and evaluating products of the client's behavior (such as items littered in a public campground; Osborne & Powers, 1980). However, such tactics raise a moral question: Is it ethical to observe individuals without their consent? The American Psychological Association (http://www.apa.org/ethics/code/code-1992.aspx) has developed a set of ethical guidelines governing all types of experiments by psychological researchers. Among the factors that these guidelines stipulate for making observations for

experimental purposes are whether (a) the person being observed or that person's guardian has signed a formal consent form, (b) the observations will aid in carrying out a therapeutic program for the person being observed, (c) the confidentiality of the observations will be maintained, and (d) specific individuals or groups can be identified from any reports stemming from the observations. Anyone contemplating recording the behavior of another person should consult the ethical guidelines of his or her professional organization and the applicable laws pertaining to privacy and confidentiality. (See also Chapter 30 of this text.)

2. The procedure that we have suggested for computing IOR during interval recording is that of dividing the number of intervals on which observers agree that the behavior occurred by the total number of intervals on which either observer recorded the occurrence of the behavior (agreements plus disagreements on the occurrence of the behavior) and multiplying by 100%. Some researchers include instances in which the observers agreed that the behavior did not occur in the measure of agreements—in other words, agreements on blank intervals. When very few behaviors have been recorded, however, this can greatly inflate a reliability score. For example, consider the 45 observation intervals given in Figure 21–6. Let's suppose that observer 1 recorded an instance of touching during interval 5 and that observer 2 recorded an instance of touching during interval 6. No other instances of touching were recorded. In such a case, the two observers would disagree completely on the occurrence of the behavior, and the IOR would be zero if it is computed as agreement only on instances in which the behavior occurred. However, if agreements on blank intervals are included, the IOR equals 43 agreements divided by 43 agreements plus 2 disagreements times 100%, which equals 95.6%. Because of this distortion, many researchers do not count agreements on blank intervals. In other words, intervals in which neither observer scores the behavior as having occurred are ignored. An acceptable exception to this would be when one is concerned with decreasing a behavior and it is important to have agreement that the behavior did not occur. These points and other comments on the complexity of computing IOR are discussed in more detail by Poling, Methot, and LeSage (1995).

Study Questions on Notes

1. What is the difference between obtrusive and unobtrusive observations?
2. When is it especially misleading to include agreement on blank intervals in computing the IOR? Give an example.
3. When might it be acceptable to include agreement on blank intervals in your computation of an IOR? Why would this be acceptable?

22

Doing Research in Behavior Modification

As described in Chapter 20, a minimal behavior modification program has four phases: a *screening phase* for clarifying the problem and determining who should treat it, an *assessment phase* for determining the causes of the problem behavior and its initial level prior to the program, a *treatment phase* in which the intervention strategy is initiated, and a *follow-up phase* for evaluating the persistence of the desirable behavioral changes following termination of the program. Many behavior modification projects go beyond these phases and demonstrate convincingly that it was indeed the treatment that caused a particular change in behavior. The value of such demonstrations might be illustrated best with a hypothetical example.

Our example involves a second-grade student's frequency of successfully completing addition and subtraction problems in daily math classes. Kelly performed at a much lower level than any of the other students and was disruptive during the class. The teacher reasoned that an increase in Kelly's performance at solving the assigned math problems might make it more pleasurable for Kelly to work at the problems and might thereby decrease the disruptive interactions with nearby students. During a one-week baseline, the teacher assigned a certain number of problems to the class and recorded the number that Kelly completed successfully during each half-hour period. Kelly averaged seven successfully completed math problems per half hour, less than half the class average of 16 problems in the same amount of time. The teacher next introduced a reinforcement program, telling Kelly that each successfully completed math problem would add an extra minute of recess for the whole class on Friday afternoon. Kelly's performance improved during the first week of the program. During the second week, Kelly exceeded the class average of 16 correct math problems per half-hour class.

Can the teacher attribute the improvement in Kelly's performance to the treatment? Our initial tendency might be to say yes because the performance is much better now than it was during the original baseline. Consider, however, that the improvement might have been the result of other factors. For example, a bad cold could have depressed Kelly's baseline performance, and the recovery from the cold may have improved the mathematical performance after the program began. Or a new student who set a good example for Kelly to model might have been seated nearby during the treatment phase but not during the baseline. Or perhaps the problems assigned during the treatment phase were easier than those assigned during baseline. Or perhaps something that the teacher could not possibly have been aware of was responsible for the improved performance. Behavior modification research attempts to demonstrate convincingly that it was the treatment, rather than some uncontrolled variable, that was responsible for any change in the target behavior.

THE REVERSAL-REPLICATION (ABAB) DESIGN

Suppose the teacher would like to demonstrate convincingly whether the treatment program was indeed responsible for Kelly's improvement. Besides satisfying the teacher's curiosity, there are several practical reasons why such a demonstration might be desirable. Such a demonstration would indicate whether to try a similar procedure with another problem Kelly might have, whether to try similar procedures with other students in the class, and whether the teacher would recommend similar procedures to other teachers. Therefore, at the end of the second week of the reinforcement program, the teacher eliminated the reinforcement and returned to the baseline condition. Suppose that the hypothetical results of this manipulation by the teacher are those shown in Figure 22–1.

By the end of the second week of return to the baseline conditions, Kelly was performing at a level approximately that of the original baseline. The teacher then reintroduced the treatment phase and Kelly's performance again improved (see Figure 22–1). The teacher had replicated both the original baseline and the original treatment effects. If some uncontrolled variable were operating, we must hypothesize that it was occurring mysteriously at exactly the same time the treatment program was operative and was not occurring when the treatment program was

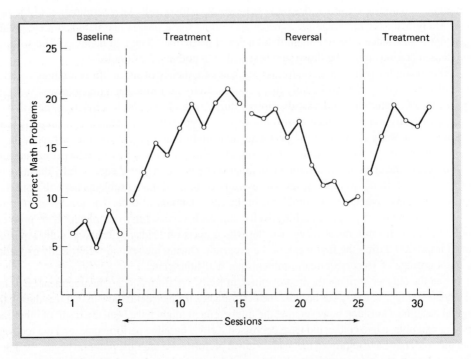

FIGURE 22–1 Hypothetical data showing a reversal-replication (ABAB) design for Kelly.

removed. This becomes much less plausible with each successful replication of the effect. We now have confidence that it was indeed the teacher's procedure that produced the desired behavioral change. Thus, the teacher demonstrated a cause–effect relationship between a particular behavior and the treatment program. In research terminology, the measure of behavior is referred to as the **dependent variable**; the treatment or the intervention is referred to as the **independent variable**. In the previous example, correctly completing math problems was the dependent variable and the teacher's program for Kelly was the independent variable. Two considerations in evaluating a possible cause–effect relationship are internal validity and external validity. A study or experiment is said to have **internal validity** if it convincingly demonstrated that the independent variable caused the observed change in the dependent variable. A study or experiment is said to have **external validity** to the extent that the finding can be generalized to other behaviors, individuals, settings, or treatments.

The type of research strategy that the teacher employed is called a **reversal-replication design**, which is an experimental design consisting of a baseline phase followed by a treatment phase, followed by a reversal back to baseline conditions, and followed by a replication of the treatment phase. The baseline is often represented as A and the treatment noted as B. Hence, this research design is also called an *ABAB design.* It has also been called a *withdrawal* design because the treatment is withdrawn during the second baseline phase (Poling, Methot, & LeSage, 1995). For an application of this design in a research study, see Ivancic, Barrett, Simonow, and Kimberly (1997).

Although the reversal-replication design appears simple at first glance, beginning students doing behavior modification research quickly have several questions that are not easy to answer. Assuming that problems of response definition, observer accuracy, and data recording (discussed in Chapter 21) have been solved, the first question is this: How long should the baseline phase last? The difficulties of answering this question might be appreciated best by viewing Figure 22–2. Which of the baselines in this figure do you consider to be the most adequate? If you selected baselines 4 and 5, we agree. Baseline 4 is acceptable because the pattern of behavior appears stable and predictable. Baseline 5 is acceptable because the trend observed is in a direction opposite to the effect predicted for the independent variable acting on the dependent variable. Ideally, then, a baseline phase should continue until the pattern of performance is stable or until it shows a trend in the direction opposite to that predicted when the independent variable is introduced.

Other considerations might lead to shortening or lengthening a baseline in an applied research project. First, scientific considerations related to the newness of the independent and dependent variables should be reviewed. We might be more comfortable conducting a shorter baseline in a new study of behavior that has already been well researched than in a study of a less explored area. Second, practical considerations might limit the length of baseline observations. The experimenter's available time, the observers' availability, the students' restrictions for completing projects on time, and any number of other factors might lead us to limit or extend the baseline for nonscientific reasons. Finally, ethical considerations often affect baseline length. For example, an extended baseline phase is ethically unacceptable when attempting to manage the self-abusive behavior of a child with a developmental disability.

Another question that a beginning student in behavior modification research has pertains to how many reversals and replications are necessary. Again, this question has no easy answer. If we observe a very large effect when the independent variable is introduced and if the area is one that has been explored before, one replication might be sufficient. Other combinations of factors might lead us to conduct several replications to convincingly demonstrate a cause–effect relationship.

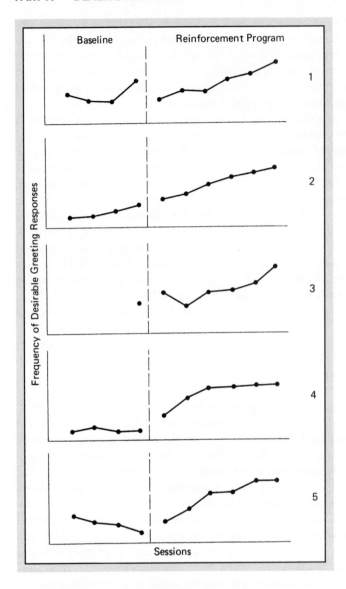

FIGURE 22-2 Hypothetical data for five children.

Although the reversal-replication design is a common behavior modification research strategy, it has limitations that make it inappropriate in certain situations. First, it might be undesirable to reverse to baseline conditions following a treatment phase. When treating a child's self-abusive behavior, for example, reversing to baseline following a successful treatment to prove that the treatment was responsible for the change in behavior would be ethically unacceptable.

Second, it might be impossible to obtain a reversal due to behavioral trapping. In Chapter 16, we described how improved behavior might become "trapped." Once a shy child has been taught to interact with peers, this interactive behavior might be maintained by attention from the peers. Once a golf pro has taught a novice to hit a golf ball over 200 yards, it is unlikely that the novice golfer will return to a swing that produced a 150-yard drive.

Study Questions

1. Briefly name and describe the four minimal components of a behavior modification program.
2. In two or three sentences, explain why we cannot necessarily claim that a change in behavior during a minimal behavior modification program was due to the treatment.
3. In two or three sentences, distinguish between a minimal behavior modification program and behavior modification research.
4. Define *dependent variable,* and give an example.
5. Define *independent variable,* and give an example.
6. Define *internal validity.*
7. Define *external validity.*
8. With reference to an example, briefly describe the four components of the reversal-replication design. What is another name for this design?
9. Ideally, how long should the baseline phase of the reversal-replication design continue?
10. In a sentence or two each, describe why Baselines 1, 2, and 3 from Figure 22–2 are inadequate.
11. What scientific, practical, and ethical considerations might lead someone to lengthen or shorten a baseline?
12. How many reversals and replications are necessary in a reversal-replication design?
13. Identify two limitations of the reversal-replication design, and give an example of each.

MULTIPLE-BASELINE DESIGNS

Returning a behavior to baseline sometimes might be impossible and reversing an improvement in behavior even for a short time is often undesirable. Multiple-baseline designs are used to demonstrate the effectiveness of a particular treatment without reversing to baseline conditions.

A Multiple-Baseline-Across-Behaviors Design

Suppose Kelly's teacher wanted to demonstrate the effects of the reinforcement procedure on the child's academic performance but did not want to do a reversal and risk losing the improvement Kelly showed. The teacher might demonstrate the treatment's effect by using a **multiple-baseline-across-behaviors design** that involves establishing baselines for two or more of an individual's behaviors followed by introducing the treatment sequentially across those behaviors. The first step for Kelly's teacher to apply this design might be to record Kelly's performance in solving math problems during math class as well as in spelling and sentence writing during language arts. The resulting baselines might have been those shown in Figure 22–3. The treatment of an extra minute of recess per correct problem might have been introduced in math class while the other baseline conditions might have been continued during language arts. If the results were those shown in Figure 22–3, the teacher might next have introduced the treatment for the second behavior by allowing an extra minute of recess for each word Kelly spelled correctly. Finally, the teacher might have introduced the treatment for the third behavior—sentence writing. If performance was as indicated in Figure 22–3, the behavior changed only when the treatment was introduced. This hypothetical example illustrates the control of a treatment over several behaviors. For an example of this design in an actual research study, see Gena, Krantz, McClannahan, and Poulson (1996).

A potential problem with this design is that the behaviors might not be independent. If Kelly's teacher had applied the treatment program to one behavior while the other two behaviors

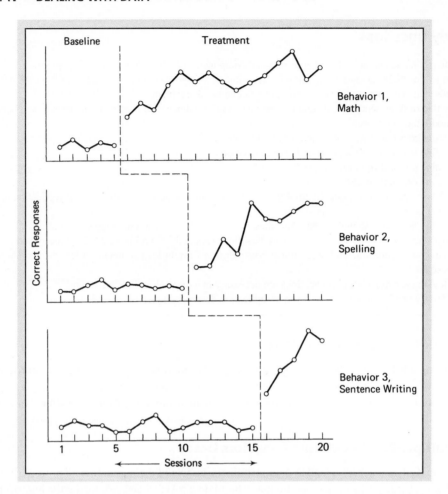

FIGURE 22–3 Hypothetical data illustrating a multiple-baseline-across-behaviors design for Kelly.

were kept at baseline conditions and if an improvement had been observed in all three behaviors concurrently, the teacher could not have confidently attributed the improvement to the treatment itself. Nordquist (1971) reported an example of such response generalization. Other limitations are that it might not be possible to find two or more suitable behaviors or sufficient observers to gather the necessary data on several behaviors. In addition, if the procedure is used with only one individual, we can conclude only that the treatment was internally valid with that individual. We must be cautious in extrapolating the results to other individuals.

A Multiple-Baseline-Across-Situations Design

A **multiple-baseline-across-situations design** involves establishing baselines for a behavior of an individual across two or more situations concurrently followed by the introduction of the treatment to the behavior sequentially across those situations. For example, Allen (1973) was concerned with decreasing bizarre verbalizations of an 8-year-old boy with minimal brain damage. While attending a sleep-away summer camp, the boy fantasized for hours about his imaginary pet penguins that he called Tug Tug and Junior Polka Dot. These verbalizations interfered with the boy's interactions with his peers and the camp counselors. During an initial baseline phase, data on the verbalizations were collected in four situations: during trail walks in the evening, in the dining hall, in the boy's cabin, and during classes. The treatment, an extinction program that ignored verbalizations, was then introduced in the first situation (trail walking) while the remaining three situations continued on baseline. Following the successful reduction of the verbalizations during trail walking, treatment was introduced to the second situation, the dining hall, and the remaining two situations continued on baseline. Eventually, the treatment was introduced sequentially across the remaining two situations. The daily number of bizarre verbalizations decreased to near zero in each situation following the introduction of treatment to that situation.

A potential problem with a multiple-baseline-across-situations design is that, when the treatment is applied to the behavior in the first situation, it might cause subsequent improvement in all situations (i.e., stimulus generalization across situations). When this happens, the experimenter is not able to conclude that the improvement was necessarily the result of the treatment. Other potential limitations are that the behavior might occur in only one situation, or there might not be sufficient observers to gather the necessary data. In addition, if the procedure is used with only one individual, we can conclude only that the treatment is effective with that individual. We must be cautious in extrapolating the result to other individuals.

A Multiple-Baseline-Across-People Design

A **multiple-baseline-across-people design** involves establishing baselines for a specific behavior across two or more people concurrently followed by the introduction of the treatment sequentially to each person. For example, Fawcett and Miller (1975) used a multiple-baseline-across-people design to demonstrate the effectiveness of a combination of procedures (called a *treatment package*) designed to improve public speaking. The public speaking skills of three individuals were recorded during initial public speaking sessions. The first individual was then given the treatment package while the others continued on baseline. Exposure to the treatment package improved the public speaking behaviors of the first individual. The treatment package was introduced sequentially to the second person and then to the third person, and each time it led to an improvement in public speaking behaviors. This demonstration of improvement in individuals who receive treatment sequentially across time is a convincing demonstration of a treatment program's effectiveness. For another application of this design, see Wanlin, Hrycaiko, Martin, and Mahon (1997).

A potential problem with the multiple-baseline-across-people design is that the first individual might explain the treatment or model the desirable behavior to the other individuals, causing them to improve in the absence of treatment (see, e.g., Kazdin, 1973). Also, it is not always possible to find either two or more individuals with the same problem with whom to do a baseline or the additional observers necessary to gather the data. Note that successfully replicating the effect across individuals demonstrates internal validity as well as a degree of external validity, and we can extrapolate the effects with some confidence to other individuals.

Study Questions

14. State an advantage of a multiple-baseline design over a reversal-replication design.
15. With reference to an example, briefly describe a multiple-baseline-across-behaviors design.
16. What are three potential limitations of a multiple-baseline-across-behaviors design?
17. With reference to an example, briefly describe a multiple-baseline-across-situations design.

18. What are three potential limitations of a multiple-baseline-across-situations design?
19. With reference to an example, briefly describe a multiple-baseline-across-people design.
20. What are three potential limitations of a multiple-baseline-across-people design?

THE CHANGING-CRITERION DESIGN

With a **changing-criterion design**, the control that a treatment exerts on an individual's behavior is evaluated by introducing successive changes in the behavioral criterion for application of the treatment. If the behavior consistently changes in the same direction each time a change is made in the criterion for application of the treatment, we can conclude that the treatment was responsible for the change in behavior.

DeLuca and Holborn (1992) used a changing-criterion design to demonstrate the effects of a token reinforcement system on exercising by 11-year-old boys, some of whom were obese and others of whom were not. First, during Phase 1 (baseline), consisting of several 30-minute exercise sessions, they assessed each boy's pedaling rate on a stationary bicycle. Based on these data, they set a criterion for reinforcement for each boy that was approximately 15% above his average baseline rate of pedaling. In Phase 2, when a boy met the criterion, he earned points (signaled by a bell ringing and a light going on) that could be exchanged later for backup reinforcers. After a boy's performance stabilized at this new higher level of pedaling, Phase 3 was initiated; its criterion for reinforcement was changed to approximately 15% above the average rate of performance in Phase 2. Similarly, each subsequent phase increased the criterion for reinforcement to 15% higher than the average pedaling rate of the preceding phase. As in Figure 22–4, which shows the data for one of the boys, performance improved with each subsequent change in the criterion for reinforcement. This pattern was demonstrated for both the three boys who were obese and the three boys who were not. To further demonstrate the experimental control of the reinforcement program, as indicated in Figure 22–4, a reversal to baseline phase was included in

FIGURE 22–4 Mean number of revolutions per minute pedaled on a stationary bicycle by a boy. After a baseline phase, token reinforcement was given at increasingly larger levels of variable ratio (VR) reinforcement (that is, the mean response requirement became increasingly larger).

Source: Figure 1 in "Effects of a Variable Ratio Reinforcement Schedule with Changing Criteria on Exercise in Obese and Non-Obese Boys" by R. V. DeLuca and S. W. Holborn, *Journal of Applied Behavior Analysis,* 25, 1992. Copyright ©1992. Reprinted by permission of Dr. Rayleen DeLuca, University of Manitoba.

this study. Although the reversal provided confirming information, such reversals are not a defining feature of the changing-criterion design.

ALTERNATING-TREATMENTS (OR MULTIELEMENT) DESIGN

The preceding experimental designs are ideally suited for demonstrating that a particular treatment was indeed responsible for a specific behavioral change. However, what if we wanted to compare the effects of different treatments for a single behavior of a single individual? Multiple-baseline designs are not well suited for this purpose. An alternative design for such a concern, first proposed by Barlow and Hayes (1979) is known as an **alternating-treatments design**, also called a **multielement design**, which involves alternating two or more treatment conditions, one condition per session, to assess their effects on a single behavior of a single individual. For example, Wolko, Hrycaiko, and Martin (1993) were concerned with comparing three treatments for improving young gymnasts' frequency of completed skills during practice on the balance beam. One treatment was the standard coaching typically applied by the gymnastics coach. The second condition was standard coaching plus public goal setting, monitoring, and coach feedback. In this condition, the coach posted written goals for a gymnast who recorded her practice performance, placed it on a graph in the gymnasium, and received feedback from the coach at the end of each practice. The third condition was standard coaching and private self-management involving a gymnast setting her own goals and keeping track of her performance in a private notebook. The three conditions were randomly alternated across practices. The results with one of the gymnasts were plotted as three cumulative graphs (see Figure 22–5). As the results for this gymnast indicate, standard coaching plus private self-management was consistently more effective than standard coaching plus public self-management and standard coaching alone (the baseline condition). For another example of the alternating-treatments design, see Daly, Martens, Kilmer, and Massie (1996).

As Sidman (1960, p. 326) suggested, it is possible to use the alternating-treatments design to study different topographies of behavior. For an example of this, see Ming and Martin (1996).

A potential problem with the alternating-treatments design is that the treatments might interact; that is, one of the treatments might produce an effect because of either contrast to the other treatments in alternating sessions or stimulus generalization across treatments. And in many studies using an alternating-treatments design, interactions have occurred (e.g., Hains & Baer, 1989).

DATA ANALYSIS AND INTERPRETATION

Researchers who employ the behavior modification experimental designs described in this chapter typically analyze their data without using control groups and statistical techniques that are more common in other areas of psychology. In general, this is so because behavior modifiers are interested in understanding and improving the behavior of individuals, not group averages (see Sidman, 1960, for justification and elaboration of this approach). The evaluation of the effect of a particular treatment is typically made on the basis of two major sets of criteria: scientific and practical. Scientific criteria are the guidelines a researcher uses to evaluate whether there has been a convincing demonstration that the treatment was responsible for producing a reliable effect on the dependent variable. This judgment is commonly made by visually inspecting the graph of the results. Problems in deciding whether a treatment produced a reliable effect on a **NOTE 1**

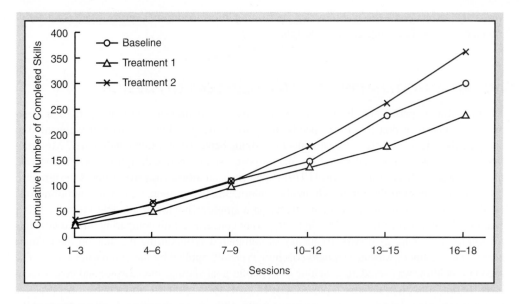

FIGURE 22–5 Frequency of completed beam skills for a gymnast under conditions of standard coaching (baseline), standard coaching plus public self-management (Treatment 1) versus standard coaching plus private self-management (Treatment 2). Each condition was in effect for six sessions with the conditions randomly alternated across a total of 18 sessions.

(*Source:* Adapted from data from K. L. Wolko, D. W. Hrycaiko, and G. L. Martin, "A Comparison of Two Self-Management Packages to Standard Coaching for Improving Practice Performance of Gymnasts," *Behavior Modification, 17* (1993), pp. 209–223.

dependent variable might best be appreciated by examining Figure 22–6. Most observers of the five graphs would probably agree that there is a clear, large effect in Graph 1, a reliable although small effect in Graph 2, and questionable effects in the remaining graphs.

Seven guidelines are commonly used for inspecting data to judge whether the treatment had an effect on the dependent variable. Confidence that an effect has been observed is greater the more times that it is replicated, the fewer the overlapping points between baseline and treatment phases, the sooner the effect is observed following the treatment's introduction, the larger the effect is in comparison to baseline, the more precisely the treatment procedures are specified, the more reliable the response measures, and the more consistent the findings with existing data and accepted behavioral theory. (For discussion of a problem of visual inspection of data, see Fisch, 1998. For a description of a visual aid and a staff training program for improving the reliabiity and validity of visual inspection of single-case designs, see Fisher, Kelley, & Lomas, 2003.)

Judging whether an effect has been demonstrated from a scientific point of view is one thing; evaluating the practical importance of behavior change to the client, other significant individuals in the client's life, and society in general is something else. In evaluating the practical impact of the treatment, we must consider more than the scientific guidelines for judging the treatment's effect on behavior. If Graph 2 in Figure 22–6 were a graph of self-abusive behavior, a reliable cause–effect relationship has been demonstrated but might be of little clinical significance. If the individual is still self-abusive during the treatment phases, those responsible for caring for that individual would not be satisfied. Judgments about the practical importance of behavioral change are referred to as *judgments of clinical effectiveness or social importance.*

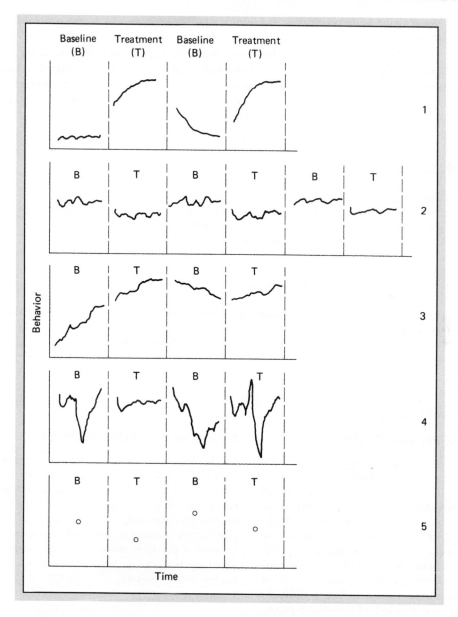

FIGURE 22–6   Some hypothetical data.

A concept related to practical importance is that of social validity. Wolf (1978) has suggested that behavior modifiers need to socially validate their work on at least three levels: (a) the extent to which the target behaviors are really the most important ones for the client and society, (b) the acceptability to the client of the particular procedures used, especially when alternative procedures can accomplish approximately the same results, and (c) the satisfaction of the consumers (the clients or their caregivers) with the results. One social validation procedure involves subjective evaluation in which clients or other significant individuals are asked about their satisfaction with the goals, procedures, and results. Another social validation procedure is to conduct preference tests to determine which of two or more alternatives clients prefer. In a third procedure, the goals as well as the results of treatment are validated socially by comparing results with clients to the average performance of some comparison group, such as normal peers. Kazdin (1977b) and Wolf discussed these strategies in more detail. Social validation helps to ensure that behavior modifiers do the best job that they can in helping individuals function fully in society. Other strategies to ensure accountability of treatment specialists are discussed in Chapter 30.

Study Questions

21. With reference to an example, briefly describe the changing-criterion design.
22. With reference to an example, briefly describe an alternating-treatments design. What is another name for this design? Explain when and why that name might be preferred.
23. Briefly describe a potential problem with the alternating-treatments design.
24. In a sentence or two each, explain the scientific and practical criteria for evaluating the effects of a particular treatment. Be sure to distinguish between the two in your answer.
25. Describe why it is difficult to draw conclusions about the effects of the treatments in Graphs 3, 4, and 5 in Figure 22–6.
26. What seven criteria would give you maximum confidence that the treatment in an ABAB design had produced an effect on the dependent variable?
27. What are the three levels of social validation, and why are they important?

Application Exercises

A. EXERCISE INVOLVING OTHERS

Suppose you are teaching some students about doing research that utilizes reversal-replication and multiple-baseline designs. Your students must do a research project in which they select a dependent variable and evaluate the effects of some treatment on that dependent variable. Your task as the teacher is to analyze the material in this chapter to prepare a guide that will help the students to select the appropriate experimental design. Your guide should take the form of a series of if–then statements that would lead to a particular design. For example, if (a) and (b), then choose a reversal design; but if (c), (d), and (e), then choose a multiple-baseline design, and so forth.

B. SELF-MODIFICATION EXERCISE

As described in Chapter 20, self-recording without any additional behavioral procedures sometimes causes reactivity—that is, the self-recording alone leads to behavioral change. Suppose you have decided to describe a self-recording procedure and then to investigate that as a treatment in a self-modification program. Describe a plausible multiple-baseline design that would enable you to assess self-recording as an effective self-control treatment.

Note and Extended Discussion

1. The experimental designs described in this chapter are referred to as *single-case, single-subject,* or *within-subject experimental designs*. In most of these designs, an individual serves as his or her own control in the sense that performance of that individual in the

absence of treatment is compared to that individual's performance during treatment. More common designs in many areas of psychology are control-group or between-subjects designs. A control-group design typically involves at least two groups, one that receives the treatment and one that does not. The average performance of the two groups is then compared according to appropriate statistical procedures. Single-case designs are more popular than control-group designs among behavior modifiers for a number of reasons (Hrycaiko & Martin, 1996). First, they focus on repeated measurement of an individual's performance across a number of sessions and therefore provide potentially valuable information on individual variation in performance. Group designs, with their emphasis on the average performance of groups, typically gather data at a single point in time rather than continuously monitoring individuals over time. Second, researchers using single-case designs typically need to locate only a few individuals with the same performance problem in order to evaluate an intervention. Researchers using group designs often find locating enough individuals with the same performance problem to form the different groups to be difficult. Third, because all individuals in a single-case design receive the intervention at one time or another, an applied researcher does not face resistance from clients (or their significant others) to participate in a no-treatment control group. Fourth, because single-case designs rely on replication logic rather than the sampling logic of the group designs (Smith, 1988), they are not hampered by some of the statistical assumptions required of group designs. Group designs, for example, assume that the dependent variable is distributed in the population in some fashion (usually normally) and that the samples are randomly selected from that population. Often, however, these assumptions are either not assessed or not met. For these and other reasons, behavior modifiers favor single-case designs. For excellent books on single-case designs, see Bailey and Burch (2002) and Johnston and Pennypacker (2009). See Martin, Thompson, and Regehr (2004) for a review of research using single-case designs in sport psychology. For a discussion of some common misunderstandings about single-case designs, see Hrycaiko and Martin. For a discussion of reasons for using between-subjects designs, see Poling, Methot, and LeSage (1995). See Brossart, Parker, Olson, and Mahedevan (2006), Ma (2006), Parker (2006), and Parker and Hagan-Burke (2007) for a discussion on statistical techniques that can be used to interpret single-case research. For a discussion of the pros and cons of using statistical inference procedures in behavior analysis research, see *The Behavior Analyst,* 2000, Vol. 22, No. 2.

Study Question on Note 1

1. List four reasons why many behavior modifiers prefer single-case designs to group designs.

23 Functional Assessment of the Causes of Problem Behavior

Throughout Part II of this book, especially in the "Pitfalls" sections, we repeatedly point out how misapplication of behavior principles can cause problem behavior. In other words, if the principles are not working for you, they will likely be working against you. Increasingly, behavior analysts are attempting to understand the causes of problem behaviors in order to treat them more effectively.

A functional assessment of the causes of a problem behavior involves asking two questions: (a) what are the antecedents (i.e., the S^Ds [see Chapter 8], the eliciting stimuli [see Chapter 14], or the motivating operations [see Chapter 19]) of the behavior and (b) what are the immediate consequences (i.e., the positive or negative reinforcement) of the behavior? More specifically, we ask: Is the behavior being evoked or elicited by particular stimuli? Is it being reinforced? Does the behavior lead to escape from aversive events? From the client's point of view, what function does the behavior serve? The answers to such questions have important implications for planning effective treatment.

FUNCTIONAL ASSESSMENT PROCEDURES

Functional assessment refers to a variety of procedures for attempting to identify antecedents and consequences for problem behaviors. In this section, we consider these procedures and discuss how knowledge of variables that are controlling specific problem behaviors can help in designing effective treatment programs. The information presented here follows logically from the basic principles and procedures discussed in the earlier chapters of this book.

Questionnaire Assessment

One way to discover antecedents and consequences that control problem behavior is to administer a questionnaire with a series of relevant questions that people familiar with the client are asked. For example, Matson and Vollmer (1995) devised a questionnaire called *Questions About Behavioral Function* to help staff determine whether problem behavior of persons with developmental disabilities was maintained by attention from others, escape from aversive conditions, sensory feedback, or tangible reinforcers. Kearney and Silverman (1990) developed a similar questionnaire, called the *School Refusal Assessment Scale,* to assess variables responsible for children refusing to attend school. Sobell, Toneatto, and Sobell (1994) reviewed questionnaires for identifying antecedents and consequences of excessive alcohol drinking. As with other indirect assessment procedures (see Chapter 20), such measures might not always be reliable (Iwata, Kahng, Wallace, & Lindberg, 2000; Sturmey, 1994).

Observational Assessment

Another way to discover a problem behavior's controlling variables is to perform an observational or descriptive assessment in which the observational assessor carefully observes and describes the antecedents and immediate consequences of the problem behavior in its natural settings. (For examples, see Table 3–3 in Chapter 3.) From these descriptions, the assessor forms hypotheses about the antecedent stimuli, motivational variables, and consequences controlling the problem behavior. Then a treatment plan based on these hypotheses is devised and implemented. If the treatment is successful, the descriptive analysis is validated. (For additional discussion and examples of observational assessment, see Iwata et al., 2000.)

Functional Analysis

A third way to discover controlling variables is to do a **functional analysis**, which is the systematic manipulation of environmental events to experimentally test their role as antecedents or as consequences in controlling and maintaining specific problem behaviors. In this procedure— also called an *experimental functional assessment*—the therapist directly assesses the effects of potential controlling variables on the problem behavior. Consider a case described by Iwata, Pace, Kalsher, Cowdery, and Cataldo (1990). Susie was a 5-year-old child with developmental disabilities who had been referred for therapy because of a high frequency of self-injurious behavior that included banging her head and slapping her face. Was this a way for Susie to get positive reinforcement in the form of adult attention (Chapter 3)? Was it a way for her to escape from demands to perform various tasks (Chapter 13)? Or were the injurious behaviors self-reinforcing? To assess these possibilities experimentally, Iwata and his colleagues examined Susie's self-abusive behavior over several sessions in a therapy room. Using an *attention condition,* the therapist approached Susie and voiced concern following instances of self-abuse (e.g., "Oh Susie, what's wrong?"). Using a *demand condition,* the therapist presented various educational tasks to Susie at a rate of one every 30 seconds. In other sessions, Susie was either left alone in an empty therapy room or was observed when the therapy room contained a number of toys and games. Across several sessions, the results were clear: Susie was frequently self-abusive in the demand condition but was rarely self-abusive in the other two conditions.

NOTE 1   Armed with this functional analysis, Iwata and his colleagues designed a treatment program in which the self-injurious escape behavior was extinguished by continuing the demand when Susie engaged in self-abuse. Instead of backing off following instances of self-abuse, the therapist physically guided Susie to complete the various educational activities as they were presented. By the fifth session, Susie's self-abuse had decreased to near zero, and she was more compliant in performing the tasks. Because the treatment was successful, we might infer that the therapist had correctly identified the cause of the problem behavior through the functional analysis. In other words, the success of the treatment validated the results of the functional analysis.

In a review of 277 published studies of functional analyses of problem behavior, 253 (91%) were with persons with developmental disabilities and 25 (9%) were with typically developing children (Hanley, Iwata, & McCord, 2003). Examples of the latter studies include finger sucking by children in their home (Ellingson et al., 2000), disruptive classroom behavior of students with emotional problems (DePaepe, Shores, Jack, & Denny, 1996), reluctant speech of an elementary school student (Mace & West, 1986), inappropriate classroom behavior of an elementary school student (Lewis & Sugai, 1996), and the emotional problems of an 11-year-old boy in the fifth grade (Kern, Childs, Dunlap, Clarke, & Falk, 1994). For a description of step-by-step procedures to guide school practitioners in conducting functional assessments of problem behaviors of children in schools and using the analyses to plan effective interventions, see Cipani and Schock (2007) and Steege and Watson (2009).

Although functional analyses can provide convincing demonstrations of the controlling variables of problem behaviors, they do have some limitations (Cone, 1997; Sturmey, 1995). First, many behavior problems (e.g. those that occur in community settings) occur at frequencies of less than one per day (Whitaker, 1993). Functional analyses for such low-frequency behaviors require a great deal of time before sufficient data can be obtained to draw valid conclusions. Second, functional analyses cannot be applied to extremely dangerous behaviors, such as suicide threats (Sturmey, 1995). Third, because functional analyses require scheduling a number of observational sessions, the expense and personnel requirements might be prohibitive. For example, in a summary of 152 functional analyses, it was reported that the length of assessments ranged from 8 to 66 sessions (2 to 16.5 hours) (Iwata, Pace, Cowdery, & Miltenberger 1994). In an attempt to minimize this limitation, several researchers have compared standard functional analyses to ones involving fewer and shorter sessions for each condition. The results suggest that valid conclusions can usually be drawn from only one or two repetitions of selected test and control conditions and with a session length usually limited to 5 minutes (see, e.g., Northup et al., 1991; Tincani, Gastrogiavanni, & Axelrod, 1999).

There is some confusion in the literature concerning the terms *functional assessment* and *functional analysis.* Some writers have used the terms interchangeably. Others (e.g., Cone, 1997; Horner, 1994) have distinguished between the terms as we have in this book. For additional discussion and examples of functional analyses, see Cipani and Schock (2007), Dunlap and Kincaid (2001), Iwata et al. (2000), and Sturmey (2007).

Study Questions

1. A functional assessment of the causes of a problem behavior involves asking what two questions?
2. Briefly describe three ways to discover controlling variables of problem behavior.
3. How does a functional analysis (as the term is used in this book) differ from other types of functional assessment?
4. Briefly describe how a functional analysis indicated that Susie's self-abusiveness was likely maintained because it enabled her to escape from demanding adults. How did the treatment condition confirm the functional analysis?
5. Describe three limitations of functional analyses.

MAJOR CAUSES OF PROBLEM BEHAVIORS

Having considered ways to detect the causes of problem behaviors, we now examine the major causes of problem behaviors and examples of the general type of treatment that might be indicated in each category. These causes can be divided into two categories: operant and respondent

	Social	Self-Stimulation	Nonsocial
Positive reinforcement	A	B	C
Negative reinforcement	D	E	F

FIGURE 23–1   Causes of operant problem behavior. (See text for explanation.)

or elicited. Causes of operant problem behavior can be further subdivided into the categories shown in Figure 23–1. We consider the subcategories of operant problem behavior first, followed by elicited or respondent problem behavior.

Problem Behaviors Maintained by Social Positive Reinforcement

As we have seen in the "Pitfalls" sections of earlier chapters, behavioral excesses often are developed and maintained by the social attention they evoke (A in Figure 23–1). Indicators that attention maintains the behavior include (a) whether attention reliably follows the behavior, (b) whether the individual looks at or approaches a caregiver just before engaging in the behavior, and (c) whether the individual smiles just before engaging in the behavior. (Attention from others can also function as an S^D for problem behavior, as Bergen, Holborn, & Scott-Huyghebart, 2002 illustrated.)

If a functional analysis indicates that attention maintains the behavior, treatment involving social reinforcement would be recommended. For example, the therapist might devise a treatment using attention when the individual is not engaging in the problem behavior (DRO; see Chapter 7) or is engaging in some behavior that is incompatible with it (DRI; see Chapter 7). The goal would be to eliminate the undesirable behavior. An alternative would be to bring the behavior under appropriate stimulus control (see Chapter 8) and then decrease it to the point that it is acceptable. This strategy is illustrated by the following case.

A CASE OF PESTERING   Lori, a girl in a treatment center for children with developmental disabilities, was small for her age.[1] Perhaps in part because of her appealing characteristics, staff attention had gradually shaped extreme persistence in her approach behavior to the point that she had become a chronic pest. The following sequence was typical. While Bonnie, the nurse in charge of the ward, sat working in her office, Lori peeked in and said, "Hi." "Hi, Lori, I'm busy now but I'll talk to you later," said Bonnie. "You busy now?" said Lori. There was no response from Bonnie, who was trying to work and to ignore Lori's pestering. "You work hard?" asked Lori. (No response from Bonnie.) "Hi," said Lori. (No response from Bonnie.) "You don't love me?" said Lori with a sad look. "Of course I love you, Lori," said Bonnie, unable to resist any longer. Although the staff attempted to ignore Lori's excessive pestering, it was almost impossible to do so consistently. An observational assessment indicated (a) that the antecedent for Lori's pestering consisted of a staff member in Lori's vicinity (within approximately 10–15 feet) and (b) that the behavior was being maintained by a schedule of intermittent positive social reinforcement.

---

[1] This example is based on an unpublished case report by G. Martin at Cedar Cottage, The Manitoba Developmental Centre, Portage la Prairie, Manitoba, Canada, 1971.

Because total elimination of the behavior would have been extremely difficult, and probably not even desirable, the staff designed a procedure for eliminating the behavior only partially—that is, eliminating it only when it was most disruptive. Because pestering appeared to be a function of social attention from staff, they decided to use this reinforcer in the program. Each staff member pinned a 2 x 4-inch card to his or her shirt or dress. The card was red on one side and green on the other. On the first morning of the procedure, a staff member walked quickly toward Lori before she had a chance to begin pestering, and said quickly and firmly, "Hi, Lori. See my card [while pointing to the card]? I can't talk to you because I'm busy and the card is red. I'll see you later." The staff member then quickly turned and walked away, leaving Lori standing in a state of stunned silence. Within a few seconds, the staff member returned with the green side of the card showing. Smiling pleasantly, she said, "Hi, Lori. See my card? It's on the green side and I'm not busy, so now I can talk to you." The staff member then proceeded to engage Lori in a brief conversation. When there was a pause in the conversation, the staff member suddenly assumed a businesslike attitude, turned the card to the red side, and said, "I can't talk to you now, Lori. My card will be red for awhile. I'll see you later." The staff member then quickly walked away before Lori had a chance to respond.

During the first few days of the procedure, the green side was usually showing, reinforcing Lori's soliciting social interaction with a staff member. When the staff had their cards turned to the red side, they consistently ignored Lori's attention-seeking behavior. Over several days, the staff introduced the red side for longer and longer periods of time. Lori quickly learned to discriminate whether or not a nearby staff member was available for conversation, and she responded appropriately. After 2 weeks, the staff managed their red and green cards individually. Over time, Lori appeared to learn more subtle discriminations, such as distinguishing between staff behaviors when they were busy versus when they were relaxing or socializing. If the staff were busy, she would refrain from pestering.

Problem Behaviors Maintained by Self-Stimulatory Positive Reinforcement

Behaviors are often reinforced by the sensory stimulation they produce. This is termed *self-stimulation* and is said to be *self-reinforcing* (B in Figure 23–1). For example, massaging one's scalp produces an enjoyable tingling sensation. Unfortunately, for persons with autism and intellectual disabilities, this type of consequence might also maintain extreme self-stimulatory behaviors such as body rocking, hand flipping, gazing at lights, and even self-injurious behaviors such as slapping or scratching one's face. Reinforcers for such behaviors might consist of sensory or perceptual feedback including vestibular sensations, visual patterns, repetitive sounds, and tactile or kinesthetic sensations (Guess & Carr, 1991; Lovaas, Newsom, & Hickman, 1987). An indicator that the behavior is self-reinforcing is that it continues unabated at a steady rate although it has no apparent effect on other individuals or the external environment. If it appears that sensory reinforcement is maintaining stereotypic or self-injurious behavior, an important component of treatment might be enriching the individual's environment to reduce deprivation of sensory stimulation. (Note that this would be a MAO; see Chapter 19.) Alternatively, extinction of a self-stimulatory behavior by altering the sensory consequences that the behavior produces might be effective as the following case illustrates.

A CASE OF FACE SCRATCHING   This case, described by Rincover and Devaney (1982), illustrates a functional analysis and treatment of a problem behavior maintained by sensory stimulation.

Sarah was a 4½-year-old child with an intellectual disability who severely scratched her face with her nails. Although her nails were cut so short that it was impossible for them to tear her skin, her scratching still resulted in worsening skin irritations and abrasions. Observations during daily 5-hour classes in a treatment center for persons with developmental disabilities indicated that the scratching occurred frequently during the day. She scratched when smiling, when upset, when interacting with others, when alone, and whether or not demands were placed on her. Clearly, the behavior appeared to be maintained by self-stimulation reinforcement rather than social reinforcement. The treatment therefore consisted of extinction of scratching by eliminating the tactile sensations that the scratching had produced. Each day her hands were covered with thin rubber gloves that did not prevent her from scratching but did eliminate the sensory stimulation and prevented her from damaging her skin. The result was an immediate and substantial decrease in the rate of scratching. Within 4 days, scratching was eliminated. During follow-up sessions, the gloves were removed, first for just 10 minutes a day, then for longer and longer intervals, until finally they were no longer needed.

Problem Behaviors Maintained by Nonsocial External Sensory Positive Reinforcement

Some problem behavior might be maintained by reinforcing sights and sounds from the nonsocial external environment (C in Figure 23–1). A child who throws toys might enjoy the loud noise when they land. The sights produced might maintain flushing items down the toilet repeatedly or letting taps run to overflow a sink. For an indicator that nonsocial external sensory stimulation is reinforcing a particular problem behavior, note whether the individual continues the behavior undiminished even though it appears to have no social consequences over numerous occasions. If a functional assessment indicates that the behavior is maintained by external sensory reinforcement, a component of the treatment program might involve sensory reinforcement of a desirable alternative behavior. The following case illustrates this.

A CASE OF FLUSHING JEWELRY DOWN THE TOILET   This case, treated by one of the authors, involved a child with intellectual disabilities who was living at home. It illustrates a problem behavior that might have been maintained by social attention, by sensory stimulation from the nonsocial external environment, or by both. Occasionally during the day and always when her mother was busy in the kitchen, the child would go to her mother's bedroom, take a piece of jewelry out of the jewelry box, carry it to the bathroom, and flush it down the toilet. She would then come and tell her mother what she had done. For the purposes of assessment and treatment, the mother's jewelry was replaced with "junk" jewelry. An observational assessment suggested two possible explanations of the problem behavior. First, the appearance of the jewelry swirling around the toilet bowl before disappearing might have functioned as a sensory reinforcer. Second, the entire sequence of activities might have been a behavioral chain that was reinforced by the mother's attention after the child emitted the sequence of steps and then told her mother what she had done. The treatment procedure that was used considered both possibilities. The girl was given several prompted trials during which, when she and her mother were both in the kitchen, the mother took the daughter by the hand, went into the bedroom, prompted her to take a piece of jewelry out of the box, and guided her to bring the jewelry into the kitchen and drop it in a jar on the kitchen table. It was thought that the tinkling sound of the jewelry as it dropped into the jar might serve as a sensory reinforcer to replace the sight of the jewelry disappearing down the toilet. In addition, the new sequence or behavioral chain was highly reinforced with praise and an occasional treat.

After several guided trials, the mother was able to initiate the new chain by instructing the child while they were both in the kitchen. During the first 2 days of treatment, the child was not given an opportunity to go into the bedroom on her own. On the start of the third day, the child was instructed that any time she wanted when mom was in the kitchen, she could get some jewelry, place it in the jar in the kitchen, and receive praise from mom. To enhance the likelihood of this new sequence, the mother took a photograph of the daughter putting the jewelry into the jar on the kitchen table and placed the picture beside the jewelry box in the bedroom. During the next 3 weeks, the child continued periodically to bring jewelry to the kitchen and to receive praise and occasional treats for doing so. Not once did she flush jewelry down the toilet. Eventually, she stopped playing with her mother's jewelry altogether.

Study Questions

6. What are three indicators that a problem behavior is probably maintained by the social attention that follows it?
7. Briefly describe the stimulus discrimination training procedure and the resulting stimulus control that enabled the staff to manage Lori's pestering.
8. What is an indicator that a problem behavior is being maintained by self-stimulatory reinforcement?
9. Describe how Rincover and Devaney applied extinction to a problem that appeared to be maintained by self-stimulatory reinforcement.
10. What is an indicator that a problem behavior is being reinforced by nonsocial external sensory stimulation? Give an example illustrating this indicator.
11. What were two plausible explanations of the behavior of the child with intellectual disabilities of flushing jewelry down the toilet? How did the treatment procedure consider both possibilities?

Problem Behaviors Maintained by Social Negative Reinforcement

Some problem behaviors are negatively reinforced by escape from demands (D in Figure 23–1; see Chapter 13). For example, when requested to answer difficult questions, some children might engage in tantrums that are strengthened by the withdrawal of the request. A strong indicator that a problem behavior is in this category is that the individual engages in the behavior only when certain types of requests are made. If your functional assessment supports this type of interpretation, it might be feasible to persist with requests or demands until compliance occurs. As illustrated in the case of Susie's self-abusive behavior earlier in this chapter, removing the escape function of a behavioral excess will cause that behavior to decrease. Alternatively, with nonverbal persons, as described in Chapter 12, you might teach the individual some other way (such as by finger tapping or hand raising) to indicate that the task is aversive. In this way, an adaptive response that has the same or similar function as the problem behavior but is more acceptable could replace the excess behavior (Mace, Lalli, Lalli, & Shey, 1993). In other situations, you might design a treatment program in which the level of difficulty of the requested behavior starts low and is gradually increased, as illustrated by the following case.

A CASE OF UNWANTED "TARZAN" NOISES   Edward was an 8-year-old child with a mild developmental disability who was in a special education class.[2] His teacher, Ms. Millan, reported

---

[2] The details of this case were provided by a student in a behavior modification course for resource teachers taught by G. Martin at the Winnipeg School Division, Winnipeg, Manitoba, Canada, January–March, 1973.

to one of the authors that Edward consistently (three or four times a day) made loud "Tarzan" noises in class. A questionnaire assessment with Ms. Millan indicated that Edward made the Tarzan noises when he was asked questions for which he did not know the answer. Rather than giving wrong answers, Edward would burst out with his Tarzan imitation, which disrupted the class. It appeared that Edward's outbursts enabled him to escape from questions that he found difficult. Therefore, the program Ms. Millan implemented at first eliminated such questions. Each day, she spent some time with Edward individually regarding the work to be done for the next day. During these sessions, she quizzed Edward on his knowledge of the subject matter. Although he would occasionally make mistakes, he did not make Tarzan noises. Because only he and Ms. Millan were present during those sessions, the behavior was apparently under the stimulus control of the presence of the other class members.

Over the next 2 weeks during class, Ms. Millan asked Edward questions to which he knew the answers and gave him a great deal of approval for correct answers. Then, over the next 2 weeks, she began asking slightly more difficult questions, each of which was prefaced with a strong prompt such as "Now, Edward, here's a question that's a little difficult. But I'm sure you can answer it, and if you can't we'll figure out the answer together, won't we, class?" Thus, if Edward gave a wrong answer, he was immediately engaged with the teacher and the rest of the class in an attempt to figure out the answer. This gave him the opportunity to receive the attention of the class for desirable behavior rather than for the undesirable Tarzan noises. The entire project required approximately 1 month of careful attention from Ms. Millan. Thereafter, Edward required no special attention. To maintain his good behavior, Ms. Millan made sure that she periodically asked Edward questions to which he knew the answers.

Problem Behaviors Maintained by Self-Stimulatory Negative Reinforcement

Consider the case of Sarah, the child who severely scratched her face. Observation indicated no underlying medical cause for this behavior, such as an allergy, an insect bite, or a toothache. However, if the child had been scratching to relieve the unpleasant sensations caused by a physical condition, this would be an example of a problem behavior maintained by self-stimulatory negative reinforcement (E in Figure 23–1). In such cases the underlying medical cause should be treated by an appropriate health care professional as discussed later in this chapter.

Problem Behaviors Maintained by Nonsocial Negative Reinforcement

Many of our behaviors are maintained by nonsocial negative reinforcement or escape from nonsocial aversive stimuli. Examples include squinting in the presence of bright light or covering your ears to escape a loud sound. Some problem behaviors might also be maintained by nonsocial negative reinforcement (F in Figure 23–1). A child might repeatedly remove her shoes because they squeeze her toes too tightly. Or an individual who is used to loose-fitting clothes but has a job that requires formal attire might frequently loosen his top button and tie. It is debatable as to whether such behaviors are undesirable.

Elicited Problem Behaviors

Some problem behaviors are respondent or elicited (see Chapter 14) rather than controlled by their consequences. Aggression can be elicited by aversive stimuli (see Chapter 12) or by withholding a reinforcer following a previously reinforced response (i.e., extinction; see Chapter 5). Emotions have elicited components (see Chapter 15). For example, if a previously neutral stimulus has occurred in close association with an aversive event, that stimulus might come to elicit anxiety. Several behavioral checklists have been published for conducting questionnaire assessments of the conditioned stimuli (CSs) that elicit the respondent components of emotions. Examples include the *Fear Survey Schedule* (Cautela, Kastenbaum, & Wincze, 1972) and the *Fear Survey for Children* (Morris & Kratochwill, 1983). A descriptive functional assessment or a functional analysis could also be conducted to determine the specific stimuli, circumstances, or thoughts that might elicit respondent components of emotions (Emmelkamp, Bouman, & Scholing, 1992). The two main indicators that a problem behavior is elicited are that it consistently occurs in a certain situation or in the presence of certain stimuli and that it is never followed by any clearly identifiable reinforcing consequence. Another indicator, as suggested by the word *elicited,* is that the behavior seems to be involuntary (i.e., the person seems unable to inhibit it). If a problem behavior appears to be elicited, the treatment might include establishing one or more responses that compete with it so that their occurrence precludes the occurrence of the undesirable response (i.e., counterconditioning; see Chapter 14) as illustrated in the following example.

A RESPONDENT CONDITIONING APPROACH TO REDUCING ANGER RESPONSES   Joel (see Schloss, Smith, Santora, & Bryant, 1989) was a 26-year-old man with a mild intellectual disability who had recently been dismissed from a dishwashing position because of his angry outbursts. A questionnaire assessment with Joel's mother and staff members of the Association for Retarded Citizens (with whom Joel was associated) and observational assessments with Joel led to the identification of three categories of CSs for respondent components of emotions. The CSs included "jokes" (humorous anecdotes told to Joel), "criticism" (especially about deficiencies in Joel's conduct or appearance), and "heterosexual talk" (discussions of dating, marriage, etc.). Within each category, a hierarchy of provoking events had been established ranging from those that caused the least anger to those that caused the most anger. The respondent components of emotions included rapid breathing, facial expression indicative of anger, and trembling. Operant components of emotion were also monitored, including talking loudly and avoiding eye contact with the person whose comments were eliciting Joel's anger. Treatment focused primarily on counterconditioning. Joel was first taught how to relax using a process called *progressive muscle relaxation* (described further in Chapter 28). Then, while in a state of relaxation, a CS for anger from one of the categories was presented. For example, a joke-related situation was described to Joel, and he was asked to imagine it while remaining relaxed. Across several sessions, more and more of the CSs for anger were introduced, gradually proceeding up each of the hierarchies from situations that caused the least anger to those that caused the most anger. (As described in Chapter 28, this procedure is referred to as *systematic desensitization.*) In addition to the clinic-based procedures, Joel was requested to listen at home to a tape recording that induced muscle relaxation and to practice relaxation exercises when he encountered CSs for anger in everyday life. Overall, the program was very successful. Anger-related responses decreased to a very low level during training sessions and generalized to natural settings for each of the categories.

MEDICAL CAUSES OF PROBLEM BEHAVIORS

Often the controlling variables with which behavior modifiers are concerned lie in the individual's external environment. Sometimes, however, a behavior that appears problematic might have a medical cause. For example, a nonverbal individual might bang his or her head against hard objects to reduce pain from an internal source, such as an ear infection (E in Figure 23–1).

A medical cause might be indicated if the problem emerges suddenly and does not seem to be related to any changes in the individual's environment.

To encourage behavior modifiers to gather all possible information about the causes of problem behaviors, Jon Bailey and David Pyles developed the concept of *behavioral diagnostics* (Bailey & Pyles, 1989; Pyles & Bailey, 1990). With this approach to behavioral assessment, the therapist diagnoses the problem after examining antecedents, consequences, and medical and nutritional variables as potential causes of problem behaviors. Based on the diagnosis, the therapist develops a treatment plan, tests the plan under controlled conditions and, if the results are successful, puts the treatment plan in place.

With the behavioral diagnostic model, examples of data that might be collected during the diagnosis phase include health/medical variables (e.g., menstrual cycles or constipation), nutrition variables (e.g., caloric intake or food allergies), medications, and, of course, the information about the kinds of antecedents and consequences of behavior illustrated in this chapter. The concept of behavioral diagnostics is broader than that of a functional assessment. Consistent with this broader view, variables that influence problem behaviors of many individuals are listed in Table 23–1. Variables that commonly act as antecedents or consequences for problem behaviors with persons with developmental disabilities are listed by Demchak and Bossert (1996).

If there is any chance that a behavior problem has a medical cause, an appropriate health care professional should be consulted prior to treating the problem. This is not to say that behavioral techniques cannot be effective if the problem has a medical cause; on the contrary, often they can. For example, hyperactivity is often treated by a combination of behavioral and medical procedures (Barkley, 1998). Such treatment, however, should be carried out in consultation with a physician (see Chapter 2 for a discussion of behavioral approaches to medical problems).

GUIDELINES FOR CONDUCTING A FUNCTIONAL ASSESSMENT

The following is a summary of important guidelines for conducting a functional assessment.

1. Define the problem behavior in behavioral terms.
2. Identify antecedent events that consistently precede the problem behavior.
3. Identify consequences that immediately (although possibly intermittently) follow the problem behavior.
4. As suggested by behavioral diagnostics, consider health/medical/personal variables that might contribute to the problem.
5. Based on Guidelines 2, 3, and 4, form hypotheses about the consequent events that maintain the problem behavior, the antecedent events that elicit it or evoke it, and/or the health/medical/personal variables that exacerbate it.
6. Take data on the behavior, its antecedents and consequences in its natural setting, and health/medical/personal variables to determine which of the hypotheses in Guideline 5 are likely to be correct.
7. If possible, do a functional analysis by directly testing the hypotheses developed in Guideline 5.
8. Incorporating the principles discussed in Part II of this text and following the guidelines for designing treatment programs in Chapter 24, develop a treatment program based on the hypothesis that is most likely to be correct as determined by Guidelines 6 and 7.
9. If the treatment is successful, accept the result of the functional assessment as confirmed. If it is not successful, redo the assessment or attempt a solution based on the principles in Part II of the book and follow the guidelines in Chapter 24.

TABLE 23–1	Factors to Consider in Assessing Causes of Problem Behavior

General Setting

Low overall level of reinforcement

Conditions that cause discomfort (e.g., hot, noisy, crowded)

Presence or absence of particular people

Organismic Variables

State of health (e.g., flu, headache, allergies)

Motivational state (e.g., hungry, thirsty)

Emotional state (e.g., angry, jealous)

Temporary bodily states (e.g., fatigue, menstrual cramps)

Task Variables

Too difficult

Improper pace (too fast, too slow)

Lack of variety

Lack of choice

Lack of perceived importance

Specific Antecedents

Sudden change in immediate surroundings

Introduction of new tasks

Excessive demands

Unclear instructions

Removal of visible reinforcers

Withholding of reinforcers following previously reinforced responses

Presentation of aversive stimuli

Instruction to wait

Observance of someone else being reinforced

Specific Consequences: Problem Behavior Leads to

Escape from demands

Attention from others

Sympathy

Getting one's way

Tangible reinforcers

Internal sensory feedback

External sensory feedback

Study Questions

12. What is a strong indicator that a problem behavior is being maintained as a way of escaping from demands? Give an example illustrating this indicator.

13. Suppose that a nonverbal child screams loudly as a way of escaping from demands by adults in various training settings. Describe two alternative strategies that the adults might follow to deal with the problem behavior.

14. What are the two main indicators that a problem behavior is a respondent behavior that is elicited by prior stimuli (versus operant behavior being maintained by reinforcing consequences)? Give an example illustrating this indicator.

15. Describe an example that is not in the text of how nonsocial negative reinforcement could produce undesirable behavior.

16. Describe the main components in the treatment of Joel's anger.

17. What is behavioral diagnostics? In what sense is this term broader than functional assessment?

18. In a sentence or two for each, outline the six major causes of operant problem behaviors described in this chapter.

Application Exercises

A. EXERCISE INVOLVING OTHERS

Identify a behavioral excess of someone you know well. (Do not identify that person.) Try to identify the stimulus control and maintaining consequences for that behavior. Based on your functional assessment, what do you think would be the best treatment procedure to decrease or eliminate that behavior?

B. SELF-MODIFICATION EXERCISE

Identify one of your own behavioral excesses. Try to identify the stimulus control and maintain consequences for that behavior. Based on your functional assessment, what do you think would be the best treatment procedure to decrease or eliminate that behavior?

Note and Extended Discussion

1. St. Peter Pipkin and Vollmer (2009) reviewed basic and applied literature indicating that knowledge of the exact schedule of reinforcement that has reinforced the problem behavior could also be important in planning a treatment program for the problem behavior. For example, an alternative to using extinction to reduce a problem behavior is to present noncontingent reinforcement (see Note 3 of Chapter 5 and Note 1 of Chapter 16). However, St. Peter Pipkin and Vollmer provide evidence that this treatment might be effective only if (a) the behavior had not previously been reinforced on an intermittent ratio like schedule and (b) the noncontingent reinforcement rate is quite different from the reinforcement rate of the schedule maintaining the problem behavior. If the intervals between reinforcements during noncontingent reinforcement are too similar to the intervals between reinforcements on the schedule maintaining the problem behavior, then instead of decreasing the problem behavior, noncontingent reinforcement might actually increase it.

Study Question on Note

1. Describe an example indicating that knowledge of the schedule of reinforcement that has maintained a problem behavior might be important before using noncontingent reinforcement as a treatment for that problem behavior.

24

Planning, Applying, and Evaluating a Behavioral Program

This chapter provides *general* guidelines that should be followed when designing a behavioral program. It assumes knowledge of the principles and procedures presented in the previous chapters. The client might be anyone—a person with autism or intellectual disabilities; a patient with psychiatric problems; a predelinquent or delinquent child or teenager; a typically developing child or teenager at home, in a classroom, or in a community setting; or a normal adult. The situation is one in which you, as a behavior modifier or a mediator (parent, teacher, etc.), would be largely responsible for carrying out a treatment program or intervention.

DECIDING WHETHER TO DESIGN A PROGRAM FOLLOWING A REFERRAL

Behavioral problems have a variety of causes, come in a variety of forms and types, and differ widely in degree of complexity and severity. The fact that a problem has been referred is not always a sufficient reason for proceeding with program design and implementation. To decide whether and where to begin, answering the following questions during the screening or intake phase of behavioral assessment is helpful (see Chapter 20).

1. *Was the Problem Referred Primarily for the Benefit of the Client?* If the problem was referred by others, you must determine whether the accomplishment of the goal will be for the benefit of the client. If its accomplishment is for the benefit of others, it should be at least neutral for the client. Ethical considerations may require that some referrals simply stop here.

2. *Is the Problem Important to the Client or to Others?* You might ask two questions to evaluate the importance of the problem: Will solving the problem lead to less aversiveness or more positive reinforcement for the client or others? Will solving the problem be likely to give rise directly or indirectly to other desirable behaviors? If the answer to either of these questions is no, you should reconsider your involvement with the problem.

3. *Can the Problem and the Goal be Specified So That You are Dealing with a Specific Behavior or Set of Behaviors That Can Be Measured in Some Way?*   Many referrals are vague, subjective, and general, such as, "Chris is a poor student," "My child is driving me up a wall," "I'm really an unorganized person." If the problem is initially vague (e.g., if it is merely labeled "aggression"), you must specify a component behavior or behaviors (e.g., kicking furniture, throwing objects inappropriately) that (a) define the problem and (b) can be measured or assessed objectively. In such cases, however, it is important to ask whether dealing with the defined component behavior(s) will solve the general problem in the eyes of the referring agent or agencies. If it is impossible to agree with the agent on the component behaviors that define the problem, then you should probably stop there. If you do achieve agreement, it should be specified in writing.

4. *Have You Eliminated the Possibility That the Problem Involves Complications That Would Necessitate Referring It to Another Specialist?*   In other words, are you the appropriate person to deal with this problem? If there is any chance that the problem has medical complications, serious psychological ramifications (e.g., the danger of suicide), or a *DSM-IV-TR* diagnosis (see Note 1 of Chapter 1) that you are not qualified to treat, the appropriate specialist should be consulted. You should then treat the problem only in a manner that the specialist recommends.

NOTE 1

5. *Is the Problem one that Would Appear to be Easily Manageable?*   To answer this question, you should consider the following: If the problem is to decrease an undesirable behavior, has the behavior been occurring for a short time, under narrow stimulus control, and with no intermittent reinforcement? A problem with these characteristics is likely to be easier to solve than an undesirable behavior that has been occurring for a long time, under the control of many situations, and with a history of intermittent reinforcement. Moreover, you should identify desirable behavior that can replace the undesirable behavior. If the problem is to teach a new behavior, you should assess whether the client has the prerequisite skills. If there is more than one problem, you should rank order them according to their priorities for treatment and begin with the problem assigned the highest priority.

If the problem involves a child with disruptive behavior, you should be aware that the child's parents may have some preconceived notions of treatment based on watching shows such as *Supernanny* and *Nanny 911*. Such shows have done a good service to behavior modification in that they talk about behavior problems in a matter-of-fact way, focus on finding effective solutions, and help parents to implement interventions that are consistent with evidence-based practice such as time out, planned ignoring, and token programs (Bailey & Burch, 2006). However, such programs may also mislead parents to believe that severe behavior problems of children can be effectively treated within a few days (Fabiano & Elkin, 2006). You need to be prepared to deal with this possibility.

6. *If the Desired Behavior Change Is Obtained, Can It Be Readily Generalized To and Maintained in the Natural Environment?*   To answer this question, you should consider how your training setting can be faded into the natural environment. You should also consider whether the natural environment has contingencies that will maintain the improved behavior, whether you can influence people in the natural environment to help maintain the improved behavior, and whether the client can learn a self-control program (discussed in Chapter 26) that will help the improved behavior persist.

7. *Can You Identify Significant Individuals (Relatives, Friends, and Teachers) in the Client's Natural Environment Who Might Help Record Observations and Manage Controlling Stimuli and Reinforcers?*   When designing programs for children, you

NOTE 2

should consider whether the parents can successfully implement and maintain the program. It makes little sense to accept a referral that would require 2 hours per day for a child in a single-parent family if you have only about 1 hour each week to spend on the project, the parent works full-time and has four other children who require parental attention, and no other adults are available to implement the program.

8. *If There Are Individuals Who Might Hinder the Program, Can You Identify Ways to Minimize Their Potential Interference?* It makes little sense for you to design a program if people are going to sabotage it by, for example, reinforcing undesirable behavior that you are trying to extinguish.

On the basis of your tentative answers to these eight questions, are your training qualifications, daily schedule, and available time adequate for you to participate in the program? You should accept referrals only for which you have the appropriate training and time to carry out an effective program.

When a behavior modifier first enters settings in which interventions are requested (a group home for persons with developmental disabilities, the home of a child with problems, or a classroom), the behavioral problems and the number and complexity of potentially disruptive influences are often staggering. For obvious reasons, it is best to start simple in order to succeed in a small way rather than to attempt too much and risk failing gloriously. A careful evaluation of the initial referral in terms of these questions and considerations can often contribute greatly to the initial success of a behavioral program.

Study Questions

1. How does a behavior modifier evaluate the importance of a problem?
2. What does a behavior modifier do when given a vague problem (such as "aggression") to work on? Illustrate with an example.
3. How does a behavior modifier evaluate the ease with which a problem might be solved?
4. Watch an episode of *Supernanny* (http://abc.go.com/primetime/supernanny). If you don't have access to this program, substitute any program that deals with a behavior problem. Is the problem that is presented one that would likely be easily managed? Justify your answer.
5. How does a behavior modifier evaluate the ease with which the desired behavioral change might be generalized to and maintained in the natural environment?
6. Assume that you are a professional behavior modifier. List four possible conditions under which you would not treat a behavioral problem that has been referred to you.

SELECTION AND IMPLEMENTATION OF A PREPROGRAM ASSESSMENT PROCEDURE

Suppose that you have decided to treat a problem that has been referred to you. You might then proceed through the following steps of implementing a preprogram assessment procedure as introduced in Chapter 20 (pp. 241–246).

1. For a reliable baseline, define the problem in precise behavioral terms.
2. Select an appropriate baseline procedure (see Chapters 20, 21, and 23) that will enable you to
   a. monitor the problem behavior
   b. identify the current stimulus control of the problem behavior

    c. identify the maintaining consequences of the problem behavior

    d. monitor relevant medical/health/personal variables

    e. identify an alternative desirable behavior

3. Design recording procedures that will enable you to log the amount of time devoted to the project by professionals (such as teachers or group home staff). This will help you to do a cost-effectiveness analysis.

4. Ensure that the observers have received appropriate training in identifying the critical aspects of the behavior, applying the recording procedures, and graphing the data.

5. If the baseline is likely to be prolonged, select a procedure for increasing and maintaining the strength of the record-keeping behavior of the data recorders.

6. After beginning to collect baseline data, analyze it carefully to select an appropriate treatment or intervention strategy and decide when to terminate the baseline phase and begin the intervention.

We reviewed the guidelines for behavioral assessment in Chapters 20, 21, and 23, and will not repeat them here. However, you as a behavior modifier should answer some additional questions during the pretreatment assessment phase:

> ***What Daily Times Can the Mediator(s) Schedule for This Project?***   If a teacher has about 10 minutes each day just before lunch to devote to the project, there is no sense in (a) designing time-sampling data sheets that require the teacher to assess behavior throughout the day or (b) gathering data that the teacher will never have time to examine.

> ***Will Others in the Situation Help or Hinder Data Collection?***   There is no sense in designing a baseline procedure to record the duration of a child's tantrumming in a home situation if a grandparent, aunt, brother, or other relative is going to give the child a candy to stop the tantrums. On the other hand, friends and relatives can often be extremely helpful, either by recording data directly or by reminding others to do so. If the help of others is to be utilized, posting data sheets and a summary of the recording procedures where everyone involved in the project can see them would be a good practice.

> ***Will the Surroundings Make Your Assessment Difficult?***   If you want to determine a baseline for the frequency and timing of a child's marking on walls throughout the day and the house has many rooms through which the child wanders, it may be difficult to immediately detect instances of the behavior. Or suppose that you want a baseline for someone's own smoking behavior but during the baseline period, that person spends time in the home of a friend who doesn't smoke. Obviously, this is not ideal for assessment procedures. If you want to assess a child's basic self-dressing skills by presenting clothing items with appropriate instructions while the child's favorite TV program is blaring in the background, your assessment is not likely to be accurate.

> ***How Frequent is the Problem Behavior?***   Is it a problem, such as thumb sucking, fingernail biting, or inattentiveness in school, that occurs often each day? Or is it one that occurs once every few weeks, such as occasional tantrums, stealing, or running away from home? In some cases, your answers to these questions might influence you to withdraw from the project. A problem behavior that occurs rarely can be extremely difficult to treat if you have limited time available for the project. Certainly, the perceived frequency of the behavior will dictate the type of recording procedure as described in Chapter 21 to be selected.

> ***How Rapidly Should the Behavior Change?***   Does the behavior require immediate attention because of its inherent danger (e.g., self-abuse)? Or is the behavior one whose

immediate change is merely convenient for those concerned (e.g., parents wanting to toilet train their child just before going on vacation)? If the behavior (e.g., smoking, excessive TV watching, and inadequate housecleaning) has been occurring for many months and if another few days or weeks more or less can be tolerated, you might be more diligent to design a detailed data-recording system to reliably assess baseline levels of performance.

Is the Presenting Problem a Behavioral Deficit or Can It Be Reformulated as Such? Even if the problem is a behavioral excess to decrease, you should try to identify a desirable alternative behavior to increase.

Study Questions

7. What five variables should an appropriate baseline procedure enable you to monitor or identify?
8. What six questions should a behavior modifier answer during the pretreatment assessment phase?

STRATEGIES OF PROGRAM DESIGN AND IMPLEMENTATION

Some behavior modifiers are skillful at designing effective programs off the top of their heads—that is, identifying the program details that are critical to success and that produce rapid desirable results. There are no guidelines that will immediately turn you into that kind of behavior modifier. Nor are there any rigid sets of guidelines to which you should adhere for every program you design. Many behaviors can be managed successfully with a minor rearrangement of existing contingencies; others require much creativity. The following guidelines will help you to design an effective program in most instances.

1. Identify the goals for target behaviors and their desired amount and stimulus control. Then answer these questions.
   a. Is the description precise?
   b. On what grounds did you choose the goal, and how is it in the client's best interest?
   c. Has the client been given all possible information about the goal?
   d. Have steps been taken to increase the client's commitment to accomplish the goal? (Commitment was discussed in Chapter 17 and is discussed later in this chapter.)
   e. What are potential side effects of accomplishing the goal for both the client and others?
   f. Do the answers to the foregoing questions suggest that you should proceed? If so, then continue.
2. Identify individuals (friends, relatives, teachers, and others) who might help to manage controlling stimuli and reinforcers. Also identify individuals who might hinder the program.
3. Examine the possibility of capitalizing on antecedent control. Can you use:
   a. rules
   b. goal setting
   c. modeling
   d. physical guidance
   e. situational inducement (rearrange the surroundings, move the activity to a new location, relocate people, or change the time of the activity)
   f. motivating operations

4. If you are developing a new behavior, will you use shaping, fading, or chaining? What MEO will you use (see Chapter 19)?

5. If you are changing the stimulus control of an existing behavior, can you select the controlling S^Ds so that they:
   a. are different from other stimuli on more than one dimension
   b. are encountered mainly in situations in which the desired stimulus control should occur
   c. evoke attending behavior
   d. do not evoke undesirable behavior

6. If you are decreasing a behavioral excess:
   a. can you remove S^Ds for the problem behavior
   b. can you withhold reinforcers that are maintaining the problem behavior or present an MAO for those reinforcers (see Chapter 19)
   c. can you apply DRL to reduce the rate of the behavior to a low but acceptable rate
   d. can you apply DRO, DRI, or DRA (note that each of these will incorporate extinction of the problem behavior assuming that you can identify and withhold maintaining reinforcers for it)
   e. should you use punishment? Remember that punishment, if used at all, is acceptable only (if at all) as a last resort and under appropriate professional supervision with appropriate ethical approval.

7. Specify the details of the reinforcement system by answering these questions.
   a. How will you select reinforcers? (See Chapter 3.)
   b. What reinforcers will you use? Can you use the same reinforcers currently maintaining a problem behavior? (See Chapter 23.)
   c. How will reinforcer effectiveness be continually monitored, and by whom?
   d. How will reinforcers be stored and dispensed, and by whom?
   e. If you use a token system or token economy, what are the details of its implementation (see Chapter 4 and 25)?

8. Specify the training setting. What environmental rearrangement will be necessary to maximize the desired behavior, minimize errors and competing behavior, and maximize proper recording and stimulus management by the mediators who will directly carry out the program?

9. Describe how you will program generality of behavior change (Chapter 16) by:
   a. Programming stimulus generalization. Can you:
      (i) train in the test situation
      (ii) vary the training conditions
      (iii) program common stimuli
      (iv) train sufficient stimulus exemplars
      (v) establish a stimulus equivalence class
   b. Programming response generalization. Can you:
      (i) train sufficient response exemplars
      (ii) vary the acceptable responses during training
      (iii) use behavioral momentum to increase low probability responses within a response class
   c. Programming behavior maintenance (generality over time). Can you:
      (i) use natural contingencies of reinforcement
      (ii) train the people in the natural environment
      (iii) use schedules of reinforcement in the training environment
      (iv) give the control to the individual

10. Specify the details of the daily recording and graphing procedures.

11. Collect the necessary materials (such as reinforcers, data sheets, graphs, and curriculum materials).

12. Make checklists of rules and responsibilities for all participants in the program (staff, teachers, parents, peers, students, the client, and others; see Figure 24–1).

13. Specify the dates for data and program reviews, and identify those who will attend.

14. Identify some contingencies that will reinforce the behavior modifiers and mediators (in addition to feedback related to the data and program reviews).

15. Review the potential cost of the program as designed (cost of materials, teacher time, professional consulting time, etc.), and judge its merit against its cost. Reprogram as necessary or desired on the basis of this review.

16. Sign a behavioral contract. A **behavioral contract** is a written agreement that provides a clear statement of what behaviors of what individuals will produce what reinforcers and who will deliver those reinforcers. Behavioral contracting was described initially as a strategy for scheduling the exchange of reinforcers between two or more individuals, such as between a teacher and students (Homme, Csanyi, Gonzales, & Rechs, 1969) or between parents and children (Dardig & Heward, 1976; DeRisi & Butz, 1975; Miller & Kelley, 1994). Treatment contracts between behavior therapists and clients are also recommended to ensure that the behavior modifier is accountable to the client (Sulzer-Azaroff & Reese, 1982). In general, a **treatment contract** is a written agreement between the client and the behavior modifier that clearly outlines the objectives and methods of treatment, the framework of the service to be provided, and contingencies for remuneration that may be forthcoming to the behavior modifier. When the agreement is signed, both the client and the behavior modifier have secured basic protections of their rights. We recommend that behavior modifiers prepare such a written agreement with the appropriate individual(s) prior to implementing a program.

17. Implement the program. The implementation of your program also requires a great deal of consideration. This might be done in two parts. First, you must be certain that those carrying out the program—the mediators—understand and agree with their roles and responsibilities. This might involve a detailed discussion and review session with the mediators. It may also involve some modeling and demonstration on your part, perhaps some role-playing on the part

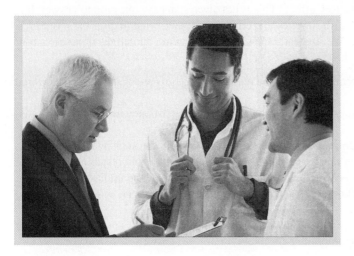

FIGURE 24–1 Behavior modification places high value on accountability for everyone involved in behavior modification programs.

of the mediators depending on the complexity of the programs, and finally some monitoring and on the spot feedback when the program is actually implemented. This ensures that parents, teachers, and/or others are encouraged to follow the program and receive reinforcement for doing so (see, e.g., Hrydowy & Martin, 1994). The second aspect of program implementation is introducing it to the client in a manner that will enhance his or her *commitment* to the program. It is very important that the client's initial contact with the program be highly reinforcing to increase the probability of further contacts. Questions to consider include: Does the client fully understand and agree with the goals of the program? Is the client aware of how the program will benefit him or her? Has the mediator spent sufficient time with the client and interacted in such a way as to gain his or her trust and confidence (see Chapter 20)? Has the program been designed so that the client is likely to experience some success quickly? Will the client come in contact with reinforcers early in the program? An affirmative answer to each of these questions greatly increases the chances that the program will be successful.

Study Questions

9. You are about to design a treatment program. After defining the target behavior and identifying its desired level of occurrence and stimulus control, what five questions should you answer before proceeding to the design?
10. If you are thinking of capitalizing on antecedent control, what six categories should you consider?
11. If you are decreasing a behavioral excess, what five questions should you ask?
12. List five considerations for programming stimulus generalization.
13. List three considerations for programming response generalization.
14. List four considerations for programming behavior maintenance.
15. What is a behavioral contract?
16. What is a treatment contract, and what should it clearly outline?
17. What five questions should be answered affirmatively to increase the client's commitment to the program?

PROGRAM MAINTENANCE AND EVALUATION

Is your program having a satisfactory effect? This is not always an easy question to answer. It is also not always easy to decide, according to some criterion or other, what to do if the program is not having a satisfactory effect. We suggest reviewing the following guidelines to assess a program that has been implemented.

1. Monitor your data to determine whether the recorded behaviors are changing in the desired direction.
2. Consult the people who must deal with the problem and determine whether they are satisfied with the progress.
3. Consult the behavioral journals, professional behavior modifiers, or others with experience in using similar procedures on similar problems to determine whether your results are reasonable in terms of the amount of behavior change during the period the program has been in effect.
4. If, on the basis of Guidelines 1, 2, and 3, the results are satisfactory, proceed directly to guideline 8.
5. If, on the basis of Guideline 1, 2, or 3, your results are unsatisfactory, answer the following questions and make the appropriate adjustment for any yes answer.

a. Have the reinforcers that are being used lost their effectiveness—in other words, has an MAO occurred with regard to the reinforcers being used?

b. Are competing responses being reinforced?

c. Are the procedures being applied incorrectly?

d. Is outside interference disrupting the program?

e. Are there any subjective variables—staff or client negative attitudes, teacher or client lack of enthusiasm, and so forth—that might be adversely affecting the program?

6. If none of the answers to these five questions is yes, check to see whether additional programming steps need to be added or removed. The data may show excessive error rates, which would suggest the need for additional programming steps. Or they may show very high rates of correct responses, which might indicate that the program is too easy and that satiation of intrinsic reinforcers or "boredom" is occurring. Add, remove, or modify steps as necessary.

7. If the results are now satisfactory, proceed to Guideline 8; otherwise consult with a colleague or consider redesigning a major aspect of the program or redoing a functional assessment to identify the antecedents and consequences controlling the target behavior.

8. Decide how you will provide appropriate program maintenance until the behavioral objective is reached (see Chapter 16).

9. Following attainment of the behavioral goal, outline an appropriate arrangement for assessing performance during follow-up observations and assessing social validity (see Chapter 22).

10. After successful follow-up observations have been obtained, determine the costs in terms of time and finances for the behavior changes that occurred (called a *cost-effectiveness analysis*).

11. When possible and appropriate, analyze your data and communicate your procedures and results to other behavior modifiers and interested professionals. Be sure to conceal the client's identity to maintain confidentiality.

Study Questions

18. After a program has been implemented, what three things should be done to determine whether it is producing satisfactory results? (See Guidelines 1, 2, and 3.)

19. Describe in detail the steps that should be followed if a program is not producing satisfactory results (see Guidelines 5, 6, and 7.)

20. If a program is producing satisfactory results, what two things should be done prior to successfully terminating it? (See Guidelines 8 and 9.)

Application Exercise

A. EXERCISE INVOLVING OTHERS

Suppose that you are a behavior modifier. The mother of a 4-year-old child asks for your help in designing a program to overcome the child's extreme disobedience. Construct realistic but hypothetical details of the behavior problem and take it through all steps in each of the following stages of programming:

1. Deciding whether you should design a program to treat the problem.

2. Selecting and implementing an assessment procedure.

3. Developing strategies of program design and implementation.

4. Establishing program maintenance and evaluation.

(*Note:* The problem will have to be fairly complex for you to take it through all the steps in each of these stages.)

Notes and Extended Discussion

1. Whether you are the appropriate person to deal with a particular problem may be influenced in part by whether you live in an urban or a rural setting. Rodrigue, Banko, Sears, and Evans (1996) identified a number of difficulties associated with providing behavior therapy services in rural areas. While rural regions have a disproportionate number of at-risk populations that are costly to serve (e.g., elderly people, children, minorities, poor persons), they typically do not offer the full array of needed mental health services and are characterized by lower availability of and accessibility to specialized services. In other words, while you may not be the ideal person to treat the problem, you may be the best person available. Before accepting the responsibility of designing a program in such a case, however, you should consult the ethical guidelines for human services of your professional organization. (See also Chapter 30 of this book.)

2. Even if significant others are not necessary to implement a program, their availability can be extremely valuable for programming generality. Consider the problem of developing effective behavioral weight-loss programs for children (see LeBow, 1991). Israel, Stolmaker, and Adrian (1985) introduced two groups of overweight children (from 8 to 12 years of age) to an 8-week intensive, multicomponent, behavioral weight-reduction program. The parents of one group were also presented a short course on behavioral child-management skills. At the end of the 8-week treatment program, both groups of children had lost approximately the same amount of weight. After a one-year follow-up, however, maintenance of improved weight status was superior for the children whose parents had been introduced to the behavioral child-management procedures.

Study Questions on Notes

1. As a behavior modifier, how might the geographic setting affect your decision to accept a referral?
2. How did Israel and colleagues demonstrate that utilizing significant others in a program can enhance generality?

25 Token Economies

Recall from Chapter 4 that a conditioned reinforcer is a stimulus that was not originally reinforcing but acquires reinforcing power from being paired appropriately with other reinforcers. Some conditioned reinforcers, such as praise, are quite brief. The stimulus is gone almost as soon as it is presented. As discussed in Chapter 4, other conditioned reinforcers called *tokens* can be accumulated and exchanged for goods and services (Hackenberg, 2009).

A behavioral program in which individuals can earn tokens for a variety of desirable behaviors and can exchange the earned tokens for backup reinforcers is called a **token economy**. Our modern society in which people perform a variety of jobs to earn money that they exchange for various items such as food, shelter, clothing, transportation, luxuries, and access to leisure time activities is a complex token economy. A system in which people purchase bus or subway tokens that they exchange for access to public transit is a somewhat simpler token economy. Token economies are also used as educational and therapeutic tools in behavior modification programs. According to Hackenberg (2009, p. 280), "Token economies are among the oldest and most successful programs in all of applied psychology."

Using token reinforcers has two major advantages. First, they can be given immediately after a desirable behavior occurs and cashed in at a later time for a backup reinforcer. Thus they can be used to "bridge" long delays between the target response and the backup reinforcer, which is especially important when delivering the backup reinforcer immediately after the behavior is impractical or impossible. Second, tokens that are paired with many different backup reinforcers are generalized conditioned reinforcers and therefore do not depend on a specific motivating operation for their strength. This makes it easier to administer consistent and effective reinforcers when dealing with a group of individuals who might be in different motivational states.

Token economies as components of behavioral programs have been used in a variety of settings. They have been used in psychiatric wards, institutions and classrooms for persons with developmental disabilities, classrooms for children and teenagers with attention-deficit hyperactivity disorder (ADHD), normal classroom settings ranging from preschool to college and university, homes for troubled children, prisons, the military, wards for the treatment of persons **NOTE 1** with drug addiction or alcoholism, nursing homes, and convalescent centers (e.g., see Boniecki & Moore, 2003; Corrigan, 1995; Dickerson, Tenhula, & Green-Paden, 2005; Filcheck, McNeil, Greco, & Bernard, 2004; Higgins, Silverman, & Heil, 2008; Liberman, 2000; Matson & Boisjoli, 2009). A token economy has also been used in a behaviorally managed experimental community of college students (Johnson, Welch, Miller, & Altus, 1991; Thomas & Miller, 1980).

Techniques used in token economies have also been extended to various community settings to decrease littering and noise pollution as well as to increase waste recycling, energy conservation, the use of mass transportation, racial integration, behaviors involved in gaining employment, and self-help behaviors in people who are disadvantaged by the economic system. In normal family homes, token economies have been used to control children's behavior and to treat marital discord. In various work settings, tokens have been used to increase safety behavior, decrease absenteeism, and enhance on-the-job performance (Kazdin, 1977a, 1985).

In this chapter, we cannot do justice to the whole range of behaviors and situations to which token economies have been applied. For more specific details on establishing a token economy in a **NOTE 2** particular setting, the reader is referred to any of the excellent books and articles (e.g., Ayllon, 1999; Myles, Moran, Ormsbee, & Downing, 1992) that are available for that purpose. What we intend to do in this chapter is to describe typical steps in the use of token economies in various settings. We will also illustrate many of the steps with reference to Achievement Place, a group home in Lawrence, Kansas, in which a very effective token program was developed for predelinquent youths—boys from 10 to 16 years of age who were typically from difficult home environments and who had been referred by the courts for committing minor crimes such as petty theft and fighting. The program uses what is termed the *Teaching-Family Model* (*TFM*) in which four to eight individuals live with a married couple in a large domestic home. Major features of the TFM include:

1. a token economy in which participants earn points for appropriate social behaviors, academic performance, and daily living skills and exchange them for privileges such as snacks, television, hobbies, games, allowance, and permission to participate in activities away from the home
2. a self-government system in which the youth participate in the development of daily living rules and the management of the program
3. an emphasis on normalization
4. ongoing evaluation of the performance of the participants

Developed in the early 1970s, the TFM has been extended to a variety of settings across the United States and in Canada and to children and adults with a variety of problem types including autism, intellectual disabilities, substance abuse, and severe mental health problems. Although further research is needed to develop strategies for long-term maintenance of gains achieved by children and adults who participate in TFM programs, the model continues to be one of the most effective approaches for the treatment of a variety of problems (Braukmann & Wolf, 1987; Fixsen, Blase, Timbers, & Wolf, 2001; Friman, 2000).

Study Questions

1. What are tokens?
2. What is a token economy?
3. What are two major advantages to using tokens as reinforcers?
4. List at least five settings in which token economies have been used.

5. List at least five behaviors that token economies have been designed to develop.

6. In a sentence, describe the type of individual whom Achievement Place was designed to help.

INITIAL STEPS IN SETTING UP A TOKEN ECONOMY

Deciding on the Target Behaviors

Target behaviors are determined largely by (a) the type of individuals involved, (b) the short- and long-range objectives to be accomplished, and (c) specific behavioral problems that interfere with achieving those objectives. For example, if you are the classroom teacher of a group of first-graders, your objectives will likely include teaching skills in reading, writing, addition, subtraction, and constructive social interaction. Your target behaviors will include these skills or ones that are prerequisite to them. The target behaviors must be clearly defined so that the students know what behaviors are expected of them and so that you can reinforce those behaviors reliably when they occur. Thus, one of your target behaviors might be sitting quietly when the teacher gives instructions. A more advanced target behavior might be correctly completing 10 addition problems.

The more homogeneous the group with which you are dealing, the easier it is to standardize the rules concerning which specific responses will be reinforced with what specific number of tokens. From this perspective, many groups for whom token economies are appropriate are fortunately composed of individuals who are at roughly the same behavioral level (e.g., individuals with severe intellectual disabilities or college students enrolled in a PSI course; see Chapter 2). Even with very homogeneous groups, having some specific reinforcement rules for certain individuals according to their respective behavioral needs is often necessary. This necessity for individualizing programs adds to the complexity of administering a token economy, but the resulting difficulties are not serious if you are not required to handle too many radically different individual programs at once. Assigning special cases to special treatment groups might be one efficient way to solve the problem of individualization in certain types of settings.

At the original Achievement Place (Phillips, 1968) described previously, target behaviors for the predelinquent youth were selected in social, self-care, and academic areas that were considered to be important to the youths both while they were at Achievement Place and in future environments when they left the group home. Both desirable and undesirable behaviors were identified, and the target behaviors and the points (which served as tokens) that they earned or lost are listed in Table 25–1.

Taking Baselines

As is done before initiating other procedures, baseline data on the specific target behaviors should be obtained before initiating a token economy. It might be that your group is already performing at a satisfactory level and that the potential benefits to be gained from setting up a token economy do not justify the time, effort, and cost involved in doing so. After the program has been started, comparing the data with the baseline data will enable you to determine the program's effectiveness.

Selecting Backup Reinforcers

The methods for selecting backup reinforcers are essentially the same as the methods for selecting reinforcers described in Chapter 3. Keep in mind, however, that a token system generally

TABLE 25–1 Behaviors and the Number of Points That They Earned or Lost at Achievement Place

Behaviors That Earned Points	Number of Points
1. Watching news on TV or reading the newspaper	300 per day
2. Cleaning and maintaining neatness in one's room	500 per day
3. Keeping one's person neat and clean	500 per day
4. Reading books	5 to 10 per page
5. Aiding the teaching-parents in various household tasks	20 to 1,000 per
6. Doing dishes	500 to 1,000 per meal
7. Being well dressed for an evening meal	100 to 500 per meal
8. Performing homework	500 per day
9. Obtaining desirable grades on school report cards	500 to 1,000 per grade
10. Turning out lights when not in use	25 per light

Behaviors That Lost Points	Number of Points
1. Failing grades on the report card	500 to 1,000 per grade
2. Speaking aggressively	20 to 50 per response
3. Forgetting to wash hands before meals	100 to 300 per meal
4. Arguing	300 per response
5. Disobeying	100 to 1,000 per response
6. Being late	10 per minute
7. Displaying poor manners	50 to 100 per response
8. Engaging in poor posture	50 to 100 per response
9. Using poor grammar	20 to 50 per response
10. Stealing, lying, or cheating	10,000 per response

(*Source:* From E. L. Phillips, "Achievement Place: Token Reinforcement Procedures in a Home-Style Rehabilitation Setting for 'Pre-delinquent' Boys." *Journal of Applied Behavior Analysis, 1,* 1968, pp. 213–223; reprinted with permission of the Society for the Experimental Analysis of Behavior.)

increases the variety of practical reinforcers that you can use because they need not be limited to those that can be delivered immediately following a desired response.

In considering reinforcers that are normally available, take extreme caution to avoid serious ethical problems that can arise. Various legislatures have enacted laws affirming the rights of mentally ill patients and residents of treatment centers to have access to meals, comfortable beds, TV, and so on. Furthermore, a number of court decisions have upheld these civil rights. Therefore, never plan a program that might involve depriving individuals of something that legally and morally belongs to them.

After establishing what backup reinforcers you are going to use and how you are going to obtain them, you should next consider the general method of dispensing them. A store or commissary is an essential feature of most token economies. In a small token economy, such as a classroom, the store can be quite simple, say, a box located on the teacher's desk or another table in the room. In a larger token economy, the store is typically much larger, perhaps occupying one or more rooms. Regardless of the size of the store, a precise method of keeping records of purchases must be devised so that an adequate inventory (especially of high-demand items) can be maintained at all times.

At Achievement Place, the backup reinforcers were items and activities that were naturally available in the group home and that appeared to be important to the youths. Their access to the backup reinforcers, referred to as *privileges,* occurred on a weekly basis. At the end of each week, the youths could trade the points that they had earned that week for privileges for the next week (see Table 25–2).

Selecting the Type of Tokens to Use

Tokens can take on any of the forms that money has assumed. These include personal "checks," entries in a "bank book," marks on a chart on the wall or in notebooks, stickers, stars, or stamps pasted in booklets—these and numerous other possibilities might suit the needs of your particular token economy.

In general, tokens should be attractive, lightweight, portable, durable, easy to handle, and, of course, not easily counterfeited (Figure 25–1). If automatic dispensers of backup reinforcement are used, you should ensure that your tokens will operate those devices. You should also ensure that you have an adequate number of tokens. For example, Stainback, Payne, Stainback, and Payne (1973) suggest that you should have on hand about 100 tokens per child when starting a token economy in a classroom.

You should also acquire the necessary accessories for handling and storing tokens. For example, schoolchildren might need boxes, bags, or purses in which to store the tokens they have earned. At Achievement Place, as indicated in Tables 25–1 and 25–2, points were used as tokens. Throughout each day, points were recorded on 3 x 5-inch index cards that the youths always carried with them. In this way, the points could be dispensed or taken away immediately following desirable or undesirable behavior.

TABLE 25–2	Backup Reinforcers That Could Be Earned Each Week with Points at Achievement Place
Privileges for the Week	**Price in Points**
Allowance	1,000
Access to bicycle	1,000
Access to TV	1,000
Access to games	500
Access to tools	500
Snacks	1,000
Permission to go downtown	1,000
Permission to stay up past bedtime	1,000
Permission to come home late after school	1,000

Source: From E. L. Phillips, "Achievement Place: Token Reinforcement Procedures in a Home-Style Rehabilitation Setting for 'Pre-delinquent' Boys." *Journal of Applied Behavior Analysis, 1,* 1968, pp. 213–223; reprinted with permission of the Society for the Experimental Analysis of Behavior.)

FIGURE 25–1   Tokens should not be easily counterfeited.

Identifying Available Help

Help from other individuals might not be essential in a small token economy, such as a classroom, but is certainly useful—especially in the initial stages of the program. In a large token economy, such as a psychiatric facility, such help is essential.

Help might be obtained from a number of sources: (a) people already assigned to work with the individuals of concern (e.g., nurse's aides, teaching assistants), (b) volunteers (e.g., homemakers, senior citizens, members of civic organizations and community action groups), (c) behaviorally advanced individuals within the institution (e.g., older students assigned to help younger students), and (d) members of the token economy itself. In some cases, individuals have been NOTE 3 taught to deliver tokens to themselves contingent on their own appropriate behavior.

After the token economy begins to function smoothly, more and more of its members will gradually become able to assume more and more responsibility in helping to achieve its goals. For example, at Achievement Place, some of the youths supervise others in carrying out routine household tasks (see Fixsen & Blase, 1993). The supervisor, or "manager," as the youth is called, has the authority to both administer and remove tokens for peers' performances. Of the several methods that were studied for selecting managers, democratic elections proved to be best in terms of the performances of the youths and their effectiveness in accomplishing their tasks (Phillips, Phillips, Wolf, & Fixsen, 1973; Wolf, Braukmann, & Ramp, 1987). In another experiment at Achievement Place, some youths earned tokens for serving as therapists for others who had speech problems. The youths performed this function with remarkable effectiveness despite having very little adult supervision and no specific training (Bailey, Timbers, Phillips, & Wolf, 1971).

In some courses that use PSI (including CAPSI—see pp. 16–17), students who master an assignment evaluate the performance of other students on that assignment and give them immediate feedback concerning their performance. Another method used in college and university PSI classes is to give the students a test on the first several sections of the course material at the beginning of the term. Each student who demonstrates the ability to readily master the course material is put in charge of a small group of students, whom the student helps to tutor and supervise throughout the remainder of the course (Johnson & Ruskin, 1977).

In deciding how you are going to obtain support to manage your token economy, you will need to consider how the helpers' behavior is to be reinforced. Your approval is, of course, a potential reinforcer that should be used generously. Permission to continue working in the token economy and to work at desired jobs is an additional potential reinforcer.

Choosing the Locations

No special locations are essential for a token economy, which is nice because the designer of a token economy often has little or no choice in its location. Some locations are better than others, however, depending on the type of token economy under consideration. For example, college instructors using token economies often arrange to have their courses scheduled in large classrooms. Movable desks are generally preferred over stationary ones because they enable students to work easily in small groups. Classrooms with token economies are often noisy places that give an initial impression of mass confusion to a casual observer. Almost all students soon adjust quite well to the noise, so the confusion doesn't prevent them from working with great efficiency. The Internet has provided a better environment for academic token economies because students can be in almost any location (e.g., Pear & Crone-Todd, 1999; Pear & Martin, 2004).

Study Questions

7. List and briefly describe six initial steps involved in setting up a token economy.
8. Identify six target behaviors for the youths at Achievement Place: three desirable and three undesirable behaviors.
9. What is the store of a token economy? Give examples.
10. What six characteristics should a token have?
11. Identify three sources of potential volunteer help in managing a token economy.
12. What do you think are some advantages in having members of the token economy themselves function as the main source of help?
13. What are two ways in which help has been obtained to manage PSI courses?

SPECIFIC IMPLEMENTATION PROCEDURES

Before and during the implementation of a token economy, as with any other new program, a number of specific procedures must be chosen and implemented. These can be categorized as follows.

Keeping Data

This procedure concerns what sort of data sheets should be used, who is to record the data, and when the data are to be recorded.

The Reinforcing Agent

It is important to decide who will administer the reinforcement and for what behaviors. Ayllon and Azrin (1968) recommended that, when several managers dispense tokens to several individuals (as in a psychiatric ward), only one person be assigned to reinforce a particular response at a particular time. Otherwise, "no one individual can be held responsible for failure to administer the reinforcement procedures properly, since any deviation, omission, or modification is easily attributed to the behavior of some other employee" (p. 136).

Care should be taken to ensure that tokens are always delivered in a positive and conspicuous manner immediately following a desired response. Friendly, smiling approval should be administered along with the token, and the individual should be told, at least in the initial stages, why he or she is receiving the token.

Number or Frequency of Tokens to Pay

Several important considerations involve the amount of tokens to give for a particular behavior. One consideration is the stage of the token economy. Stainback, Payne, Stainback, and Payne (1973) recommended that from 25 to 75 tokens per child is not excessive on the first day of a token economy in a classroom. They recommended further that the number be decreased gradually to an average of about 15 to 30 each day. Other considerations are the therapeutic value of the behavior being reinforced and the likelihood that the individuals will engage in it without tokens. As an example of the latter consideration, the number of tokens that college students at the University of Kansas Experimental Living Project could earn for doing chores in their residence was related to the amount of time required to perform the chore (Johnson, Welch, Miller, & Altus, 1991).

Managing the Backup Reinforcers

How frequently backup reinforcers will be available to be purchased must be determined. In the beginning, the frequency should probably be quite high and then decreased gradually. For schoolchildren, Stainback et al. (1973) recommended that store time be held once or twice per day for the first three or four days and then decreased gradually in frequency until it is held only once each week (Friday afternoon) by the third week of the token economy.

It is also necessary to decide on the price of each backup reinforcer. In addition to the monetary cost, which is the most obvious consideration in assigning token values to backup reinforcers, two other factors should be considered. One is supply and demand. That is, the price should be higher for items whose demand exceeds the supply and less for items whose supply exceeds the demand. This will help to maintain an adequate supply of effective reinforcers and promote optimal utilization of the reinforcing power of each backup reinforcer. The other factor to consider is the therapeutic value of the backup reinforcer. An individual should be charged very little for a backup reinforcer that is beneficial to him or her. This will help to induce the individual to partake of the reinforcer. For example, an individual whose social skills need improving might be charged only a few tokens for admission to a party because of the valuable behavior that participating in this event might help to develop.

Possible Response-Cost Punishment Contingencies

The use of tokens provides the possibility of using fines as punishment for inappropriate behavior (see, e.g., Table 25–1; Lippman & Motta, 1993; Sullivan & O'Leary, 1990). This type of punishment might be preferable from an ethical point of view to physical punishment and time out. As with all forms of punishment, it should be used sparingly and only for clearly defined behaviors (see Chapter 12).

If fines are used in a token economy (e.g., see Table 25–1), it might be necessary to add training contingencies that teach individuals how to accept fines in a relatively nonemotional, nonaggressive manner. Phillips, Phillips, Fixsen, and Wolf (1973) described such contingencies for their token economy at Achievement Place with predelinquent youths. In that economy, the contingencies related to fines probably helped to teach youths an important social skill: how to accept reprimands from law enforcers in society.

Monitoring and Training Staff or Helpers

The managers of a token economy are also subject to the laws of behavior. They must receive frequent reinforcement for appropriate behavior, and their inappropriate behavior must be corrected if the token economy is to function effectively. Their duties must therefore be specified clearly, and they must be monitored in performing those duties. The importance of doing so was made clear to Montrose Wolf and his colleagues when they attempted to replicate the first (and very successful) Achievement Place. As expressed by Wolf, Kirigin, Fixsen, Blase and Braukmann (1995), to train a couple as house parents to start a new group home, they put the couple in

> the "best" academic masters degree program we could design. Their courses included behavior theory, child and adolescent development, and other abstract courses. Unfortunately, those courses contained nothing specific about how to treat youths in a group home. . . . We will never forget that emotionally harrowing summer when we sent that misled, misguided, and mistrained couple into their group home, so doomed to fail. (pp. 27–28)

The developers thus redesigned their training program for the teaching-parents and successfully replicated the TFM at the state level. When they attempted to extend the model to the national level, they again met with failure. Eventually, they realized that this was a result of their being unable to personally provide the "amount of monitoring, specification of behaviors, and skill teaching that could occur in the Kansas homes compared to the distant homes around the country where these functions did not occur at all" (Wolf et al., 1995, p. 39). To serve these and other functions at the national level, the developers established the Teaching-Family Association (TFA):

> TFA is designed to serve many functions, including the mediation of educational, professional, recreational, vocational, and social reinforcers for its members. However, TFA's most important function is quality refinement: To specify behavior, monitor, and provide skill-teaching to every training site that is associated with it. (Wolf et al., 1995, p. 46)

TFA has evolved into an international organization with many regional member sites. According to the organization's website (www.teaching-family.org), TFA is "[t]he only entity in North America that defines and implements standards and reviews procedures related to the actual performance and quality of treatment and service delivery systems at all organizational levels."

Handling Potential Problems

In the design of a token economy, as with any complex procedure, it is wise to plan for potential problems. Some problems that often arise are (a) confusion, especially during the first few days after the initiation of the economy, (b) staff or helper shortages, (c) attempts by individuals to get tokens they have not earned or backup reinforcers for which they do not have enough tokens, (d) individuals playing with tokens and manipulating them in distracting ways, and (e) failure to purchase backup reinforcers. These and other problems that might arise can often be managed by careful planning beforehand.

However, as these initial failures in extending the TFM indicate, careful planning beforehand is not always sufficient to prevent problems from occurring. The developers of Achievement Place attribute overcoming this to the development and use of subjective feedback questionnaires given to consumers of the program and online staff, which helped the developers identify and solve unanticipated problems that occurred (Wolf et al., 1995).

Study Questions

14. Before and during the implementation of a token economy, what seven specific procedures must be decided on and implemented?
15. What are some of the advantages and disadvantages of assigning only one person to reinforce a particular response at a particular time in a token economy in an institutional ward?
16. How should tokens be delivered?
17. How many tokens should you have for each student in the group?
18. How often should store time be held in a token economy with schoolchildren?
19. Describe three problems that are likely to occur during the initial days of a token economy.

PREPARATION OF A MANUAL

The final stage to complete before implementing the token economy is to prepare a manual or written set of rules describing exactly how the economy is to run. This manual should explain in detail what behaviors are to be reinforced, how they are to be reinforced with tokens and backup reinforcers, the times at which reinforcement is to be available, what data are to be recorded, how and when they are to be recorded, and the responsibilities and duties of every staff member and helper. Each rule should be reasonable and acceptable to all involved. Each person delivering tokens should receive a copy of the manual or a clear and accurate version of those portions of it pertaining to his or her specific duties and responsibilities. If feasible, each individual on the token economy should be given a clear and accurate version of those portions of the manual pertaining to him or her. If the individual is not able to read fluently but can understand the spoken language, a clear explanation of the relevant portions of the manual should be provided.

The manual should include definite procedures for evaluating whether the rules are being followed adequately and procedures for ensuring that they are. The manual should include methods for arbitrating disputes concerning the rules, and the participation in the arbitration procedures should be provided to the greatest extent that is practical and consistent with the token economy's goals. Effecting such participation on the token economy by the individuals is a step toward developing behaviors that are highly prized in the natural environment. To this end, it is desirable at some stage in the token economy to have the individuals themselves participate in constructively revising the rules and designing new ones. The rules should also be capable of modification when evidence indicates that a change is desirable. Sudden and drastic changes, however, can generate undesirable emotional behavior. Moreover, individuals might be disinclined to follow the rules when they are changed frequently or arbitrarily. So that rule modifications might occur in the smoothest manner possible, it is advisable to have the manual itself specify the basis on which it will be revised. Advance notification of impending rule changes should be given to all concerned, and revisions and additions to the manual should be explained, discussed, justified, put in writing, and disseminated prior to being put into effect.

One of the consequences regarding the difficulty in replicating Achievement Place described previously was that the researchers developed explicit and detailed training manuals so that teaching-parents would know exactly what to do under a wide range of circumstances (Braukmann & Blase, 1979; Phillips, Phillips, Fixsen, & Wolf, 1974). These training manuals provide a good model for developing the training manuals for establishing and operating token economies in a variety of settings.

GENERALITY PROGRAMMED TO THE NATURAL ENVIRONMENT

While token economies are sometimes regarded only as ways in which to manage problem behavior within institutional settings, their more important function is to help individuals adjust to the natural environment. Kazdin (1985) summarized a large amount of data indicating that token economies are effective with diverse populations and that the gains achieved with these economies are often maintained for several years following the termination of the program. However, NOTE 4 because social reinforcement, not tokens, prevails in the natural environment, a token economy should be designed so that social reinforcement gradually replaces token reinforcement.

Two general ways of weaning an individual from tokens are used. One is to eliminate them gradually. The second is to decrease their value gradually. The first alternative can be accomplished by gradually (a) making the token delivery schedule more and more intermittent, (b) decreasing the number of behaviors that earn tokens, or (c) increasing the delay between the target behavior and token delivery. Alternative (b) can be accomplished by gradually decreasing the amount of backup reinforcement that a given number of tokens can purchase or by gradually increasing the delay between token acquisition and the purchase of backup reinforcers. At present, we cannot say which method or combination of methods produces the best results. In addition, all considerations involved in programming generality (discussed in Chapter 16) should be reviewed.

Gradually transferring control to the individuals so that they plan and administer their own reinforcements is another step in preparing them for the natural environment. An individual who can evaluate her or his own behavior, decide rationally what changes need to be made in it, and program effectively for these changes is clearly in a good position to cope with almost any environment. Methods for establishing these skills are discussed in Chapter 26.

ETHICAL CONSIDERATIONS

Token economies involve the systematic application of behavior modification techniques on a relatively large scale. The possibilities of abusing the techniques, even unintentionally, are thereby magnified, and precautions must be taken to avoid such abuse. One such precaution is to make the system completely open to public scrutiny, provided that such openness is subject to the approval of the individuals in the program or their advocates. An important source of ethical control for the TFM, for example, is the TFA's rigorous standards and procedures for certifying programs that claim to use the TFM. Ethical considerations involving all behavior modification programs are discussed extensively in Chapter 30.

A SUMMARY OF CONSIDERATIONS NECESSARY IN DESIGNING A TOKEN ECONOMY

1. Review some appropriate literature.
2. Identify your target behaviors.
   a. List short-range and long-range objectives.
   b. Arrange your objectives in order of priority.
   c. Select those objectives that are most important for the individuals in the program and that are prerequisites for later objectives.
   d. Identify several of the priority objectives on which to start, emphasizing those that can be accomplished quickly.
   e. Determine a number of target behaviors for each of the starting objectives.
3. Take a baseline of your target behaviors.
4. Select your backup reinforcers.
   a. Use reinforcers that are usually effective with the population of interest.
   b. Use the Premack principle (see Chapter 3).
   c. Collect verbal information from the individuals in the program concerning their reinforcers.
   d. Give the individuals in the program catalogs that will help them to identify reinforcers.
   e. Ask individuals in the program what they like to do when they have free time away from work or other demands.
   f. Identify natural reinforcers that could be programmed.
   g. Consider ethics and legalities regarding the reinforcers on your list.
   h. Design an appropriate store to keep, display, and dispense your backup reinforcers.
5. Select the most appropriate type of token. (They should be attractive, lightweight, portable, durable, easy to handle, and difficult to counterfeit.)
6. Identify those who are available to help manage the program:
   a. existing staff
   b. volunteers
   c. university students
   d. residents of the institution
   e. members of the token economy
7. Obtain an appropriate location and necessary equipment.
   a. Accept the location with the larger(est) space.
   b. Choose equipment and furnishings that are easily movable.
   c. Rearrange the setting so that target behaviors can be detected most easily and reinforced immediately.

8. Decide on specific implementation procedures.

    a. Design appropriate data sheets and determine who will take data and how and when it will be recorded.

    b. Decide who is going to administer reinforcement, how it will be administered, and for what behaviors it will be provided.

    c. Decide on the number of tokens that can be earned per day.

    d. Establish "store" procedures and determine the token value of backup reinforcers.

    e. Be wary of punishment contingencies. Use them sparingly: only for clearly defined behaviors and only when it is ethically justifiable to do so.

    f. Ensure that staff and helper duties are clearly defined and that a desirable schedule of monitoring and reinforcement is implemented.

    g. Plan for potential problems.

9. Prepare a token economy manual for the individuals in the program, the staff, and the helpers.

10. Institute your token economy.

11. Plan strategies for obtaining generality to the natural environment.

12. Monitor and practice relevant ethical guidelines at each step.

Study Questions

20. Describe two general methods of weaning individuals from tokens when transferring behavior to the natural environment.

21. If one decides to effect a gradual decrease in the number of behaviors that earn tokens, what general guidelines might be followed in deciding which behaviors no longer require token reinforcement? That is, on which behaviors do you start?

22. What is one precaution to help ensure high ethical standards for a token economy?

Application Exercises

A. EXERCISES INVOLVING OTHERS

1. For a group of individuals of your choosing, identify five plausible goals for a token economy.

2. Define precisely the target behaviors related to each of the five goals listed in Exercise 1.

3. Describe things you might do to identify backup reinforcers for the group of individuals you chose in Exercise 1.

Notes and Extended Discussion

1. Token economies in the classroom have taken a new turn with the rise of classroom mini-economies in which teachers use play money to teach children basic principles of economics and personal finances (e.g., Day & Ballard, 2005). Children in classroom mini-economies earn play money, which they can exchange later for items in a class store, for (a) working at classroom jobs, (b) running classroom businesses, and (c) engaging in desired academic and classroom management behaviors. Classroom jobs include custodian (cleaning bookshelves, boards, erasers), attendance officer (taking daily attendance), and horticulture specialist (taking care of classroom plants). Classroom businesses include making things that other children can purchase (e.g., artwork, craft items, class newspaper) and providing services to other children (e.g., tutoring, desk cleaning, singing telegrams). Desired academic and classroom management behaviors include completing assignments on time, showing improvement in schoolwork, and lining up quietly in the hallway. Thus, while standard classroom token economies have focused on desired academic behavior, classroom mini-economies address the broader goal of preparing children to fruitfully engage in the economy of the natural environment.

2. Much of the material in this chapter is covered in greater detail in the following major works on token economies: Ayllon and Azrin (1968) and Glynn (1990), which deal with token economies for psychiatric patients; Stainback et al. (1973), which discusses token economies in elementary school classrooms; Welch and Gist (1974), which primarily addresses token economies in sheltered workshops; Ayllon and Milan (1979), which describes token programs in prisons; and Kazdin (1977a), which presents a comprehensive review of token-economy research. For more information on token systems for children and teens with ADHD, see Barkley (1996). See Keller and Sherman (1982) and Chapter 2 of this book for additional information on the use of token-economy procedures in college and high school courses in which systems incorporating these procedures are sometimes called *Personalized System of Instruction* (*PSI*). For a review and discussion of token reinforcement procedures and concepts in relation to general principles of behavior, see Hackenberg (2009).

3. Rae, Martin, and Smyk (1990) designed a program to pay tokens to individuals with developmental disabilities in a sheltered workshop for improved on task performance. The tokens could be redeemed for items in the workshop cafeteria. However, the workshop had insufficient staff to reliably keep track of individuals who were on task and those who were not. A solution was to teach the workers to self-monitor their own on task performance. A pencil and a sheet with squares on it were placed in front of each worker. The workers were taught that when a buzzer sounded, they should mark an X on one of the squares if they were on task. The buzzer was set to go off at six random times during half a day. Upon earning six X's, a worker could exchange them for a token. The total program proved to be effective for increasing the on task behavior of the workers on a variety of workshop tasks.

4. With regard to the TFM's program generality, research shows that it is effective for managing the behavior of predelinquent youth when they are in the program (e.g., Kirigin, Braukmann, Atwater, & Wolf, 1982); however, it is less clear that it is effective after they leave the program. In fact, several initial studies purported to show that there is no difference between recidivism rate of predelinquents who had been in TFM programs and those who had been in traditional programs (e.g., Fonagy, Target, Cottrell, Phillips, & Kurtz, 2002; Jones, Weinrott, & Howard, 1981; Kirigin et al., 1982; Wilson & Herrnstein, 1985). Kingsley (2006), however, argued that these studies are methodologically and statistically flawed and that, moreover, a number of more recent studies indicate that the TFM does meaningfully reduce recidivism (e.g., Friman et al., 1992; Larzelere et al., 2001; Larzelere, Daly, Davis, Chmelka, & Handwerk, 2004; Lipsey, 1992, 1999a, 1999b; Lipsey & Wilson, 1998; Thompson et al., 1996). Clearly, more research is needed on this. Perhaps more important, research is needed to determine effective methods for transferring the gains made in the program to the environment in which individuals in the program will live when they graduate from the program.

Study Questions on Notes

1. What is a classroom mini-economy?
2. How is a classroom mini-economy similar to and how does it differ from a standard classroom token economy?
3. Would you expect children in a classroom mini-economy to show more or less generalization to the natural environment than if they had not participated in the mini-economy? Explain.
4. Describe a token program in which individuals in a sheltered workshop administered tokens to themselves.

26

Helping an Individual to Develop Self-Control[1]

Al and Mary have just finished having doughnuts and coffee in the campus cafeteria. "I think I'll have another doughnut," said Al. "They look so delicious! I just don't have the willpower to resist. Besides," he added, while patting his protruding midsection, "one more won't make any difference."

Many problems of self-control involve self-restraint—learning to decrease excessive behaviors that have immediate gratification—such as excessive smoking, eating, drinking, and TV watching. Other problems of self-control require behavioral change in the opposite direction—responses that need to be increased—such as studying, exercising, being assertive, and performing household chores. Many people speak as though some magical force within us—called *willpower*—is responsible for overcoming such problems. People believe this, in part because others are always saying things like, "If you had more willpower, you could get rid of that bad habit," or "If you had more willpower, you could improve yourself." Most of us have heard such advice many times. Unfortunately, it's usually not very helpful advice because the person offering it almost always neglects to tell us how we can get more of this so-called willpower. It is more useful to look at how problems of self-control stem from differences between effective versus ineffective consequences of a behavior. From such a starting point, we proceed to a model for self-control. Finally, we describe how most successful **self-control programs** proceed through five basic steps. Such programs are also called **self-management** or **self-modification**, a strategy for using principles of behavior modification to change or control one's own behavior.

CAUSES OF SELF-CONTROL PROBLEMS

"I just *can't* resist having an extra dessert."

"I *really* should get into an exercise program. I wish I weren't so lazy."

---

[1] Material in this chapter was described by Martin and Osborne (1993) and is paraphrased with permission.

"My term paper is due, I have a big midterm, and I have to finish writing up my lab assignment. What am I doing at this bar? Why am I not home studying?"

Do any of these sound familiar? If you're like most people, you've probably said such things many times. These are the times when we are tempted to talk about not having enough willpower. Let's see how such problems can be explained by examining how immediately significant, delayed, cumulatively significant, and improbable consequences affect or fail to affect behavior.

Problems of Behavioral Excesses

One type of self-control problem consists of behavioral excesses—doing too much of something. Examples are overeating, watching TV excessively, and drinking too much coffee. All such behavioral excesses lead to immediate reinforcers (e.g., tasty food, enjoyable scenes on TV). Even though the excesses might eventually lead to negative consequences, the latter are often ineffective. Let's see why.

IMMEDIATE REINFORCERS VERSUS DELAYED PUNISHERS FOR A BEHAVIOR   Suppose that a teenager wants to go out with friends but still has homework to be done. When the parents ask about the homework, the teenager lies and is allowed to leave with friends. Lying is immediately reinforced. The lie is not discovered until later, and the consequent punishment (e.g., being grounded, failing the assignment) is long delayed from the instance of lying. If a behavior leads to immediate reinforcers but delayed punishers, the immediate reinforcers often win out. Many problems of self-control stem from this fact (Brigham, 1989ab). The immediate backslapping and laughter of friends after someone "chugs" a pitcher of beer may override the delayed punishing consequences of a hangover. The immediate reinforcing consequences from sexual behavior with a friend's spouse may override the delayed hurt and emotional anguish when the friend finds out and is no longer a friend.

IMMEDIATE REINFORCERS VERSUS CUMULATIVELY SIGNIFICANT PUNISHERS FOR A BEHAVIOR   Consider the problem of eating too many sweets. Eating an extra dessert is immediately reinforced by the taste. Although the negative effects (e.g., excess cholesterol) of the extra dessert are immediate, they are too small to have an effect. Rather, it is the accumulation of extra desserts on many occasions that causes a health problem. Consider the problem of smoking. The immediate consequences of smoking (e.g., nicotine effects) are positive for smokers. Although negative effects (e.g., tar deposited on the smoker's lungs) are immediate, the harmful outcomes from a single cigarette are too small to counteract the enjoyment of smoking. Rather, it is the accumulation of the effects of hundreds of cigarettes that results in shortness of breath, sore throat, coughing, and possible lung cancer. Thus, for many self-control problems, the immediate reinforcement for consumption of harmful substances (nicotine, cholesterol, etc.) wins out over the unnoticeable immediate negative effects that are only cumulatively significant (Malott, 1989).

IMMEDIATE REINFORCERS FOR PROBLEM BEHAVIOR VERSUS DELAYED REINFORCERS FOR ALTERNATIVE DESIRABLE BEHAVIOR   Let's suppose it's a Thursday evening in the middle of your term. Your roommate just rented a movie that you would like to watch but you have an exam tomorrow. Do you watch the movie now and receive a low grade on the exam later, or do you study for three hours and receive a higher grade later? Unfortunately, many students choose the movie. Consider the case of a worker who receives a large Christmas bonus from the company.

Will the worker spend the bonus on something that is immediately pleasurable, like a ski trip, or invest it in a tax-free retirement fund? Which would you choose if you were the worker? For self-control problems involving a choice between two alternative behaviors, both with positive outcomes, the one that produces the immediate reinforcer often wins out (Brigham, 1989b).

Problems of Behavioral Deficits

Another type of self-control problem consists of responses that need to be increased, such as flossing your teeth, taking good lecture notes, and exercising regularly. Such behaviors usually lead to small, immediate punishers. And even though there might be positive outcomes if the behaviors occur or major negative outcomes if the behaviors don't occur, both of these outcomes are often ineffective. Let's see why.

IMMEDIATE SMALL PUNISHERS FOR A BEHAVIOR VERSUS CUMULATIVELY SIGNIFICANT REINFORCERS   For nonexercisers, an initial exercising session can be quite unpleasant (e.g., time consuming, tiring, stressful). Even though an instance of exercising may have immediate benefits (e.g., increased blood circulation, better removal of waste products), such outcomes are too small to be noticed. Rather, it is the accumulation of the benefits of exercising on many occasions that is eventually noticeable. Many people fail to follow desirable health practices (exercising, taking prescribed medications, etc.) because doing so leads to immediate small punishers whereas the positive effects, though immediate, are too small to be effective until they have accumulated over many trials (Malott, 1989).

IMMEDIATE SMALL PUNISHER FOR A BEHAVIOR VERSUS IMMEDIATE BUT IMPROBABLE MAJOR PUNISHER IF THE BEHAVIOR DOES NOT OCCUR   Most people know that wearing eye protection when playing racquetball can prevent serious eye damage and that wearing a helmet when riding a bicycle could prevent brain damage from a serious accident. Why, then, do many people not wear goggles when playing racquetball or helmets when riding bicycles? First, such behaviors usually lead to immediate mild punishers (the goggles and the helmet may be hot and uncomfortable). Second, although the major punishers for not performing the behavior would be immediate, they are improbable. The longer and more often one engages in these behaviors, however, the more likely the punishers become according to the laws of probability.

IMMEDIATE SMALL PUNISHER FOR A BEHAVIOR VERSUS DELAYED MAJOR PUNISHER IF THE BEHAVIOR DOES NOT OCCUR   Why do many people avoid exercising, put off going for a dental checkup, or fail to take good lecture notes? This type of self-control problem has immediate weak punishers. Exercising can make you hot and uncomfortable. The sound of the dentist's drill is unpleasant. Your fingers get tired while taking good lecture notes. Moreover, all of these activities take time from more reinforcing activities. While the delayed consequences such as major dental problems can be extremely aversive, they occur long after many missed preventive opportunities. In such scenarios, the immediate punishing consequences often win out. In other words, by avoiding a weak aversive stimulus now, one eventually receives a strong aversive consequence later.

Study Questions

1. What do people seem to mean when they talk about willpower? Is willpower a useful concept? Why or why not?

2. Describe a problem of a behavioral excess in which an immediate reinforcer wins out over a delayed punisher for the behavior.

3. Describe a problem of a behavioral excess in which an immediate reinforcer wins out over a cumulatively significant punisher for the behavior.

4. Describe a problem of a behavioral excess in which an immediate reinforcer (for the problem behavior) wins out over a delayed reinforcer (for an alternative desirable behavior).

5. Describe a problem of a behavioral deficiency that occurs because the behavior leads to immediate small punishers that win out over cumulatively significant reinforcers for the behavior.

6. Describe a problem of a behavioral deficiency that occurs because immediate small punishers for the behavior win out over immediate but highly improbable major punishers if the behavior does not occur.

7. Describe a problem of a behavioral deficiency that occurs because an immediate small punisher for the behavior wins out over a delayed major punisher if the behavior does not occur.

A BEHAVIORAL MODEL FOR SELF-CONTROL

An effective model of self-control must deal satisfactorily with the causes of self-control problems described in the preceding section. The model that we describe here is a behavioral model with two parts. The first part requires clearly specifying the problem as a behavior to be controlled. The second part requires that you apply behavioral techniques to manage the problem. A **behavior model of self-control** is a statement that self-control occurs when an individual behaves in some way that arranges the environment to manage his or her own subsequent behavior. This means emitting a *controlling behavior* to effect a change in a *behavior to be controlled* (Skinner, 1953). See Figure 26–1.

In examples in the previous chapters, one person emitted the behavior to be controlled, and one or more other people emitted the controlling behaviors—manipulating antecedents and applying reinforcing or punishing consequences for the behavior. In instances of self-control, however, the same person emits the behavior to be controlled and the controlling behaviors. This raises the problem of *controlling the controlling behavior*. That is, because self-control implies that some behavior of a person controls other behavior of that person, the question arises as to

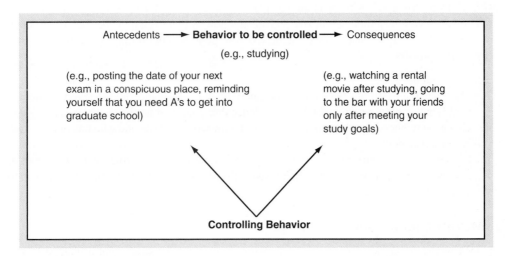

FIGURE 26–1 A model for self-control.

what controls or causes the controlling behavior. The answer is other people or society. The society in which we live teaches us various controlling behaviors (see Skinner, 1953, p. 240). You may have been taught, for example, to emit controlling behaviors such as setting goals for studying, giving yourself reminders for meeting those goals, and keeping track of your progress in doing so. If your efforts in emitting such behaviors are successful and your behaviors to be controlled do in fact occur (e.g., your studying improves), society provides maintaining contingencies for your efforts (e.g., receiving better grades, getting the kind of job that you want, being able to talk intelligently with other people, and so forth).

We now turn to self-control strategies that have been successful for many individuals.

STEPS IN A SELF-CONTROL PROGRAM

For our discussion of self-control strategies, "you" could be anyone who wants to change some aspect of her or his own behavior. Assume that you have decided to use behavior modification to treat one of your self-control problems. We will describe how to do so by using the following steps: (a) specify the problem and set goals, (b) make a commitment to change, (c) take data and assess the causes of the problem, (d) design and implement a treatment plan, and (e) prevent relapse and make your gains last.

1. Specify the Problem and Set Goals

What is it that you would like to change? How will you know if you have succeeded? To answer these questions, you need to try to specify the problem and set some goals in quantitative terms. For Al (at the beginning of this chapter), this was relatively easy. His goal was to lose 30 pounds (about 14 kg). Stated more precisely, he wanted to use about 1,000 calories more each day than he consumed to give a weight loss of about 2 pounds (about 1 kg) each week. Many problems of self-control can be easily specified in quantitative terms. It's relatively easy, for example, to set specific goals in the areas of weight control and exercise. In contrast, other self-improvement goals, such as "having a more positive attitude toward school," "becoming less tense," or "improving a relationship," are more difficult to measure. Mager (1972) refers to such vague abstractions as "fuzzies." A *fuzzy* is an acceptable starting point for identifying a self-control goal; however, you must then "unfuzzify" the abstraction by identifying the performance(s) that would cause you to agree that you have achieved your goal. Mager outlined a number of useful steps for this process.

    a. Write out the goal.
    b. Make a list of the things that you should say or do that clearly indicates that you've met the goal. That is, what would you take as evidence that your goal has been achieved?
    c. Given a number of people with the same goal, how would you decide who has met the goal and who has not?
    d. If your goal is an outcome—such as achieving a certain weight, saving a certain amount of money, or having a clean room—then make a list of specific behaviors that will help you to achieve that outcome.

2. Make a Commitment to Change

NOTE 1   **Commitment to change** refers to your statements or actions that indicate that it is important to change your behavior, that you recognize the benefits of doing so, and that you will work toward doing so. Perri and Richards (1977) demonstrated that both a commitment to change and knowl-edge of change techniques were important for successfully accomplishing self-modification projects by undergraduate psychology students. In problem areas such as eating, smoking, study-ing, or dating, Perri and Richards found that successful self-managers both had a stronger commit-ment to change and used more behavior change techniques than did unsuccessful self-managers.

A high probability of success in changing your behavior requires actions to keep your commitment strong. First, list all of the benefits for changing your behavior. Write them out and post them in a conspicuous place. Second, make your commitment to change public (Hayes et al., 1985; Seigts, Meertens, & Kok, 1997). Increasing the number of people who can remind you to stick to your program increases your chances of success (Passman, 1977). Third, rearrange your environment to provide frequent reminders of your commitment and your goal (Graziano, 1975). You could write your goals on index cards and leave them in conspicuous places, such as taped to the door of your fridge or on the dashboard of your car. Or you might creatively use photographs to remind you of your goal. Also make sure that those reminders are associated with the positive benefits of reaching your goal. Fourth, invest considerable time and energy in ini-tially planning your project (Watson & Tharp, 2007). Prepare a list of statements related to your investment in your project so that you can use those statements to help strengthen and maintain your commitment (e.g., "I've put so much into it, it would be a shame to quit now"). Fifth, because you will undoubtedly encounter temptations to quit your project, plan ahead for various ways to deal with them (Watson & Tharp, 2007).

Study Questions

8. Describe the behavioral model of self-control.
9. Consider the model of self-control illustrated in Figure 26–1. In that model, what controls the control-ling behavior? Discuss.
10. List the steps that Mager recommends to "unfuzzify" a vaguely stated problem or self-control goal.
11. How does this book define *commitment*?
12. Describe five steps that you could take to strengthen and maintain your commitment to a program of self-control.

3. Take Data and Analyze Causes

The next step is to take data on the occurrence of the problem behavior—when, where, and how often it occurs. This is especially important when the goal is to decrease excessive behaviors. As indicated in Chapter 20, a number of reasons for keeping track of the problem behavior exist, not the least of which is to provide a reference point for evaluating progress. For many self-control projects, an index card and a pencil can be used to tally instances of the problem as they occur throughout the day. You could use a number of techniques to increase the strength of record keep-ing. If the problem behavior is smoking, you should record each cigarette before you smoke it so that the behavior will reinforce recording it. You might set external reinforcers that other people control. For example, you might give control of your spending money to someone who can moni-tor your behavior continuously for extended periods of time and return your money contingent upon consistent data taking. You might also get other people to reinforce your recording behavior by (a) telling friends about your self-modification project, (b) keeping your recording chart or graph in an obvious place to increase the likelihood of feedback from friends, and (c) keeping your friends informed on how the project and results are progressing. Contingencies mediated by other people are important sources of maintenance for your controlling behaviors.

In some cases (as pointed out in Chapter 20), recording and graphing the behavior may be all that is needed to bring about improvement. Maletsky (1974) made a convincing demonstration of this effect. Three of the five cases that he studied were completed successfully, even though he was careful not to introduce any treatment other than the counting and graphing of unwanted behaviors. One successful case concerned repetitive scratching that resulted in unsightly lesions on the arms and legs of a 52-year-old woman; another concerned a 9-year-old boy's repetitive hand raising in class whether or not he knew the answers to the teacher's questions; and the third involved the out-of-seat behavior in school of an 11-year-old girl. In all three cases, the behavior decreased over a six-week period as a result of daily self-counting and graphing. In some cases, counting each thought, desire, or urge to emit a behavior before the behavior occurs might even be possible. McFall (1970) reported a study in which recording each urge to have a cigarette was sufficient to decrease not only the likelihood of subsequently taking a cigarette but also the number of urges. Additional examples of beneficial effects of self-monitoring can be found in Cone (1999), Latner and Wilson (2002), and Wood, Murdock, and Cronin (2002).

When recording the frequency of the problem during these initial observations, you should take a close look at the antecedents that might be S^Ds or S^Δs for the problem behavior and at the immediate consequences that might be maintaining the problem. Suggestions for successful programming strategies often arise from this exercise.

Recall Al at the beginning of the chapter. When he began examining the circumstances in which he typically snacked, he made a surprising finding. The great majority of instances of eating were followed immediately by some other reinforcing event:

a bite of a doughnut and then a sip of coffee

another potato chip while watching TV—his favorite basketball player just scored another basket

another candy to munch on while in his car—the stoplight turns green and Al drives away

Al ate while drinking coffee, drinking beer, talking to friends, talking on the phone, riding in a car—in other words, while coming into contact with a wide variety of reinforcing events in the natural environment. As we indicated in earlier chapters, the effects of reinforcers are automatic and do not depend on an individual's awareness. Moreover, aspects of the different settings became cues for Al's excessive eating. No wonder Al had trouble with self-control.

Thus, during preliminary observations, it is important to analyze antecedents for the undesired behavior, immediate consequences that might maintain the undesired behavior to be eliminated, and the immediate consequences (or lack of them) of the behavior that you wish to develop. This information can be very useful in the next step of your program.

4. Design and Implement a Treatment Plan

Throughout your life, in the presence of certain *antecedents,* certain *behaviors* have had certain *consequences*. Each of these three variables provides a fertile area for selecting self-control techniques.

MANAGE THE ANTECEDENTS   As indicated in Chapters 17, 18, and 19, it is helpful to think of major classes of antecedents that control our behavior: instructions, modeling, physical guidance, our immediate surroundings, other people, the time of day, and motivating operations.

Instructions.   Meichenbaum (1977) suggested that almost every self-modification program should include some self-instructions. They have been used in formal self-management projects to increase exercise and study behavior (Cohen, DeJames, Nocera, & Ramberger, 1980), reduce fears (Arrick, Voss, & Rimm, 1981), reduce nail biting (Harris & McReynolds, 1977), and improve a variety of other behaviors (Watson & Tharp, 2007). Before planning instructions for your self-control program, we encourage you to review the guidelines for using rules and goals in Chapter 17. We also discuss self-instructional strategies further in Chapter 27.

Modeling.   Modeled behavior is another class of stimulus events that is useful in self-control programs. For example, if you want to improve your skills at introducing yourself at social gatherings, find someone who's good at it, observe that person's behavior, and imitate it. A procedure called *participant modeling* (described more fully in chapter 28) is an especially effective method for reducing fears. With this procedure, the fearful person observes a model interacting with the fear-inducing stimulus and then imitates the model.

Physical Guidance.   In Chapter 18, we described how behavior modifiers use physical contact to induce an individual to go through the motions of the desired behavior. Examples of using physical contact to guide your own behavior are difficult to identify because if you could guide your behavior easily, you would probably not engage in the problem behavior. However, in his classic analysis of self-control, Skinner (1953) described how individuals use physical restraint to control their own behavior. You might, for example, keep your hands in your pockets to avoid nail biting, bite your tongue to avoid making a rude comment, or clasp your hands together to avoid striking someone in a moment of anger.

Our Immediate Surroundings.   Do you have trouble studying at home? Try going to the library, where studying is a high-probability behavior (Brigham, 1982). Many people have a particular behavior they would like to decrease that occurs in particular situations. A useful strategy is to rearrange the environment to present cues for the desirable alternative behaviors (see Chapter 18).

Other People.   As we said earlier, observing models is one way of providing strong prompts for you to engage in some behavior. Another strategy is simply to change the people around you. You've learned to behave in one way with some people and in other ways with other people. In some cases, your self-control program will consist of increasing contact with certain people and minimizing it with others. For example, you may be less likely to swear when in conversation with a highly religious person but more likely to swear when shooting the breeze with the gang. Marlatt and Parks (1982) have indicated that people with addictive behaviors are more likely to relapse if they hang out with others engaging in those behaviors.

The Time of Day.   Sometimes it's possible to achieve successful self-control by changing the time of the activity. For example, many students are more alert in the evening, but and spend their time then socializing. Students might accomplish self-control of studying by moving socializing to mornings and studying to evenings.

Motivating Operations.   Recall from Chapter 19 that motivating operations are events that influence the strength of consequences as reinforcers or punishers and that influence behaviors affected by those consequences. In self-control programs, a strategy for increasing desirable behavior is to introduce an MEO for reinforcers that influence that behavior. For example, when one of the authors and his wife were visiting Brazil in the early years of their marriage, he took a picture of his wife jogging on the beach in Rio de Janeiro. In later years, when his wife looked at an enlargement of the photo posted on the closet door in their bedroom, it motivated her to continue her jogging program to maintain her slim figure. MAOs also can be used in self-control programs to decrease the likelihood of undesirable behavior. A strategy that Al could use to decrease his doughnut consumption when having coffee with Mary in the campus cafeteria would be to eat a couple of carrots before going to the cafeteria. This would function as an MAO for food and decrease the likelihood of his purchasing doughnuts with his coffee.

MANAGE THE BEHAVIOR   If the behavior of concern is relatively simple, such as swearing, you're likely to focus more on antecedents and consequences. If the behavior is complex, you need to spend some time focusing on the behavior itself. If your goal is to acquire some complex skills, it is helpful to consider task analysis and mastery criteria. **Mastery criteria** are performance requirements for practicing a skill so that if the criteria are met, the behavior has been learned. Consider, for example, learning to play golf. Simek and O'Brien (1981) task analyzed a golf game into 22 components. They arranged these in a behavioral progression for instructional purposes and identified mastery criteria for each component (see Table 26–1). Then they taught a

---

TABLE 26–1   A Behavioral Progression and Mastery Criteria for Learning Golf

Complete Golf Chain and Mastery Criterion

Step	Shot	Mastery Criterion
1.	10-inch putt	4 putts consecutively holed
2.	16-inch putt	4 putts consecutively holed
3.	2-foot putt	4 putts consecutively holed
4.	3-foot putt	4 putts consecutively holed
5.	4-foot putt with some break	2 holed, 2 of 4 within 6 inches
6.	6-foot putt	4 consecutively within 6 inches
7.	10-foot putt	4 consecutively within 12 inches
8.	15-foot putt	4 consecutively within 15 inches
9.	20-foot putt	4 consecutively within 18 inches
10.	30-foot putt	4 consecutively within 24 inches
11.	35-foot chip, 5 feet off green, seven-iron	4 of 6 within 6 feet
12.	35-foot chip, 15 feet off green, wedge	4 of 6 within 6 feet
13.	65-foot chip	4 of 6 within 6 feet
14.	25-yard pitch	4 of 6 within 10 feet
15.	35-yard pitch	4 of 6 within 15 feet
16.	50-yard pitch	4 of 6 within 15 feet
17.	75-yard shot	4 of 6 within 30 feet
18.	100-yard shot	4 of 6 within 40 feet
19.	125-yard shot	4 of 6 within 45 feet
20.	150-yard shot	4 of 6 within 54 feet
21.	175-yard shot	4 of 6 within 66 feet
22.	200-yard shot (if within your range)	4 of 5 within 90 feet

(*Source:* T. C. Simek and R. M. O'Brien, *From Total Golf: A Behavioral Approach to Lowering Your Score and Getting More of Your Game.* Huntington, NY: B-Mod Associates, 1981, p. 2. Copyright 1981 by T. C. Simek and R. M. O'Brien. Reprinted with permission.)

group of novices by first starting with 10-inch putts rather than by teaching them to swing a club as is often done by golf instructors. Why? One reason was the general rule to start with the simple and proceed to the complex. Another reason was that it incorporated a powerful natural reinforcer for performing the response correctly—namely, hitting the ball into the hole (note that this is similar to the argument for using backward chaining; see Chapter 11). Gradually, as mastery criteria for simple responses were met, the length of the shot was increased to longer putts, then to short chip shots, to longer chip shots, to short pitch shots, to longer pitch shots, to middle iron shots, eventually to hitting fairway woods, and finally to using a driver. But how well did they score when put on a golf course, you might ask. In a study with 12 novice golfers, six of them completed the behavioral progression and mastery criteria in eight lessons. The other six golfers received eight lessons of traditional instruction from a golfer who had taught golf for several years. All 12 then played a complete 18-hole round of golf. The behavioral progression group "whipped" the traditional group handily, beating them by an average of 17 strokes.

Shaping is another procedure for focusing on the behavior, and it is useful for self-improvement projects in which your ultimate goal involves a large behavioral change from your starting point. Important rules of thumb to keep in mind include starting small, meeting mastery criteria before moving up a step, and keeping progressive steps small. Studies of dieters, for example, have reported that those who set small, gradual shaping steps for reducing calories were more likely to develop self-control of binge eating (Gormally, Black, Daston, & Rardin, 1982; Hawkins & Clement, 1980).

Another manipulation that requires you to focus on the behavior is to consider the energy expenditure needed to perform the behavior, generally referred to as *effort*. One strategy for decreasing a problem behavior is to arrange conditions so that it requires more effort to perform that behavior. For example, Susan typically studies in a carrel in the library. Frequently, she interrupts her studying to call her friends. With her cell phone clearly visible in the study carrel, picking it up and dialing involves very little effort. Leaving her cell phone in a locker at the entrance to the library, however, would greatly increase the effort involved in making a call and would likely decrease the instances of doing so. Altering response requirements to decrease the effort needed to emit a behavior can also be used to increase desirable behavior. David decided that his daily water consumption was too low, and he set a goal of going to a water fountain at least four times a day. However, doing so required considerable effort, and he rarely met his goal. He therefore decided to purchase a water bottle to keep with him. His water consumption increased considerably. Although these examples involve manipulating response effort, note that they might also be described as managing antecedents by manipulating the immediate surroundings.

Study Questions

13. Describe two strategies for increasing the likelihood of keeping records of a problem behavior to be changed.
14. Describe an example that illustrates how recording and graphing of a problem behavior was all that was needed to bring about improvement.
15. Describe how Al was inadvertently reinforced for eating numerous times throughout the day.
16. List seven major classes of antecedents that you might consider when planning how to manage the situation in a self-control program.
17. Describe an example that indicates how the manipulation of a motivating operation was an effective self-control strategy.
18. Define *mastery criterion,* and describe an example that is not in the text.

19. Describe an example that illustrates how the manipulation of energy expenditure or effort needed to perform a behavior is an effective self-management strategy. Would you say that the example involved the manipulation of a motivating operation? Why or why not?

MANAGE THE CONSEQUENCES   One strategy for manipulating consequent events is to eliminate certain reinforcers that may inadvertently strengthen a particularly undesirable behavior in a specific situation. When Al analyzed his eating problem, he noticed that, in addition to the taste of food itself, other reinforcers (TV, pleasant conversation, etc.) were usually associated with eating. A major feature of Al's dieting control program, therefore, should be to disassociate eating from these other activities. Recommendations by LeBow (1981) to accomplish this include (a) eating only in the kitchen when at home, (b) using the same eating utensils and placemats at each meal, (c) eating only at designated times, and (d) keeping food out of every room but the kitchen.

A second strategy for manipulating consequences is recording and graphing the target behavior (see, e.g., Watson & Tharp, 2007). Seeing a graph that shows gradual improvement can serve as a prompt for a variety of positive thoughts about your progress. It can also serve as a prompt for others to give you extra social attention for sticking to the self-control program.

A third strategy for manipulating consequences involves arranging to receive specific reinforcers when you show improvement or even for just sticking to the program (see Watson & Tharp, 2007). This is especially important if your desired behavior will lead to small but cumulatively significant or improbable reinforcers or if failure to perform your desired behavior will lead to small but cumulatively significant or improbable punishers. Three ways of arranging for reinforcers to be received in a self-control program include (a) asking others to manage them for you, (b) reminding yourself of delayed natural reinforcers, and (c) managing reinforcers yourself. This last way may seem the most obvious considering that we are talking about *self*-control; however, there is a problem with it, as you will see.

Asking others to manage reinforcers for you is an effective way to receive reinforcers in self-control programs (Watson & Tharp, 2007). For example, Mary decided to initiate a jogging program. She also decided that she would receive money immediately after jogging. Also, if she jogged every day, she could select and engage in one of several possible social activities with her husband. If she met her goals, Mary's husband dispensed the reinforcers (Kau & Fischer, 1974).

The second way to receive reinforcers—reminding yourself of delayed natural consequences for a behavior immediately after it occurs—can be illustrated by the problem of shopping for holiday presents. Suppose that you set a goal of buying presents early during the year rather than waiting until the last minute. Doing so has sizable natural consequences. You can buy presents on sale, saving a significant amount of money. You can avoid the holiday rush, minimizing the stress and hassles that typically accompany holiday shopping. A better selection of presents is available, and you have more time to select the best present for each person on your gift list. However, the positive consequences of giving the presents, such as the recipients' joyful reactions, are long delayed after the behavior of shopping early. A solution, therefore, is to increase the saliency of such delayed reinforcers right after the behavior to be controlled. Immediately after you purchase a gift during a fall sale, for example, you might record the amount saved and post it in a conspicuous place. You could look at a photograph of the gift's future recipient and imagine how happy that person will be when the present is opened. You could also make a list of nonshopping activities you will be able to enjoy during the holiday rush.

The third way to receive reinforcers in self-control programs is for individuals to manage consequences for their own behavior (Watson & Tharp, 2007). Suppose, for example, that you

FIGURE 26–2 Does self-reinforcement work?

decide to allow yourself to surf the Internet only after studying for an exam. This seems like an example of self-reinforcement. However, in such circumstances, you can always access the reinforcer without emitting the desired behavior as illustrated in Figure 26–2. What would prevent you from doing so? We suspect that in this and other such examples of self-reinforcement, other contingencies are operating in addition to self-reinforcement. Perhaps just before studying you worried about the likelihood of failing the exam, and studying enabled you to escape from such worrying. Perhaps, immediately after studying, you thought about the likelihood of getting an A. Or perhaps other factors influenced your studying. Thus, while it is certainly possible for you to give yourself a reinforcer only after emitting some behavior, it is not clear that this contingency alone is responsible for the improved behavior. For further discussion of conceptual problems involving the concept of self-reinforcement, see Catania (1975), Goldiamond (1976), and Mace, Belfiore, and Hutchinson (2001).

Some guidelines for incorporating reinforcers into your program include (a) make it possible for you to earn specific reinforcers on a daily basis, (b) set up bonuses that you can earn for progress on a weekly basis, (c) vary the reinforcers from one day to the next and one week to the next to prevent boredom with the entire system, (d) if possible and desirable, have other individuals dispense the reinforcers to you for meeting your goals, and (e) tell others about your progress.

Recall from Chapter 3 the Premack principle, which states that any activity that you are likely to perform can be used to reinforce a behavior that you are less likely to perform. You can use this strategy in self-control programs. High-frequency behaviors used in documented cases of self-improvement have involved making telephone calls (Todd, 1972), urinating (Johnson, 1971), opening the daily mail at the office (Spinelli & Packard, 1975), and sitting on a particular chair (Horan & Johnson, 1971).

5. Prevent Relapse and Make Your Gains Last

Suppose you've made good progress on your self-control program: Perhaps you've lost weight, haven't had a cigarette in three months, or your studying has paid off and you got an A on your last two exams. Now the question is: Will the changes last? Will you be able to maintain your gains over the long run? Unfortunately, relapses are common in self-control programs (Marlatt & Parks, 1982). By **relapse**, in a self-control program we mean going back to the unwanted behavior at approximately its same level as before you started your program. Just as the three variables of *antecedents, behaviors,* and *consequences* were valuable areas to consider when designing your program, they also provide a useful framework for analyzing causes of relapses and how to prevent them.

CAUSES OF RELAPSE IN ANTECEDENTS   A strategy for preventing relapses is to recognize their possible causes and to take steps to minimize them. Let's look at some examples involving antecedents.

Avoidable Setback Antecedents.   A common cause of relapses in self-control programs is a failure to anticipate *setback antecedents*—that is, antecedents that increase one's risk for returning to earlier unwanted behavior patterns. Some setback antecedents can simply be avoided until you are better able to cope with them. For example, Carla decided to quit smoking. Initially, she believed that she couldn't resist the temptation to smoke while playing poker with her friends on Friday nights. Her strategy was simply not to play poker for the first month of the program. Fred decided to go on a diet, to eat healthier foods, and to consume fewer calories. But he knew that he couldn't resist the banana splits at the supermarket where he usually bought groceries. His solution: He changed the place where he shopped. If you can successfully avoid setback antecedents until you have achieved some success with your self-control program, you may then be better able to cope with situations that provide strong antecedents for the problem behavior.

Unavoidable Setback Antecedents.   Some setback antecedents simply can't be avoided. A strategy to prevent relapse is to anticipate unavoidable setback antecedents and to take steps to cope with them. Consider John's case. He had faithfully followed his exercise program for a month and a half, but he was about to embark on a camping trip. He knew that the complete change in routine and the duties each night around the campground were not conducive to exercising. His solution was to obtain his traveling companions' approval to stop traveling each night half an hour early. While the others relaxed in the campground, John exercised. They then all shared in the campground duties. The more that you can recognize unavoidable setback antecedents before you encounter them, the better are your chances for planning coping strategies.

Overreaction to Occasional Setbacks.   After 2 weeks of sticking faithfully to her schedule for studying, Janice rented five movies and watched them for 10 hours straight. Fred, following a month of successful dieting, had a banana split three days in a row. Very few people achieve successful self-control without experiencing an occasional setback. However, temporary setbacks are not a problem if you get right back into your program. When you suffer a setback, don't dwell on it. Instead, review the many occasions when you have stuck to your program as a prompt to set new goals and to make a renewed commitment.

Counterproductive Self-Talk.   When people attempt to change, they are bound to encounter stumbling blocks. When these happen, counterproductive self-talk can exacerbate the problem and may lead to a relapse. People who have difficulty dieting may say things like, "I'm too hungry to wait until dinner. I'll have a snack to tide myself over." That type of self-talk is a cue to eat.

What kinds of self-talk in your self-control program might lead to a relapse? For each example that you can think of, identify desirable alternative self-talk that might have the opposite effect. Dieters, for example, might tell themselves things like, "I feel hungry, but I'm not starving. I'll just focus on something to take my mind off food."

CAUSES OF RELAPSE IN THE SPECIFICATION OF THE RESPONSE   Sometimes relapses occur because individuals do not pay sufficient attention to the response component of their self-control program. Let's look at some examples.

A Fuzzy Target Behavior.   Tracy wanted to improve her golf skills. After a month of regular practice at the driving range, however, she wasn't sure if she was improving. The problem was that "wanting to improve" was too vague. She had not specified her target behavior precisely enough. If Tracy's goal had been to hit five drives in a row over 175 yards, to hit three 7-irons in a row within 30 feet of the 100-yard marker, or to make four 3-foot putts in a row, she would have been able to evaluate her progress more easily (Martin & Ingram, 2001). As we described earlier, a fuzzy goal is an acceptable starting point, but you must then "unfuzzify" your target behavior by describing it in such a way that you and others can easily recognize it when it occurs.

A Long-Term Target Behavior.   Suppose that you set for yourself a long-term goal of earning an A in a particular course. Your goal is clear, but it's a long way away. For such projects, you should set short-term goals that provide specific progress checks along the way. With respect to your goal of earning an A, you might set a short-term goal of studying the material for that course for a minimum of 1 hour every day. Another short-term goal might be to answer a certain number of study questions each day. Daily short-term goals should be precisely stated and realistic and should move you in the direction of your long-term goal.

Trying Too Much Too Soon.   Some self-control projects never get off the ground because they are too ambitious. Wanting to eat more healthily, exercise more, floss your teeth regularly, manage your money more wisely, and get better grades are admirable goals, but trying to improve in all areas at once is a formula for failure. If you've identified several areas to improve, prioritize them in order of their personal value to you. From the top two or three priority areas, select one as your focus. Starting small increases your likelihood of success.

CAUSES OF RELAPSE IN CONSEQUENCES   Recall our model of self-control. It involves emitting a *controlling behavior* to manage a *behavior to be controlled*. Inadequate or poorly scheduled consequences for either of these behaviors can lead to a relapse. Let's look at some examples.

Failure to Incorporate Everyday Rewards into Your Program.   Many people begin self-control programs with a great deal of enthusiasm. After awhile, the extra work from recording, graphing, rearranging the environment, and so forth can become quite burdensome. One way to prevent relapse is to link your self-control program to everyday rewarding activities. One person we know linked his exercise program to watching movies on his DVD player. His goal was to exercise a minimum of four times a week. On average, he also rented movies about four nights a week.

He therefore signed a contract with his wife that he would watch a movie only if he first walked to the rental store to pick up the movie—a distance of approximately 1.5 miles (2.4 km). Examine ways that you can incorporate daily rewarding activities into the support of your self-control program.

Consequences That Are Only Cumulatively Significant. Suppose that your dieting program has been successful. You decide that your new slim body can easily handle an extra dessert. One dessert is not a problem. Rather, it is the accumulation of extra desserts on many occasions that will put the weight back on. As described earlier, for many self-control problems, the immediate reinforcement for consumption of harmful substances is likely to win out over the negative consequences from those substances because the negative effects are noticeable only after they have accumulated over many trials. Individuals with these types of self-control problems are very likely to experience a relapse. One strategy to prevent relapse in such situations is to set specific dates for postchecks and to list specific strategies to follow if the postchecks are unfavorable. For example, if your self-control program was one of weight reduction, you might agree with a friend that you will weigh yourself in your friend's presence once a week. If your weight increases to a specified level, then you will immediately return to your program.

ADDITIONAL STRATEGIES TO MAKE IT LAST   Additional strategies to prevent relapse and maintain your gains over the long term involve all three factors of antecedents, responses, and consequences. One strategy is to practice the self-control steps outlined in this chapter to improve additional behaviors. You are more likely to continue using self-control techniques if you practice them on more than one self-control project (Barone, 1982). Moreover, you are more likely to be able to deal with a relapse if you are skillful in the self-control techniques that brought about the improvement in the first place.

Perhaps the most effective way to make your gains last is to involve supportive others in your program, both in the short term and in the long term. One strategy is to set up a buddy system. When you start your project, you might find a friend or relative with a similar problem and set mutual maintenance goals. Once a month, you could get together and check each other's progress. If your progress has been maintained, you could celebrate in a previously agreed-upon way. In a study of smokers, Karol and Richards (1978) found that those who quit with a buddy and who telephoned encouragement to each other showed more reduction of smoking in an 8-month follow-up than did smokers who tried to quit on their own.

A particularly effective strategy is to sign a behavioral contract with supportive others. Behavioral contracts, which were discussed in Chapter 24, have been used to strengthen desirable target behaviors with children (e.g., Miller & Kelly, 1994) and adults (e.g., Dallery, Meredith, & Glenn, 2008; Leal & Galanter, 1995). A contract usually involves two or more people, although "self-contracts" have also been used (e.g., Seabaugh & Schumaker, 1994). A form that you might use for your contract is presented in Table 26–2.

A contract serves at least four important stimulus control functions:

1. It ensures that all parties involved agree to the goals and procedures and that they do not lose sight of them during the course of the treatment.
2. Because the goals are specified behaviorally, the contract also ensures that throughout the program, all parties will agree on how close they are to reaching the goals.
3. The contract provides the client a realistic estimate of the cost of the program in time, effort, and money.
4. The signatures on the contract help to ensure that all parties will faithfully follow the specified procedures because in our society signing a document indicates a commitment.

TABLE 26–2	A Form for a Behavioral Contract

My specific goals for my self-control program are:

_____

_____

_____

Short-term goals for my self-control program include:

_____

_____

_____

To observe, record, and graph my behavior, I will:

_____

_____

_____

To minimize the causes of the problem, I will:

_____

_____

_____

The details of my treatment plan include:

1. Steps to manage the situation:

_____

_____

_____

2. Steps to manage consequences:

_____

_____

_____

3. Steps to deal with or change complex behavior:

_____

_____

_____

4. Rewards that I can earn for sticking to and/or completing my project:

_____

_____

_____

(continued)

TABLE 26–2   *(Continued)*

Additional steps that I will take to increase and maintain my commitment to the project and to prevent relapse include:

_____

_____

_____

Schedule for review of progress:

_____

_____

_____

Signatures of all involved and the date of the agreement:

| _____ | _____ | _____ |
| (Date) | (Your signature) | (Supporter's signature) |

As we have stressed in previous chapters, behavior modification procedures should be revised in appropriate ways when the data indicate that they are not producing satisfactory results. Thus, your contract should be open to renegotiation at any time. If you find that you simply cannot meet some commitment specified in your contract, you should inform the other signatories at your next meeting with them. You can discuss the difficulty and if it seems desirable, you can draft and sign a new contract replacing the previous one. Before doing so, however, you might examine the following troubleshooting guide for behavior contracts.

Troubleshooting Guide[2]

The following questions may help you to spot the problems in your contracting system.

The Contract

1. Was the target behavior specified clearly?
2. If the target behavior was complex, did the contract ask for small approximations to the desired behavior?
3. Were specific deadlines identified for the target behavior?
4. Did the contract clearly identify situations in which the target behavior should occur?
5. Did the contract provide for immediate reinforcement? Are the reinforcers still important and valuable to you?
6. Could reinforcers be earned often (daily or weekly)?
7. Did the contract call for and reward accomplishment rather than obedience?
8. Was the contract phrased in a positive way?
9. Do you consider the contract to be fair and in your best interests?

---

[2] Adapted from DeRisi and Butz, *Writing Behavioral Contracts: A Case Simulation Practice Manual* (Champaign, IL: Research Press, 1975), pp. 58–60.

The Mediator (your cosigner)

1. Did the mediator understand the contract?
2. Did the mediator dispense the kind and amount of reinforcement specified in the contract?
3. Did the mediator meet with you on the dates specified in the contract?
4. Is a new mediator required?

Measurement

1. Are the data accurate?
2. Is your data collection system too complex or too difficult?
3. Does your data collection system clearly reflect your progress in achieving the target behavior?
4. Do you need to improve your data collection system?

CIRCUMVENTION OF THE THERAPIST

Obviously, some personal problems require help from a therapist (as discussed further in Chapters 27 and 28). It should be clear from the preceding sections in this chapter, however, that many people who have mastered some behavior modification principles can use them to control their own behavior. A person who has mastered this book probably does not need a therapist for many behavior problems, such as decreasing smoking, nail biting, or swearing or enhancing studying, exercising, or eating healthy foods. That person knows how to take data, how to plan a program and evaluate its effectiveness, how to apply a large number of behavior modification principles and techniques, and how to use a behavioral contract to maintain the controlling **NOTE 2** behavior. In short, many people can be their own behavior modifiers.

Study Questions

20. List the five steps that characterize many programs of self-control (they start on p. 324).
21. Describe three different strategies for manipulating consequences in self-control programs in a sentence or two for each.
22. Describe three different ways of arranging for reinforcers to be received in a self-control program in a sentence or two for each.
23. Is self-reinforcement an effective self-control strategy? Discuss.
24. What is the meaning of *relapse* in a self-control program?
25. Briefly describe four possible causes of relapse in situations, and indicate how each might be handled.
26. Briefly describe three possible causes of relapse in the specification of the response, and indicate how each might be handled.
27. Briefly describe two possible causes of relapse in consequences, and indicate how each might be handled.
28. What is a behavioral contract? Describe its essential features.
29. What important stimulus–control functions does a behavioral contract serve?
30. Is it plausible to suggest that many individuals can become their own behavior therapists? Justify your answer.

Application Exercises

A. EXERCISE INVOLVING OTHERS

Describe a self-control problem experienced by someone that you know. Is the problem best characterized as a behavioral deficiency or a behavioral excess? What seems to be the cause of the problem?

B. SELF-MODIFICATION EXERCISES

1. Using the information in this and the preceding chapters, describe how you might go about following all five steps of a self-control program for bringing about successful self-adjustment for a behavior of yours that you would like to change.

2. Implement your program and take data for a minimum of 3 weeks. Then write a summary report of the results (approximately 5 to 10 pages plus graphs).

Notes and Extended Discussion

1. A verbal commitment to do something is verbal behavior that corresponds to other behavior that one later engages in if the commitment is kept. A number of studies have been conducted on training a correspondence between stated intentions (commitments) and later behavior (Lloyd, 2002). For example, Ward and Stare (1990) prompted a group of kindergarten children to state that they were going to play in a certain designated area prior to playing there (*correspondence training*). Specifically, the children were prompted to say, "I'm going to play at the workbench today." The children received a token if they made this statement. After 4 minutes of play, children who played at the workbench received another token for playing there after saying that this is what they would do. Compared to a group of children who simply received tokens for playing in the designated area, the group that received correspondence training showed more instances of following through on stated intentions to engage in another activity (playing with toys) even though they received no tokens for following through on this commitment. The results thus showed that correspondence training on one response can generalize to a new response. This tendency to generalize correspondence training may be what makes it possible for us to keep commitments for behavior change that we have made to ourselves. Correspondence training is also one way that humans learn self-awareness or self-knowledge (Dymond & Barnes, 1997).

2. How effective are self-help manuals? Although a review by Rosen (1987) found major limitations to their usefulness, meta-analysis—a statistical procedure for combining the data analysis of many studies—suggests that somewhat more positive conclusions are in order (Den Boer, Wiersma, & Van Den Bosch, 2004; Hirai & Clum, 2006; Gould & Clum, 1993; Gregory, Canning, Lee, & Wise, 2004; Scogin, Bynum, Stephens, & Calhoon, 1990). That does not mean that all self-help books in book stores have been evaluated. However, experiments that examined sophisticated, complex self-help manuals based on behavioral principles indicated that self-administered treatments stand a good chance of success. The most successful targets for improvement involved study habits, depression, parenting skills, social skills, and overcoming anxiety and fears. Less successful self-treatment programs occurred with the control of alcohol drinking, smoking, and overeating (Gould & Clum, 1993 Seligman, 1994; Watkins & Clum, 2008). Also, a number of studies have demonstrated that university students who have read various editions of the self-modification book by David Watson and Ronald Tharp were more successful at completing self-improvement projects than students who have not read the book (Watson & Tharp, 2007). For a list of specific

self-help books that have been found to be effective for a specific clinical problem in one or more randomized control studies, see Malouff and Rooke (2007). For a discussion of strategies for integrating self-help formats into psychotherapy, see Norcross (2006).

Study Questions on Notes

1. What is correspondence training? Briefly describe how generalized correspondence was demonstrated in kindergarten children.
2. With which behavior problems are self-help manuals most effective and least effective?

27

Cognitive Behavior Therapy, Self-Directed Coping Methods, and ACT

Behavior modification, as described in the preceding chapters, began to emerge in the 1950s and 1960s (this early history is discussed further in Chapter 29). During that time, behaviorally oriented therapists began to treat clients who typically received traditional types of psychotherapy, such as psychoanalysis. The new approach was called *behavior therapy,* and the professionals who applied it were known as *behavior therapists.* The initial focus of behavior therapy was the treatment of clients with fear and anxiety, but soon it was being used to treat a wide variety of clinical problems—anxiety disorders, obsessive-compulsive disorders, stress-related problems, depression, marital problems, and sexual dysfunction—discussed further in Chapter 28. In 1966, the Association for Advancement of Behavior Therapy (AABT), an interdisciplinary organization committed to the advancement of a scientific approach to the understanding and treatment of psychological problems, was established.

Publications that described another new approach to therapy, called *cognitive therapy,* appeared in the 1960s and 1970s (Beck, 1970; Ellis, 1962). **Cognitive processes** refer to covert verbalizations and/or imagery that are frequently called *believing, thinking, expecting,* or *perceiving.* Accordingly, cognitive therapists tend to help clients overcome difficulties by getting rid of unproductive, debilitating thoughts or beliefs and adopting more constructive ones.

Early behavior modifiers noted certain similarities between the goals and procedures of cognitive therapists and their own. Cognitive therapists, in turn, adopted some behavior modification methods. Out of this mutual appreciation grew an area that came to be known as *cognitive behavior modification* or *cognitive behavior therapy.* Of these latter two terms, in the 1970s and 1980s the term *cognitive behavior modification* was commonly used (e.g., Mahoney, 1974; Meichenbaum, 1977, 1986), whereas during the last two decades, the term *cognitive behavior therapy* became the more common of the two terms (e.g., Bjorgvinsson & Rosqvist, 2009; Hofmann & Otto, 2008; Lam, 2008). In 2005, AABT was renamed the Association for Behavioral and Cognitive Therapies (ABCT). Both cognitively oriented and behaviorally oriented therapists have learned from each other and agree on many issues (see, e.g., DiGiuseppe, 2008; Dougher, 1997; Hawkins & Forsyth, 1997; Wilson, Hayes, & Gifford, 1997).

In addition, both approaches are firmly committed to the view that the criterion for judging the effectiveness of any treatment is the amount of measurable improvement that occurs in the client's behavior.

Stephen Hayes (2004) referred to early behavior therapy as the first wave of behavioral approaches to therapy and to cognitive behavior therapy as the second wave. Hayes also described what he called the *third wave of behavior therapy*: therapeutic approaches based on behavior analysis that incorporate the concepts of *mindfulness, acceptance,* and *values.* The purpose of this chapter is to describe briefly some of the procedures referred to as *cognitive behavior therapy* or *cognitive behavior modification* as well as procedures from the third wave. Representative of this third wave is a therapy developed by Hayes and colleagues called *acceptance and commitment therapy* (ACT; Hayes, Strosahl, & Wilson, 1999). In accordance with the first part of the subtitle of this book, we will teach you what cognitive behavior therapy and ACT are but not how to do them. We will not attempt to teach you how to conduct therapy with individuals with clinical problems. Such therapy must be undertaken only by qualified professional therapists.

We have organized the different procedures of cognitive behavior therapy and ACT into three categories: (a) treatments that emphasize cognitive restructuring to decrease maladaptive thoughts that are assumed to cause troublesome emotions, (b) self-directed strategies to enhance overt coping skills, and (c) treatments that include "mindfulness," "acceptance," and "values" as important components of therapy.

COGNITIVE RESTRUCTURING METHODS

Cognitive therapy has two underlying major theoretical assumptions: (1) Individuals interpret and react to events by forming cognitions—beliefs, expectations, attitudes—on the basis of the perceived significance of those events, and (2) defective or maladaptive cognitions can cause emotional and behavioral disorders. It follows from these assumptions that the primary focus of therapy is to fundamentally change a client's cognitions. As stated by the well-known cognitive behavior therapist Robert Leahy, "[t]he therapist's role is to help the patient recognize his or her idiosyncratic style of thinking and modify it through the application of evidence and logic" (Leahy, 2003, p. 1). Stated simply, cognitive therapists believe that faulty thinking is the cause of emotional and behavioral problems, and thus the primary focus of the cognitive approach to therapy is to help clients recognize and change faulty thinking. Strategies for recognizing maladaptive thinking and replacing it with adaptive thinking are often referred to as **cognitive restructuring**. From the point of view of this book, cognitive approaches deal mainly with the client's private verbal behavior and imagery (see Chapter 15). However, a person's verbal behavior and imagery can affect his or her emotional and overt behavior, so the difference between cognitive and behavioral approaches are not as great as it might at first appear. (We elaborate on this point toward the end of this chapter.) Moreover, therapists who use cognitive techniques generally also include behavior modification components in their treatments.

Study Questions

1. What are cognitive processes?
2. For what do the letters ABCT stand?
3. What are the three waves of behavior therapy described by Hayes?
4. What are the two major assumptions of cognitive therapy?

5. Stated simply, what do some cognitive therapists believe to be the cause of emotional and behavioral problems, and what is the primary focus of their approach to therapy?
6. Briefly, what is cognitive restructuring?

Rational-Emotive Behavior Therapy

Do you ever find yourself saying, "I always screw things up," "I'm such a klutz," or "I never do things right"? The well-known cognitive therapist Albert Ellis considered such self-statements to be irrational—after all, you don't always screw up, you're not always clumsy, and you do some things right. Ellis believed that such irrational thoughts can cause anxiety, sadness, anger, or other troublesome emotions. His approach to therapy was to help people identify such irrational thoughts or beliefs and to replace them with more rational self-statements (e.g., Ellis, 1962; Ellis & Bernard, 1985; Ellis & Dryden, 1997).

The original name for Ellis's approach, *rational-emotive therapy* (*RET*), was based on the premise that most everyday emotional problems and related overt behaviors stem from irrational interpretations that people make of events in their lives. People tend to think in *absolute terms,* such as a student thinking, "I *must* do well in *all* of my courses." People tend to *overgeneralize,* such as a student thinking after getting a poor mark on one exam, "I'll *never* be a good student." People also tend to *catastrophize*: They tell themselves that things are so horrible they can't possibly stand it. For example, Jim had slept through his alarm and was going to be late for class. Rushing to get ready, he cut himself while shaving and thought, "I'm a walking disaster! I always screw things up." Later, he got caught in a traffic jam. "Why does the worst always happen to me?" He felt angry and frustrated. Ellis considered such self-statements ("I'm a walking disaster," "The worst always happens to me") to be at the root of emotional problems (e.g., Jim's anger and frustration).

Basically, the RET approach is to teach clients to counteract such irrational self-statements with more positive and realistic statements. This is accomplished in three main phases. First, the therapist helps the client identify troublesome thoughts that are based on irrational beliefs, such as Jim's thoughts that he is a walking disaster. Second, in a very confrontational, argumentative way, the RET therapist vigorously challenges the client's irrational beliefs that are thought to be the basis for the problematic self-talk. For example, Jim might be harboring the irrational belief that he *must* never be late for class, a type of irrational thinking that Ellis referred to as "muster-bation." To Jim, an RET therapist might say, "Sooner or later everyone living in a city will get caught in a traffic jam and have other events happen that make them late. What makes you so special?" or "What do you mean that you always screw things up? You told me that you got an A on your last computer assignment." Third, the client is taught through modeling and homework assignments to replace the irrational self-statements with statements based on rational beliefs. For example, Jim might be taught to tell himself that there are far worse things than being late for class and that even though things could be better, they could certainly be a lot worse. His situation might be annoying or inconvenient, but it is not catastrophic. (One hopes, however, that Jim would still be able to recognize a real catastrophe, unlike the cartoon character in Figure 27–1.)

Ellis (1993) later added the word *behavior* to the name of his therapy, and it is now called **rational-emotive behavior therapy (REBT)**. He did so because, despite being a cognitive therapist, Ellis frequently used behavioral "homework" assignments. For example, Jim might be told to write down each time he performs a complex action, such as working at his computer, to prove to himself that he is not a walking disaster. The homework assignments are usually designed to help the client challenge irrational beliefs and confront troublesome emotions. (For a practical guide to REBT, see Dryden, 1999.)

FIGURE 27–1 An exaggerated example of rational-emotive therapy.

EVALUATION OF REBT To the extent that Ellis's approach is successful, is it because the therapist disputes the client's irrational beliefs (a "cognitive" component)? Or is it because the homework assignments influence the client to confront anxiety-evoking situations in real life, which might lead to extinction of the anxiety (behavioral components)? (See Chapter 28.) Or is the improvement the result of a combination of both the correction of faulty thinking and the homework assignments? Examination of studies of REBT that do not include a behavioral component suggests that a big part of the success of REBT might be due to the homework assignments rather than to the disputation of irrational beliefs (Gossette & O'Brien, 1989, 1992).

Beck's Cognitive Therapy

Independently of Ellis, Aaron T. Beck (1976) developed a cognitive therapy procedure that is similar to REBT. His cognitive therapy was originally developed for the treatment of depression. However, he subsequently applied it to a wide variety of other problems, including manic states, anxiety disorders, hysteria, obsessional disorders, psychosomatic disorders, and phobias (see Beck,

Emery, & Greenberg, 1985). In addition, Beck wrote a self-help book for couples that shows how they can use cognitive therapy to improve their relationships (Beck, 1988). Kingdon and Turkington (1994) have extended the approach to cases of schizophrenia.

According to Beck (1976), people with emotional disorders engage excessively in aberrant, fallacious, or dysfunctional thinking, and this is what causes or exacerbates their problems. Among the various types of dysfunctional thinking are the following.

1. *Dichotomous thinking*, which is thinking in absolute terms; for example, assuming that one is a failure if one gets any grade less than an A
2. *Arbitrary inference*, which is drawing a conclusion on the basis of inadequate evidence; for example, misinterpreting a frown on the face of a passerby as the passerby's disapproval
3. *Overgeneralization*, which is reaching a general conclusion on the basis of a few instances; for example, assuming that a single failure means that one cannot succeed at anything
4. *Magnification*, which is exaggerating the meaning or significance of a particular event; for example, believing that it is terrible or catastrophic not to obtain something that one wants very badly

Beck's procedure involves three general components. First, clients identify the dysfunctional thoughts and maladaptive assumptions that might be causing debilitating emotions. This is usually accomplished through a series of visualization exercises and easily answered questions. For example, a client might be encouraged to recall or imagine situations that elicited such emotions and to focus on the thoughts experienced in those situations. Second, once a thought or dysfunctional assumption has been identified, several methods can be used to counteract it. Beck used one such method, reality checking or hypothesis testing. After the client has identified the dysfunctional belief or thought and has learned to distinguish it as a hypothesis rather than as a reality, he or she then tests it empirically through homework assignments. For example, if a client believes that everyone he meets turns away from him in disgust, the therapist might help him devise a system for judging other people's facial expressions and body language so that the client can determine objectively whether the thoughts behind the problem are indeed accurate. As another example, clients might be encouraged to participate in role-playing sessions. A client who believed that store clerks thought she was inept changed this negative view of herself when she played the role of a salesclerk waiting on her. Third, Beck frequently uses additional homework assignments that contain liberal doses of behavior modification procedures to develop various desirable daily activities. For example, depressed individuals frequently neglect routine tasks such as showering or bathing, bed making, and housecleaning. Homework assignments might be directed toward reestablishing these behaviors. (For a description of procedures for conducting Beck's cognitive therapy with individuals with depression, see Young, Rygh, Weinberger, & Beck, 2008).

COMPARISON OF THE APPROACHES OF ELLIS AND BECK   Some obvious similarities exist between Beck's approach and Ellis's REBT. Both approaches assume that the client's difficulty is caused by some type of inappropriate thought pattern, such as a tendency to exaggerate or catastrophize unpleasant events. Both focus on changing a client's irrational thinking, and both use various behavioral homework assignments. A difference is that Beck does not emphasize the tendency of clients to catastrophize or "awfulize" nearly as much as Ellis did. A second difference is that transcripts of sessions with clients conducted by Beck versus those by Ellis suggest that Beck took a gentler, less confrontational approach than Ellis did when discussing clients' irrational beliefs. A third difference in their approaches is the way they attempt to change irrational beliefs. Ellis attempted to change them by disputing them aggressively through relentless logical arguments. Beck frequently attempted to change them by helping the client develop homework assignments to test them experimentally.

EVALUATION OF BECK'S COGNITIVE THERAPY   Although Beck and his colleagues have applied their approach to a variety of disorders, they consider it to be especially effective for depressed individuals (Beck et al., 1985). Cognitive therapy has been shown to be at least as effective as medication for acute episodes of depression (Antonuccio, Danton, & DeNelsky, 1995), although less effective than medication for chronic depression (Thase et al., 1994). Dobson (1989), using a technique called *meta-analysis,* concluded that Beck's cognitive therapy was the best treatment available for unipolar depression.

However, another meta-analysis of published, randomized control trials for treatment of mildly to moderately depressed outpatients found overall effectiveness to be just 46.6% for cognitive therapy compared to 55.3% for behavior therapy and 52.3% for interpersonal psychotherapy (Depression Guideline Panel, 1993). Moreover, evidence from a large-scale, multisite study conducted by the National Institute of Mental Health found that Beck's cognitive therapy was no more effective than a control condition for persons suffering from depression (Elkin et al., 1989). However, that study has been criticized for having a number of methodological flaws, including the use of newly trained cognitive therapists who might not have been adequately supervised (Elkin, 1994; Otto, Pava, & Sprich-Buckminster, 1995).

Although Young et al. (2008) state that "evidence demonstrating the efficacy of cognitive behavior therapy in the treatment of unipolar and bipolar depression continues to mount" (p. 297), the aforementioned evidence on the overall effectiveness of Beck's cognitive therapy that has been reviewed is mixed. Because it might be effective, the question arises as to what its active ingredients or effective components are. Component analyses of Beck's cognitive therapy for treating depression suggest that cognitive restructuring might not be a necessary component in the treatment of depression (Dimidjian et al., 2006; Dimidjian, Martell, Addis, & Herman-Dunn, 2008; Gortner, Golan, Dobson, & Jacobson, 1998; Jacobson et al., 1996; Martell, Addis, & Dimidjian, 2004).

Along the same lines, Andrew Sweet and his colleagues examined 29 studies that compared purely behavioral treatments to those same treatments with added cognitive components for a variety of disorders including depression. They reported that 83% of the studies showed that no more beneficial outcome was achieved by adding therapy components that focused specifically on cognitive restructuring (Latimer & Sweet, 1984; Sweet & Loizeaux, 1991). Thus, while the addition of cognitive restructuring techniques to behavioral treatments might improve outcomes with some individuals suffering from various disorders, the preceding studies suggest that it often does not do so. Nevertheless, as discussed in Chapter 28, cognitive behavior therapy has been shown to be effective for a wide variety of disorders (Butler, Chapman, Forman, & Beck, 2006).

Study Questions

 7. What are the three main phases of rational-emotive behavior therapy? Who developed it?
 8. Why did Ellis change the name of his therapy from RET to REBT?
 9. According to Beck, what causes problems for individuals with neuroses? Describe three examples.
 10. Describe the three major components of Beck's cognitive therapy.

11. Describe three similarities and three differences between the approaches of Beck and Ellis.

12. Studies in the 1980s indicated that cognitive behavior therapy was the treatment of choice for unipolar depression. Is that therapy effective because of the cognitive restructuring or because of the behavioral homework assignments? Discuss.

SELF-DIRECTED COPING METHODS

The previous section discussed cognitive restructuring, which focuses on substituting rational thoughts and appraisal of information for irrational or dysfunctional thinking. Other strategies focus on teaching self-instructional and problem-solving strategies to help clients emit overt behaviors to cope with difficult and stressful situations.

Self-Instructional Training

Meichenbaum and Goodman (1971) initially developed self-instructional training to help children control impulsive behavior. Self-instructional training with children typically proceeds through these five steps:

1. *Adult Demonstrates Self-Instructing*   For example, an adult might say, "My job is to draw a 10. First I'll draw a straight line like this, and then I'll draw an oval beside it" (while drawing a 10). "I did a good job."

2. *Child Performs While Adult Verbalizes*   For example, the adult would give the child the pencil and repeat the instructions from Step 1 (and subsequent praise) while the child draws a 10.

3. *The Child Performs the Task and Verbalizes Out Loud*   For example, the child would initiate the behavior illustrated by the adult in Step 1.

4. *Overt Self-Instructions Fade*   Over two or three trials, the child is encouraged to repeat the task while saying the instructions and self-praise more and more softly.

5. *Task Performance Is Performed with Covert Self-Instructions*   Finally, the child is prompted to perform the task while saying the instructions and the self-praise silently so that the teacher can't hear them.

An impulsive child receiving self-instructional training would first be encouraged to practice the steps with simple tasks, such as drawing a 10, and then progress to more complex tasks appropriate for the child's developmental level, such as adding and subtracting.

Meichenbaum (1986) and others have since extended self-instructional training strategies to help adult clients as well as children develop coping skills for dealing with stressful situations that are largely out of their control. Often, the emphasis in this approach is more on teaching the client to cope with the negative emotions than on completely eliminating them. For example, following treatment, one phobic client said,

> [Self-instructing] makes me able to be in the situation, not to be comfortable, but to tolerate it. I don't talk myself out of being afraid, just out of appearing afraid. You immediately react to the things you're afraid of and then start to reason with yourself. I talk myself out of panic. (Meichenbaum, 1986, p. 372)

The first step in Meichenbaum's approach is to teach a client to cope with stress by helping the client identify certain internal stimuli produced by the stressful situation and by negative self-statements the client makes (e.g., "I can't deal with this," "I'm no good"). The client learns to use these internal stimuli as S^Ds for engaging in appropriate self-instruction. Next, through modeling and behavioral rehearsal, the client learns self-talk to counteract negative self-statements in the presence of the stressful situation (e.g., "The fact that I'm anxious just before giving a speech doesn't mean I'm going to blow it—my anxiety is just a way of preparing me to be alert and do a good job"). Third, the client is taught to self-instruct the steps for taking appropriate action (e.g., "I'll take three deep breaths, smile, then follow my notes and give my speech" while performing those actions). Finally, the client is instructed to make self-reinforcing statements immediately after he or she has coped successfully with the stressful situation (e.g., "I did it! Wait 'til I tell my therapist about this!").

STRESS INOCULATIONS   Meichenbaum (1985) developed a strategy that he called "stress inoculations." It typically proceeds through three phases. In the *reinterpretation phase,* clients are taught that it's not the stressor (such as a student having to give a talk in class) that is the cause of their nervousness or stress reaction; rather, it is the way they view that event. Clients are also taught to verbalize that they are capable of learning to take steps to deal with the situation. In the *coping training phase,* clients learn a variety of appropriate coping strategies, such as relaxation, self-instruction, and self-reinforcement. Finally, in the *application phase,* clients practice their self-talk and coping skills to stressful stimuli, such as having an arm immersed in freezing water, watching a gruesome film, or recalling a stressful visit to the dentist. Just prior to and during exposure to such stressful situations, the client practices appropriate coping skills. Research indicates that stress inoculations can be particularly helpful for clients with anxiety or stress problems (Meichenbaum & Deffenbacher, 1988).

EVALUATION OF SELF-INSTRUCTIONAL METHODS   A large number of studies indicate that self-instructional training strategies are effective for such relatively specific tasks as controlling impulsiveness, increasing assertiveness, and improving leisure skills (Meichenbaum, 1986; Spiegler & Guevremont, 2003). Applications to more complex issues, such as social anxiety and personality disorders, have been less successful (Spiegler & Guevremont). As we describe later in this chapter, self-instructional training appears to rely largely on rule-governed behavior. And as indicated in Chapter 17, rules are often effective when they describe specific circumstances and deadlines for specific behavior that lead to sizable and probable outcomes even when the outcomes are delayed. Rules that are deficient in any of these components are less likely to be effective.

Problem-Solving Methods

Problem-solving methods focus on teaching people how to proceed through logical reasoning to satisfactory solutions to personal problems. D'Zurilla and Goldfried (1971) outlined the following six general steps in personal problem solving.

1. *General Orientation*   The client is encouraged to recognize problems and to realize that it is possible to deal with them by acting systematically rather than impulsively. For example, when faced with a problem, the client might be taught to make statements such as "I know I can work this out if I just proceed step-by-step" or "Let me see how I can rephrase this as a problem to be solved."

2. *Problem Definition*   When asked to specify the problem, most clients reply in vague terms—for example, "I've been very upset lately." By specifying the history of the problem

and the variables that seem to be controlling it, it is generally possible to define the problem more precisely. For example, a close analysis might indicate that what is upsetting the client is feeling forced to live in a mess created by an untidy roommate.

3. *Generation of Alternatives*   After defining the problem precisely, the client is instructed to brainstorm possible solutions—that is, to "let one's mind run free" and to think of as many solutions as possible, no matter how far-fetched. For example, possible solutions might be to (a) move, (b) learn to accept messiness, (c) speak assertively to the roommate about keeping the place neat, (d) try to shape neat behavior in the roommate, (e) negotiate a behavioral contract with the roommate, (f) throw the roommate's things out the window, and (g) throw the roommate out the window.

4. *Decision Making*   The next step is to examine the alternatives carefully, eliminating those that are obviously unacceptable, such as (f) and (g). The client should then consider the likely short-term and long-term consequences of the remaining alternatives. Writing out the positives and negatives of various alternatives has been demonstrated to improve satisfaction with decision making, to increase the likelihood of sticking to decisions, and to lead to more productive choices and fewer regrets (Janis & Mann, 1977; Janis & Wheeler, 1978). On the basis of these considerations, the client should select the alternative that seems most likely to provide the optimum solution.

5. *Implementation*   Initially with the help of the therapist, the client devises a plan for carrying out the best solution to the problem. Sometimes this requires learning new skills. If, for example, the client who decided that the best alternative from those listed in Step 3 was (e), then the client might need to learn about behavioral contracting (see pp. 334–337).

6. *Verification*   When the plan is put into effect, the client is encouraged to keep track of progress to ensure that it solves the problem. If it doesn't, the problem-solving sequence must be restarted and another solution attempted.

EVALUATION OF PROBLEM-SOLVING METHODS   Foxx and Faw (1990) described a program for teaching problem-solving skills to psychiatric patients and discussed how generalization of these skills might be enhanced. In addition, D'Zurilla and Nezu (1999) described how the problem-solving approach might be applied to a variety of clinical problems. Although evidence indicates that adults and children can readily learn problem-solving skills, they do not always apply them appropriately to achieve satisfactory solutions to personal problems.

Study Questions

13. Briefly list the five steps of self-instructional training that Meichenbaum and others used with children.

14. Briefly describe the three phases of Meichenbaum's stress inoculation training.

15. In a sentence each, outline the six steps of problem solving described by D'Zurilla and Goldfried.

MINDFULNESS AND ACCEPTANCE STRATEGIES

Recall the mindfulness-based intervention for aggression that was taught to James (the lead case in Chapter 18). When he experienced anger, he would focus on the sensations that he felt in the soles of his feet. From a behavioral point of view, **mindfulness** involves nonjudgmental awareness, observation, and description of one's covert or overt behaviors as they occur and, in some cases, observation of the antecedents and consequences of those behaviors.

Mindfulness is an ancient concept considered to be "at the heart of Buddha's teachings" (Nhat Hanh, 1998, p. 59). It involves paying close attention to the sights, smells, tastes, and tactile sensations of an experience as it occurs. Suppose that you made arrangements to meet your friend Sasha at a particular restaurant at noon. At 12:30, Sasha still hasn't arrived. Feeling angry, you might think to yourself, "This really upsets me. I hate it when Sasha's late! I can't stand it when Sasha's so unreliable! Why do I put up with this? The people in the restaurant must think I'm an idiot for standing here for half an hour." Alternatively, you might practice mindfulness, thinking to yourself, "I'm standing in front of a restaurant. I notice that my heart is beating faster. I feel a queasiness in my stomach. I'm clenching my fists and my forearms feel tense. I'm wondering what people in the restaurant are saying about me. I'm visualizing Sasha apologizing to me." As this example illustrates, mindfulness involves becoming fully aware of one's sensations, thoughts, feelings, and observable behavior on a moment-to-moment basis.

Acceptance, also called **experiential acceptance** to distinguish it from other types of acceptance in psychotherapy (see Block-Lerner, Wulfert, & Moses, 2009), refers to refraining from judging one's sensations, thoughts, feelings, and behaviors as good or bad, pleasant or unpleasant, useful or useless, and so on. Mindfulness and acceptance go hand in hand. While mindfulness focuses on one's behaviors and sensations, acceptance focuses on not judging those behaviors and sensations. One's thoughts are viewed as just responses, just passing events. Feelings, both positive and negative, are accepted as part of life. Acceptance-based procedures are used to teach individuals that they can feel their feelings and think their thoughts, even though they might be aversive, and still take constructive action that is consistent with their values and life goals. An excellent manual for the layperson to learn and practice mindfulness and acceptance-based techniques is the book by Williams, Teasdale, Segal, and Kabat-Zinn (2007) titled *The Mindful Way Through Depression: Freeing Yourself from Chronic Unhappiness.*

In 1990, Jon Kabat-Zinn published an excellent manual for helping individuals use mindfulness techniques to cope with stress. In the late 1980s and early 1990s, several therapists began incorporating mindfulness and acceptance-based procedures into behavior therapy (Hayes, Jacobson, Follette, & Dougher, 1994; Linehan, 1993; Teasdale, Segal, & Williams, 1995). As indicated earlier, therapists who incorporate such experiential change strategies in therapy have been described as the third wave of behavior therapists (Hayes, 2004; Hayes, Follette, & Linehan, 2004). One such approach to treatment is acceptance and commitment therapy (ACT).

Acceptance and Commitment Therapy (ACT)

ACT, developed by Hayes and colleagues (Hayes, Strosahl, & Wilson, 1999), proceeds through three main phases. First, through the use of metaphors, paradox, stories, and other verbal techniques presented by the therapist, the client learns that past attempts to control troublesome thoughts and emotions have often served only to increase the frequency of such thoughts and emotions. If someone tells you not to think of a pink elephant, what are you likely to think about? A pink elephant. Similarly, if someone tells you or you tell yourself to stop thinking a particular debilitating thought, you are likely to think it even more. Second, through the use of mindfulness training and acceptance exercises, the client learns to experience and nonjudgmentally embrace thoughts and emotions, including those that are troublesome. In one such exercise, for example, a client is encouraged to imagine his or her thoughts as they "float by like leaves on a stream" (Hayes, 2004). Thus, rather than trying to recognize and change troublesome thoughts and feelings as might occur in cognitive restructuring, the goal of mindfulness and acceptance training is to simply "be with" one's worrisome thoughts and unpleasant feelings. A phrase recommended for clients to repeat to themselves is, "It's OK. . .whatever it is, it's already here: Let me feel it" (Williams et al., 2007, p. 84). This is the acceptance portion of ACT. Third, regardless of whether the troublesome thoughts and emotions are eliminated, clients are encouraged to identify values in various life domains, such as work, family, health, intimate relationships, and so forth. The client is then encouraged to translate these values into achievable, concrete goals, and to identify and emit specific behaviors to achieve those goals. This is the commitment portion of ACT: Clients are encouraged to identify valued goals in their lives and commit to actions to pursue those goals.

NOTE 1

ACT differs from the cognitive therapy (CT) of Ellis and Beck in several ways. First, CT assumes that troublesome thoughts constitute the primary cause of disturbing emotions whereas ACT considers both thoughts and emotions simply as responses and assumes that both are caused by various environmental contingencies. Second, a major focus of CT is the use of cognitive restructuring to change troublesome thoughts directly while ACT teaches the client to embrace and accept various thoughts and emotions. ACT also teaches clients that, in spite of experiencing troublesome thoughts and aversive feelings, they can still take constructive action to pursue valued goals. A third difference is the focus of the behavioral homework assignments. With CT, a primary purpose of behavioral homework assignments is to help the client overcome distorted thinking. With ACT, behavioral homework assignments are used to build larger patterns of effective action in the pursuit of valued goals. For these reasons, we consider ACT to be a form more of behavior therapy than of cognitive therapy.

NOTE 2

EVALUATION OF ACT   ACT is a relatively new approach to therapy, and considerable research is needed to clearly establish its efficacy. Nevertheless, early studies have been positive. For example, it has been shown to be equivalent to systematic desensitization (described in Chapter 28) in treating math anxiety (Zettle, 2003), equivalent to cognitive therapy for treating anxiety and depression (Forman, Herbert, Moitra, Yeomans, & Geller, 2007), effective for reducing stress in the workplace (Bond & Bunce, 2000), and effective as a treatment for obsessive-compulsive disorder (Twohig, Hayes, & Masuda, 2006). Other outcome studies were reviewed by Hayes, Masuda, Bissette, Luoma, and Guerrero (2004), Ost (2008), and Powers, Zum Vörde Sive Vörding, and Emmelkamp (2009).

NOTE 3

Study Questions

16. What is *mindfulness* as Buddhists and cognitive behavior therapists use the term?
17. What is *acceptance* as cognitive behavior therapists use the term?
18. Briefly describe the three phases of ACT.
19. What are three differences between cognitive therapy and ACT?

A BEHAVIORAL INTERPRETATION OF COGNITIVE RESTRUCTURING, SELF-DIRECTED COPING METHODS, AND ACT

As indicated in Chapter 14, two important categories of behaviors are operant and respondent. As discussed in Chapter 15, much of what we call "thinking" and "feeling" in everyday life can be described in terms of these two fundamental behavioral categories. Also, as indicated in Chapter 15, we assume that the principles and procedures of operant and respondent conditioning apply to private as well as to public behavior. In a number of examples in this book, private behavior was modified to bring about desired changes in public behavior. In no case, however, was it necessary to assume that private behavior is fundamentally different from public behavior. On the contrary, the treatments used were based on the assumption that the same general principles and procedures are applicable to both private and public behavior. From this point of view, we reexamine some cognitive procedures.

Why Might Cognitive Restructuring Be Effective?

You will recall that some cognitive therapists believe that faulty thinking is the cause of emotional and behavioral problems and that the primary focus of cognitive restructuring is to change faulty thinking. As discussed in Chapter 15, it's certainly plausible to suppose that some self-statements can function as CSs to elicit the respondent components of anxiety, anger, and other emotions. Consider the case of Jim, the student who overslept, cut himself while shaving, and later got stuck in traffic. Instances of Jim's irrational self-talk (e.g., "I'm a walking disaster! Why does the worst always happen to me?") might function as CSs to elicit the respondent components of anxiety or anger. His self-statements might also be analyzed in terms of rule-governed behavior. You will recall from Chapter 17 that a *rule* is a description of a contingency in which in a given situation a certain response will produce certain consequences. The statement of a rule (e.g., "If I study my behavior modification text for 3 hours tonight, I'll do well on my behavior modification test tomorrow") can exert control over behavior (it can influence you to study your behavior modification text for 3 hours). From a behavioral perspective, cognitive restructuring deals largely with rule-governed behavior (Poppen, 1989; Zettle & Hayes, 1982). Jim's irrational self-talk might be thought of as faulty rules. His statement "I always screw up" implies the rule: "If I attempt this task I will encounter failure." Such a rule might cause him to avoid a variety of tasks that he is capable of performing. A cognitive therapist might dispute such irrational self-statements, challenge Jim to replace them with rational self-statements, and give him homework assignments that would support rational thinking. For example, Jim might rehearse such rules as "I do some things quite well. I'll follow the computer assignment instructions carefully so that I can complete the assignment by the deadline." Such rules would counteract his irrational self-talk ("I always screw up") and would likely lead to behavior that will be reinforced. The therapist will have helped Jim to replace inaccurate rules with more accurate ones, and the natural environment is likely to maintain behavior appropriate to the more accurate rules.

Now consider other types of irrational thinking. According to Ellis and Grieger (1977), irrational thinking also includes categories referred to as "awfulizing" (e.g., "It's absolutely awful that I lost my job") and "musterbation" (e.g., "I must get a job or I'm a rotten person"). When a client expresses such thoughts, an REBT therapist might challenge the client ("Why is it awful?" or "Just because you don't have a job doesn't make you a rotten person"). And even though a client might learn to express that being without work is not awful she still is out of work. In such cases, cognitive restructuring is unhelpful (e.g., see Figure 27–1). The client has not been given a set of rules (e.g., "I'll check the want ads," "I'll go to the employment agency") that are likely to lead to effective action that the natural environment will maintain. Even if the client has been given clear rules for effective behavior, he or she might be deficient in the necessary behaviors (time management, assertiveness, persistence, etc.) needed to find a job. Thus, in some cases of cognitive restructuring, the rules might be ineffective because (a) they don't identify specific circumstances for specific behaviors that lead to supportive environmental consequences or (b) the client is deficient in the behaviors specified by the rules.

In summary, cognitive restructuring techniques from a behavioral point of view might be effective when (a) they decrease the frequency of irrational self-statements that elicit the respondent component of troublesome emotions and (b) they teach a client to rehearse rules through verbal discourse and homework assignments that identify specific circumstances for specific behaviors that are likely to be maintained in the natural environment.

Why Might Self-Instruction and Problem-Solving Training Be Effective?

We suggest that these approaches teach rule-governed behavior that leads to effective consequences. Teaching a student who is nervous about giving a speech in class (a) to recognize the fact that she is nervous, (b) to emit some coping self-statements, and (c) to self-instruct the steps for taking appropriate action is essentially giving the student a set of rules to follow. If the rules govern the behavior successfully (the student gives the speech and receives positive feedback), then the use of those rules will have been strengthened. Because there is a focus on performing the behavior successfully, there is a greater chance of successful behavior change than if the focus had just been on self-instructions alone. Similarly, in problem solving, whereas the first three steps (general orientation, problem definition, and generation of alternatives) involve self-talk, the last three steps (decision making, implementation, and verification) require the individual to take action and solve the problem. Once again, self-talk that is appropriately linked to overt behaviors and to supportive environmental consequences is more likely to be effective than self-talk that is not.

Why Might ACT Be Effective?

Why are mindfulness and acceptance-based procedures therapeutic? One possibility is that nonjudgmentally observing ongoing sensations displaces the behavior of irrational thinking and the negative emotions elicited by it. In Jim's case, if he had observed mindfully how his heart was racing, how tightly he was gripping the steering wheel, and so forth when he was stuck in traffic, he might have been less likely to make irrational statements to himself (e.g., "Why does the worst always happen to me?") that had previously elicited negative emotions. As another example, in the lead case in Chapter 18 in which James was taught to mindfully focus on the soles of his feet when he felt anger, doing so likely replaced the thoughts that elicited angry feelings.

A second possibility relates to the differences between contingency-shaped and rule-governed behavior. Mindfulness and acceptance involve exposure to natural contingencies, and the awareness and nonjudgmental acceptance of one's sensations would appear to be largely contingency-shaped behavior (Hayes, 2004). In contrast, cognitive restructuring deals largely with rule-governed behavior. Contingency-shaped behavior has been described as natural, reactive, and intuitive (Baldwin & Baldwin, 2001) whereas rule-governed behavior tends to be inflexible and rigid (Hayes, 1989). Thus, when a client can accept the sensations characteristic of troublesome thoughts and emotions as experiences to be embraced, exposure to natural contingencies is more likely to modify such behavior.

A third possibility is that once the client accepts the sensations characteristic of troublesome thoughts and emotions as simply responses and nothing more, that person might then be more amenable to identifying various life values, articulating concrete goals (i.e., rules) that represent those values, and committing to specific behaviors to achieve those goals. Stated simply, it might be that once a client accepts irrational thinking and troublesome emotions as "no big deal," then in spite of them, the person can more easily "get on with life." Thus, it appears that ACT uses strategies to enhance contingency-shaped behavior in the first two phases of therapy and then capitalizes on both rule-governed and contingency-shaped behavior in the third phase of therapy.

CONCLUDING COMMENTS

Although the behavioral applications we have described briefly in this chapter are usually called *cognitive,* and although they are often said to be directed toward modifying thoughts, beliefs, and attitudes, their distinguishing characteristic seems to be that they deal with private verbal behavior and imagery as well as with public behavior. They do not appear to involve any behavior principles besides those discussed in the previous chapters of this book. All behavior practitioners should be open to innovative procedures for helping people change their behavior. At the same time, as this chapter has pointed out, looking at such procedures from a consistent behavioral viewpoint has practical as well as theoretical advantages. In addition, it is especially important that, whenever possible, practitioners use procedures that have been validated in the research literature and avoid those that have not been validated.

Study Questions

20. Describe an example that illustrates how a person's self-statements (operant thinking) can function as CSs to elicit the respondent components of an emotion. (You might want to review Chapter 15.)
21. Describe an example that illustrates how a person's self-statements might exert rule-governed control over that person's behavior. (You might want to review Chapter 17.)
22. Describe an example that illustrates how cognitive therapists capitalize on rule-governed behavior to help their clients.
23. From a behavioral point of view, summarize why cognitive restructuring techniques might be effective.
24. What is one explanation of why both self-instruction and problem-solving training might be effective?
25. Briefly describe three behavioral explanations that might explain why mindfulness and acceptance-based procedures are therapeutic.
26. Discuss whether reputable behavior modifiers deny the existence and importance of thoughts and feelings.

Application Exercise

SELF-MODIFICATION EXERCISE

Consider a situation in which you sometimes experience negative thinking (e.g., thinking about your future, a social relationship, work, your performance in a course). In a sentence, describe the general theme around which negative thinking occurs. Then write down 10 different types of thoughts (these could be self-statements, images, or a mixture of the two) that you experience when thinking negatively about that particular topic or theme. Next, for each negative thought, describe an alternative positive thought or coping self-statement that you might practice to counteract the negative thought. Your coping thoughts should be realistic, positive, and specific, and should relate to specific positive outcomes.

Notes and Extended Discussion

1. ACT is based on an approach to the understanding of human language and cognition referred to as *relational frame theory* (RFT; Hayes, Barnes-Holmes, & Roche, 2001). RFT builds on research on forming equivalence classes discussed in Chapter 8. In general, relational framing is responding in certain ways to a set of arbitrary stimuli that are related to each other by some linguistic phrase or "frame" (e.g., a dime *is worth more than* a nickel). In other words, even though a dime is smaller than a nickel in terms of actual size, we have arbitrarily designated the dime as being worth more. Relational frames exhibit three characteristics. First, they exhibit *bidirectionality* (also referred to as *mutual entailment*). For example, if you have learned that two nickels equal a dime, then you will also have learned that a dime equals two nickels. This bidirectionality is involved in all relational frames, such as smaller than and bigger than, slower than and faster than, duller than and brighter than, and so on. Second, relational frames show *combinatorial entailment*. For example, if a child learns a dime is worth more than a nickel and a quarter is worth more than a dime, the child will also have learned that a quarter is worth more than a nickel. (Note that the transitivity relationship of stimulus equivalence, discussed in Note 1 of Chapter 8, is an example of combinatorial entailment). Third, relational frames display *transformation of stimulus functions*. Suppose through training that the written word *dog,* the spoken word *dog,* and an actual dog have become a stimulus equivalence class for a child. Suppose further that a dog approaches the child and barks loudly, scaring the child. The sight of the dog now functions to cause fear. That function will also be transferred to related stimuli so that the child will now feel fear when hearing someone say "dog" or when reading the word *dog.* For Hayes and colleagues, relational framing is the essence of verbal behavior and is the characteristic that sets humans apart from other animals. Nonhuman animals show stimulus generalization to different stimuli provided that the stimuli have some physical characteristic in common, such as learning the concepts red, tree, or people (see Chapter 8). Humans, however, show stimulus generalization across members of an equivalence class even though the members are very different physically. This effect, along with the transformation of stimulus functions among related stimuli, leads to relational framing, which allows us to talk and think about events that are not present, to analyze pros and cons of possible outcomes, and to select courses of action to solve problems. Unfortunately, relational framing can also cause troublesome emotions with respect to stimuli that are not present, such as excessive regret or remorse about events in the remote past and excessive and unproductive worrying about potential events in the distant future. For reviews of RFT, see Volume 19 (2003) of *The Analysis of Verbal Behavior* and Palmer (2004).

2. Another method for treating persistent disturbing thoughts is *thought-stopping* (Wolpe, 1958). Consider the case of Carol (Martin, 1982). After being engaged for 3 years, Carol's fiancé, Fred, left her for another woman. Carol suffered from frequent, obsessive thoughts about Fred. She agreed to try thought-stopping. To teach Carol how to use this process, the therapist first instructed her to close her eyes, think about Fred, and raise her finger when she was beginning to feel unhappy. When she did so, the therapist yelled, "Stop!" Carol was startled, immediately opened her eyes, and thoughts about Fred ceased. The therapist and Carol repeated this routine twice more. The therapist then instructed Carol to think about Fred, and when she visualized him clearly, she should yell, "Stop!" herself. Carol followed this routine, and once again, thoughts of Fred immediately ceased. Carol followed this routine on two more trials, which taught her that she could at least temporarily cease thinking about Fred by yelling "Stop!" The therapist then instructed Carol to once more think about Fred, but this time, when clearly visualizing him, she should imagine yelling "Stop!" silently to herself. Carol followed this instruction successfully and repeated it on

two more trials. The therapist then explained to Carol that thought-stopping involves two phases: (a) first terminating the distressing thoughts (which Carol had learned to do) and (b) then thinking competing adaptive thoughts. To implement these phases, Carol agreed that each time she experienced a thought characteristic of those that upset her, she would stop doing what she was doing, clasp her hands, close her eyes, and silently yell "Stop!" to herself. Then she would open her eyes and take from her purse five photographs of herself in a happy mood or situation. She would look at each of the photographs, one at a time, and then turn them over and read statements on the back that prompted her to think positive thoughts. The therapist also instructed her to vary the positive thoughts when viewing the photographs at different times. After following this procedure for several weeks, thoughts about Fred decreased to a very low level, and Carol decided that she no longer needed help. Thought-stopping is often used as part of a treatment package for decreasing troublesome thoughts.

3. At the beginning of this chapter, we indicated that behavior therapy had been referred to as the *first wave* of behavioral approaches to therapy, cognitive behavior therapy as the *second wave*, and ACT as the *third wave*. What do representatives of each wave think about the other waves? Two representatives of each wave participated in a panel discussion at the annual meeting of the Association for Behavioral and Cognitive Therapies in 2007. Their comments reflect some very interesting agreements and disagreements, which can be found in the Winter, 2008 issue (No. 8) of the *Behavior Therapist* (see DiGiuseppe, 2008; Hayes, 2008; Leahy, 2008; Moran, 2008; O'Brien, 2008; and Salzinger, 2008). Points of contention included whether there really are three clearly defined waves of behavior therapy as Hayes (2004) has contended, whether there is convincing evidence that ACT is more effective than other forms of cognitive or cognitive behavior therapy, and whether ACT is defined with sufficient rigor to be reliably applied and scientifically tested.

Study Questions on Notes

1. With an example, illustrate the bidirectionality aspect of relational framing.
2. With an example, illustrate the combinatorial entailment aspect of relational framing.
3. With an example, illustrate how relational framing involves transformation of stimulus functions among related stimuli.
4. Briefly describe the three steps that a therapist might follow in teaching a client to use thought-stopping to terminate distressing thoughts.
5. How would Carol's problem have been treated with ACT?

28

Areas of Clinical Behavior Therapy

In this chapter, we give a brief overview of the ways in which behavior therapists and cognitive behavior modifiers are applying the principles and techniques described in the preceding chapters to treat some of the most frequently encountered adult psychological disorders. Partly under the instigation of third-party payers (such as insurance companies and governments), the empha-

NOTE 1 sis in clinical psychology has shifted to **empirically supported therapies (ESTs)**—therapies that have proved to be effective in scientifically conducted clinical trials. Typically, ESTs are behavioral or cognitive behavioral treatments, primarily because—as discussed in Chapter 1—the behavioral approach emphasizes basing treatments on well-established principles, measuring the outcomes of treatments in objectively defined behaviors, and altering treatments that are not producing satisfactory results. As discussed in the previous chapter, we consider cognitive procedures to be directed toward private or covert behavior in a way that is generally consistent with operant and Pavlovian conditioning theory. Thus, although we use the terms *behavioral* and *cognitive* procedures in this chapter, this is merely for convenience to reflect common usage rather than indicating any sort of fundamental distinction.

Our intention is not to teach you how to assess, diagnose, or treat the disorders discussed in this chapter. This is beyond the scope of this text, and these activities must be done only by trained professionals. Instead, our purpose is to provide general information about how qualified behavior therapists treat these disorders and to relate that information to the behavioral principles and procedures discussed in previous chapters. Behavioral and cognitive behavioral treatments of the disorders discussed in this chapter have received more detailed coverage in other books (e.g., Antony & Barlow, 2004; Barlow, 2008; Lambert, 2004).

It should be noted that pharmaceutical treatments are available for some of the problems covered in this chapter. While drugs alone can sometimes be effective treatment, many studies show that they are often more effective in combination with behavior therapy or cognitive behavior therapy. Given that drugs often have unwanted side effects, it is usually considered desirable to avoid their use when behavioral or cognitive behavior therapy is a viable alternative. See Flora (2007) for an excellent discussion of how drugs are frequently overused in the treatment of psychological problems that would be more safely and effectively treated by behavioral procedures alone.

The clinical disorders covered in this chapter are representative of the types of disorders that behavior therapists treat. Because these clinical problems are not independent, clients often have more than one at the same time—a condition known as *co-morbidity*. Treatment is generally not as straightforward when co-morbidity is present as when it is not present. For simplicity, this chapter assumes that the client suffers from only one of the conditions discussed.

SPECIFIC PHOBIAS

Many people have such intense fears that they become virtually incapacitated by these fears. A person might have such an intense fear of heights that walking up a single flight of stairs or looking out a second-story window causes acute anxiety. Another person might be unable to go into public places because of being terrified of crowds. Trying to convince these people that their fears are irrational often has no beneficial effect. They usually know that their fears have no rational basis and would like to eliminate them, but they cannot because the fears are automatically elicited by specific stimuli. An intense, irrational, incapacitating fear of a stimulus class is called a *specific phobia*. Specific phobias are classed as animal type (e.g., fear of dogs, birds, spiders), natural environment type (e.g., fear of heights, storms), blood–injury–injection type (e.g., fear of seeing blood, having an operation), situational type (e.g., enclosed spaces, flying), and other type (any specific phobia not included in the preceding).

Specific phobias are classified by the *DSM-IV-TR* (See Note 1 of Chapter 1) as a type of anxiety disorder. We start with a discussion of specific phobias because several well-known behavioral treatments have been developed to treat them. We discuss other anxiety disorders later in this chapter.

Study Questions

1. What are empirically supported therapies (ESTs)?
2. Why do empirically supported therapies often turn out to be behavioral or cognitive-behavioral therapies?
3. What is a specific phobia?
4. List three classes of specific phobias, and give two examples of each.

Systematic Desensitization

Joseph Wolpe (1958) developed the earliest behavioral treatment for specific phobias. He hypothesized that the irrational fear characteristic of a phobia is a respondently conditioned response to the feared object or situation (described in Chapter 15). From this hypothesis, Wolpe reasoned that he could eliminate the irrational fear response if he could establish a response to the feared stimulus that counteracted or opposed the fear response. You may recall from Chapter 14 that this process is called *counterconditioning*. A fear-antagonistic response that Wolpe found suitable for this purpose was relaxation. He further reasoned that when counterconditioning the fear response, the therapist should be careful not to elicit the fear response all at once in its full intensity because too much fear in the therapy session would interfere with the process. Given this rationale, Wolpe might have called his treatment *systematic counterconditioning*. However, he gave it the name *systematic desensitization*.

Systematic desensitization is a procedure for overcoming a phobia by having a client in a relaxed state successively imagine the items in a fear hierarchy. A **fear hierarchy** is a list of fear-eliciting stimuli arranged in order from the least to the most fear-eliciting.

In the first phase of systematic desensitization, the therapist helps the client construct a fear hierarchy of approximately 10 to 25 stimuli related to the feared stimulus. See Table 28–1 for an actual example of a fear hierarchy constructed with a client.

In the next phase, the client learns a deep-muscle relaxation procedure that requires tensing and relaxing a set of muscles. This tension–relaxation strategy is applied to muscles of all major areas of the body (e.g., arms, neck, shoulders, and legs) and, after several sessions, enables an individual to relax deeply in a matter of minutes. During the third phase, the actual therapy begins. At the direction of the therapist, the client while relaxing clearly imagines the least fear-eliciting scene in the hierarchy for a few seconds and then stops imagining it and continues relaxing for about 15 to 30 seconds. This is repeated. Then the next scene is presented and repeated in the same way. This continues over sessions until the last scene in the hierarchy is presented. If at any point the client experiences anxiety (communicated to the therapist by raising the index finger), the therapist returns the client to a previous step or inserts an intermediate scene. When all of the scenes in the hierarchy have been imagined, the client can usually encounter the feared stimuli without distress. The positive reinforcement the client then receives for interacting with the previously feared stimuli helps to maintain continued interactions with those stimuli.

Although systematic desensitization is normally carried out by having the client imagine the feared stimuli, it can also be conducted *in vivo*—from the Latin "in life" or, in other words, in the presence of the actual stimuli that elicit fear in the natural environment. *In vivo* exposure is often used when clients have difficulty imagining scenes. It also has the advantage of eliminating the need to program generalization from imagined scenes to actual situations. However, it is usually less time consuming and less costly for a client to imagine feared scenes in a hierarchical order than to arrange *in vivo* hierarchical exposure to them.

During the last decade, for reasons that are not entirely clear given its proven effectiveness in numerous studies, systematic desensitization has lost popularity among therapists. One reason might be its emphasis on covert or private behavior (i.e., imagery) in the treatment as opposed to overt behavior, which behaviorists tend to favor. In addition, because of its stimulus–response emphasis, systematic desensitization does not appeal to cognitively oriented therapists. (For further discussion of these points, see McGlynn, Smitherman, & Gothard, 2004.)

Flooding

Flooding is a method for extinguishing fear by exposure to a strongly feared stimulus for an extended period of time. Whereas the model for systematic desensitization is counterconditioning, the model for flooding is extinction. That is, the basic assumption behind flooding is that if the client is exposed to the feared stimulus and is not allowed to escape from it, but no aversive event follows, the fear response to that stimulus will extinguish. Flooding is carried out either *in vivo* or through imagery. Whereas *in vivo* compared to imagery is generally preferred because in theory it should maximize generalization, there is evidence that both methods are equally effective (Borden, 1992).

As the name *flooding* suggests, the treatment involves eliciting the fear at or close to its full intensity. However, the procedure might involve graded levels of exposure if the distress

TABLE 28–1   Example of a Fear-of-Flying Hierarchy

1. The plane has landed and stopped at the terminal. I get off the plane and enter the terminal, where I am met by friends.

2. A trip has been planned, and I have examined the possible methods of travel and decided "out loud" to travel by plane.

3. I have called and told the travel agent of my plans. The agent gives me the times and flight numbers.

4. It is the day before the trip, and I pack my suitcase, close it, and lock it.

5. It is 10 days before the trip, and I receive the tickets in the mail. I note the return address, open the envelope, and check the tickets for the correct dates, times, and flight numbers.

6. It is the day of the flight; I'm leaving home. I lock the house, put the bags in the car, and make sure that I have the tickets and money.

7. I am driving to the airport for my flight. I am aware of every plane I see. As I get close to the airport, I see several planes—some taking off, some landing, and some just sitting on the ground by the terminal.

8. I am entering the terminal. I am carrying my bags and tickets.

9. I proceed to the airline desk, wait in line, and have the agent check my tickets and then weigh and check my bags.

10. I am in the lounge with many other people, some with bags, also waiting for flights. I hear the announcements over the intercom and listen for my flight number to be called.

11. I hear my flight number announced, and I proceed to the security checkpoint with my hand luggage.

12. I approach the airline desk beyond the security checkpoint, and the agent asks me to choose a seat from the "map" of the plane.

13. I walk down the ramp leading to the plane and enter the door of the plane.

14. I am now inside the plane. I look at the interior of the plane and walk down the aisle, looking for my seat number. I then move in from the aisle and sit down in my assigned seat.

15. The plane is in flight, and I decide to leave my seat and walk to the washroom at the back of the plane.

16. I notice the seat-belt signs light up, so I fasten my seat belt and I notice the sound of the motors starting.

17. Everyone is seated with their seat belts fastened, and the plane slowly moves away from the terminal.

18. I notice the seat-belt signs are again lighted, and the pilot announces that we are preparing to land.

19. I am looking out the window and suddenly the plane enters clouds and I cannot see out the window.

20. The plane has stopped at the end of the runway and is sitting, waiting for instructions to take off.

21. The plane is descending to the runway for a landing. I feel the speed and see the ground getting closer.

22. The plane has taken off from the airport and banks as it changes direction. I am aware of the "tilt."

23. The plane starts down the runway, and the motors get louder as the plane increases speed and suddenly lifts off.

Source: This example is based on a case described by Roscoe, Martin, and Pear (1980).

experienced by the client is too overwhelming. A fear of heights, for example, might be treated by having the client look out the window on the first floor, then the third floor, then the seventh floor, and finally the top of a 10-story building. Thus, except for the absence of an explicit relaxation procedure, flooding can be very similar to desensitization.

Participant Modeling

Participant modeling is a method for decreasing fear in which a client imitates another individual approaching a feared object. As the procedure's name suggests, both the client and therapist are participating together in the feared situation. Participant modeling is typically carried out in a graded fashion. For example, if a client has a fear of birds, the client observes a budgie in a cage from about 10 feet away. The client is then encouraged to imitate this behavior and is praised for doing so. After several trials, the process is repeated at a distance of 5 feet from the bird, then 2 feet, then beside the cage, then with the cage door open, and finally ending with the budgie perched on the client's finger.

Nonexposure Approaches

NOTE 2 Systematic desensitization, flooding, and participant modeling are *exposure-based therapies*; that is, they involve the client's exposure—either in imagination or *in vivo*—to the feared stimulus or stimuli. Cognitive therapy has been used effectively in combination with exposure-based approaches. For example, if an individual with claustrophobia (fear of being in closed spaces, such as elevators) is making self-statements such as "I'm going to be trapped" or "I'm going to suffocate," cognitive therapy might reduce the believability of these self-statements and thus eliminate or greatly reduce the phobia (Booth & Rachman, 1992; Shafran, Booth, & Rachman, 1993).

ACT, described in Chapter 27, has also been used in the treatment of specific phobias. Forsyth and Eifert (2007) have prepared a self-help guide for individuals to use ACT to overcome anxiety, phobias, and excessive worrying. Antony and Norton (2009) have described step-by-step strategies for individuals suffering from anxiety problems, including phobias, to use cognitive behavioral procedures to overcome their anxiety problems.

Outcome Comparisons of Treatments for Specific Phobias

Comparison studies of systematic desensitization, flooding, and participant modeling has not demonstrated any clear differences in outcome among these different treatments (Borden, 1992). As indicated in Chapter 27, ACT was as effective as systematic desensitization in the treatment of a specific phobia (Zettle, 2003).

Study Questions

5. What is a fear hierarchy?
6. Define *systematic desensitization.*
7. Using an example, briefly describe the three phases of systematic desensitization of a specific phobia.
8. Describe the fundamental difference between flooding and systematic desensitization.
9. Briefly describe an example of how *in vivo* flooding might be used to treat a specific phobia.
10. Briefly describe an example of how participant modeling might be used to treat a specific phobia.
11. What is the defining characteristic of exposure-based therapies? Give an example of a nonexposure-based therapy.

OTHER ANXIETY DISORDERS

According to the *DSM-IV-TR,* anxiety disorders are characterized by (a) fear/anxiety that results in physiological changes such as sweaty hands, trembling, dizziness, and heart palpitations, (b) the escape and/or avoidance of situations in which the fear is likely to occur, and (c) interference by the unwanted behaviors with the individual's life. For a discussion of how contemporary learning principles and research can explain the etiology of anxiety disorders, see Mineka and Zinbarg (2006). The *DSM-IV-TR* classifies anxiety disorders into several broad categories including specific phobias, panic disorder and agoraphobia, generalized anxiety disorder, obsessive-compulsive disorder, and posttraumatic stress disorder. Having already considered specific phobias, we now consider the other four types.

Panic Disorder and Agoraphobia

Panic disorder is a susceptibility to panic attacks, which are intense fear experiences that seem to come "out of the blue" with no precipitating stimulus or cue. These attacks include four or more of the following symptoms: (a) heart-rate abnormalities, including extremely rapid heart beat, heart palpitations, and pounding heart, (b) sweating, (c) trembling, (d) shortness of breath or feeling of being smothered, (e) feelings of choking, (f) chest pain or discomfort, (g) nausea or extreme abdominal discomfort, (h) dizziness or feeling light-headed or faint, (i) feeling of unreality, (j) numbness or tingling sensation, (k) chills or hot flushes, (l) fear of going crazy or losing control, and (m) fear of dying.

Agoraphobia—which literally means fear of the marketplace—is an intense fear of going out in public or leaving the confines of one's home. People who suffer from panic disorder frequently also have agoraphobia because they are afraid of having a panic attack in public or outside their home. This can lead to a self-fulfilling prophecy in which the fear of having a panic attack actually generates the attack. To paraphrase Franklin D. Roosevelt's famous words, what a person with panic disorder fears most is fear itself.

TREATMENT   In general, exposure-based therapy carried out *in vivo* is an effective treatment for panic disorder with agoraphobia (Bouman & Emmelkamp, 1996). This might be accomplished by having the client first make short trips from home, followed by gradually longer and longer trips. Alternatively, for an excellent example of contingency management to treat panic disorder, see Guilhardi (2004). Cognitive behavioral treatment is also effective for panic disorder with agoraphobia (Craske & Barlow, 2008). Cognitive behavioral treatment typically includes a behavioral component involving exposure to feared situations and a cognitive component to help change the client's misconceptions about panic attacks. For example, a client might believe that a panic attack will precipitate a heart attack whereas in fact this outcome is extremely unlikely. In addition, the client might be taught relaxation and thought-stopping techniques to lessen the intensity of a panic attack. (Thought-stopping was described in Note 2 of Chapter 27).

Generalized Anxiety Disorder

A person with *generalized anxiety disorder* is constantly worrying and feeling intensely anxious over things, events, and potential events that most people would consider trivial, unimportant, or unlikely. Such a person is so consumed with anxiety that it interferes with normal functioning, often including the ability to sleep at night.

TREATMENT   The most effective therapies for this problem are treatment packages that combine cognitive and behavioral strategies (Borkovec & Sharpless, 2004; Dugas & Robichaud, 2006). One of the behavioral components is usually exposure therapy. The therapist teaches the client relaxation techniques (like those used in systematic desensitization) and then has the client use the start of worrying (i.e., exposure to worry itself) as a stimulus to relax, which competes with or suppresses worrying. It is difficult to worry while relaxed. In addition, cognitive techniques might be used to challenge and change the client's belief in the importance or likelihood of the things worried about. Acceptance techniques (see Chapter 27) might also help the client realize that worrying or not worrying will not make bad events more likely to occur—that is, the client is taught to make self-statements to the effect that worry by itself has no effect on things worried about.

Obsessive-Compulsive Disorder

A person suffering from an *obsessive-compulsive disorder* might experience unwanted intrusive thoughts (called an *obsession*) or feel impelled to engage in unproductive repetitive behaviors (called a *compulsion*), or both. Unlike a person with generalized anxiety disorder, a person with obsessive-compulsive disorder obsesses or worries about a specific thing. In addition, obsessions and compulsions tend to go together because obsessions seem to cause anxiety that can be reduced only by engaging in compulsive behavior. For example, a person might worry about someone breaking into the office overnight, feel anxious about it, and then check and recheck that the office door is locked before leaving. A person with obsessive-compulsive disorder, however, is not satisfied with merely rechecking once but will recheck many times before finally leaving.

Some other common examples of obsessive-compulsive behaviors are obsessing about catching a terrible disease from germs, resulting in constant hand washing; obsessing about hitting a pedestrian, leading to constantly retracing one's route while driving to make sure no injured pedestrians are lying on or beside the road; and obsessing about hurting one's children, leading to avoiding using knives and other potentially dangerous objects in their presence.

TREATMENT   An effective treatment for obsessive-compulsive disorder is *in vivo* exposure and response prevention (Franklin & Foa, 2008). The client is encouraged to engage in behavior leading to the obsession while being prevented from engaging in the compulsive behavior. Suppose that a client experiences obsessive thoughts about germs when touching unwashed objects, which causes considerable anxiety. Suppose further that engaging in a variety of compulsive washing rituals appears to be maintained by anxiety reduction. An exposure-and-response-prevention treatment would involve asking the client to touch particular "contaminated" objects while refraining from performing the washing ritual. The rationale behind this approach is that having the obsession occur without the subsequent anxiety-reducing compulsive behavior allows the anxiety elicited by the obsession to occur in full strength and hence to extinguish. Often a graduated approach is used. For example, a parent who is obsessed with the fear of harming his children with a knife might be encouraged to first hold a butter knife in the presence of the children, then a table knife, then a paring knife, and finally a butcher knife.

Cognitive therapy might also be used to change the self-statements the client makes that help to maintain the obsession (Taylor, Thordarson, & Sochting, 2004). For example, a person who is deathly afraid of germs might be taught to say privately that proper hand washing for 20 seconds is sufficient to protect against germs. Acceptance procedures (see Chapter 27) might help an individual learn that thoughts are not powerful controllers of behavior. The parent who obsesses about harming his children might be taught to regard these thoughts simply as normal "mental garbage" or "mental background noise" that have no bearing on the parent's actual feelings or behavior toward his children.

Posttraumatic Stress Disorder

The classic cases of posttraumatic stress disorder (PTSD) occurred during World War I when many soldiers exposed to artillery bombardment exhibited what was then called *shell shock*. The ability of these soldiers to function was extremely impaired, and many were branded as cowards. It is now recognized that not only battlefield conditions but also any extraordinary stressful or traumatic event—such as being physically or sexually abused, being in a serious traffic accident, or witnessing a catastrophic event—can produce PTSD. It has a number of symptoms including re-experiencing the intense fear that occurred during the traumatic event; exhibiting other intense psychological reactions such as depression, difficulty sleeping, and lack of concentration; and impaired daily functioning. The impaired functioning by someone with this disorder appears to be due to the individual's attempts to avoid thinking about the traumatic event or events and hence to avoid stimuli that remind the individual of the event. Because there are many such stimuli, the effort to avoid them consumes a large proportion of the individual's time and energy.

TREATMENT   One effective treatment for PTSD is long-term vicarious exposure to the event or events that caused the problem (Foa, 2000). This might be done in imagination, talking about the traumatic event(s) with a therapist, writing about the traumatic event(s), or both. In this way, the emotionality elicited by stimuli related to the trauma will extinguish and the debilitating attempts to avoid those stimuli will decrease. Another effective treatment is referred to as *cognitive processing therapy* (Resick & Schnicke, 1992). This approach combines exposure with cognitive therapy. The cognitive component is directed toward helping the client learn to challenge faulty thinking about the traumatic event(s) and to generate alternative, more balanced thoughts. (Resick, Monson, & Rizvi, 2008, reviewed research on these and other variations of behavioral treatments for PTSD.)

Study Questions

12. List and briefly describe four types of anxiety disorder.
13. Briefly describe an effective treatment for panic disorder with agoraphobia.
14. What is the distinction between obsessions and compulsions, and how might they be related?
15. Briefly describe an effective treatment for obsessive-compulsive disorder.
16. With reference to an example, briefly describe how cognitive therapy might be used in the treatment of an obsessive-compulsive disorder.
17. With reference to an example, briefly describe how acceptance procedures might be used in the treatment of an obsessive-compulsive disorder.
18. In several sentences, describe an effective treatment for posttraumatic stress disorder.

DEPRESSION

Everyone has felt depressed at some point. Usually the feeling occurs when some significant reinforcer or potential reinforcer has been removed from our lives. For example, a poor grade on a test might cause a student to feel depressed because of the potential loss of a good grade in a course. Most people get over their depressions fairly quickly as they find other reinforcers to compensate for the lost reinforcers. Some people, however, suffer from what is referred to as a *major depressive episode,* a period of at least two weeks during which there is a loss of interest in nearly all activities (American Psychiatric Association, 2000b). Such individuals experience appetite reduction; decreased energy and increased fatigue; impaired ability to think, concentrate, or make decisions; and often a sense of worthlessness or guilt.

Given what we know about depression in normal individuals, a reasonable theory about individuals with a major depressive episode is that they lack daily reinforcers. A behavioral theory called *behavioral activation,* states that "individuals become depressed when there is an imbalance of punishment to positive reinforcement in their lives" (Martell, 2008, p. 40). (For a discussion of a behavioral analysis of the causes of depression, see Kantor, Busch, Weeks, & Landes, 2008.)

TREATMENT   Behavioral approaches in the 1970s demonstrated some success treating depression by increasing the contingent reinforcers in chronically depressed individuals' lives (Ferster, 1973; Lewinsohn, 1975). One way they did that was by encouraging depressed individuals to seek out reinforcers (e.g., take up hobbies, read books, and go to movies). Behavior therapists have tried enlisting significant others, such as spouses, to reinforce the behavior of seeking and sampling new reinforcers as another strategy. Many of our reinforcers are social, that is, they come from other people, and it takes a certain amount of social skills to access these reinforcers. People with depression often lack these skills. Thus, a component of therapy for depression often involves teaching the client social skills.

Although a behavioral approach to the treatment of depression had a promising start in the 1970s, that approach lost momentum in the 1980s when Beck's famous cognitive therapy became popular. Beck, Rush, Emery, and Shaw (1979) hypothesized that depression results from core beliefs called *cognitive schemas* that lead to negative interpretation of life events. As described in Chapter 27, a major component of Beck's cognitive therapy for depression is cognitive restructuring to help clients overcome faulty thinking. However, in the late 1990s in the wake of studies (e.g., Gortner, Golan, Dobson, & Jacobson, 1998; Jacobson et al., 1996) indicating that the effective ingredient of Beck's cognitive therapy was the homework assignments, not the cognitive restructuring component, the behavioral approach to the treatment of depression experienced a resurgence (Dimidjain et al., 2006; Dimidjian, Martell, Addis, & Herman-Dunn, 2008; Martel, 2008; Martell et al., 2004; Jacobson, Martell, & Dimidjain, 2001; Martell, Addis, & Jacobson, 2001). This approach, called *behavioral activation,* begins with performing a functional analysis (see Chapter 23) of "the antecedents, behaviors, and consequences that form elements of the client's repertoire contributing to depression" (Martel, p. 42). In a step-by-step procedure, the treatment is designed to block avoidance behaviors that prevent the individual from coming into contact with reinforcing contingencies and to encourage the client to engage in activities identified in functional analysis as reinforcing. Research indicates that behavioral activation is at least as effective as cognitive therapy in the treatment of depression and prevention of relapse (Dimidjian et al., 2006; Dobson et al., 2008).

Encouraging persons with clinical depression to participate in exercise programs is also an effective treatment (Tkachuk & Martin, 1999). Also, as indicated in Chapter 27, ACT has also been shown to be an effective treatment for depression (Forman, Herbert, Moitra, Yeomans, & Geller, 2007). For a comparison of behavioral activation and ACT in the treatment of depression, see Kantor, Baruch, and Gaynor (2006).

ALCOHOL PROBLEMS

Excessive alcohol consumption is a major health problem that costs the economy billions of dollars each year in poor job performance and absenteeism (Taylor, 2003). Most alcohol treatment agencies distinguish between problem drinkers and alcoholics (Taylor). *Problem drinkers* experience substantial social, occupational, or medical problems resulting from alcohol consumption. In addition to these problems, *alcoholics* also show alcohol dependence and withdrawal symptoms. Making a similar distinction, the *DSM-IV-TR* distinguishes between alcohol abuse and alcohol dependence. To be diagnosed with *alcohol abuse,* one must show problems in at least one of four areas: (a) failure to fulfill major social obligations, (b) repeatedly drinking in a way that creates the potential for harm, (c) continuing to drink despite known social or interpersonal problems caused by drinking, and (d) incurring repeated alcohol-related legal consequences. To be diagnosed with *alcohol dependence,* an individual must exhibit at least three of the following seven symptoms: (a) a persistent desire or attempt to cut down or stop, (b) consumption of larger amounts over longer periods of time, (c) necessity of an increasing amount to produce the same effects, (d) withdrawal symptoms if the individual stops drinking, (e) neglect of other activities, (f) increased time spent using alcohol, and (g) continued use despite knowledge of problems related to use.

TREATMENT   The well-known organization Alcoholics Anonymous (AA) has developed a program of social support that has had success in helping individuals with alcohol problems. Not everyone with an alcohol problem, however, is willing to accept the philosophy and regimen of AA, which includes the goal of abstinence for life. Fortunately, research shows that behavior therapy can be as or more effective than AA (Emmelkamp, 2004).

Behavioral treatment procedures have been successful in helping problem drinkers to learn to drink in moderation (Emmelkamp, 2004; Walters, 2000). Sobell and Sobell (1993) developed a program that teaches problem drinkers to use goal setting to drink in moderation, to control "triggers" (either SDs or establishing operations) for drinking, to learn problem-solving skills to avoid high-risk situations, to engage in self-monitoring to detect triggers and maintaining consequences of drinking behaviors, and to practice all of these techniques with various homework assignments.

Behavioral programs have utilized a number of components to treat alcoholics or alcohol **NOTE 3** dependency including (a) a *motivational interview* in which the therapist asks the client questions about the problem, the answers to which act as motivational-establishing operations for change (i.e., reduced drinking of alcohol becomes reinforcing and therefore strengthens behavior that leads to reduced drinking) (Arkowitz, Westra, Miller, & Rollnik, 2008; Miller, 1996), (b) *functional analysis* (see Chapter 23) to identify the antecedents and consequences that prompt and maintain alcohol drinking (McCrady, 2008), (c) *coping-skills training* to teach clients to deal with stressors that are thought to cause excessive alcohol consumption, (d) *contingency contracting* (see Chapter 26) to provide reinforcers for work, social, and recreational activities that do not involve alcohol, and (e) strategies to prevent relapse (see Chapter 26). For discussions of these strategies, see Emmelkamp (2004) and McCrady (2008).

EATING DISORDERS

Several distinct eating disorders have been identified: (a) *bulimia nervosa,* (b) *anorexia nervosa,* (c) *binge eating disorder,* and (d) *obesity.* With the first two, the client is malnourished and obsessed with being thin. An individual with obesity is sufficiently overweight to have health problems. The chief difference between individuals with bulimia and those with anorexia is that the former have frequent episodes of binge eating followed by purges, which consist of self-induced vomiting, taking laxatives or enemas, or engaging in exercise or long periods of fasting in an attempt to counteract the effects of binging, whereas individuals with anorexia rarely eat or eat very little. (For a discussion of causes of eating disorders, see Farmer & Latner, 2007).

TREATMENT   Bulimia and anorexia have been extremely resistant to treatment. Some success has been achieved with bulimia by starting with behavioral procedures followed by cognitive procedures (Fairburn, 2008; Fairburn, Cooper, Shafran, & Wilson, 2008). The behavioral procedures involve reinforcement for going between binges for a specified amount of time, which is gradually increased, and for eating regular meals at specified times. The cognitive procedures involve attempts to counteract the client's unrealistic beliefs about food, weight, and appearance. Most individuals with bulimia and anorexia have poor body images. They see themselves as fat when in fact they are usually thin to the point of being malnourished. Both behavioral and cognitive procedures have been considerably less effective with anorexia. This might be because individuals with anorexia tend to experience extreme anxiety at any attempt to get them to behave in a way that would be less than perfect in their belief systems.

Whether they binge or not, behavioral procedures are effective in weight reduction for overweight and obese clients (Craighead, 2004; Faith, Fontaine, Cheskin, & Allison, 2000; Lundgren, 2006). These procedures focus on long-term lifestyle changes in eating habits and exercise and in attitudes toward both (Faith et al.). The programs tend to be more effective if the emphasis is on choosing the right foods rather than on calorie reduction. Behavioral components of such programs are likely to involve (a) *self-monitoring,* including daily records of foods eaten and their caloric contents and body weight, (b) *stimulus control,* such as restricting eating at home to a specific location (e.g., the kitchen table), (c) *the changing of the rate of eating* by having clients put down utensils between bites or take short breaks between courses, (d) *behavioral contracting,* such as having clients sign a contract in which they agree to lose a certain amount of weight in a specified period of time in return for some desired reinforcer (see Chapter 26), and (e) *relapse prevention strategies* (such as those discussed in Chapter 26).

COUPLE DISTRESS

Couple distress occurs when one or both individuals in an intimate (e.g., marital) relationship experience dissatisfaction with it. There are probably as many specific reasons for couple distress as there are distressed relationships. Behavior therapists, however, generally start with the premise that the underlying cause is that the relationship has more negative than positive interactions or communications. For example, while communicating, one partner might tend to make sarcastic or other hostile statements that the other partner reciprocates with hostile statements, leading to a breakdown in communication (or worse) between the two individuals.

TREATMENT   Behavioral couple therapy typically involves a number of components including the following (Snyder & Abbott, 2004): (a) *instigation of positive exchanges*—each individual is asked to increase behaviors that are pleasing to the other partner (e.g., displaying affection, showing respect, expressing appreciation; see Figure 28–1), (b) *communication training*—each individual is taught to express thoughts and feelings concerning what is liked and appreciated

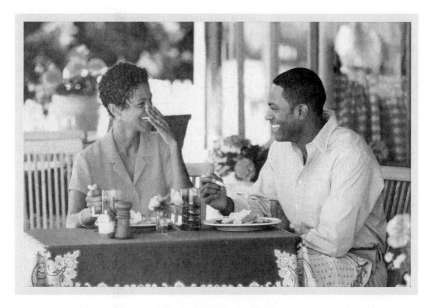

FIGURE 28–1   What behavioral strategies might be used to help couples increase their rate of positive interactions and decrease their rate of negative interactions with each other?

about the other to help the other express his or her feelings and to be an effective listener, (c) *problem-solving training*—couples learn to use their communication skills to systematically identify and solve problems and conflicts in their relationship (see problem-solving training in Chapter 27), and (d) *programming generality*—clients learn to monitor their relationship for specific critical signs of a relapse and to continue using the problem-solving and conflict-resolution techniques that they learned in therapy. In an approach called *integrative behavioral couple therapy,* some therapists also incorporate acceptance procedures and exercises (see Chapter 27) to teach partners to accept emotional responses that each partner has to the other (Christensen, Sevier, Simpson, & Gattis, 2004; Christensen, Wheeler, & Jacobson, 2008).

SEXUAL DYSFUNCTION

There are several types of sexual dysfunction. In males, the major types are (a) inability to have an erection and (b) premature ejaculation. In females, the major types are (a) vaginismus (involuntary spasms of the vagina musculature that interfere with sexual intercourse), (b) dyspareunia (genital pain related to sexual intercourse), (c) inhibited orgasm, and (d) low sexual desire.

TREATMENT   A reasonable working hypothesis for many cases of sexual dysfunction is that anxiety is an important factor. In males, the anxiety might be fear of performing poorly, which therefore becomes a self-fulfilling prophecy. In females, the anxiety might be fear of the sex act. In either case, exposure programs appear to be most effective. Based on pioneering work by Masters and Johnson (1970), therapists generally recommend that the couple engage in pleasurable stimulation of each other in a relaxing atmosphere without expectation of, or pressure to, engage in intercourse (Leiblum & Rosen, 2000; Wincze & Carey, 2001). Masturbation by the woman might also be encouraged to help her learn to experience orgasm if that is one of the issues. Thus, both partners shift the goal from performance to that of experiencing pleasure.

Although a common theoretical assumption is that sexual responses are learned (Plaud, 2007) and although behavioral homework assignments have proven effective in treating many cases of sexual dysfunction, we caution against taking an oversimplistic view of this problem. Sexual dysfunction can result from many causes including medical diseases, relationship difficulties, lifestyle factors, and age-related changes. Wiegel, Wincze, and Barlow (2004) and Wincze, Bach, and Barlow (2008) have described a range of assessments that a therapist should use before attempting to treat a case of sexual dysfunction. We should also point out that, because the development of Viagra and other drugs, sexual dysfunction treatment has become increasingly medicalized (Wiegel et al., 2004). Future research is needed to compare the effects of behavior therapies and medical interventions for a variety of sexual dysfunctions.

HABIT DISORDERS

Many people suffer from frequent and repetitive behaviors that are inconvenient and annoying. These include nail biting, lip biting, knuckle cracking, hair twirling, hair plucking, excessive throat clearing, muscle tics, and stuttering. In many cases, these behaviors are similar to the compulsions described earlier in this chapter except that they are not linked to obsessive thoughts. Many individuals cope with such behaviors on a daily basis. Sometimes, however, such behaviors occur with a sufficient frequency or intensity to cause the individual to seek treatment. When that happens, the behavior is referred to as a *habit disorder* (Hansen, Tishelman, Hawkins, & Doepke, 1990).

TREATMENT   A method called *habit reversal* has been used effectively to treat a number of habit disorders (Azrin & Nunn, 1973; Miltenberger, Fuqua, & Woods, 1998). This method typically consists of three components. First, the client learns to describe and identify the problem behavior. Second, the client learns and practices a behavior that is incompatible with or competes with the problem behavior. The client practices the competing behavior daily in front of a mirror and engages in it immediately after an occurrence of the problem behavior. Third, for motivation, the client reviews the inconvenience caused by the disorder, records and graphs the behavior, and has a family member provide reinforcement for engaging in the treatment.

Study Questions

19. Briefly describe the behavioral characteristics of a major depressive episode.

20. Describe a behavioral theory about the cause of depression and how this theory suggests a treatment for depression.

21. What are the components of Sobell and Sobell's program for problem drinkers?

22. Briefly describe four components of a behavioral treatment for alcohol dependency.

23. Briefly describe four types of eating disorders. With which has behavior therapy been most effective?

24. List and briefly describe four behavioral strategies for treating obesity.

25. List and briefly describe four components of behavioral couples therapy.

26. Describe a general behavioral approach to the treatment of sexual dysfunction.

27. Describe the three components of habit reversal used to treat a habit disorder.

Notes and Extended Discussion

1. The evolution of managed care organizations, such as the U.S. health management organizations (HMOs), and their influence in determining whether psychologists should be paid for providing treatment has put pressure on psychologists to develop cost-effective treatments for a variety of psychological disorders. In 1993, the Division of Clinical Psychology of the American Psychological Association developed a task force to identify empirically supported psychotherapies, create lists of such therapies, and disseminate that information to various stakeholders (e.g., HMOs). This task force has become a standing committee known as the Committee on Science and Practice and has published several reports. This committee established guidelines for a treatment to be judged as an *empirically supported treatment* (EST). Using these guidelines and considering the research evidence, the committee has identified two levels of ESTs: well established and probably efficacious. Treatments considered to be well established must meet the following criteria: (a) at least two well-controlled studies with random assignment of participants have demonstrated that the treatment is more effective than a medical or psychological placebo (either a therapeutically ineffective pill or psychological procedure) or at least as effective as an established treatment, (b) the treatment is described precisely in a manual that other therapists can use to perform the procedure consistently, (c) client characteristics in the research were clearly specified, and (d) research was conducted in at least two independent research settings. The latest list of ESTs can be viewed at http://pantheon.yale.edu/~tat22/empirically_supported/treatments.htm.

    While efforts to establish a list of therapies that have proved to be effective in scientifically conducted clinical trials is laudatory, the effort has been criticized and has led to recommendations to improve the scientific viability of the process. Discussion of these topics can be found in a special issue of *Behavior Modification* (2003, Vol. 27, No. 3). Also, it is one thing to have a list of ESTs; it is another thing to influence practitioners to learn about those ESTs. For discussions of challenges facing the dissemination of ESTs, see Kazdin (2008), Rego et al. (2009), Siev, Huppert, and Chambless (2009), and a special issue of *Behavior Modification* (2009, Vol. 33, No. 1).

2. A form of exposure therapy that has become increasingly popular over the past decade as the cost of computer technology has fallen is virtual reality therapy. This involves exposing individuals to realistic computer-generated anxiety-eliciting stimuli (such as images of numerous crawling spiders to treat cases of arachnophobia). Although this form of therapy is new, the results so far are encouraging (Lamson, 1997; North, North, & Coble, 1997; Riva, Wiederhold, & Molinari, 1998; Rothbaum et al., 1995; Rothbaum et al., 2006; Wiederhold & Wiederhold, 2004; Winerman, 2005).

3. An approach that is receiving increasing attention as an effective treatment for alcohol and substances addiction is straightforward operant conditioning. This approach, called *contingency management* (CM), requires developing ways to measure abstinence and acquiring a reinforcer that is powerful enough to compete with the addictive substance. Addictions that have been treated with CM include alcohol, drugs such as cocaine and heroin, and nicotine. Breath analysis is used as a measure of whether the individual has been abstinent from alcohol over a given period of time. Analysis of CO levels in the breath is used as a measure of whether an individual has refrained from smoking because smoking temporarily increases CO levels in the lungs. Urine samples are used to measure abstinence from opiate drugs. Common reinforcers in CM programs are lottery tickets, money, and vouchers that can be exchanged for goods and services. Data indicate that CM increases

abstinence dramatically in many individuals with substance abuse problems. Because CM can be expensive and labor intensive, however, much research in this area has focused on creative ways to economically measure abstinence and to obtain effective reinforcers. For more information on CM therapy, see the *Journal of Applied Behavior Analysis* (2008, Vol. 41, No. 4), "Special Issue on the Behavior Analysis and Treatment of Drug Addiction," or Higgins et al. (2008).

Study Questions on Notes

1. What criteria must a treatment meet to be considered a well-established empirically supported treatment (EST) by the American Psychological Association?
2. What is virtual reality therapy?
3. Briefly outline a CM approach to alcohol addiction. How does this approach differ from Sobell and Sobell's program described in the text? What are some practical problems of the CM approach?

PART VI

A HISTORICAL PERSPECTIVE
AND ETHICAL ISSUES

29 Giving It All Some Perspective: A Brief History

This chapter traces some of the highlights of the remarkable early growth of the field of behavior modification. It should be read with the following qualifications in mind:

1. Although we describe behavior modification as developing primarily through two major separate lines of influence, there are obvious cross-influences, blends, and offshoots.
2. We identify what we consider to be major highlights of the development of behavior modification during its formative years: the 1950s and 1960s. We also include some highlights **NOTE 1** of the 1970s. For more complete histories of behavior modification, see Kazdin (1978) and Pear (2007).
3. We describe mainly historical highlights in North America. **NOTE 2**
4. Some instructors require their students to read this chapter early in the course. Therefore, we have prepared this chapter to stand alone.

In this chapter, we first consider two major orientations: one that emphasizes Pavlovian or respondent conditioning and one that emphasizes operant conditioning. Then we discuss mixtures of these with other orientations.

THE PAVLOVIAN AND WOLPEAN ORIENTATION

Late in the 19th century, Russian physiologist Ivan P. Pavlov, using dogs as experimental subjects, conducted groundbreaking experiments on digestion. These experiments, which won him the Nobel Prize in Medicine in 1904, involved measuring the secretions of the salivary glands and the other digestive glands including those of the stomach, pancreas, and small intestines. Pavlov observed that the presentation of food to a dog elicited a chain of digestive secretions beginning with salivation. He soon also noticed that the mere sight and smell of food and even the sounds of it being prepared for the experiment elicited digestive gland secretions. Believing in the potential importance of this observation for studying the higher activity of the brain, he decided to use the secretions of the salivary glands as a basis for studying the process by which new reflexes are acquired. He discovered that if a stimulus such as a tone that did not initially elicit salivation was paired with food several times, the presentation of the tone alone would come to elicit salivation. Pavlov called the food–salivation reflex an *unconditional reflex* (i.e., one that is unlearned or not conditional on any pairing process) and the tone–salivation reflex a *conditional reflex* (i.e., one that is learned or conditional on a pairing process). Thus, he embarked on a systematic study of what is now called *Pavlovian, classical,* or *respondent conditioning* (see Chapter 14). Results of this work were published in a classic book titled in its English translation, *Conditioned Reflexes: An Investigation of the Physiological Activity of the Cerebral Cortex* (Pavlov, 1927). In that book, Pavlov's "unconditional reflexes" and "conditional reflexes" were translated into English as *unconditioned reflexes* and *conditioned reflexes,* respectively, which are the terms used today.

Prior to 1913, psychology was defined as the "science of the mind." In 1913, the American psychologist John B. Watson advocated an alternative approach that he called *behaviorism.* Asserting that psychology should be redefined as the science of behavior, he published an influential paper in which he argued that most human activities could be explained as learned habits. After becoming familiar with the work of Pavlov and possibly Vladimir M. Bechterev, another Russian physiologist who studied learned reflexes independently of Pavlov, Watson (1916) adopted the conditioned reflex as the unit of habit. He argued that most complex activities were due to Pavlovian conditioning. Watson followed his 1916 paper with a classic experiment in collaboration with Rosalie Rayner that demonstrated Pavlovian conditioning of a fear response in an 11-month-old infant. In that experiment, Watson and Rayner first demonstrated that the child was not afraid of a white rat. Then, after several pairings of the white rat with a loud noise that caused the infant to cry and show other indications of fear, the child exhibited a conditioned reflex of fear to the rat (Watson & Rayner, 1920; see also Chapter 15).

During the next 20 years, a number of somewhat isolated reports of the application of Pavlovian conditioning procedures to various behaviors appeared in the literature (for a list of many of these, see Yates, 1970). None of these applications, however, appears to have had any sustained impact on the development of behavior modification as we know it today.

Within this Pavlovian tradition, two significant developments occurred in the 1950s. One development happened in South Africa where Joseph Wolpe began some research that drew heavily on Pavlovian conditioning and the work of J. B. Watson, Mary Cover Jones, and British physiologist Sir Charles Sherrington. Following up on the Watson and Rayner study, Jones (1924) demonstrated the elimination of a child's fear reactions to a rabbit by gradually moving the rabbit closer to the child over trials while the child was engaging in pleasurable activities. Sherrington (1947) noted that if one group of muscles is stimulated, an antagonistic muscle group will be inhibited, and vice versa. He called this *reciprocal inhibition* and postulated it to be a general process acting throughout the nervous system. Wolpe extended the principle of reciprocal inhibition to state that if a response that is incompatible with a learned fear or anxiety can be made to occur to a stimulus that had been conditioned to produce that fear, then that stimulus will cease to elicit the fear reaction. Wolpe developed the earliest behavioral treatment for specific phobias, which (as described in Chapter 28) are intense irrational fears, such as a fear of heights. In 1958, Wolpe published his first book on reciprocal inhibition. It was to provide a major force in launching the modern era of the Pavlovian tradition of behavior therapy. Wolpe typically used relaxation responses to inhibit a learned fear or anxiety in a procedure called *systematic desensitization* (see Chapter 28).

Also during the 1950s, the British psychologist Hans Eysenck was influential in criticizing traditional Freudian psychoanalytic treatment and in advocating learning-theory or conditioning procedures as alternatives. In 1960, Eysenck published a book of readings, *Behaviour Therapy and the Neuroses*. In that book, he presented a number of case histories in which variations of reciprocal inhibition and Pavlovian conditioning procedures were used in clinical therapy. The Pavlovian-conditioning orientation of behavior therapy has occasionally been referred to as the *Wolpe–Eysenck school.*

In the early 1960s, Wolpe moved to the United States where he began a program at Temple University in which he trained therapists in systematic desensitization. In 1963, Eysenck founded the journal *Behaviour Research and Therapy*. On June 30, 1984, the behavior therapy unit at Temple University Medical Center ceased to exist. Wolpe (1985) attributed termination of the unit to misunderstanding of behavior therapy by psychodynamic psychotherapists. Nevertheless, Wolpe continued to contribute actively to the field of behavior therapy until his death in 1997.

The highlights of the development of the Pavlovian–Wolpe orientation prior to the 1980s are presented in the bottom panel of Table 29–1.

Study Questions

1. Describe how Pavlov demonstrated Pavlovian conditioning with dogs.
2. What are two other names for Pavlovian conditioning?
3. Describe how Watson and Rayner demonstrated Pavlovian conditioning of a fear response in an 11-month-old infant.
4. How did Joseph Wolpe extend the principle of reciprocal inhibition?
5. What did Wolpe call his procedure for using relaxation to inhibit a learned fear?
6. What role did Hans Eysenck play in the development of behavior therapy in the 1950s?

THE OPERANT-CONDITIONING ORIENTATION: APPLIED BEHAVIOR ANALYSIS

Pavlovian conditioning is a type of learning that involves reflexes—automatic responses to prior stimuli. However, much of our behavior is influenced by its consequences rather than by prior stimuli. B. F. Skinner was the first psychologist to make a clear distinction between behavior that is elicited by stimuli and behavior that is controlled by its consequences. The former he termed *respondent behavior* and the latter he termed *operant behavior*. Hence, Skinner's term for Pavlovian conditioning was *respondent conditioning* (which is the term that we consistently use for Pavlovian conditioning in the other chapters of this text and in the remainder of this chapter).

Skinner was strongly influenced by Watson's behaviorism and by Pavlov's experimental approach but believed that a different methodology was needed to study operant behavior. In 1932, he described an apparatus that contained a lever that a laboratory rat could press and a mechanism for dispensing food pellets to reinforce the rat's lever pressing. Others have since called his experimental chamber a *Skinner box.*

In 1938, B. F. Skinner described his research in the book *The Behavior of Organisms: An* NOTE 3 *Experimental Analysis* in which he outlined the basic principles of operant conditioning—a type of learning in which behavior is modified by its consequences. This pioneering work influenced other experimental psychologists to begin studying operant conditioning.

In 1950, Fred S. Keller and William N. Schoenfeld wrote an introductory psychology text, *Principles of Psychology: A Systematic Text in the Science of Behavior.* This text differed from NOTE 4 other introductory psychology texts in that it discussed traditional topics in psychology—such as

TABLE 29–1	Some Historical Highlights of Behavior Modification and Behavior Therapy Prior to 1980		
	Pre-1950s	**1950s**	**Early and Middle 1960s**
THE OPERANT CONDITIONING ORIENTATION: APPLIED BEHAVIOR ANALYSIS	Some basic research and theory (Skinner, 1938)	Two major texts (Keller & Schoenfeld, 1950; Skinner, 1953) Some human studies and applications: profoundly retarded (Fuller, 1949), schizophrenics (Lindsley, 1956), psychotics (Ayllon & Michael, 1959), verbal conditioning (Greenspoon, 1955), stuttering (Flanagan, Goldiamond, & Azrin, 1958) A basic operant research journal, with some applications (*Journal of the Experimental Analysis of Behavior*, 1958–)	Some major university training centers Several books of readings (e.g., Ulrich, Stachnik, & Mabry, 1966) More applications, many to "resistant" populations: e.g., retardation (Birnbrauer, Bijou, Wolf, & Kidder, 1965; Girardeau & Spradlin, 1964), autism (Ferster & DeMyer, 1962; Lovaas, 1966; Wolf, Risley, & Mees, 1964), hyperactivity (Patterson, 1965), delinquency (Schwitzgebel, 1964), psychotics (Isaacs, Thomas, & Goldiamond, 1960; Haughton & Ayllon, 1965) Child development (Bijou & Baer, 1961)
OFFSHOOTS AND MIXTURES			Premack Principle (Premack, 1965) Coverant control (Homme, 1965) Precision teaching (Lindsley, 1966) Modeling (Bandura & Walters, 1963) A major book of readings (Ullmann & Krasner, 1965) An applied journal (*Behavior Research and Therapy*, 1963–) Covert sensitization (Cautela, 1966)
THE PAVLOVIAN–WOLPEAN ORIENTATION	Some basic research and theory (Pavlov, 1927; Watson & Rayner, 1920) An early application of fear desensitization (Jones, 1924) An early application of assertion training (Salter, 1949)	Two major texts (Dollard & Miller, 1950; Wolpe, 1958) Applications of systematic desensitization, assertion training, and aversion therapy to a variety of phobias and behavioral excesses Comparisons of behavior therapy and psychotherapy (Eysenck, 1959)	Some major university training centers Several books of readings (e.g., Eysenck, 1960; Franks, 1964) More applications of systematic desensitization, assertion training, and aversion therapy to a variety of classic neurotic behaviors and sexual disorders

TABLE 29–1	(Continued)	

Late 1960s	1970s
Additional major university training centers	Many "how-to-do-it" books in a variety of areas
Isolated undergraduate and graduate courses in many universities	Behavior modification procedures described for many "traditional" areas of psychology (e.g., social, developmental, personality, abnormal, and clinical)
Additional books describing applied research and procedures applicable to a variety of areas: e.g., education (Skinner, 1968), parenting (Patterson & Gullion, 1968), community work (Tharp & Wetzel, 1969), mental hospitals (Schaefer & Martin, 1969)	Many other helping professions adopting behavior modification procedures (see Chapter 2)
	Wide variety of individual, institutional, and community applications and research
Additional applications to a variety of areas, including self-control, delinquency, university teaching, marriage counseling, sexual behaviors, and academic skills	
An applied journal (Journal of Applied Behavior Analysis, 1968–)	
Token economies (Ayllon & Azrin, 1968)	Emergence of cognitive behavior modification, social learning theory, and eclectic behavior therapy
Contingency contracting (Homme, Csanyi, Gonzales, & Rechs, 1969)	Numerous behavior modification–behavior therapy conferences and workshops
Formulation of social learning theory (Bandura, 1969)	Concern for behavior modification–behavior therapy as a profession, and for controls against misapplications
Two major books (Bandura, 1969; Franks, 1969)	
Implosive therapy (Stampfl & Levis, 1967)	Mixed paraprofessional and professional organizations (e.g., Association for Behavior Analysis, 1974–)
	Professional organizations (Association for the Advancement of Behavior Therapy, 1970–; Behavior Research and Therapy Society, 1970–; European Association of Behavior Therapy, 1971–)
	More journals specializing in behavior modification (see Note 2 in Chapter 2)
Several major university training centers	Many additional books, publications, and training workshops; much additional research
Additional books (e.g., Wolpe, 1969)	
More applications to phobias, anger, asthmatic attacks, frigidity, homosexuality, insomnia, speech disorders, exhibitionism, and other behaviors	

learning, perception, concept formation, motivation, and emotion—in terms of operant and respondent conditioning principles. Keller and Skinner had been graduate students together at Harvard University, and the Keller and Schoenfeld text was inspired largely by the work and writings of Skinner. *Principles of Psychology* had an important impact within the operant tradition.

In 1953, Skinner published his book *Science and Human Behavior*. Like the Keller and Schoenfeld text, this book was also written as an introductory psychology text; however, it extended to topics—such as government and law, religion, economics, education, and culture—not usually covered in introductory psychology texts. In this book, he offered his interpretation of how the basic behavior principles (see Part II of this text) influence the behavior of people in all kinds of situations. Although little supporting data existed for Skinner's generalizations to humans at that time, his interpretations influenced others to begin examining the effects of reinforcement variables on human behavior in a number of basic and applied research studies.

NOTE 5

Many of the reports in the 1950s were demonstrations that consequences affect human behavior in predictable ways or single-case demonstrations that an application of a behavioral program could effect a desired behavior change. For example, Fuller (1949) reported a case in which an institutionalized bedridden adult with profound intellectual disability was taught to raise his arm to a vertical position when arm movements were reinforced with a warm sugar-milk solution. Joel Greenspoon (1955) demonstrated that a simple social consequence (saying "mmm-hmm") could influence college students to say certain types of words. Nathan Azrin and Ogden Lindsley (1956), two of Skinner's graduate students, demonstrated that jelly bean reinforcement could influence pairs of young children to cooperate in playing a simple game. Each of these experiments demonstrated that consequences influence human behavior in predictable ways. None of these experiments, however, was primarily practically oriented. One of the first published reports of the 1950s that concerned practical, applied problems was that of Teodoro Ayllon and Jack Michael (1959). With Michael as his Ph.D. dissertation advisor, Ayllon conducted a number of behavioral demonstrations at the Saskatchewan Hospital, a psychiatric institution in Weyburn, Saskatchewan, Canada. These demonstrations showed how staff could use behavioral procedures to modify patient behaviors such as delusional talk, refusals to eat, and various disruptive behaviors.

Following Ayllon and Michael's article and several subsequent papers published by Ayllon and his colleagues from their work at Weyburn, similar demonstrations of behavioral control began to appear with some frequency in the early 1960s (see the top panel in Table 29–1). This early work was characterized by two features: (a) Much of it was done with very resistant populations, such as persons with intellectual disabilities, children with autism, and severely regressed psychiatric patients who had not received a great deal of successful input from traditional psychology and (b) many of the applications took place in institutional or highly controlled settings. A notable exception to this early trend is Sidney Bijou and Donald Baer's (1961) interpretation of child development from a strictly behavioral perspective.

In 1965, Leonard Ullmann and Leonard Krasner published an influential collection of readings, *Case Studies in Behavior Modification*. This was the first book with "behavior modification" in its title. In addition to collecting a number of case histories and research reports by other authors, Ullmann and Krasner compared two models of abnormal behavior. The *behavioral model of abnormal behavior* suggests that abnormal behavior is a function of specifiable environmental causes and that it is possible to rearrange the environment in such a way that the behavior can be changed or improved. They found in contrast that Sigmund Freud's proposed *medical model of abnormal behavior* viewed abnormal behavior as a symptom of an underlying disturbance in a personality mechanism with the implication that one must treat the underlying personality disturbance through Freudian psychoanalysis rather than treating the observed symptoms by rearranging the environment. Freud's model of abnormal behavior was adapted from the model in physical medicine in which germs, viruses, lesions, and other disturbances lead to the production of symptoms in the functioning of normal humans. The Ullmann and Krasner book included studies from both operant and the Pavlovian orientations, and it undoubtedly had a significant impact on furthering behavior modification and providing, in a single source, information on much of the preliminary work in this area. In 1965, Krasner and Ullmann followed up their previous book with an edited book of research studies titled *Research in Behavior Modification.*

In the late 1960s, the operant conditioning orientation began to spread throughout the Western Hemisphere. Several university training centers were developed; many universities initiated at least one or two courses in behavior modification at both the graduate and undergraduate levels, and applications spread to normal school settings, university teaching, homes, and other populations and locations.

By the 1970s, the operant orientation had grown considerably. As discussed in Chapter 1, this approach is frequently referred to as *applied behavior analysis*. It is surprising to find contemporary textbooks that suggest that this approach has been used primarily on client populations with "limited cognitive capacity" and where considerable environmental control is a potential characteristic of the treatment procedures. Although this was true in the 1950s and 1960s, applications now occur with virtually all populations and settings (see Chapters 2, 27, and 28).

It has also been claimed that behavior analysts ignore the causes of problem behavior. In the early stages of behavior modification, there was some justification for this charge because behavior analysts emphasized that managing consequences could alleviate problem behavior regardless of its causes. During the 1970s, some behavior analysts (e.g., Carr, 1977; Johnson & Baumeister, 1978; Rincover, 1978; Rincover, Cook, Peoples, & Packard, 1979) began to stress the importance of understanding the causes of—that is, the conditions producing or maintaining—problem behavior. Indeed, the first edition of this text, published in 1978, contained a section titled "It Helps to Know the Causes of Behavior" in a chapter that evolved into Chapter 23 of this edition.

The growing emphasis on understanding the causes of problem behavior led to the pioneering of functional analysis by Brian Iwata and his colleagues (Iwata, Dorsey, Slifer, Bauman, & Richman,1982). Functional analysis is the discovery of controlling variables (antecedents and consequences) for behavior by directly assessing their effects on behavior. A number of prominent behavior analysts hailed functional analysis as a major new development in the field. In 1994, the *Journal of Applied Behavior Analysis* published a special issue (Vol. 27, No. 2) devoted to functional analysis approaches to behavioral assessment and treatment (discussed in Chapter 23), and this area continues to be a highly active area of research and application (e.g., Dufrene, Watson, & Kazmerski, 2008; Hanley, Iwata, & McCord, 2003; Langdon, Carr, & Owen-DeSchryver, 2008). It should be noted that the causes that functional analysis uncovers are environmental causes, not hypothetical inner causes of the medical model that are often speculated about by nonbehavioral (e.g., psychoanalytic) approaches.

The highlights of the development of the operant orientation prior to the 1980s are presented in the top panel of Table 29–1.

Study Questions

7. What is operant conditioning?
8. In what way was the Keller and Schoenfeld book *Principles of Psychology* unlike other introductory psychology texts of its day?
9. How did Skinner's *Science and Human Behavior* influence the initial development of behavior modification?
10. Many of the early reports in the operant tradition in the 1950s were straightforward experiments that demonstrated that consequences influence human behavior. Briefly, describe two such experiments.
11. Briefly describe one of the first published reports (a very influential one) that concerned practical applications within the operant tradition.
12. The publications of the early 1960s within the operant orientation seem to have been characterized by two features. What were they?
13. Was the influential book *Case Studies in Behavior Modification* strictly within the operant orientation? Why or why not?
14. Distinguish between the behavioral model and the medical model of abnormal behavior.
15. What is another name for the operant orientation?

MIXTURES AND OFFSHOOTS OF THE TWO MAJOR ORIENTATIONS

Much of the early history of behavior modification and behavior therapy clearly falls within either the operant orientation or the Pavlovian–Wolpean orientation. Most other early developments tended to be offshoots of one or the other of these traditions or fall in a gray area somewhere between (see the middle panel of Table 29–1).

One major "mixture" was *social learning theory,* first outlined by Julian Rotter in 1954 in his book *Social Learning and Clinical Psychology.* The most influential of the social learning theorists, however, has been Albert Bandura (1969, 1977, 1986, 1996). His approach is "social" in the sense that it places great emphasis on the social contexts in which behavior is acquired and maintained. In addition to basic principles of respondent and operant conditioning, Bandura has strongly emphasized the importance of *observational learning.* By watching other people act and by observing what happens to them, we can then imitate their behavior (see the discussion of modeling in Chapter 18). Bandura also emphasizes cognitive processes as an important influence on behavior. *Cognitive processes* refer to things that we say to ourselves or imagine, which are frequently called "believing," "thinking," and "expecting." An important cognitive process, for example, is what Bandura calls *self-efficacy* (Bandura, 1982, 1996). This refers to a belief that a person can perform adequately in a particular situation. In Bandura's words, "Given appropriate skills and adequate incentives . . . efficacy expectations are a major determinant of peoples' choices of activities, how much effort they will expend, and how long they will sustain effort in dealing with stressful situations" (1977, p. 194). (See Chapter 27 for discussion of how cognitions can be explained in terms of operant and respondent conditioning.)

Another mixture that emerged in the 1960s and 70s is referred to as *cognitive behavior modification* or *cognitive behavior therapy* (see Chapter 27). Therapists such as Albert Ellis (1962) and Aaron Beck (1970) believed that faulty cognitive processes (i.e., faulty thinking) causes emotional and behavioral problems. Ellis and Beck independently developed approaches to therapy that focused on helping clients recognize and change faulty thinking.

Cognitive behavior modification, now more commonly called *cognitive behavior therapy,* is to be distinguished from social learning theory. Social learning theory, with its emphasis on the regulation of behavior by Pavlovian conditioning, operant conditioning, and cognitive processes, provides a way of explaining behavior. Cognitive behavior therapy has focused mainly on explaining maladaptive behaviors in terms of dysfunctional thinking and includes a method called *cognitive restructuring* as the primary treatment component for modifying dysfunctional thinking.

In addition to these theoretical models of behavior modification—the Pavlovian–Wolpean orientation, the operant orientation, and the mixtures and offshoots of each—some early practicing behavior therapists subscribed to an eclectic approach that includes more traditional components. Arnold Lazarus is representative of this position. Referring to what he called *multimodal behavior therapy,* Lazarus (1971, 1976) argued that practicing clinicians should not restrict themselves to a particular theoretical framework but should use a variety of behavioral and nonbehavioral techniques provided that the techniques have some empirical support.

As indicated by this brief discussion of various conceptualizations of behavior modification, although there is some disagreement among behavior modifiers on theoretical issues, there is also considerable agreement.

Study Questions

16. What are the names of two major behavior modification/behavior therapy journals first published in the 1960's (see Table 29–1)?
17. What does the term *cognitive processes* mean?
18. Briefly, how did cognitive therapists Ellis and Beck explain emotional problems, and how did they propose to treat them?
19. What is a major emphasis of social learning theory, and who was its most influential proponent?

THE TERMS BEHAVIOR MODIFICATION, BEHAVIOR THERAPY, COGNITIVE BEHAVIOR MODIFICATION, AND APPLIED BEHAVIOR ANALYSIS

Some writers use the terms *behavior modification* and *behavior therapy* interchangeably. Other writers use *applied behavior analysis* when referring to the principles discussed in Chapters 3 through 15. What is the historical use of these terms? It appears that Lindsley, Skinner, and Solomon (1953) were the first to use the term *behavior therapy.* They did so in a report describing some research in which psychotic patients in a mental hospital were reinforced with candy or cigarettes for pulling a plunger. (For a discussion of the early laboratory contributions of Lindsley and Skinner to the formation of behavior therapy, see Reed & Luiselli, 2009.) However, those within the operant orientation subsequently made little use of the term (at least, until the 1970s). Although Lazarus (1958) next used the term *behavior therapy* when he applied it to Wolpe's reciprocal inhibition framework, the term became popular among those within the Pavlovian–Wolpean orientation after Eysenck (1959) used it to describe procedures published by Wolpe.

The first use of the term *behavior modification* appears to be as a section heading in a chapter by R. I. Watson (1962). In the 1960s and 70s, many writers distinguished between behavior modification, with its roots in operant conditioning, and behavior therapy, with its roots in Pavlovian conditioning. Others, however, did not make that distinction consistently. For example, Ullmann and Krasner (1965) frequently used *behavior modification* and *behavior therapy* interchangeably.

There are some interesting historic connections between behavior modification and humanistic psychology. Watson (1962) credited Carl Rogers, a founder of humanistic psychology, with having "launched the research approach in behavioral modification through psychotherapy" (p. 21); and Ullmann (1980), reflecting on his and Krasner's decision to use *behavior modification* in the title of their case-studies book, credited Rogers for the idea to use that term as opposed to behavior therapy.

Skinner's subtitle for his 1938 book *The Behavior of Organisms* was *An Experimental Analysis*. The words *behavior* and *analysis* were to become prominent in the operant orientation. In 1957, a group of Skinner's followers founded the Society for the Experimental Analysis of Behavior (SEAB). In 1958, SEAB began to publish the *Journal of the Experimental Analysis of Behavior,* which, as stated in the inside cover of each issue, "is primarily for the original publication of experiments relevant to the behavior of individual organisms." In 1968, SEAB began to publish the *Journal of Applied Behavior Analysis,* which, as stated in the inside cover of each issue, "is primarily for the original publication of experimental research involving applications of the experimental analysis of behavior to problems of social importance." In 1974 in Chicago, a group of psychologists interested in behavior analysis founded the Midwestern Association of Behavior Analysis, which, as its membership expanded, became the Association for Behavior Analysis (ABA) in 1978 and finally the Association for Behavior Analysis International (ABAI) in 2007. ABAI publishes several journals: *The Behavior Analyst* (begun in 1978), *The Analysis of Verbal Behavior* (purchased by ABAI in 1994), and *Behavior Analysis in Practice* (begun in 2008). In 1991, recognizing the importance of upholding certain standards in the training of behavior analysts, ABA established a process for accrediting graduate programs in behavior analysis. In 1998, another group of behavior analysts established a nonprofit corporation called the Behavior Analysis Certification Board, whose purpose, as stated on its website (www.bacb.com), is "to meet professional credentialing needs identified by behavior analysts, governments, and consumers of behavior analysis services."

Some of the distinctions that have tended to characterize the uses of the terms *behavior therapy, behavior modification, cognitive behavior modification,* and *applied behavior analysis* are presented in Table 29–2.

In spite of the historical distinctions, the terms are often used interchangeably. In our view, *behavior modification* has acquired a broader meaning than the other terms. *Behavior therapy* and *cognitive behavior therapy* are clearly less appropriate than *applied behavior analysis* or *behavior modification* when dealing with nondysfunctional behavior. As indicated in Chapter 1, we suggest that the term *behavior modification* subsume *cognitive behavior therapy, behavior therapy,* and *applied behavior analysis*. Behavior therapy or *cognitive behavior therapy* is behavior modification carried out on dysfunctional behavior, generally in a clinical setting. *Applied behavior analysis* emphasizes the application of operant conditioning principles and is behavior modification in which there often is an attempt to analyze or clearly demonstrate controlling variables of the behavior of concern. *Behavior modification* includes cognitive behavior therapy and applied behavior analysis. It includes all explicit applications of behavior principles to improve specific behavior—whether or not in clinical settings and whether or not controlling variables have been explicitly demonstrated—which is how we have used the term in this book.

TABLE 29–2	A Comparison of the Uses of the Terms *Behavior Therapy, Cognitive Behavior Modification, Behavior Modification,* and *Applied Behavior Analysis*

1960s and 1970s

Behavior Therapy/ Cognitive Behavior Modification	Behavior Modification
1. Terms used most often by followers of the Pavlovian–Wolpean orientation and followers of the cognitive orientation	1. Term used most often by followers of the operant orientation
2. Terms tended to be used by behavioral psychologists and psychiatrists who were concerned primarily with treatment in traditional clinical settings; for a historical time line of behavior therapy in psychiatric settings, see Malatesta, AuBuchon, and Bluch, 1994	2. Term tended to be used by behavior specialists in schools, homes, and other settings that were not primarily the domain of the clinical psychologist and psychiatrist
3. Terms tended to be used to refer to behavioral treatments conducted in the therapist's office by means of verbal interaction ("talk therapy") between therapist and client	3. Term tended to be used for behavioral treatments carried out in the natural environment as well as in special training settings
4. Terms were associated with an experimental foundation that was based primarily on human studies in clinical settings	4. Term was associated with an experimental foundation in basic operant research with animals and humans in addition to experimental studies in applied settings

1980s to the Present

- The terms **behavior therapy** and **cognitive behavior modification** have generally been replaced by the term **cognitive behavior therapy**, which continues to be used as described in the left column.
- The term **applied behavior analysis** is used increasingly by followers of the operant orientation as described in the right-hand column.
- The term **behavior modification** tends to have a somewhat broader meaning and includes behavior therapy, cognitive behavior therapy, and applied behavior analysis.

THE FUTURE OF BEHAVIOR MODIFICATION

Behavior modification has been applied to a wide variety of individual and social problems. In addition, more and more of these applications have been concerned with the prevention and amelioration of existing problems. There is no doubt that the helping professions including social work, medicine, rehabilitation, nursing, education, dentistry, psychiatry, public health, and clinical and community psychology are increasingly adopting behavior modification procedures. Applications are also occurring with increasing frequency in areas such as business, industry, sports, recreation, and the promotion of healthy lifestyles (see Chapter 2). Someday a thorough knowledge of behavioral techniques might become an accepted necessity in our culture. Children will grow up to see a world in which the positive applications of behavior principles will result in an informed, skillful, productive society without war, poverty, or pollution.

Study Questions

20. Who first used the term *behavior therapy* and in what context?

21. Describe four differences in the usage of the terms *behavior therapy/cognitive behavior modification* versus *behavior modification* during the 1960s and 1970s (see Table 29–2).

22. In a sentence for each, distinguish between the terms *behavior therapy, applied behavior analysis,* and *behavior modification* as they tend to be used today.

Notes and Extended Discussion

1. The history of behavior modification is as long as the history of psychology from which it emerged. For a complete discussion of the early history of psychology and the major systems that developed during the 20th and early 21st centuries, see Pear (2007). Some of the more important precursors to the emergence of behavior modification are identified next.

Plato (427–347 B.C.) attributed behavior to something called the *psyche* (soul), which he believed is separate from the body and continues to exist even after death. His student Aristotle (384–322 B.C.) argued that the soul is the "form" or functioning of the body including its behavior. Plato's view of the soul had a greater influence than Aristotle's did on early Western European theologians and philosophers.

The French philosopher René Descartes (1595–1650) was the first to articulate a clear distinction between the body and the soul. He maintained that the body is essentially a machine operating on the basis of reflexes and guidance from a *mente* (soul or mind) comprised of an immaterial, nonspatially extended substance. A long line of philosophers in Britain—from John Locke (1632–1704) to John Stuart Mill (1806–1873)—known as the *British empiricists* contested his philosophy. In their discourses, these individuals replaced the word *soul* with the more scientific-sounding word *mind,* which stems from an Old English word pertaining to memory or thought.

A group of physiologists known as the *Russian reflexologists* or *psychoreflexologists*—most notably Ivan M. Sechenov (1829–1905) and his followers Ivan P. Pavlov (1849–1936) and Vladimir M. Bechterev (1857–1927)—picked up on Descartes' concept of reflexes and the British empiricists' focus on associations. Bechterev and Pavlov independently performed experiments on establishing new reflexes, which Bechterev called "association reflexes" and Pavlov called "conditional reflexes."

In the United States, a group of psychologists called *functionalists,* led primarily by William James (1842–1910) at Harvard and John Dewey (1859–1952) at the University of Chicago, basing their approach on Darwin's theory of evolution, advocated studying the mind's role in the adaptation of the individual to the environment. This included both animal and human studies on learning, such as those of E. L. Thorndike (1874–1949).

John B. Watson (1878–1958) took functionalism a step further. He asserted that psychology, rather than being about the mind, should be purely the science of behavior. Following Watson's exit from academic psychology, the behavioral approach opened to a new generation of leaders.

2. In the 1950s, important historical developments in behavior modification occurred concurrently in three countries: in South Africa, where Wolpe conducted his pioneering work on systematic desensitization; in England, where Eysenck spurred on the behavior modification movement by emphasizing dissatisfaction with traditional methods of psychotherapy; and in the United States, where Skinner and his colleagues were working within the operant conditioning orientation. During the 1960s and 1970s, however, most of the major books and research papers in behavior modification and behavior therapy were based on developments in the United States. For example, three of the first four major behavior therapy journals were published in the United States, and most of their articles were written in the United States (*Journal of Applied Behavior Analysis,* 1968–the present); *Behavior Therapy,* 1970; *Behavior Therapy and Experimental Psychiatry,* 1970–the present). Although the fourth journal (*Behaviour Research and Therapy,* 1963–the present) was edited by Eysenck in England, it too contained a large number of U.S. research reports. Since the 1970s, however, behavior modification has become a truly worldwide movement. Significant developments have occurred in Argentina (Blanck, 1983); in Asia (Oei, 1998); in Australia (Brownell, 1981; King, 1996; Schlesinger, 2004); in Brazil (Ardila, 1982; Grassi, 2004); in Canada (Martin, 1981); in Chile (Ardilla, 1982); in Colombia (Ardilla, 1982; Lopez & Aquilar, 2003); in Costa Rica (Pal-Hegedus, 1991); in Cuba (Dattilio, 1999); in the Dominican Republic (Brownell, 1981); in England (Brownell, 1981); in France (Agathon, 1982; Cottraux, 1990); in Germany (Stark, 1980); in Ghana (Danguah, 1982); in Holland (Brownell, 1981); in Hungary (Tringer, 1991); in Israel (Brownell, 1981; Zvi, 2004); in Italy (Moderato, 2003; Sanivio, 1999; Scrimali & Grimaldi, 1993); in Ireland (Flanagan, 1991); in Japan (Sakano, 1993; Yamagami, Okuma, Morinaga, & Nakao, 1982); in Mexico (Ardilla, 1982); in New Zealand (Blampied, 1999, 2004); in Norway (Brownell, 1981); in Poland (Kokoszka, Popiel, & Sitarz, 2000; Suchowierska & Kozlowski, 2004); in Romania (David & Miclea, 2002); in Singapore (Banerjee, 1999); in Spain (Caballo & Buela-Casal, 1993); in South Korea (Kim, 2003); in Sri Lanka (DeSilva & Simarasinghe, 1985); in Sweden (Brownell, 1981; Carter, 2004); in Thailand (Mikulis, 1983); in the United Kingdom (Dymond, Chiesa, & Martin, 2003); in Uruguay (Zamora & Lima, 2000); and in Venezuela (Ardila, 1982). In the September, 2009 issue of *Inside Behavior Analysis,* discussion can be found of behavior analysis in Brazil, China, Colombia, India, Ireland, Israel, Italy, Japan, Mexico, New Zealand, the Philippines, Poland, Sweden, Taiwan, and the United Kingdom.

3. Burrhus Frederick Skinner (1904–1990) had a remarkable career and received numerous awards, including the Distinguished Scientific Award from the American Psychological Association (1958), the President's National Medal of Science (1968), and the Humanist of the Year Award from the American Humanist Society (1972). In addition to his basic theoretical and experimental contributions, Skinner published a utopian novel, *Walden Two* (1948b), worked on a project to teach pigeons to guide missiles during World War II (Skinner, 1960), and developed the concept of programmed instruction and teaching machines (Skinner, 1958). He continued to be active throughout his academic career, publishing his last book in 1989.

4. Fred S. Keller (1899–1996), B. F. Skinner's friend and colleague, made other major contributions. In 1961, he accepted a position at the University of São Paulo, Brazil, where he established the first operant conditioning course and developed the personalized system of instruction, a behavior modification approach to university teaching (see Chapter 2). Keller contributed immeasurably to the development of behavior modification in Brazil. Former students of his, their students, and so on, continue to advance behavioral psychology in that country (e.g., see Grassi, 2004).

5. Clark Hull (1884–1952), an early contemporary of Skinner, developed a learning theory that meshed together operant and respondent conditioning into a theory that did not distinguish between the two types of conditioning. According to Hull (1943, 1952), reinforcement was involved in respondent as well as in operant conditioning. Hull did not attempt to interpret a wide variety of human behavior to the extent done by Skinner (1953, 1957). Two other psychologists, John Dollard and Neal Miller (1950), however, translated Freudian

psychodynamic concepts into the language of Hull's learning theory. Dollard and Miller's book and the writings of another learning theorist, Edwin Guthrie (1935) were influential mainly in the Pavlovian and Wolpean orientation.

Study Questions on Notes

1. How did Aristotle's view of the soul differ from that of Plato's?
2. Briefly state a contribution each of the following made to the behavioral approach:
   a. Descartes
   b. the British empiricists
   c. the Russian reflexologists
   d. the functionalists
3. Name three countries that were important in the development of behavior modification in the 1950s and the person most associated with this development in each of these countries.
4. Cite three of Skinner's contributions other than his basic research and theoretical writings.
5. In what Latin American country did Keller accept an academic position in 1961, and what contribution did he make to behavior modification while there?
6. To which of the two major orientations did Hull, and Dollard and Miller mainly contribute?

30 Ethical Issues

Throughout this book, we have emphasized the ethical or moral concerns that one should always bear in mind when applying behavior modification. It would be a great tragedy if this powerful scientific technology were used in ways that harmed rather than helped humanity. Because this is a real danger, it is fitting that we devote the final chapter of this book to a more detailed discussion of ethical concerns.

The history of civilization is a continuous story of the abuse of power. Throughout the ages, powerful people have used the reinforcers and punishers at their disposal to control the behavior of people who had fewer reinforcers and punishers to deliver or the means to deliver them contingent on selected target behaviors. The effect of this tradition has been to increase the reinforcements occurring to the more powerful at the expense of those occurring to the less powerful. From time to time, as the proportion of total reinforcement allotted to them steadily dwindled, people subjected to this abuse of power have successfully revolted against their oppressors and have modified existing social structures or established new ones to check or eliminate the possibility of future abuses. Constitutions, bills of rights, and related political documents of modern states can be viewed as formal specifications of contingencies designed to control the behavior of those who control the behavior of others. In Western democracies, for example, we have moved from the era of the divine right of monarchs to one of "government by laws." Moreover, with the introduction of periodic popular elections, people who are controlled by those who make the laws can exert a certain measure of reciprocal control. They can vote them out of office. In socialist and communist countries, the revolutionary process concentrated on eliminating economic abuses. In the absence of democracy, other abuses developed, and many former communist countries have become more democratic. Nevertheless, the new social designs and practices that have emerged thus far have invariably fallen short of their objective; power continues to be abused throughout the world.

Because of this cultural history and because of people's personal experiences with others who have abused their power, people have learned to react negatively to overt attempts to manage behavior. It should not be surprising, therefore, that in its early years, the term *behavior modification* evoked many negative reactions ranging from suspicion to outright hostility. These early reactions were exacerbated by the tendency to mistakenly equate behavior modification with such invasive procedures as electroconvulsive shock therapy, brainwashing, and even torture. For example, a survey of the *New York Times* indicated that over a 5-year period in the 1970s, the term *behavior modification* was used incorrectly approximately 50% of the time (Turkat & Feuerstein, 1978). Today, as reports in newspapers, television, and movies illustrate, the general public is more aware that behavior modification including cognitive behavior therapy and applied behavior analysis (discussed in Chapters 1 and 29) helps individuals manage their behavior.

Systematic applications of learning principles and techniques are based on two assumptions: (a) behavior can be controlled and (b) it is desirable to do so to achieve certain objectives. Whether behavior is completely or only partially determined by environmental and genetic factors makes for interesting philosophical discussions. From a practical point of view, however, it makes little difference one way or the other. The important point is that the amount of potential control over behavior is steadily increasing as a result of new discoveries in behavioral science, refinements in behavioral technology, and advances in Internet communication that makes these discoveries increasingly available to more and more people around the world.

Extreme wariness is a healthy reaction to any new advance in science or technology. Perhaps civilization would be in less danger today if more precautions had been taken early in the development of atomic energy. The solution to the present problems stemming from scientific and technological advances, however, does not lie in attempting to turn the clock back to a seemingly more secure, prescientific era. Science and technology are not the problem. They are merely highly sophisticated means that people have developed for solving problems. The real problem is that people frequently misuse these tools. This is, of course, a behavioral problem. It would seem, therefore, as Skinner (1953, 1971) argued, that the science of behavior is the logical key to the solution of that problem. As with other powerful sciences and technologies, however, behavior modification can be misused. It therefore is important to have ethical guidelines to ensure that it is used for the good of society. In the next section, we discuss ethics from a behavioral perspective. Then we examine some common arguments against deliberately changing behavior. Finally, we turn to the question of how safeguards can be imposed on behavior modification to ensure that it will always be used in the best interests of humanity.

Study Questions

1. Describe in behavioral terms how the history of civilization is a story of the continuous abuse of power. From your knowledge of history or current events, give an example of this abuse.
2. From your knowledge of history or current events, give an example of what often happens when the reinforcements occurring to one group in a society fall below a certain critical level relative to the reinforcements occurring to another group in that society.
3. From a behavioral point of view, how might we account for constitutions, bills of rights, and related political documents of modern states?
4. Explain why we tend to react negatively to all overt attempts to control our behavior.
5. Why and how do people who would control our behavior disguise their aims? Give an example of this that is not in the text.
6. State two propositions on which behavior modification is based.
7. Why is extreme wariness a healthy reaction to any new development in science or technology? Discuss an example of this.

A BEHAVIORAL VIEW OF ETHICS

From a behavioral point of view, the term *ethics* refers to certain standards of behavior that a culture developed to promote the survival of that culture (Skinner, 1953, 1971). For example, stealing is considered unethical or wrong in many cultures because of the disruptive effect it has on the culture. Many ethical guidelines, such as "stealing is wrong," likely evolved during prehistoric times. It might be that among a number of cultures that existed before recorded history, respecting the possessions of others happened to be socially reinforced and stealing happened to be punished in some of these cultures but not in others. Cultures in which respecting others' possessions was not reinforced, however, tended not to survive. There are a number of possible reasons for this. Perhaps the members of cultures that did not reinforce respecting others' possessions put so much effort into fighting each other that they were vulnerable to invasions from other cultures or they did not have enough time or energy to provide an adequate amount of food for themselves. Perhaps these cultures were so unreinforcing to their members that the members defected in large numbers to other groups, so that their former cultures became extinct due to lack of membership. Whatever the case, many cultures that reinforced respecting others' possessions—that is, cultures that considered not stealing ethical or right and stealing unethical or wrong—survived.

Thus, ethics evolved as part of our culture in much the same way that parts of our bodies evolved; that is, ethics contributed to the survival of our culture in much the same way that fingers and an opposable thumb have contributed to the survival of our species. This is not to say that people do not, at times, deliberately decide to formulate ethical rules for their culture. It is part of a cultural evolutionary process that at some point members of a culture begin to engage in such behavior because they have been conditioned to work toward the survival of their culture. One way in which to work toward the survival of one's culture is to formulate and enforce a code of ethics that strengthens that culture through reinforcement as well as punishment.

Ethical guidelines are important sources of behavioral control when immediate reinforcers influence an individual to behave in a way that leads to aversive stimuli for others. For example, whereas a thief is immediately reinforced by possession of the stolen goods, loss of those goods is aversive to the victims. To influence its members to be honest with each other, a culture might therefore develop and enforce the ethical guideline "You shall not steal." Sometimes such guidelines are formulated into rules that specify legal contingencies (e.g., "If you steal, you will be fined or sent to jail"). Sometimes such guidelines are formulated into rules that imply contingencies based on religious beliefs (e.g., "If you obey God's commandment to not steal, you will go to heaven when you die"). When members of a culture learn to follow such ethical guidelines, the guidelines exert rule-governed control over behavior (see Chapter 17). This is one way that people learn to emit behavior that is ethical and to refrain from behavior that is unethical.

With this behavioral view of ethics in mind, let's now examine whether behavior modifiers should attempt to deliberately change the behavior of others.

ARGUMENTS AGAINST DELIBERATELY CONTROLLING BEHAVIOR

As we indicated earlier, because of our knowledge of the abuse of power throughout history and because of our personal experience with others who have abused their power, we have learned to react negatively to overt attempts to change our behavior. Perhaps for these reasons it is some-   **NOTE 1** times argued that all attempts to control behavior are unethical. However, a little reflection shows that the goal of any social help profession (e.g., education, psychology, and psychiatry) can be achieved only to the extent that the practitioners of that profession exert control over behavior. For example, the goal of education is to change behavior so that students respond differently to their environment. To teach a person to read is to change the way that person responds to signs, newspapers, books, email, and other items containing written or printed words. The goals of counseling, psychological treatment, and psychiatry likewise involve changing people's behavior so that they can function more effectively than they did prior to receiving professional help.

Perhaps because of people's negative reactions to overt attempts to change behavior, many members of the helping professions do not like to think that they are controlling behavior. They prefer to see themselves as merely helping their clients achieve control over their own behavior. Establishing self-control, however, is also a form of behavioral control. One teaches someone to emit behavior that controls that individual's other behavior in some desired fashion (see Chapter 26). To do this, it is necessary to manage the behavior involved in self-control. The helping practitioner might object that this is nevertheless not control because the external influence over the client's behavior is withdrawn as soon as the practitioner is sure that the client is able to manage his or her own behavior. Actually, as we emphasize repeatedly throughout this book, the practitioner has shifted the control to the natural environment. One may speak of this as "withdrawing control," but the control still continues although its form has changed. If the practitioner has been successful in achieving the behavioral objectives, the desired behavior will be maintained and in that sense, the practitioner's initial influence over the behavior will persist.

Some people argue that deliberately planning to change behavior is "cold" and "mechanical" and believe that it interferes with "warm," "loving," "spontaneous" relationships that should exist between persons. Determining where this objection to planning comes from is difficult because we know of no logical or empirical evidence that supports it. On the contrary, most behavior modification programs that we know about are characterized by friendly, warm interactions between the individuals involved. Good behavior modifiers are genuinely interested in people and find the time to interact with their clients on a personal level just as other helping practitioners do. Moreover, in the absence of an empathic relationship, clients will resist complying with behavior therapists' requests for conducting various self-monitoring and homework assignments (Hersen, 1983; Martin & Worthington, 1982; Messer & Winokur, 1984). Although some people in all professions appear to be cold and mechanical, it is our impression that such people are no more common among behavior modifiers than they are among any other group in the helping professions.

Conversely, a lack of planning can be disastrous. For illustrations of this, refer to the "Pitfalls" sections in Part II in which we give numerous examples of how behavior principles and processes can work to the disadvantage of those who are ignorant of them or who do not plan for them. A practitioner who is not skillful in constructing programs for developing desirable behavior is apt to unwittingly introduce contingencies that develop undesirable behavior.

While it is often necessary to change, manage, influence, or otherwise control behavior, *it is also necessary to ensure that this is done ethically*. We have argued throughout this book that we are likely to achieve desirable behavioral change if we practice research-based principles and procedures of behavior modification. We turn now to ethical guidelines for doing so.

Study Questions

8. From a behavioral point of view, what does the term *ethics* mean?

9. Describe how ethics has evolved as a part of our culture.

10. In a sentence explain when, from a behavioral point of view, ethical guidelines represent an important source of behavioral control.

11. Using an example, explain how ethical guidelines involve rule-governed control over behavior.

12. Explain why all helping professions are involved in the control of behavior whether or not their practitioners realize it. Give an example.

13. Discuss the relative merits of planning versus not planning for behavior change.

ETHICAL GUIDELINES

Having a set of guidelines that describe ethical applications of behavior modification is important. However, simply resolving to treat various individuals and groups in ethical ways is not a sufficient guarantee that they will be so treated. Contingencies of reinforcement must be arranged to make this happen. One way to arrange such contingencies is through *countercontrol.* This is "the reciprocal of control; it is the influence the controllee has on the controller by virtue of access to suitable reinforcers" (Stoltz & Associates, 1978, p. 19). For example, in a democracy, voters exert countercontrol over elected officials because they can vote them out of office. Similarly, a client can stop seeing a therapist as a form of countercontrol if the therapist does not conform to prearranged treatment guidelines. Some individuals in treatment programs, however, such as children, psychiatric patients, geriatric patients, and persons with severe developmental disabilities, might lack meaningful forms of countercontrol. In such cases, other ethical safeguards are necessary. These safeguards require that the behavior modifier be held accountable to a recognized individual or group for applying acceptable procedures and producing satisfactory results.

Various groups and organizations have addressed the ethical issues involved in the application of behavior modification. Three highly reputable organizations that have done so are the Association for the Advancement of Behavior Therapy (AABT), now called the Association for Behavioral and Cognitive Therapies (ABCT), the American Psychological Association (APA), and the Association for Behavior Analysis (ABA), now called the Association for Behavior Analysis International (ABAI).

In 1977, in its journal *Behavior Therapy,* the AABT published a set of basic ethical questions that should always be asked with regard to any behavioral program. These questions are reprinted in Table 30–1. Most of these points are made frequently throughout this book, especially in Chapter 24. If you are carrying out a behavior modification program and answer no to any of these questions, it is extremely likely that the ethics of what you are doing would be considered questionable by any recognized group of behavior modifiers or behavior therapists. It should be noted that these ethical questions are relevant not only to behavior modifiers, cognitive behavior therapists, and applied behavior analysts but also to all providers of human services.

In 1978, a commission appointed by the APA published a comprehensive report (Stolz & Associates, 1978) on the ethical issues involved in behavior modification. A primary conclusion of the commission was that persons engaged in any type of psychological intervention should subscribe to and follow the ethics codes and standards of their professions. For members of the APA and the Canadian Psychological Association, the current version of the ethics code is the APA's *Ethical Principles of Psychologists and Code of Conduct* (2002). This document includes a set of general principles that are intended to guide psychologists toward the very highest ethical ideals of the profession and a detailed set of standards to encourage ethical behavior by psychologists and their students.

TABLE 30–1   Ethical Issues for Human Services

The focus of this statement is on critical issues of central importance to human services. The statement is not a list of prescriptions and proscriptions.

On each of the issues described, ideal interventions would have maximum involvement by the person whose behavior is to be changed, and the fullest possible consideration of societal pressures on that person, the therapist, and the therapist's employer. It is recognized that the practicalities of actual settings sometimes require exceptions and that there certainly are occasions when exceptions can be consistent with ethical practice.

In the list of issues, the term "client" is used to describe the person whose behavior is to be changed; "therapist" is used to describe the professional in charge of the intervention; "treatment" and "problem," although used in the singular, refer to any and all treatments and problems being formulated with this checklist. The issues are formulated so as to be relevant across as many settings and populations as possible. Thus, they need to be qualified when someone other than the person whose behavior is to be changed is paying the therapist, or when that person's competence or the voluntary nature of that person's consent is questioned. For example, if the therapist has found that the client does not understand the goals or methods being considered, the therapist should substitute the client's guardian or other responsible person for "client," when reviewing the issues listed.

A   Have the goals of treatment been adequately considered?
1   To ensure that the goals are explicit, are they written?
2   Has the client's understanding of the goals been assured by having the client restate them orally or in writing?
3   Have the therapist and client agreed on the goals of therapy?
4   Will serving the client's interests be contrary to the interests of other persons?
5   Will serving the client's immediate interests be contrary to the client's long term interest?

B   Has the choice of treatment methods been adequately considered?
1   Does the published literature show the procedure to be the best one available for that problem?
2   If no literature exists regarding the treatment method, is the method consistent with generally accepted practice?
3   Has the client been told of alternative procedures that might be preferred by the client on the basis of significant differences in discomfort, treatment time, cost, or degree of demonstrated effectiveness?
4   If a treatment procedure is publicly, legally, or professionally controversial, has formal professional consultation been obtained, has the reaction of the affected segment of the public been adequately considered, and have the alternative treatment methods been more closely reexamined and reconsidered?

C   Is the client's participation voluntary?
1   Have possible sources of coercion on the client's participation been considered?
2   If treatment is legally mandated, has the available range of treatments and therapists been offered?
3   Can the client withdraw from treatment without a penalty or financial loss that exceeds actual clinical costs?

D   When another person or an agency is empowered to arrange for therapy, have the interests of the subordinated client been sufficiently considered?
1   Has the subordinated client been informed of the treatment objectives and participated in the choice of treatment procedures?
2   Where the subordinated client's competence to decide is limited, have the client as well as the guardian participated in the treatment discussions to the extent that the client's abilities permit?

TABLE 30-1	(Continued)

3 If the interests of the subordinated person and the superordinate persons or agency conflict, have attempts been made to reduce the conflict by dealing with both interests?

E Has the adequacy of treatment been evaluated?
  1 Have quantitative measures of the problem and its progress been obtained?
  2 Have the measures of the problem and its progress been made available to the client during treatment?

F Has the confidentiality of the treatment relationship been protected?
  1 Has the client been told who has access to the records?
  2 Are records available only to authorized persons?

G Does the therapist refer the clients to other therapists when necessary?
  1 If treatment is unsuccessful, is the client referred to other therapists?
  2 Has the client been told that if dissatisfied with the treatment, referral will be made?

H Is the therapist qualified to provide treatment?
  1 Has the therapist had training or experience in treating problems like the client's?
  2 If deficits exist in the therapist's qualifications, has the client been informed?
  3 If the therapist is not adequately qualified, is the client referred to other therapists, or has supervision by a qualified therapist been provided? Is the client informed of the supervisory relation?
  4 If the treatment is administered by mediators, have the mediators been adequately supervised by a qualified therapist?

Note: Adopted May 22, 1977, by the board of directors of the Association for Advancement of Behavior Therapy. This statement on Ethical Issues for Human Services was taken from the Membership Directory of the Association for Advancement of Behavior Therapy and is reprinted by permission of the association.

In 1988, in its journal *The Behavior Analyst,* the ABA published a statement of clients' rights (Van Houten et al., 1988) to direct both the ethical and appropriate application of behavioral treatment. The following discussion points for the ethical application of behavior modification are based on the reports by Stoltz & Associates (1978) and Van Houten and colleagues (1988).

1. Qualifications of the Behavior Modifier

Behavior modifiers must receive appropriate academic training. They must also receive appropriate supervised practical training to ensure competence in behavioral assessment, designing and implementing treatment programs, evaluating their results, and ensuring a thorough understanding of professional ethics. In cases in which a problem or treatment is complex or might pose risks, Van Houten and colleagues (1988) argue that clients have a right to direct involvement by an appropriately trained doctoral-level behavior modifier. Regardless of the level of training, the behavior modifier should always ensure that the procedures being used are consistent with the most up-to-date literature in the recognized behavior modification, behavior therapy, and applied behavior analysis journals.

If you want to carry out a behavior modification project and are not a recognized professional, you should obtain supervision from a recognized professional in the field. Such professionals are likely to be members of ABAI or ABCT and certified by the Behavior Analysis Certification Board (BACB; for more information, go to www.abainternational.org, abct.org, and www.bacb.com). Alternatively, practitioners can be certified in behavioral psychology by the

American Board of Behavioral Psychology, an affiliated board of the American Board of Professional Psychology (Nezu, 2000). The American Board of Professional Psychology develops the examination content and examination instrument used by all 50 states in the United States to license psychologists. For an excellent discussion of the BACB ethical guidelines, including practical advice on how to adhere to them illustrated with numerous examples, see Bailey and Burch (2005).

2. Definition of the Problem and Selection of Goals

NOTE 2
Target behaviors selected for modification must be those that are the most important for the client and society. The emphasis should be on establishing functional, age-appropriate skills that will enable the client greater freedom to pursue preferred activities. For individuals with severe handicaps especially, the focus should be on teaching skills that promote independent functioning. Even when improved functioning requires the elimination of problem behaviors, the goals should include developing desirable alternative behaviors. The goals should also be consistent with the basic rights of the client to dignity, privacy, and humane care.

Defining the problem and selecting the goals depend on the values of the individuals involved. For example, some people consider overt gay or lesbian tendencies to be behavior that should be modified; others do not. One form of countercontrol, therefore, is to require the behavior modifier to clearly specify his or her values relating to the client's problems. Ideally, the values on which the goals are based should be consistent with those of the client and with the long-term good of society. A second form of countercontrol is for the client to be an active participant in selecting goals and identifying target behaviors. In situations in which this is not possible (such as cases of persons with severe developmental disabilities), competent impartial third parties (e.g., ombudspersons, representatives of the community) authorized to act on behalf of a client can ensure accountability by being involved in crucial decisions concerning the selection of goals and the intervention methods.

3. Selection of Treatment

Behavior modifiers should use the most effective, empirically validated intervention methods with the least discomfort and fewest negative side effects. It is generally agreed that behavior modifiers should use the least intrusive and restrictive interventions wherever possible; however, there is no clear agreement on a continuum of intrusiveness or restrictiveness. These terms appear to be used in at least three ways.

First, interventions based on positive reinforcement are generally considered to be less intrusive and restrictive than interventions based on aversive control. That does not mean that aversive procedures should never be used. It might not be in the client's best interest for behavior modifiers to apply a slow-acting procedure if available research indicates that more aversive procedures would be more effective. As Van Houten and colleagues (1988, p. 114) expressed, "In some cases, a client's right to effective treatment might dictate the immediate use of quicker-acting, but temporarily more restrictive procedures."

Second, *intrusive* and *restrictive* sometimes refer to the extent to which clients are given choices and allowed freedom of movement in a therapeutic environment. In a work-training program for persons with developmental disabilities, for example, the assignment of specific tasks might be considered more intrusive or restrictive than allowing clients to choose among several optional work activities.

Third, *intrusive* and *restrictive* sometimes refer to the extent to which consequences are deliberately managed as opposed to naturally occurring. As indicated in Chapter 3, natural reinforcers are unprogrammed reinforcers that occur in the normal course of everyday living. Chapter 16 and elsewhere in this text stress the desirability of using natural contingencies of reinforcement whenever possible. If it is necessary to use contrived or deliberately programmed reinforcers early in a program, the behavior modifier should transfer control to natural reinforcers as quickly as possible.

While recognizing the desirability of selecting treatments that are the least intrusive and restrictive based on the three meanings of those terms previously discussed, we must remember that the most effective treatment is likely to be one that is based on a functional assessment of the causes of problem behavior as discussed in Chapter 23. As expressed by Pyles and Bailey (1990), if the causes of an individual's problem behavior can be identified through functional analysis, and if those causes can be used to implement an effective treatment, undue concern for the intrusiveness/restrictiveness issue might not be particularly helpful.

One way to ensure countercontrol is to stipulate that no program is to be carried out on a client who has not given informed consent to participate in that program (i.e., consent based on knowledge of the procedures to be used and their probable effects). Stated differently, the behavior modifier should explain alternative treatments that could be used, state their pros and cons, and give the client a choice. This collaboration between the behavior modifier and an informed client is an essential element of behavior modification, and one that serves to protect clients' rights. A mechanism to facilitate informed consent is the signing of a treatment contract that clearly outlines the objectives and methods of treatment, the framework for the service to be provided, and the contingencies for the remuneration that might be forthcoming to the therapist (as described in Chapter 24). There is, however, a problem with the concept of informed consent; namely, it involves verbal behavior that, like other behavior, is under the control of the environment. Hence, verbal behavior might be manipulated in a particular fashion that might not be in the best interests of the client. The stipulation of informed consent thus provides only a partial check on the ethics of a program. In addition, for many individuals, informed consent is inapplicable (e.g., individuals with severe developmental disabilities). Therefore, an additional way to help ensure that clients' rights are protected is by having ethical review committees composed of professionals and members of the community evaluate the ethics of proposed programs.

4. Record Keeping and Ongoing Evaluation

An important component of ensuring ethical treatment of clients is the maintenance of accurate data throughout a program. This includes a thorough behavioral assessment before the intervention is developed; ongoing monitoring of target behaviors as well as possible side effects; and appropriate follow-up evaluation after the treatment is concluded. Whereas behavior modifiers should always take good records, they should exercise utmost discretion in whom they permit to see those records. Confidentiality must be respected at all times.

Given the preceding caution, an important form of countercontrol is to provide frequent opportunities for a client to discuss with the behavior modifier the data that tracks progress throughout the program. For this, of course, the client must have access to his or her own records. Another strategy is for the behavior modifier (with the client's permission) to share the client's records with those who are directly concerned with the client's progress. Feedback on the program's effectiveness from those who are concerned directly with the client's welfare is an important accountability mechanism. As indicated in Chapter 1, the most important characteristic of behavior modification is its strong emphasis on defining problems in terms of behavior that can be measured in some way and using changes in the behavioral measure of the problem as the best indicator of the extent to which the problem is being helped. Sharing these data with all concerned parties and periodic evaluation of the data by all concerned is the cornerstone for ensuring ethical and effective treatment programs by the behavior modifiers.

CONCLUSIONS

Behavior modification has great potential to be used for the good of society. An important responsibility of behavior modifiers is to develop ethical safeguards to ensure that behavior modification is always used wisely and humanely and does not become a new tool in the oppression that has thus far characterized the human species. Of all the safeguards discussed, the most fundamental is countercontrol. Perhaps the best way for behavior modifiers to help develop effective countercontrol throughout society is to spread their skills as widely as possible and to help educate the general public with respect to behavior modification. It should be difficult to use behavioral science to the disadvantage of any group whose members are well versed in the principles and tactics of behavior modification.

Study Questions

14. Discuss countercontrol. Why is it important?
15. What was a primary conclusion of the comprehensive report by Stolz & Associates on the ethical issues involved in behavior modification?
16. What steps can be taken to help ensure that a behavior modifier is appropriately qualified?
17. State two countercontrol measures regarding the definition of problems and selection of goals.
18. In a sentence, what should be the characteristics of the intervention methods used by behavior modifiers?
19. Discuss three possible meanings of *intrusive* and *restrictive* interventions.
20. Describe a mechanism to facilitate informed consent.
21. What constitutes the cornerstone for ensuring ethical and effective treatment programs by behavior modifiers?
22. Briefly explain why it should be difficult to use behavior modification to the detriment of any group whose members are well versed in the principles and tactics of behavior modification.

Notes and Extended Discussion

1. Skinner (1971) argued that we can trace the negative reaction to behavior control, at least in part, to the influence of 18th-century revolutionaries and social reformers. To counteract the aversive control utilized by tyrants, these activists developed the concept of freedom as a rallying cry. It was, said Skinner, a worthwhile concept in its time, for it helped to spur people to break away from aversive forms of control. Now, however, we have moved into an era in which positive reinforcement is a more predominant means of control and will perhaps become increasingly so with the growth of behavior modification. The concept of freedom has therefore outlived its social usefulness. Indeed, it is harmful, in that it tends to

prevent us from seeing how our behavior is controlled by positive reinforcement. For example, many states and provincial governments in North America have turned to lotteries and casinos as ways to raise funds. Most people who happily buy lottery tickets or gamble in a casino feel that they are "free" to do so and fail to recognize that their behavior is being controlled to the same extent as it would be if they were being "forced" to pay the same amount in taxes. But the mechanism of control is different (i.e., positive reinforcement versus avoidance conditioning). Moreover, the concept of freedom encourages the view that some people deserve more "dignity" than others because of their achievements, whereas in actuality one's achievements or lack thereof are due to one's conditioning history and genetic predispositions. Hence, Skinner titled his book *Beyond Freedom and Dignity* (1971).

2. Prilleltensky (2008) has argued that psychologists (specifically community psychologists – see Chapter 2) who truly wish to help their clients should not focus only on the presenting problem of individual clients. He argues that psychologists should also focus on two other levels: the relational level and the political level. The relational level consists of the members of the community with whom the client interacts. The political level consists of the laws and regulations that affect the client. Clients who are seen by community psychologists are typically members of disadvantaged groups—i.e., groups with less power, as discussed in this chapter, than the more dominant groups in the culture. By working only at the individual level, Prilleltensky argues, psychologists tend to maintain the status quo in which the clients remain permanently disadvantaged. In contrast, by working at all three levels psychologists may be able to help shift the balance of power more toward their clients, thereby truly helping them to function more fully in society.

Study Questions on Notes

1. Discuss Skinner's view that we must go "beyond freedom and dignity" if civilization is to solve some of its most difficult problems.
2. Describe an example illustrating how governments use positive reinforcement to control behavior without citizens feeling that they are being controlled.
3. Discuss Prilleltensky's approach to community psychology.

GLOSSARY

(The following are the main technical terms used in behavior modification. Please note that many of these terms differ from their standard English dictionary definitions. For further information about these terms, check the index of this text.)

ABAB design. See *reversal-replication design.*

Acceptance. See *experiential acceptance.*

Adventitious chain. A behavioral chain that has some components that are functional in producing the reinforcer and at least one component (called the *superstitious component*) that is not.

Adventitious reinforcement. Strengthening of behavior accidentally when it is followed by a reinforcer even if the behavior did not actually produce the reinforcer.

Alternating-treatments design. An experimental design that involves rapidly alternating two or more treatment conditions. Also called a *multielement design.*

Applied behavior analysis. Behavior modification that emphasizes the application of operant conditioning principles, and in which there often is an attempt to analyze or clearly demonstrate controlling variables of the behavior of concern.

Aversive stimulus. Either a punisher or a negative reinforcer.

Avoidance conditioning, principle of. See *principle of avoidance conditioning.*

Backup reinforcer. A stimulus that is deliberately associated with other stimuli to cause them to become conditioned reinforcers.

Backward chaining. A method for establishing a behavioral chain in which the last step of the chain is taught first, then the next-to-last step is linked to the last step, and so on, until the entire chain is learned.

Behavior. Any muscular, glandular, or electrical activity of an organism.

Behavior analysis. The scientific study of the laws that govern the behavior of humans and animals.

Behavior model of self-control. A statement that self-control occurs when an individual behaves in some way that arranges the environment to manage his or her subsequent behavior.

Behavior modification. The systematic application of learning principles and techniques to assess and improve individuals' covert and overt behaviors in order to enhance their daily functioning.

Behavior therapy/cognitive behavior therapy. Behavior modification carried out on dysfunctional behavior, generally in a clinical setting.

Behavioral assessment. The collection and analysis of information and data in order to (a) identify and describe target behaviors, (b) identify possible causes of the behavior, (c) guide the selection of an appropriate behavioral treatment, and (d) evaluate treatment outcome.

Behavioral chain. A consistent sequence of stimuli and responses that occur closely to each other in time and in which the last response is typically followed by reinforcement. Also called a *stimulus-response chain.*

Behavioral contract. A written agreement that provides a clear statement of what behaviors of which individuals will produce what consequences and who will deliver those consequences.

Behavioral deficit. Too little behavior of a particular type.

Behavioral excess. Too much behavior of a particular type.

Behavioral rehearsal. A client rehearses particular behaviors (plays a role) in a practice setting to increase the likelihood that the client will emit those behaviors appropriately in the real world.

Behavioral trap. A contingency in which behavior that has been developed by programmed reinforcers is "trapped" (i.e., maintained) by natural reinforcers.

Chain. See *behavioral chain.*

Changing-criterion design. A research design in which the control that a treatment exerts on an individual's behavior is evaluated by introducing successive changes in the behavioral criterion for application of the treatment.

Classical conditioning. See *respondent conditioning.*

Cognition. Covert verbalizations and imagery; frequently called *believing, thinking,* and *expecting.*

Cognitive behavior modification. An approach to treatment that focuses mainly on changing overt behavior by modifying covert behavior such as dysfunctional thinking.

Cognitive processes. Covert verbalizations and/or imagery that are frequently called *believing, thinking, expecting,* or *perceiving.*

Cognitive restructuring. Strategies for recognizing maladaptive thinking and replacing it with adaptive thinking.

Commitment to change. Statements or actions by an individual that indicate that it is important to change his/her behavior, that the individual recognizes the benefits of doing so, and will work toward doing so.

Common-element stimulus class. A set of stimuli, all of which have some physical characteristics in common.

Competing behaviors. See *incompatible behaviors.*

Concurrent schedules of reinforcement. When each of two or more behaviors is reinforced on different schedules at the same time.

Conditioned aversive stimulus. See *warning stimulus.*

Conditioned punisher. A stimulus that is a punisher as a result of having been paired with another punisher.

Conditioned reflex. A stimulus-response relationship in which a stimulus elicits a response because of prior respondent conditioning.

Conditioned reinforcer. A stimulus that was not originally reinforcing, but has become a reinforcer from being paired or associated with another reinforcer.

Conditioned response (CR). Either a response elicited by a conditioned stimulus or an operant response that has been strengthened by reinforcement.

Conditioned stimulus (CS). A stimulus that elicits a response because that stimulus has been paired with another stimulus that elicits that or a similar response.

Conditioning. Establishing a response through either respondent or operant conditioning.

Contingency-shaped behavior. Behavior that develops because of its immediate consequences.

Contingent. Said of a reinforcer with respect to a behavior if the behavior must occur before the reinforcer will occur.

Continuous recording. Recording every instance of a behavior during a designated observation period.

Continuous reinforcement. An arrangement in which each instance of a particular response is reinforced.

Counterconditioning. Eliminating a conditioned response by conditioning a new response that is incompatible with the conditioned response to the conditioned stimulus at the same time that the former conditioned response is being extinguished.

CR. *See conditioned response.*

CS. *See conditioned stimulus.*

Dependent variable. A measure of behavior that is studied as a function of an independent variable.

Deprivation. A period of time during which an individual does not experience the reinforcer.

Differential reinforcement of alternative (DRA) behavior. Extinction of a problem behavior combined with reinforcing a behavior that is topographically dissimilar to but not necessarily incompatible with the problem behavior.

Differential reinforcement of incompatible (DRI) responding. Withholding reinforcers for a particular response and reinforcing an incompatible response.

Differential reinforcement of low (DRL) rates. A reinforcer is presented *only* if a particular response occurs at a low rate; can be programmed as limited-responding DRL or space-responding DRL.

Differential reinforcement of other (DRO) responding. See *differential reinforcement of zero responding.*

Differential reinforcement of zero (DR0) responding. A reinforcer is presented *only* if a specified response does *not* occur during a specified period of time. Also called *differential reinforcement of other responding.*

Dimensions of applied behavior analysis. (a) a focus on measurable behavior that is socially significant; (b) a strong emphasis on the learning principles frequently referred to as *operant conditioning* to develop treatment strategies; (c) an attempt to clearly demonstrate that the applied treatment was responsible for the improvement in the behavior that was measured; and (d) a demonstration of generalizable and long-lasting improvements in behavior.

Direct assessment. Judgment based on information about a behavior by directly observing it.

Direct effect of a reinforcer. Strengthening of a response that is followed immediately by a reinforcer.

Discriminative stimulus (S^D). A stimulus in the presence of which a response will be reinforced.

Discriminative stimulus (S^Δ). A stimulus in the presence of which a response will not be reinforced.

Discriminative stimulus (S^{Dp}). A stimulus in the presence of which a response will be punished.

DRA. See *differential reinforcement of alternative behavior*.

DRI. See *differential reinforcement of incompatible responding*.

DRL. See *differential reinforcement of low rates*.

DRO. See *differential reinforcement of zero responding*.

Echoic. A vocal imitative response that is developed and maintained by social reinforcement.

Effective stimulus control. A strong correlation between the occurrence of a particular stimulus and a particular response. Also called *good stimulus control*.

Empirically supported therapies (ESTs). Therapies that have proved to be effective in scientifically conducted clinical trials.

Error. A response to an S^Δ or a failure to respond to an S^D.

Errorless discrimination training. The use of a fading procedure to establish a stimulus discrimination so that no errors occur. Also called *errorless learning*.

Errorless learning. See *errorless discrimination training*.

Escape conditioning. A contingency in which an aversive stimulus is removed immediately following a response. Also called *negative reinforcement*.

Escape conditioning, principle of. See *principle of escape conditioning*.

Establishing operation. See *motivating establishing operation*.

ESTs. See *empirically supported therapies*.

Exclusionary timeout. Removal of an individual briefly from a reinforcing situation contingent on a response.

Experiential acceptance. Refraining from judging one's thoughts, sensations, feelings, and behaviors as good or bad, pleasant or unpleasant, useful or useless, etc.. Also called *acceptance*.

External validity. The extent to which a finding of a study or experiment can be generalized to other behaviors, individuals, settings, or treatments.

Extinction burst. An increase in responding during extinction.

Extinction (operant). The withholding of a reinforcer following a previously reinforced response that weakens the response.

Extinction (operant), principle of. See *principle of extinction (operant)*.

Extinction (respondent). Presenting a CS while withholding the US with the result that the CS gradually loses its capability of eliciting the CR.

Fading. The gradual change over successive trials of an antecedent stimulus that controls a response so that the response eventually occurs to a partially changed or completely new stimulus.

FD schedule. See *fixed-duration schedule*.

Fear hierarchy. A list of fear-eliciting events arranged in order from the least to the most fear-eliciting.

FI/LH. See *fixed-interval-with-limited-hold schedule*.

Final desired behavior. In a shaping program a behavior that does not currently occur but is targeted or desired to do so at the end of the shaping process. Also called the *target behavior*.

Final desired stimulus. In a fading procedure the stimulus that does not currently evoke the response but is targeted or desired to do so at the end of the fading process. Also called the *target stimulus*.

FI schedule. See *fixed-interval schedule*.

Fixed-duration (FD) schedule. A reinforcer is presented only if a behavior occurs continuously for a fixed period of time.

Fixed-interval (FI) schedule. A reinforcer is presented following the first instance of a specific response after a fixed period of time.

Fixed-interval-with-limited-hold (FI/LH) schedule. A schedule of reinforcement in which a limited hold has been added to a fixed interval schedule.

Fixed-ratio (FR) schedule. A reinforcer occurs each time a fixed number of responses of a particular type are emitted.

Flooding. A method for extinguishing fear by exposure to a strongly feared stimulus for an extended period of time.

Forward chaining. A method for establishing a behavioral chain in which the initial step of the chain is taught first, then the initial step is linked to the second step, and so on until the entire chain is learned.

Frequency of behavior. The number of instances of a behavior that occurs in a given period of time. Also called *rate of behavior*.

Functional analysis. The systematic manipulation of environmental events to experimentally test their role as antecedents or as consequences in controlling and maintaining specific problem behaviors.

Functional assessment. A variety of procedures for attempting to identify antecedents and consequences of problem behaviors.

Generalized conditioned reinforcer. A conditioned reinforcer that is paired with more than one kind of backup reinforcer.

Generalized imitation. Occurs when, after learning to imitate a number of behaviors (perhaps with some shaping, fading, physical guidance, and reinforcement), an individual imitates a new response on the first trial without reinforcement.

Good stimulus control. See *effective stimulus control*.

Higher-order conditioning. A procedure in which a stimulus becomes a conditioned stimulus by being paired with another conditioned stimulus instead of with an unconditioned stimulus.

Independent variable. A treatment or intervention introduced to study its influence on a dependent variable.

Indirect effect of a reinforcer. Strengthening of a response that is followed by a reinforcer even though the reinforcer is delayed.

Intermittent reinforcement. An arrangement in which a behavior is reinforced only occasionally rather than every time it occurs.

Internal validity. Said of a study or experiment if it convincingly demonstrated that the independent variable caused the observed change in the dependent variable.

Interobserver reliability (IOR). A measure of the extent to which two observers agree on the occurrences of a behavior after independently observing and recording it during a specified period of time.

Interval recording. A recording method that logs the behavior as either occurring or not occurring during short intervals of equal duration during the specified observation period.

Latency. The time between the occurrence of a stimulus and the beginning of a behavior.

LH. See *limited hold*.

Limited hold (LH). A finite amount of time after a reinforcer becomes available that a response will produce it.

Limited-responding DRL. A schedule that specifies the maximum allowable number of responses during a certain time interval in order for reinforcement to occur.

Mand. A verbal response that is under the control of a motivating operation and is reinforced by the corresponding reinforcer or removal of the corresponding aversive stimulus.

MAO. See *motivating abolishing operation*.

Mastery criterion. A specific guideline for performing a skill so that if the guideline is met, the skill is likely to be mastered.

MEO. See *motivating establishing operation*.

Method of successive approximations. See *shaping*.

Mindfulness. Awareness, observation, and description of one's covert and overt behaviors as they occur in a nonjudgmental way; in some cases, observation of the antecedents and consequences of those behaviors.

MO. See *motivating operation*.

Modeling. Demonstrating a sample of a given behavior to an individual to induce that individual to engage in a similar behavior.

Motivating abolishing operation (MAO). An event or operation that temporarily decreases the effectiveness of a reinforcer or punisher and decreases the likelihood of behaviors that normally lead to that reinforcer or increases the likelihood of behaviors that lead to that punisher.

Motivating establishing operation (MEO). An event or operation that temporarily increases the effectiveness of a reinforcer or punisher and increases the likelihood of behaviors that lead to that reinforcer or decreases the likelihood of behaviors that lead to that punisher.

Motivating operation (MO). An event or condition that (a) temporarily alters the effectiveness of a reinforcer or punisher, and (b) influences behavior that normally leads to that reinforcer or punisher.

Multielement design. See *alternating-treatments design.*

Multiple-baseline-across-behaviors design. A research design that involves establishing baselines for two or more of an individual's behaviors followed by introducing the treatment sequentially across those behaviors.

Multiple-baseline-across-people design. A research design that involves establishing baselines for a specific behavior across two or more individuals followed by introducing the treatment sequentially to each individual.

Multiple-baseline-across-situations design. A research design that involves establishing baselines for a behavior of an individual across two or more situations followed by introducing the treatment to the behavior sequentially across those situations.

Natural environment. Setting in which natural reinforcers occur.

Natural reinforcers. Unprogrammed reinforcers that occur in the normal course of everyday living.

Negative reinforcement, principle of. See *principle of escape conditioning.*

Negative reinforcer. A stimulus whose removal immediately after a response causes the response to be strengthened or to increase in frequency.

Noncontingent. Said of a reinforcer if it is presented at a particular time regardless of the preceding behavior.

Nonexclusionary timeout. Introducing into the situation a stimulus associated with less reinforcement contingent on a response.

Operant behaviors. Behaviors that operate on the environment to generate consequences and are in turn influenced by those consequences.

Operant conditioning. The process of strengthening a behavior by reinforcing it or weakening it by punishing it.

Operant extinction. See *extinction (operant).*

Operant responses. See *operant behaviors.*

Pain-inducing punisher. A stimulus immediately following a behavior that activates pain receptors or other sense receptors that typically evoke feelings of discomfort. Also called a *physical punisher.*

Participant modeling. A method for decreasing fear in which a client imitates another individual approaching a feared object.

Pavlovian conditioning. See *respondent conditioning.*

Physical guidance. The application of physical contact to induce an individual to go through the motions of a desired behavior. Also called a *physical prompt.*

Physical prompt. See *physical guidance.*

Physical punisher. See *pain-inducing punisher.*

Positive reinforcement, principle of. See *principle of positive reinforcement.*

Positive reinforcer. A stimulus which, when presented immediately following a behavior, causes the behavior to increase in frequency.

Premack principle. The opportunity to engage in a highly probable behavior can be used to reinforce a behavior that has a lower probability of occurring.

Principle of avoidance conditioning. A contingency in which a response prevents an aversive stimulus from occurring, thereby resulting in an increase in the frequency of that response.

Principle of escape conditioning. The removal of certain stimuli, called aversive stimuli, immediately after the occurrence of a response will increase the likelihood of that response. Also called *principle of negative reinforcement.*

Principle of extinction (operant). (a) if, in a given situation, somebody emits a previously reinforced response and that response is not followed by a reinforcer, (b) then that person is less likely to do the same thing again when next encountering a similar situation.

Principle of negative reinforcement. See *principle of escape conditioning.*

Principle of positive reinforcement. If, in a given situation, somebody does something that is followed immediately by a positive reinforcer, then that person is more likely to do the same thing again when he or she next encounters a similar situation.

Principle of punishment. If, in a given situation, someone does something that is immediately followed by a punisher, then that person is less likely to do the same thing again when she or he next encounters a similar situation.

Principle of respondent conditioning. If a neutral stimulus is followed closely in time by an unconditioned stimulus that elicits a specific unconditioned response, then the previously neutral stimulus will also tend to elicit that response in the future.

Programmed reinforcers. Reinforcers that are arranged systematically in behavior modification programs.

Prompt. A supplemental antecedent stimulus provided to increase the likelihood that a desired behavior will occur but that is not a part of the final desired stimulus to control that behavior.

Punisher. A stimulus whose presentation immediately after a behavior causes that behavior to decrease in frequency.

Punishment. Presentation of a punisher immediately following a behavior with the effect that the behavior decreases in frequency. Also see *principle of punishment*.

Punishment, principle of. See *principle of punishment*.

Rate of behavior. See *frequency of behavior*.

Relapse. The return of a treated behavior to its level prior to treatment.

Relative duration of behavior. The length of time that a behavior occurs within some period.

Reprimand. Negative verbal stimuli presented contingent on behavior.

Respondent behaviors. Behaviors elicited by prior stimuli and that are not affected by their consequences.

Respondent conditioning. Establishing a response to a new stimulus by pairing that stimulus with another stimulus that elicits that response. Also called *Pavlovian conditioning* and *classical conditioning*.

Respondent conditioning, principle of. See *principle of respondent conditioning*.

Respondent extinction. See *extinction (respondent)*.

Response cost. The removal of a specified amount of reinforcer immediately following a particular behavior.

Response generalization. Increased probability of a response as a result of the reinforcement of a another response.

Response topography. The specific movements involved in making a response.

Reversal-replication design. An experimental design consisting of a baseline phase, followed by a treatment phase, followed by a reversal back to baseline, followed by replication of the treatment phase. Also called an *ABAB design*.

Role-playing. See *behavioral rehearsal*.

Rule. A statement describing a three-term contingency of reinforcement (antecedent–behavior–consequence).

Rule-governed behavior. Behavior controlled by the presentation of a rule.

S^D. See *discriminative stimulus (S^D)*.

S^Δ. See *discriminative stimulus (S^Δ)*.

S^{Dp}. See *discriminative stimulus (S^{Dp})*.

Satiation. Condition in which an individual has experienced a reinforcer to such an extent that it is temporarily no longer reinforcing.

Schedule of reinforcement. A rule specifying which occurrences of a given behavior, if any, will be reinforced.

Self-control program. A strategy for using principles of behavior modification to change or control one's own behavior. Also called a *self-management program* and a *self-modification program*.

Self-management program. See *self-control program*.

Self-modification program. See *self-control program*.

Shaping. The development of a new behavior by the reinforcement of successive approximations of that behavior and the extinction of earlier approximations of that behavior until the new behavior occurs. Also called the *method of successive approximations*.

Simple conditioned reinforcer. A conditioned reinforcer paired with a single backup reinforcer.

Spaced-responding DRL. A specified behavior must not occur during a specified interval, and after the interval has passed, an instance of that behavior must then occur for a reinforcer to occur. Also see *differential reinforcement of low rates*.

Spontaneous recovery. The reappearance of an extinguished behavior following a rest.

Starting behavior. In a shaping procedure a behavior that reliably occurs and is an approximation of the final desired behavior, and is used to begin the process of developing the final desired behavior.

Starting stimulus. In a fading procedure a stimulus that reliably evokes the response and is used to begin the process of bringing the response under the control of the final desired stimulus.

Stimuli. Plural of *stimulus*; the people, animals, objects, and events currently present in an one's immediate surroundings that impinge on one's sense receptors and that can affect behavior.

Stimulus. Singular of *stimuli*.

Stimulus control. The degree of correlation between an antecedent stimulus and a subsequent response.

Stimulus discrimination. A response occurs to an S^D and not to an S^Δ.

Stimulus discrimination training. The procedure of reinforcing a response in the presence of an S^D and extinguishing that response in the presence of an S^Δ.

Stimulus equivalence class. A set of completely dissimilar stimuli that an individual has learned to group or match together.

Stimulus generalization. Refers to the *procedure* of reinforcing a response in the presence of a stimulus or situation and the *effect* of the response becoming more probable in the presence of another stimulus or situation.

Stimulus-response chain. See *behavioral chain*.

Superstitious behavior. Behavior that is strengthened by adventitious reinforcement.

Systematic desensitization. A procedure for overcoming a phobia by having a client while in a relaxed state successively imagine the items in a fear hierarchy.

Tact. A naming response that is developed and maintained by social reinforcement. (See Skinner, 1957, for a more precise definition.)

Target behaviors. Behaviors to be improved in a behavior modification program. Also see *final desired behavior*.

Target stimulus. See *final desired stimulus*.

Task analysis. The process of breaking a task down into smaller steps or component responses to facilitate training.

Time sampling recording. An observational procedure in which a behavior is scored as occurring or not occurring during very brief observation intervals that are separated from each other by a much longer period of time.

Timeout. A period of time immediately following a particular behavior during which an individual loses the opportunity to earn reinforcers.

Token economy. A behavioral program in which individuals in a group can earn tokens for a variety of desirable behaviors and can cash in their tokens for backup reinforcers.

Token system. A behavior modification program in which an individual can earn tokens for performing desirable behaviors and can cash in the tokens for various backup reinforcers.

Tokens. Conditioned reinforcers that can be accumulated and exchanged for backup reinforcers.

Topography. See *response topography*.

Total-task presentation. A chaining method in which an individual attempts all of the steps from the beginning to the end of the chain on each trial until that person learns the chain.

Treatment contract. A written agreement between the client and the behavior modifier that clearly outlines the objectives and methods of treatment, the framework of the service to be provided, and contingencies for remuneration that may be forthcoming to the behavior modifier.

Unconditioned punisher. A stimulus that is a punisher without prior learning.

Unconditioned reflex. A stimulus-response relationship in which a stimulus automatically elicits a response apart from any prior learning.

Unconditioned reinforcer. A stimulus that is reinforcing without prior learning or conditioning.

Unconditioned response (UR). A response elicited by an unconditioned stimulus.

Unconditioned stimulus (US). A stimulus that elicits a response without prior learning or conditioning.

UR. *See unconditioned response.*

US. *See unconditioned stimulus.*

Variable-duration (VD) schedule. A reinforcer is presented only if a behavior occurs continuously for a fixed period of time, and the interval of time from reinforcer to reinforcer changes unpredictably.

Variable-interval (VI) schedule. A reinforcer is presented following the first instance of a specific response after an interval of time, and the length of the interval changes unpredictably from one reinforcer to the next.

Variable-interval-with-limited-hold schedule (VI/LH). A variable-interval schedule with an added limited hold.

Variable-ratio (VR) schedule. A reinforcer occurs after a certain number of a particular response, and the number of responses required for each reinforcer changes unpredictably from one reinforcer to the next.

VD. See *variable-duration schedule.*

VI/LH schedule. See *variable-interval-with-limited-hold schedule.*

VI schedule. See *variable-interval schedule.*

VR schedule. See *variable-ratio (VR) schedule.*

Warning stimulus. A stimulus that signals a forthcoming aversive stimulus. Also called a *conditioned aversive stimulus.*

REFERENCES

Ader, R., & Cohen, N. (1982). Behaviorally conditioned immunosuppression and murine systemic lupis erythematosus, *Science, 215,* 1534–1536.

Ader, R., & Cohen, N. (1993). Psychoneuroimmunology: Conditioning and stress. *Annual Review of Psychology, 44,* 53–85.

Agathon, M. (1982). Behavior therapy in France: 1976–1981. *Journal of Behavior Therapy and Experimental Psychiatry, 13,* 271–277.

Agnew, J. L. (1998). The establishing operation in organizational behavior management. *Journal of Organizational Behavior Management, 18,* 7–19.

Agras, W. S., Taylor, C. B., Feldman, D. E., Losch, M., & Burnett, K. F. (1990). Developing computer-assisted therapy for the treatment of obesity. *Behavior Therapy, 21,* 99–109.

Airapetyantz, E., & Bykov, D. (1966). Physiological experiments and the psychology of the subconscious. In T. Verhave (Ed.), *The experimental analysis of behavior* (pp. 140–157). New York: Appleton-Century-Crofts.

Alberto, P. A., & Troutman, A. C. (2008). *Applied behavior analysis for teachers* (8th ed.). Upper Saddle River, NJ: Prentice Hall/Simon & Schuster.

Albion, F. M., & Salzburg, C. L. (1982). The effects of self-instruction on the rate of correct addition problems with mentally retarded children. *Education and Treatment of Children, 5,* 121–131.

Allen, G. J. (1973). Case study: Implementation of behavior modification techniques in summer camp settings. *Behavior Therapy, 4,* 570–575.

Allen, K. D., & Stokes, T. F. (1987). Use of escape and reward in the management of young children during dental treatment. *Journal of Applied Behavior Analysis, 20,* 381–390.

Allen, K. D., & Warzak, D. J. (2000). The problem of parental nonadherence in clinical behavior analysis: Effective treatment is not enough. *Journal of Applied Behavior Analysis, 33,* 373–391.

American Association on Mental Retardation (AAMR). (1990). Revised policy on aversive procedures. *AAMR News and Notes, 3*(4), 5.

American Association on Mental Retardation (AAMR). (2002). *Mental retardation: Definition, classification, and systems of supports* (10th ed.). Washington, DC: Author.

American Psychiatric Association. (1952). *Diagnostic and statistical manual of mental disorders: DSM-I.* Washington, DC: Author.

American Psychiatric Association. (1968). *Diagnostic and statistical manual of mental disorders: DSM-II* (2nd ed.). Washington, DC: Author.

American Psychiatric Association. (1980). *Diagnostic and statistical manual of mental disorders: DSM-III* (3rd ed.). Washington, DC: Author.

American Psychiatric Association. (1987). *Diagnostic and statistical manual of mental disorders: DSM-III–R* (3rd ed.). Washington, DC: Author.

American Psychiatric Association. (1993). Practice guidelines for major depressive disorder in adults. *American Journal of Psychiatry, 150*(Suppl. 4), 1–26.

American Psychiatric Association. (1994). *Diagnostic and statistical manual of mental disorders: DSM-IV* (4th ed.). Washington, DC: Author.

American Psychiatric Association. (2000). *Diagnostic and statistical manual of mental disorders: DSM-IV-TR* (4th ed.). Washington, DC: Author.

American Psychological Association (APA). (2002). *Ethical principles in the conduct of research with human participants.* Washington, DC: Author.

Anderson, C. M., & Freeman, K. A. (2000). Positive behaviour support: Expanding the application of applied behaviour analysis. *The Behavior Analyst, 23*, 85–94.

Antonuccio, D. O., Danton, W. G., & Denelsky, G. Y. (1995). Psychotherapy versus medication for depression: Challenging the conventional wisdom with data. *Professional Psychology: Research and Practice, 26*, 574–585.

Antony, M. M., & Barlow, D. H. (Eds.). (2004). *Handbook of assessment and treatment planning for psychological disorders.* New York: Guilford Press.

Antony, M. M., & Norton, P. (2009). *The anti-anxiety workbook.* New York: Guilford Press.

Ardila, R. (1982). International developments in behavior therapy in Latin America. *Journal of Behavior Therapy and Experimental Psychiatry, 13*, 15–20.

Arkowitz, H., Westra, H., Miller, W. R., & Rollnick, S. (2008). *Motivational interviewing in the treatment of psychological problems.* New York: Guilford Press.

Arnal, L., Fazzio, D., Martin, G. L., Yu, C. T., Keilback, L., & Starke, M. (2007). Instructing university students to conduct discrete-trials teaching with confederates simulating children with autism. *Developmental Disabilities Bulletin, 35*, 131–147.

Arrick, C. M., Voss, J., & Rimm, D. C. (1981). The relative efficacy of thought-stopping and covert assertion. *Behaviour Research and Therapy, 19*, 17–24.

Asch, S. E. (1948). The doctrine of suggestion, prestige and imitation in social psychology. *Psychological Review, 55*, 250–276.

Ash, D. W., & Holding, D. H. (1990). Backward versus forward chaining in the acquisition of a keyboard skill. *Human Factors, 32*, 139–146.

Aubuchon, P. G., Haber, J. D., & Adams, H. E. (1985). Can migraine headaches be modified by operant pain techniques? *Journal of Behavior Therapy and Experimental Psychiatry, 16*, 261–263.

Austin, J. (2000). Performance analysis and performance diagnostics. In J. Austin & J. E. Carr (Eds.), *Handbook of applied behavior analysis* (pp. 449–472). Reno, NV: Context Press.

Austin, J., & Carr, J. E. (Eds.). 2000. *Handbook of applied behavior analysis.* Reno, NV: Context Press.

Austin, L. (2000). Behavioral approaches to college teaching. In J. Austin & J. E. Carr (Eds.), *Handbook of applied behavior analysis* (pp. 321–350). Reno, NV: Context Press.

Ayllon, T. (1999). *How to use token economy and point systems,* (2nd ed.). Austin, TX: Pro-Ed, Inc.

Ayllon, T., & Azrin, N. H. (1968). *The token economy: A motivational system for therapy and rehabilitation.* New York: Appleton-Century-Crofts.

Ayllon, T., & Michael, J. (1959). The psychiatric nurse as a behavioral engineer. *Journal of the Experimental Analysis of Behavior, 2,* 323–334.

Ayllon, T., & Milan, M. A. (1979). *Correctional rehabilitation and management: A psychological approach.* New York: Wiley.

Azrin, N. H. (1967). Pain and aggression. *Psychology Today, 1*(1), 27–33.

Azrin, N. H. (1976). Improvements in the community-reinforcement approach to alcoholism. *Behavior Research and Therapy, 14*, 339–348.

Azrin, N. H., & Lindsley, O. R. (1956). The reinforcement of cooperation between children. *Journal of Abnormal and Social Psychology, 52*, 100–102.

Azrin, N. H., & Nunn, R. G. (1973). Habit reversal: A method of eliminating nervous habits and tics. *Behaviour Research and Therapy, 11*, 619–628.

Azrin, N. H., Ruben, H., O'Brien, F., Ayllon, T., & Roll, D. (1968). Behavioral engineering: Postural control by a portable operant apparatus. *Journal of Applied Behavior Analysis, 1*, 99–108.

Azrin, N. H., Sisson, R. W., Meyers, R., & Godley, N. (1982). Alcoholism treatment by disulfiram and community reinforcement therapy. *Journal of Behavior Therapy and Experimental Psychiatry, 13*(2), 105–112.

Babel, D., Martin, G. L., Fazzio, D., Arnal, L., & Thomson, K. (2008). Assessment of the reliability and validity of the Discrete-Trials Teaching Evaluation Form. *Developmental Disabilities Bulletin, 36,* 67–80.

Baer, D. M., Peterson, R. F., & Sherman, J. A. (1967). The development of imitation by reinforcing behavioral similarity to a model. *Journal of the Experimental Analysis of Behavior, 10,* 405–416.

Baer, D. M., & Wolf, M. M. (1970). The entry into natural communities of reinforcement. In R. Ulrich, T. Stachnik, & J. Mabry (Eds.), *Control of human behavior* (Vol. 2, pp. 319–324). Glenview, IL: Scott Foresman.

Baer, D. M., Wolfe, M. M., & Risley, T. R. (1968). Some current dimensions of Applied Behavior Analysis. *Journal of Applied Behavior Analysis, 1,* 91–97.

Bailey, J. S. (1992). Gentle teaching: Trying to win friends and influence people with a euphemism, metaphor, smoke, and mirrors. *Journal of Applied Behavior Analysis, 25,* 879–883.

Bailey, J. S., & Burch, M. R. (2002). *Research methods in applied behavior analysis.* Thousand Oaks, CA: Sage.

Bailey, J. S., & Burch, M. R. (2005). *Ethics for behavior analysts: A practical guide to the Behavior Analyst Certification Board Guidelines for Responsible Conduct.* Mahwah, NJ: Lawrence Erlbaum Associates.

Bailey, J. S., & Burch, M. R. (2006). *How to think like a behavior analyst.* Mahwah, NJ: Lawrence Erlbaum Associates.

Bailey, J. S., Hughes, R. G., & Jones, W. E. (1980). *Applications of backward chaining to air-to-surface weapons delivery training.* Williams Airforce Base, AZ: Operations training division, Human Resources Laboratory.

Bailey, J. S., & Pyles, D. A. M. (1989). Behavioral diagnostics. *Monographs of the American Association on Mental Retardation, 12,* 85–106.

Bailey, J. S., Timbers, G. D., Phillips, E. I., & Wolf, M. M. (1971). Modification of articulation errors of pre-delinquents by their peers. *Journal of Applied Behaviour Analysis, 3,* 265–281.

Baldwin, J. D., & Baldwin, J. I. (2000). *Behavior principles in everyday life* (4th ed.). Upper Saddle River, NJ: Prentice Hall.

Bambara, L. M., & Kern, L. (2005). *Individualized supports for students with problem behaviors: Designing positive behavior plans.* New York, NY: Guilford Press.

Bandura, A. (1965). Influence of models' reinforcement contingencies in the acquisition of imitative responses. *Journal of Personality and Social Psychology, 1,* 589–595.

Bandura, A. (1969). *Principles of behavior modification.* New York: Holt, Rinehart & Winston.

Bandura, A. (1977). *Social learning theory.* Upper Saddle River, NJ: Prentice Hall.

Bandura, A. (1982). Self-efficacy mechanism in human agency. *American Psychologist, 37,* 122–147.

Bandura, A. (1986). *Social foundations of thought and action: A social-cognitive theory.* Upper Saddle River, NJ: Prentice Hall.

Bandura, A. (2004). Health promotion by social cognitive means. *Health Education and Behavior, 31,* 143–164.

Bandura, A., & Walters, R. H. (1963). *Social learning and personality development.* New York: Holt, Rinehart & Winston.

Banerjee, S. P. (1999). Behavioral psychotherapy in Singapore. *The Behavior Therapist, 22,* 80, 91.

Barkley, R. A. (1998). *Attention-deficit hyperactive disorder: A handbook for diagnosis and treatment* (2nd ed.). New York: Guilford Press.

Barkley, R. A. (1996). 18 ways to make token systems more effective for ADHD children and teens. *The ADHD Report, 4,* 1–5.

Barlow, D. H. (Ed.). (2008). *Clinical handbook of psychological disorders: A step-by-step treatment manual* (14th ed.) New York: Guilford Press.

Barlow, D. H., & Hayes, S. C. (1979). Alternating-treatments design: One strategy for comparing the effects of two treatments in a single subject. *Journal of Applied Behavior Analysis, 12,* 199–210.

Barone, D. F. (1982). Instigating additional self-modification projects after a personal adjustment course. *Teaching of Psychology, 9,* 111.

Barrios, B. A., & Hartmann, D. P. (1986). The contributions of traditional assessment: Concepts, issues, and methodologies. In R. O. Nelson & S. C. Hayes (Eds.), *Conceptual foundations of behavioral assessment* (pp. 81–110). New York: Guilford Press.

Batra, M., & Batra, V. (2005/2006). Comparison between forward chaining and backward chaining techniques in children with mental retardation. *The Indian Journal of Occupational Therapy, 37,* 57–63.

Beck, A. T. (1970). Cognitive therapy: Nature and relation to behavior therapy. *Behavior Therapy, 1,* 184–200.

Beck, A. T. (1976). *Cognitive therapy and the emotional disorders*. New York: International Universities Press.

Beck, A. T. (1988). *Love is never enough: How couples can overcome misunderstandings, resolve conflicts, and solve relationship problems through cognitive therapy*. New York: Harper & Row.

Beck, A. T., Emery, G., & Greenberg, R. L. (1985). *Anxiety disorders and phobias: A cognitive perspective*. New York: Basic Books.

Beck, A. T., Rector, N. A., Stolar, N., & Grant, P. (2008). *Schizophrenia: Cognitive theory, research, and therapy*. New York: Guilford press.

Beck, A. T., Rush, A. J., Shaw, B. F., & Emery, G. (1979). *Cognitive therapy of depression*. New York: Guilford Press.

Bellack, A. S. (1986). Schizophrenia: Behavior therapy's forgotten child. *Behavior Therapy, 17,* 199–214.

Bellack, A. S., & Hersen, M. (1993). *Clinical behavior therapy with adults*. In A. S. Bellack & M. Hersen (Eds.), *Handbook of behavior therapy in the psychiatric setting* (pp. 3–18). New York: Plenum Press.

Bellack, A. S., & Hersen, M. (Eds.). (1998). *Behavioral assessment: A practical handbook* (4th ed.). New York: Allyn & Bacon.

Bellack, A. S., & Muser, K. T. (1990). Schizophrenia. In A. S. Bellack, M. Hersen, & A. E. Kazdin (Eds.), *International handbook of behavior modification and behavior therapy* (2nd ed., pp. 353–376). New York: Plenum Press.

Bellack, A. S., Muser, K. T., Gingerich, S., & Agresta, J. (Eds.). (1997). *Social skills training for schizophrenia*. New York: Guilford Press.

Bellamy, G. T., Horner, R. H., & Inman, D. P. (1979). *Vocational habilitation of severely retarded adults: A direct service technology*. Baltimore: University Park Press.

Bentall, R. P., Lowe, C. F., & Beasty, A. (1985). The role of verbal behavior in human learning. II: Developmental differences. *Journal of the Experimental Analysis of Behavior, 47,* 165–181.

Bergen, A. E., Holborn, S. W., & Scott-Huyghebart, V. C. (2002). Functional analysis of self-injurious behavior in an adult with Lesch–Nyhan Syndrome. *Behavior Modification, 26,* 187–204.

Berkowitz, L. (1988). Frustrations, appraisals, and aversively stimulated aggression. *Aggressive Behavior, 14,* 3–11.

Berkowitz, L. (1989). Frustration-aggression hypothesis: Examination and reformulation. *Psychological Bulletin, 106,* 59–73.

Bierman, K. L., Miller, C. L., & Stabb, S. D. (1987). Improving the social behavior and peer acceptance of rejected boys: Effects of social skill training with instructions and prohibitions. *Journal of Consulting and Clinical Psychology, 55,* 194–200.

Bijou, S. W., & Baer, D. M. (1961). *Child development: A systematic and empirical theory* (Vol. 1). New York: Appleton-Century-Crofts.

Bijou, S. W., & Baer, D. M. (1965). *Child development II: Universal stage of infancy*. Upper Saddle River, NJ: Prentice Hall.

Birnbrauer, J. S., Bijou, S. W., Wolf, M. M., & Kidder, J. D. (1965). Programmed instruction in the classroom. In L. P. Ullmann & L. Krasner

(Eds.), *Case studies in behavior modification* (pp. 358–363). New York: Holt, Rinehart & Winston.

Bjorgvinsson, T., & Rosqvist, J. (2009). *Cognitive behavioral therapy for depression: A practical guide to management and treatment.* New York: Routledge.

Blampied, N. (1999). Cognitive-behavior therapy in Aotearoa, New Zealand. *The Behavior Therapist, 22,* 173–178.

Blampied, N. (2004). The New Zealand Association for Behavior Analysis. *Newsletter of the International Association for Behavior Analysis, 27*(2), 27.

Blanck, G. (1983). *Behavior therapy in Argentina.* Buenos Aires: AAPC Ediciones.

Blimke, J., Gowan, G., Patterson, P., & Wood, N. (1984). Sport and psychology: What ethics suggest about practice. *Sports Science Periodical on Research and Technology in Sport.* Ottawa, Ont: Coaching Association of Canada.

Block-Lerner, J., Wulfert, E., & Moses, E. (2009). ACT in context: An exploration of experiential acceptance. *Cognitive and Behavioral Practice, 16,* 443–456.

Blount, R. L., Drabman, R. S., Wilson, N., & Stewart, D. (1982). Reducing severe diurnal bruxism in two profoundly retarded females. *Journal of Applied Behavior Analysis, 15,* 565–571.

Blum, N., & Friman, P. (2000). Behavioral pediatrics. In J. Austin & J. E. Carr (Eds.), *Handbook of applied behavior analysis* (pp. 161–186). Reno, NV: Context Press.

Bond, F. W., & Bunce, D. (2000). Mediators of change in emotion-focused and problem-focused work site stress management interventions. *Journal of Occupational Health Psychology, 5,* 156–163.

Boniecki, K. A. & Moore, S. (2003). Breaking the silence: Use of the token economy to reinforce classroom participation. *Teaching of Psychology, 30,* 224–227.

Booth, R., & Rachman, S. (1992). The reduction of claustrophobia: I. *Behaviour Research and Therapy, 30,* 207–221.

Borkovec, T. D., & Sharpless, B. (2004). Generalized anxiety disorder: Bringing cognitive-behavioral therapy into the valued present. In S. C. Hayes, V. M. Follette, & M. M. Linehan (Eds.), *Mindfulness and acceptance: Expanding the cognitive-behavioral tradition.* New York: Guilford Press.

Borden, J. W. (1992). Behavioral treatment of simple phobia. In S. M. Turner, K. S. Calhoun, & H. E. Adams (Eds.), *Handbook of clinical behavior therapy* (pp. 77–94). New York: Wiley.

Borrego, J., Ibanez, E. S., Spendlove, S. J., & Pemberton, J. R. (2007). Treatment acceptability among Mexican American parents. *Behavior Therapy, 38,* 218–227.

Bouchard, S., Vallieres, A., Roy, M., & Maziade, M. (1996). Cognitive restructuring in the treatment of psychotic symptoms in schizophrenia: A critical analysis. *Behavior Therapy, 27,* 257–277.

Bouman, T. K., & Emmelkamp, P. M. G. (1996). Panic disorder and agoraphobia. In V. B. Van Hasselt & M. Hersen (Eds.), *Sourcebook of psychological treatment manuals for adult disorders* (pp. 23–64). New York: Plenum Press.

Bovjberg, D. H., Redd, W. H., Maier, L. A., Holland, J. C., Lesko, L. M., Niedzwiecki, D., et al. (1990). Anticipatory immune suppression in women receiving cyclic chemotherapy for ovarian cancer. *Journal of Consulting and Clinical Psychology, 58,* 153–157.

Braam, C., & Malott, R. W. (1990). "I'll do it when the snow melts": The effects of deadlines and delayed outcomes on rule-governed behavior in preschool children. *Analysis of Verbal Behavior, 8,* 67–76.

Brantner, J. P., & Doherty, M. A. (1983). A review of time-out: A conceptual and methodological analysis. In S. Axelrod & J. Apsche (Eds.), *The effects of punishment on human behavior* (pp. 87–132). New York: Academic Press.

Braukmann, C. J., & Blase, K. B. (Eds.). (1979). *Teaching-parent training manuals* (2 vols.). Lawrence, KS: University of Kansas Printing Service.

Braukmann, C., & Wolf, M. (1987). Behaviorally based group homes for juvenile offenders.

In E. K. Morris & C. J. Braukmann (Eds.), *Behavioral approaches to crime and delinquency: A handbook of application, research, and concepts* (pp. 135–160). New York: Plenum Press.

Brigham, T. A. (1982). Self-management: A radical behavioral perspective. In P. Karoly & F. H. Canfer (Eds.), *Self-management and behavior change: From theory to practice* (pp. 32–59). New York: Pergamon Press.

Brigham, T. A. (1989a). *Managing everyday problems.* New York: Guilford Press.

Brigham, T. A. (1989b). *Self-management for adolescents: A skills training program.* New York: Guilford Press.

Briscoe, R. V., Hoffman, D. B., & Bailey, J. S. (1975). Behavioral community psychology: Training a community board to problem-solve. *Journal of Applied Behavior Analysis, 8,* 157–168.

Bromfield, R., Bromfield, D., & Weiss, B. (1988). Influence of the sexually abused label on perceptions of a child's failure. *Journal of Educational Research, 82,* 96–98.

Bromfield, R., Weisz, J. R., & Messer, T. (1986). Children's judgments and attributions in response to the "mentally retarded" label: A developmental approach. *Journal of Abnormal Psychology, 95,* 81–87.

Brossart, D. F., Parker, R. I., Olson, E. A., & Mahadevan, L. (2006). The relationship between visual analysis and five statistical analyses in a simple AB single-case research design. *Behavior Modification, 30,* 531–563.

Brown, R. (1973). *A first language: The early years.* Cambridge, MA: Harvard University Press.

Brown, W. H., Pfeiffer, K., Mciver, K. L., Dowda, M., Almeida, J., & Pate. R. R. (2006). Assessing preschool children's physical activity: An Observational System for Recording Physical Activity in Children—Preschool version (OSRPAC-P). *Research Quarterly for Exercise and Sport, 77,* 167–176.

Brownell, K. D. (1981). Report on international behavior therapy organizations. *The Behavior Therapist, 4,* 9–13.

Bruzek, J. L., Thompson, R. H., & Peters, L. C. (2009). Resurgence of infant caregiving responses. *Journal of the Experimental Analysis of Behavior, 92,* 327–343.

Bush, J. P., & Ciocco, J. E. (1992). Behavioral coding and sequential analysis: The portable computer systems for observational use. *Behavioral Assessment, 14,* 191–197.

Butler, A., Chapman, J. M., Forman, E. M., & Beck, A. T. (2006). The empirical status of cognitive behavioral therapy: A review of meta-analyses. *Clinical Psychology Review, 26,* 17–31.

Buzas, H. P., & Ayllon, T. (1981). Differential reinforcement in coaching skills. *Behavior Modification, 5,* 372–385.

Caballo, V. E., & Buela-Casal, G. (1993). Behavior therapy in Spain. *Behavior Therapist, 16,* 53–54.

Caldwell, L. (1971). Behavior modification with children. Paper presented at the 1st Manitoba Behavior Change Conference, Portage la Prairie, Manitoba, Canada.

Cameron, J., Banko, K. M., & Pierce, W. D. (2001). Pervasive negative effects of rewards on intrinsic motivation: The myth continues. *The Behavior Analyst, 24,* 1–44.

Carr, E. G. (1977). The origins of self-injurious behavior: A review of some hypotheses. *Psychological Bulletin, 84,* 800–816.

Carr, E. G., & Durand, V. M. (1985). Reducing behavior problems through functional communication training. *Journal of Applied Behavior Analysis, 18*(2), 111–126.

Carr, E. G., Newsom, C. D., & Binkoff, J. A. (1980). Escape as a factor in the aggressive behavior of two retarded children. *Journal of Applied Behavior Analysis, 13,* 101–117.

Carr, J. E., Coriaty, S., & Dozier, C. L. (2000). Current issues in the function-based treatment of aberrant behavior in individuals with developmental disabilities. In J. Austin & J. E. Carr (Eds.), *Handbook of applied behavior analysis* (pp. 91–112). Reno, NV: Context Press.

Carr, J. E., & Sidener, T. M. (2002). In response: On the relation between applied behavior analysis and positive behavior support. *The Behavior Analyst, 25*(1), 425–253.

Carter, N. (2004). Swedish Association for Behavior Analysis. *Newsletter of the International Association for Behavior Analysis, 27*(2), 29.

Catania, A. C. (1975). The myth of self-reinforcement. *Behaviorism, 3,* 192–199.

Cattell, R. B., Eber, H. W., & Tatsuoka, M. M. (1970). *Handbook for the 16-Personality Factor Questionnaire.* Champaign, IL: Institute for Personality and Ability Testing.

Cautela, J. R. (1966). Treatment of compulsive behavior by covert desensitization. *Psychological Record, 16,* 33–41.

Cautela, J. R. (1981). *Behavior analysis forms for clinical intervention* (Vol. 2). Champaign, IL: Research Press.

Cautela, J. R., Kastenbaum, R., & Wincze, J. (1972). The use of the Fear Survey Schedule and the Reinforcement Survey Schedule to survey possible reinforcing and aversive stimuli among juvenile offenders. *Journal of Genetic Psychology, 121,* 255–261.

Cautela, J. R., & Kearney, A. (1993). *The covert conditioning handbook.* Pacific Grove, CA: Brooks/Cole.

Charlop, M. H., Burgio, L. D., Iwata, B. A., & Ivancic, M. T. (1988). Stimulus variation as a means of enhancing punishment effects. *Journal of Applied Behavior Analysis, 21,* 89–95.

Chen, C. P. (1995). Counseling applications of RET in a Chinese cultural context. *Journal of Rational-Emotive and Cognitive Behavior Therapy, 13,* 117–129.

Chomsky, N. (1959). A review of B. F. Skinner's *Verbal Behavior. Language, 35,* 26–58.

Christensen, A., Sevier, M., Simpson, L. E., & Gattis, K. S. (2004). Acceptance, mindfulness, and change in couple therapy. In S. C. Hayes, V. M. Follette, & M. M. Linehan (Eds.), *Mindfulness and acceptance: Expanding the cognitive behavioural tradition.* New York: Guilford Press.

Christensen, A., Wheeler, J. G., & Jacobson, N. S. (2008). Couple distress. In D. H. Barlow (Ed.), *Clinical handbook of psychological disorders: A step-by-step treatment manual* (4th ed.). New York: Guilford Press.

Christner, R. W., Stewart, J., & Freeman, A. (Eds.). (2007). *Handbook of cognitive-behavior group therapy with children and adolescents: Specific settings and presenting problems.* New York: Routledge Mental Health.

Christophersen, E. R., & Mortweet, S. L. (2001). *Treatments that work: Empirically supported treatments for managing child behavior problems.* Washington, DC: American Psychological Association.

Chung, S. H. (1965). Effects of delayed reinforcement in a concurrent situation. *Journal of the Experimental Analysis of Behavior, 8,* 439–444.

Cipani, E. (2004). *Punishment on trial.* Reno, NV: Context Press.

Cipani, E., & Schock, K. M. (2007). *Functional behavioral assessment, diagnosis, and treatment.* New York: Springer Publishing Company.

Clarke, I., & Wilson, H. (2008). *Cognitive Behavior Therapy for acute in-patient mental health units.* London: Routledge.

Cohen, R., Dejames, P., Nocera, B., & Ramberger, M. (1980). Application of a simple self-instruction procedure on adult exercise and studying: Two case reports. *Psychological Reports, 46,* 443–451.

Cone, J. D. (1997). Issues in functional analysis in behavioral assessment. *Behavior Research and Therapy, 35,* 259–275.

Cone, J. D. (Ed.). (1999). Special section: Clinical assessment applications of self-monitoring. *Psychological Assessment, 11,* 411–497.

Conyers, C., Martin, T. L., Martin, G. L., & Yu, D. C. T. (2002). The 1983 AAMR manual, the 1992 AAMR manual, or the Developmental Disabilities Act: Which is used by researchers?

Education and Training in Mental Retardation and Developmental Disabilities, 37, 310–316.

Conyers, C., Miltenberger, R., Maki, A., Barenz, R., Jurgens, M., Sailor, A., Haugen, N., & Kopp, B. (2004). A comparison of response cost and differential reinforcement of other behavior to reduce disruptive behavior in a preschool classroom. *Journal of Applied Behavior Analysis, 37,* 411–415.

Coon, D. W., & Thompson, L. W. (2002). Family caregivers for older adults: Ongoing and emergent themes for the behavior therapist. *The Behavior Therapist, 25,* 17–20.

Corrigan, P. W. (1995). Use of a token economy with seriously mentally ill patients: Criticisms and misconceptions. *Psychiatric Services, 46.* 1258–1263.

Cottraux, J. (1990). "Cogito ergo somme": Cognitive behavior therapy in France. *Behavior Therapist, 13,* 189–190.

Cowdery, G. E., Iwata, B. A., & Pace, G. M. (1990). Effects and side-effects of DRO as treatment for self-injurious behavior. *Journal of Applied Behavior Analysis, 23,* 497–506.

Cox, B. S., Cox, A. B., & Cox, D. J. (2000). Motivating signage prompts: Safety belt use among drivers exiting senior communities. *Journal of Applied Behavior Analysis, 33,* 635–638.

Cracklen, C., & Martin, G. (1983). To motivate age-group competitive swimmers at practice, "fun" should be earned. *Swimming Techniques, 20*(3), 29–32.

Craighead, L. W. (2004). Obesity and eating disorders. In M. M. Antony & D. H. Barlow (Eds.), *Handbook of assessment and treatment planning for psychological disorders.* New York: Guilford Press.

Craske, M. G., & Barlow, D. H. (2008). Panic disorder and agoraphobia. In D. H. Barlow (Ed.), *Clinical handbook of psychological disorders: A step-by-step treatment manual* (4th ed.). New York: Guilford Press.

Crosbie J., & Glenn, K. (1993). A computer based personalized system of instruction in applied behavior analysis. *Behavior Research Methods, Instruments and Computers, 25,* 366–370.

Crowell, C. R., Quintanar, L. R., & Grant, K. L. (1981). Proctor: An online student evaluation and monitoring system for use with PSI format courses. *Behavior Research Methods and Instrumentation, 13,* 121–127.

Cummings, N. A., O'Donohue, W. T., & Ferguson, K. E. (2003). *Behavioral health as primary care: Beyond efficacy to effectiveness.* Reno, NV: Context Press.

Cuvo, A. J., & Davis, P. K. (2000). Behavioral acquisition by persons with developmental disabilities. In J. Austin & J. E. Carr (Eds.), *Handbook of applied behavior analysis* (pp. 39–60). Reno: NV: Context Press.

Cuvo, A. J., Davis, P. K., O'Reilly, M. F., Mooney, B. M., & Crowley, R. (1992). Promoting stimulus control with textual prompts and performance feedback for persons with mild disabilities. *Journal of Applied Behavior Analysis, 25,* 477–489.

Dallery, J., Meredith, S., & Glenn, I. M. (2008). A deposit contract method to deliver abstinence reinforcement for cigarette smoking. *Journal of Applied Behavior Analysis, 41,* 609–615.

Daly, E. J., III, Martens, B. K., Kilmer, A., & Massie, D. R. (1996). The effects of instructional match and content overlap on generalized reading performance. *Journal of Applied Behavior Analysis, 29,* 507–518.

Danaher, B. G. (1977). Research on rapid smoking: Interim summary and recommendations. *Addictive Behavior, 2,* 151–166.

Danguah, J. (1982). The practice of behavior therapy in West Africa: The case of Ghana. *Journal of Behavior Therapy and Experimental Psychiatry, 13,* 5–13.

Daniels, A. C., & Daniels, J. E. (2005). *Performance management: Changing behavior that drives organizational effectiveness.* Atlanta, GA: Performance Management Publications.

Dardig, J. C., & Heward, W. L. (1976). *Sign here: A contracting book for children and their parents.* Kalamazoo, MI: Behaviordelia.

Daruna, J. H. (2004). Introduction to psycho-neuroimmunology. St. Louis, MO: Elsevier, Academic Press.

Dattilo, F. M. (1999). Cognitive behavior therapy in Cuba. *The Behavior Therapist, 22,* 78, 91.

David, D., & Miclea, M. (2002) Behavior therapy in Romania: A brief history of theory, research, and practice. *The Behavior Therapist, 25,* 181–183.

Day, H. R., & Ballard, D. (2005). *The Classroom Mini-Economy.* New York: NY: National Council for Economic Education.

Deci, E. L., Koestner, R., & Ryan, R. M. (1999). A meta-analytic review of experiments examining the effects of extrinsic rewards on intrinsic motivation. *Psychological Bulletin, 125,* 627–668.

Deitz, S. M., & Repp, A. C. (1973). Decreasing classroom misbehavior through the use of DRL schedules of reinforcement. *Journal of Applied Behavior Analysis, 6,* 457–463.

Dekker, E., & Groen, J. (1956). Reproducible psychogenic attacks of asthma: A laboratory study. *Journal of Psychosomatic Research, 1,* 58–67.

Deleon, I. G., & Iwata, B. A. (1996). Evaluation of a multiple-stimulus presentation format for assessing reinforcer preferences. *Journal of Applied Behavior Analysis, 29,* 519–533.

Deluca, R. V., & Holborn, S. W. (1992). Effects of a variable ratio reinforcement schedule with changing-criteria on exercise in obese and non-obese boys. *Journal of Applied Behavior Analysis, 25,* 671–679.

Demchak, M. (1990). Response prompting and fading methods: A review. *American Journal on Mental Retardation, 94,* 603–615.

Demchak, M. A., & Bossert, K. W. (1996). *Innovations: Assessing problem behaviors.* Washington, DC: American Association on Mental Retardation.

Den Boer, P. C., Wiersma, D., & Van Den Bosche, R. J. (2004). Why is self-help neglected in the treatment of emotional disorders? A meta-analysis. *Psychological Medicine, 34,* 959–971.

Depaepe, P. A., Shores, R. E., Jack, S. L., & Denny, R. K. (1996). Effects of task difficulty on the disruptive and on-task behavior of students with severe behavior disorders. *Behavioral Disorders, 21,* 216–225.

Depression Guideline Panel. (1993). *Depression in primary care: Vol. 2. Treatment of major depression* (Clinical Practice Guideline, No. 5, AHCPR Pub. No. 93–0551). Rockville, MD: U.S. Department of Health and Human Services, Public Health Service, Agency for Health Care Policy and Research.

Derenne, A., & Baron, A. (2002). Behavior analysis and the study of aging. *The Behavior Analyst, 25,* 151–160.

Dericco, D. A., & Niemann, J. E. (1980). In vivo effects of peer modelling on drinking rate. *Journal of Applied Behavior Analysis, 13,* 149–152.

Derisi, W. J., & Butz, G. (1975). *Writing behavioral contracts: A case simulation practice manual.* Champaign, IL: Research Press.

Desilva, P., & Simarasinghe, D. (1985). Behavior therapy in Sri Lanka. *Journal of Behavior Therapy and Experimental Psychiatry, 16,* 95–100.

Devries, J. E., Burnette, M. M., & Redmon, W. K. (1991). AIDS prevention: Improving nurses' compliance with glove wearing through performance feedback. *Journal of Applied Behavior Analysis, 24,* 705–711.

Dickerson, F. B., Tanula, W. N. & Green-Paden, L. D. (2005). The token economy for schizophrenia: Review of the literature and recommendations for future research. *Schizophrenia Research, 75,* 405–416.

Dick-Siskin, L. P. (2002). Cognitive-behavioral therapy with older adults. *The Behavior Therapist, 25,* 3–4, 6.

Didden, R. (2007). Functional analysis methodology in developmental disabilities. In P. Sturmey (Ed.), *Functional analysis in clinical treatment* (pp. 65–86). London: Elsevier.

Digiuseppe, R. (2008) Surfing the waves of behavior therapy. *The Behavior Therapist, 31,* 154–155.

Dimidjian, S., Hollon, S. D., Dobson, K. S., Schmaling, K. B., Kohlenberg, R. J., Addis, M. E., et al. (2006). Randomized trial of behavioral activation, cognitive therapy, and antidepresssant medication in the acute treatment of adults with major depression. *Journal of Consulting and Clinical Psychology, 74,* 658–670.

Dimidjian, S., Hollon, S., Dobson, K., Schmaling, K., Kohlenberg, R., McGilinchey, J., et al. (2003, November). Behavioral activation, cognitive therapy, and antidepressant medication in the treatment of major depression: Design and acute phase outcomes. Presented at the 37th Annual Convention of the Association for Advancement of Behavior Therapy, Boston.

Dimidjian, S., Martell, C. R., Addis, M. E., & Herman-Dunn, R. (2008). In D.H. Barlow (Ed.), *Clinical handbook of psychological disorders: A step-by-step treatment manual* (4th ed., pp. 328–364). New York: Guilford Press.

Dobson, K. S. (1989). Meta-analysis of the efficacy of cognitive therapy for depression. *Journal of Consulting and Clinical Psychology, 57,* 414–419.

Dobson, K. S., Hollon, S. D., Dimidjian, S., Schmaling, K. B., Kohlenberg, et al. (2008). Randomized trial of behavioral activation, cognitive therapy, and antidepressant medication in the prevention of relapse and recurrence in major depression. *Journal of Consulting and Clinical Psychology, 76,* 468–477.

Doleys, D. M., Meredith, R. L., & Ciminero, A. R. (Eds.). (1982). *Behavioral psychology and medicine and rehabilitation: Assessment and treatment strategies.* New York: Plenum Press.

Dollard, J., & Miller, N. E. (1950). *Personality and psychotherapy.* New York: McGraw-Hill.

Dorsey, M. F., Iwata, B. A., Ong, P., & McSween, T. E. (1980). Treatment of self-injurious behavior using a water mist: Initial response suppression and generalization. *Journal of Applied Behavior Analysis, 13,* 343–353.

Dougher, M. J. (1997). Cognitive concepts, behavior analysis, and behavior therapy. *Journal of Behavior Therapy and Experimental Psychiatry, 28,* 65–70.

Dougher, M. J. (Ed.). (2000). *Clinical behavior analysis.* Reno, NV: Context Press.

Drash, P. W., & Tudor, M. (1993). A functional analysis of verbal delay in preschool children: Implications for prevention and total recovery. *The Analysis of Verbal Behavior, 11,* 19–29.

Dryden, W. (1999). *Rational-emotive behavior therapy: A training manual.* New York: Springer.

Dufrene, B.A., T. Watson, T. S., & Kazmerski, J. S. (2008). Functional analysis and treatment of nail biting. *Behavior Modification, 32,* 913–927.

Dugas, M. J., & Robichaud, M. (2006). *Cognitive-behavioral treatment for generalized anxiety disorder: From science to practice.* New York: Routledge.

Dunlap, G., & Kincaid, D. (2001). The widening world of functional assessment: Comments on four manuals and beyond. *Journal of Applied Behavior Analysis, 34,* 365–377.

Dymond, S., & Barnes, D. (1997). Behavior analytic approaches to self-awareness. *The Psychological Record, 47,* 181–200.

Dymond, S., Chiesa, M., & Martin, N. (2003). An update on providing graduate level training in applied behavior analysis in the UK. *Newsletter of the International Association for Behavior Analysis, 26*(3), 10.

Dymond, S., & Rehfeldt, R. A. (2000). Understanding complex behavior: The transformation of stimulus functions. *The Behavior Analyst, 23,* 239–254.

D'Zurilla, T. J., & Golfried, M. R. (1971). Problem-solving and behavior modification. *Journal of Abnormal Psychology, 78,* 107–126.

D'Zurilla, T. J., & Nezu, A. M. (1999). *Problem-solving therapy, 2nd ed.: A social competence approach to clinical intervention.* New York: Springer.

Ekman, P. (1972). *Universal and cultural differences in facial expressions of emotions.* In J. K. Cole (Ed.), Nebraska Symposium on Motivation (Vol. 19). Lincoln: University of Nebraska Press.

Elkin, I. (1994). The NIMH Treatment of Depression Collaborative Research Program: Where we began and where we are. In A. E. Bergin & S. L. Garfield (Eds.), *Handbook of psychotherapy and behavior change* (4th ed., pp. 114–139). New York: Wiley.

Elkin, I., Shea, M. T., Watkins, J. T., Imber, S. D., Sotsky, S. M., Collins, J. F., et al. (1989). National Institute of Mental Health Treatment of Depression Collaborate Research Program: General effectiveness treatments. *Archives of General Psychiatry, 46,* 971–982.

Ellingson, S. A., Miltenberger, R. G., Stricker, J. M., Garlinghouse, M. A., Roberts, J., & Galenski, T. L. (2000). Analysis and treatment of finger sucking. *Journal of Applied Behavior Analysis, 33,* 41–52.

Ellis, A. (1962). *Reason and emotion in psychotherapy.* New York: Lyle Stewart.

Ellis, A. (1993). Changing rational-emotive therapy (RET) to rational-emotive behavior therapy (REBT). *The Behavior Therapist, 16,* 257–258.

Ellis, A., & Bernard, M. E. (Eds.). (1985). *Clinical applications of rational-emotive therapy.* New York: Plenum Press.

Ellis, A., & Dryden, W. (1997). *The practice of rational-emotive behavior therapy* (2nd ed.). New York: Springer.

Ellis, A., & Grieger, R. (1977). *Handbook of rational-emotive therapy.* New York: Springer.

Elwood, R. W., & Appel, M. (2009). Pain experience in hermit crabs? *Animal Behaviour, 77,* 1243–1246.

Emmelkamp, P. M. G. (2004). Behavior therapy with adults. In M. J. Lambert (Ed.), *Bergin and Garfield's handbook of psychotherapy and behavior change* (5th ed., pp. 393–446). New York: Wiley.

Emmelkamp, P. M. G., Bouman, T. K., & Scholing, A. (1992). *Anxiety disorders: A practitioner's guide.* Chichester, UK: Wiley.

Engelman, K. K., Altus, D. E., Mosier, M. C., & Mathews, R. M. (2003). Brief training to promote the use of less intensive prompts by nursing assistants in a dementia-care unit. *Journal of Applied Behavior Analysis, 36,* 129–132.

Ervin, R. A., & Ehrhardt, K. E. (2000). Behavior analysis and school psychology. In J. Austin & J. E. Carr (Eds.), *Handbook of applied behavior analysis* (pp. 113–136). Reno, NV: Context Press.

Eysenck, H. J. (1959). Learning theory and behavior therapy. *Journal of Mental Science, 105,* 61–75.

Eysenck, H. J. (Ed.). (1960). *Behaviour therapy and the neuroses.* London: Pergamon.

Fabiano, G. A., & Elkin, T. D. (2006). Dissemination of behavior therapy techniques through television. *The Behavior Therapist, 29,* 3–4.

Fabiano, G. A., Pelham, W. E., Jr., Manos, M. J., Gnagy, E. M., Chronis, A. M., Onyango, A. N., et al. (2004). An evaluation of three time-out procedures for children with attention-deficit/ hyperactive disorder. *Behavior Therapy, 35,* 449–469.

Fairburn, C. G. (2008). *Cognitive behavior therapy and eating disorders.* New York: Guilford Press.

Fairburn, C. G., Cooper, Z., Shafran, R., & Wilson, G. T. (2008). Eating disorders: A transdiagnostic protocol. In D. H. Barlow (Ed.), *Clinical handbook of psychological disorders: A step-by-step treatment manual* (4th ed.). New York: Guilford Press.

Faith, M. S., Fontaine, K. R., Cheskin, L. J., & Allison, D. B. (2000). Behavioral approaches to the problems of obesity. *Behavior Modification, 24,* 459–493.

Fantino, E. (2008). Choice, conditioned reinforcement, and the Prius effect. *The Behavior Analyst, 31,* 95–111.

Fantino, E., & Logan, C. A. (1979). *The experimental analysis of behavior.* San Francisco: Freeman.

Farmer, R. F., & Latner, J. D. (2007). Eating disorders. In P. Sturmey (Ed.), *Functional analysis in clinical treatment* (pp. 379–402). London: Elsevier.

Farrell, A. D. (1991). Computers and behavioral assessment: Current applications, future possibilities, and obstacles to routine use. *Behavioral Assessment, 13,* 159–179.

Favell, J. E., Azrin, N. H., Baumeister, A. A., Carr, E. G., Dorsey, M. F., Forehand, R., et al. (1982). The treatment of self-injurious behavior. *Behavior Therapist, 13,* 529–554.

Fawcett, S. B., & Miller, L. K. (1975). Training public-speaking behavior: An experimental analysis and social validation. *Journal of Applied Behavior Analysis, 8,* 125–135.

Fazzio, D., Martin, G. L., Arnal, L., & Yu, D. (2009). Instructing university students to conduct discrete-trials teaching with children with autism. *Journal of Autism Spectrum Disorders, 3,* 57-66.

Feldman, M. A. (1990). Balancing freedom from harm and right to treatment in persons with developmental disabilities. In A. Repp and N. N. Singh (Eds.), *Current perspectives in use of nonaversive and aversive interventions with developmentally disabled persons.* Sycamore, IL: Sycamore Press.

Fellner, D. J., & Sulzer-Azaroff, B. (1984). A behavioral analysis of goal setting. *Journal of Organizational Behavior Management, 6,* 33–51.

Ferster, C. B. (1993). A functional analysis of depression. *American Psychologist, 28,* 857–870.

Ferster, C. B., & Demyer, M. K. (1962). A method for the experimental analysis of the behavior of autistic children. *The American Journal of Orthopsychiatry, 32,* 89–98.

Ferster, C. B., & Skinner, B. F. (1957). *Schedules of reinforcement.* New York: Appleton-Century-Crofts.

Filcheck, H. A., McNeil, C. B., Greco, L. A., & Bernard, L S. (2004). Using a whole-class token economy and coaching of teacher skills in a preschool classroom to manage disruptive behavior. *Psychology in the Schools, 41,* 351–361.

Filter, K. J. (2007). Positive behavior support: Considerations for the future of a model. *The Behavior Analyst, 30,* 87–89.

Fisch, G. S. (1998). Visual inspection of data revisited: Do the eyes still have it? *The Behavior Analyst, 21,* 111–123.

Fischer, J., & Corcoran, K. (1994). *Measures for clinical practice: A source book* (2nd ed., Vols. 1 and 2). New York: Free Press.

Fisher, W. W., Kelley, M. E., & Lomas, J. E. (2003). Visual aids and structured criteria for improving visual inspection and interpretation of single-case designs. *Journal of Applied Behavior Analysis, 36,* 387–406.

Fixsen, D. L., & Blase, K. A. (1993). Creating new realities: Program development and dissemination. *Journal of Applied Behavior Analysis, 26,* 597–615.

Fixsen, D. L., Blase, K. A., Timbers, G. D., & Wolf, M. M. (2001). In search of program implementation: 792 replications of the teaching-family model. In G. A. Bernfeld, D. P. Farrington, & A. W. Leschied (Eds.), *Offender rehabilitation in practice: Implementing and evaluating effective programs* (pp. 149–166). London: Wiley.

Flanagan, B., Goldiamond, I., & Azrin, N. (1958). Operant stuttering: The control of stuttering behavior through response-contingent consequences. *Journal of the Experimental Analysis of Behavior, 1,* 173–177.

Flanagan, C. (1991). Behavior therapy and cognitive therapy in Ireland. *The Behavior Therapist, 14,* 231–232.

Flora, S. R. (1990). Undermining intrinsic interest from the standpoint of a behaviorist. *The Psychological Record, 40,* 323–346.

Flora, S. R. (2000). Praise's magic: Reinforcement ratio five-one gets the job done. *Behavior Analyst Today [Online], 1*(4), 64–69. Available: www.behavior.org.

Flora, S. R. (2007). *Taking America off drugs: Why behavior therapy is more effective for treating ADHD, OCD, depression, and other psychological problems.* New York: State University of New York Press.

Flora, S. R., & Flora, D. B. (1999). Effects of extrinsic reinforcement for reading during childhood on reported reading habits of college students. *The Psychological Record, 49,* 3–14.

Foa, E. B. (2000). Psychosocial treatment of post-traumatic stress disorder. *Journal of Clinical Psychiatry, 61*(Suppl. 5), 43–48.

Fombonne, E. (2007). Epidemiological surveys of pervasive developmental disorders. In F. Volkmar (Ed.), *Autism and pervasive developmental disorder* (2nd ed., pp. 33–68). Cambridge, UK: Cambridge University Press.

Fonagy, P., Target, M, Cottrell, D., Phillips, J., Kurtz, Z. (2002). *What works for whom? A critical review of treatments for children and adolescents.* New York: Guilford Press.

Forman, E. M., Herbert, J. D., Moitra, E., Yeomans, P. D., & Geller, P. A. (2007). A randomized controlled effectiveness trial of Acceptance and Commitment Therapy and Cognitive Therapy for anxiety and depression. *Behavior Modification, 31,* 772–799.

Forsyth, J. P., & Eifert, G. H. (2007). *The mindfulness and acceptance workbook for anxiety: A guide to breaking free from anxiety, phobias, and worry using Acceptance and Commitment Therapy.* Oakland, CA: New Harbinger.

Foxx, R. M., & Faw, G. D. (1990). Problem-solving skills training for psychiatric inpatients: An analysis of generalization. *Behavioral Residential Treatment, 5,* 159–176.

Foxx, R. M., & Shapiro, S. T. (1978). The timeout ribbon: A non-exclusionary timeout procedure. *Journal of Applied Behavior Analysis, 11,* 125–136.

Franklin, M. E., & Foa, E. B. (2008). Obsessive compulsive disorder. In D. H. Barlow (Ed.), *Clinical handbook of psychological disorders: A step-by-step treatment manual.* New York: Guilford Press.

Franks, C. M. (1964). *Conditioning techniques in clinical practice and research.* New York: Springer.

Franks, C. M. (Ed.). (1969). *Behavior therapy: Appraisal and status.* New York: McGraw-Hill.

Frea, W. D., & Vittimberga, G. L. (2000). Behavior interventions for children with autism. In J. Austin & J. E. Carr (Eds.), *Handbook of applied behavior analysis* (pp. 247–274). Reno, NV: Context Press.

Frederick, L. D., Deitz, S. M., Bryceland, J. A., & Hummel, J. H. (2003). *Behavior analysis, education, and effective schooling.* Reno, NV: Context Press.

Frederiksen, L. W., & Lovett, F. B. (1980). Inside organizational behavior management: Perspectives on an emerging field. *Journal of Organizational Behavior Management, 2,* 193–203.

Friman, P. C. (2000). Behavioral family-style residential care for troubled out-of-home adolescents: Recent findings. In J. Austin and J. E. Carr (Eds.), *Handbook of Applied Behavior Analysis.* Reno, NV: Context Press.

Friman, P. C., Osgood, D. W., Smith, G., Shanahan, D., Thompson, R. W., Larzelere, R., & Daly, D. L. (1996). A longitudinal evaluation of prevalent negative beliefs about residential placement for troubled adolescents. *Journal of Abnormal Child Psychology, 24,* 299–324.

Friman, P. C., & Poling, A. (1995). Making life easier with effort: Basic findings and applied research on response effort. *Journal of Applied Behavior Analysis, 28,* 583–590.

Friman, P. C., & Vollmer, D. (1995). Successful use of the nocturnal urine alarm for diurnal enuresis. *Journal of Applied Behavior Analysis, 28,* 89–90.

Fuller, P. R. (1949). Operant conditioning of a vegetative human organism. *American Journal of Psychology, 62,* 587–590.

Gelfand, D. M., Hartmann, D. P., Lamb, A. K., Smith, C. L., Mahan, M. A., & Paul, S. C. (1974). Effects of adult models and described alternatives on children's choice of behavior management techniques. *Child Development, 45,* 585–593.

Geller, E. S., Winett, R. A., & Everett, P. B. (1982). *Preserving the environment: New strategies for behavior change.* New York: Plenum Press.

Gena, A., Krantz, P. J., McClannahan, L. E., & Poulson, C. L. (1996). Training and generalization of effective behavior displayed by youth with autism. *Journal of Applied Behavior Analysis, 29,* 291–304.

Gershoff, E. T. (2002). Corporal punishment by parents and associated child behaviors and experiences: A meta-analytic and theoretical review. *Psychological Bulletin, 128,* 539–579.

Ghezzi, P. M., Williams, W. L., & Carr, J. E. (Eds.). (1999). *Autism: Behavior analytic perspectives.* Reno, NV: Context Press.

Gimpel, G. A., & Holland, N. L. (2003). *Emotional and behavioral problems of young children.* New York: Guilford Press.

Girardeau, F. L., & Spradlin, J. E. (1964). Token rewards on a cottage program. *Mental Retardation, 2,* 345–351.

Glenwick, D. S. (1990). Commentary on the special issue: The adolescent identity development of behavioral community psychology. *The Community Psychologist, 23,* 14–16.

Glynn, S. N. (1990). Token economy approaches for psychiatric patients: Progress and pitfalls over 25 years. *Behavior Modification, 14,* 383–407.

Glynn, E. L., & Thomas, J. D. (1974). Effect of cueing on self-control of classroom behavior. *Journal of Applied Behavior Analysis, 7,* 299–306.

Goetz, E. M., & Baer, D. M. (1973). Social control of form diversity and the emergence of new forms in childrens' block building. *Journal of Applied Behavior Analysis, 6,* 105–113.

Goldiamond, I. (1965). Self-control procedures in personal behavior problems. *Psychological Reports, 17,* 851–868.

Goldiamond, I. (1976). Self-reinforcement. *Journal of Applied Behavior Analysis, 9,* 509–514.

Gormally, J., Black, S., Daston, S., & Rardin, D. (1982). The assessment of binge eating severity among obese persons. *Addictive Behaviors, 7,* 47–55.

Gortner, E. T., Golan, J. K., Dobson, K. S., & Jacobson, N. S. (1998). Cognitive behavior treatment for depression. *Relapse Prevention, 66,* 377–384.

Gossette, R. L., & O'Brien, R. M. (1989, May). Efficacy of rational-emotive therapy with children: Fact or artifact? Paper presented at the meeting of the Association for Behavior Analysis, Nashville, TN.

Gossette, R. L., & O'Brien, R. M. (1992). The efficacy of rational-emotive therapy in adults: Clinical fact or psychometric artifact? *Journal of Behavior Therapy and Experimental Psychiatry, 23,* 9–24.

Gould, D. (1998). Goal-setting for peak performance. In J. M. Williams (Ed.), *Applied sport psychology: Personal growth to peak performance* (3rd ed.). Mountainview, CA: Mayfield.

Gould, R. A., & Clum, G. A. (1993). A meta-analysis of self-help treatment approaches. *Clinical Psychological Review, 13,* 167–189.

Graaf, I. D., Speetjens, P., Smit, F., Wolff, M. D., & Tavecchio, L. (2008). Effectiveness of the Triple P Positive Parenting Program on behavioral program in children: A meta-analysis. *Behavior Modification, 32,* 714–735.

Grassi, T. C. C. (Ed.). (2004). *Contemporary challenges in the behavioral approach: A Brazilian overview.* Santo André, Brazil: Esetec Editores Associados.

Graziano, A. M. (1975). Futurants, coverants and operants. *Behavior Therapy, 6,* 421–422.

Graziano, A. M. (2002). *Developmental disabilities: Introduction to a diverse field.* Boston: Allyn & Bacon.

Greenspoon, J. (1951). The effect of verbal and nonverbal stimuli on the frequency of members of two verbal response classes. Unpublished doctoral dissertation, Indiana University, Bloomington.

Greenspoon, J. (1955). The reinforcing effect of two spoken words on the frequency of two responses. *American Journal of Psychology, 68,* 409–416.

Greenspoon, J. (1976). *The sources of behavior: Abnormal and normal.* Monterey, CA: Brooks/Cole.

Gregory, R. J., Canning, S. S., Lee, T. W., Wise, J. C. (2004). Cognitive bibliotherapy: A meta-analysis. *Professional Psychology: Research and Practice, 35,* 275–280.

Gresham, F. M., & MacMillan, D. L. (1997). Autistic recovery? An analysis and critique of the empirical evidence on the early intervention project. *Behavioral Disorders, 22,* 185–201.

Griffen, A. K., Wolery, M., & Schuster, J. W. (1992). Triadic instruction of chained food preparation responses: Acquisition and observational learning. *Journal of Applied Behavior Analysis, 25,* 193–204.

Griffith, R. G., & Spreat, S. (1989). Aversive behavior modification procedures and the use of professional judgment. *Behavior Therapist, 12*(7), 143–146.

Guess, D., & Carr, E. (1991). Emergence and maintenance of stereotopy and self-injury. *American Journal on Mental Retardation, 96,* 299–319.

Guess, D., Helmstetter, E., Turnbull, H. R., III, & Knowlton, S. (1986). *Use of aversive procedures with persons who are disabled: An historical review and critical analysis.* Seattle, WA: Association for Persons with Severe Handicaps.

Guess, D., Sailor, W., Rutherford, G., & Baer, D. M. (1968). An experimental analysis of linguistic development: The productive use of the plural morpheme. *Journal of Applied Behavior Analysis, 1,* 297–306.

Guevremont, D. C., Osnes, P. G., & Stokes, T. F. (1986). Preparation for effective self-regulation: The development of generalized verbal control. *Journal of Applied Behavior Analysis, 19,* 99–104.

Guilhardi, H. J. (2004). Coercive control and anxiety—A case of "panic disorder" treated by therapy by contingencies of reinforcement. In T. Grassi (Ed.), *Contemporary challenges in the behavioral approach: A Brazilian overview.* Santo André, Brazil: Esetec Editores Associados.

Guthrie, E. R. (1935). *The psychology of human learning.* New York: Harper & Row.

Hackenberg, T. D. (2009). Token reinforcement: A review and analysis. *Journal of the Experimental Analysis of Behavior, 91,* 257–286.

Hagopian, L. P., Piazza, C. C., Fisher, W. W., Thibault Sullivan, M., Acquisto, J., & Leblanc, L. A. (1998). Effectiveness of functional communication training with and without extinction and punishment: A summary of 21 inpatient cases. *Journal of Applied Behavior Analysis, 12*(2), 273–282.

Hains, A. H., & Baer, D. M. (1989). Interaction effects in multi-element designs: Inevitable, desirable, and ignorable. *Journal of Applied Behavior Analysis, 22,* 57–69.

Hanley, G. P., Iwata, B. A., & McCord, B. E. (2003). Functional analysis of problem behavior: A review. *Journal of Applied Behavior Analysis, 36,* 147–185.

Hanley, G. P., Piazza, C. C., Fisher, W. W., Maglieri, K. A. (2005). On the effectiveness of and preference for punishment and extinction components of function-based intervenetions. *Journal of Applied Behavior Analysis, 38*(1), 51–65.

Hansen, D. J., Tishelman, A. C., Hawkins, R. P., & Doepke, K. (1990). Habits with potential as disorders: Prevalence, severity, and other characteristics among college students. *Behavior Modification, 14,* 66–88.

Hantula, D. A., Boyd, J. H., & Crowell, C. I. (1989). Ten years of behavioral instruction with computers: Trials, tribulations, and reflections. *Proceedings of the Academic Microcomputer Conference* (pp. 81–92). Indianapolis, IN: Author.

Hardy, L., Martin, G., Yu, D., Leader, C., & Quinn, G. (1981). *Objective behavioral assessment of the severely and moderately mentally handicapped: The OBA.* Springfield, IL: Charles C Thomas.

Haring, T. G., & Kennedy, C. H. (1990). Contextual control of problem behavior in students with severe disabilities. *Journal of Applied Behavior Analysis, 23,* 235–243.

Harris, B. (1979). What happened to little Albert? *American Psychologist, 34,* 151–160.

Harris, C. S., & McReynolds, W. T. (1977). Semantic cues and response contingencies in self-instructional control. *Journal of Behavior Therapy and Experimental Psychiatry, 8,* 15–17.

Harris, F. R., Wolf, M. M., & Baer, D. M. (1964). Effects of adult social reinforcement on child behavior. *Young Children, 20,* 8–17.

Hatch, M. L., Friedman, S., & Paradis, C. M. (1996). Behavioral treatment of obsessive-compulsive disorder in African Americans. *Cognitive and Behavioral Practice, 3,* 303–315.

Haughton, E., & Ayllon, T. (1965). Production and elimination of symptomatic behavior. In L. P. Ullmann & L. Krasner (Eds.), *Case studies in behavior modification* (pp. 94–98). New York: Holt, Rinehart & Winston.

Hawkins, G. H., & Cooper, D. H. (1990). Adaptive behavior measures in mental retardation research: Subject description in AJMD/AJMR articles (1979–1987). *American Journal of Mental Retardation, 94,* 654–660.

Hawkins, R. C., & Clement, P. (1980). Development and construct validation of a self-report measure of binge eating tendencies. *Addictive Behaviors, 5,* 219–226.

Hawkins, R. P. (1979). The functions of assessment: Implications for selection and development of devices for assessing repertoires in clinical, educational, and other settings. *Journal of Applied Behavior Analysis, 12,* 501–516.

Hawkins, R. P., & Dotson, V. A. (1975). Reliability scores that delude: An Alice in Wonderland trip through the misleading characteristics of interobserver agreement scores in interval recording. In E. Ramp & G. Semp (Eds.), *Behavior analysis: Areas of research and application* (pp. 359–376). Upper Saddle River, NJ: Prentice Hall.

Hawkins, R. P., & Forsyth, J. P. (1997). Bridging barriers between paradigms: Making cognitive concepts relevant for behavior analysis. *Journal of Behavior Therapy and Experimental Psychiatry, 28,* 3–6.

Hawkins, R. P., Mathews, J. R., & Hamdan, L. (1999). *Measuring behavioral outcomes.* Norwell, MA: Kluwer Academic/Plenum Publishers.

Hayes, S. C. (1989). *Rule-governed behavior: Cognition, contingencies, and instructional control.* New York: Plenum Press.

Hayes, S. C. (2004). Acceptance and commitment therapy, relational frame theory, and the third wave of behavior therapy. *Behavior Therapy, 35,* 639–666.

Hayes, S. C. (2008). Avoiding the mistakes of the past. *The Behavior Therapist, 31,* 150–153.

Hayes, S. C., Barnes-Holmes, D., & Roche, B. (Eds.). (2001). *Relational frame theory: A post-Skinnerian account of human language and cognition.* New York: Plenum Press.

Hayes, S. C., & Bissett, R. T. (2000). Behavioral psychotherapy and the rise of clinical behavior analysis. In J. Austin & J. E. Carr (Eds.), *Handbook of applied behavior analysis* (pp. 231–245). Reno, NV: Context Press.

Hayes, S. C., Follette, V. M., & Linehan, M. M. (Eds.). (2004). *Mindfulness and acceptance: Expanding the cognitive behavioral tradition.* New York: Guilford Press.

Hayes, S. C., Jacobson, N. S., Follette, V. M., & Dougher, M. J. (Eds.). (1994). *Acceptance and change: Content and context in psychotherapy.* Reno, NV: Context Press.

Hayes, S. C., Masuda, A., Bissette, R., Luoma, J., & Guerrero, L. F. (2004). DBT, FAP, and ACT: How empirically oriented are the new behavior therapy technologies. *Behavior Therapy, 35,* 35–54.

Hayes, S. C., Rosenfarb, I., Wulfert, E., Munt, E. D., Korn, D., & Zettle, R. D. (1985). Self-reinforcement effects: An artifact of social standard setting? *Journal of Applied Behavior Analysis, 18,* 201–214.

Hayes, S. C., Strosahl, K. D., & Wilson, K. G. (1999). *Acceptance and commitment therapy: An experiential approach to behavior change.* New York: Guilford Press.

Haynes, S. N. (1998). The changing nature of behavioral assessment. In A. S. Bellack & M. Hersen (Eds.), *Behavioral assessment: A practical handbook* (4th ed., pp. 1–21). Boston: Allyn & Bacon.

Hefferline, R. F., Keenan, B., & Harford, R. A. (1959). Escape and avoidance conditioning in human subjects without their observation of the response. *Science, 130,* 1338–1339.

Henrich, J., & Gil-White, F. J. (2001). The evolution of prestige: Freely conferred deference as a mechanism for enhancing the benefits of cultural transmission. *Evolution and Human Behavior, 22,* 165–196.

Hermann, J. A.. Demontes, A. I., Dominguez, B., Montes, F., & Hopkins, B. L. (1973). Effects of bonuses for punctuality on the tardiness of industrial workers. *Journal of Applied Behavior Analysis, 6,* 563–570.

Herrnstein, R. J. (1961). Relative and absolute strength of response as a function of frequency of reinforcement. *Journal of the Experimental Analysis of Behavior, 4,* 267–272.

Herrnstein, R. J., & Devilliers, P. A. (1980). Fish as a natural category for people and pigeons. In G. H. Bower (Ed.), *The psychology of learning and motivation* (Vol. 14, pp. 60–97). New York: Academic Press.

Herrnstein, R. J., & Loveland, D. H. (1964). Complex visual concept in the pigeon. *Science, 146,* 549–551.

Herrnstein, R. J., Loveland, D. H., & Cable, C. (1976). Natural concepts in pigeons. *Journal of Experimental Psychology: Animal Behavior Processes, 2,* 285–302.

Hersen, M. (1976). Historical perspectives in behavioral assessment. In M. Hersen & A. S. Bellack (Eds.), *Behavioral assessment: A practical handbook* (pp. 3–17). New York: Pergamon Press.

Hersen, M. (Ed.). (1983). *Outpatient behavior therapy: A clinical guide.* New York: Grune & Stratton.

Hersen, M., & Last, C. G. (Eds.). (1999). *Child behavior therapy casebook.* New York: Kluwer Academic Publishers/Plenum Press.

Higgins, S. T., Silverman, K., & Heil, S. H. (Eds.). (2008). *Contingency management in substance abuse treatment.* New York: Guilford Press.

Hildebrand, R. G., Martin, G. L., Furer, P., & Hazen, A. (1990). A recruitment of praise package to increase productivity levels of developmentally handicapped workers. *Behavior Modification, 14,* 97–113.

Hile, M. G. (1991). Hand-held behavioral observations: The Observer. *Behavioral Assessment, 13,* 187–196.

Hirai, M., & Clum, G. A. (2006). A meta-analytic study of self-help interventions for anxiety problems. *Behavior Therapy, 37,* 99–111.

Hofmann, S. G., & Otto, M. W. (2008). *Cognitive behavioral therapy for social anxiety disorder: Evidence-based and treatment-specific treatment techniques (Practical clinical guidelines).* New York: Routledge Mental Health.

Homme, L. E. (1965). Perspectives in psychology: XXIV. Control of coverants, the operants of the mind. *Psychological Record, 15,* 501–511.

Homme, L. E., Csanyi, A. P., Gonzales, M. A., & Rechs, J. R. (1969). *How to use contingency contracting in the classroom.* Champaign, IL: Research Press.

Honig, W. K., & Stewart, K. (1988). Pigeons can discriminate locations presented in pictures. *Journal of the Experimental Analysis of Behavior, 50,* 541–551.

Horan, J. J., & Johnson, R. G. (1971). Covariant conditioning through a self-management application of the Premack principle: Its effect on weight reduction. *Journal of Behavior Therapy and Experimental Psychiatry, 2,* 243–249.

Horner, R. H., Dunlap, G., Koegel, R. L., Carr, E. G., Sailor, W., Anderson, J., Albin, R. W., & O'Neil, R. E. (1990). Toward a technology of "nonaversive" behavioral support. *Journal of the Association for Persons with Severe Handicaps, 15,* 125–132.

Horner, R. D., & Keilitz, I. (1975). Training mentally retarded adolescents to brush their teeth. *Journal of Applied Behavior Analysis, 8,* 301–309.

Horner, R. H. (1994). Functional assessment: Contributions and future directions. *Journal of Applied Behavior Analysis, 27,* 401–404.

Horner, R. H., Sprague, T., & Wilcox, B. (1982). General case programming for community activities. In B. Wilcox & G. T. Bellamy (Eds.), *Design of high school programs for severely handicapped students* (pp. 61–98). Baltimore: Paul Brookes.

Hrycaiko, D., & Martin, G. L. (1996). Applied research studies with single-subject designs: Why so few? *Journal of Applied Sport Psychology, 8,* 183–199.

Hrydowy, E. R., & Martin, G. L. (1994). A practical staff management package for use in a training program for persons with developmental disabilities. *Behavior Modification, 18,* 66–88.

Huang, W., & Cuvo, A. J. (1997). Social skills training for adults with mental retardation in job-related settings. *Behavior Modification, 21,* 3–44.

Hull, C. L. (1943). *Principles of behavior.* New York: Appleton-Century-Crofts.

Hull, C. L. (1952). *A behavior system.* New Haven, CT: Yale University Press.

Hume, K. M., Martin, G. L., Gonzales, P., Cracklen, C., & Genthon, S. (1985). A self-monitoring feedback package for improving freestyle figure skating performance. *Journal of Sport Psychology, 7,* 333–345.

Hur, J., & Osborne, S. (1993). A comparison of forward and backward chaining methods used in teaching corsage making skills to mentally retarded adults. *The British Journal of Developmental Disabilities, 39* (Part 2, No. 77), 108–117.

Irey, P. A. (1972). Covert sensitization of cigarette smokers with high and low extraversion scores. Unpublished master's thesis, Southern Illinois University, Carbondale.

Israel, A. C., Stolmaker, L., & Adrian, C. A. G. (1985). The effects of training parents in general child management skills on a behavioral weight loss program for children. *Behavior Therapy, 16,* 169–180.

Issacs, W., Thomas, J., & Goldiamond, I. (1960). Application of operant conditioning to reinstate verbal behavior in psychotics. *Journal of Speech and Hearing Disorders, 25,* 8–12.

Ivancic, M. T., Barrett, G. T., Simonow, A., & Kimberly, A. (1997). A replication to increase happiness indices among some people with profound developmental disabilities. *Research in Developmental Disabilities, 18,* 79–89.

Iwamasa, G. Y. (1999). Behavior therapy and Asian Americans: Is there a commitment? *The Behavior Therapist, 10,* 196–197, 205–206.

Iwamasa, G. Y., & Smith, S. K. (1996). Ethic diversity in behavioral psychology: A review of the literature. *Behavior Modification, 20,* 45–59.

Iwata, B. A., Dorsey, M. F., Slifer, K. J., Bauman, K. E., & Richman, G. S. (1982). Toward a functional analysis of self-injury. *Analysis and Intervention in Developmental Disabilities, 2,* 3–20.

Iwata, B. A., Kahng, S. W., Wallace, M. D., & Lindberg, J. S. (2000). The functional analysis model of behavioral assessment. In J. Austin & J. E. Carr (Eds.), *Handbook of applied behavior analysis* (pp. 61–90). Reno, NV: Context Press.

Iwata, B. A., Pace, G. M., Cowdery, G. E., & Miltenberger, R. G. (1994). What makes extinction work: An analysis of procedural form and function. *Journal of Applied Behavior Analysis, 27,* 131–144.

Iwata, B. A., Pace, G. M., Dorsey, M. F., Zarcone, J. R., Vollmer, T. R., Smith, R. G., et al. (1994). The functions of self-injurious behavior: An experimental-epidemiological analysis. *Journal of Applied Behavior Analysis, 27,* 215–240.

Iwata, B. A., Pace, G. M., Kalsher, M. J., Cowdery, G. E., & Cataldo, M. F. (1990). Experimental analysis and extinction of self-injurious escape behavior. *Journal of Applied Behavior Analysis, 23,* 11–27.

Izard, C. E. (1991). *The psychology of emotions.* New York: Plenum Press.

Jackson, D. A., & Wallace, R. F. (1974). The modification and generalization of voice loudness in a 15-year-old retarded girl. *Journal of Applied Behavior Analysis, 7,* 461–471.

Jacobs, H. (2000). Brain injury rehabilitation. In J. Austin & J. E. Carr (Eds.), *Handbook of applied behavior analysis* (pp. 211–230). Reno, NV: Context Press.

Jacobson, N. S., Dobson, K. S., Truax, P. A., Addis, M. E., Koerner, K., Gollan, J. K., et al. (1996). A component analysis of cognitive behavioral treatment for depression. *Journal of Consulting and Clinical Psychology, 64,* 295–304.

Jacobson, N. S., Martell, C. R., & Dimidjian, S. (2001). Behavioral activation for depression: Returning to contextual roots. *Clinical Psychology: Science & Practice, 8,* 255–270.

Jacobson, J. W., Mulick, J. A., & Green, G. (1998). Cost-benefit estimates for early intensive behavioral intervention for young children with autism: General model and single state case. *Behavioral Interventions, 13,* 201–226.

Janis, I., & Mann, L. (1977). *Decision-making.* New York: Free Press.

Janis, I., & Wheeler, D. (1978). Thinking clearly about career choices. *Psychology Today, 11*(12), 66–76, 121–122.

Jensen, B. J., & Haynes, S. N. (1986). *Self-report questionnaires and inventories.* In A. R. Ciminero, K. S. Calhoun, & H. E. Adams (Eds.), *Handbook of behavioral assessment* (2nd ed.). New York: Wiley.

Johnson, C. M., Redmon, W. K., & Mawhinney, T. C. (Eds.). (2001). *Handbook of organizational performance: Behavior analysis and management.* New York: Haworth Press.

Johnson, C. R., Hunt, F. M., & Siebert, M. J. (1994). Discrimination training in the treatment of pica and food scavenging. *Behavior Modification, 18,* 214–229.

Johnson, K. R., & Ruskin, R. S. (1977). *Behavioral instruction: An evaluative review.* Washington, DC: American Psychological Association.

Johnson, S. P., Welch, T. M., Miller, L. K., & Altus, D. E. (1991). Participatory management: Maintaining staff performance in a university housing cooperative. *Journal of Applied Behavior Analysis, 24,* 119–127.

Johnson, W. G. (1971). Some applications of Homme's coverant control therapy: Two case reports. *Behavior Therapy, 2,* 240–248.

Johnson, W. L., & Baumeister, A. (1978). Self-injurious behavior: A review and analysis of methodological details of published studies. *Behavior Modification, 2,* 465–484.

Johnston, J. M. (2006). "Replacing" problem behavior: An analysis of tactical alternatives. *The Behavior Analyst, 29,* 1–11.

Johnston, J. M., Foxx, R. M., Jacobson, J. W., Green, G., & Mulick, J. A. (2006). Positive behavior support and Applied Behavior Analysis. *The Behavior Analyst, 29,* 51–74.

Johnston, J. M., & Pennypacker, H. S. (Eds.). (2009). *Strategies and tactics of behavioral research* (3rd ed.). New York: Routledge.

Jones, M. C. (1924). The elimination of children's fears. *Journal of Experimental Psychology, 7,* 383–390.

Jones, R. R., Weinrott, M. R., & Howard, J. R. (1981). *The national evaluation of the teaching family model.* Final Report R01 MH Grants 25631 and MH 31018 awarded by the Center for Studies of Crime and Delinquency, National Institute of Mental Health. Eugene, OR: Evaluation Research Group, Inc.

Jones, R. S. P., & McCaughey, R. E. (1992). Gentle teaching and applied behavior analysis: A critical review. *Journal of Applied Behavior Analysis, 25,* 853–867.

Juliano, L. M., Donny, M., Houtsmuller, E. J., & Stitzer, M. L. (2006). Experimental evidence for a causal relationship between smoking lapse and relapse. *Journal of Abnormal Psychology, 11,* 166–173.

Kabat-Zinn, J. (1990). *Full catastrophe living: Using the wisdom of your body and mind to face stress, pain, and illness.* New York: Dell Publishing.

Kahng, S. W., & Iwata, B. A. (1998). Computerized systems for collecting real-time observational data. *Journal of Applied Behavior Analysis, 31,* 253–261.

Kahng, S. W., And Iwata, B. A. (2000). Computer systems for collecting real-time observational data. In T. Thompson, D. Felce, & F. Symons (Eds.), *Behavioral observation: Technology and applications in developmental disabilities* (pp. 35–46). Baltimore. MD: Brookes.

Kantor, J. W., Baruch, D. E., & Gaynor, S. T. (2006). Acceptance and Commitment Therapy and behavioral activation for the treatment of depression: Description and comparison. *The Behavior Analyst, 29,* 161–185.

Kantor, J. W., Busch, A. M., Weeks, C. E., & Landes, S. J. (2008). The nature of clinical depression: Symptoms, syndromes, and behavioral analysis. *The Behavior Analyst, 31,* 1–21.

Karol, R. L., & Richards, C. S. (1978, November). Making treatment effects last: An investigation of maintenance strategies for smoking reduction. Paper presented at the meeting of the Association for the Advancement of Behavior Therapy, Chicago.

Kau, M. L., & Fischer, J. (1974). Self-modification of exercise behavior. *Journal of Behavior Therapy and Experimental Psychiatry, 5,* 213–214.

Kazdin, A. E. (1973). The effect of vicarious reinforcement on attentive behavior in the classroom. *Journal of Applied Behavior Analysis, 6,* 72–78.

Kazdin, A. E. (1977a). *The token economy: A review and evaluation.* New York: Plenum Press.

Kazdin, A. E. (1977b). Assessing the clinical or applied importance of behavior change through social validation. *Behavior Modification, 1,* 427–451.

Kazdin, A. E. (1978). *History of behavior modification.* Baltimore: University Park Press.

Kazdin, A. E. (1985). The token economy. In R. M. Turner & L. M. Ascher (Eds.), *Evaluating*

behavior therapy outcome (pp. 225–253). New York: Springer.

Kazdin, A. E. (2008). Evidence-based treatment and practice: New opportunities to bridge clinical research and practice, enhance the knowledge base, and improve patient care. *American Psychologist, 63,* 146–159.

Kazdin, A. E., & Erickson, L. M. (1975). Developing responsiveness to instructions in severely and profoundly retarded residents. *Journal of Behavior Therapy and Experimental Psychiatry, 6,* 17–21.

Kazdin, A. E., & Polster, R. (1973). Intermittent token reinforcement and response maintenance in extinction. *Behavior Therapy, 4,* 386–391.

Kearney, C. A., & Silverman, W. K. (1990). A preliminary analysis of a functional model of assessment and treatment for school refusal behavior. *Behavior Modification, 14,* 340–366.

Keller, F. S. (1968). Good-bye, teacher . . . *Journal of Applied Behavior Analysis, 1,* 79–89.

Keller, F. S., & Schoenfeld, W. N. (1950). *Principles of psychology.* New York: Appleton-Century-Crofts.

Keller, F. S., & Sherman, J. G. (1982). *The PSI handbook: Essays on personalized instruction.* Lawrence, KS: T.R.I. Publications.

Kendall, P. C. (Ed.). (2000). *Child and adolescent psychotherapy: Cognitive behavioral procedures* (2nd ed.). New York: Guilford Press.

Kern, L., Childs, K. E., Dunlap, G., Clarke, S., & Falk, G. D. (1994). Using assessment based curricular intervention to improve the classroom behavior of a student with emotional and behavioral challenges. *Journal of Applied Behavior Analysis, 27,* 7–19.

Kim, J. (2003). History of Korean ABA. *Newsletter of the International Association for Behavior Analysis, 26,* (3), 20–21.

King, N. (1996). The Australian Association for Cognitive and Behavior Therapy. *The Behavior Therapist, 19,* 73–74.

Kingdon, D. G., & Turkington, D. (1994). *Cognitive-behavioral therapy of schizophrenia.* New York: Guilford Press.

Kingsley, D. E. (2006). The Teaching-Family Model and post-treatment recidivism: A critical review of the conventional wisdom. *International Journal of Behavioral and Consultation Therapy, 2,* 481–497.

Kinsner, W., & Pear, J. J. (1988). Computer-aided personalized system of instruction for the virtual classroom. *Canadian Journal of Educational Communication, 17,* 21–36.

Kirby, F. D., & Shields, F. (1972). Modification of arithmetic response rate and attending behavior in a seventh grade student. *Journal of Applied Behavior Analysis, 5,* 79–84.

Kircher, A. S., Pear, J. J., & Martin, G. (1971). Shock as punishment in a picture-naming task with retarded children. *Journal of Applied Behavior Analysis, 4,* 227–233.

Kirigin, K. A., Braukmann, C. J., Atwater, J. D., & Wolf, M. M. (1982). An evaluation of Teaching-Family (Achievement Place) group homes for juvenile offenders. *Journal of Applied Behavior Analysis, 15,* 1.

Knight, M. F., & McKenzie, H. S. (1974). Elimination of bedtime thumb-sucking in home settings through contingent reading. *Journal of Applied Behavior Analysis, 7,* 33–38.

Koegel, R. L., & Williams, J. A. (1980). Direct versus indirect response-reinforcer relationships in teaching autistic children. *Journal of Abnormal Child Psychology, 8,* 537–547.

Kohler, F. W., & Greenwood, C. R. (1986). Toward technology of generalization: The identification of natural contingencies of reinforcement. *The Behavior Analyst, 9,* 19–26.

Kohn, A. (1993). *Punished by rewards: The trouble with gold stars, incentive plans, A's, praise, and other bribes.* New York: Houghton Mifflin.

Kokoszka, A., Popiel, A., & Sitarz, M. (2000). Cognitive-behavioral therapy in Poland. *The Behavior Therapist, 23,* 209–216.

Komaki, J., & Barnett, F. T. (1977). A behavioral approach to coaching football: Improving the play execution of the offensive backfield on a youth football team. *Journal of Applied Behavior Analysis, 7,* 199–206.

Konarski, E. A., Jr., Favell, J. E., & Favell, J. E. (Eds.). (1997). *Manual for the assessment and treatment of the behavior disorders of people with mental retardation.* Morganton, NC: Western Carolina Center Foundation.

Koop, S., Martin, G., Yu, D., & Suthons, E. (1980). Comparison of two reinforcement strategies in vocational-skill training of mentally retarded persons. *American Journal of Mental Deficiency, 84,* 616–626.

Krasner, L., & Ullmann, L. T. (Eds.) (1965). *Research in Behavior Modification.* New York: Holt, Rinehart, & Winston.

Kulik, C.-L., Kulik, J. A., & Bangert-Drowns, R. L. (1990). Effectiveness of mastery learning programs: A meta-analysis. *Review of Educational Research, 60,* 265–299.

Lalli, J. S., Vollmer, T. R., Progar, P. R., Wright, C., Borrero, J., Daniel, D., et al. (1999). Competition between positive and negative reinforcement in the treatment of escape behavior. *Journal of Applied Behavior Analysis, 32,* 285–296.

Lam, D. C. K. (2008). *Cognitive behavior therapy: A practical guide to helping people take control.* New York: Routledge.

Lambert, M. J. (Ed.). (2004). *Bergin & Garfield's Handbook of psychotherapy and behaviour change.* New York: Wiley.

Lamson, R. (1997). *Virtual therapy.* Montreal, Canada: Polytechnic International Press.

Langdon, N. A., Carr, E. G., & Owen-Deschryver, J. S. (2008) Functional Analysis of precursors for serious problem behavior and related intervention. *Behavior Modification, 32,* 804–827.

Laraway, S., Snycerski, S., Michael, J., & Poling, A. (2003). Motivating operations and terms to describe them: Some further reinfinements. *Journal of Applied Behavior Analysis, 36,* 407–414.

Larkin, K. T., & Zayfert, C. (1996). Anger management training with essential hypertensive patients. In V. B. Van Hasselt & M. Hersen (Eds.), *Sourcebook of psychological treatment manuals for adult disorders* (pp. 689–716). New York: Plenum Press.

Larzelere, R. E., Daly, D. L., Davis, J. L., Chmelka, M. B., & Handwerk, M. L. (2004). Outcome evaluation of Girls and Boys Town's Family Home Program. *Education and Treatment of Children, 27,* 130–149.

Larzelere, R. E., Dinges, K., Schmidt, M. D., Spellman, D. F., Criste, T. R., & Connell, P. (2001). Outcomes of residential treatment: A study of the adolescent clients of Girls and Boys Town. *Child & Youth Care Forum, 30,* 175–184.

Laties, V. G., & Mace, F. C. (1993). Taking stock: The first 25 years of the *Journal of Applied Behavior Analysis. Journal of Applied Behavior Analysis, 26,* 513–525.

Latimer, P. R., & Sweet, A. A. (1984). Cognitive vs. behavioral procedures in cognitive behavior therapy: A critical review of the evidence. *Journal of Behavior Therapy and Experimental Psychiatry, 15,* 9–22.

Latner, J. D., & Wilson, G. T. (2002). Self-monitoring and the assessment of binge eating. *Behavior Therapy, 33,* 465–477.

Lattal, K. A., & Metzger, B. (1994). Response acquisition by Siamese fighting fish with delayed visual reinforcement. *Journal of the Experimental Analysis of Behavior, 61,* 35–44.

Lazarus, A. A. (1958). New methods in psychotherapy: A case study. *South African Medical Journal, 32,* 660–664.

Lazarus, A. A. (1971). *Behavior therapy and beyond.* New York: McGraw-Hill.

Lazarus, A. A. (1976). *Multi-model behavior therapy.* New York: Springer.

Leahy, R. L. (2003). *Cognitive therapy techniques: A practitioner's guide.* New York: Guilford Press.

Leahy, R. L. (2008). A closer look at ACT. *The Behavior Therapist, 31,* 148–150.

Leal, J., & Galanter, M. (1995). The use of contingency-contracting to improve outcome in methadone maintenance. *Substance Abuse, 16,* 155–167.

LeBow, M. C. (1989). *Adult obesity therapy.* New York: Pergamon Press.

LeBow, M. D. (1981). *Weight control: The behavioral strategies.* New York: Wiley.

LeBow, M. D. (1991). *Overweight children: Helping your child to achieve lifetime weight control.* New York: Insight Books/Plenum Press.

Lehrer, P. M., Woolfolk, R. L., & Sime, W. E. (Eds.). (2007). *Principles and practice of stress management* (3rd ed.). New York: Guilford Press.

Leiblum, S. R., & Rosen, R. C. (Eds.). (2000). *Principles and practice of sex therapy: Third edition.* New York: Guilford Press.

Lennox, D. B., Miltenberger, R. G., & Donnelly, D. (1987). Response interruption and DRL for the reduction of rapid eating. *Journal of Applied Behavior Analysis, 20,* 279–284.

Lerman, D. C., & Iwata, B. A. (1995). Prevalence of the extinction burst and its attenuation during treatment. *Journal of Applied Behavior Analysis, 28,* 93–94.

Lerman, D. C., & Iwata, B. A. (1996). Developing a technology for the use of operant extinction in clinical settings: An examination of basic and applied research. *Journal of Applied Behavior Analysis, 29,* 345–382.

Lerman, D. C., Iwata, B. A., Shore, B. A., & Deleon, I. G. (1997). Effects of intermittent punishment on self-injurious behavior: An evaluation of schedule thinning. *Journal of Applied Behavior Analysis, 30,* 187–201.

Lerman, D. C., Iwata, B. A., Shore, B. A., & Kahng, S. (1996). Responding maintained by intermittent reinforcement: Implications for the use of extinction with problem behavior in clinical settings. *Journal of Applied Behavior Analysis, 29,* 153–171.

Lerman, D. C., Iwata, B. A., & Wallace, M. D. (1999). Side effects of extinction: Prevalence of bursting and aggression during the treatment of self-injurious behavior. *Journal of Applied Behavior Analysis, 32,* 1–8.

Lerman, D. C., & Vorndran, C. M. (2002). On the status of knowledge for using punishment: Implications for treating behavior disorders. *Journal of Applied Behavior Analysis, 35,* 431–464.

Leslie-Toogood, A., & Martin, G. L. (2003). Do coaches know the mental skills of their athletes? Assessments from volleyball and track. *Journal of Sport Behavior, 26,* 56–68.

Lewinsohn, P. M. (1975). The behavioral study and treatment of depression. In M. Hersen, R. M. Eisler, & P. M. Miller (Eds.), *Progress in behavior modification* (Vol. 1, pp. 19–65). New York: Academic Press.

Lewis, T., J., & Sugai, G. (1996). Descriptive and experimental analysis of teacher and peer attention and the use of assessment-based intervention to improve pro-social behavior. *Journal of Behavioral Education, 6,* 7–24.

Liberman, R. P. (2000). The token economy. *American Journal of Psychiatry, 157,* 1398.

Lindsley, O. R. (1956). Operant conditioning methods applied to research in chronic schizophrenia. *Psychiatric Research Reports, 5,* 118–139.

Lindsley, O. R. (1966). An experiment with parents handling behavior at home. *Johnstone Bulletin, 9,* 27–36.

Lindsley, O. R., Skinner, B. F., & Solomon, H. C. (1953). *Studies in behavior therapy: Status report. I.* Waltham, MA: Metropolitan State Hospital.

Linehan, M. M. (1993). *Cognitive behavioral treatment of borderline personality disorder.* New York: Guilford Press.

Lines, J. B., Schwartzman, L., Tkachuk, G. A., Leslie-Toogood, S. A., & Martin, G. L. (1999). Behavioral assessment in sport psychology consulting: Applications to swimming and basketball. *Journal of Sport Behavior, 4,* 558–569.

Linscheid, T. R., Iwata, B. A., Ricketts, R. W., Williams, D. E., & Griffin, J. C. (1990). Clinical evaluation of the Self-Injurious Behavior Inhibiting System (SIBIS). *Journal of Applied Behavior Analysis, 23,* 53–78.

Linscheid, T. R., Pejeau, C., Cohen, S., & Footo-Lenz, M. (1994). Positive side-effects in the treatment of SIB using the Self-Injurious Behavior Inhibiting System (SIBIS): Implications for operant and biochemical explanations of SIB. *Research in Developmental Disabilities, 15,* 81–90.

Lippman, M. R., & Motta, R. W. (1993). Effects of positive and negative reinforcement on daily living skills in chronic psychiatric patients in community residences. *Journal of Clinical Psychology, 49,* 654–662.

Lipsey, M. (1999a). Juvenile delinquency treatment: A meta-analytic inquiry into the viability of effects. In T. D. Cook, H. Cooper, D. Cordray, H. Hartman, L. V. Hedges, R. J. Light, T. A. Louis, & F. Mosteller (Eds.), *Meta-analysis for evaluation: A casebook* (pp. 83–128). New York: Russell Sage Foundation.

Lipsey, M. W. (1999b). Can intervention rehabilitate serious delinquents? *Annals of the American Academy of Political and Social Science(s), 564,* 142–199.

Lipsey, M. W., & Wilson, D. B. (1998). Effective intervention for serious juvenile offenders: A synthesis of research. In R. Loeber & D. P. Farrington (Eds.), *Serious and violent juvenile offenders: Risk factors and successful interventions* (pp. 315–345). Thousand Oaks, CA: Sage.

Lloyd, K. E. (2002). A review of correspondence training: Suggestions for a revival. *The Behavior Analyst, 25,* 57–73.

Locke, E. A., & Latham, G. P. (1990). *A theory of goal setting and task performance.* Upper Saddle River, NJ: Prentice Hall.

Loewenstein, G., Brennan, T. A., & Volpp, K. G. (2007). Asymmetric paternalism to improve health behaviors. *Journal of the American Medical Association, 298,* 2415–2417.

Logue, A. W. (1995). *Self-control: Waiting until tommorow for what you want today.* Upper Saddle River, NJ: Prentice Hall.

Lopez, W. L., & Aguilar, M. C. (2003). Reflections on the history of ABA Columbia: Five years of experience and development. *Newsletter of the International Association for Behavior Analysis, 26*(3), 14–15.

Lovaas, O. I. (1966). A program for the establishment of speech in psychotic children. In J. K. Wing (Ed.), *Early childhood autism* (pp. 115–144). Elmsford, NY: Pergamon Press.

Lovaas, O. I. (1977). *The autistic child: Language development through behavior modification.* New York: Irvington.

Lovaas, O. I. (1987). Behavioral treatment and normal educational and intellectual functioning in young autistic children. *Journal of Consulting and Clinical Consulting, 55,* 3–9.

Lovaas, O. I., Newsom, C., & Hickman, C. (1987). Self-stimulatory behavior and perceptual development. *Journal of Applied Behavior Analysis, 20,* 45–68.

Lowe, C. F., Beasty, A., & Bentall, R. P. (1983). The role of verbal behavior in human learning: Infant performance on fixed interval schedules. *Journal of the Experimental Analysis of Behavior, 39,* 157–164.

Lubetkin, B. S., Rivers, P. C., & Rosenberg, C. N. (1971). Difficulties of disulfiram therapy with alcoholics. *Quarterly Journal of Studies on Alcohol, 32,* 118–171.

Lubow, R. E. (1974). High-order concept formation in pigeons. *Journal of the Experimental Analysis of Behavior, 21,* 475–483.

Luce, S. C., Delquadri, J., & Hall, R. V. (1980). Contingent exercise: A mild but powerful procedure for suppressing inappropriate verbal and aggressive behavior. *Journal of Applied Behavior Analysis, 13,* 583–594.

Ludwig, A. M., Levine, J. A., & Stark, L. H. (1970). *LDS and alcoholism.* Springfield, IL: Charles C Thomas.

Lundgren, J. D. (2006). Behavior therapy and its contributions to obesity treatment. *The Behavior Therapist, 29,* 28–29.

Lutz, J. (1994). *Introduction to learning and memory.* Pacific Grove, CA: Brooks/Cole.

Ma, H. (2006). An alternative method for quantitative synthesis of single-subject researches: Percentage of data points exceeding the median. *Behavior Modification, 30,* 598–617.

Mace, F. C., & Belfiore, P. (1990). Behavioral momentum in the treatment of escape-motivated stereotypy. *Journal of Applied Behavior Analysis, 23,* 507–514.

Mace, F. C., Belfiore, P. J., & Hutchinson, J. M. (2001). Operant theory and research on self-regulation. In B. J. Zimmerman & D. H. Schunk (Eds.), *Self-regulated learning and academic achievement: Theoretical perspectives* (2nd ed., pp. 39–65). Mahwah, NJ: Lawrence Erlbaum Associates.

Mace, F. C., Hock, M. L., Lalli, J. S., West, B. J., Belfiore, P., Pinter, E., et al. (1988). Behavioral momentum in the treatment of noncompliance. *Journal of Applied Behavior Analysis, 21,* 123–141.

Mace, F. C., Lalli, J., Lalli, E. P., & Shey, M. C. (1993). Function analysis and treatment of aberrant behavior. In R. Van Houten & S. Axelrod (Eds.), *Behavior analysis and treatment* (pp. 75–99). New York: Plenum Press.

Mace, F. C., McCurdy, B., & Quigley, E. A. (1990). A collateral effect of reward predicted by matching theory. *Journal of Applied Behavior Analysis, 23,* 197–205.

Mace, F. C., & West, B. J. (1986). Analysis of demand conditions associated with reluctant speech. *Journal of Behavior Therapy and Experimental Psychiatry, 17,* 285–294.

Madsen, C. H., Becker, W. C., Thomas, D. R., Koser, L., & Plager, E. (1970). An analysis of the reinforcing function of "sit down" commands. In R. K. Parker (Ed.), *Readings in educational psychology* (pp. 71–82). Boston: Allyn & Bacon.

Madsen, C. H., Jr., & Madsen, C. R. (1974). *Teaching discipline: Behavior principles towards a positive approach.* Boston: Allyn & Bacon.

Mager, R. F. (1972). *Goal analysis.* Belmont, CA: Fearon.

Mahoney, K., Vanwagenen, K., & Meyerson, L. (1971). Toilet training of normal and retarded children. *Journal of Applied Behavior Analysis, 4,* 173–181.

Mahoney, M. J. (1974). *Cognition and behavior modification.* Cambridge, MA: Ballinger.

Maier, S. F., Watkins, L. R., & Fleshner, M. (1994). Psychoneuroimmunology: The interface between behavior, brain, and immunity. *American Psychologist, 49,* 1004–1017.

Malatesta, V. J., Aubuchon, P. G., & Bluch, M. (1994). A historical timeline of behavior therapy in psychiatric settings: Development of a clinical science. *Behavior Therapist, 17,* 165–168.

Maletsky, B. M. (1974). Behavior recording as treatment: A brief note. *Behavior Therapy, 5,* 107–111.

Malott, R. W. (1989). The achievement of evasive goals: Control by rules describing contingencies that are not direct-acting. In S. C. Hayes (Ed.), *Rule-governed behavior: Cognition, contingencies, and instructional control* (pp. 269–324). New York: Plenum Press.

Malott, R. W. (1992). A theory of rule-governed behavior and organizational behavior management. *Journal of Organizational Behavior Management, 12,* 45–65.

Malott, R. W., & Whaley, D. L. (1983). *Psychology.* Holmes Beach, FL: Learning Publications.

Malott, R. W. (2008). *Principles of behavior* (6th ed.). Upper Saddle River, NJ: Pearson Prentice-Hall.

Malouff, J. M., & Rooke, S. E. (2007). Empirically supported self-help books. *The Behavior Therapist, 30,* 29–131.

Marion, C., Vause, T., Harapiak, S., Martin, G. L., Yu, D., Sakko, G., et al. (2003). The hierarchical relationship between several visual and auditory discriminations and three verbal operants among individuals with developmental disabilities. *The Analysis of Verbal Behavior, 19,* 91–105.

Marlatt, G. A., & Parks, G. A. (1982). Self-management of addictive disorders. In P. Karoly & F. H. Kanfer (Eds.), *Self-management and behavior change: From theory to practice* (pp. 443–488). New York: Pergamon Press.

Marr, M. J. (2003). The stitching and the unstitching: What can behavior analysis have to say about creativity? *The Behavior Analyst, 26,* 15–27.

Martell, C. R. (2008). Behavioral activation treatment for depression. In W. O'Donohue & J. E. Fisher (Eds.), *Cognitive behavior therapy: Applying empirically supported techniques in your practice* (2nd ed., pp. 40–45). Hoboken, NJ: John Wiley & Sons.

Martell, C., Addis, M., & Dimidjian, S. (2004). Finding the action in behavioral activation: The search for empirically supported interventions and mechanisms of change. In S. C. Hayes, V. M. Follette, & M. M. Linehan (Eds.), *Mindfulness and acceptance: Expanding the cognitive behavioral tradition* (pp. 152–167). New York: Guilford Press.

Martell, C. R., Addis, M. E., & Jacobson, N. S. (2001). *Depression in context: Strategies for guided action.* New York: Norton.

Martin, G. A., & Worthington, E. L. (1982). Behavioral homework. In M. Hersen, R. M. Isler, & P. M. Miller (Eds.), *Progress in behavior modification* (Vol. 13, pp. 197–226). New York: Academic Press.

Martin, G. L. (1981). Behavior modification in Canada in the 1970's. *Canadian Psychology, 22,* 7–22.

Martin, G. L. (1982). Thought stopping and stimulus control to decrease persistent disturbing thoughts. *Journal of Behavior Therapy and Experimental Psychiatry, 13*(3), 215–220.

Martin, G. L. (1992). Applied behavior analysis in sport and physical education: Past, present and future. In R. P. West & L. A. Hammerlynk (Eds.), *Designs for excellence in education: The legacy of B. F. Skinner* (pp. 223–287). Longmont, CO: Sopris West.

Martin, G. L. (2007). *Sport psychology: Practical guidelines from behavior analysis* (3rd ed.). Winnipeg, Canada: Sport Science Press.

Martin, G. L., England, G. D., & England, K. G. (1971). The use of backward chaining to teach bed-making to severely retarded girls: A demonstration. *Psychological Aspects of Disability, 18,* 35–40.

Martin, G. L., England, G., Kaprowy, E., Kilgour, K., & Pilek, V. (1968). Operant conditioning of kindergarten-class behavior in autistic children. *Behaviour Research and Therapy, 6,* 281–294.

Martin, G. L., & Ingram, D. (2001). *Play golf in the zone: The psychology of golf made easy.* San Francisco: Van der Plas.

Martin, G. L., Koop, S., Turner, C., & Hanel, F. (1981). Backward chaining versus total task presentation to teach assembly tasks to severely retarded persons. *Behavior Research of Severe Developmental Disabilities, 2,* 117–136.

Martin, G. L., & Osborne, J. G. (Eds.). (1980). *Helping in the community: Behavioral applications.* New York: Plenum Press.

Martin, G. L., & Osborne, J. G. (1993). *Psychological adjustment and everyday living* (2nd ed.). Upper Saddle River, NJ: Prentice Hall.

Martin, G. L., & Pear, J. J. (1978). *Behavior modification: What it is and how to do it.* Upper Saddle River, NJ: Prentice Hall.

Martin, G. L., Thompson, K., & Regehr, K. (2004). Studies using single-subject designs in sport psychology: 30 years of research. *The Behavior Analyst, 27,* 263–280.

Martin, G. L., Thorsteinsson, J. R., Yu, C. T., Martin, T. L., & Vause, T. (2008). The Assessment of Basic Learning Abilities Test for predicting learning of persons with intellectual disabilities: A review. *Behavior Modification, 32,* 228-247.

Martin, G. L., & Tkachuk, G. (2000). Behavioral sport psychology. In J. Austin & J. E. Carr (Eds.), *Handbook of applied behavior analysis* (pp. 399–422). Reno, NV: Context Press.

Martin, G. L., & Toogood, A. (1997). Cognitive and behavioral components of a seasonal psychological skills training program for competitive figure skaters. *Cognitive and Behavioral Practice, 4,* 383–404.

Martin, G. L., Toogood, S. A., & Tkachuk, G. A. (Eds.). (1997). *Behavioral assessment forms for sport psychology consulting.* Winnipeg, Canada: Sport Science Press.

Martin, T. L., Pear, J. J., & Martin, G. L. (2002a). Analysis of proctor grading accuracy in a computer-aided personalized system of instruction course. *Journal of Applied Behavior Analysis, 35,* 309–312.

Martin, T. L., Pear, J. J., & Martin, G. L. (2002b). Feedback and its effectiveness in a computer-aided personalized system of instruction course. *Journal of Applied Behavior Analysis, 35,* 427–430.

Masia, C. L., & Chase, P. N. (1997). Vicarious learning revisited: A contemporary behavior analytic interpretation. *Journal of Behavior Therapy and Experimental Psychiatry, 28,* 41–51.

Masters, J. C., Burrish, T. G., Hollon, S. D., & Rimm, D. C. (1987). *Behavior therapy: Techniques and empirical findings* (3rd ed.). Orlando, FL: Harcourt Brace Jovanovich.

Masters, W. H., & Johnson, V. E. (1970). *Human sexual inadequacy.* Boston: Little, Brown.

Mathews, J. R., Friman, P. C., Barone, V. J., Ross, L. V., & Christophersen, E. R. (1987). Decreasing dangerous infant behavior through parent instruction. *Journal of Applied Behavior Analysis, 20,* 165–169.

Matsen, J. L., Bielecki, J., Mayville, E. A., Smolls, Y., Bamburg, J. W., & Baglio, C. S. (1999). The development of a reinforcer choice assessment scale for persons with severe and profound mental retardation. *Research in Developmental Disabilities, 20,* 379–384.

Matson, J. L., & Boisjoli, J. A. (2009). The token economy for children with intellectual disability and/or autism: A review. *Research in Developmental Disabilities, 30,* 240–248.

Matson, J. L., & Smith, K. R. M. (2008). Current status of intensive behavioral interventions of young children with autism and PDD-NOS. *Research in Autism Spectrum Disorders, 2,* 60–74.

Matson, J. L., & Vollmer, T. R. (1995). *User's guide: Questions About Behavioral Function (QABF).* Baton Rouge, LA: Scientific Publishers.

Mattaini, M. A., & McGuire, M. S. (2006). Behavioral strategies for constructing non-violent cultures with youth: A review. *Behavior Modification, 30,* 184–224.

Mazaleski, J. L., Iwata, B. A., Vollmer, T. R., Zarcone, J. R., & Smith, R. G. (1993). Analysis of the reinforcement and extinction components in DRO contingencies with self injury. *Journal of Applied Behavior Analysis, 26,* 143–156.

Mazur, J. E. (1991). Choice with probabilistic reinforcement: Effects of delay and conditioned reinforcers. *Journal of the Experimental Analysis of Behavior, 55*(1), 63–77.

McCrady, B. S. (2008). Alcohol use disorders. In D. H. Barlow (Ed.), *Clinical handbook of psychological disorders: A step-by-step treatment manual* (4th ed.). New York: Guilford Press.

McEachin, J. J., Smith, T., & Lovaas, O. I. (1993). Long-term outcome for children with autism who received early intensive behavioral treatment. *American Journal on Mental Retardation, 97,* 359–372.

McFall, R. M. (1970). The effects of self-monitoring on normal smoking behavior. *Journal of Consulting and Clinical Psychology, 35,* 135–142.

McGee, J. J., Menolascino, F. J., Hobbs, D. C., & Menousek, P. E. (1987). *Gentle teaching: A nonaversive approach for helping persons with mental retardation.* New York: Human Sciences Press.

McGill, P. (1999). Establishing operations: Implications for the assessment, treatment, and prevention of problem behavior. *Journal of Applied Behavior Analysis, 32,* 393–418.

McGinnis, J. C., Friman, P. C., & Carlyon, W. D. (1999). The effect of token rewards on "intrinsic" motivation for doing math. *Journal of Applied Behavior Analysis, 32,* 375–379.

McGlynn, F. D., Smitherman, T. A., & Gothard, K. D. (2004). Comment on the status of systematic desensitization. *Behavior Modification, 28,* 194–205.

McIver, K. L., Brown, W. H., Pfeiffer, K. A., Dowda, M., & Pate, R. R. (2009). Assessing children's physical activity in their homes: The Observational System for Recording Physical Activity in Children—Home. *Journal of Applied Behavior Analysis, 42,* 1–16.

McKinney, R., & Fiedler, S. (2004). Schizophrenia: Some recent advances and implications for behavioral intervention. *The Behavioral Therapist, 27,* 122–125.

Meadows, S. (1996). *Parenting behavior and childrens' cognitive development.* Hillsdale, NJ: Erlbaum.

Meany-Daboul, M. G., Roscoe, E. M., Bourret, J. C., & Ahearn, W. H. (2007). A comparison of momentary time sampling and partial-interval recording for evaluating functional relations. *Journal of Applied Behavior Analysis, 40,* 501–514.

Meichenbaum, D. H. (1977). *Cognitive behavior modification: An integrative approach.* New York: Plenum Press.

Meichenbaum, D. H. (1985). *Stress inoculation training.* New York: Pergamon Press.

Meichenbaum, D. H. (1986). Cognitive behavior modification. In F. H. Kanfer & A. P. Goldstein (Eds.), *Helping people change: A textbook of methods* (3rd ed., pp. 346–380). New York: Pergamon Press.

Meichenbaum, D., & Deffenbacher, J. L. (1988). Stress inoculation training. *Counselling Psychologist, 16,* 69–90.

Meichenbaum, D. H., & Goodman, J. (1971). Training impulsive children to talk to themselves: A means of developing self-control. *Journal of Abnormal Psychology, 77,* 115–126.

Messer, S. B., & Winokur, M. (1984). Ways of knowing and visions of reality in psychoanalytic therapy and behavior therapy. In H. Arkowitz & S. B. Messer (Eds.), *Psychoanalytic therapy and behavior therapy: Is integration possible?* (pp. 63–100). New York: Plenum Press.

Michael, J. (1982). Distinguishing between discriminative and motivational functions of stimuli. *Journal of the Experimental Analysis of Behavior, 37,* 149–155.

Michael, J. (1986). Repertoire-altering effects of remote contingencies. *Analysis of Verbal Behavior, 4,* 10–18.

Michael, J. (1987). Symposium on the experimental analysis of human behavior: Comments by the discussant. *Psychological Record, 37,* 37–42.

Michael, J. (1988). Establishing operations and the mand. *The Analysis of Verbal Behavior, 6,* 3–9.

Michael, J. (1991). A behavioral perspective on college teaching. *Behavior Analyst, 14,* 229–239.

Michael, J. (1993). Establishing operations. *Behavior Analyst, 16,* 191–206.

Michael, J. (2000). Implications and refinements of the establishing operation concept. *Journal of Applied Behavior Analysis, 33,* 401–410.

Michael, J. (2007). Motivating operations. In J. O. Cooper, T. E. Heron, & W. L. Heward (Eds.), *Applied behavior analysis* (2nd ed., pp. 374–391). Upper Saddle River, NJ: Prentice Hall/Merrill.

Midgley, M., Lea, S. E. G., & Kirby, R. M. (1989). Algorithmic shaping and misbehavior in the acquisition of token deposit by rats. *Journal of the Experimental Analysis of Behavior, 52,* 27–40.

Mikulis, W. L. (1983). Thailand and behavior modification. *Journal of Behavior Therapy and Experimental Psychiatry, 14,* 93–97.

Miller, D. L., & Kelley, M. L. (1994). The use of goal setting and contingency contracting for improving children's homework. *Journal of Applied Behavior Analysis, 27,* 73–84.

Miller, W. R. (1996). Motivational interviewing: Research, practice and puzzles. *Addictive Behaviors, 21,* 835–842.

Miltenberger, R. G., Fuqua, R. W., & Woods, D. W. (1998). Applying behavior analysis to clinical problems: Review and analysis of habit reversal. *Journal of Applied Behavior Analysis, 31,* 447–469.

Miltenberger, R. G. (2008). *Behavior modification: Principles and procedures* (4th ed.) Delmont, CA: Thompson Wadworth.

Mineka, S., & Zinbarg, R. (2006). A contemporary learning theory perspective on the etiology of anxiety disorders: It's not what you thought it was. *American Psychologist, 61,* 10–26.

Ming, S., & Martin, G.L. (1996). Single-subject evaluation of a self-talk package for improving figure skating performance. *The Sport Psychologist, 10,* 227–238.

Moderato, P. (2003). Behaviorism and behavior analysis in Italy. *Newsletter of the International Association for Behavior Analysis, 26*(3), 17–19.

Mohr, B., Muller, V., Mattes, R., Rosin, R., Federmann, B., Strehl, U., et al. (1996). Behavioral treatment of Parkinson's disease leads to improvement of motor skills and to tremor reduction. *Behavior Therapy, 27,* 235–255.

Moran, D. J. (2008). Charting a collaborative course. *The Behavior Therapist, 31,* 155–157.

Moran, D. J., & Malott, R. W. (Eds.). (2004). *Evidence-based educational methods* (pp. 223–243). San Diego, California: Elsevier Academic Press.

Morris, R. J., & Kratochwill, T. R. (1983). *Treating children's fears and phobias: A behavioral approach.* New York: Pergamon Press.

Mulaire-Cloutier, C., Vause, T., Martin, G. L., & Yu, D. (2000). Choice, task preference, task performance, and happiness indicators with persons with severe developmental disabilities. *International Journal of Practical Approaches to Disability, 24,* 7–12.

Myerson, J., & Hale, S. (1984). Practical implications of the matching law. *Journal of Applied Behavior Analysis, 17,* 367–380.

Myles, B. S., Moran, M. R., Ormsbee, C. K., & Downing, J. A. (1992). Guidelines for establishing and maintaining token economies. *Intervention in School and Clinic, 27,* 164–169.

National Institute of Mental Health. Retrieved January 1, 2009, from www.nimh.nih.gov/health/publications/schizophrenia/what-is-schizophrenia.shtml.

Neef, N. A., Mace, F. C., & Shade, D. (1993). Impulsivity in students with serious emotional disturbances: The interactive effects of reinforcer rate, delay, and quality. *Journal of Applied Behavior Analysis, 26,* 37–52.

Neef, N. A., Mace, F. C., Shea, M. C., & Shade, D. (1992). Effects of reinforcer rate and reinforcer quality on time allocation: Extensions of the matching theory to educational settings. *Journal of Applied Behavior Analysis, 25,* 691–699.

Neef, N., & Northup, J. (2007). Attention-deficit-hyperactivity disorder. In P. Sturmey (Ed.), *Functional analysis in clinical treatment* (pp. 87–110). London, UK: Elsevier.

Neef, N. A., Shade, D., & Miller, M. S. (1994). Assessing influential dimensions of reinforcers on choice in students with serious emotional disturbance. *Journal of Applied Behavior Analysis, 27,* 575–583.

Nelson, R. O. (1983). Behavioral assessment: Past, present, and future. *Behavioral Assessment, 5,* 195–206.

Nevin, J. A. (1988). Behavioral momentum and the partial reinforcement effect. *Psychological Bulletin, 103,* 44–56.

Nevin, J. A. (1992). An integrative model for the study of behavioral momentum. *Journal of the Experimental Analysis of Behavior, 57,* 301–316.

Nevin, J. A., & Grace, R. C. (2000). Behavioral momentum and the law of effect. *Behavioral and Brain Sciences, 23,* 73–130.

Nezu, A. (2000). It's official: To be behavioral is to be special. *The Behavior Therapist, 23,* 181–184, 206.

Nhat Hanh, T. (1998). *The heart of the Buddha's teaching: Transforming suffering into peace, joy, and liberation.* Berkeley, CA: Parallax Press.

Nisbet, E. K. L., & Gick, N. L. (2008). Can health psychology help the planet? Applying theory and models of health behavior to environmental actions. *Canadian Psychology, 49,* 296–403.

Norcross, J. C. (2006). Integrating self-help into psychotherapy: Sixteen practical suggestions. *Professional Psychology: Research & Practice, 37,* 383–393.

Nordquist, D. M. (1971). The modification of a child's enuresis: Some response-response relationships. *Journal of Applied Behavior Analysis, 4,* 241–247.

North, M. M., North, S. M., & Coble, J. R. (1997). Virtual reality therapy for fear-of-flying. *American Journal of Psychiatry, 154,* 130.

Northup, J., Wacker, D., Sasso, G., Steege, M., Cigrand, K., Cook, J., et al. (1991). A brief functional analysis of aggressive and alternative behavior in an out-clinic setting. *Journal of Applied Behavior Analysis, 24,* 509–522.

O'Brien, R. M. (2008). What would have happened to CBT if the second wave had preceded the first? *The Behavior Therapist, 31,* 153–154.

O'Brien, S., & Repp, A. C. (1990). Reinforcement-based reductive procedures: A review of 20 years of their use with persons with severe or profound retardation. *Journal of the Association for Persons with Severe Handicaps, 15,* 148–159.

O'Connor, R. (1969). Modification of social withdrawal through symbolic modeling. *Journal of Applied Behavior Analysis, 2,* 15–22.

O'Donnell, J. (2001). The discriminative stimulus for punishment or S^{Dp}. *The Behavior Analyst, 24,* 261–262.

O'Donnell, J., Crosbie, J., Williams, D. C., & Saunders, K. J. (2000). Stimulus control and generalization of point-loss punishment with humans. *Journal of the Experimental Analysis of Behavior, 73,* 261–274.

Oei, T. P. S. (Ed.). (1998). *Behavior therapy and cognitive behavior therapy in Asia.* Glebe, Australia: Edumedia.

Ohman, A., Dimberg, U., & Ost, L. G. (1984). Animal and social phobias. In S. Reiss & R. Bootzin (Eds.), *Theoretical issues in behavior therapy* (pp. 210–222). New York: Academic Press.

Okouchi, H. (2009). Response acquisition by humans with delayed reinforcement. *Journal of the Experimental Analysis of Behavior, 91,* 377–390.

O'Leary, K. D. (1984). The image of behavior therapy: It is time to take a stand. *Behavior Therapy, 15,* 219–233.

Olenick, D. L., & Pear, J. J. (1980). Differential reinforcement of correct responses to probes and prompts in picture-naming training with severely retarded children. *Journal of Applied Behavior Analysis, 13,* 77–89.

Olsen, R., Laraway, S., Austin, J. (2001). Unconditioned and conditioned establishing operations in organizational behavior management. *Journal of Organizational Behavior Management, 21,* 7–35.

O'Neill, G. W., & Gardner, R. (1983). *Behavioral principles in medical rehabilitation: A practical guide.* Springfield, IL: Charles C Thomas.

Osborne, J. G., & Powers, R. B. (1980). Controlling the litter problem. In G. L. Martin & J. G. Osborne (Eds.), *Helping in the community: Behavioral applications* (pp. 103–168). New York: Plenum Press.

Ost, L. G. (2008). Efficacy of the third wave of behavioral therapies: A systematic review and meta-analysis. *Behavior Research and Therapy, 46,* 296–321.

Otto, M. W., Pava, J. A., & Sprich-Buckminster, S. (1995). Treatment of major depression: Applications and efficacy of cognitive behavior therapy. In M. H. Pollack, M. W. Otto, & J. E. Rosenbaum (Eds.), *Challenges in psychiatric treatment: Pharmacological and psychosocial strategies* (pp. 31–52). New York: Guilford Press.

Otto, T. L., Torgrud, L. J., & Holborn, S. W. (1999). An operant blocking interpretation of instructed insensitivity to schedule contingencies. *The Psychological Record, 49,* 663–684.

Page, T. J., Iwata, B. A., & Neef, N. A. (1976). Teaching pedestrian skills to retarded persons: Generalization from the classroom to the natural environment. *Journal of Applied Behavior Analysis, 9,* 433–444.

Paggeot, B., Kvale, S., Mace, F. C., & Sharkey, R. W. (1988). Some merits and limitations of hand-held computers for data collection. *Journal of Applied Behavior Analysis, 21,* 429.

Pal-Hegedus, C. (1991). Behavior analysis in Costa Rica. *Behavior Therapist, 14,* 103–104.

Palmer, D. C. (1991). A behavioral interpretation of memory. In L. J. Hayes & P. N. Chase (Eds.), *Dialogues on verbal behavior* (pp. 259–286). Reno, NV: Context Press.

Palmer, D. C. (2004). Data in search of a principle: A review of Relational Frame Theory: A post-Skinnerian account of human language and cognition. *Journal of the Experimental Analysis of Behavior, 81,* 189–204.

Paradis, C. M., Friedman, S., Hatch, M. L., & Ackerman, R. (1996). Cognitive behavioral treatment of anxiety disorders in orthodox Jews. *Cognitive and Behavioral Practice, 3,* 271–288.

Parker, R. I. (2006). Increased reliability for single-case research results: Is the bootstrap the answer? *Behavior Therapy, 37,* 326–338.

Parker, R. I., & Hagan-Burke, S. (2007). Useful effect-size interpretations for single-case research, *Behavior Therapy, 38,* 95–105

Pascarella, E. T., & Terenzini, P. T. (1991). *How college affects students: Findings and insights from 20 years of research.* San Francisco: Jossey-Bass.

Passman, R. (1977). The reduction of procrastinative behaviors in a college student despite the "contingency fulfillment problems": The use of external control in self-management techniques. *Behavior Therapy, 8,* 95–96.

Patterson, G. R. (1965). An application of conditioning techniques to the control of a hyperactive child. In L. P. Ullmann & L. Krasner (Eds.), *Case studies in behavior modification* (pp. 370–375). New York: Holt, Reinhart & Winston.

Patterson, G. R., & Gullion, M. E. (1968). *Living with children: New methods for parents and teachers.* Champaign, IL: Research Press.

Pavlov, I. P. (1927). *Conditioned reflexes: An investigation of the physiological activity of the cerebral cortex* (G. V. Anrep, Trans.). London: Oxford University Press.

Pear, J. J. (1983). Relative reinforcements for cognitive and behavioral terminologies. *Psychological Record, 33,* 20–25.

Pear, J. J. (2001). *The science of learning.* Philadelphia: Psychology Press.

Pear, J. J. (2004). A spatiotemporal analysis of behavior. In J. E. Burgos & E. Ribes (Eds.), *Theory, basic and applied research and technological applications in behavior science: Conceptual and methodological issues* (pp. 131–149). Guadalajara: University of Guadalajara Press.

Pear, J. J. (2007). *A historical and contemporary look at psychological systems.* Mahwah, NJ: Lawrence Erlbaum Associates.

Pear, J. J., & Crone-Todd, D. E. (1999). Personalized System of Instruction in cyberspace. *Journal of Applied Behavior Analysis, 32,* 205–209.

Pear, J. J., & Crone-Todd, D. E. (2002). A social constructivist approach to computer-mediated instruction. *Computers & Education, 38,* 221–231.

Pear, J. J., & Eldridge, G. D. (1984). The operant–respondent distinction: Future directions. *Journal of the Experimental Analysis of Behavior, 42,* 453–467.

Pear, J. J., & Kinsner, W. (1988). Computer-aided Personalized System of Instruction: An effective and economical method for short and long distance education. *Machine-Mediated Learning, 2,* 213–237.

Pear, J. J., & Legris, J. A. (1987). Shaping of an arbitrary operant response by automated tracking. *Journal of the Experimental Analysis of Behavior, 47,* 241–247.

Pear, J. J., & Martin, T. L. (2004). Making the most of PSI with computer technology. In D. J. Moran & R. W. Malott (Eds.), *Evidence-based educational methods* (pp. 223–243). San Diego: Elsevier Academic Press.

Pear, J. J., & Novak, M. (1996). Computer-aided Personalized System of Instruction: A program evaluation. *Teaching of Psychology, 23,* 119–123.

Pelios, L., Morren, J., Tesch, D., & Axelrod, S. (1999). The impact of functional analysis methodology on treatment choice for self-injurious and aggressive behavior. *Journal of Applied Behavior Analysis, 32*(2), 185–195.

Perin, C. T. (1943). The effect of delayed reinforcement upon the differentiation of bar responses in white rats. *Journal of Experimental Psychology, 32,* 95–109.

Perri, M. G., & Richards, C. S. (1977). An investigation of naturally occurring episodes of self-controlled behaviors. *Journal of Consulting Psychology, 24,* 178–183.

Perry, A., Pritchard, E. A., & Penn, H. E. (2006). Indicators of quality teaching in intensive behavioral intervention: A survey of parents and professionals. *Behavioral Interventions, 21,* 85-96.

Phillips, E. L. (1968). Achievement Place: Token reinforcement procedures in a home-style rehabilitation setting for "pre-delinquent" boys. *Journal of Applied Behavior Analysis, 1,* 213–223.

Phillips, E. L., Phillips, E. A., Fixsen, D. L., & Wolf, M. M. (1973). Behavior shaping works for delinquents. *Psychology Today, 7*(1), 75–79.

Phillips, E. L., Phillips, E. A., Fixsen, D. L., & Wolf, M. M. (1974). *The teaching family handbook* (2nd ed.). Lawrence, KS: University of Kansas Printing Service.

Phillips, E. L., Phillips, E. A., Wolf, M. M., & Fixsen, D. L. (1973). Achievement Place: Development of the elected manager system. *Journal of Applied Behavior Analysis, 6,* 541–546.

Pinker, S. (1994). *The language instinct: How the mind creates language.* New York: William Morrow.

Plaud, J. J. (2007). Sexual disorders. In P. Sturmey (Ed.), *Functional analysis in clinical treatment* (pp. 357–378). London: Elsevier.

Plaud, J. J., & Gaither, G. A. (1996). Behavioral momentum. *Behavior Modification, 20,* 183–201.

Plimpton, G. (1965). Ernest Hemingway. In G. Plimpton (Ed.), *Writers at work: The Paris Review interviews* (2nd series, pp. 215–239). New York: Viking.

Poche, C., Brouwer, R., & Swearingen, M. (1981). Teaching self-protection to young children. *Journal of Applied Behavior Analysis, 14,* 169–176.

Poche, C., Yoder, P., & Miltenberger, R. (1988). Teaching self-protection skills to children using television techniques. *Journal of Applied Behavior Analysis, 21,* 253–361.

Polenchar, B. F., Romano, A. G., Steinmetz, J. E., & Patterson, M. M. (1984). Effects of US parameters on classical conditioning of cat hindlimb flexion. *Animal Learning and Behavior, 12,* 69–72.

Poling, A. (2001). Comments regarding Olsen, Laraway, and Austin (2001). *Journal of Organizational Behavior Management, 21,* 47–56.

Poling, A., Dickinson, A., Austin, J., & Normand, M. (2000). Basic and behavioral research in organizational behavior management. In J. Austin & J. E. Carr (Eds.), *Handbook of applied behavior analysis* (pp. 295–320). Reno, NV: Context Press.

Poling, A., Methot, L. L., & Lesage, M. G. (1995). *Fundamentals of behavior analytic research.* New York: Plenum Press.

Poppen, R. L. (1989). Some clinical implications of rule-governed behavior. In S. C. Hayes (Ed.), *Rule-governed behavior: Cognition, contingencies, and instructional control* (pp. 325–357). New York: Plenum Press.

Potter, B. A. (1980). *Turning around: The behavioral approach to managing people.* New York: AMACOM.

Pouthas, V., Droit, S., Jacquet, A. Y., & Wearden, J. H. (1990). Temporal differentiation of response duration in children of different ages: Developmental changes in relations between verbal and nonverbal behavior. *Journal of the Experimental Analysis of Behavior, 53,* 21–31.

Powers, R. B., & Osborne, J. G. (1976). *Fundamentals of behavior.* St. Paul, MN: West.

Powers, M. B., Zum Vörde Sive Vörding, M. B., & Emmelkamp, P. M. G. (2009). Acceptance and commitment therapy: A meta-analytic review. *Psychotherapy and Psychosomatics, 78(2),* 73–80.

Premack, D. (1959). Toward empirical behavioral laws. I: Positive reinforcement. *Psychological Review, 66,* 219–233.

Premack, D. (1965). Reinforcement theory. In D. Levin (Ed.), *Nebraska Symposium on Motivation* (pp. 123–180). Lincoln: University of Nebraska.

Prilleltensky, I. (2008). The role of power in wellness, depression, and liberation: The promise of psycho-political validity. *Journal of Community Psychology, 36,* 116–136.

Public Law, 98-517, October 19, 1984: Developmental Disabilities Act of 1984. Washington, D. C.: U.S. Government.

Purcell, D. W., Campos, P. E., & Perilla, J. L. (1996). Therapy with lesbians and gay men: A cognitive behavioral perspective. *Cognitive and Behavioral Practice, 3,* 391–415.

Pyles, D. A. M., & Bailey, J. S. (1990). Diagnosing severe behavior problems. In A. C. Repp & N. N. Singh (Eds.), *Perspectives on the use of nonaversive interventions for persons with developmental disabilities* (pp. 381–401). Sycamore, IL: Sycamore Press.

Quarti, C., & Renaud, J. (1964). A new treatment of constipation by conditioning: A preliminary report. In C. M. Franks (Ed.), *Conditioning techniques in clinical practice and research* (pp. 219–227). New York: Springer.

Rae, A. (1993). Self-paced learning with video for undergraduates: A multimedia Keller Plan. *British Journal of Educational Technology, 24,* 43–51.

Rae, S., Martin, G. L., & Smyk, B. (1990). A self-management package versus a group exercise contingency for increasing on-task behavior of developmentally handicapped workers. *Canadian Journal of Behavioral Science, 22,* 45–58.

Rasey, H. W., & Iversen, I. H. (1993). An experimental acquisition of maladaptive behavior by shaping. *Journal of Behavior Therapy and Experimental Psychiatry, 24,* 37–43.

Reed, D. D., & Luiselli, J. K. (2009). Antecedents to a paradigm: Ogden Lindsley and B. F. Skinner's founding of "behavior therapy." *The Behavior Therapist, 32,* 82–85.

Rego, S. A., Barlow, D. H., McCrady, B. S., Persons, J. B., Hildebrandt, T. B., & McHugh, R. K. (2009). Implementing empirically supported treatments in real-world clinical settings: Your questions answered! *The Behavior Therapist, 32,* 52–58.

Reid, D. H., & Parsons, M. B. (2000). Organizational behavior management in human service settings. In J. Austin & J. E. Carr (Eds.), *Handbook of applied behavior analysis* (pp. 275–294). Reno, NV: Context Press.

Repp, A. C., Deitz, S. M., & Deitz, D. E. (1976). Reducing inappropriate behaviors in classrooms and individual sessions through DRO schedules of reinforcement. *Mental Retardation, 14,* 11–15.

Repp, A. C., Karsh, K. G., Felce, D., & Ludewig, D. (1989). Further comments on using hand-held computers for data collection. *Journal of Applied Behavior Analysis, 22,* 336–337.

Resick, P. A., Monson, C. M., & Rizvi, S. L. (2008). Post-traumatic stress disorder. In D. H. Barlow (Ed.), *Clinical handbook of psychological disorders: A step-by-step treatment manual* (4th ed.). New York: Guilford Press.

Resick, P. A., & Schnicke, M. K. (1992). Cognitive processing therapy for sexual assault victims. *Journal of Consulting and Clinical Psychology, 60,* 748–756.

Reynolds, L. K., & Kelley, M. L. (1997). The efficacy of a response-cost based treatment package for managing aggressive behavior in preschoolers. *Behavior Modification, 21,* 216–230.

Richard, D. C. S., & Bobicz, K. (2003). Computers and behavioral assessment: Six years later. *The Behavior Therapist, 26,* 219–223.

Richman, G. S., Reiss, M. L., Bauman, K. E., & Bailey, J. S. (1984). Training menstrual care to mentally retarded women: Acquisition, generalization, and maintenance. *Journal of Applied Behavior Analysis, 17,* 441–451.

Rincover, A. (1978). Sensory extinction: A procedure for eliminating self-stimulatory behavior in psychotic children. *Journal of Abnormal Child Psychology, 6,* 299–310.

Rincover, A., Cook, R., Peoples, A., & Packard, D. (1979). Sensory extinction and sensory reinforcement principles for programming multiple adaptive behavior change. *Journal of Applied Behavior Analysis, 12,* 221–233.

Rincover, A., & Devaney, J. (1982). The application of sensory extinction procedures to self-injury. *Analysis and Intervention in Developmental Disabilities, 2,* 67–81.

Riva, G., Wiederhold, B. K., & Molinari, E. (1998). *Virtual environments in clinical psychology and neuroscience. Methods and techniques in advanced patient-therapist interaction.* Amsterdam, the Netherlands: IOS Press.

Roane, H. S. (2008). On the applied use of progressive-ratio schedules of reinforcement. *Journal of Applied Behavior Analysis, 41,* 155–161.

Roberts, R. N. (1979). Private speech in academic problem-solving: A naturalistic perspective. In G. Zevin (Ed.), *The development of self-regulation through private speech* (pp. 295–323). New York: Wiley.

Roberts, R. N., & Tharp, R. G. (1980). A naturalistic study of children's self-directed speech in academic problem-solving. *Cognitive Research and Therapy, 4,* 341–353.

Rodrigue, J. R., Banko, C. G., Sears, S. F., & Evans, G. (1996). Old territory revisited: Behavior therapists in rural America and innovative models of service delivery. *The Behavior Therapist, 19,* 97–100.

Roscoe, B., Martin, G. L, & Pear, J. J. (1980). Systematic self-desensitization of fear of flying: A case study. In G. L. Martin & J. G. Osborne (Eds.), *Helping in the community: Behavioral applications* (pp. 345–352). New York: Plenum Press.

Rosen, G. M. (1987). Self-help treatment books and the commercialization of psychotherapy. *American Psychologist, 42,* 46–51.

Rothbaum, B. O., Anderson, P., Zimand, E., Hodges, L., Lang, D., & Wilson, J. (2006). Virtual reality exposure therapy and standard (in vivo) exposure therapy in the treatment of fear of flying. *Behavior Therapy, 37,* 80–90.

Rothbaum, B. O., Hodges, L. F., Kooper, R., et al., (1995), Effectiveness of computer-generated (virtual reality) graded exposure in the treatment of acrophobia. *American Journal of Psychiatry, 152,* 626–628.

Rotter, J. B. (1954). *Social learning and clinical psychology.* Upper Saddle River, NJ: Prentice Hall.

Rovetto, F. (1979). Treatment of chronic constipation by classical conditioning techniques. *Journal of Behavior Therapy and Experimental Psychiatry, 10,* 143–146.

Sajwaj, T., Libet, J., & Agras, S. (1974). Lemon-juice therapy: The control of life-threatening rumination in a six-month-old infant. *Journal of Applied Behavior Analysis, 7,* 557–563.

Sakano, Y. (1993). Behavior therapy in Japan: Beyond the cultural impediments. *Behavior Change, 10,* 19–21.

Salend, S. J., Ellis, L. L., & Reynolds, C. J. (1989). Using self-instructions to teach vocational skills to individuals who are severely retarded. *Education and Training in Mental Retardation, 24,* 248–254.

Salmon, D. J., Pear, J. J., & Kuhn, B. A. (1986). Generalization of object naming after training with picture cards and with objects. *Journal of Applied Behavior Analysis, 19,* 53–58.

Salter, A. (1949). *Conditioned reflex therapy.* New York: Creative Age Press.

Salzinger, K. (2008). Waves or ripples? *The Behavior Therapist, 31,* 147–148.

Sanivio, E. (1999). Behavioral and cognitive therapy in Italy. *The Behavior Therapist, 22,* 69–75.

Sarwer, D. B., & Sayers, S. L. (1998). Behavioral interviewing. In A. S. Bellack & M. Hersen (Eds.), *Behavioral assessment: A practical handbook* (4th ed., pp. 63–78). Boston: Allyn & Bacon.

Schaefer, C. E., & Briesmeister, J. M. (Eds.). (1998). *Handbook of parent training: Parents as co-therapists for children's behavior.* New York: Wiley.

Schaefer, H. H., & Martin, P. L. (1969). *Behavioral therapy.* New York: McGraw-Hill.

Schleien, S. J., Wehman, P., & Kiernan, J. (1981). Teaching leisure skills to severely handicapped adults: An age-appropriate darts game. *Journal of Applied Behavior Analysis, 14,* 513–519.

Schlesinger, C. (2004). Australian Association for Cognitive and Behavior Therapy. *Newsletter of the International Association for Behavior Analysis, 27*(2), 20–21.

Schlinger, H. D., Derenne, A., & Baron, A. (2008). What 50 years of research tell us about pausing under ratio schedules of reinforcement. *The Behavior Analyst, 31,* 39–60.

Schloss, P. J., & Schloss, M. A. (2004). *Applied behavior analysis in the classroom* (2nd ed.). Boston: Allyn & Bacon.

Schloss, P. J., Smith, M., Santora, C., & Bryant, R. (1989). A respondent conditioning approach to reducing anger responses of a dually-diagnosed man with mild mental retardation. *Behavior Therapy, 20,* 459–464.

Schreibman, L. (1975). Effects of within-stimulus and extra-stimulus prompting on discrimination learning in autistic children. *Journal of Applied Behavior Analysis, 8,* 91–112.

Schroeder, H. E., & Black, M. J. (1985). Unassertiveness. In M. Hersen & A. S. Bellack (Eds.), *Handbook of clinical behavior therapy with adults* (pp. 509–530). New York: Plenum Press.

Schunk, D. H. (1987). Peer models and children's behavioral change. *Review of Educational Research, 57,* 149–174.

Schwartz, M. S., & Andrasic, F. (1998). *Biofeedback: A practitioner's guide.* New York: Guilford Press.

Schwitzgebel, R. L. (1964). *Streetcorner research: An experimental approach to juvenile delinquency.* Cambridge, MA: Harvard University Press.

Scogin, F., Bynum, J., Stephens, G., & Calhoon, S. (1990). Efficacy of self-administered treatment programs: Meta-analytic review. *Professional Psychology: Research and Practice, 21,* 42–47.

Scott, M. A., Barclay, B. R., & Houts, A. C. (1992). Childhood enuresis: Etiology, assessment, and current behavioral treatment. In M. Hersen, R. N. Eisler, & P. M. Miller (Eds.), *Progress in behavior modification* (Vol. 28, pp. 84–119). Sycamore, IL: Sycamore Press.

Scott, R. W., Peters, R. D., Gillespie, W. J., Blanchard, E. B., Edmundson, E. D., & Young, L. D. (1973). The use of shaping and reinforcement in the operant acceleration and deceleration of heart rate. *Behaviour Research and Therapy, 11,* 179–185.

Scrimali, T., & Grimaldi, L. (1993). Behavioral and cognitive psychotherapy in Italy. *The Behavior Therapist, 16,* 265–266.

Seabaugh, G. O., & Schumaker, J. B. (1994). The effects of self-regulation training on the academic productivity of secondary students with learning problems. *Journal of Behavioral Education, 4,* 109–133.

Searight, H. R. (1998). *Behavioral medicine: A primary care approach.* Philadelphia: Brunner-Mazel.

Seigts, G. H., Meertens, R. M., & Kok, G. (1997). The effects of task importance and publicness on the relation between goal difficulty and performance. *Canadian Journal of Behavioural Science, 29,* 54–62.

Seligman, M. E. P. (1971). Phobias and preparedness. *Behavior Therapy, 2,* 307–321.

Seligman, M. E. P. (1994). *What you can change and what you can't.* New York: Knopf.

Semb, G., & Semb, S. A. (1975). A comparison of fixed-page and fixed-time reading assignments in elementary school children. In E. Ramp & G. Semb (Eds.), *Behavior analysis: Areas of research and application* (pp. 233–243). Upper Saddle River, NJ: Prentice Hall.

Serketich, W. J., & Dumas, J. E. (1996). The effectiveness of behavioral parent training to modify antisocial behavior in children: A meta-analysis. *Behavior Therapy, 27,* 171–186.

Shafran, R., Booth, R., & Rachman, S. (1993). The reduction of claustrophobia: II. Cognitive analyses. *Behaviour Research and Therapy, 31,* 75–85.

Shahan, T. A., Bickel, W. K., Madden, G. J., & Badger, G. J. (1999). Comparing the reinforcing efficacy of nicotine containing and denicotinized cigarettes: A behavioral economic analysis. *Psychopharmacology, 147,* 210–216

Sherrington, C. S. (1947). *The integrative action of the central nervous system.* Cambridge, UK: Cambridge University Press.

Shimoff, E., Matthews, B. A., & Catania, A. C. (1986). Human operant performance: Sensitivity and pseudosensitivity to contingencies. *Journal of the Experimental Analysis of Behavior, 46,* 149–157.

Sidman, M. (1953). Avoidance conditioning with brief shock and no exteroceptive warning signal. *Science, 118,* 157–158.

Sidman, M. (1960). *Tactics of scientific research.* New York: Basic Books.

Sidman, M. (1994). *Equivalence relations and behavior: A research story.* Boston: Authors Cooperative.

Siedentop, D. (1978). The management of practice behavior. In W. F. Straub (Ed.), *Sport psychology: An analysis of athletic behavior* (pp. 42–61). Ithaca, NY: Mouvement.

Siedentop, D., & Tannehill, D. (2000). *Developing teaching skills in physical education* (4th ed.). Mountain View, CA: Mayfield.

Siev, J., Huppert, J., & Chambless, D. L. (2009). The dodo bird, treatment technique, and disseminating empirically supported treatments. *The Behavior Therapist, 32,* 69–76.

Simek, T. C., & O'Brien, R. M. (1981). *Total golf: A behavioral approach to lowering your score and getting more out of your game.* Huntington, NY: B-Mod Associates.

Singer, G. H., Singer, J. S., & Horner, R. H. (1987). Using pretask requests to increase the probability of compliance for students with severe disabilities. *Journal of the Association for Persons with Severe Handicaps, 12,* 287–291.

Singh, N. N., Wahler, R. G., Adkins, A. D., & Myers, R. E. (2003). Soles of the feet: A mindfulness-based self-control intervention for aggression by an individual with mild mental retardation and mental illness. *Research in Developmental Disabilities, 24*(1), 58–169.

Sirard, J. R., & Pate, R. R. (2001). Physical activity assessment in children and adolescents. *Sports Medicine, 31,* 439–454.

Skinner, B. F. (1938). *The behavior of organisms.* New York: Appleton-Century-Crofts.

Skinner, B. F. (1948a). "Superstition" in the pigeon. *Journal of Experimental Psychology, 38,* 168–172.

Skinner, B. F. (1948b). *Walden Two.* New York: Macmillan.

Skinner, B. F. (1953). *Science and human behavior.* New York: Macmillan.

Skinner, B. F. (1957). *Verbal behavior.* New York: Appleton-Century-Crofts.

Skinner, B. F. (1958). Teaching machines. *Science, 128,* 969–977.

Skinner, B. F. (1960). Pigeons in a pelican. *American Psychologist, 15,* 28–37.

Skinner, B. F. (1968). *The technology of teaching.* New York: Appleton-Century-Crofts.

Skinner, B. F. (1969). *Contingencies of reinforcement: A theoretical analysis.* New York: Appleton-Century-Crofts.

Skinner, B. F. (1971). *Beyond freedom and dignity.* New York: Knopf.

Skinner, B. F. (1974). *About behaviorism.* New York: Knopf.

Skinner, B. F. (1977). Why I am not a cognitive psychologist. *Behaviorism, 5,* 1–10.

Skinner, B. F. (1989). *Recent issues in the analysis of behavior.* Columbus, OH: Charles E. Merrill.

Skinner, B. F., & Vaughan, N. E. (1983). *Enjoy old age: A program of self-management.* New York: W. W. Norton.

Smith, M. T., Perlis, M., Park, A., Smith, M. S., Pennington, J., Giles, G. E., et al. (2002). Comparative meta-analysis of pharmacotherapy and behavior therapy for persistent insomnia. *American Journal of Psychiatry, 159*(1), 5–11.

Smith, R. E. (1988). The logic and design of case study research. *The Sport Psychologist, 2,* 1–12.

Smith, R., Michael, J., & Sundberg, M. L. (1996). Automatic reinforcement and automatic punishment in infant vocal behavior. *The Analysis of Verbal Behavior, 13,* 39–48.

Snyder, D. K., & Abbott, B. V. (2004). Couple distress. In M. M. Antony & D. H. Barlow (Eds.), *Handbook of assessment and treatment planning for psychological disorders.* New York: Guilford Press.

Snyder, J., Schrepferman, L., & St. Peter, C. (1997). Origins of antisocial behavior: Negative reinforcement and affect disregulation of behavior as socialization mechanisms in family interaction. *Behavior Modification, 21,* 187–215.

Sobell, L. C., Toneatto, T., & Sobell, M. B. (1994). Behavioral assessment and treatment planning for alcohol, tobacco, and other drug problems: Current status with an emphasis on clinical applications. *Behavior Therapy, 25,* 533–580.

Sobell, M. B., & Sobell, L. C. (1993). *Problem drinkers: Guided self-change treatment.* New York: Guilford Press.

Sommer, R. (1977, January). Toward a psychology of natural behavior. *APA Monitor, 8,* 13–14.

Spiegler, M. D., & Guevremont, D. C. (2003). *Contemporary behavior therapy* (4th ed.). Belmont, CA: Wadsworth/Thompson Learning.

Spinelli, P. R., & Packard, T. (1975, February). Behavioral self-control delivery systems. Paper presented at the National Conference on Behavioral Self-Control, Salt Lake City, UT.

Spira, A. P., & Edelstein, B. A. (2006). Behavioral interventions for agitation in older adults with dementia: An evaluative review. *International Psychogeriatrics, 18,* 195–225.

Spooner, F. (1984). Comparisons of backward chaining and total task presentation in training severely handicapped persons. *Education and Training of the Mentally Retarded, 19,* 15–22.

Sprague, J. R., & Horner, R. H. (1984). The effects of single-instance, multiple-instance, and general case training on generalized vending machine use by moderately and severely handicapped students. *Journal of Applied Behavior Analysis, 17,* 273–278.

Springer, C. R., & Pear, J. J. (2008). Performance measures in courses using computer-aided personalized system of instruction. *Computers and Education, 51,* 829–835.

Staats, A. W. (1996). *Behavior and personality.* New York: Springer.

Staats, A. W., Staats, C. K., & Crawford, H. L. (1962). First-order conditioning of meaning and the parallel conditioning of a GSR. *Journal of General Psychology, 67,* 159–167.

Stainback, W. C., Payne, J. S., Stainback, S. B., & Payne, R. A. (1973). *Establishing a token economy in the classroom.* Columbus, OH: Charles E. Merrill.

Stampfl, T. G., & Levis, D. J. (1967). Essentials of implosive therapy: A learning-theory-based psychodynamic behavioral therapy. *Journal of Abnormal Psychology, 72,* 496–503.

Stark, M. (1980). The German Association of Behavior Therapy. *Behavior Therapist, 3,* 11–12.

Steege, M. W., & Watson, T. S. (2009). *Conducting school-based functional behavioral assessments: A practitioner's guide, 2nd edition.* New York: Guilford Press.

Stephens, C. E., Pear, J. J., Wray, L. D., & Jackson, G. C. (1975). Some effects of reinforcement schedules in teaching picture names to retarded children. *Journal of Applied Behavior Analysis, 8,* 435–447.

Stokes, T. F., & Baer, D. M. (1977). An implicit technology of generalization. *Journal of Applied Behavior Analysis, 10,* 349–367.

Stokes, T. F., & Osnes, P. G. (1986). Programming the generalization of children's social behavior. In P. S. Strain, M. J. Guralnick, & H. Walker (Eds.), *Children's social behavior: Development, assessment, and modification* (pp. 407–443). Orlando, FL: Academic Press.

Stokes, T. F., & Osnes, P. G. (1989). An operant pursuit of generalization. *Behavioral Therapy, 20,* 337–355.

Stolz, S. B., & Associates. (1978). *Ethical issues in behavior modification.* San Francisco: Jossey-Bass.

Stone, A. A., Turkkan, J. S., Bachrach, C. A., Jobe, J. B., Kurtzman, H. S., Cain, V. S. (2000). *The Science of Self-Report: Implications for Research and Practice.* Mahwah, N. J.: Lawrence Erlbaum Associates.

St. Peter Pipkin, C., & Vollmer, T. R. (2009). Applied implications of reinforcement history effects. *Journal of Applied Behavior Analysis, 42,* 83–103.

Stromer, R., Mackay, H. A., & Remington, B. (1996). Naming: The formation of stimulus classes, and applied behavior analysis. *Journal of Applied Behavior Analysis, 29,* 409–431.

Stromer, R., McComas, J. J., & Rehfeldt, R. A. (2000). Designing interventions that include delayed reinforcement: Implications of recent laboratory research. *Journal of Applied Behavior Analysis, 33,* 359–371.

Stuart, R. B. (1971). Assessment and change of the communication patterns of juvenile delinquents and their parents. In R. D. Rubin, H. Fernsterheim, A. A. Lazarus, & C. M. Franks (Eds.), *Advances in behavior therapy* (pp. 183–196). New York: Academic Press.

Sturmey, P. (1994). Assessing the functions of aberrant behaviors: A review of psychometric instruments. *Journal of Autism and Developmental Disabilities, 24,* 293–303.

Sturmey, P. (1995). Analogue baselines: A critical review of the methodology. *Research in Developmental Disabilities, 16,* 269–284.

Sturmey, P. (Ed.). (2007). *Functional analysis in clinical treatment.* London, UK: Elsevier.

Suchowierska, M., & Kozlowski, J. (2004). Behavior analysis in Poland: A few words on Polish ABA. *Newsletter of the International Association for Behavior Analysis, 27*(2), 28–29.

Sullivan, M. A., & O'Leary, S. G. (1990). Maintenance following reward and cost token programs. *Behavior Therapy, 21,* 139–149.

Sulzer-Azaroff, B., & Reese, E. P. (1982). *Applying behavior analysis: A program for developing professional competence.* New York: Holt, Rinehart & Winston.

Sundberg, M. L. (2004). A behavioral analysis of motivation and its relation to mand training. In W. L. Williams (Ed.), *Advances in developmental disabilities: Etiology, assessment, intervention, and integration* (pp. 199–220). Reno, NV: Context Press.

Sundberg, M. L., & Michael, J. (2001). The benefits of Skinner's analysis of verbal behavior for children with autism. *Behavior Modification, 25,* 698–724.

Sundberg, M. L., Michael, J., Partington, J. W., & Sundberg, C. A. (1996). The role of automatic reinforcement in early language acquisition. *The Analysis of Verbal Behavior, 13,* 21–37.

Sundberg, M. L., & Partington, J. W. (1998). *Teaching language to children with autism and other developmental disabilities.* Pleasant Hill, CA: Behavior Analysts.

Svenningsen, L. An examination of the effect of CAPSI as a learning system in developing knowledge and critical thinking in two blended learning courses. Unpublished doctoral dissertation, University of Manitoba, Winnipeg, Manitoba.

Sweet, A. A., & Loizeaux, A. L. (1991). Behavioral and cognitive treatment methods: A critical comparative review. *Journal of Behavior Therapy and Experimental Psychiatry, 22,* 159–185.

Tanaka-Matsumi, J., & Higginbotham, H. N. (1994). Clinical application of behavior therapy across ethnic and cultural boundaries. *The Behavior Therapist, 17,* 123–126.

Tanaka-Matsumi, J., Higginbautham, H. N., & Chang, R. (2002). Cognitive behavioral approaches to counselling across cultures: A functional analytic approach for clinical applications. In P. B. Pedersen, J. G. Draguns, W. J. Lonner, & J. E. Trimble (Eds.), *Counselling across cultures* (5th ed., pp. 337–354). Thousand Oaks, CA: Sage.

Taylor, C. B., Fried, L., & Kenardy, J. (1990). The use of real-time computer diary for data acquisition and processing. *Behavior Research and Therapy, 28,* 93–97.

Taylor, S. E. (2003). *Health psychology* (5th ed.). New York: McGraw-Hill.

Taylor, S., Thordarson, D. S., & Sochting, I. (2004). Obsessive-compulsive disorder. In M. M. Antony & D. H. Barlow (Eds.), *Handbook of assessment and treatment planning for psychological disorders.* New York: Guilford Press.

Taub, E., Crago, J. E., Burgio, L. D., Groomes, T. E., Cook, E. W., III, Deluca, S. C., & Miller, N. E. (1994). An operant approach to rehabilitation medicine: Overcoming learned nonuse by shaping. *Journal of the Experimental Analysis of Behavior, 61,* 281–293.

Teasdale, J. D., Segal, Z. V., & Williams, J. M. G. (1995). How does cognitive therapy prevent depressive relapse and why should attentional control (mindfulness) training help? *Behavior Research and Therapy, 33,* 25–39.

Terenzini, P. T., & Pascarella, E. T. (1994, January/February). Living with myths: Undergraduate education in America. *Change,* 28–32.

Tews, L. (2007). Early intervention for children with autism: Methodologies critique. *Developmental Disabilities Bulletin, 35,* 148–168.

Tharp, R. G., & Wetzel, R. J. (1969). *Behavior modification in the natural environment.* New York: Academic Press.

Thierman, G. J., & Martin, G. L. (1989). Self-management with picture prompts to improve quality of household cleaning by severely mentally handicapped persons. *International Journal of Rehabilitation Research, 12,* 27–39.

Thiessen, C., Fazzio, D., Arnal, L., Martin, G. L., Yu, C. T., & Kielback, L. (2009). Evaluation of a self-instructional manual for conducting discrete-trials teaching with children with autism. *Behavior Modification, 33,* 360–373.

Thomas, D. L., & Miller, L. K. (1980). Helping college students live together. Democratic decision-making versus experimental manipulation. In G. L. Martin & J. G. Osborne (Eds.), *Helping in the community: Behavioral applications* (pp. 291–305). New York: Plenum Press.

Thompson, R. H., & Iwata, B. A. (2000). Response acquisition under direct and indirect contingencies of reinforcement. *Journal of Applied Behavior Analysis, 33,* 1–11.

Thompson, R. H., Iwata, B. A., Conners, J., & Roscoe, E. M. (1999). Effects of reinforcement for alternative behavior during punishment of self-injury. *Journal of Applied Behavior Analysis, 32,* 317–328.

Thompson, R. W., Smith, G. L., Osgood, D. W., Dowd, T. P., Friman, P. C., & Daly, D. L. (1996). Residential care: A study of short- and long-term educational effects. *Children and Youth Services Review, 18,* 221–242.

Thompson, T., Felce, D., & Symons, F. (Eds.). (2000). *Behavioral observation: Technology* *and applications in developmental disabilities.* Baltimore. MD: Brookes.

Thomson, K., Martin, G. L., Arnal, L., Fazzio, D., & Yu, C. T. (2009). Instructing individuals to deliver discrete-trials teaching to children with autism spectrum disorders: A review. *Research in Autism Spectrum Disorders, 3,* 590-606.

Thorndike, E. L. (1911). Animal intelligence: An experimental study of the associative processes in animals. *Psychological Review Monograph Supplement 2,* Whole No. 8.

Tiffany, S. T., Martin, C., & Baker, R. (1986). Treatments for cigarette smoking: An evaluation of the contributions of aversion and counselling procedures. *Behavior Research and Therapy, 24,* 437–452.

Timberlake, W., & Allison, J. (1974). Response deprivation: An empirical approach to instrumental performance. *Psychological Review, 81,* 146–164.

Timberlake, W., & Farmer-Dougan, V. A. (1991). Reinforcement in applied settings: Figuring out ahead of time what will work. *Psychological Bulletin, 110,* 379–391.

Tincani, M. J., Gastrogiavanni, A., & Axelrod, S., (1999). A comparison of the effectiveness of brief versus traditional functional analyses. *Research in Developmental Disabilities, 20,* 327–338.

Tingstrom, D. H., Sterling-Turner, H. E., & Wilczynski, S. M. (2006). The Good Behavior Game: 1969–2002. *Behavior Modification, 30,* 225–253.

Tkachuk, G.A., & Martin, G.L. (1999). Exercise therapy for psychiatric disorders: Research and clinical implications. *Professional Psychology: Research and Practice, 30,* 275–282.

Todd, F. J. (1972). Coverant control of self-evaluative responses in the treatment of depression: A new use for an old principle. *Behavior Therapy, 3,* 91–94.

Torgrud, L. J., & Holborn, S. W. (1990). The effects of verbal performance descriptions on nonverbal operant responding. *Journal of the Experimental Analysis of Behavior, 54,* 273–291.

Tringer, L. (1991). Behavior therapy in Hungary. *The Behavior Therapist, 14,* 13–14.

Tucker, M., Sigafoos, J., & Bushell, H. (1998). Use of non-contingent reinforcement in the treatment of challenging behavior. A review and clinical guide. *Behavior Modification, 22,* 529–547.

Turk, D. C., & Okifuji, A. (1997). Evaluating the role of physical, operant, cognitive, and affective factors in the pain behaviors of chronic pain patients. *Behavior Modification, 21,* 259–280.

Turkat, I. D., & Feuerstein, M. (1978). Behavior modification and the public misconception. *American Psychologist, 33,* 194.

Turner, J. R., Cardon, L. R., & Hewitt, J. K. (1995). *Behavior genetic approaches in behavioral medicine.* New York: Plenum Press.

Twohig, M. P., Hayes, S. C., & Masuda, A. (2006). Increasing willingness to experience obsessions: Acceptance and Commitment Therapy as treatment for obsessive-compulsive disorder. *Behavior Therapy, 37,* 3–13.

Tyron, W. W. (1998). Behavioral observation. In A. S. Bellack & M. Hersen (Eds.), *Behavioral assessment: A practical handbook* (4th ed., pp. 79–103). Boston: Allyn & Bacon.

Tyron, W. W., & Cicero, S. D. (1989). Classical conditioning of meaning—I. A replication and higher order extension. *Journal of Behavior Therapy and Experimental Psychiatry, 20,* 137–142.

Ullmann, L. P. (1980). This week's citation classic, *Case Studies in Behavior Modification. Current Contents/Social and Behavioral Sciences* (No. 11), 255. (Available online at http://garfield .library.upenn.edu/classics.html).

Ullmann L. P., & Krasner, L. (Eds.). (1965). *Case studies in behavior modification.* New York: Holt, Rinehart & Winston.

Ulrich, R., Stachnik, T., & Mabry. J. (Eds.). (1966). *Control of human behavior* (Vol. 1). Glenview, IL: Scott Foresman.

Upper, D., Cautela, J. R., & Brook, J. M. (1975). Behavioral self-rating checklist. In M. Hersen, R. M. Eisler, & P. M. Miller (Eds.), *Progress in* *behavior modification* (Vol. 1, pp. 275–305). New York: Academic Press.

Van Houten, R. (1983). Punishment: From the animal laboratory to the applied setting. In S. Axelrod & J. Apsche (Eds.), *The effects of punishment on human behavior* (pp. 13–44). New York: Academic Press.

Van Houten, R., Axelrod, S., Bailey, J. S., Favell, J. E., Foxx, R. M., Iwata, B. A., et al. (1988). The right to effective behavioral treatment. *Journal of Applied Behavior Analysis, 21,* 381–384.

Van Houten, R., & Doleys, D. M. (1983). Are social reprimands effective? In S. Axelrod & J. Apsche (Eds.), *The effects of punishment on human behavior* (pp. 45–70). New York: Academic Press.

Vaughan, M. (1989). Rule-governed behavior in behavior analysis: A theoretical and experimental history. In S. C. Hayes (Ed.), *Rule-governed behavior: Cognition, contingencies, and instructional control* (pp. 97–118). New York: Plenum Press.

Vaughan, M. E., & Michael, J. L. (1982). Automatic reinforcement: An important but ignored concept. *Behaviorism, 10,* 217–227.

Vaughan, W., Jr., & Herrnstein, R. J. (1987). Choosing among natural stimuli. *Journal of the Experimental Analysis of Behavior, 47,* 5–16.

Vause, T., Regher, K., Feldman, M., Griffiths, D., & Owen, F. (2009). Right to behavioral treatment for individuals with intellectual disabilities: Issues of punishment (219–239). In F. Owen & D. Griffiths (Eds.), *Challenges to the human rights of people with intellectual disabilities.* London & Philadelphia: Jessica Kingsley Publishers.

Vause, T., Yu, C. T., & Martin, G. L. (2007). The Assessment of Basic Learning Abilities Test for persons with intellectual disability: A valuable clinical tool. *Journal of Applied Research in Intellectual Disabilities, 20, 483-489.*

Verbeke, A. K., Martin, G. L., Thorsteinsson, J. R., Murphy, C., & Yu, C. T. (2009). Does mastery of ABLA Level 6 make it easier for individuals with developmental disabilities to learn to name objects? *Journal of Behavioral Education, 18,* 229-244.

Verbeke, A. K., Martin, G. L., Yu, C. T., & Martin, T. L. (2007). Does ABLA test performance predict picture name recognition with persons with severe developmental disabilities? *The Analysis of Verbal Behavior, 23,* 35–39.

Vollmer, T. R., & Iwata, B. A. (1992). Differential reinforcement as treatment for behavior disorders: Procedural and functional variations. *Research in Developmental Disabilities, 13,* 393–417.

Vollmer, T. R., Iwata, B. A., Zarcone, J. R., Smith, R. G., & Mazaleski, J. L. (1993). The role of attention in the treatment of attention-maintained self-injurious behavior: Non-contingent reinforcement and differential reinforcement of other behavior. *Journal of Applied Behavior Analysis, 26,* 9–21.

Vollmer, T. R., Roane, H. S., Ringdahl, J. E., & Marcus, B. A. (1999). Evaluating treatment challenges with differential reinforcement of alternative behavior. *Journal of Applied Behavior Analysis, 32,* 9–23.

Vygotsky, L. S. (1978). *Mind and society.* Cambridge, MA: Harvard University Press.

Wahler, R. G. (2007). Chaos, coincidence, and contingency in the behavior disorders of childhood and adolescence. In P. Sturmey (Ed.), *Functional analysis in clinical treatment* (pp. 111–128). London, UK: Elsevier.

Wahler, R. G., Winkel, G. H., Peterson, R. F., & Morrison, D. C. (1965). Mothers as behavior therapists for their own children. *Behaviour Research and Therapy, 3,* 113–124.

Walker, H. M., & Buckley, N. K. (1972). Programming generalization and maintenance of treatment effects across time and across setting. *Journal of Applied Behavior Analysis, 5,* 209–224.

Wallace, I. (1971). *The writing of one novel.* Richmond Hill, Ont., Canada: Simon & Schuster.

Wallace, I., & Pear, J. J. (1977). Self-control techniques of famous novelists. *Journal of Applied Behavior Analysis, 10,* 515–525.

Walls, R. T., Zane, T., & Ellis, W. D. (1981). Forward and backward chaining, and whole task methods. *Behavior Modification, 5,* 61–47.

Walters, G. D. (2000). Behavioral self-control training for problem drinkers: A meta-analysis of randomized control studies. *Behavior Therapy, 31,* 135–149.

Wanlin, C., Hrycaiko, D., Martin, G. L., & Mahon, M. (1997). The effects of a goal-setting package on performance of speed skaters. *Journal of Sport Psychology, 9,* 212–228.

Ward, P. (2005). The philosophy, science, and application of behavior analysis in physical education. In D. Kirk, D. MacDonald, & M. O'Sullivan (Eds.), *The Handbook of Physical Education.* Thousand Oaks, CA: Sage.

Ward, W. D., & Stare, S. W. (1990). The role of subject verbalization in generalized correspondence. *Journal of Applied Behavior Analysis, 23,* 129–136.

Warren, S. F. (2000). Mental retardation: Curse, characteristic, or coin of the realm? *American Association on Mental Retardation News and Notes, 13,* 10–11.

Watson, D. L., & Tharp, R. G. (1997). *Self-directed behavior: Self-modification for personal adjustment* (7th ed.). Monterey, CA: Brooks/Cole.

Watson, D. L., & Tharp, R. G. (2007). *Self-directed behavior: Self-modification for personal adjustment* (9th ed.). Monterey, CA: Brooks/Cole.

Watson, J. B. (1913). Psychology as the behaviorist views it. *Psychological Review, 20,* 158–177.

Watson, J. B. (1916). The place of the conditioned reflex in psychology. *Psychological Review, 23,* 89–116.

Watson, J. B. (1930). *Behaviorism* (rev. ed.). Chicago: University of Chicago Press.

Watson, J. B., & Rayner, R. (1920). Conditioned emotional reactions. *Journal of Experimental Psychology, 3,* 1–14.

Watson, R. I. (1962). The experimental tradition and clinical psychology. In A. J. Bachrach (Ed.), *Experimental foundations of clinical psychology* (pp. 3–25). New York: Basic Books.

Wearden, J. H. (1988). Some neglect problems in the analysis of human operant behavior. In G. Davey & C. Cullen (Eds.), *Human operant conditioning and behavior modification* (pp. 197–224), Chichester, UK: Wiley.

Welch, M. W., & Gist, J. W. (1974). *The open token economy system: A handbook for a behavioral approach to rehabilitation.* Springfield, IL: Charles C Thomas.

Welch, S. J., & Pear, J. J. (1980). Generalization of naming responses to objects in the natural environment as a function of training stimulus modality with retarded children. *Journal of Applied Behavior Analysis, 13,* 629–643.

Wetherell, J. L. (2002). Behavior therapy for anxious older adults. *The Behavior Therapist, 25,* 16–17.

Wexler, D. (1981). *Manual for the Wexler Adult Intelligence Scale—Revised.* New York: Psychological Corporation.

Whaley, D. L., & Malott, R. W. (1971). *Elementary principles of behavior.* Upper Saddle River, NJ: Prentice Hall.

Whitaker, S. (1993). The reduction of aggression in people with learning disabilities: A review of psychological methods. *British Journal of Clinical Psychology, 32,* 1–37.

Whitman, T. L., Spence, B. H., & Maxwell, S. (1987). A comparison of external and self-instructional teaching formats with mentally retarded adults in a vocational training setting. *Research in Developmental Disabilities, 8,* 371–388.

Wiederhold, B. K., & Wiederhold, M. D. (2004). *Virtual reality therapy for anxiety disorders: Advances in evaluation and treatment.* Washington, DC: American Psychological Association.

Wiegel, M., Wincze, J. P., & Barlow, D. H. (2004). Sexual dysfunction. In M. M. Antony & D. H. Barlow (Eds.), *Handbook of assessment and treatment planning for psychological disorders.* New York: Guilford Press.

Wilder, D. A., & Wong, S. E. (2007). Schizophrenia and other psychotic disorders. In

P. Sturmey (Ed.), *Functional analysis in clinical treatment* (pp. 283–306). London: Elsevier.

Williams, B., Myerson, J., & Hale, S. (2008). Individual differences, intelligence, and behavioral analysis. *Journal of the Experimental Analysis of Behavior, 90,* 219–231.

Williams, C. D. (1959). The elimination of tantrum behavior by extinction procedures. *Journal of Abnormal and Social Psychology, 59,* 269.

Williams, J. E., & Cuvo, A. J. (1986). Training apartment upkeep skills to rehabilitation clients: A comparison of task analysis strategies. *Journal of Applied Behavior Analysis, 19,* 39–51.

Williams, M., Teasdale, J., Segal, Z., & Kabat-Zinn, J. (2007). *The mindful way through depression: Freeing yourself from chronic unhappiness.* New York: Guilford Press.

Williams, W. L. (Ed.). (2004). *Advances in developmental disabilities: Etiology, assessment, intervention, and integration.* Reno, NV: Context Press.

Williams, W. L., Jackson, M., & Friman, P. C. (2007). Encopresis and enuresis. In P. Sturmey (Ed.), *Functional analysis in clinical treatment* (pp. 171–192). London: Elsevier.

Wilson, G. T. (1991). Chemical aversion conditioning in the treatment of alcoholism: Further comments. *Behavior Research and Therapy, 29,* 415–419.

Wilson, K. G., Hayes, S. C., & Gifford, E. V. (1997). Cognition in behavior therapy: Agreements and differences. *Journal of Behavior Therapy and Experimental Psychiatry, 28,* 53–63.

Wilson, J. Q., & Herrnstein, R. J. (1985). *Crime and human nature.* New York, NY: Simon & Schuster.

Wincze, J. P., Bach, A. K., & Barlow, D. H. (2008). Sexual dysfunction. In D. H. Barlow (Ed.), *Clinical handbook of psychological disorders: A step-by-step treatment manual* (4th ed.). New York: Guilford Press.

Wincze, J. P., & Carey, M. P. (2001). *Sexual dysfunction, second edition: A guide for assessment and treatment.* New York: Guilford Press.

Winerman, L. (2004). Back to her roots. *Monitor on Psychology, 35*(8), 46–49.

Winerman, L. (2005). Fighting phobias: A virtual cure. *Monitor on Psychology, 36*(7), 87–89.

Wisocki, P. A. (1999). *Handbook of clinical behavior therapy with the elderly client.* New York: Kluwer/Plenum.

Witt, J. C., & Wacker, D. P. (1981). Teaching children to respond to auditory directives: An evaluation of two procedures. *Behavior Research of Severe Developmental Disabilities, 2,* 175–189.

Wolf, M. M. (1978). Social validity: The case for subjective measurement or how applied behavior analysis is finding its heart. *Journal of Applied Behavior Analysis, 11,* 203–214.

Wolf, M. M., Braukmann, C. J., & Remp, K. A. (1987). Serious delinquent behavior as part of a significantly handicapping condition: Cures and supportive environments. *Journal of Applied Behavior Analysis, 20,* 347–359.

Wolf, M. M., Hanley, E. L., King, L. A., Lachowicz, J., & Giles, D. K. (1970). The timer-game: A variable interval contingency for the management of out-of-seat behavior. *Exceptional Children, 37,* 113–117.

Wolf, M. M., Kirigin, K. A., Fixsen, D. L., Blase, K. A., & Braukmann, C. J. (1995). The teaching-family model: A case study in data-based program development and refinement (and dragon wrestling). *Journal of Organizational Behavior Management, 15,* 11–68.

Wolf, M. M., Risley, T., & Mees, H. (1964). Application of operant conditioning procedures to the behavior problems of an autistic child. *Behavior Research and Therapy, 1,* 305–312.

Wolfe, V. F., & Cuvo, A. J. (1978). Effects of within-stimulus and extra-stimulus prompting on letter discrimination by mentally retarded persons. *American Journal of Mental Deficiency, 83,* 297–303.

Wolfensberger, W. (Ed.). (1972). *Normalization: The principle of normalization in human services.* Toronto: National Institute of Mental Retardation.

Wolko, K. L., Hrycaiko, D. W., & Martin, G. L. (1993). A comparison of two self-management packages to standard coaching for improving practice performance of gymnasts. *Behavior Modification, 17,* 209–223.

Wolpe, J. (1958). *Psychotherapy by reciprocal inhibition.* Stanford, CA: Stanford University Press.

Wolpe, J. (1969). *The practice of behavior therapy.* Elmsford, NY: Pergamon Press.

Wolpe, J. (1982). *The practice of behavior therapy* (3rd ed.). New York: Pergamon Press.

Wolpe, J. (1985). Requiem for an institution. *Behavior Therapist, 8,* 113.

Wolpe, J. (1990). *The practice of behavior therapy* (4th ed.). New York: Pergamon Press.

Wood, S. J., Murdoch, J. Y., & Cronin, M. E. (2002). Self-monitoring and at-risk middle-school students: Academic performance improves, maintains, and generalizes. *Behavior Modification, 25,* 605–626.

Wyatt, W. J., Hawkins, R. P., & Davis, P. (1986). Behaviorism: Are reports of its death exaggerated? *Behavior Analyst, 9,* 101–105.

Yamagami, T., Okuma, H., Morinaga, Y., & Nakao, H. (1982). Practice of behavior therapy in Japan. *Journal of Behavior Therapy and Experimental Psychology, 13,* 21–26.

Yates, A. J. (1970). *Behavior therapy.* New York: Wiley.

Young, J. E., Rygh, J. L., Weinberger, A. D., & Beck, A. T. (2008). Cognitive therapy for depression. In D. H. Barlow (Ed.), *Clinical handbook of psychological disorders: A step-by-step treatment manual* (4th ed., pp. 250–305). New York: Guilford Press.

Yu, D., Martin, G. L., Suthons, E., Koop, S., & Pallotta-Cornick, A. (1980). Comparisons of forward chaining and total task presentation formats to teach vocational skills to the retarded. *International Journal of Rehabilitation Research, 3,* 77–79.

Zamora, R., & Lima, J. (2000). Cognitive behavioral therapy in Uruguay. *The Behavior Therapist, 23,* 98–101.

Zettle, R. D. (2003). Acceptance and commitment therapy (ACT) versus systematic desensitization in treatment of mathematics anxiety. *Psychological Record, 53,* 197–215.

Zettle, R. D., & Hayes, S. C. (1982). Rule-governed behavior: A potential theoretical framework for cognitive behavioral therapy. In P. C. Kendall (Ed.), *Advances in cognitive behavioral research and therapy* (Vol. 1, pp. 73–118). New York: Academic Press.

Ziegler, S. G. (1987). Effects of stimulus cueing on the acquisition of groundstrokes by beginning tennis players. *Journal of Applied Behavior Analysis, 20,* 405–411.

Zvi, M. B. (2004). IABA: The new Israeli ABA Chapter. *Newsletter of the International Association for Behavior Analysis, 27*(2), 24–25.

AUTHOR INDEX

SUBJECT INDEX